THE COMPLETE
SECRET ARMY

THE UNOFFICIAL AND UNAUTHORISED
GUIDE TO THE CLASSIC TV SERIES

THE COMPLETE SECRET ARMY

THE UNOFFICIAL AND UNAUTHORISED
GUIDE TO THE CLASSIC TV SERIES

ANDY PRIESTNER

CLASSIC
TV PRESS

First published in England in December 2008 by

Classic TV Press

103 High Street, Cherry Hinton, Cambridge, CB1 9LU, England

ISBN: 978-0-9561000-0-9 (paperback)

The Complete Secret Army © 2008 Andy Priestner

Foreword © 2008 Michael E. Briant

The moral rights of the author have been asserted.

Internal design and layout by Classic TV Press

Printed and bound by CPI Antony Rowe, Eastbourne

Printed in England

1 2 3 4 5 6 7 8 9 10 11 12 13 14 15

British Library Cataloguing in Publication Data

A catalogue record for this book is available from the British Library

ACKNOWLEDGEMENTS

First and foremost I would like to thank my wife, Marisa, whose knowledge of *Secret Army* is now almost as extensive as mine, for contributing so much of her time to this book. Not only did she proof the whole manuscript – often while simultaneously jiggling our newborn on her knee – but she comprehensively edited it too, offering many excellent ideas and suggestions that were immediately incorporated. She has also been my faithful companion on several location scouting trips, both here in the UK and in Belgium. Grateful thanks are also due to the regular cast of *Secret Army*, who are some of the friendliest and most down-to-earth people I have ever met. I must make particular mention of Angela Richards, Juliet Hammond-Hill, Clifford Rose, Jan Francis, Terrence Hardiman and Hazel McBride, all fantastically gifted actors who have been incredibly generous with their time and support. I am also extremely grateful for the assistance of several of *Secret Army*'s talented directors, including Viktors Ritelis, Paul Annett, Tristan de Vere Cole, Andrew Morgan and Roger Jenkins, but especially Michael E. Briant who has very kindly provided a foreword. I am also indebted to Joan Glaister, wife of the late great Gerry, who has been supportive of the project since the outset, and lead designer Austin Ruddy, who provided so much information about designing the Candide. I must also thank the many, many other *Secret Army* and *Kessler* personnel who made a contribution: Bernard Hepton, Michael Culver, Paul Shelley, Nigel Williams, Stephan Chase, Robin Langford, Godfrey Johnson, Trisha Clarke, Rachel Beasley, Michael Burrell, Michael Minchin, John Fabian, Lex Tudhope, John Hurst, Alison Glennie, Nicholas Young, Alan Dobie and Sheila Orgar. Grateful thanks to: Maria and Malcolm Leel, Kevin and Robert Ashley and Mark Smith (of Castor) for intrepid location hunting and the resulting photographs; Anders Oliver Magnuson for historical leads and Swedish theatre information; Ann-Sofie Berg for the Blithe Spirit programme; Dave Hofstetter for vintage photos of the Candide; Ian Clarke for sending the Behind the Scenes document all the way from Madrid; Olive Bird for giving her kind permission to use the draft *Bridgehead* script; and the numerous photographers who agreed to the inclusion of actor photos. Thanks are also due to: Sayara Thompson for translating Russian dialogue; Louise North of the BBC Written Archives Centre; David Edgar of the British Film Insitute library; Dave Rice for contacts; Josey and Tony Carpenter for finally buying the DVDs; Carol Langham for enjoying *Secret Army* almost as much as *The Wire*; Rich Cross for not writing this book with me (I jest); Brian Bowen for listening to me banging on as usual; Anna Park for making me laugh very hard by raising doubts about the whole premise of the show; Alex Allinson for having 'Natalie Chantrens hair' back in the day; Hugh Priestner for remembering Reinhardt; and my mother, Carol George, for letting me watch the *Secret Army* repeat season back in 1981 at a time when I was all too ready to lose myself in another world.

for

John Alexander Priestner

TABLE OF CONTENTS

FOREWORD

Secret Army was one of the most important series that the BBC Television Drama department was making at that time. Drama series were frequently excellent, having a 10-day rehearsal period then two full days in a studio. Because there were generally only 13 episodes annually, it was possible to have well-prepared scripts and time for the actors and directors to explore the motivation of the characters and delve into the storylines. When I was asked to direct episodes of the second and third series by producer Gerry Glaister, I was thrilled and delighted. Once I started work and entered the rehearsal room, I felt I had 'come of age' as a director.

The cast of regular leading actors was an impressive array of talent. Led by Bernard Hepton, Angela Richards and Clifford Rose, the rehearsal room was a place of invention, creation and the most enjoyable working atmosphere imaginable. I couldn't wait to get to work each day. It was interesting that there were in fact several leading characters, each with their own separate storylines, motivations and character development. Each of them had their own group of supporting players. Kessler, with Brandt or Reinhardt, portrayed professional German officers who loved their country and believed, without doubt or hesitation, in the future of the Fatherland and its expansionist policies. Their honest trust in the integrity of Nazi Germany was occasionally offset by Reinhardt's cynicism. The 'true love', beyond 'lust', which developed between the Sturmbannführer, later Standartenführer, Ludwig Kessler and the local Belgian woman Madeleine, was fascinating. At first just two lonely people wanting company, the 'Madeleine-Ludwig' relationship created a wonderful picture of the problems of an occupying force, far from home.

In the Candide, Monique was apparently able to overcome her loathing of the Nazi horde whilst playing hostess and singing German songs to Gestapo Officers whilst Natalie waited at table. Albert, always the realist, was always

on his guard and never prepared to take risks. He was the professional in the Lifeline organisation who would prefer to see an entire RAF crew be captured by the Germans, than risk any member of his own group. He had to earn a living by running a profitable business which was heavily financed by his clientele of German officers. Albert was a pragmatist – Monique a romantic, I think.

Above: Michael E. Briant outside 'Le Candide'

1

With three central storylines, which frequently entwined only at the tables of the restaurant, rehearsals were often separated into two or three groups after the first readthrough. The complete company would come together again on the last day of rehearsal, when run-throughs in story order would happen in the morning so I could judge the overall effect and again in the afternoon for the Producer. Gerry would follow the action of each scene as it was played out between marker posts and tape lines on the floor, rattling coins in his pocket and without an expression on his face. He had a nose for overacting or untruthful performances, so as a director I never felt I had to ham the show up, just find the most truthful way of presenting the drama. Unlike many producers who would dictate copious notes to their secretary during a Producer's Run, Gerry would wait till the end, give a couple of little snorts then perhaps give only one note. It was invariably astute and to the point.

During filming of the final series in the Grand Place, I had had one corner decorated with huge swastika flags and Nazi emblems. German staff cars drove past the exterior of Le Candide and our actors in German uniforms of the Gestapo, SS and Luftwaffe strolled in the sun towards the place where Monique would entertain them and the culinary delights of an excellent restaurant awaited. Real-life tourists would come up to Clifford and Terrence and ask if they could have their photo taken with them, explaining that their husband, uncle, father, whatever, had served in World War II in the SS, Luftwaffe or Gestapo in Brussels and it would be lovely to have a souvenir. Why not?

Because the framework of stories followed the historical evolution of the war there clearly was going to be an end to the series sooner rather than later. The only dramatic questions were who would survive the Allied invasion and liberation of Belgium and possibly what happened to them after the war. It was with this in mind that the infamous episode fourteen of the last series was written by John Brason. It was a return to the Candide twenty-five years later with all the principal actors required to age up for the occasion. Apparently it simply did not work. Gerry looked at it, decided it was not of sufficient quality and insisted it was pulled. It was written off together with all its costs. Therefore episode thirteen, *The Execution*, became the final episode instead of a series which had achieved considerable artistic and popular acclaim.

I recently reviewed the episodes of *Secret Army* that I had directed and felt pleased. Decades later it still looks good. The acting is excellent and the stories, for the most part, are thoughtful and believable. It stands up. That Andy Priestner has written a book about it and asked me to contribute with this foreword makes me feel proud to have been associated with a show that is still entertaining viewers today.

Michael E. Briant
Saujon, France, August 2008

INTRODUCTION

Secret Army was one of the most popular BBC television series of the 1970s, regularly drawing audiences of over 16 million viewers. Despite its age – thirty years old at the time of writing – it remains captivating viewing to this day and has earned a reputation as one of the finest TV dramas of all time. First broadcast in the UK between 1977 and 1979, *Secret Army* told the story of the members of a Brussels-based resistance organisation, Lifeline, engaged in the hazardous activity of helping downed Allied airmen to return home, and of the senior German officers charged with halting their activities. *Secret Army* was created by legendary television producer Gerard (Gerry) Glaister, at a time in his career when he already had an impressive string of drama credits to his name, including *The Expert* (1968-71, 1976), *Colditz* (1972-4) and *The Brothers* (1972-6). This new series would prove once again that Glaister, who would also produce *Secret Army*, had an innate understanding of what the British public wanted to watch.

As he had done so successfully with his previous World War II series, *Colditz*, Glaister would seek to base a great many of *Secret Army*'s stories and characters around real-life historical incidents and people. He drew particularly upon the dangerous activities of the Comète evasion line, led by the diminutive but formidable Andrée De Jongh (Dédée), which between 1940 and 1943 saved over 800 airmen from captivity. However, such was *Secret Army*'s impact on its audience, particularly in its second and third series, that its settings, events and principal characters became so familiar and popular with viewers that they arguably became just as real and resonant as the actual persons and happenings on which they were based. This is one of the reasons why it spawned a spin-off, *Kessler* (1981), which concluded the story of one of *Secret Army*'s most memorable characters some thirty years after the war. Another less fortunate measure of its success was the wholesale spoofing of the series by the sitcom *'Allo! 'Allo!* (1982-92), which effectively wiped *Secret Army* from the collective memory of the British public.

Despite its deceptively simple premise, over three years and forty-two episodes, *Secret Army* develops into far more than just another wartime series. As well as the typically faithful recreation of the period – a hallmark of BBC drama in the Seventies – the series boasts brilliantly conceived scripts which not only provide a challenging examination of life and morality during war, but also of human nature in all its complexity. Its characters are similarly well-conceived and although they are split into two distinct groups – Lifeline and their German oppressors – the series takes a radical and groundbreaking approach to their depiction. The series's 'bad guys' are presented as human beings first and members of the Third Reich second. While their actions and beliefs are not condoned, they are examined and explained in a way which helps the viewer to better understand the reasons for both their outlook and behaviour. We even get to glimpse the more human side of the ostensible

3

villain of the piece, Sturmbannführer Kessler, through his relationship with his Belgian mistress, Madeleine. He may be the most hated and feared man of the Low Countries, but *Secret Army* nevertheless commendably strives to present him as a three-dimensional person rather than a well-worn stereotype in an SS uniform. The series's 'good guys', while clearly seeking an end to hostilities through incredibly daring and courageous acts, are not always above making morally questionable decisions themselves, and the much touted excuse of the continued security of the evasion line does not always convince. The motivation of the central Lifeline character, Albert Foiret, is particularly dubious and he is gradually revealed to be a lot less altruistic than he first appears. *Secret Army* positively revels in presenting uncomfortable and awkward truths and, as a rule, its situations and characters, rather than being black and white, more often than not exhibit shades of grey.

One of the principal reasons why *Secret Army* succeeds where other dramas fail is undoubtedly the strength of its ensemble cast. To name just a handful of the series's performers is to do something of a disservice to their fellow regular cast members, however Bernard Hepton, Angela Richards and Clifford Rose are widely acknowledged to be particularly outstanding in the roles with which they will forever be associated.

Another memorable component of the series is Robert Farnon's haunting theme music which, combined with Alan Jeapes's BAFTA-winning title sequence, is hugely atmospheric and sets the scene perfectly for the type of gripping edge-of-the-seat action which came to characterise the drama. Equally in keeping are the songs performed by Richards in the episodes themselves, many of which she also wrote and which, due to their frequent repetition, effectively become a soundtrack to the series. Glaister and series script editor and principal scriptwriter, John Brason, carefully refined *Secret*

© Henri Denis

Army's formula as it progressed, which is precisely why, unlike so many long-running British drama series, it improves series on series, offering increasingly accomplished episodes throughout its three-year run and ever-more rewarding character development. At times, such immense highs are achieved that it is difficult to imagine that such standards can possibly continue to be maintained, but maintained they are, and by the time *Secret Army* reaches its third and final series, set against the unbearably tense backdrop of the last few months of the German Occupation of Brussels, it is difficult to think of a better written, performed and constructed series than this. When the series finally bowed out on Saturday 15 December 1979, more than a third of the population of Britain tuned in to find out if reconciliation was possible between Albert and Monique and whether Kessler would be brought to justice.

© Viktors Ritelis

Although selected episodes from the second and third series of *Secret Army* were repeated in 1981, the same year in which its sequel *Kessler* was first broadcast, it has never received a complete repeat run on UK terrestrial television, possibly another side effect of *'Allo! 'Allo!*'s almost permanent presence in the schedules since 1982. Apart from a VHS release, exclusive to retailer WHSmith, which contained a selection of episodes, *Secret Army* did not again become available in the public domain until satellite channels like UK Gold had the good sense to dust off the drama, and from the mid-90s it (and latterly its sister channel UK Drama) regularly showed the series in its entirety, barring some edits – serious in places – due to pre-watershed time slots, for several years. *Secret Army* finally enjoyed a full and unedited release on DVD and VHS, in 2003-4, a move which prompted a notable revival of interest in the series and an overwhelmingly positive reappraisal of its merits online, in newspapers and magazines and in books on classic television. Perhaps the most glowing review to appear since its DVD release can be found in Sangster and Condon's comprehensive tome *TV Heaven*, in which the authors describe *Secret Army* as 'the single greatest popular drama series ever produced by the BBC,' adding that they would 'fight anyone who dares disagree'! Their words echoed those of Paul Cornell et al in the 1996 2nd edition of *The Guinness Book of Classic TV*, who chose to describe it as 'the best ever example of an on-going drama series', believing that since its broadcast 'it had lost little of its tension' and that 'the strength of the performances and the quality of much of the writing [was] still shining through.'[1] While this book was in preparation, interest was again reignited in late 2007 when digital channel UK TV History began the first of several re-runs of the series. The second run was so enthusiastically received that the channel also elected to clear *Kessler* for subsequent broadcast, in order to satisfy the number of requests for its transmission from new *Secret Army* devotees.

As well as providing reasons as to why *Secret Army* still enthralls and enchants viewers in equal measure, this book intends to provide an in-depth behind-the-scenes guide to all three series, documenting the production process and profiling the key figures responsible for its success both in front of and behind the camera. Alongside cast lists and episode synopses, it also offers thorough analysis and opinion of each and every one of the series's 42 episodes, as character development, production values, continuities, individual performances and emerging themes are all examined in some detail. The real-life people and historical events which inspired *Secret Army*'s rich and authentic storylines are also uncovered and outlined. The book is liberally sprinkled with interview testimony and trivia, new and old, from the series's cast and crew and illustrated with many of their photographs. There is also an extensive UK and Brussels location guide for use by the more intrepid reader who may want to follow in the footsteps of the characters themselves.

This book is no hagiography. Although it will be readily apparent that it is written by a long-term fan of the series, *The Complete Secret Army* nevertheless seeks to be a critical work and will not always be as reverential as might be expected. If you do find yourself disagreeing with certain opinions herein, particularly in the individual episode reviews, then take comfort in the fact that they are just that: opinions, and therefore entirely subjective.

Despite its critical pretensions, above all else this book is intended to be a celebration of a series which, although critically acclaimed, also, quite paradoxically, manages to be largely forgotten. If this work goes some way towards redressing this balance then it has done its job.

'It was the BBC's golden era.
What I regret is that no-one told me at the time.'

VIKTORS RITELIS

SERIES ONE
(1977)

REGULAR CAST

Albert Foiret
BERNARD HEPTON

Lisa 'Yvette' Colbert
JAN FRANCIS

Flt Lt John Curtis
CHRISTOPHER NEAME

Monique Duchamps
ANGELA RICHARDS

Sturmbannführer Ludwig Kessler
CLIFFORD ROSE

Major Erwin Brandt
MICHAEL CULVER

Natalie Chantrens
JULIET HAMMOND-HILL

Alain Muny
RON PEMBER

Dr Pascal Keldermans
VALENTINE DYALL

Andrée Foiret
EILEEN PAGE

Gaston Colbert
JAMES BREE

Louise Colbert
MARIA CHARLES

Jacques Bol
TIMOTHY MORAND

Corporal Veit Rennert
ROBIN LANGFORD

Yvonne
HENRIETTA BAYNES

CREW

Producer
GERARD GLAISTER

Script Editor
JOHN BRASON

Technical Advisor
GRP CPT WILLIAM RANDLE CBE AFC DFM

Writers
WILLIS HALL (1, 6, 11)
JOHN BRASON (2, 3, 14, 16)
ARDEN WINCH (4)
JAMES ANDREW HALL (5, 13)
N. J. CRISP (7, 8, 15)
ROBERT BARR (9)
SIMON MASTERS (10)
MICHAEL CHAPMAN (12)

Directors
KENNETH IVES (1, 6, 11, 12, 15)
VIKTORS RITELIS (2, 4, 9, 10, 13, 16)
PAUL ANNETT (3, 5, 7, 8, 14)

Designers
AUSTIN RUDDY (1, 3 - Studio, 4 - Studio, 11, 12, 15)
KEN LEDSHAM (1, 2, 6 - Studio, 9 - Film)
RAY LONDON (2, 6 - Film, 9 - Studio, 10 - Studio, 13, 16)
PETER BLACKER (3 - Film, 5, 7, 8, 14),
SUSAN SPENCE (4 - Film, 6 - Studio, 7, 8, 10 - Film)
JAMES HATCHARD (8)

Production Assistants
DEREK NELSON (1, 6, 11, 12, 15)
TONY VIRGO (2, 4, 9, 10)
RALPH WILTON (3, 5, 7, 8)
MICHAEL OWEN MORRIS (13, 16)
TERRY DEVANEY (14)

Production Unit Managers
FRANK PENDLEBURY (1-11, 14)
JOHN FABIAN (7, 12-16)

11

Costume Designer
ANDREW MACKENZIE

Make-Up Artists
JUDITH NEAME
DERRY HAWS

Film Cameramen
GODFREY JOHNSON (1-3, 5-9, 12, 16)
DAVID SOUTH (4, 10)
FRED HAMILTON (11)

Film Recordists
BASIL HARRIS (1-3, 5-9, 12, 16)
JOHN GATLAND (4, 10)
ALAN COOPER (11)

Film Editors
SHEILA S. TOMLINSON (1, 2, 4-10, 12, 16)
HOWARD BILLINGHAM (3)
GRAHAM DEAN (6)
RICHARD TREVOR (11)

Studio Lighting
ALAN HORNE (1-11)
PETER WINN (12-16)

Studio Sound
TREVOR WEBSTER (1-4, 9, 12-16)
JOHN HOWELL (5-8, 10)
MIKE JONES (11)

Videotape Editor
STEVE MURRAY (14)

Consultant
WILFRED GREATOREX

Title Design
ALAN JEAPES
MICHAEL SANDERS

Theme Music
ROBERT FARNON

'Memories Come Gently' composed by
ANGELA RICHARDS, LESLIE OSBORNE, NORMAN WARREN

SERIES 1 - PRODUCTION

'The contribution to the war effort made by the men and women who organised the escape lines was incalculable. This was their battle against the enemy who had invaded their country and like front line uniformed soldiers, many hundreds died in battle, seized by the Gestapo, the French Secret Police, or betrayed by collaborators amongst their countrymen. They were tortured, executed, or sent to concentration camps where many died slow deaths from starvation and constant ill treatment, but always when one was captured another took their place... These were the people who provided a lifeline for aircrew who came down in their country. It is their story that the series will tell...'

(Extract from a two-page document written by Gerry Glaister in 1976, outlining the proposed background for an idea for a new BBC TV series entitled *Life-Line*.)

Tremendous Possibilities

By 1976, Gerry Glaister, whose long career at the BBC had started back in 1957 when he left repertory theatre, was widely regarded as one of TV's most successful and influential producers. His recent critical successes had included the incredibly popular prisoner-of-war drama *Colditz*, created with Brian Degas, which ran for two series between 1972 and 1974 and was nominated for a BAFTA for Best Drama Series/Serial in 1973, and the addictive family business saga *The Brothers*, which he had devised with N. J. Crisp, and had become a

© Joan Glaister

regular fixture of Sunday night television from the early- to mid-Seventies. Both series were considered to be groundbreaking in different ways: *Colditz* because of its admirable realism, hard-hitting plots and sympathetic depiction of the castle's unnamed Kommandant, played by Bernard Hepton; *The Brothers* for storylines which were deemed scandalous and risqué at the time and for its examination of the changing face of UK business.

Glaister chose to follow this success with an idea which owed far more to *The Brothers* than to *Colditz*: the gritty North Sea drama *Oil Strike North*. Once again created with Crisp, Glaister spent two years researching and developing the programme which was eventually made in the first half of 1975. Unfortunately, when the series was aired in the autumn, it was not greeted with the same enthusiasm or acclaim as his previous productions and it was not recommissioned. It was shortly after this comparative failure that Glaister was asked by the BBC's then Head of Drama Series, Ronnie Marsh, if he had any further ideas for new series. Clearly keen to see Glaister create and produce a series as popular as *Colditz* had been, Marsh specifically wanted him to have a think "about something to do with the Second World War." Glaister, who had spent the war as an RAF pilot and had been decorated with the DFC (Distinguished Flying Cross) for his daring photo reconnaissance missions, was more than happy with the idea of returning to the wartime genre, especially as it would afford him the opportunity to draw upon his own experiences. He had first done this back in 1963 when he was one of two producers on the World War II

Location filming for *Moonstrike* in 1963
© Unknown

series *Moonstrike*. Created by Robert Barr, *Moonstrike* was based on the true stories of the missions of No. 161 Squadron, based at RAF Tempsford in Bedfordshire, whose pilots flew agents into and out of Occupied France via Lysander aircraft during full moon periods. A decade later, when producing the phenomenally successful *Colditz*, Glaister had been able to apply his knowledge of the mindset and behaviour of Allied servicemen. However, for *Life-Line*, his third wartime series, Glaister stated – when interviewed in 1977 – that he wanted to turn his attention from those men who had become prisoners of war to those who actually evaded capture, and given his own war career, specifically to the evasion of aircrew. Another difference to the *Colditz* format was his decision not to approach this new drama from the perspective of the Allied servicemen, but rather from that of the resistance operatives who helped them to escape, having always considered there to be "tremendous possibilities in a series dealing with the people who took the aircrew after they had bailed out."[1] He was particularly struck by the fact that these brave men and women had not been deterred by the fact that they faced certain death if they were discovered to be assisting evaders and that a staggering total of 3,500 servicemen – of which 2,803 were airmen – made it home because of their courageous actions.

Ronnie Marsh gave the 'green light' to Glaister's idea pretty much immediately, authorising him to start pre-production with a view to broadcast of the series the following year (1977). Unfortunately, as Glaister was a BBC employee who had come up with the concept while at TV Centre, an unfairly bureaucratic interpretation of policy by Marsh (which was undoubtedly motivated by a desire to cut costs) led to him being refused a creator credit for the series. It

14

was a decision which understandably angered Glaister (and which incidentally later enabled the BBC to go ahead with *'Allo! 'Allo!*, a turn of events which made him feel yet more aggrieved).

Initial Outline

After successfully pitching his idea, Glaister's first step was to produce an outline of the premise and scope of his new drama, which initially comprised an account of the work of the evasion lines. This document would be rewritten at a later date and the differences between the two versions are interesting for several reasons. For one thing, Glaister's original title for the series was *Life-Line*, a name he chose because it was about 'the people who provided a life-line to the aircrew who came down in their country.' However, as this earliest surviving document has the title *Life-Line* scribbled out, in favour of *The Secret Army* in Glaister's handwriting, it seems likely that this initial name did not last very long. Glaister would later tell *Radio Times* the reason why he settled on this new name: "We chose this title because, although these people were not a resistance group, they saw themselves as an army."[2] Another difference is the document's marked interest in how the evasion lines first came about due to the evacuation of Dunkirk and the subsequent assistance of the survivors ('They were given refuge by the ordinary people of the countries that had been overrun'), perhaps suggesting an original intention to begin the drama in 1940 rather than 1942.

Equally interesting is the very strong emphasis placed upon the role of women in the evasion lines, which would be somewhat played down in the later revision: 'Many of the bravest, cleverest and most able organisers were young attractive women. They were among the best guides. Their courage and physical stamina was outstanding.'

© Jan Olav Flatmark

Script Editor

As his ideas about the series became clearer, Glaister decided to recruit John Brason (right) to work alongside him as his script editor. Glaister knew Brason through his scripts for *Colditz*, which had arguably been among the best of the series. His episodes included the award-winning *Tweedledum*, which featured a BAFTA-nominated performance from Michael Bryant as a man who feigns insanity in order to get out of Colditz with terrible consequences, and the two-parter *Gone Away*, the memorable finale to the first series, in which Robert Wagner's and Jack Hedley's characters attempt to reach neutral Switzerland (which was later edited together to form the TV Movie *Escape from Colditz*). Since *Colditz*, he had written several episodes for the BBC's slow-moving sci-fi drama *Moonbase 3* (1973), a critically acclaimed 1974 episode of *Special Branch* (1969-74) about a cross-dressing hitman (featuring Tony Beckley and Jacqueline Pearce) entitled *Catherine the Great* and Yorkshire TV's high quality children's drama *Boy Dominic* (later just *Dominic*) (1974, 1976). Brason, who would also become *The Secret Army*'s principal scriptwriter, shared with Glaister a passion for television with broad appeal and a realistic approach to the business of broadcasting. When interviewed during the series's first month of production, he stated: "It is a commercial business, making television series. We're making them for a large section of the public, therefore it has to appeal to a large section of the public. We are making something which has to have by that very nature popular appeal. We're not writing for the eggheads."[3]

Randle and Dédée

Before progressing the scope and structure of the series any further, Glaister and Brason immersed themselves in available literature on the period and the evasion lines specifically. This was partly in order to understand what made these men

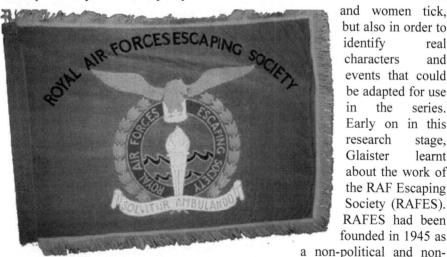

and women tick, but also in order to identify real characters and events that could be adapted for use in the series. Early on in this research stage, Glaister learnt about the work of the RAF Escaping Society (RAFES). RAFES had been founded in 1945 as a non-political and non-sectarian society which could offer financial support to surviving members of escape line organisations and to the dependants of those who died. In 1976, the Chairman of RAFES was former evader, Group Captain William (Bill) Randle

CBE AFC DFM.

Randle owed his life to the most successful escape organisation of them all, Comète (so called because of the speed by which it returned evaders home), and more specifically to its fearless founder and leader, the indomitable Andrée De Jongh, who preferred to go by the name Dédée. Between September and October 1942, Dédée escorted the 21-year-old Randle from Namur (where the photo to the right was taken of him), where he had taken refuge  for some time in a Carmelite monastery, to Brussels, where he was reunited with two of his missing crew members. From there, she took them on to Paris and then the long journey down to St Jean de Luz, via Biarritz. After guiding the group over the Pyrenees – with the assistance of legendary Basque guide Florentino – and into Spain, Dédée finally delivered them safely into the hands of the British Consul in San Sebastian.

Just three months later, Dédée was arrested by the Gestapo, having been caught red-handed with three RAF evaders at a farm in the foothills of the Pyrenees. Several Comète members planned to rescue her from the prison in Southern France where she was originally incarcerated, but the Germans moved her on before they had the chance to put the plan into action. During her subsequent interrogation in a Paris prison, she openly admitted that she was the leader of the entire evasion line. However, neither the Gestapo nor the Luftwaffe could credit an operation of the size and complexity of Comète to a woman, especially to one as young and diminutive as Dédée. Despite the loss of Dédée and later her father Frédéric (code name Paul) who was also an active member of the Line, and further terrible betrayals – notably by Jacques Desoubrie masquerading as Jean Masson – and arrests, the Line managed to stay in business until the Normandy landings effectively closed off the route they had established to Spain. In total, Comète delivered an incredible 800 airmen and soldiers to safety making an important contribution to the Allied victory in the process. Dédée would once again prove her redoubtable spirit by surviving the horrors of Ravensbrück concentration camp, and in 1946, after recovering from this ordeal, was awarded the George Medal, the highest award that can be given to a civilian in Great Britain. Dédée died in Brussels, aged 91, in October 2007. (Right: Dédée during WWII.)

Glaister was fascinated by Randle's evasion story and the exploits of Dédée and Comète, and realised that elements of both could be incorporated into *The Secret Army* to great dramatic effect. Aside from his familiarity with how the evasion lines operated, Glaister also recognised that the Group Captain's knowledge of RAF history – he was at that time attempting to revive the fortunes of the RAF Museum in Hendon and was a former Chairman of AI9 (the peacetime successor to MI9) – would also be of immense value to his new series. As a result, just as he had employed former prisoner Major Pat Reid on *Colditz*, in August 1976 Glaister asked Randle if he would consider becoming Technical Advisor on *The Secret Army*, in the first instance until May 1977. Randle, who waived all rights to a fee, agreed, despite the fact that his concurrent work for the RAF Museum dictated that he would have to work on the series at home in his spare time. (Above left: Bill Randle's return to the River Bidassoa in 1977, 35 years after he waded it with Dédée, Florentino and his fellow evaders, in order to cross from France into Spain.)

The Writers' Bible

After a further period of research, Glaister discussed with Brason the content of a 'Writers' Bible' for the series. A similar document had proved very useful when putting *Colditz* together and Glaister was therefore keen to have one for this new series. Glaister's original background piece, modified in line with decisions made regarding the direction, feel and scope of the series, opened the document. Several significant additions to the original text, which would all come to be reflected in the series itself, included: the fact that evasion lines became both organised and sophisticated; that they were 'led and inspired by spirited *men* and women'; and a single sentence stressing that the work in which they were involved was 'a nerve-testing game.' This latter interpolation undoubtedly arose from Glaister's desire to approach this new drama first and foremost as a tense thriller series. As well as being a devotee of the genre, Glaister, who especially admired the work of Alfred Hitchcock, had produced and directed several popular thriller serials such as *Wideawake* (1959) and *The Dark Island* (1962) in the early part of his TV career. Glaister clearly viewed *The Secret Army* as another opportunity to emulate Hitchcock's unrivalled control of pace and suspense. However, perhaps the most interesting change was that made to the original text's final sentence, which had stated that the series would tell the story of 'the people who provided a lifeline for the aircrew who came down in their country' and was altered to be far more inclusive and specific: 'It is this story – one of the escape organisers, their enemies on the Continent and their allies in Whitehall, as well as some of the evaders – that we shall be telling in *The Secret Army*.' This mention of Whitehall suggests that, initially at least, there was an intention to also depict the British side of the equation; however, as it would turn out, only the establishing episode would feature any London-based scenes.

A brand new paragraph at the end of this opening section revealed that, in lieu of using it as the series's title, the evasion line would be called Lifeline and, as with the Comète Line, it would begin in Brussels and be run by Belgians. This decision was apparently in keeping with the historical reality, which was tartly observed by Bill Randle in 2004: "There were no French escape routes because they couldn't trust each other! All the escape routes that mattered were Belgian."[4] The paragraph ended by describing the Line as having been started as early as 1940 and being 'a small-scale escape line' by the Spring of 1941, and by listing those working against Lifeline as Gestapo Unit XI, the Luftwaffe Special Police and the French and Belgian secret police. A final sentence, which it is clear from the larger typeface must be a late addition, states that the series's narrative would begin in 1942.

The remainder of the Writers' Bible is prefaced as 'Script Editor's Notes: background information and guides for writers'. However, it was by no means the product of John Brason alone. Brason certainly compiled the material, as Glaister by his own admission was not one for paperwork, but the latter nevertheless made a significant contribution to its content. Interviewed in 1977, Brason made it very apparent that Glaister was the man in charge, stating that he only put this document together after: "...having discussed it with the producer so that I am clear what he has in mind, because it is his series."[5] It is worth noting that Randle too had a hand in its content, on matters of historical background and accuracy.

A Few Basic Guidelines

The first two-page section of Brason's 'Script Editor's Notes', entitled 'A few basic guidelines for writers', provides such a firm steer on the series's tone, content and conventions that it is clear that he and Glaister were very certain by the time it was written of the elements which they wanted to come to characterise the series; however, as will later be revealed, it seems clear that the pair did not reach this point without going up a few blind alleys first.

One of the recurring themes of these statutes is a determination for writers to avoid obvious clichés. The very first guideline is that scripts should not contain 'overt heroics', because it was felt that 'the fact that these people [escape line agents] did what they did at all is heroic enough.' The guidelines also dispel the myth that all Belgians and French were patriots during wartime and that in fact many 'thoroughly disliked the British and didn't give a damn about 'the cause of freedom'.' However, it is noted that they 'didn't much like the Germans either'! Similarly dispelled is the myth that the German presence was ubiquitous in the countries they occupied, specifically the idea, propagated by many war films, that every road and bridge was patrolled by guards and that there were 'suspicious leather-clad Gestapo figures crouching in every shadow.' Instead it is made clear that: 'The German genius was to make conquered peoples police and subjugate themselves.' The guidelines are also intent on stressing that those Germans that were posted in occupied countries 'behaved as well as did the average Tommy' and that 'rape and pillage were not rife, nor was sadism part of the German character.' Further attempts to get away from a 'broad brush' approach are obvious in a paragraph about how the series would portray its opposing camps: 'Without going so far as to say "Whatever is the cliché – do the opposite," let us ensure that the 'goodies' are just as clumsy as the 'baddies' and that mistakes and gaffes are made.' Furthermore, the guidelines encourage the idea that the German characters could be made to appear more menacing than they otherwise might, by showing them to be as efficient as they really had been, and include the sobering thought that on the strength of this attribute they should have won the war.

The guidelines are also intent on conveying important details and practicalities that the writers needed to be aware of, such as the fact that evaders ate a great deal, that foodstuffs had to be sourced from the black market and that, given the numbers of evaders in transit, this was an expensive business. Less practical, but just as factual, is the interesting sociological observation that attitudes were less sophisticated at the time that the series is set than at the time of writing (1976) and that scripts should attempt to reflect this simplicity.

Some of the conventions and core principles of the series are also detailed here, such as the rule that the Lifeline personnel are to be considered by the writers to be the main characters, 'NOT the evaders,' and that violence could only 'be implied not shown' (unless there was an exceptional circumstance of such that was deemed vital to a plot, although it is stated that this would 'take some selling to the production'!). The guidelines are similarly prescriptive about the use of language in the series. Unlike *Colditz*, in which the leads (with the obvious exception of the Kommandant, Mohn and Ulmann) were all British, *The Secret Army* was set to feature main characters who were Belgian and therefore whose first languages were either French or Flemish. Glaister and Brason chose to deal with this issue by electing to have 'everyone speaking English regardless of nationality,' and as 'our principal characters (and therefore principal speakers) are Belgian we must have them deliver their lines 'straight'.' The only exceptions to this rule were the lead German characters who, as in *Colditz*, would be permitted to 'suggest an accent.'

One of the most illuminating guidelines concerns the tone which Glaister and Brason were seeking for the series: 'We would like to try and maintain a background sense of *A Family at War* in Occupied Europe, but these are people living in constant fear, and at this time largely without hope. The sense of claustrophobia should hang almost visibly over the whole thing.' *A Family at War* (1970-2) was a popular Granada Television drama series, created by John Finch, which ran for 52 hour-long episodes and centred on the lives and loves of the Liverpool-based Ashton family just before and during the Second World War. The idea that *The Secret Army*'s prospective writers should seek to emulate it, at least in part, suggests a desire to incorporate a strong and addictive running background story featuring the sort of well-drawn and carefully developed regular characters and relationships which had come to characterise the Granada drama. The main difference would be in that the troubles faced by the members of Lifeline would be considerably more threatening and distressing than those experienced by the Ashtons, simply by virtue of their direct involvement in evasion operations and their day-to-day existence in an occupied country. The sentence concerning almost visible claustrophobia once again hints at Hitchcockian overtones of all-pervading tension and suspense.

The final basic guideline given is an entirely practical directive regarding the typical make-up of an episode in terms of the ratio between telecine (location filming) and studio recording. In this regard, writers were requested to confine the former to only 10% of the episode's total runtime – a standard percentage for BBC dramas at the time.

The Line and its Safe-houses

A less vital, but nevertheless important element of the Script Editor's Notes is the extensive number of pages devoted to the exact geography of the series's evasion line. This was conveyed through a series of maps of Brussels, Belgium and France, together with text describing each distinct stage of the journey and descriptions of the (fictitious) safe-houses in operation along the route which could be utilised by writers in their scripts and provide 'occasional locales and recurring characters.' Despite the level of detail offered on this element of the series, it is interesting to note that, aside from Keldermans's surgery, only the Senlis and St Etienne safe-houses and their respective personnel would ever be

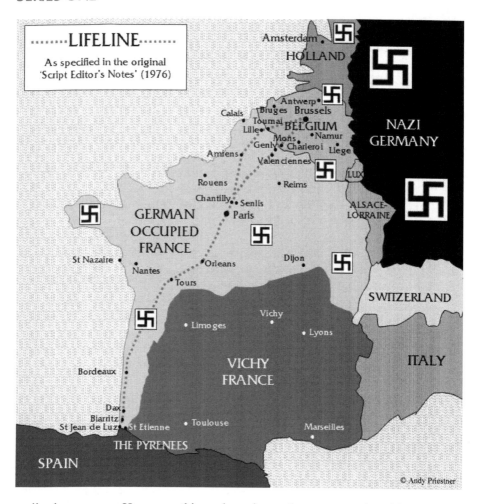

realised on-screen. However, this perhaps has rather more to do with Glaister's and Brason's decision to concentrate much more of the action in Brussels than was originally anticipated, than with an unwillingness of the series's writers to run with their suggestions. The 'Notes' also detail aspects of life within a safe-house, which Brason states 'should be noted (though they are largely common sense) and made use of to give the sense of authenticity that makes for good drama.' These notes included the facts that evaders walked around in socks or bare feet, that lavatories were flushed sparingly, cigarette butts were burned in the fireplace and that evaders ate ALL their food and that said food was selected so that no tell-tale leftovers such as bones could give outsiders clues to their presence in a safe-house.

Although Glaister always described Lifeline as being based upon a number of escape organisations not just one, in terms of its geography it nevertheless followed the same phenomenally successful route as that of the Comète Line:

from Brussels to the Spanish border via Paris and Biarritz. However, Brason details several modifications to the route in deference to dramatic and technical considerations. Rather than attempting to realise Paris on a BBC budget, he and Glaister wisely elected instead to locate a significant safe-house in Senlis, a town on the outskirts of the French capital. Brason explained this by stating: 'The aim was to take evaders expeditiously into and out of the capital without staying there if possible. French police and Gestapo checks in Paris were common and thorough. Provincial checks in Occupied France were not. It also makes filming in the UK much easier!' Brason also admitted that 'for purely filmic purposes,' the Lifeline route was adapted to include a tributary of the river Sambre nearer to the Franco-Belgian border than it actually was, in order that river-swimming/wading could be incorporated into the series's plots (ultimately, only one scene – in Series Two's *Little Old Lady* – would utilise this opportunity).

The Evader

The route established, the Script Editor's Notes next turn their attention to the evaders who Lifeline's agents would guide along its route. Once again, Brason, Glaister and Randle were keen to deliver the facts instead of the clichés: 85% of RAF evaders were Non-Commissioned Officers; most were 'very young, straight from grammar school, inexperienced in living therefore, and totally ignorant of the continent apart from what they had been taught in school;' and, more significantly in terms of prospective scripts, 'most were very frightened when shot down and took some time to calm down... then oddly enough, became rather blasé.' The 'Notes' also detail the 'collection routine':

   a) Attend to the medical needs of the evader
   b) Interrogate to prove authenticity (for which the onus was upon the evader)
   c) Escape training (to knock British mannerisms out of them)
   d) The actual escape

However, the point which is made most emphatically is that 'despite the obvious fact that a fully-trained air-crew man was immensely valuable to the British forces and should be returned as soon as possible, priorities showed beyond any question that the escape guide was infinitely more valuable and many evaders would be sacrificed to save one guide,' and furthermore that once they had discarded their uniform and adopted a new identity, then they were 'no longer a serviceman with the protection of the Geneva convention' and could therefore be shot as a spy.

Some general notes on escape lines and considerable background information on the situation in Holland and France, but curiously not Belgium, follow, together with: a 10-page chronology of the war comparing major events, events in occupied countries, activities of the French Resistance and those of Resistance in other countries, photocopied from an uncredited source; the routine of a wireless operator; basic information received by RAF servicemen on evasion; and the contents of their 'escape kits'.

Running Characters

Easily the most interesting remaining sections of the document are those dealing with the series's principal – consistently referred to as 'running' – characters, detailing their motives, outlook and traits, and the anticipated 'general running background' of the first series. For the most part, these sections describe the characters and situations almost exactly as they transferred to the broadcast episodes. However, there are several interesting exceptions which deserve mention.

Lisa Colbert (Yvette)

From an early stage, due to their fascination with the real-life leader of the Comète Line, Andrée De Jongh, code name Dédée, Glaister and Brason were set on having a female character running Lifeline, naming her Lisa Colbert, code name Yvette. Unlike Dédée, it was decided to give Lisa a more explicit motive for her patriotism and bravery, namely the deaths of her loved ones during the German invasion of Belgium in May 1940. However, it was decided that this incident would not be dwelt upon in the series in any great depth.

YVETTE (code name)

Real name: LISA COLBERT
Age: 23/4

- Father, mother and sole boyfriend Pieter, killed in German advance. Now lives with Gaston and wife in Brussels.
- Born in Opteren, near frontier. Mining area.
- Profession: Schoolteacher.
- Is registered as nurse to Dr Keldermans (but seldom performs any duties) which makes it possible for her not to be drafted into other activities or German labour forces.
- Her motives in running Lifeline are not clear... partially personal, partially patriotic, NOT political.
- Reluctant to involve herself emotionally with anyone after the harrowing loss of those dear to her in one shock moment.
- Will not relinquish any sovereignty in Lifeline to Curtis or anyone.

In his *Secret Army* novel (published on 17 November 1977), which serves as a prequel to the first series, John Brason fleshes out Lisa's back story and motivation further. Therein he relates her quiet pre-invasion existence in the town of Biem, the sudden death of her boyfriend, 27-year-old Pieter Coecke, and her parents, and her subsequent experiences as a refugee in the town of St Truiden and the loss to the Germans of two people who gave her shelter there, café owner – Eulalie Moreelse and cripple Pieter Pynas. It is these latter events in particular that are presented as the primary catalyst for her subsequent actions: 'Something was changing inside Lisa. She no longer merely accepted, meekly and fearfully. A hidden steel was quietly being bared. This further affront and pain in the loss of Eulalie and Pieter Pynas was too much. The reaction inside her was fermenting, waiting only for the moment when hate could find outlet in positive action.'[6] This moment comes when Lisa is petitioned for help by an RAF navigator on the run, Sergeant Tom Wetherby, and she decides to help him. The novel goes on to explain Lisa's decision to live with her Uncle Gaston and Aunt Louise in Brussels so that she can use it as a base from which to take further evaders down to Spain; her subsequent discovery that Gaston is also engaged in resistance work; and her introduction (via Gaston) to Albert Foiret. It is during her first meeting with Albert that Lisa explains – in a speech that pulls no punches – why she feels that patriotism is not enough of a motivation for her resistance work: 'For me it has to be deep-rooted hatred of the German and everything his disgusting regime stands for. Preferably a personal hatred, with scars that even time cannot heal. I want people who can kill those beasts with their bare hands if necessary, and have the courage to kill their own friends and neighbours if there is danger of betrayal.'[7] It is a speech which surprises Albert and prompts him to join forces with her, and so Lifeline is effectively born.

Frédéric and Andrée De Jongh

Throughout the novel Brason describes Lisa as pretty and petite, a fact which also suggests direct inspiration from Dédée and which Glaister would keep in mind when it came to casting the part. A further piece of background information on Lisa is offered by the identity card for her character, which was produced for use in the series itself and for pre-broadcast publicity. This reveals that she was born on 14 August 1918, making her 23 when the series begins, that she lives at No. 17 Chaussée de St Jean Baptiste (the home of her aunt and uncle) and that as a nurse she specialises in physiotherapy.

Albert Foiret

Glaister and Brason settled upon restaurateur Albert Foiret as the series's lead male character. Although he is an undeniably more unique creation than Lisa, enjoying no direct parallel with any real-life person, in his protectiveness towards her there are shades of Frédéric De Jongh's relationship with his daughter, while his status as restaurant proprietor brings another Brussels-based hero of the Comète Line to mind: Baron Jean Greindl (code name Nemo) of the Swedish Canteen. However, their characters are quite different, especially in terms of their respective selflessness.

ALBERT FOIRET

Age: 47/8

- Proprietor (full owner) of Restaurant Candide (bistro).
- The most responsible (after Yvette) for Lifeline. His job gives him curfew privileges, enemy contacts, and a glossed-over right to participate in black market offerings.
- Has a reluctant loyalty to his invalid and bitter wife, a curious sort of compassion for her and a deep sense of guilt about his relationship with his mistress. Over the years his wife's bitterness and bitchiness has soured that regard but he remains loyal.
- Though not cast in any special heroic mould, he is probably the most courageous, the toughest, and most responsible member of the Line after Yvette.
- His motives are purely patriotic and anti-German.

What is striking about this description is the statement that Albert's motives are purely patriotic and anti-German. While this may be true of the Albert we first meet, as the series progresses it becomes abundantly clear that his motives have become far more self-serving than patriotic. His description as second to Lisa in terms of toughness and courage is also notable. Although Lisa is presented as surprisingly tough and cold-hearted on occasion, Albert is shown to be infinitely more ruthless and prone to seemingly callous expedient action. Similarly interesting is Albert's description as the undisputed number two in terms of the Lifeline hierarchy, especially given his superior leadership qualities. As the first series progresses this line of command becomes somewhat blurred, particularly when yet another natural leader, Curtis, is added into the mix and it becomes clear that there are 'too many chiefs and not enough indians'. This situation effectively compromises Lisa's position as Lifeline's sole leader and has occasionally been criticised as a chauvinistic development that was at odds with historical reality. One surprising omission from this initial description of Albert is his tendency towards miserliness, a trait which sees him consistently put business, namely his restaurant, before anything else.

Albert's ID card gives his place of birth as Brussels and his date of birth as 15 December 1895, making him 47 at the start of the series. It gives his address as Café Candide (although the establishment is in fact called 'Le Restaurant Candide'), 9 Rue Deschanel, Brussels.

Monique Duchamps

In an attempt to increase the tension of the series further, on a more personal level, and in line with the intention to emulate the feel of *A Family at War*, Glaister and Brason elected to incorporate a tried-and-tested dramatic standard into the series: a 'love triangle'. The unhappily married Albert would be this love triangle's somewhat unlikely object of affection, while his invalid wife Andrée and the character of Monique Duchamps, the Candide's barmaid, would be the women vying for his attention. Monique's involvement in this plotline aside, it was also decided that she should fulfil the function of an 'everyman' (in fact 'everywoman') character in the ongoing narrative, offering a way in to the series in the sense that she would be the person with whom the audience would sympathise the most, both in terms of her unsatisfactory relationship with Albert and her instinctive reactions to such unconscionable incidents as expedient murder.

MONIQUE DUCHAMPS

Age: 28/30

- Native of Brussels. Highly attractive barmaid... the main attraction at the bistro, but her free-and-easy manner belies her character.
- She is totally true to Albert whom she adores.
- Though sometimes irritated by Albert's refusal to do anything about their relationship, she still continues as his mistress and puts up with Andrée's bitter and twisted harangues.
- She knows the sort of man she has, and genuinely respects and admires him.
- She is very female (as opposed to feminine)... something of the young Signoret...

In his prequel novel, Brason gives further details about Monique's relationship with Albert, revealing how they first met when she began work as a barmaid at his previous establishment, the 'tiny Chanterelle' in the 'tatty Boulevard Maeterlinck' in 1934 (by which time Andrée was already an invalid): 'After the initial intimacy Monique had assumed Albert would 'forget' her, but he hadn't. The relationship remained – clandestine and unlovely – until Monique packed her bags one Saturday and simply left.' Brason goes on to relate how, just prior to the Occupation, Albert bought the Candide, and after he became involved in Lifeline 'sought out Monique and asked her to come back to him' because he 'needed a barmaid whom he could trust totally.' Unfortunately this sequence of events is not followed strictly throughout the series and it is stated at one point that Monique and Albert first met when she came into the Candide one day. Brason's novel also seeks to explain why Monique subsequently resumed her relationship with Albert despite the fact that she recognises that he is 'nobody's idea of Adonis.' The reason given is that Monique believes that the war and his evasion line work has wrought a change in Albert, bringing out and developing a side of his character that otherwise might have 'remained unknown': 'Albert showed command, strength, courage and sheer manliness that awoke the remainder of Monique to his sexual advances, and they became lovers in a way that they had not hitherto.'[8]

It is interesting that Monique's character sketch in the 'Writers' Bible' tells us nothing about how she fits into the work of Lifeline, suggesting either that this had yet to be determined, or alternatively that it was not important enough to be detailed. Either way this fits in with the rather haphazard depiction of her role in the opening half of the first series. However, in his novel Brason is explicit about her function within Lifeline, when during Lisa's first meeting with her, she declares: 'You will help *me* Monique. I need someone I can rely upon to act as liaison within the group. Someone who can move about easily, and at the same time have sound reason to remain here and hold the fort at all times.'[9]

The description of Monique as having 'something of the young Signoret' about her is the only hint that we have of a specific inspiration for her character. Simone Signoret (1921-1985) was a French Jew who became an Academy Award winning actress. During the Occupation, the young Signoret (left) hung out with a group of bohemian writers and actors who met at the Café De Flore in the Saint-Germain-des-Pres quarter of Paris. It was during this period in her life that she decided to become an actress. Another possible inspiration for Monique was the fearless real-life Comète agent, Elvire de Greef, code-name Tante Go, a Belgian woman who successfully operated in the South of France throughout the war. In his book about Dédée and Comète, *Little Cyclone*, Airey Neave described Elvire as 'a strong and vital character' who 'looked at the most 35' and showed her finest qualities when facing bitter disaster.[10]

Monique's ID card gives her middle name as Alice, her place of birth as Alost and her date of birth as 4 March 1907, which would make her 34 at the start of the series and therefore several years older than the age given in her initial description. This difference that can be explained by the fact that the ID cards were produced after the parts had been cast and that the actress chosen to play Monique was a little older than was originally anticipated.

John Curtis

Originally named Royce, the character of RAF liaison man, Flight Lieutenant John Curtis, whose presence in Brussels would provoke much antagonism and mistrust from members of Lifeline was devised in particularly close conjunction with Series Advisor, Group Captain Bill Randle. Curtis's fake identity was based directly on the cover given to Randle during his evasion: that of a commercial traveller (a reserved occupation) with responsibilities for Belgium, France and Switzerland, who could therefore travel easily around Western Europe. The only difference was the name used: Randle's cover name being André de Vougelaar, Curtis's being Monsieur Moreelse (which incidentally was also the surname Brason gave to the woman who first helps Lisa in his *Secret Army* novel).

FLIGHT LIEUTENANT JOHN CURTIS

Age: 28/30

- Has a flair for languages, specialising in French which he perfected during exchange 'pen-pal' visits prior to the war.
- Quick-thinking, initially extrovert, and sharp-eyed, he is potentially suited to his task.
- After his initial experience as a shot-down pilot (almost completed first tour of operation), he makes himself eminently suitable for 'field' operations within Occupied Europe. Is sent back to Belgium as liaison-man between the evasion lines and London (MI9)... also acts as paymaster and trouble-shooter for London.
- His influence and effort is responsible for making the individual evasion lines cooperate with each other... and for making sure the Resistance movements do not interfere with evasion.
- Dating from his own evasion Curtis has a subdued and unstated yen for Yvette. He never comes out with it, and it comes to nothing but she is perhaps aware of the interest and will not permit herself to reciprocate.
- His purposes (directed by London) he does not communicate to anyone. He remains for a long time, highly suspect to the evasion lines.
- His uncommunicativeness and his peripheral involvement with Lifeline's activities give him the position within the group of the 'mysterious lodger'. Whenever he has consolidated his position with them something goes awry and the suspicion is renewed.
- He learns quickly... but he commences the role as a comparative novice and makes many mistakes... eventually he becomes competent and ruthless.
- He operates in Belgium. A travelling representative of the Boutts Chemical Industries of Antwerp (specialising in fertilisers).

It is clear from the above description that the function that Curtis would fulfil in the series was planned in more detail than that of any other character. Aside from the aforementioned links with Randle, it is possible that the production team also drew upon the wartime role of MI9 agent Airey Neave (right), who after escaping from Colditz and returning to England was recruited by MI9, sent on field operations in Occupied Europe and charged with the task of aiding the evasion lines. It seems all the more likely that they had Neave in mind when you consider that the actor cast as Curtis, Christopher Neame, had previously played a British character (Player) in Glaister's *Colditz* who escaped from the castle during a theatrical production just as

Neave had done. Neame and Neave therefore link the two characters.

Contrary to the above description, Curtis's 'yen for Yvette' does not remain unstated for very long at all and she becomes painfully aware of his attentions. Similarly, although it 'comes to nothing' for a considerable amount of time, a change of heart on the part of the production team ensured that his advances were finally reciprocated in the last episode of the first series. There is evidence from the 'Running Background' section of the 'Writer's Bible' that one of the reasons why so much detail is provided on Curtis is that Glaister and Brason were concerned that his function would not be clear to viewers, especially as the decision had already been taken not to have the series return to the UK after the first episode (as this would mean 'introducing new characters and a whole new can of beans in MI9'), hence the decision to spell it out even more explicitly to the writers via another page of notes:

'Royce [Curtis] has become one of 'our men in Europe' with particular responsibility for escape-lines. His function is therefore:

1) To act as paymaster towards the evasion line operatives.

    a) performed by physically taking cash from the UK to outlets.

    b) added to by arranging the funding via Allied interests blocked in Europe and deviously transferred into the pipeline.

    c) checked by keeping careful tabs on possible misappropriations of funds.

2) To act as liaison officer between various independently run evasion lines, and organising the inter-switching at crisis periods as the war progresses and the Gestapo, etc., become more efficient.

3) To endeavour to urge London-based control of the entire operations system.

4) To assist in any way, as and when requested.

5) To ensure that SOE (Special Operations Executive) and other organisations do not usurp and misuse the evasion lines for extraneous purposes.

These notes go on to explain that 'in effect only 1) and 2) are actually carried out without positive hindrance. 3) is steadfastly refused by most evasion line organisations, especially Lifeline. While 4) can only prove difficult without inviting 3) and 5) and is avoided wherever possible.' It is also made clear that it is only because of his 'personality and affection for Yvette' that any of the above strategies are at all possible and that there is a 'deep and running basis for friction' between Curtis and the escape lines.

Further information was prepared for Curtis relating to his background in England, which revealed that his middle name was Maitland (which was his mother Nora's maiden name), his RAF No. was 013727, that he was born in Leeds on 22 July 1911 (making him 31 at the start of the series), that his religion is Church of England and that his mother lives at 34 Newsome Rise, Leeds.

Natalie Chantrens

Just as Dédée could not possibly have operated as Comète's only guide, the production team decided that Yvette should be likewise joined in her dangerous work by another young female guide: Natalie Chantrens. Natalie was not directly inspired by any one real-life person, instead she was an amalgam of several celebrated Comète guides: Elsie Marechal who regarded Dédée with the deepest admiration; Peggy Van Lier who assisted Nemo in Brussels; and the impulsive Micheline Dumont, known as 'Michou', who kept the Line running long after Dédée was imprisoned by the Germans. In his novel, Brason details

Yvette's first encounter with Natalie at the Candide, when she recruits the young girl to her cause: 'You and I will be the principal guides. We will take the evaders down the Line from safe-house to safe-house. We will act as Guardian Angels right from Brussels down through Paris, to the Pyrenees, and if necessary take them over to Spain. You and I alone will know the entire route... that way there is maximum security.'[11]

NATALIE CHANTRENS

Age: 18/19

- Young, petite, with all youth's penchant for adventure and danger per se.
- Inclined to militancy.
- She is Yvette's left hand (Albert being the right hand).
- Cool, courageous and unaffected by violence and death. She has no qualms about killing... nor does she enjoy it... it just simply 'is'.
- Relationship with Yvette is close and very fond... which eventually becomes an embarrassment to her (second series) when Yvette returns from prison to find the Line has changed to a political leftist organisation.

What is most striking about this initial character sketch is the confidence felt by the production team that there would be a second series even before scripts had been written for the first! This plan to have Yvette imprisoned from a point in the first series, only to return in the second series to discover that Natalie had changed the Line immeasurably in the interim was dropped, not because of the decision to write Lisa out of the series (which came much later), but because it was decided to take Natalie in a different direction altogether. Ironically, Natalie would later be presented as the most fervently anti-Communist member of Lifeline and the threat of a leftist takeover would be levelled by a different character entirely.

31

Originally envisaged as equally petite as Lisa, after the part was cast, Natalie would become more statuesque and be a little older than first anticipated. When Brason introduces Natalie in his novel, he clearly does so after Juliet Hammond-Hill had been confirmed in the part: 'Her touch of Central Asian physiognomy, was highly attractive. Not that her look was in any way oriental. It wasn't. Just a certain something about the shape of the face, and above all the eyes, hinted at the fabled Circassian.' He goes on to suggest that: 'Many a young man had bit the dust thanks to those eyes, and many an older one had prayed for rejuvenation when held momentarily in their steady gaze... neither arch nor impertinent but promising, with a touch of mockery.'[12] When casting the part, a notable exception was made to the rule about the Lifeline regulars delivering their lines 'straight' without a continental accent. Hammond-Hill would be permitted to use her natural French accent, although strangely enough it was decided that her character should be of Dutch origin rather than French.

Erwin Brandt

Like Yvette, Major Erwin Brandt of the Luftwaffe Polizei was a character who was based, at least in part, on a specific real-life figure: Hanns Joachim Scharff.

 Scharff (left), who interrogated downed RAF men in Frankfurt rather than Brussels, was described by his former captives as a genial, clever man who believed that a man could resist brutality more easily than he can resist kindness and who, as a result of this belief, extricated at least one piece of information from every prisoner he interrogated, whether or not the man realised it. Scharff would apparently think nothing of taking his interrogation subjects from solitary confinement to civilian restaurants for dinner or for an afternoon of swimming at Frankfurt's public pool. In so doing he often had to spirit men out of the hands of the Gestapo and into his own. After Germany's defeat, Scharff, who moved to Los Angeles, understandably played up his techniques as only a matter of kindness; nevertheless he was regarded as one of the most effective interrogators of the war and the information he retrieved would of course have contributed to Germany's war effort. In Scharff, Glaister and Brason had found exactly what they wanted their Luftwaffe character to be: a figure that was a direct contrast to the well-worn stereotype of the brutal Nazi interrogator.

ERWIN BRANDT

Age: 35

- Rank: Major (Luftwaffe). Old school in general and political convictions. No supreme supporter of extreme Nazism, but reluctantly approving of Hitler's achievements for Germany.

- Father ex-Navy and personal friend of Admiral Canaris (Head of Abwehr).
- Now incapacitated from flying by injury taken over England in 1940.
- Though disillusioned about the war, he is, so far, loyal to Germany. Later (second series) he conceives it his duty to act against the Nazi regime and becomes involved with Canaris in an anti-Hitler plot.
- Gentlemanly, intelligent, but tough and unemotional, he devises most of the intelligent ideas to catch evaders.
- He despises (and fears, though not personally) the Gestapo and has a continuous 'duel of wits' with Kessler. He cannot accept the Gestapo's torturing methods and will go to considerable risks (to his career) to extract RAF personnel from Kessler's clutches.
- Married. Two children.

Although Scharff's character forms a significant element of this character sketch, in Brandt the production team elected to develop a more complex individual who, unlike the allegedly cheerful Scharff, would be a troubled man who would continually question his loyalties to the Reich and who would be locked in direct combat with his Gestapo counterpart in Brussels due to his moral and political convictions.

As with Natalie's sketch, there is also a confident assertion here that there will be a second series, which would see Brandt finally throw in his hand with the anti-Hitler plotters. However, once again, by the time the second series came around, the production team would have revised this plotline somewhat. Also waiting for Series Two to come around would be Brandt's (as yet unnamed) wife, a conscious decision having been made that there was not room for her in the already over-populated first series.

Brason's novel provides further interesting background on Brandt, revealing how flying had been his life since he was a boy, how he first learned to fly at a gliding club near Wuppertal and, when the Luftwaffe was born, then transferred painlessly to single-engine monoplanes. It also charts his disenchantment with the new Germany, how his 'mind revolted against the Blitzkreig tactics,' and how Admiral Canaris, who 'vehemently disliked the Nazis and everything they stood for,' took him under his wing after his father's death, prompting him to perceive the cracks in the surface of the Nazi regime. Nevertheless it also presents the fact that everybody likes to be on the winning side and that Brandt was no exception and, despite his misgivings, 'felt the surge of power and triumph as Germany swept all before it.' The injury which permanently grounded him took place six weeks after the Battle of Britain, when he came too near to an anti-aircraft burst: 'The blast had not only crippled his plane and forced an immediate return to base, it had given him substantial head injuries and shattered his right eardrum.' The narrative goes on to relate that as well as all the medals he had been awarded, 'he also had a scarred mind that was no longer at peace with his conscience,' and that this was his mental state when he received his posting as General Staff Officer in Brussels.[13]

It is possible that the surname Brandt was chosen due to one Colonel Heinz Brandt, an officer who lost his life during the 20 July 1944 Hitler bomb plot. Col. Brandt reportedly moved the briefcase containing Stauffenberg's bomb further away from the Führer in order to get a better look at a map that was under discussion at the time, and inadvertently saved Hitler's life in the process. However, Col. Brandt himself had died in the explosion. He had previously become unknowingly involved in another plot to assassinate Hitler in March 1943, when he had carried a bomb disguised as a bottle of brandy onto the Führer's plane – a bomb which failed to detonate.

Ludwig Kessler

Although Brandt would pose a serious threat to Lifeline, it was loyal Nazi, Sturmbannführer Ludwig Kessler, who Glaister and Brason would fashion as the ostensible villain of the piece. Although they had little choice but to give Kessler some unavoidably Nazi characteristics, nevertheless they were both keen to ensure that he did not become too much of an obvious stereotype (e.g. he was not going to be portrayed as a sadist). One aspect of his character that appears in the initial character sketch but was quickly dropped was a suggestion of homosexuality, perhaps because this too was considered to be a somewhat clichéd Nazi officer trait.

LUDWIG KESSLER

Age: Early thirties

- Rank: Major (Gestapo). His high (for Gestapo) rank is due to service with the SD (and a part in the Gleiwitz raid in 1939).
- Kessler is a survivor (within the Nazi party as well as everyday life). He stepped neatly from SD into Gestapo.
- He is quite soft-spoken, not a sadist in any overt sense, not highly intelligent or cultured, but has a basic shrewdness which carries him through.
- His dislike of Brandt is more a dislike of what he stands for (establishment, upper-class, gentlemanliness) which admits his own inferiority complex.
- Quiet and unassuming out-of-office, he is ruthless, hard and petty within his job.
- There is a shadowy side to Kessler's nature which hints at perversion, possibly of a homosexual nature. Not very much is to be made of this aspect… but the hint of it might be present. (In any event the actor cast for the part will hopefully be subtle about the inference).
- Normally dressed in civvies…he will wear his rank in SS uniform when called to formal occasions, and if he ever needs to make an impression.
- NOTE: Gestapo rarely needed to pull rank on ANYONE. A Gestapo Sergeant could interrogate and detain a Wehrmacht General without the interference of rank or position.

Although not based on any one historical figure, two names have been regularly cited as the possible inspiration for Kessler: Sturmbannführer Ernst Ehlers who was the Head of Gestapo in Brussels, and Obersturmführer Kurt Asche, his subordinate who headed up the Gestapo's 'Jewish Section' there. In his book *The German Occupation of Belgium 1940-1944*, Werner Warmbrunn profiles the latter: 'Asche was a self-educated man without completed secondary education who had worked in a drugstore before joining the S.A. in 1931. He was a fanatical anti-Semite and participated in the Kristallnacht action of November 1938. He had been a member of the Special SS Task Forces (Einsatzgruppen) in Poland since 1939 and arrived in Brussels at the end of 1940.'[14] The main difference between Kessler and Asche is the fact that Kessler is never presented as an anti-Semite – in fact in *Kessler*, at a point at which he has no reason to lie, he tells Mical and Bauer that he has never had anything against the Jews – although of course, as Head of Gestapo, he did comply with the unconscionable deportation of Jews from the Low Countries to death camps in Eastern Europe. The reason why Ehlers has been linked with Kessler is probably nothing more than the fact that he too was the Head of Gestapo in Brussels. However, it is interesting to note that, like Kessler, Ehlers and Asche were also brought to justice at the start of the Eighties. While Ehlers committed suicide on the eve of his trial, Asche was tried and sentenced to seven years in prison. The fact that Clifford Rose, the actor who came to play Kessler, does not recall that he was based on any particular figure, with neither the names Asche nor Ehlers sounding familiar to him, suggests that Kessler was instead a composite character boasting both Nazi attributes and unique characteristics of his own.

In the above character summary and Brason's novel, we learn that Kessler had a hand in the Gleiwitz raid. Taking place on 31 August 1939, this incident saw German operatives, masquerading as anti-German Polish saboteurs, seize and broadcast from the Gleiwitz radio station in Upper Silesia, near the German border with Poland. Twenty other staged incidents took place along the border at the same time, in order to give the impression of Polish aggression against Germany. These staged attacks, dubbed 'Operation Himmler', were used to justify the German invasion of Poland which took place the very next day. In his novel, Brason describes how Kessler was the last to leave the Gleiwitz radio station: 'Schanführer Ludwig Kessler glanced around the entrance and the small area inside the wire perimeter. Three men wearing Polish uniforms were lying dead, judiciously placed to give credence to the raid... he bent over the one by the gate and rearranged him to one side. He thought that the corpse looked excessively stiff for someone newly dead, but after all it was not his province. He'd done his job, and quite enjoyed the doing of it.'[15] It is also clear from the novel that Kessler's loyalty to the Nazi party goes back as far as 'the early days in Munich.'[16]

Kessler's appointment to the position of Head of Gestapo in Brussels is detailed in the novel through his meetings with key players in the Nazi regime such as Reichsführer Himmler and Admiral Canaris. These set pieces define

Kessler's character further (Himmler: "You have a natural grasp of priorities"[17]; 'Kessler's muscles were housed between his ears, and they were formidable.'[18]), and set up the series-long rivalry between the Gestapo and the Luftwaffe Polizei as played out between Kessler and Brandt (and later Reinhardt) with Himmler telling Kessler: "For the moment you will work alongside the Luftwaffe police without authority over them," quickly adding: "Eventually it may be necessary to eliminate any interference" and that "Brandt's loyalties are suspect, but as yet there is no evidence against them."[19] Certain passages hint at a Nazistic take on racial purity: he observes children at play in Berlin 'with the desired features of a Hitlerknabe,'[20] while others suggest a rather limited existence: 'He neither smoked nor drank in excess – though he did both. He had no dependents, no hobbies, no specific interests outside his work. He had neither fiancée nor mistress. He was in fact alone, and cocooned in his job. The State was his family, and its purposes his purposes.'[21] Incidentally, it was precisely these limitations which would later encourage Glaister to elect to broaden Kessler's horizons for fear that the character might end up becoming two-dimensional. The novel closes as Kessler arrives in Brussels in secret in order to acclimatise to the city, but also to ensure that his new colleagues are subjected to 'his most cherished weapons': 'fear and surprise', as he prepares to remould and reshape the German regime, particularly in respect of the troublesome evasion lines, in the Belgian capital.[22]

It is possible that Glaister decided to name the character Kessler as he had previously used it for another villain, played by Edward Brooks, in his children's adventure serial *The Long Chase* (1972).

Alain Muny

Radio operators were crucial members of escape organisations as their difficult and dangerous work directly affected their ongoing operation and security. In *The Secret Army* it was decided that this role would be filled by a patriotic working class farmer named Alain Muny.

ALAIN MUNY

Age: 52/54

- Farm worker with his own share in a family farm (one fifth).
- Is the radio operator for Lifeline… and has so far evaded all detection.
- Overt sense of humour and given to joking and general light spirits… but totally reliable.
- Unmarried.

Originally intended to be unmarried, Alain would eventually be given a wife, Estelle, and two children, whose young ages suggested that he had married late in life. The idea of presenting him as a farm worker rather than farm owner was similarly shelved. It is likely that he was initially conceived as the latter in order to explain why he was able to spend so much time engaged on Lifeline business. As it is, in the series itself, his regular abandonment of his own farm remains unexplained until the introduction (in the second series) of Gil Muny, his live-in younger brother, who has apparently taken on the day-to-day operation of the farm. It is interesting to note that Alain's planned 'overt sense of humour' is perhaps not quite as overt as it was originally intended to be, although his wit is indeed employed to alleviate the occasional tense scene.

In Brason's novel, Alain is introduced when Lisa makes her very first visit to the Candide and she orders him (and Jacques Bol) to sever all their connections with other resistance groups: "Once we are operational there will be no time for divided loyalties, and no time to hold up our own progress while you run about doing sabotage that does little good and equally little damage." Although he is initially reluctant to function as a radio operator only ("Well I don't know…"), Lisa characteristically ignores him and assumes his agreement.[23]

Although it is not specified in the Script Editor's Notes, Brason and Glaister decided that Alain, like Natalie and several other 'supporting' characters, would not appear in every single episode of the first series.

Gaston Colbert

As well as fulfilling the important plot function of introducing his niece to Albert Foiret and therefore giving birth to Lifeline (depicted in Brason's prequel novel, not in the series itself), Gaston also serves as the evasion line's chief forger. However, perhaps more significantly, Gaston would become the first regular character to suffer a tragic exit from the series. The production team planned Gaston's demise from the outset, partly in order to flag up the possibility that the series's regulars might not always survive to fight another day, but also to make it clear that the work in which Lifeline's agents are engaged is very perilous indeed.

GASTON FREDERIC COLBERT

Age: 52/56

- Assistant bank manager. A mild, short-sighted man of courteous manners and kindness.
- Well-liked and respected in both place-of-work and the community.
- His friends and acquaintances are generally well-placed… hence his ability to act as go-between and obtain documents, ration cards, identity cards, curfew-permits, or blank forms when necessary.
- He does what he does out of simple patriotism and concern for his niece, Yvette.
- He is slightly timorous and nervous, but courageous when put to it.
- He is 'tumbled' and eventually executed.

In his prequel novel, Brason filled in some more background detail on Gaston and his wife, Louise, relating that they had lived at No. 17 Chaussée de St Jean

Baptiste, Ixelles, for twenty-two years, ever since Gaston took his position at the Brussels Bank and that they previously lived in Liege.

Although wise, Gaston would also display a naïve streak. In the novel, Brason depicts him as determined to continue with his resistance activity but totally unprepared for the approach to the work advocated by the much tougher Lisa and Albert. He is horrified by a speech she makes on first meeting the restaurateur, about "killing friends and neighbours if necessary" if there is a danger of betrayal: 'Gaston's face was one of mild horror and pity.'[24]

Louise Colbert

Gaston's wife, Louise, was conceived as an eternal worrier, whose fears for her husband and niece would eventually be seen to be perfectly reasonable, if profoundly irritating. She would be set to vocalise her fears so often that her husband's eventual downfall would come to feel almost inevitable.

LOUISE COLBERT

Age: 54

- Does not like living in Brussels... does not like being 'involved' but merely wishes to be left alone.
- Wholly disapproves of Yvette's activity 'whatever it may be', and is shocked and frightened to learn that her husband is involved.
- But she adores Yvette as her own child, and is deeply fond of her husband.
- When...(in Episode 7) both Yvette and Gaston are arrested, though unable to <u>do</u> much, she makes her own protests in her own way.

Keen to add an extra depth to what could otherwise be a rather two-dimensional character, Brason decided to hint in her character sketch to an inner strength which she is only moved to demonstrate after her husband's death. Although he states that she is unable to <u>do</u> much, in the first series's penultimate episode Louise's timely and intelligent action ultimately saves Lifeline. As with many other characters in the series, Louise would be shown to be unable to choose to opt out of the war despite her strong desire not to be 'involved'.

Dr Pascal Keldermans

As they had learned through their research, and from Randle, that resistance-friendly doctors were vital to the ongoing operation of the evasion lines due to the fact that the downed airmen often came into their care in an injured state, Glaister and Brason elected to create the semi-regular character of Dr Keldermans.

DR PASCAL KELDERMANS

Age: 70 (or late sixties)

- Brussels medical practitioner (equivalent of Harley Street) with large house and practice.
- Active in helping evasion lines and gives regular safe-house facilities to evaders.
- Stern, but kindly, and probably highly efficient doctor.
- Married. No children.

He is introduced in Brason's prequel novel as: 'A tall, elderly man with a small greying beard. His aspect was commanding though his eyes were kind.'[25] As in the series, Brason provides him with an engaging turn of phrase. When he first tells Lisa that she must call him Pascal, he states: "I have an inbuilt objection to attractive young ladies eyeing me with awe and deference because I happen to be a doctor and older than I would wish." In line with the Hippocratic Oath, Brason also has Keldermans declare that: "I treat human beings, whatever their race, creed or nationality," but that the Oath "does not influence my personal sympathies. I like to think of myself as a patriot."[26] As Lisa would come to be placed as a nurse at his surgery as a cover, it was decided that the pair would enjoy a particularly strong bond, with the elderly doctor coming to regard her in a paternal fashion as the series progressed.

Andrée Foiret

Given that it was decided that Andrée would rarely appear in the series – she would be heard more often than seen – it is a little surprising that such a detailed initial character sketch was prepared for the character. The explanation for this is that though she rarely features in person, her debilitating presence is tangible throughout the first series, particularly insofar as it affects Albert and Monique.

ANDRÉE FOIRET

Age: 45/6

- Wife of Albert.
- Invalid and semi-paralysed wife, confined to her bed. She is totally incapable of movement from the waist down.
- Her sense of inadequacy and the injustice of fate brought about by her affliction has been subtly changed in her mind into bitterness and a smouldering sense of betrayal and injustice.
- She is inclined to 'make allowances' for Albert, soon to be swallowed by anger, but her feelings for Monique, the mistress, are those of utter hatred.
- Once her jealous imagining and suspicions have been confirmed, she goes over the top in her hatred and informs upon Monique… not even thinking of the possible consequences to Albert, the others and herself.
- Her emotional state is therefore responsible for the temporary fall of Lifeline, the destruction of the bistro and her own death.
- We HEAR but seldom SEE Andrée until the last two episodes of Series One.

Appropriately enough, in Brason's novel she is introduced not in person but by the sound of pronounced knocking on the back room ceiling and the comment by Jacques: "Poor Albert. One day he will strangle her, and it will be the end"[27] (interestingly this comment foreshadows the murder charge that is eventually levelled in the final series). The above character sketch is not specific about Andrée's condition other than the fact that she is paralysed. However, in his novel Brason has Keldermans diagnose her as suffering from General Paralysis of the Insane caused by the effect of syphilis on the central nervous system, meaning that she would have become paralysed eventually even if she had not been involved in a car accident. He also realises that the condition will eventually affect her sight too. The fact that Keldermans makes no such diagnosis in the series is very odd.

A hugely significant difference between the above character sketch and Andrée's involvement in the transmitted episodes is her informing upon Monique, an action which was originally intended to lead to the 'temporary fall of Lifeline' and the destruction of the original Candide in a great fire. However, Andrée herself would still die, although not in the blaze.

Jacques Bol

Given that he turns out to be a rather inconsequential and little-seen member of Lifeline, Jacques is described surprisingly early in the character summaries section of the Script Editor's Notes (between Natalie and Curtis), perhaps suggesting that Glaister and Brason originally intended to make far more use of the dark-haired cycle shop owner.

JACQUES BOL

Age: 36/40

- Runs a small bicycle shop not far from the Gare du Midi. Able therefore to move about... deal in tyres... keep a workshop etc.
- Once (1937-9) a champion European cyclist. Hip injury due to cycling but not greatly affecting.
- Tendency to leftist ideas... but loyal to Yvette.
- Unmarried.

As with Natalie, the idea of making more of his leftist sympathies as the series progressed was dropped. Nevertheless, reference would be made to his difficulty in accepting Lisa's edict that he could only work for Lifeline, thus hinting at his Communist leanings.

Veit Rennert

Rennert is a lightly sketched character who, in line with the fact that he is Kessler's unquestioning adjutant, is somewhat necessarily a 'faceless nothing' who lives to obey orders and keep his master happy.

VEIT RENNERT

Age: 34

- Rank: Gefreiter.
- Subdued, rat-like, wholly subservient, timorous assistant.
- Treated badly by Kessler because he accepts the treatment.
- Not a Uriah Heep… just a faceless nothing.

Initially conceived as a rather older character, he would become a very young soldier who was barely out of his teens and therefore far more likely to behave in a 'subservient' and 'timorous' manner. In his novel, Brason indicates that Rennert has already seen battle and suggests that if Kessler kicked or struck the young Gefreiter it might be less painful to him than the Sturmbannführer's frequent looks of cold disapproval.[28]

Sophie and Madeleine Chantal

Sophie and Madeleine Chantal were directly inspired by two elderly ladies who really did operate a safe-house in Paris up until Autumn 1943, at which point they escaped to England (see the review of *Invasions*). Their inclusion in the running characters section of the Script Editor's Notes suggests that the production team originally intended that the sisters would, like Jacques, feature more regularly than was ultimately the case.

SOPHIE and MADELEINE CHANTAL

Ages: 75 and 78 approx.

- Two gentlewomen spinsters who run the major safe-house in Senlis, their home, 30 kilometres north of Paris.
- They are the 'seigneurs' of Senlis, and live in a large eighteenth century house on the outskirts.
- Sophie is overtly sweet, kind and gentle… and absent-minded.
- Madeleine is tall, thin, ram-rod like, commanding and intimidating.
- Both are patriots to the point of jingoism.

Brason spends significant time building up their characters in his prequel novel, particularly in respect of how they are perceived by the locals: 'These two enormously dignified gentlewomen held sway over Senlis and its environs in a way not seen since the feudal days of the Counts of Chantilly'[29] Although Brason intended that the Chantals' safe-house and home should be an 18th century chateau, their circumstances would appear to be far more modest in the series itself, unless of course the local Nazis had requisitioned their grand home for themselves by the time that the series opened (in 1942).

The General Running Background

In a section entitled 'The General Running Background', Brason detailed the general content of the series's first fifteen episodes, explaining that: 'Without wishing to be too specific about this, and also encouraging writers to inject any ideas of their own, it is obvious that certain general paths must be followed in order to keep overall tabs on the happenings of our running characters.'

Specific direction was given once again regarding Lisa not responding to Royce's (Curtis's) advances, while it is also made more explicit that Albert 'will not abandon or be other than gentle with his bitch of an invalid wife' and that, despite this, Monique 'though weary of the (love) triangle, is loyal to him.' In line with Andrée's character profile, it is stated that ultimately 'this triangle causes the near-collapse of the Line as Andrée, in a fit of unthinking jealousy, betrays Monique (and therefore the others)' in the final fifteenth episode. It is not made clear whether it was intended that Monique (and the others) would survive this betrayal, although we know from Natalie's character profile, that at the very least, it was planned that Lisa would be imprisoned for some time as a result of Andrée's actions. These additional background notes also reveal a plan to have Lisa temporarily imprisoned at a time concurrent to her Uncle's capture and interrogation (what would become the events of *Too Near Home*) and also make it clearer that, after the loss of Gaston, Louise 'acquits herself with courage and fortitude.'

Brason briefly details that 'Natalie has one serious affair of the heart… with an evader who turns out to be a German 'plant'' whom she ultimately executes herself. This plot (the premise of the episode *A Question of Loyalty*) would ultimately be given to Monique instead, with Albert becoming the infiltrator's executioner. Of Royce (Curtis), Brason explains that he 'will slowly become tougher, harder and even heartless and ruthless.' He also directs that the antagonism between Kessler and Brandt will continue to grow: 'They do not actually thwart each other, but there is NO cooperation of any value. Kessler already anti-[Brandt], becomes suspicious of Brandt's allegiances.'

On a more general note, Brason also stresses that 'safe-houses and personnel may be 'lost'' but that he and Glaister want to retain Keldermans's surgery, the Chantals' house in Senlis and the Spanish frontier houses, and that reference can be made to other evasion lines but 'there is no point in complicating the issue by having episodes other than on or about our established Lifeline!'

Although Brason is open here about writers having the freedom to bring their own ideas and creativity to the table, it is clear from this and other sections of the Writer's Bible that he and Glaister already had very firm ideas about the narrative boundaries of their series and exactly how they wanted it to develop. Indeed, it is also clear that they even had a rough idea as to the plots of many specific episodes. This 'hold' on the series's content and direction would in no way slacken as the series progressed into its second and third years; in fact, writers would rarely be commissioned for a script for which the premise had not already been drafted by the production team.

The Original Episode One

Apart from Glaister's initial outline, the Writers' Bible stands as one of the earliest surviving documents relating to the genesis of *Secret Army*. However, one other document reveals that there may well have been an earlier version of the Script Editor's Notes, or at least that the characters, situations and approach that are detailed therein were not arrived at immediately and instead evolved over a period of time: a draft script by writer Wilfred Greatorex for the original episode one.

Greatorex was another former RAF man, who had first achieved television success with his ATV boardroom drama *The Plane Makers* (1963-65), which would later become *The Power Game* (1965-6, 1969), acting as 'series editor' and occasional writer on both. Greatorex went on to create: arms-dealer drama *Hine* (1971), featuring Barrie Ingham in the title role; the mini-series *Man from Haven* (1972), featuring Ian Holm as a blackmailer; and the HTV series *The Inheritors* (1974), with Peter Egan, which concerned the future of a vast family estate. In 1975 and 1976 he penned episodes of Glaister's *Oil Strike North* and *The Mackinnons*, and it was during this time that the pair discussed the former's plans for *The Secret Army* and the latter's for a post-war set series entitled *Airline*, which concerned the fortunes of a former World War Two sergeant-pilot who starts his own airline service.

Greatorex must have been commissioned by Glaister very early on in the planning stages in the Autumn of 1976, as his script, which was entitled *Homing Pigeon*, reveals that several characters had not yet been created, had different names, or indeed were entirely different to how they would eventually be realised on screen. As this is the case it seems that Greatorex only had the bare bones of the new series to go on at the time and as a result, although it may not have been Glaister and Brason's intention, his script ended up helping them to decide on a rather different approach to the series and prompted them to refine and realign the characters they had created (in a way that would be ultimately detailed in the Writers' Bible). It is entirely possible, but unknown, whether other writers were commissioned at the same time as Greatorex. If they were, and their scripts did go on to make it into the first series, then they would most certainly have undergone some radical revision.

Homing Pigeon is essentially a retread of Bill Randle's October 1942 evasion journey from Belgium to Spain (for a full synopsis of the episode see Appendices). Several characters are as they appear in the Writers' Bible: Lisa, Curtis (but still called by his original name: Royce), Brandt, Gaston and Louise Colbert, whereas others are subtly different. Kessler for instance, who is already in situ at the start of the episode is described as 'a sturdy major in the Gestapo' who at 46 'isn't likely to rise much higher.' He is also an openly sadistic and violent character, taking pleasure in torture and at one point even striking an evader, and is therefore a more stock 'nasty Nazi' that he would eventually turn out to be. Spookily though, one description suggests the role was tailor-made for its eventual incumbent, Clifford Rose: 'He has the face of a worried Puritan.' Elsewhere, Albert is married to an invalid and still has Monique as his mistress. However, the pair are described respectively as a 'weedy, seedy' 38-year-old who 'wears a permanent Gitane [French cigarette] at his lips,' and a 'bright as a button' 20-year-old with 'a figure from heaven.' Both Albert's description and the wider age gap between him and Monique give a very different, rather grubby feel to their relationship. The Candide too is presented in a more sleazy light: 'A decadent maelstrom alive with German troops and German good-time girls,' so it resembles a 'knocking shop' rather more than a backstreet café. Another significantly different character is Alain, who is described as a 28-year-old 'slight, but strong' patriot with 'peasant's clothes and spectacles.' He is far more strait-laced than 'our Alain' and even expresses concern that Lisa chooses to visit a place like the Candide and associate with Albert. Furthermore he is gobsmacked to learn that Monique is his mistress. The regular characters that do not feature in *Homing Pigeon* at all – one of the main reasons why his draft script must have been completed before the end of 1976 – include Natalie, Dr Keldermans and Jacques. One character who does not make it from Greatorex's script into the series, and was intended to be a Lifeline regular (the script states that he will be important to evaders in the series) is a 'jowly monk in his early fifties' called Père Michel, who is clearly based on the monk who assisted Randle: Father Marcel. In the event the dramatisation of the authentic assistance of evasion lines by monks would be limited to a single episode, John Brason's *Good Friday*.

The script concentrates almost wholly upon Royce's experiences, as he: flies out on a night bombing mission; bails out after being hit and parachutes down; is interrogated by Belgian patriots; meets Alain and Lisa; arrives at a succession of safe-houses; is reunited with his fellow crew members; is coached on acting European; takes several train journeys through France; goes over the Pyrenees and makes the crossing into Spain with Lisa and a Basque guide called Tollo (based on the infamous Florentino) before saying a passionate goodbye Lisa. With all of this going on, apart from Lisa, the Lifeline regulars barely get a look in. Albert and Monique, for instance, only have a handful of lines between them. Conversely, Royce and his fellow evaders, particularly Willis and Godley, take the limelight. In this way, *Homing Pigeon* differs crucially from the approach of the series proper as it dramatises events chiefly from the evader's perspective rather than from that of the agents of Lifeline. Although Glaister and Brason's initial reaction to receiving Greatorex's script is unknown, it is clear that they ultimately decided that it took the series in a direction that they did not want to pursue. As Glaister had said from the outset, the story he wanted the series to tell was of 'the people who provided a lifeline for aircrew' (hence the original name *Life-Line*) rather than that of the evaders who passed through their hands. It is unclear whether Greatorex refused to alter his script – apart from anything else it would have had to be significantly redrafted due to its sheer length (it is almost double that of a typical *Secret Army* script) – but whatever the exact turn of events, the writer certainly left the series under a cloud. What *is* known is that the Script Editor's Notes were subsequently altered to reinforce what the series was about ('Our Lifeline personnel are our main characters, NOT the evaders') so that other writers would not follow the same approach as Greatorex. The fact that his script was now officially considered 'unusable' perhaps explains why Randle's fascinating evasion story was effectively off limits to other writers, something which seems ironic given its pertinence and the fact that he was the series's Technical Advisor. There is also the possibility that *Homing Pigeon* made Glaister and Brason decide that the series needed a later starting point, in both a historical and narrative sense. Certainly historically it was shifted from beginning in Autumn 1941 to the start of 1942 instead. As for the regulars, Glaister and Brason felt that they needed work too. Albert and Monique would become older, and the age gap between them would decrease. Kessler, meanwhile, would become more controlled and therefore far more menacing, while Alain would be revised completely. Although the Candide would still appear as a lively 'maelstrom' when first visited, Greatorex's 'good time girls' would be absent from this rather more reputable establishment.

Although Greatorex's script was not used, he would receive significant recompense for his contribution, far more than being simply paid off for the script as was typical at the time. This was perhaps because the BBC judged that despite the fact that Greatorex's script was not taken up, as it was for the opening episode of *The Secret Army* it was considered to have made a difference to the series's development, something that Glaister himself always hotly denied. The situation was further complicated by the fact that Glaister was by this time simultaneously acting as a kind of consultant on Greatorex's *Airline*. Taking both elements into account, Glaister's BBC bosses decided that a deal should be struck whereby Greatorex's and Glaister's names would appear as 'consultant' on each other's programmes. Glaister was very unhappy with this decision and was only somewhat ameliorated later on when agreement was reached for Greatorex's name to be removed from the credits from Series Two onwards. In contrast to Greatorex, when *Airline* was finally made and broadcast in 1982 – incidentally featuring *Colditz* regulars Anthony Valentine and Richard Heffer – Glaister insisted that his name did not appear on the series's credits.

The Writers

Once the Writers' Bible was completed, Glaister and Brason set about recruiting the writers who would be working within their carefully delineated guidelines. Brason himself, who had been recruited as the series's principal scriptwriter as well as script editor, would pen four of the fifteen episodes that had been allocated to the series, including the crucial final instalment, which was an eleventh-hour replacement for another unusable script.

N. J. Crisp

Glaister asked his long-term collaborator N. J. (Norman James) Crisp to write a total of three scripts for his new series. Crisp had worked with Glaister on numerous previous occasions. Together they had created no less than four series including: *The Expert*, which concerned the investigations of forensic pathologist Dr John Hardy, played by Marius Goring; thirteen-part children's adventure series *The Long Chase*, which was shot entirely on film and starred Jan Francis and Glyn Houston; the tremendously popular boardroom-to-bedroom saga *The Brothers*; and the gritty *Oil Strike North* starring Nigel Davenport. As well as writing many episodes for the above series, Crisp had also written five episodes for Glaister's *Colditz*, including the opening instalment of the second series: *Arrival of a Hero*, which introduced the sadistic Major Mohn. During this period, the prolific Crisp also found time to script many episodes of the long-running police drama *Dixon of Dock Green* (1955-76), having been recruited by its producer to help rid the series of its cosy image by penning hard-hitting scripts with tougher criminals. Crisp was a founding member of the Writers' Guild – formed in 1959 – serving as its chairman from 1968 to 1971, negotiating the first £1,000 fee to be paid to a writer for a television drama and persuading the ITV companies to make a pension contribution with each script commissioned.

In 1975, at the age of 51, Crisp was diagnosed with a malformation of the spinal cord, which left him partially disabled and caused his eyesight to gradually fail (by 1983 he was registered blind); however, he would continue to write for television and film well into the Eighties. Crisp, like Glaister, was a former RAF man, serving from 1943 to 1947, a factor which, his considerable writing credentials aside, made him an obvious choice to deliver scripts for *The Secret Army*.

Robert Barr

For the important mid-series script in which it had already been decided that Lisa would be imprisoned and Gaston would meet his end, Glaister turned to veteran television writer Robert Barr. Barr had been one of four reporters chosen to shadow General Dwight D. Eisenhower from D-Day through to the end of the war. In his attempts to get news of specific offensives back to London, on one particular occasion he travelled by Jeep and hitch-hiked to the recently liberated Brussels to radio from there, however, on his way back to the Front, due to a sudden German advance, he found himself behind enemy lines and lost his transmitter in the process.

After the war, he wrote and produced the very first television documentary for the BBC entitled *Germany Under Control* (1946), which he followed with *Report on Germany* (1948). Barr established the corporation's Documentary Section before dipping his toe in live broadcast drama for the first time, adapting and producing an hour-long version of *The Time Machine* in 1949. He subsequently became a pioneer of a new genre: drama-documentary, with works such as *War on Crime* (1950), *Flying Ambulance* (1958) and *Medico* (1959) for which he was awarded the Prix Italia. Barr is probably best known for the BBC drama *Spycatcher* (1959-61), which was based on the wartime exploits of counter-espionage agent Lt Col. Oreste Pinto, played by Bernard Archard, and ran to four series. He went on to script the acclaimed Hebrides-set thriller *The Dark Island* (1962) starring Robert Hardy, which was produced and directed by Glaister. He would work with Glaister again the following year on the wartime drama, *Moonstrike*. Later that decade, Barr began a lengthy involvement with the long-running police drama *Z Cars* (1962-78) as writer and executive producer, subsequently contributing to its various spin-offs: *Softly Softly* (1966-70), *Softly Softly: Task Force* (1970-6) and *Barlow at Large* (1971, 1973). In 1968 he also created the local newspaper drama *Gazette* (1968), which became *Hadleigh* (1969-76). The Cold War series *Spy Trap* (1972-5), with Paul Daneman, was another success for Barr in the early Seventies.

In 1976, Barr was approached to write for the Highlands-set drama series *The Mackinnons* (1977), which Glaister was producing. It was soon after submitting this script (entitled *The Inheritance*) that Glaister asked Barr to write for *The Secret Army*.

Arden Winch

Another established writer who would also be approached for a single script was Arden Winch. Winch, who would later make his name in the TV thriller genre with the tense Glaister-produced serials *Blood Money* (1980), *Skorpion* (1983) and *Cold Warrior* (1984), began his career in television in the early Sixties, writing for the BBC's *Television Playhouse* and the ITV *Play of the Week*. He subsequently scripted the thriller series *The Paradise Makers* (1967) featuring Michael Bryant as ex-spy and physicist Dr James Creig, and the police drama *Something to Hide* (1968) with Charles Gray as Detective Inspector Waugh, before contributing single episodes to *Manhunt* (*What Did You Do in the War, Daddy?*) (1970), *The Regiment* (1972-3) and, like John Brason, *Moonbase 3*, for which he wrote the series finale: *View of a Dead Planet*. He first worked for Glaister on *Colditz*, penning three episodes in total, including the well-received *Lord Didn't It Rain* and *Odd Man In*.

When Winch was asked by Glaister to write for *The Secret Army*, he had recently completed a number of scripts for another BBC RAF series, *Wings*

(1977) – on which he was one of the principal writers – which was due to air early the following year.

Michael Chapman

When he was asked to consider writing for the *The Secret Army*, Michael Chapman was taking initial steps towards getting his own wartime drama series onto the screen: *Enemy at the Door* (1978-80), for London Weekend Television. Chapman's early work included the ABC crime series *The Protectors* (1964) (not the Robert Vaughn series) and sci-fi series *Undermind* (1965), also for ABC, which saw a man and his sister-in-law, Drew and Anne Heriot, try to thwart an alien force. Chapman went on to produce the supernatural drama *Haunted* (1967) with Patrick Mower, the detective dramas *Public Eye* (1965-75) and *Van Der Valk* (1972-3, 1977), contributing scripts to both series, and the 8-part crime serial *The Life and Death of Penelope* (1976), which he also wrote.

Immediately before writing for *The Secret Army*, he, like Glaister, worked as a producer on the Scottish drama *The Mackinnons*, the commissioning of his script being as a result of this connection.

Willis Hall

Easily the most accomplished writer approached to work on the new series was Willis Hall. Hall's writing career began whilst in the armed forces in the Far East, when he wrote a play about the army set in Malaya. Originally presented as an amateur production at the Edinburgh Fringe with the title *Disciplines of War*, for its eventual West End run in 1959 the play would be retitled *The Long and the Short and the Tall*, with a film version following in 1961. In 1960, Hall and Keith Waterhouse, who was to become his long-term collaborator, adapted the latter's novel, *Billy Liar*, into another successful play. Hall and Waterhouse would collaborate again on the hugely successful films *Whistle Down the Wind* (1961), *A Kind of Loving* (1962) and a revised *Billy Liar* (1963), and were quickly heralded as pioneers of British 'New Wave' cinema as a result.

Around this time, as well as penning screenplays, Hall and Waterhouse began to write for television and increasingly turned their attention to comedy, working on *That Was the Week That Was* (1962), *BBC 3* (1965) and *The Frost Report* (1966), before scripting the situation comedies *Inside George Webley* (1968-70) with Roy Kinnear and *Queenie's Castle* (1970-2) with Diana Dors, and episodes of the comedy drama *Budgie* (1971-2). After a successful television adaptation of *Billy Liar* (1973-4), Hall wrote solo on the anthology series *Village Hall* (1974-5) and the short-lived suburban drama *The Crezz* (1976). In 1976, he was busy devising a new police drama *The Fuzz* (1977), when he was asked by the production team to submit two scripts for *The Secret Army*.

It is clear that Hall was commissioned to write these episodes well before it was decided that Greatorex's *Homing Pigeon* was to be abandoned, as after delivering his first two scripts, which would become *Growing Up* and *A Question of Loyalty* (both of which were felt to hit exactly the right tone), he was approached to also pen the replacement episode one. Although he agreed to take it on, he had definite misgivings about the fact that Glaister and Brason wanted him to pack so much into it.

James Andrew Hall

37-year-old James Andrew Hall was at an early point in his career when he was asked to work on the series, but nevertheless already had several television writing credits under his belt, such as episodes of *Public Eye*, *New Scotland Yard* (1972) and *Dial M for Murder* (1974). Perhaps his most thought-provoking works to that date had been five plays in the *Handle with Care* (1974-6) series, produced for students of sociology, which featured central performances from Rachel Davies, John Alkin and Lalla Ward. He would later become the Andrew Davies of his day, adapting successful productions of *The Mill on the Floss* (1978), *The History of Mr Polly* (1980), *Dombey and Son* (1983), *The Invisible Man* (1984), *The Prisoner of Zenda* (1984) and *David Copperfield* (1986). Like Willis Hall, James would be asked to supply two scripts for the new series.

Simon Masters

Simon Masters, a young writer who had not yet had a television script accepted but who had been working for several years as a BBC script editor on Robert Barr's *Spy Trap*, Glaister's *The Brothers* and the tremendously successful first series of *Poldark* (1975), tried his hand at scripting an episode and won his first commission.

By mid-January 1977, a total of seven writers were deeply immersed in writing the fifteen scripts which would make up the first series. Each writer would have to contend with: a thorough technical check of the script by Bill Randle, who remembers how he '...worked on the scripts at home, often well into the night and always returned them, with comment where necessary, within 24 hours'[30]; and meetings with John Brason, who as script editor was responsible for tightening the scripts up, developing running themes, maintaining continuity and ensuring that the series had a unified feel.

When interviewed at the time about the preparation of his scripts for *Secret Army*, Willis Hall explained the particular problems that he and the other writers faced: "Of course with a series that's already been on, you know who the actors are and it's quite easy to write for them, but if you're writing in this sort of vacuum where none of the parts have been cast and you know that half a dozen people are also writing for these six faceless people, it's worrying at the beginning." However, he went on to state that: "It's always extraordinary how the scripts do come together and on second draft the running characters suddenly begin to form not only in your mind, but in the minds of the other six writers."[31]

The Regular Cast

Gerard Glaister rarely resorted to a formal auditioning process and instead, when casting the lead roles in his series, much preferred to take likely candidates out to lunch, over which he would ascertain whether they had what he was looking for.

Jan Francis (Lisa "Yvette" Colbert)

For the central part of Lisa Colbert (code-name Yvette), Glaister was keen to cast an actress who was as pretty, young and diminutive as Dédée and therefore just as unlikely a leader of a complex escape organisation. One actress who he felt sure fitted the bill had worked with him previously on his 1972 adventure series *The Long Chase*: Jan Francis.

Born in Streatham, London, in 1951, Janet Stephanie Francis had performed as a ballerina with the Royal Ballet, both at Covent Garden and on tour, during

her teenage years. However, her ballet career came to an abrupt halt after she injured her right knee during a performance. After recovering from her injury, she returned to ballet for a short time, notably to feature in a production of *Swan Lake* with Margot Fonteyn, but had decided during her recuperation period to pursue a new long-term career goal. In 1969 she left the Royal Ballet behind in order to become an actress, joining the Cheltenham Repertory Company for a season of plays. By 1971 she had won her first acting role on television, playing Shirley Matthews in an episode of LWT's *The Fenn Street Gang* (1971-3), and was by now calling herself Jan rather than Janet. Aged 21, Francis took her first regular role as Anne Shirley's best friend, Diana Barry, in a popular BBC adaptation of *Anne of Green Gables* (1972), a role she would later reprise in its sequel *Anne of Avonlea* (1975) again with Kim Braden in the title role. After the first *Anne*, Francis won her second regular role as Susan Frazer in Glaister's *The Long Chase* later that year. Francis's other notable early roles included: Sophie in *The Four Beauties* – an episode of the first series of *Country Matters* (1972-3), which won the 1973 BAFTA for Best Drama Series; Mabel Dunham, nicknamed 'Magnet', in the Sunday serial *Hawkeye: The Pathfinder* (1973) (a sequel to the popular 1971 BBC dramatisation of *The Last of the Mohicans*) with Patrick Troughton; the headstrong Lizzie in the well-received *Play for Today: The Lonely Man's Lover* (1974); and Mathilde Kschessinska, the first love of Tsar Nicholas II (played by Charles Kay), in an episode of the acclaimed drama series *Fall of Eagles* (1974) entitled *The Last Tsar*. As Kschessinska had been Russia's first prima ballerina, this role also gave Francis the opportunity to demonstrate her dance background.

By the mid-Seventies, Francis was becoming a familiar face on television, guest-starring as: Zora in the one-off children's drama *The Carpet Weaver of Samarkand* (1974); Captain Jane Ashley in *The Hanged Man* (1975); Lesley Galbraith in *Sutherland's Law* (1973, 1975-6); and in several editions of *Play of the Month*, including *London Assurance* (1976), in which she appeared opposite two of her future colleagues: James Bree and Clifford Rose.

A year before starting *Secret Army*, Francis auditioned for the role of Purdey in *The New Avengers*, making the short-list before losing out to Joanna Lumley, and took the prominent guest role of femme fatale Irene Baker in two consecutive episodes of the popular Saturday night drama *The Duchess of Duke Street* (1976-7), in which she ensnared Christopher Cazenove's Charlie Haslemere. At the end of 1976, she also recorded an edition of *Jackanory Playhouse* called *The Golden Samurai* (1977) with Peter Davison. Francis's final role before production began on *Secret Army* in April 1977 was that of the coquettish Netje van der Berg in an episode of *Raffles* (1975-7) entitled *A Bad Night*.

Francis was one of the first actors to be formally contracted, on 3 February 1977.

Bernard Hepton (Albert Foiret)

Bernard Hepton's measured performance as the sympathetic German Kommandant in *Colditz*, for which he was nominated for a BAFTA award in 1974, had impressed Glaister so much that when he conceived *The Secret Army* Hepton was the only serious contender for the lead role of restaurateur Albert Foiret.

Born in Bradford in 1925, Bernard Heptonstall became interested in acting and theatre when he was in his teens during the war: "I was a teenage 'fire-watcher' and it was very boring, and the lady in charge of us all decided to bring some little one-act plays in, and I didn't even know what a play was. I had been to the theatre once, and that was when I was very tiny, to see a pantomime, and we started reading these plays, and as we read them, so doors began to open for me and a sort of magic land was there behind the doors, and I became fascinated by it, absolutely fascinated."[32] As a result, the young Hepton joined the Bradford Civic Playhouse, where he met

Esme Church, a well-known actress and director from the Old Vic, and subsequently became her first student when she opened a theatre school there: "For two years I was a student, and I was in absolute heaven and the education went on and on and on and I was filled with delight. Then I was asked to go to York Rep and I was there for two years, again I thought this was just wonderful."[33] After hearing many good things about Sir Barry Jackson's Birmingham Repertory company, Hepton became determined to join it and, after two years getting by as a draughtsman, he eventually won two little parts in *Henry VI Part III* in 1952. After winning larger roles and arranging several fight scenes for a variety of Shakespeare productions, Hepton let it be known that he was keen to have a go at directing and Sir Barry decided to give him the opportunity. Hepton subsequently enjoyed many happy years directing at Birmingham in the late Fifties and early Sixties, working with many of Britain's top actors along the way, such as Ian Richardson, Rosemary Leach and Derek Jacobi, in countless acclaimed productions. After the death of Sir Barry, a loss which Hepton felt changed the whole atmosphere of the place, he elected to leave Birmingham and take over the Liverpool Rep (where one of his first plays was *Celebration* by none other than Willis Hall). However, Hepton was soon deeply unhappy in his new post, as he no longer had the freedom that he had had at Birmingham and was working for people who he believed were "resistant to what was happening in the theatre."[34]

Leaving Liverpool behind him, Hepton joined the BBC as part of a fresh intake of up-and-coming directors and producers for the new BBC2. After realising that he wanted to produce rather than direct ("I wanted to say: 'I would like that, you write it and you direct it.'"), Hepton produced the popular soap *Compact* (1962-5), editions of *Thursday Theatre* and the *Wednesday Thriller*, and adaptations of *The Wings of the Dove*, *The Naked Island* and *Coriolanus*, between 1965 and 1966. However, after producing at the BBC for two years, he decided that he was "not a company man"[35] and promptly left it all behind.

At this point in his career, he remembers that "nobody knew me as an actor then so I had to rely on one or two friends to sort of push me around a bit and give me some parts."[36] However, roles soon materialised: as Lord Portmanteau in *The Play of the Month: Devil's Eggshell* (1966); Wemmick in a ten-part adaptation of *Great Expectations* (1967); the Rev. Mr Farebrother in *Middlemarch* (1968); and Dr Crippen in *Detective: Crime of Passion* (1968). After playing Chauvelin in the mini-series *The Elusive Pimpernel* (1969), Hepton was to take a role for which he would become famous: that of Archbishop Thomas Cranmer in the classic series *The Six Wives of Henry VIII* (1970), a part he would reprise in the similarly well-received *Elizabeth R* (1971) and the film *Henry VIII and His Six Wives* (1972). In 1973, Hepton played Herbert Starling opposite Francesca Annis in *A Pin to See the Peepshow*, a drama which incidentally featured his future *Secret Army* co-star, Ron Pember, as his father-in-law. After twenty-four episodes of *Colditz* as the Kommandant between 1972-4, he changed direction entirely to 'play it for laughs' as Mr Fletcher ('the Lecher') in Eric Chappell's *The Squirrels* (1974 (pilot), 1975-7) and Norman Potter in Jack Rosenthal's *Sadie, It's Cold Outside* (1975).

His last few roles before accepting the part of Albert included: Palmer in the award-winning *Orde Wingate* (1976) with Barry Foster; the machiavellian freedman Pallas in the equally feted *I, Claudius* (1976), in which he would work with Derek Jacobi again; and a final series of *The Squirrels*, which aired early in 1977.

Hepton was formally contracted to play Albert on 4 February 1977 and was to be the highest paid actor on the series by some considerable margin.

Angela Richards (Monique Duchamps)

In 1976, Bernard Hepton had the same agent, Bryan Drew, as 33-year-old actress and singer Angela Richards, who was enjoying great success in musical theatre in London's West End. Richards remembers that Drew 'knew that the casting was going on for *Secret Army* and he rang Gerry Glaister and he said "I think you should see my client."' Glaister followed up his suggestion, taking her to lunch at the BBC canteen in Television Centre in mid-January 1977. Of this meeting, Richards recalls: "I just talked and Gerry talked. And I obviously charmed the socks off him as I got the part!"

© Bennett Studios

Richards, born Angela Twigg in December 1944, had wanted to be an actress from a young age: "I was too shy at school to actually stand up and recite anything, but I always knew that I could. I never went to a theatre until I was about fifteen. I suppose I wanted to be an actress because I knew that I was good at mimicking people, and if you could make people laugh you could usually get yourself out of trouble, either at school or with your Mum and Dad."[37]

In 1964, while Richards was in her final year at RADA (the Royal Academy of Dramatic Art), theatrical producer and film director Wendy Toye was putting together a new West End show called *Robert and Elizabeth*. With music by Ron Grainer, the operetta was about the romance and elopement of poets Robert Browning and Elizabeth Barrett, who were to be played by Keith Michell and June Bronhill respectively. Toye needed to find a young actress who could sing to play Elizabeth's younger sister, Henrietta, and in this regard approached RADA principal John Fernald, who told her that he thought Richards would be suitable for the role. Toye went to see her in her end of year musical *Once Upon A Time* and subsequently auditioned her for the role, which she duly won. As Richards recalls, this meant that, rather unusually, she "didn't ever go into repertory theatre. I went straight from drama school into rehearsals in the West End." Some time after the show's debut in October 1964, one evening June Bronhill fell suddenly ill at the end of the very first scene and, as her understudy was on holiday, Richards (as second understudy) was propelled into the limelight. It was her performance that night that secured her the key role of Kathie in *On the Level* in 1966, an unusual musical about high school examinations which was put together by the same team as *Robert and Elizabeth*. This was the same year in which Richards made her TV debut in the Christmas Day BBC1 pantomime, in the title role of *Aladdin* with Roy Castle, Mary Millar and Arthur Askey. Further major West End musicals followed, including *Annie* in 1967 (not the musical with the red-haired orphan) – of which Michael Billington said: 'Angela Richards brings charm, good looks and an excellent voice to the part of a love-lorn

Stockport girl'[38] – and *The Beggar's Opera* in 1968, as well as straight acting roles in plays at the Old Vic and Nottingham Playhouse. Richards also took more roles on television, playing Ginevra Fanshawe in *Vilette* (1970) and Gloria Fleming in *The Closed Shop* (1970). Highlights of the next few years included: the roles of Lucy Lockett in *The Beggar's Opera* and Jennifer Dubedat (taking over from Joan Plowright) in *The Doctor's Dilemma* at the Chichester Festival in 1972; appearing opposite Lauren Bacall as the scheming Eve Harrington in *Applause* (in 1972-3) – the musical version of *All About Eve* – for which she won rave reviews; playing Cunegonde opposite Ian Ogilvy in the BBC's *Play of the Month: Candide* (1973); and the Cole Porter tribute musical *Cole* in 1974. 1975 would be another successful year for Richards, in which she would take the role of Celia in the Oxford Playhouse production of *As You Like It*, which also featured Frances de la Tour as Rosalind, and star as the indefatigable Hallelujah Lil in the Brecht/Weill musical *Happy End* with Bob Hoskins, in which her performance was described as 'fervent' and 'virtuoso' by reviewers. At the end of the year, together with Richard Stilgoe, she also contributed music and sketches to a BBC five-part discussion programme fronted by Ludovic Kennedy about the changing role of women in society, called *Women: Which Way Now?* (1975-6).

In 1976, almost exactly a year before she started *Secret Army*, Richards took the title role in a brand new musical entitled *Liza of Lambeth* – adapted very loosely by Willie Rushton and Bernie Stringle from the W. Somerset Maugham novel of the same name – at the Shaftesbury Theatre, which also featured Patricia Hayes and Michael Robbins. After the curtain came down on *Liza of Lambeth* after 110 performances, Richards went on to make the surreal HTV children's drama *King of the Castle*, in which she and her fellow adult actors – who included Fulton Mackay and Talfryn Thomas – took dual roles, which aired from May-June 1977 while the first series of *Secret Army* was in production.

Like Jan Francis, Richards was also formally contracted on 3 February 1977.

Christopher Neame (Flt Lt John Curtis)

As had been the case with Bernard Hepton, Glaister was prompted to think of Christopher Neame for the part of Flight Lieutenant John Curtis due to his earlier work on *Colditz*. Born in London in 1947, Neame was in his early twenties when he began to win his first roles on film and in television. His earliest film credits are: as Locke in *No Blade of Grass* (1970), the bleak adaptation of the John Christopher novel *The Death of Grass*, which concerned the breakdown of society in England after industrial pollution ravages the world's crops; and Hans in the Hammer Horror film *Lust for a Vampire* (1970). Early television roles included: the part of Daniel Dirk in the Granada play *Giants and Ogres* (1971) with Lee Montague and Ann Bell, which was part of the *ITV Saturday Night Theatre* strand; and Captain Junot in the mini-series *Napoleon and Love* (1972), which also featured *Secret Army*'s Clifford Rose and Stephen Yardley. After appearing as Lt Raeburn in *The Regiment* and the Earl of Warwick in the ten-part Tudor drama *The Shadow of the Tower* (1972), Neame took what was effectively the lead role in another Hammer Horror film, *Dracula AD 1972* (1972), which was set in modern day London and saw Neame play Dracula's disturbed disciple Johnny Alucard (Dracula backwards!) who resurrects the Count and kidnaps the beautiful Jessica van Helsing (Stephanie Beacham) in order to make her Dracula's undead bride. 1972 also saw Neame begin his two-year association with *Colditz*, in which he played naval officer Lt Dick Player in a total of 17 episodes over two series. Neame very much enjoyed making the show, in which his character's stand-out episodes were *Lord Didn't it Rain*, which almost solely followed Player's adventures while on the run; the two-part first series finale *Gone Away*, in which he and several fellow prisoners escape; and the episode *Frogs in the Well*, in which Player finally breaks out of Colditz for good, in the same manner as Airey Neave did in real life.

At the start of 1973, Neame made the newspaper headlines when talks were held between Granada Television and the Independent Broadcasting Authority about a television film entitled *A Point in Time* (1972) that had been made in Sardinia the previous year. The talks revolved around a scene in which Neame was stripped naked by three nude girls, which was putting its broadcast in doubt. However, the matter was eventually resolved and the film was shown in late February. *Times* critic Leonard Buckley praised Neame's performance ('Played with a dignity at once gentle and intense') and the whole dreamlike style of the piece ('Full of puzzlement. Beautiful to watch and studded with impressive moments').

Guest roles followed as: Sydney Wing in *The Rivals of Sherlock Holmes* (1973), playing opposite Bernard Hepton's Detective Laxworthy in the episode *The Secret of the Magnifique*; Bailey in *Blockbuster*, the final episode of *The Protectors* (1972-4) together with Ron Pember; and Myers in the *Quiller* (1975) episode *The Thin Red Line*.

In the years immediately preceding *Secret Army*, Neame took two major roles: that of Kaiser Wilhelm II in the award-winning ATV mini-series *Edward the Seventh* (1975), and as Romeo in a new eight-part Thames Television version of *Romeo and Juliet* (1976) directed by Joan Kemp-Welch – who had previously worked with Neame on *The Shadow of the Tower* – which was aimed primarily at schools and also featured Anne Hasson, Simon MacCorkindale and Clive Swift.

Neame was contracted to play Curtis on 10 March 1977.

Juliet Hammond-Hill (Natalie Chantrens)

Undoubtedly the character whom Gerry Glaister found the most difficult to cast was that of young guide Natalie Chantrens, who looks-wise he knew would have

© Ros Drinkwater

to be in contrast to Angela Richards and Jan Francis. After seeing many actresses over several weeks, Glaister was still no closer to finding a suitable candidate, until that was, in early March 1977, he auditioned a 23-year-old actress named Juliet Hammond-Hill. At that time, Hammond-Hill, had only been out of drama school (the Webber Douglas Academy of Dramatic Art) for eight months, but – by her own admission – being of a somewhat impetuous disposition back then, was already becoming disillusioned by her choice of career due to the number of knock-backs she had received from several repertory companies ("I used to get the brown envelope back every time!"). After seeing an article about *Secret Army* in *Public Casting Report*, she decided that a letter to the BBC seeking a part in the new series would effectively be her last ditch effort to secure acting work: "I thought that if I don't get a positive result I'm actually just going to give up and do something else." She recalls that she sent what she remembers to be a good photograph and a "not too sycophantic" letter to Glaister in which she made sure to mention that she was French-educated and had an affinity for French people, in the hope that this might make her more suitable for a role.

This approach did the trick and Hammond-Hill soon found herself invited to an audition at the BBC, but she was completely stunned when she discovered that she was under serious consideration for one of the lead roles. Hammond-Hill was soon invited back for a second audition – which John Brason also sat in on – at which she remembers giving a poor reading. However, she was subsequently invited back for a third and final audition at which she was offered the part of Natalie. Hammond-Hill was later told by Glaister's then secretary that the producer had actually declared "I've found my Natalie" after their very first meeting.

Although overjoyed to win the part, Hammond-Hill recalls feeling pretty daunted, especially as this was her first acting role since leaving drama school: "I remember going to a party, possibly at Gerry's, and all the leading actors were there and I knew some of them by reputation and some by name, and I remember thinking 'I'm totally inexperienced here, I'm just a little novice, and they knew that as well and it was really quite hard for them to accept that I was going to be a lead role with no experience at all." Nevertheless, Hammond-Hill would soon find her feet and quickly felt comfortable in the role.

Hammond-Hill was formally contracted to play Natalie on 18 March 1977.

Michael Culver (Major Erwin Brandt)

38-year-old Michael Culver, another actor whom Gerry Glaister held in high regard, was cast as Major Erwin Brandt. Son of well-known actor Roland Culver, Michael trained at LAMDA (the London Academy of Music and Dramatic Art) and subsequently performed in the late Fifties and early Sixties as part of the London Old Vic company alongside Judi Dench and Maggie Smith, and the Dundee repertory company with Edward Fox and Glenda Jackson. His early television work included episodes of *Maigret* (1960-3), the anthology series *Studio Four* (1962) and police drama *Silent Evidence* (1962), as well as uncredited appearances in the James Bond films *From Russia With Love* (1963) and *Thunderball* (1965). His role in the first episode of the Glaister-produced wartime drama *Moonstrike*, *Home By Four*, won him the cover of the *Radio Times* in February 1963. Parts followed in: *Play of the Month: The Devil's Eggshell* (1966) with Bernard Hepton; *The Avengers* (1961-9); *Man in a Suitcase* (1967-8); and as Lt Bailes in the film *The Body Stealers* (1969). Culver subsequently began to win recurring roles in series such as *The First Churchills* (1969), *Goodbye Mr Chips* (1969), *Elizabeth R* (1971), *Persuasion* (1971) and

© Roger Eaton

The Befrienders (1972). After a stint in the new soap *Emmerdale Farm*, also in 1972, he took the role of Squire Armstrong in several episodes of the popular LWT/Talbot children's serial *The Adventures of Black Beauty* (1972-4) and a lead role, opposite Sarah Badel, in the anthology series *Seven Faces of Woman* (1974). 1975 was a busy year for Culver, seeing him guest star in episodes of popular series such as *Thriller* (1973-6), *Within These Walls* (1974-8), *The Main Chance* (1969-75), *Softly, Softly* and *Space:1999* (1975-7).

In the year prior to *Secret Army*, Culver played Dennis Jenkins in the Thames Television series *Couples* (1976), Major Farjeon in several episodes of the popular BBC drama *The Duchess of Duke Street* and, most prominently, the role of Donald Maclean in BAFTA-nominated one-off ITV spy drama *Philby, Burgess and Maclean* (1977), which also starred Derek Jacobi and was broadcast in May 1977.

Culver was one of the very last of the regular cast to be contracted, on 31 March 1977, suggesting that, as with Natalie, it took the production team some time to find the right actor to play the part.

Clifford Rose (Sturmbannführer Ludwig Kessler)

Selected to play opposite Culver in the crucial role of Kessler was seasoned actor Clifford Rose. One of three sons, John Clifford Rose was born to Percy and Violet Rose in 1929 while they were living in Hamnish Clifford, near Leominster, Herefordshire, hence Clifford. Rose recalls: "My father was a smallholder and had had ambitions to be a lay preacher. They kept poultry and grew vegetables and flowers for market. My mother had been a nurse and involved in St John Ambulance. She was also very musical and gave piano lessons, as well as organising a small orchestra."[39] Clifford boarded at St Michael's College, Tenbury Wells, and went on a scholarship to King's School, Worcester. It was here that Clifford first discovered his interest in acting. One particular source of inspiration was the school trips to Stratford to see Shakespeare: "They took us to Stratford regularly. The first production I saw was in 1944: *The Merry Wives of Windsor*."[40] Around this time, Rose began to take parts in school plays. He modestly remembers that: "My headmaster directed the school plays and was very encouraging. He gave me a very nice report saying something about 'exceptional talent'. He directed me in the title role of *Macbeth* in my final year –

I don't think my biology teacher thought taking part was the best idea!"[41] Rose had been intent on becoming a doctor, but recalls that, although he "studied all the sciences," he "didn't get into medical school. It was just post-war and places were rationed in favour of ex-servicemen."[42] As his parents were still keen for him to get a degree, Rose went on to study English at King's College, London; however, by this time he already knew that he wanted to follow in his brother David's footsteps – David had already gone to RADA – and go into the theatre. As a result, he remembers: "I got involved as much as I could in both college and university drama productions."[43] After finishing his degree, when he was still unsure of how good he was, he wrote to the Old Vic. Although an audition with them did not lead to a place, he was subsequently recommended to the new Elizabethan Theatre Company which had just been launched.

© Mark Gudgeon

In 1960, Rose would become one of the founder members of the Royal Shakespeare Company, staying with them throughout the decade. It was during these years that Rose befriended fellow actor Terrence Hardiman, who would later join him on *Secret Army*. Among the most acclaimed RSC productions of its first ten years – in which he performed alongside some of Britain's best known actors – were: Clifford Williams's *Comedy of Errors* in which he played Dromio of Ephesus, which was also televised; Peter Hall's *Wars of the Roses* (Duke of Exeter); Peter Brook's *Marat/Sade* (Monsieur Coulmier) – a production which was also filmed – and *US*; and Trevor Nunn's *The Revenger's Tragedy* (Antonio).

In 1969, partly because he wasn't getting the leading roles, Rose decided to leave the RSC behind in order to pursue a television career. By this time, he had already appeared in an episode of *Mystery and Imagination* in 1968 and made his debut as the occasional character Dr Snell, a sinister psychiatrist, in the hard-hitting drama series *Callan* (1969-74) with Edward Woodward. Other early television parts included: a 1970 episode of *A Family at War*; Jacques in several episodes of the epic Sartre drama *Roads to Freedom* (1970); Egerton in the classic drama *Elizabeth R*; Mr Pritchard in the Lord Peter Wimsey mystery *The Unpleasantness at the Bellona Club* (1972); and Emperor Franz-Josef of Austria in the mini-series *Napoleon and Love* (1972). As the Seventies continued, further notable roles followed, including: General Koller in *The Death of Adolf Hitler* (1973); creepy cockney journalist Quintus Slide in ten episodes of the BBC's mammoth Anthony Trollope serial *The Pallisers* (1974); schoolmaster Mr Jonas in *How Green Was My Valley* (1975); Mr Johnson in a musical version of

Elizabeth Gaskell's *Cranford* (1976); and guest roles in *Play of the Month*; Boyet in *Love's Labours Lost* (1975) and Cool in *London Assurance* (1976). His final television roles before beginning *Secret Army* were in episodes of *Warship*, *Van der Valk* and the week-long series *Rooms*, all of which were broadcast in 1977. Rose believes that it was actually his roles in *Callan* and *How Green Was My Valley* that chiefly contributed to him winning the part of Kessler. Dr Snell in *Callan* was a man "who interrogated drugged suspects and he was a very sinister sort of man, in fact one of the other characters in the series described him as a 'breast-fed Nazi'!", while Mr Jonas in *How Green Was My Valley* was "a rather sadistic Welsh schoolmaster who in fact was so nasty that the class ganged up on him and one of the parents' friends actually came in one day in the middle of class and put him up on the desk and beat him with a stick." Despite the similarities than can be drawn between Kessler and these characters, Rose concedes that the real answer as to why he was cast was only really known by Gerard Glaister himself.

Rose was formally contracted to play Kessler on 25 February 1977.

Ron Pember (Alain Muny)

Cast as Alain Muny was 43-year-old character actor and director, Ron Pember. A true Eastender, born in Plaistow, London, Pember began his acting career – as Ronald rather than Ron – in a 1949 touring production of *Twelfth Night* in which he played Fabian. In the Fifties he worked extensively with the Clacton, Bexhill and Eastbourne repertory companies, before making his London debut as Harry in

© Peter Cartwright

Treasure Island at the Mermaid Theatre, which had just opened, in 1959. This was the start of Pember's long association with the Mermaid Theatre and its manager Bernard Miles, with whom he had a good working relationship despite the latter's well-known eccentricity. Pember secured his first television roles in *Dixon of Dock Green* and *Armchair Theatre* in 1961, before taking the role of Bird in *Blitz!* at the Adelphi Theatre the following year.

Between 1965 and 1968, Pember became a member of Laurence Olivier's first National Theatre company at the Old Vic, taking roles in *Othello*, *Rosencrantz and Guildenstern Are Dead* and *Much Ado About Nothing* among others. During this time, Pember also took more roles on television, notably Mr Jones in *Cathy Come Home*, and minor parts in films such as *Poor Cow* (1967) and *Curse of the Crimson Altar* (1968). By now, Pember had begun to direct at the Mermaid Theatre: *The Goblet Game* (1968); *Lock Up Your*

Daughters (1969); *Treasure Island* (1969) again – which would transfer to New York and several cities in Canada later that year; *Henry IV Parts 1 and 2;* and a production of *Dick Turpin*, which he had co-written.

The early Seventies would see him take more and more character parts in television series such as *Randall and Hopkirk (Deceased)*, *A Family at War* and *Softly, Softly*, and in films including *Young Winston* (1971) and *Death Line* (1972). Prominent TV roles followed in 1973 in *A Pin to See the Peepshow* (with Bernard Hepton) and *Crown Court*, the same year in which he wrote the musical *Jack the Ripper* which opened at the Ambassador's Theatre in 1974 and transferred to the Cambridge Theatre in 1975. It was during this period that Pember enjoyed a sojourn with the RSC, making a particularly notable performance as Feste in a long-running production of *Twelfth Night* for which he was nominated for an award. In 1975 he would appear in more television, including *The Naked Civil Servant*, and the film *The Land That Time Forgot*. In the years immediately preceding *Secret Army*, as well as performing opposite his future co-star Angela Richards in the musical *Liza of Lambeth* (1976) in which he played pearly king Fingers Philips, he would return to the Mermaid to co-direct *King and Country* (1976) and direct and co-adapt *The Point!* (1977), which featured former Monkees, Davy Jones and Mickey Dolenz. As well as his role as Alain in *Secret Army*, 1977 would also see Pember play Mr Snawley in the BBC's new production of *Nicholas Nickleby* with Nigel Havers in the title role and the recurring character of the mortuary attendant in the Stephen Yardley ITV drama *The XYY Man*.

James Bree (Gaston Colbert)

Like Clifford Rose, character actor James Bree, who was cast as Lisa's Uncle Gaston was another former RSC actor. In fact, Bree and Rose had appeared together in several productions in the early Sixties, including *The Duchess of Malfi* and *The Taming of the Shrew* in 1960, alongside such acting greats as Peter O'Toole, Sian Phillips, Eric Porter, Peggy Ashcroft and Diana Rigg. Bree stayed with the RSC for three years, his final production being *A Penny for a Song* (1962) with Marius Goring and Judi Dench, in which he played the key role of Lamprett Bellboys. Bree left the RSC to break into television. His notable roles during the Sixties included: Miller in *The Avengers* episode *Immortal Clay* (1963); Professor Chernev in *R3* (1965); Davis in *The Power Game* (1966); Lucius Chad in *The Wednesday Play: A Brilliant Future Behind Him* (1967); Villers in the classic episode of *The*

61

Prisoner: Don't Forsake Me, Oh My Darling (1968); Wilkington in another *Avengers: Killer* (1968); and episodes of *The Troubleshooters* and *Z Cars*. In 1969, Bree appeared as Blofeld's Swiss lawyer Gebruder Gumbold in the Bond film *On Her Majesty's Secret Service*, and the villainous Security Chief in the epic ten-part *Doctor Who* yarn *The War Games*.

The early Seventies saw Bree in consistent demand, appearing in dramas such as *Codename, A Family at War, Roads to Freedom* in 1970, and *Upstairs Downstairs, The Persuaders!* and popular comedies such as *Please Sir!* and *On the Buses* in 1971, while in 1972 he played a Major masquerading as a woman in the three-part *Ace of Wands* adventure *Sisters Deadly*. Prominent roles followed in *The Donati Conspiracy* (1973), *Spy Trap* (in 1975), *Madame Bovary* (1975) and *The Glittering Prizes* (1976). In the Seventies, Bree continued to concurrently work in the theatre, appearing, for instance, between 1974-5 in Chekhov's *Three Sisters* and William Inge's *Bus Stop* at the Watford Palace Theatre. In 1976, prior to joining *Secret Army*, he played Montanus in *I, Claudius*, Ross in *The Duchess of Duke Street*, Malcolm Yorke in the horror film *Satan's Slave*, and the wonderfully named Adolphus Spanker in *London Assurance*.

Maria Charles (Louise Colbert)

Cast as Lisa's fretting Aunt Louise was character actress Maria Charles. Charles made her London acting debut during the Second World War in *Pick-up Girl* at the Prince of Wales Theatre at the age of 14. After training at RADA, she went on to work extensively in regional theatre before creating the part of 'boop-a-doop'

Dulcie in the original London production of Sandy Wilson's *The Boyfriend* at Wyndham's Theatre in 1954, and later also featuring in its sequel, *Divorce Me Darling* (1965). Her television roles in the Sixties included: Dorinda in *The Curious Adventures of Miss Jane Rawley* (1968); Dorcas Tindal in *The Timorous Rake* (1969); and a spell in *Crossroads* as Lorelei Macefield. She went on to win many more television roles in the Seventies, including Mrs Higgins in *Polyanna* (1973); Sara Pocket in *Great Expectations* (1974); and Mrs Blewitt in *Anne of Avonlea* (1975) alongside Jan Francis. However, her career-defining role came along in 1976 when she played Jewish mother Rita Green in Jack Rosenthal's award-winning *Play for Today*:

Bar Mitzvah Boy, a performance that undoubtedly contributed to her casting as Louise Colbert the following year.

Valentine Dyall (Dr Pascal Keldermans)

Due to his sinister performances on film, television and especially radio, velvet-toned Valentine Dyall was an unusual choice for the part of the benevolent Dr Keldermans. Born in 1908, Valentine was the son of another noted actor, Franklin Dyall. Valentine was educated at Harrow and went on to study law at Christ Church College, Oxford. During his time in Oxford he was secretary of the Oxford University Dramatic Society.

After being noticed by John Gielgud, he made his professional debut at the Old Vic in 1930 and spent that decade in supporting roles in the West End. He made his radio debut in 1936, but his career didn't really take off until he began work on the BBC Radio weekly horror series *Appointment with Fear*, which he introduced and narrated as 'the Man in Black'. This spine-chilling series was hugely successful during its twelve-year run between 1941 and 1953 and, as radio had millions of listeners at the time, made Dyall into a national celebrity.

In his first few films, Dyall played a succession of stock Nazis in *The Silver Fleet*, *The Life and Death of Colonel Blimp* and *Yellow Canary* (all 1943). He went on to feature as Alec's friend in *Brief Encounter* (1945), Sir George Bell in *Night Boat to Dublin* (1946) and the title role in the Hammer film *Dr Morelle: the Case of the Missing Heiress* (1949). It was roles like this which would eventually contribute to Dyall becoming known as 'the British Vincent Price'.

His early television work included roles in drama serials such as *Treasure Island* (1951) and comedy series like *The Idiots Weekly: Price 2D* and *A Show Called Fred* (both 1956). In the same decade, Dyall would also irregularly flex his comedic muscles on *The Goon Show* in which his 'Man in Black' persona was mercilessly parodied. More horror films followed such as *The City of the Dead* (1960) and *The Haunting* (1963), as did more television including *The Cheaters* (1960), *The Devil in the Fog* (1968) and *The Avengers* (in 1968). Although he was uncredited on both films, in 1967 Dyall would play the Voice of God in *Bedazzled* and two different roles in *Casino Royale*. Perhaps his most notable performances in the early Seventies were in the 1974 films *The Beast Must Die* (directed by *Secret Army* director and writer Paul Annett) in which he narrated 'the Werewolf break' and *The Great McGonagall* in which he played no less than an army sergeant, a doctor, a native messenger, a policeman, a fop and Alfred Lord Tennyson! One of his last roles before joining *Secret Army* was in the popular retelling of Cinderella: *The Slipper and the Rose* (1976). Dyall bore his relative celebrity as a regular supporting player with some humour, once stating: "I am the longest shining small star in the business."

Eileen Page (Andrée Foiret)

Eileen's acting career began in repertory theatre in the early Sixties. Later in the decade she would take her first television roles which included episodes of *No Hiding Place* (1966) and *The First Lady* (1969), and her first film role in *I Can't...I Can't* (1969).

Although she still spent the majority of the time in the theatre, which has always been Page's favourite dramatic medium (like Hammond-Hill she would join the RSC after her time on *Secret Army*), a few more television parts came up, such as an episode of *Affairs of the Heart* (1974), before she was seen for the part of Andrée.

The *Behind the Scenes* documentary

As pre-production gathered pace, Glaister and Brason found themselves visited ever more frequently by another BBC team who had themselves started production some months earlier. Led by Tony Roberts, this was a team working on a new documentary series entitled *Behind the Scenes*. Commissioned by the BBC several months earlier, this five-part production would seek to examine how television drama was being made in the mid-Seventies, and specifically how the BBC's newest wartime series would translate from script to screen. The *Behind the Scenes* team initially set out to achieve this aim by sitting in on pre-production script meetings in January 1977. However, they would continue to return at regular intervals as the production process continued, to: talk to the series's leads; follow rehearsals at the BBC's Acton site; attend trips to costumiers; visit a soundstage at Ealing; and eventually observe overseas location filming in Belgium.

The series was also set to feature a rather too liberal sprinkling of camera interviews with a multitude of former-RAF talking heads relating anecdotes about their wartime evasion experiences – a nice idea which ultimately did not sit well with the surrounding material, especially as this was ostensibly a series about television production. *Behind the Scenes* was eventually broadcast partway through the first run of *Secret Army* late on Sunday evenings in November-December 1977 and therefore, unfortunately, not in tandem with the episodes upon which they ended up principally concentrating: *Lisa – Code Name: Yvette*, *Radishes with Butter* and *Growing Up*. The series would be presented and narrated by Michael Molyneux, an educational broadcaster and journalist who was best known at the time for fronting 'The Legal Desk' slot on the magazine programme *Nationwide* and as an on-screen participant in *Out of Court*.

In 1980, the series was repeated during the day as part of a BBC Media Studies course for UK schools. An accompanying guide for teachers suggested discussion of such matters as: typecasting ('Ask students if they could easily accept Clifford Rose who plays Kessler in a sympathetic part as say a beat policeman or a village doctor?'); the authenticity of the series ('Does *Secret Army* succeed in giving a sense of period and place in its mix of studio props and outside locations?'); and the likely perils of location filming ('Try to give students some idea of the difficulties of marshalling groups of people and equipment on location.').[44]

Michael Molyneux © Unknown

Broadcast details:

1. *"We are not writing Hamlet"*   (11.40pm, Sunday 13 November 1977)
2. *"All those people were heroes"*   (11.30pm, Sunday 20 November 1977)
3. *"I enjoy it when it's over"*   (11.40pm, Sunday 27 November 1977)
4. *"A problem of authenticity"*   (11.25pm, Sunday 04 December 1977)
5. *"A boy? A ten-year-old boy?"*   (11.15pm, Sunday 11 December 1977)

Directors

As well as tightening up the scripts and casting the regulars, and fending off the dogged *Behind the Scenes* team, Glaister and Brason also spent Spring 1977 briefing their new production crew, including, most crucially, the three directors assigned to bring the world of *Secret Army* to life.

Kenneth Ives

Although he had only been directing television for three years, by the time Kenneth Ives was approached to direct *Secret Army* he already had an impressive array of credits to his name. Prior to becoming a director, Ives had been a successful actor. His early television appearances included episodes of *Adam Adamant Lives!* between 1966-7 and a leading role in the eternally popular *Doctor Who*, playing the sadistic Toba in the story *The Dominators* (1969). He went on to play Wratislaw in *The First Churchills* (1969), the Interviewer in the Dennis Potter-scripted *Play for Today: Angels Are So Few* (1970) and Ulm in *Arthur of the Britons* (1973). However, he is perhaps best known as an actor for playing the central role of Hawkeye in the acclaimed 1971 BBC production of *The Last of the Mohicans* opposite John Abineri and Patricia Maynard.

Ives switched to directing in 1973, his first project being a short television play called *All Who Sail In Her*, featuring none other than Ron Pember. He went on to direct: half a dozen episodes of popular police series *Softly, Softly: Taskforce* between 1973-4; an episode of the BBC *Bedtime Stories* (1974) anthology series, scripted by Andrew Davies, entitled *The Water Maiden*; and, in 1975, five consecutive episodes of the immensely popular first series of *Poldark*. In the year prior to *Secret Army* he helmed the *BBC Playhouse* production: *The Button Man* (1976) and two episodes of the gritty Birmingham underworld drama *Gangsters* (1976-7). In 1977, as well as working on his five episodes of *Secret Army*, Ives also found time to direct an episode of the 'near future' BBC2 drama *1990* (*Health Farm*), a series which coincidentally had been created by Wilfred Greatorex.

Paul Annett

Paul Annett was another director whom Glaister had not yet worked with. His directing career began at the end of the Sixties with shows such as *The Worker* (1965-70) and *Fraud Squad* (1969-70), and a documentary about the making of the film *The Battle of Britain*, entitled *The Battle for the Battle of Britain* (1969), for LWT. In the early Seventies, he went on to direct a play for LWT called *Mr Pargiter* (1971), featuring Michael Culver's father Roland in the title role, episodes of the police series *New Scotland Yard* (in 1972-3); and a *Crown Court* serial (in 1973). In 1974, he directed: the feature film *The Beast Must Die* starring Peter Cushing, which would subsequently win cult status; and, in stark contrast, the Fay Weldon-scripted *Poor Baby* and episodes of the LWT women's prison drama *Within These Walls*. Further work on television drama followed, this time for the BBC, including the final series of Robert Barr's *Spy Trap* and, like Kenneth Ives, the first series of *Poldark*, directing a total of six episodes. Just prior to his work on *Secret Army*, Annett notably directed a six-part adaptation of the classic novel *Little Lord Fauntleroy* (1976).

Viktors Ritelis

Of the three directors selected to direct the first series of *Secret Army*, Glaister knew Latvian-born Viktors Ritelis the best, having collaborated with him on and off since his directing debut in 1967 on a series that Glaister was producing called *This Man Craig*, a drama about a Scottish schoolmaster.

Ritelis had begun his career behind the camera in the early Sixties, working as a BBC production assistant on series such as *Doctor Who*, on the story *The Crusade* (1965) – in which he famously doubled for actor William Russell in a scene involving live ants – and the twelve part Dalek epic *The Daleks' Masterplan* (1965-6). Ritelis became a fully-fledged director in 1967, and some of his early directing includes episodes of *Softly, Softly* (in 1967/8) *The Troubleshooters* (in 1968) and *Sir Arthur Conan Doyle's Sherlock Holmes* (1968) with Peter Cushing, all for the BBC. In 1969, as well as directing an episode of

The Expert for Glaister, Ritelis helmed horror film *The Corpse* (1969) for Abacus and London Cannon Films, which centred on the undead corpse of a tyrannical stockbroker played by Michael Gough.

In the early Seventies, Glaister recruited Ritelis to direct: the opening episode of his spy series *Codename* (1970); several more episodes of the 1971 series of *The Expert*; and, in 1972, three episodes of his new drama *Colditz*, including the second episode *Missing, Presumed Dead* (which introduced David McCallum's Flt Lt Carter) and the chilling *The Traitor* (featuring Patrick Troughton as a Catholic priest). Around this time, Ritelis also directed episodes of such fondly-remembered classics as *The Onedin Line* (the very first series in 1971), *The Regiment* (in 1972) and the Cretan-set *The Lotus Eaters* (the second series in 1973). In the latter, Ritelis's emerging directorial style is particularly discernible, especially in a beach-set dream sequence featuring Wanda Ventham's character, a cameo appearance by series creator Michael J. Bird and a heck of a lot of mirrorlon. In 1973, Ritelis directed a further three instalments of *Colditz* for Glaister, including the episode based around Airey Neave's real-life exit from the prison (*Frogs in the Well*) and the series finale (*Liberation*). Like Paul Annett, he would also work on *Spy Trap* (in 1973). 1975 was a busy year for Ritelis as he took on episodes of *The Sweeney* and another spy show, *Quiller*, with Michael Jayston, as well as two instalments of *Play for Today*: Willy Russell's *The Death of a Young, Young Man* and *Children of the Sun*. Before Glaister recalled him for *Secret Army*, Ritelis joined Ives as one of the directors on the series *Gangsters*.

In 2004, when Ritelis looked back on the many hours of wartime drama that he had directed for Glaister (which would later include *The Fourth Arm* (1983) as well), he mused that it was: "…rather interesting seeing as I survived Hitler's Germany, that there I was helping Gerry restage World War II on three different series."

Glaister was keen that his new series should have a coherent look and feel and for this reason elected to divide up the episodes between the three directors in such a way that they rarely helmed episodes that would be broadcast consecutively, in order to prevent the domination of distinct directorial styles. However, in practice those episodes directed by Viktors Ritelis were set to stand out a mile due to their stark European realism and more filmic style. Glaister's other reason for dividing up the episodes in this way was simply in order to balance their workload so that they had sufficient time to prepare for and work on their allotted episodes before they had to move on to the next one. Only one episode would be reassigned during production: episode eight (*Guilt*), which was not originally allocated to Paul Annett despite the fact that it was effectively the second instalment of a two-part story. Annett objected to the decision and his request to direct *Guilt* as well as the preceding episode (*Lost Sheep*) was granted. Each director was set to helm five episodes each, until that was the production team were told that the series would need to fill a sudden gap in the Autumn production schedule, which led to a sixteenth episode being hurriedly commissioned and allocated to Ritelis.

Glaister summarised the role of his directors to the *Behind the Scenes* team: "As producer I cast the principal regular characters, then, with them [the directors], I discuss the scripts at length and we agree what the aims are and what the intention of the script is, and how we're going to treat it. We discuss the casting of the non-regular parts that come into each script separately and, from there on, he acts totally on his own, with reference to me as required over things to do with finance and filming and so on. But he directs the actors at rehearsal, he directs the cameras and the actors in the studio."[45] Around the same time, Kenneth Ives, who had by now started casting non-regulars for *Growing Up*, shared his modest views on the relative significance of the script, casting and the director: "I think probably 50% of the success ingredient is having a good script, 40% is casting it well, and the other 10% is what the director can do."[46]

Semi-Regular Cast

As well as being tasked with the casting of non-regulars, the directors were also required to cast those characters who were due to appear irregularly in a handful of episodes, such as: Jacques Bol, Corporal Rennert and the Chantal sisters. Interestingly, of the Series One supporting cast, only two characters would be cast by a director for a single episode and subsequently be deemed successful enough to make return appearances in a following series: bargee Hans van Broecken and his wife Lena.

Timothy Morand (Jacques Bol)

Timothy had previously appeared in Glaister's *Colditz* as the French Captain, Marquand, in the second series episodes *Odd Man In* and *Frogs in the Well* in 1974. He had also worked with Kenneth Ives before, having played Vicomte de Maresi in the first series of *Poldark*. Morand's first television credit was as Adams in Thames Television's *Six Days of Justice* in 1972; since then, Morand had appeared in episodes of *Dial M for Murder* (1974), *Marked Personal* (1974), *Coronation Street* (1974) and *Late Call* (1975). Immediately prior to *Secret Army*, he would feature as a British Corporal in the Richard Attenborough war film *A Bridge Too Far* (1977).

Robin Langford (Corporal Veit Rennert)

Robin Langford had lots of work as a child actor under his belt by the time that the opportunity came along to play Rennert in *Secret Army*. Langford, who was born and brought up in the Cotswolds, remembers how he was "seduced away from a doubtful scholarly life" at the tender age of nine and "entered the exciting world of the theatre as an actor" discovering his "love for its magical atmosphere." His first television appearance was in 1966 in an edition of *The Wednesday Play* entitled *The Head Waiter*, written by John Mortimer, in which he featured prominently as a boy who is neglected by his parents but entertained by a storytelling Head Waiter played by Donald Pleasance. The following year, at the age of twelve, he joined the RSC, playing Young Marcius in a production of *Coriolanus* with Ian Richardson in the title role, and Fleance in a Peter Hall-directed *Macbeth* with Paul Scofield. Later that year he took his first film role playing Elizabeth Taylor's son in the film *The Comedians* (which also featured Richard Burton, Alec Guinness and Peter Ustinov). More television followed, including episodes of *A Family at War*, *Tom Brown's Schooldays* (both in 1971) and *War and Peace* (1972). From 1972-3 he played the young lead, Richard Shelton, in

Southern Television's adventure series *Black Arrow*, based on the book by Robert Louis Stevenson. After jewel thief drama *Diamonds on Wheels* (1974), Langford appeared in a 1976 episode of *The Brothers*. His final TV appearance before beginning work on *Secret Army*, aged 22, was as Eddie Sturgess in the *Duchess of Duke Street* episode *A Lesson in Manners*. Langford remembers that his audition for the part of Rennert, with director Viktors Ritelis, simply extended to his pronunciation of the phrase "Herr Sturmbannführer" and that the most challenging part of the role turned out to be getting to grips with when to click his heels after entering Kessler's office!

Mary Barclay (Sophie Chantal)

Mary Barclay was cast as the more eccentric of the two Chantal sisters and was set to make four separate appearances in the series. Barclay studied at the Guildhall School of Music and Drama, toured with Donald Wolfit's travelling Shakespeare company, appeared in her first film in 1948 (the Canadian-made *Sins of the Fathers*) and featured in two Agatha Christie plays on Broadway, before settling permanently in the UK. Her most prominent television role was as the domineering Stella Dane in *Crossroads* between 1972-3. Other television included *Dixon of Dock Green* (in 1964) and *Steptoe and Son* (in 1973). Her notable film roles included: 'A's Mother' in *The Revolutionary* (1970), in which Jon Voight

played 'A'; and Martha Thompson in the Oscar-winning *A Touch of Class* (1973). Just prior to playing Sophie in *Secret Army*, she appeared as Lady Wingham in the 1976 *Wodehouse Playhouse* episode *Strychnine in the Soup*. Barclay was cast by Viktors Ritelis who had worked with her before on the 1972 *Spy Trap* episode *Desperate Men* and a *Play for Today* entitled *Children of the Sun* (1970).

Ruth Gower (Madeleine Chantal)

Ruth Gower, who would notch up a total of three episodes of *Secret Army*, had previously featured in the television plays *Dinner at Eight* and *Claudia* (both 1951), in series such as *Life with the Lyons* (in 1958), *No Hiding Place* (in 1963) and *Z Cars* (in 1967), and in the films *The Family Way* (1966) and *Oh What a Lovely War!* (1969). In 1960, she toured Australia in a theatre production of *The Marriage-Go-Round*, in which she was the leading lady to Basil Rathbone's leading man. Gower, like Barclay, was also cast by Ritelis, however she had not worked with him previously.

Gunnar Möller (Hans van Broecken)

Although he was only set to appear in just one episode of the first series and was therefore not mentioned in Brason's Script Editor's Notes, Natalie's Uncle Hans,

a German bargee masquerading as a Dutchman, would ultimately appear, albeit irregularly, in all three series. The actor cast to play him was Gunnar Möller. Born in Berlin in 1928, Möller, who was eleven years old when the Second World War began, became, like many German boys of his age, a member of the Hitler Youth. His first experience of acting was in the propaganda-oriented cinema of the Third Reich, beginning in 1940 with the feature *Unser Fräulein Doktor*, and films such as *Junge Adler* (1944) which was intended to encourage younger viewers to consider working in aviation production at an early age.

Despite the passing of Nazi Germany, the German film industry soldiered on and Möller continued acting in films throughout the late Forties and the Fifties, as well as appearing in theatre in Berlin and Munich. It was in the Fifties that his popularity with the German cinema-going audience was cemented with roles in acclaimed films such as: the romantic comedy *Heidelberger Romanze* (1951); love story *Ich denke oft an Piroschka* (1955), which was considered to be his greatest success; *Hunde, wollt ihr ewig leben* (1958), which was set during the war and concerned a man distrustful of Nazi ideology and *Nacht fiel über Gotenhafen* (1959) which was set in 1945 and depicted the flight of millions of Germans from the Russian Army.

The Sixties saw him branch out more into TV and theatre, but he still appeared in a steady stream of films, such as *Saison in Salzburg* (1961), *Maibritt, das Mädchen von den Inseln* (1964) and *Liselotte von der Pfalz* (1966). In 1973, Möller played Adolf Hilter himself in the award-winning films *Dny zrady I* and *Dny zrady II*, written and directed by Otakar Vávra. In 1974 he featured in his first international film, playing Karl Braun in *The Odessa File*. After several more German TV series, Vávra approached Möller to play Hitler again, this time in the film *Osvobození Prahy* (1976). In the same year that Möller made his first *Secret Army* episode, for which he was cast by Paul Annett, he also made the Francis Durbridge crime mini-series *Die Kette* (1977) playing Inspector Tim Everson.

Marianne Stone (Lena van Broecken)

Like Hans, Lena van Broecken, Natalie's Dutch aunt, would appear only once in the first series but would be set to return on several further occasions. By the time she joined *Secret Army*, London-born Stone had amassed a huge number of British film credits (in fact by the time she made her last film in 1985 she was rumoured to have more film credits to her name than any other British actress), albeit largely in minor roles: a succession of unnamed waitresses, shop assistants, factory workers, cleaners and secretaries. A selection of her early credits include playing a waitress in the classic *Brighton Rock* (1947), a nurse in *The Quatermass Xperiment* (1955), a stewardess in *A Night to Remember* (1958) and a hospital administrator in *The 39 Steps* (1959). One of her most prominent roles in the Sixties was as Vivian Darkbloom in *Lolita* (1962). The decade also saw the start of her long association with the *Carry On...* series.

By the Seventies, Stone was also beginning to make more appearances on television as well as film, featuring in episodes of *Bless This House* (in 1972), *Public Eye* (in 1971 and 1973) and *Seven Faces of Woman* (in 1977). Three other TV roles in the Seventies, in episodes of the series *Dead of Night* (in 1972), *Crown Court* (in 1973) and *Little Lord Fauntleroy*, saw Stone directed by Paul Annett. It was Annett who would choose to cast her again in *Secret Army*, for what was set to be one of her career's most demanding and dramatic roles.

Building characters

In early March 1977, the regular cast began to receive the first scripts for the series, along with – just as the writers had been given – a fair amount of background material explaining both the historical context of the series and the dramatic approach and tone which Glaister and Brason were hoping to strike. However, due to the fact that Greatorex's scene-setting script for episode one had been rejected, the actors would have to wait some time for Willis Hall to finish its replacement. This presented a particular problem to the regulars, as they were naturally hoping to find clues to their characters in the opening instalment. When interviewed by *Behind the Scenes* in March 1977, Jan Francis commented: "I haven't received it as yet, the first script, which is obviously going to be very important because it's going to set up the character for me... when I've got all the scripts here, I'll be able to see there'll be threads running through, giving me a clue." She went on to relate that: "At the moment I've got vague ideas as to what she's like, but I'm deliberately not fixing anything in my mind, because it's jolly hard to eradicate those." However, what she did know by this stage was that Lisa was "very different" from her, principally because "she is a marvellous organiser and I'm not," adding that it was "interesting to be cast differently to your own personality, as it makes you think harder."[47] Francis remembers today how thrilled she was at the time at the prospect of the series, as she could quickly tell that a great deal of time and care had been taken, especially over the premise and historical background.

Bernard Hepton was also looking for clues in the script to the character of Albert in March 1977: "I'm just gathering ideas, letting them sift through and waiting for the next script so that I can put another bit of jigsaw in. But the point is I've got to do this quickly before we start rehearsal, because one of the great difficulties of being in a series is that you have to make all those decisions before you start." What Hepton did feel he knew about Albert at that time was that he was a hero, "because all those people on the escape lines were heroes." On a more mundane note, Hepton had by now grown a moustache, because "I have a funny feeling at the back of my mind – a vision that Belgians of my age all have big moustaches," although he recognised that this was not building his character, merely "getting the feel of it."[48]

Clifford Rose, meanwhile, tried to get into the mindset of Kessler by carrying out his own research: "I spent quite a lot of time at the Imperial War Museum in London, researching the war and in particular the German SS and the Gestapo, and I found that extremely illuminating and very useful." He also remembers "Reading accounts of people who had conducted interrogations, what had happened during them and also something of what some of them were like outside of their work: their families, their children, their wives... and one realised that these men were not just professional soldiers, killers... but that they had another side to them." Rose knew early on that as an actor Kessler was going to be a fascinating character to play, because he, like all fanatics, was "very complicated and interesting" and "showed human nature at its most extreme". He also felt that it was very important that people like Kessler "need to be explored and explained" through drama such as *Secret Army*. As well as his trips to the Imperial War Museum, Rose found Brason's technical documentation about uniforms, flashes, insignia and the equivalent German and British ranks very useful, so that he could understand more clearly where his character, as Sturmbannführer, fitted in the Third Reich hierarchy.

Costume and Make-up

Also occupied with such matters was costume designer Andrew Mackenzie, who would be responsible for costumes for the entire first series and had previously produced costumes for *Are You Being Served* and *The Dick Emery Show*. Soon after starting work on *Secret Army*, Mackenzie made a worrying discovery: "I found, to my horror, that our own BBC stock had been depleted dramatically because, would you believe, there were five productions actually at work based in the period 1935 to 1945 at the BBC alone. So that raised a certain alarm within me. I raced up to the costumiers to find that they too were being besieged by requests for civilian clothes of the period."[49] When Mackenzie later returned to costumier Berman's and Nathan's with Valentine Dyall in April 1977 in order to find suitable attire for Dr Keldermans, the trip was recorded for use in *Behind the Scenes*.

Similarly concerned with making the actors look authentically period was make-up artist Judy Neame (née Clay), the wife of Christopher Neame, whom she had met when they had worked on *Colditz* together. Derry Haws would be the series's other principal make-up artist. Due to the period nature of the production, both Neame and Haws were set to have trouble with male supporting artists over the length of their hair, which most young men wore long in the Seventies and was therefore entirely inappropriate for the parts of British airmen or the Luftwaffe Polizei. Jan Francis recalls that "there were lots of fights about hair with the make-up girls" because the actors concerned were worried about getting post-*Secret Army* work and their 'pulling power'! However, there was still far less trouble than there had been on *Colditz*, when mutinous male supporting artistes had led to a despairing Glaister devising a special clause to be written into their contracts: 'The artist agrees to hair adjustments according to the BBC's requirements.' The 'hair clause' was retained for *Secret Army*.

Titles and Music

As well as Judy Neame, Glaister recruited several other crew members whom he had previously used on *Colditz*, such as film recordist Basil Harris and graphic designer Alan Jeapes. Jeapes's title sequence for *Colditz* had won the 1973 Royal Television Society Award for Best Graphic Design and he was eager to repeat this success on *Secret Army*. The *Colditz* title sequence consisted of various exterior and interior stills of the castle and cross-fades with the Nazi swastika.

Glaister, who always got very involved in this element of production, approved of Jeapes's decision to use stills again, but this time in a more specific narrative sequence, so that prior to each episode the stills would convey an airman's fall from the sky near a farm and subsequent journey by track, road and rail to a safe-house in Brussels while the closing sequence would show the airman's journey down the evasion line, eventually ending at the sea and so to freedom. For many, the stark, coldly beautiful vistas of cobbled roads, chalk paths and rail tracks would be one of the most memorable elements of the series, especially when married to Robert Farnon's haunting theme music. Jeapes's *Colditz* titles had also been accompanied by a Farnon composition, 'The Colditz March' (the salient parts of which were reportedly written on the back of an envelope during a twenty-minute taxi ride between BBC TV Centre and his hotel!), which had won the composer his third Ivor Novello award. Canadian-born Farnon, who passed away in April 2005 and is now regarded as one of the greatest ever composers of Light Orchestral music, took a different approach when Glaister asked him to write the theme for *Secret Army*, electing to return to a piece he had composed previously entitled 'Wall of Fear'. However, Farnon rearranged the composition especially for its use in the series, and in May 1977 conducted 35 musicians playing his new orchestration.

Angela Richards remembers the first time that she saw the completed title sequence: "I gave a sudden intake of breath… I knew then that the show was going to be exciting"; while Jan Francis recalls: "Once we saw the titles and music, we thought it had to work. We were thrilled with those."

Design

Due to the complexity of the authentic recreation of the period and the vast number of sets and furniture required for a series of such length, it was decided that *Secret Army* required a total of six separate designers, with several episodes even being allocated two designers: one to deal with film design, the other with studio design. Austin Ruddy, who had also worked with Glaister on *Colditz*, was selected to be the series's lead designer and therefore responsible for the creation of all the 'stock' sets, required for the majority of the episodes of the run, including: the Restaurant Candide (more commonly referred to as the Café Candide in production material); the Candide's back room; Kessler's office; Brandt's office; Gaston and Louise's lounge; Dr Keldermans's waiting room; and Andrée's bedroom. The Candide sets were unmistakably the most important of these due to their intensive use in the programme and Ruddy was given a completion/delivery date for them of 3 June 1977, a few days before studio recording would begin.

Into Production

By the end of March, Willis Hall had delivered the final draft of the opening episode, which after considerable discussion over a suitable title was formally confirmed, as Hall had suggested, as *Lisa – Code Name Yvette*. Scripting the episode had not been an easy task for Hall, who felt that it had been akin to fitting a large-scale feature film into a 50-minute television programme. Glaister and Brason were certainly anxious that it ticked a number of boxes: introducing all of the regular characters and all of the main settings; establishing the series's premise and intention; setting the right atmosphere and tone; and, most importantly, being sufficiently compelling to ensure that viewers would tune in again the following week. Glaister and Brason felt that Hall had achieved this, but the writer was nevertheless certain that his other two scripts for the series – *Growing Up* and *A Question of Loyalty* – were superior, principally due to the fact that they did not have to juggle so many elements and because he simply had enjoyed far more freedom when putting them together.

Due to the presence of Randle's RAF Escaping Society exhibition at the RAF Museum in Hendon, Glaister and Brason decided that this would be the ideal venue at which their regular cast could be brought together for the very first time to meet each other and presumably engender some camaraderie. The visit, for which Randle acted as tour guide, took place at the very start of April 1977, and although many of the cast already knew each other from previous acting jobs, the trip was a great success. Jan Francis remembers it as a "bonding experience", but felt that Rose and Culver should not have been invited as the exhibit gave away all of Lifeline's secrets! Not long afterwards, the lead cast members were making final preparations for production. For Francis, this meant a trip to Vidal Sassoon where she spent a rather "traumatic" day having her beloved waist-length locks cut short, permed and coloured. Conversely, Bernard Hepton was having hair added, in the form of a hair-piece. Meanwhile, Clifford Rose and Michael Culver decided to meet in a central London pub in order to try out their German accents on each other.

As was and still is the practice, the series would be divided into several production blocks. Episodes 1-6 would form the first block, with episodes 7-11 and 12-16 making up the second and third recording blocks respectively. However, it would transpire that several of the first six episodes to go into production – *Lisa – Code Name Yvette*, *Sergeant on the Run*, *Radishes with Butter*, *Growing Up*, *Too Near Home* and *Second Chance* – originally intended to be broadcast in that selfsame order, would ultimately be shifted around for reasons of narrative flow, continuity and pace. *Growing Up* would become episode six, *Too Near Home*, episode nine, and *Second Chance*, episode five, while Arden Winch's *Child's Play* (the first episode to be recorded in block two) would be brought forward to become episode four, chiefly in order to introduce the viewers to the geography of the evasion line earlier in the series.

It was decided that the majority of the first production block's UK telecine sequences would be filmed first in April, while those scenes that had to be filmed abroad would be tackled in May. The remainder of the UK-based filming would follow in June. In an ideal world, all of the series's location sequences would have been filmed overseas, but the costs involved were far too prohibitive. From an early stage, Glaister was set on foreign location filming actually in the country in which the series was set, Belgium, and more specifically, in Brussels. He sought to make this objective more achievable financially and to ease the burden on his directors and their teams by negotiating a deal with the Belgian television company Belgische Radio en Televisie (BRT), based in Brussels, whereby *Secret Army* would be produced in association with them. In practical production terms, this arrangement would ensure that foreign location filming in the city, and around Belgium in general, would be a much easier prospect, particularly in respect of hiring equipment and extras and finding suitable locations. However, the arrangement, which BRT agreed to in early Spring 1977, was not without its problems. For one thing, initially no co-production money materialised, while further down the line troubles often arose because of the division between Flemish- and French-speaking Belgians. BRT television centre consisted of parallel buildings linked by one bridge, and the personnel in the 'French building' refused to acknowledge that the 'Flemish building' even existed and vice versa. This meant that during their dealings with them the production team had to effectively treat BRT as two separate companies!

In Search of the Candide

On 6 April 1977, several key members of *Secret Army*'s production team, including script editor John Brason, lead designer Austin Ruddy and production unit manager Frank Pendlebury – who had the difficult task of keeping an eye on the overall budget – began a recce of central Brussels. This trip was taken in part to meet with their new colleagues at BRT – principally a liaison man named Wim Bergers who is remembered as a great source of knowledge as well as a vital interpreter and translator – and discuss their specific operational requirements; as well as to locate suitable locations for all the Belgian exterior film sequences for the first six episodes, but also in order that designer Austin Ruddy could potentially locate a suitably unchanged period café interior on which he could model his Candide set. Ruddy remembers that: "We scouted Brussels for a

'traditional' café, but most were very modernised. But the last night we were there, with the construction drawings due date looming frighteningly close, we came upon perfection!"

'Perfection' was the small Café de la Chaussée, run by an elderly couple who

76

were due to retire soon: "Imagine our luck when we came upon this wonderful elderly couple… Imagine *their* luck when we said we'd like to buy all their chairs, tables, ashtrays, Belgian darts set, shove-ha'penny board (below) etc. – I'd like to believe they couldn't believe their luck!" Ruddy was particularly taken with the wood panelling around the café walls, which he felt "oozed atmosphere and must have seen many a story." It was series prop-buyer Bob Sutton who had the job of negotiating a fair sum with the couple and organising the transportation of the whole consignment back to London. Ruddy had a perfect template for his Candide set and a large number of authentic props with which to dress it, although he recalls adapting its shape so that the cameras and sound crew could move around it easily.

Door to the telephone cubicle with lettering later reproduced in the studio. Note Ruddy's reflection in the mirror © Austin Ruddy

Austin Ruddy's finished Candide set © Austin Ruddy

John Brason, Frank Pendlebury and Wim Bergers with the café owners © Austin Ruddy

The front window of a Brussels café actually called 'Le Candide' © Austin Ruddy

Although the name for the restaurant, 'Le Candide', had already been chosen by this point, Ruddy recalls that the team were pleased to actually find a bistro with that exact name during their trip. A photograph was taken of the front of this 'Candide' and the exact Gothic style and colouring of the lettering (with the capital 'L' and 'C' in red and the remaining letters in black) was later copied onto the wall behind the bar on the studio set – such were the lengths that Ruddy and his fellow designers went to in order to ensure authenticity.

Ruddy also took several photographs of period architecture, including rows of houses and rooftops, some of which would later be referred to by scenic artists so that they could paint backcloths for studio sets. The Brussels recce ended on 10 April 1977.

Reference photo of period houses for the scenic artists © Austin Ruddy

The Cameras Roll…

After various scouting trips, the production team decided that due to its similarity to much of Belgium, the flat and low-lying countryside to the west of Peterborough, with its many white-washed farm buildings and poplar trees, would be the locale used for the majority of the series's UK location filming. The presence of the Nene Valley Railway (right) in the area, a preserved railway with a large quantity of European rolling stock and station buildings and platforms that could easily be dressed to appear period, also contributed to its appeal.

The cameras finally started to roll in on *Secret Army* on 17 April 1977, in various fields and farm buildings, under the direction of Kenneth Ives. The very first scenes featured Norman Eshley playing seriously wounded evader Clifford

Howson, and Max Harris as bright Belgian boy Jean-Paul Dornes, for the episode *Growing Up*. The first regular cast members to film scenes, this time in and around Waternewton mill, were Michael Culver and Juliet Hammond-Hill for the opening scenes of the first episode, *Lisa – Code Name Yvette*, which involved Brandt raiding a farm involved in resistance work and Natalie hiding from him and his troops on the farmhouse roof. Hammond-Hill remembers being nervous, not only because this was her first television, but because she had to be harnessed to the roof for the scene. However, a crew was also positioned behind her as an additional safety measure. Later that week, Bernard Hepton and Jan Francis arrived on location for their first scenes, which saw them horse-riding together, once again for *Growing Up*, of which Francis remembers neither were particularly comfortable or confident and that when it came to dismounting, she managed to slide off, but Bernard's horse just kept on going, across the remainder of the field and out onto a nearby road! Other days that week were given over to the manoeuvres scenes from episode one and the first sequences to use the Nene

Wansford Station, Nene Valley Railway
© Mark Smith

Valley Railway. Filming was not without its problems for Ives's assistant Patricia Preece, particularly in respect of the supporting artists: she recorded that two men hired to play 'pursuers' were not available for the shoot as one had become sick, while another 'went to the location, but also went to the pub, and was not around when required,' while a third who was due to pay a Luftwaffe Policeman could not be used as he refused to have his hair cut and therefore did not fulfil the conditions of his contract (due to the aforementioned 'hair clause'). During this week and subsequent months, the whole unit would be plagued by particularly unseasonal weather, the summer of 1977 being in complete contrast to the scorching summer of the previous year.

81

On 24 April, Glaister decided that the definite article should now be dropped from the series's title, to simply become *Secret Army*; however, the original name would continue to persist on scripts and documentation throughout its three-year life.

Towards the end of the month, the production team arrived first at Rossway, Berkhamstead, before moving on to Chislehurst Caves for two days' filming, again with Eshley, Harris, Francis and Hepton, then going on to Wycombe Air Park for the scenes in which Curtis arrives back in Belgium by Lysander aircraft.

Filming in London...

At the very end of April filming began in London, as Paul Annett directed scenes in Ealing for *Radishes with Butter* – including the scenes in which Lisa and Curtis visit the Schliemann family – and at the Society of Genealogists in Kensington, the exterior of which would be used for Dr Keldermans's surgery. Viktors Ritelis took up the reins on 1 May for filming in and around Covent Garden, which was closed for refurbishment at the time, for both *Sergeant on the Run* and *Too Near Home*. For the former this included all of the Brussels-set bistro and street market scenes, including the deaths of Walker's colleagues. Ritelis remembers: "We had a great time there because the area for shooting was sizeable. There were no worries about 'shooting off', which is something we always battled with in the studio. However, there was a problem with dressing the area on time." He also recalls that the sequences with the flies on fly-paper, which were his own idea and not in John Brason's script, were time consuming to implement and that sourcing large flies at short notice proved to be a particular challenge. For *Too Near Home*, Covent Garden was used for the scenes set in Senlis in which Lisa meets with Julius at his garage and is subsequently arrested by Inspector Landre. Jan Francis remembers enjoying most of the shoot, particularly as Covent Garden was her old stomping ground, having previously worked nearby as a member of the Royal Ballet at the Royal Opera House, but the experience was marred for her by Ritelis's decision during filming to slap the actress in the face without warning in order to get a particular reaction shot that he wanted! Kenneth Ives also briefly

Dr Keldermans's Surgery
© Andy Priestner

used this location for the scenes in which Howson departs by ambulance at the end of *Growing Up*.

...and Belgium

From 5 May, the first scenes to be filmed in Belgium were shot, sequences such as: Sergeant Walker's flight through Brussels via the Place du Petit Sablon and the canal at Boulevard de Nieuport; Alain's rendezvous with Lisa at the Place St Catherine market; and the comings and goings outside Jacques Bol's cycle shop.

Godfrey Johnson (left) and Viktors Ritelis (pointing) during filming in Brussels in May 1977 © Viktors Ritelis

However, the most complex endeavour of the first overseas filming block was a long shoot at Les Tiers near Liege from 10 May, under the direction of Kenneth Ives, for *Growing Up*. Sequences included the funeral procession for Anna Dornes, for which the *Behind the Scenes* team were once again present, and her subsequent cemetery burial. Brian Glover and Max Harris were joined by a large number of Flemish-speaking extras for both sequences, meaning that Ives and his team were relying on BRT liaison more than ever. Austin Ruddy recalls that there was some humour at the graveside when Ives requested a re-shoot of the scene in which the coffin was lowered, as the real-life undertakers taking part commented that they'd never been asked to raise any coffins out of the ground before. The *Behind the Scenes* team interviewed several crew members about their roles during the shoot at Les Tiers. During a filming break on the funeral procession scene, experienced film cameraman Godfrey Johnson detailed the "infinite number of variables" that could work against him lining the shots up accurately: "We've got horses that can move, a carriage that could come off line, we've got me on a dolly and gib, and we've got actors. They've all got to be in the right place at the right time – all the time – during the shot and that's tricky to get right. Having got that right, the sun's got to be in for that shot otherwise we'd be in our own shadow. Added to that we've got problems with sound… an aeroplane could go over – it's a domino effect."[50] Production Assistant Derek Nelson meanwhile explained his role on the shoot: "I coordinate everything; organise it from start to finish, which means finding the locations, getting the caterers, booking hotels, scheduling what should be done per day and in the overall period. I arrive on site – normally – before everybody else. I try to get the crews working, to get a full day's work out of them."[51] With all the required scenes for the first production block in the can, the first Belgian shoot concluded on 13 May.

Back in the UK

The following week UK location filming resumed as scenes were shot outside the Department of the Environment and Romney House. During the recording of a scene for *Sergeant on the Run* on 20 May, there was a minor collision of two vehicles when 'Albert's van' was driven too close to a German lorry which it was being filmed overtaking, but this was the least of Gerry Glaister's worries at the time, as it was the same day that his wife Joan gave birth to their daughter Isla.

By this time, the pace at the workshops where the sets were being constructed was becoming increasingly frantic, as carpenters and other craftsmen worked towards their looming June delivery dates for the stock sets required for the beginning of studio recording in a few weeks' time. Austin Ruddy and his fellow designers had long since provided drawings to the workshops in order for them to start building the sets, together with as much detailed additional information as possible in order to pre-empt any questions they might have during construction. Only one set was not destined to be transported to a studio at BBC TV Centre: an extensive roof-top structure designed by Ruddy for an important night-set sequence in *Radishes with Butter* featuring Curtis and Lisa. Instead this set was

taken to pieces in numbered sections and transported to Film Stage 2 at Ealing Film Studios where it was required for filming on 24 May. For director Paul Annett, the most challenging aspect of

Original sketches of the roof-top sequence © Austin Ruddy

the scenes to be shot on this set was the long-held plan to use the technique of Front Axial Projection (FAP) for a nerve-wracking moment in which Lisa loses

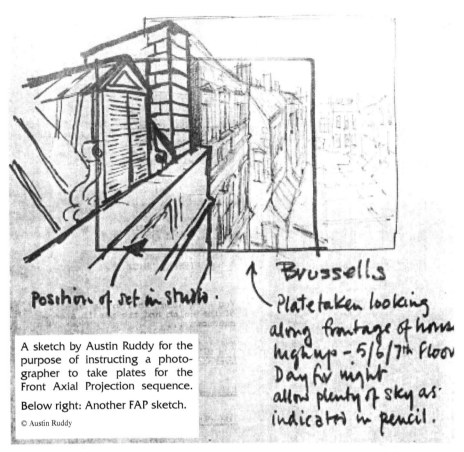

A sketch by Austin Ruddy for the purpose of instructing a photographer to take plates for the Front Axial Projection sequence.

Below right: Another FAP sketch.

© Austin Ruddy

Brussells ↑

Plate taken looking along frontage of house high up - 5/6/7th Floor Day for night allow plenty of sky as indicated in pencil.

Position of set in studio.

her balance on the roof due to a loose piece of leading, falls backwards, is grabbed by the wrist by Curtis and hangs suspended in mid-air over the street six storeys below, before she is pulled back to safety. Ruddy had previously instructed a photographer to take plates for the FAP during the Brussels recce, now Annett had to ensure that the shots lined up and looked convincing on the film stage. In essence FAP was a version of back projection for which a picture on film (a plate) was projected from beneath the camera through a half-silvered mirror at the same axis as the camera lens onto a beaded screen. The screen would reflect light only in the direction from which it had come – back into the camera – while

Position of set in studio in darker lines. View of houses on opposite side of street (narrow) Day for night to avoid blackout problems.

85

any light falling from the lights above the film stage on to the screen would be reflected back and therefore not diminish the clarity of the pictures on the screen. As well as overseeing this process, Annett was also charged with the task of describing the process on camera to the *Behind the Scenes* team. Although the set was not actually six storeys high, it was still pretty treacherous due to the fact that it had been sprayed with water in order to make it look authentic. For the shot of the fall itself, Jan Francis was replaced by stunt girl Veronica Griffith, however Francis still had to suffer the discomfort of being pulled back on to the 'roof' by Neame. There was reportedly some consternation about the overtly passionate nature of the subsequent kiss between Curtis and Lisa, with Glaister infamously commenting: "We didn't kiss like that during the war!" It was during a break in the recording of these scenes that Annett shared his views with the *Behind the Scenes* team about how vital it was that *Secret Army* should strive to be authentic as possible: "It's such recent and such important and vast history, indelibly burnt into so many people's memories, and we're also presenting it to a younger generation as an event they didn't live through, but which they're learning about. As such it's a great responsibility."[52] One actor on whom this responsibility weighed heavily was Michael Burrell, who played Schliemann in the same episode: 'For *Radishes with Butter*, I was fully screen-tested. When my then agent, June Epstein, put me forward for the part, she was asked if I was Jewish. "No," came the answer. The Beeb then said: "Well there are lots of Jewish actors, so it would be better if…" to which June responded: "Trust me, I'm the daughter of a Rabbi, he can play it!" Hence they saw me; I did the test in full costume and make-up, at the TV Centre in Wood Lane. And while we were doing it, Paul Annett said: "If you play it, you will be standing in for six million people."' Despite this pressure, Burrell was more than happy to take the role when it was offered to him: 'You can't do that sort of thing without being moved… Everything was thoughtfully done, to create an accurate sense, as far as we could, of what reality had been like.'

By this stage, the vast majority of the telecine sequences for the first six episodes were in the can. Exceptions included several scenes from *Second Chance* (Annett would direct these scenes a few weeks later, between 10-13 June, at Weybridge, the London Canal and the back lot of Shepperton Studios – a location he had previously used for his feature film *The Beast Must Die*) and others featuring Max Harris that were eventually shot on 8 July, well after studio recording had begun.

All of the rushes – the film shot on location – for the first six episodes were now examined by film editors Sheila Tomlinson (1-2, 4-5), Howard Billingham (3) and Graham Dean (6) in a viewing theatre, in order to check for 'hairs in the gate', exposure and anything else relating to picture quality. After that they worked on the film in the cutting room, synched it up with sound/dialogue and then assembled it according to the instructions of the director concerned. The director would then come and have a look at this first 'rough cut' and compare it with how he had originally envisaged the sequences tturning out. Kenneth Ives described it as a question of the film editor contributing their ideas and him contributing his and "hoping that the two of us will meet."[53] Glaister was also very involved at this stage, keen to see from the rushes how his new series was shaping up and making suggestions and decisions accordingly.

The Rehearsal Process

At 10.00am on 26 May, Glaister, Brason, the regular and guest (studio) cast and episode writer Willis Hall gathered in Room 603 of the Television Rehearsal Block at North Acton – commonly referred to as the Acton Hilton – for the read-through of *Lisa – Code Name Yvette*. The next seven days there would be devoted to rehearsals for that episode with its director, prior to the production going into the studio. To aid all parties, the dimensions of the sets as they would be in the studio were taped out on the floor, and as well as tables and chairs, boxes were used to simulate walls and larger pieces of furniture. Bernard Hepton, who of course also had experience of working as a director, recalls the rehearsal process: "Then you start blocking, you decide where the actors are going to move, you break each scene up, talking about the object of each scene – if you like, the 'wants' of the characters involved so that everyone knows what exactly they are apparently trying to do when saying a particular line," adding that, as a director, "When you start rehearsing you don't come with any stereotyped ideas which you impose from outside. It's essential to let the actor express his ideas as well – and both these things are pooled. You then have an actor who is free to experiment."[54] Francis concurs with Hepton's view, stating: "I like it if they let me do what I feel to start with."[55] Director Kenneth Ives, meanwhile, recognised the need for the director to be flexible: "It's important for the director to bring an overall plan which he can change. He must be adaptable all the time."[56]

Looking back on *Secret Army* today, the cast recognise that the rehearsal period – a resource not available to television series today – afforded them the time to feel their way into their roles and to gradually discover how they should interact with the characters around them. To take one example, the fact that for the majority of the first series Monique is Curtis's only 'champion' at the Candide was something that emerged and developed solely out of rehearsals rather than the scripts. Angela Richards fondly recalls that: "The rehearsal process was a routine you very much got into and enjoyed." Kenneth Ives, no doubt partly due to his experiences as an actor as well as a director, strongly believed that: "You don't want acting on the 'box', you want being,"[57] and that the rehearsal period made the latter more likely to happen. Viktors Ritelis also saw rehearsals as time for invention and exploration, but for him this also inevitably meant cutting and adding lines here and there which led to his regularly crossing swords with Brason and Glaister. As Jan Francis recalls, even Glaister himself "didn't change anything in the script without putting a phone call through to John Brason."

On the sixth day of rehearsals the Technical Run took place, during which the lighting and sound supervisors observed all the artists' positions throughout the episode and made plans for the forthcoming studio recording. Studio lighting engineer, Alan Horne, drew a 'lighting plot' – effectively drawing the position of every lamp he wanted to use on a plan – which he then sent off to the rigging crews to arrange in the studio. Horne would have previously discussed with Ives the time of day and level of light on the episode's telecine sequences, so he could later attempt to seamlessly match this with the levels in the studio. The camera crew which would work in the studio on *Secret Army*'s first two series was Crew 19, headed up by Senior Cameraman Roger Fenna who, despite his preference for Light Entertainment, had pitched for the drama series as he felt that his crew – for whom recent work had included *The Val Doonican Show* and *Tonight* – needed wider experience. At that time, it was still a bit of a novelty for even a Senior Cameraman to attend the Technical Run; however, on this occasion, the requirement of hand-held footage in the episode necessitated the additional presence of a camera operator as well, so John Corby also attended to run through this technically demanding sequence.

The day after the Technical Run, the Producer's Run took place, during which Glaister made his feelings known about all aspects of the episode's studio scenes, and after which Ives duly implemented the changes suggested.

Into the Studio

On the afternoon of 6 June 1977, the director and his cast went to BBC TV Centre to begin studio rehearsals. After taking in the completed sets for the first time – with which they would become very familiar during the next six months – from 2.30 to 6.30pm the actors rehearsed *in situ* while camera blocking was determined. There were five cameras in total, the positions of which would be marked on the studio floor. After an hour-long supper, 'camera rehearsal', as it was termed, resumed from 7.30 to 10.00pm. On 7 June 1977, while preparations were made for street parties across the UK and more than one million people lined the streets of London to watch the Royal Family on their way to St Paul's Cathedral at the start of the Queen's Silver Jubilee celebrations, the cast and crew of *Secret Army* were preparing for the first studio recording session, which would finally take place that afternoon and evening. The Jubilee had not affected the studio recording as much as it had other BBC productions. While *Secret Army* was allocated TC8 – officially designated as a Light Entertainment studio due to its retractable audience seating – in order that Jubilee programming, specifically the live *Jubilee Fair* edition of *Nationwide*, could take place in the other Television Centre studios, series like *Doctor Who* were moved as far afield as Birmingham's Pebble Mill studios. TC8, like TCs 1, 2 and 3, was known by some BBC technical crew members as a 'long bar' studio, while the others were 'short bar', a description which had nothing to do with the spec of the studios themselves but rather referred to their distance from the BBC Club!

Unlike the rest of the series, the studio recording for the first episode would, at the request of Kenneth Ives, incorporate two additional hours, making four-

and-a-half hours in total. This was as a result of prolonged negotiations which had begun in mid-May. At first, Ives had asked his producer for three extra hours and specifically referred to the time being needed due to their intention to use a hand-held camera for the scenes in which Curtis is confronted by Lisa and Albert in the Candide. Glaister sent him a note stating that 'only in exceptional circumstances should extra recording time be allocated' and that use of a hand-held camera was 'not sufficient grounds.' After reducing his request to two extra hours, Ives sent a note back stating that if this time was not made available, then: '...it is my considered opinion that at ten o'clock the play will not have been completed and I would like now to disclaim any responsibility for this eventuality.' Glaister subsequently relented and wrote to the BBC Head of Series, stating that Ives had a point and that he would be happier himself: '...if I felt that the first episode was not in danger of being rushed, when we might then cause a certain amount of damage to performances for, as you know, artists do tend to get rather jittery on the recording of a first episode.'

After two camera rehearsal periods, lunch and pre-recording – a portion of time that was used to record any particularly tricky scenes out of sequence – recording proper began with the two extra hours that had been granted. It was during this period that the hand-held sequence was to prove even more problematic than Ives had anticipated, as John Corby, the operator who had attended the Technical Run, had fallen ill and Crew 19's Second Cameraman, Michael Minchin, suddenly had to step into the breach. Minchin recalls that: "Ives's principal intention in using the hand-held was to differentiate 'innocent' activity from 'undercover' activity and, most importantly, impart a sense of danger when Curtis was taken into the back room of the Candide." Minchin also remembers that the camera, a Bosch Fernseh, often broke down, required another man to follow him around with the camera's 'back pack', and was prone to lens flare. These technical difficulties aside, Minchin ended up less than happy with the finished sequence, as he was not convinced that the unsteady camera made Ives's 'covert action' agenda obvious and would have liked more time to "mull over how the action was to be shot." However, on a more positive note, he recalls that: "Having that camera allowed me to do something that used to not happen that often. Regular old-style cameras tend to act as a wall between crew and cast, but this time I was mostly on a wide-angle lens and peeking around the side of it, in among the actors, and it made it much easier to get to know them." The episode's telecine sequences were played in live during this and the following recording period rather than afterwards in an editing room – an added pressure for all concerned as it was a process which required split-second timing. After supper, recording concluded between 7.30 and 10pm. Viktors Ritelis remembers that, when actors dried during recording, "their frailties would have to be logged in a book that went upstairs to explain why we'd gone five minutes into an overrun - the most heinous of crimes." However, given the extra time won by Ives, and despite the fact that Minchin was thrown in at the deep end, there was no danger of an overrun on *Lisa – Code Name Yvette*. Work on the first episode

An accurate reproduction of the front page of the script for *Lisa – Code Name Yvette*

OPENING TITLES

(ON TK - 35 mm)

LISA - CODE NAME YVETTE
by
WILLIS HALL

Starring

BERNARD HEPTON

JAN FRANCIS

CHRISTOPER NEAME

ANGELA RICHARDS

MICHAEL CULVER

CLIFFORD ROSE

with

JULIET HAMMOND-HILL

VALENTINE DYALL

RON PEMBER

and

JAMES BREE

MARIA CHARLES

was now complete, bar the VT (videotape) edit and Sypher Dub sessions – when incidental music and sound effects were added – which would take place later in June. After one day off, the regular cast returned to the Acton Hilton to go through the whole process again for episode two.

As it happens, the extra recording time allocated to *Lisa – Code Name Yvette* was precedent-setting for *Secret Army*, and many subsequent episodes were recorded in both the afternoon and evening of the second day in the studio; in fact, *Growing Up* would be granted even more, not only due to the substantial number of scenes featuring child actor Max Harris, but also because of the presence of the *Behind the Scenes* team, who wanted to feature the studio recording process in one of their programmes.

Production continues…

The only interruptions to this pattern for the series's rehearsals and studio recording, which would last until mid-December, were for further bouts of location filming in the UK and Belgium at the start of the remaining two production blocks in early August and mid-October. These periods would include filming in Kent (doubling as the

Viktors Ritelis directing the mudflat sequence for *Identity in Doubt*
© Viktors Ritelis

South of France) for *Child's Play* and in Norfolk for the memorable mudflat sequences in *Identity in Doubt*. The latter episode's director, Viktors Ritelis, remembers that he wanted to "add interest to what was scripted as a standard chase sequence." He recalled seeing a mudflat during a location recce and "thought wouldn't it be wonderful for the chase to take place through waist-deep mud!...The wardrobe people freaked, the actors freaked, the camera people thought I'd lost a marble or two, which I probably had, but I wouldn't let go and I talked, and talked, and talked." Ritelis got his way and counts the filming there in early August 1977 as: "physically the hardest thing I'd ever done." Juliet Hammond-Hill, who was also required to wade into the mud, remembers: "I went straight in and gave it 100%" and emerged later "with lice, maggots and snake-y things crawling all over me." Ritelis recalls that she looked like she'd stepped out of a Hammer horror film!

Of the second period of Belgian filming, director Paul Annett recalls that the locals did

not take at all kindly to the crew's recreation of Nazi-Occupied Belgium, and some found the production "difficult to comprehend." Ironically, the extras playing Germans, who were occasionally spat at and called "Boche," were also locals being paid for their part in the show. Jan Francis recalls a particular morning "in a square on the outskirts of Brussels, where the residents woke up to find themselves thirty years back in time and were nearly demented at the return of the Nazi swastikas, German vehicles and soldiers." She thinks that "money may even have changed hands to calm the situation down" and that the crew perhaps had not "thought enough about the emotive impact the filming would have."

Due to budgetary constraints, it was decided that not all of the series's sixteen episodes would incorporate location filming. Ultimately, *Bait*, *Good Friday* and *Suspicions* would be entirely studio-bound. While for the latter this would lend proceedings a fittingly claustrophobic tone, attempts to stage an entire street parade for the Führer's birthday were inevitably less than successful for the former.

As production continued, an obvious divide was quickly discernible between the regular cast members. Clifford Rose remembers: "The two camps rarely mixed during rehearsals... we did sit at separate tables, but it was not unfriendly, it was more that if we got too familiar with the regular Candide characters that it would somehow rub off on your character – it just wasn't done." Angela Richards puts it down to the fact that, particularly in the first series: "The Candide regulars had all their scenes together and the Germans had theirs." She believed it created a *frisson* of "interesting wariness" between the two groups: "It created that thing that you might have with people of a different race, a different culture, or a different attitude." Juliet Hammond-Hill recalls: "In Series One, I don't think Michael Culver and I exchanged a word! It was not that we were clique-y, but the Germans had a particular quality of intensity... I never got to know Michael and Clifford as I would have liked. There was this natural instinctive segregation that happened." Glaister was not at all perturbed by this development as he had observed the selfsame behaviour amongst his *Colditz* cast members. Even when he had held parties at his home, the actors playing Germans did not mix with those playing the Allied prisoners! Meanwhile, within the two disparate groups, a definite chemistry was developing between the cast members. Angela Richards recalls that amongst the Lifeline regulars there was "an almost unfelt, an almost unspoken, comfortableness, and as we progressed, it became even more comfortable." Clifford Rose also remembers that he and Michael were "very comfortable together," and that: "He was/is a self-critical actor and to some extent I am as well, so we hit it off. It was a joy to work with him." As time went on, the actors also began to feel more comfortable in their new surroundings. Jan Francis felt that: "The [Candide] back room was home, really. We knew it very well, better than our own home, because we worked so hard in it!" Despite the fact that she was seeing very little of her home and her fiancé, Francis nevertheless married in the Summer of 1977; however, the honeymoon would have to wait, as she was only given one solitary day off for the event.

During the first series, Glaister and Brason had planned for only one character to be killed off mid-run: James Bree's Gaston Colbert. However, Gaston did last longer than originally intended, due to the fact that *Too Near Home* was moved further down the transmission schedule. Bree's departure was keenly felt by the cast, and particularly by his screen niece Jan Francis. She recalls that: "When there were tensions, he was there to make us all see sense and to calm us down. It was so sad when he went; he was a very vital person and an important member of the group."

Guest Stars

Glaister, Brason and their team of directors were delighted to attract a large number of high calibre actors to guest in the series. Peter Barkworth (below), who would win the 1978 Best Actor BAFTA award for his performances in two other 1977 dramas (Tom Stoppard's *Play of the Week: Professional Foul* and the *Play for Today: The Country Party*) and a Royal Television Society performance award in 1978 that also acknowledged his role in *Secret Army*, was pleased with the quality of N. J. Crisp's two scripts for the series in which he would play flawed novelist Hugh Neville. Other well-known faces included: Maurice Denham, familiar to audiences at the time due to his regular roles in *The Lotus Eaters* and *Porridge* (1973-7), who guested as Father Girard in *Good Friday*; and John Carson who concurrently to his appearance as Van Reijn in the episode *Hymn to Freedom*, could be seen as Colonel Heatherstone

© John Haynes

in a new adaptation of *The Children of the New Forest* (1977). However, Clifford Rose admits to being most impressed by the arrival at the Acton rehearsal rooms of Kathleen Byron, principally because of her unforgettable performance as the deranged Sister Ruth in the classic Powell and Pressburger film *Black Narcissus* (1946) some thirty years earlier. Byron would feature in two episodes, *Bait* and *Good Friday*, albeit in a relatively minor role, as the interfering Celeste Lekeu.

Production concludes

The final five episodes (12-16) were rehearsed and studio-recorded between the end of October and mid-December. These were all filmed in order, with the exception of *Good Friday* and *Suspicions* which switched places. This meant that *Good Friday* ended up being recorded on Tuesday 6 December, just eight days before its broadcast! As the cast and crew reached the final episode of the first series, John Brason's *Be the First Kid in Your Block to Rule the World* – a title that the writer had always wanted to use one day and which thoroughly perplexed the cast – a few problems beset the production. Firstly, there was some behind-the-scenes wrangling between Brason and the episode's director Viktors Ritelis. Ritelis did not like the script and criticised various elements and suggested some changes, but Brason dug his heels in, refusing to accept the director's point of view. Far more serious however, was the incredibly sudden incapacity of Michael Culver, who had contracted appendicitis the day before studio recording. The episode had been written with a typical number of two-hander scenes between Brandt and Kessler, so it was far too late in the day to change the script. The production team's solution was to hire another actor to effectively play the Brandt part for one episode, albeit with a different name: Reinecke. Cast to play him was character actor Michael Wynne, who would later return in the third series episode *Prisoner* as the similarly named, but infinitely more vile, Reisener. Studio recording on *Be the First Kid* was completed on 16 December 1977, the last day of production on the first series.

Scheduling and Promotion

Some three months earlier, in early September 1977, after studio recording had been completed on a total of eight episodes, *Secret Army* debuted on BBC1. Unfortunately the series received neither the slot nor the promotion that Glaister had hoped for.

Between 1973 and 1976, Glaister's long-running boardroom saga *The Brothers* had become a staple part of Sunday night viewing (only its first 1972 series went out on Fridays – in fact Glaister opted to delay transmission of this series, which had completed production several months earlier, in order for such a slot to materialise) and he was keen to secure a weekend slot for his new series too. However, for their new BBC1 Autumn Season, from Saturday 3 September, the programme schedulers elected to transmit the second series of the popular *The Duchess of Duke Street*, after established Saturday night fare such as *Doctor Who* and *The Generation Game*, while from 11 September, Sunday evenings would be home to the equally long-awaited second series of *Poldark*. Another drama series returning to BBC1, for its third series, from Thursday 8 September was North East period drama *When The Boat Comes In* (1976-7, 1981), while the coveted Friday night slot was filled by tough new police show *Target* (1977-8) from 9 September, preceded by comedy favourite *The Liver Birds* (1969-79). The schedulers ultimately decided upon a mid-week slot for *Secret Army* of

Wednesdays at 8.05pm, crucially opposite the hugely popular *The Benny Hill Show* (1969-89) on ITV.

Glaister was thwarted further by a decision taken by BBC Publications, who published the *Radio Times* – the UK's best-selling magazine which, despite its name, contains BBC television listings as well as radio listings – to go with a front cover which promoted *Target* for the 3-9 September 1977 issue (Vol 216, No 2808), showing Patrick Mower as Detective Superintendent Steve Hackett, rather than *Secret Army*. As it would turn out *Secret Army* would be the only one of Glaister's long-running series never to receive the accolade of a *Radio Times* cover. The series fared a little better inside, with a preview on the contents page ('not a documentary but by no means frivolous fiction'[58]) and a page-long article which summarised the background to the series and interviewed Glaister. The series's creator and producer talked about the organisers of the evasion lines, stating that what they had in common was "an intense, but rational patriotism and immense courage" and that "the dangers they faced were much greater than those facing the people they were helping. As civilians they could be – and were – tortured, shot or sent to concentration camps."[59] The article went on to briefly introduce the main characters, before concluding with Glaister touching on the difficult problem of creating the right atmosphere and attitudes for the series: "A lot of values seem comic if you use the jargon of the day. Just because people said 'I say, old chap. I had a prang,' they were not half-wits. But you just don't use those expressions."[60] The article was accompanied by images of the ID cards for Albert, Monique and Lisa, together with information about Curtis and, as a finishing touch to the page, a red German Feldkommandantur stamp. Looking at the opposite page it is obvious that the *Radio Times* design team were going for a documentation theme, as DS Hackett's police record form was reproduced to accompany the article about *Target*. On the Wednesday page, a quarter-page feature above the listing for the first episode of *Secret Army*, included a map of the Lifeline evasion route from Belgium through to Spain, and an interview with Technical Advisor Bill Randle giving further detail about the evasion lines, including their *raison d'etre* ("We want to help win this war and the best means we have is to get RAF aircrew back to their units where they can get on with the bombing of Germany."), their divisions of responsibilities ("finding the shot down aircrew; holding them in safe-houses where they were made well, interrogated and briefed on their new identities and made ready to travel; and finally guiding them down the route"), before detailing the numbers of aircrew who survived ("There is no accurate figure of the numbers who were executed or died in the concentration camps, but they vastly exceeded the 2,803 aircrew who were brought to safety"). Randle concluded by referring to the Royal Air Forces Escaping Society: "It is today very active, still proud to be in contact with more than 4,300 survivors of the Secret Army."[61] Although the above *Secret Army* features were informative and interesting, alas they were a far cry from the five full pages (three in colour) devoted to the new series of *The Duchess of Duke Street*. Looking back over the pages and listings of this edition of the *Radio Times* today, it is clear that *Secret Army* had stiff competition from a whole swathe of other high-quality period dramas during its first run, and that this was indeed, the golden age of the genre. However, as director Viktors Ritelis recounts: "What I regret is that no-one told me at the time!"

Lisa – Code Name Yvette went out on BBC1 at 8.06pm on 7 September 1977 after an edition of *It's a Championship Knockout* (from the following week, *Secret Army* would follow a new series of the European *It's a Knockout – Jeux sans Frontieres* (games without borders), an interesting scheduling choice given the staggering contrast between the Europe's being depicted in each programme!). BBC2 competition came in the form of live studio debate show *Brass Tacks*, but Glaister was of course far more troubled by the concurrent presence of Benny Hill on ITV.

Critical Reception

After the transmission of its first episode, *Secret Army* received a mixed response from the critics. To a large extent this was something that did not concern Gerry Glaister unduly. When interviewed in 2004, Glaister said that this was because he was always far more interested in what the audience thought of his programmes than in what the newspaper critics said, and recounted that, eight years later, when his soap-y sun and sailing drama *Howards' Way* premiered, it received a real drubbing in the press and yet went on to arguably become his most popular, and certainly his longest running, series. That said, *Secret Army*'s debut was received a great deal more warmly by the critics than *Howards' Way* was.

The *Sunday Times* television critic had seen a preview copy of *Lisa – Code Name Yvette* and on 4 September, in an article entitled *Shades of Colditz*, was the first to report on *Secret Army*'s obvious links with Glaister's earlier wartime series, specifically citing Hepton and Neame and designer Austin Ruddy. However, he was not informed enough to know that *Secret Army*'s premise and plots were just as historically accurate as those of *Colditz*, believing that the latter was 'based much more closely on actual experiences.' However, he was wise enough to recognise the series's potential, acknowledging that 'Over the longish run from now till Christmas it could attract the same devoted following as *Colditz*.' In the *Daily Mail* on Thursday 8 September, Shaun Usher penned a very cynical review of the new series, stating that its production team were seeking to attract an audience based on 'brand image' and familiar faces: 'It couldn't be an accident that *Secret Army* is such a son of *Colditz* project, from the same stable, with much the same kind of doom-laden signature tune and even a brace of the original stars.' Why he was so offended by the superficial similarities between the programmes is unclear, especially as he went on to praise Glaister for keeping his new series 'well in touch with unromantic reality' and for depicting Lifeline's agents as 'real people with human frailties and livings to earn,' a move which he thought added an extra dimension to what would otherwise be a 'stock war thriller.' Usher concluded his piece by commenting: 'It can only improve and it's not at all bad in the first place.' The *Daily Telegraph*'s Sean Day-Lewis (son of Poet Laureate Cecil Day-Lewis and brother of actor Daniel) followed the same, and rather lazy, vein of his contemporaries by describing *Secret Army* as 'a short step down the road from *Colditz*.' His observation that 'our high-spirited chaps are once again outwitting the humourless Hun' ignored the fact that the series's heroes are chiefly Belgian. However, it seems that he had at least noticed the Belgian characters, as he stated that viewers 'would have less difficulty than the enemy in distinguishing the helpful Belgian from the less helpful since the former are either pretty (in such shapely forms as Jan Francis and Angela Richards) or personable, while the latter are either craven or sinister.' Day-Lewis also couldn't stop himself from poking fun by drawing attention to the inevitable language difficulties inherent in such a series: 'In London there is some worry about the inability of aircrew evaders to speak French, but in Brussels and the surrounding countryside, everybody speaks Willis Hall's clear direct English and even the Germans are quite moderate with their guttural explosions.' He finished his review, like Usher, by rather grudgingly admitting that 'all those who became addicted to *Colditz* will probably find this competent extension equally acceptable.'

The most favourable review of the series – and incidentally the most in-depth – was published in *The Stage and Television Today* on 15 September. Its writer, Hazel Holt, believed that although 'that rich ore-bearing seam, the Second World War, is still being mined assiduously by the BBC... this latest series may still yield a few further nuggets.' She thought that: 'The production's judicious mixture of location filming and studio work looks as if it will achieve a high degree of visual authenticity – which is half the battle in a series like this.' She reserved specific praise for 'the interior designs by Austin Ruddy (scrupulously observed, right down to the Continental light switches),' which 'heightened the realism, as did the use of what seemed to be a genuine old Lysander and some very nice Mauser rifles.' Holt too picked up on the language issue: 'It was a pity that all the Germans had to speak with broken accents, while the British and Belgians spoke impeccable BBC standard.' She felt that Hall's script was 'good' and 'taut', while she praised Ives's direction for its 'inventive touches' and 'neatly juxtaposed exposition and tension.' Moving on to the series's cast, she felt sure that Bernard Hepton was 'going to give one of those sympathetic studies for which he is noted,' and correctly guessed that, 'torn between a jealous, invalid wife and a lively young mistress, who works with him in the underground organisation, there should be plenty of scope for subtleties of characterisation in future episodes.' She found Christopher Neame to be an 'effective RAF liaison officer,' Michael Culver to be making the most of playing 'the statutory "good" German,' and 'the excellent actor Clifford Rose' to be 'revelling in the part of the clinically cold Sturmbannführer Kessler.' She was also pleased to see Valentine Dyall again 'lending his fine features and noble voice to the part of a partisan doctor.' Of the series's actresses, once she had worked out which was which ('they all look rather alike with their early 1940s hair-styles'), Holt felt that 'they will prove to be excellent.' She ended the piece on an upbeat note, predicting that 'Secret Army will be a success' and 'of a sufficiently high standard, honestly and painstakingly made, to satisfy the purist and entertain the casual viewer.' Bernard Davies, writing for his regular 'One Man's Television' column in Broadcast magazine on 19 September, took the position that it was time for such wartime dramas to cease, concluding his review with the exclamation: 'Let us – please! – get Secret Army out of our systems and then forget World War II and its automatic heroes and villains,' this despite the fact that earlier in the article he had noted that the series's 'baddies are not all bad and some goodies are various shades of off-white.' Davies felt that the subject matter of the series did 'deserve commemoration' but objected to the fact that 'the trouble about reviving old heroisms is that we also revive old enmities and old attitudes whose proper place is in the history books and in other places where they can be dispassionately evaluated.' Despite this strong stance, three years down the line Davies was still watching and enjoying Secret Army, and in 1979 eventually felt compelled to write that he had been mistaken in his initial 1977 review.

Viewing Figures and Audience Appreciation

Secret Army's first episode attracted a modest 6.7 million viewers, amounting to 13.2% of the UK population, a figure which was arguably due to its poor time-slot. By contrast The Benny Hill Show on ITV secured 31.3% of the UK population (15.8m viewers) and was therefore one of the most watched programmes of the week. As the series progressed, figures would fall to 6.3m for Sergeant on the Run and further still to just 5.8m for Radishes with Butter. Thereafter, the number of viewers climbed to 7.8m for both Second Chance and Growing Up, before reaching a first series high of 9.5m for Lost Sheep. The figures would subsequently tail off to a steady 6-7 million, before the series recorded its second highest figure of 8.7m for the finale, Be the First Kid in Your Block to Rule the World, in Christmas week 1977.

Although viewing figures, which were based on the results of the BBC's Survey of Listening and Viewing, were important to the BBC's commissioning editors, and figures of 8 and 9 million would certainly have contributed to the final decision to give Secret Army's production team a green light for a second series (especially given the fierce ITV competition in the time-slot), other factors were taken into account, such as the content of the research reports produced by the BBC's dedicated Audience Research Department. The department produced around 700 reports each year on BBC programmes, analysing the reactions of between 230-260 viewers to elements such as plot, acting and production quality. A score was also assigned, known as a Reaction Index, which measured the audience's overall appreciation, with each surveyed viewer being asked to rate the programme from a high of A+ to a low of C-. Among the programmes to be analysed in September 1977 was the opening episode of Secret Army. The Reaction Index was a very healthy score of 69, resulting from over two-thirds of those surveyed scoring the episode as either an A+ or an A. Although *Lisa – Code Name Yvette* was recognised as a 'scene-setter,' most viewers felt that it was 'a very good opening episode.' The characters and situations were deemed 'convincing and realistic' ('they were all ordinary people, as we were, doing extraordinary things'), while the production was 'widely praised for cleverly catching what was felt to be the authentic atmosphere of wartime Europe,' with Andrew Mackenzie's costumes and Judy Neame's make-up particularly singled out. However, there were, inevitably, some criticisms of the programme. A few felt it was 'predictable' and 'just another variation on the same old theme,' while one respondent commented: "I'm sick and tired of World War II series, so how do the Germans feel?" Others felt that some of the characters were a bit clichéd and 'wondered why the heroes were always good looking.' However, an overwhelming majority felt that it was 'well acted and most realistic' and that 'it augured well for the future.'

The next report would measure appreciation, halfway through the series, for the eighth episode, N. J. Crisp's *Guilt*, which had attracted 7.5 million viewers and a Reaction Index of 71. Most respondents 'thoroughly enjoyed' the episode, finding it to be 'exciting, compulsive viewing which "kept them guessing until the end,"' regarding the climax as 'well-written, interesting and "deeply human"' and as such 'typical of Mr Crisp's work.' A very small minority complained of 'unconvincing acting' and thought that the second part had failed to live up to the promise of the first (*Lost Sheep*), but these 'few reporting viewers... tended to be those who disapproved of war films of any kind whatsoever.' The vast majority had nothing but praise for the acting: 'this cast made 'a solid reliable team'... that were now beginning to develop their characters with some degree of success.' Hepton, Francis and Neame were all singled out for specific praise, while guest star Peter Barkworth was 'repeatedly commended' with one respondent stating that he gave a "quiet and powerful performance which brought the story to life." The episode's 'choice of locations' were also appreciated and it was felt that props, costumes and sets 'contributed greatly to the highly convincing wartime atmosphere.' However, the comments that would have cheered Glaister and Brason the most, given the definite tone and approach that they had wanted *Secret Army* to deliver from the outset, were from those viewers that 'approved of the way in which the War and the resistance movement in particular were presented... in realistic and often nasty terms, rather than [in] the more usual glamorised and romanticised manner.'

The final episode to come under the scrutiny of the Audience Research Department was the series finale, *Be the First Kid in Your Block to Rule the World*. Despite the very high standards set by *Guilt*, in terms of audience appreciation this episode would manage to raise the bar even higher. An exceptional Reaction Index of 78 was recorded, meaning that 80% of respondents scored the episode as either an A+ or an A. They felt that it was 'an exciting conclusion to an enjoyable series,' and there were hopes not only that the series would be repeated, but also that 'a new one would be made.' Bernard Hepton was specifically mentioned by several viewers, but praise was more commonly reserved for the entire cast, with whom the audience were 'highly impressed.' There was also some analysis of how many respondents had seen all or most of the sixteen episodes of the first series (50%) and how many had seen less than half (26%). This report also revealed an average Reaction Index for the entire series (which also covered several episodes other than those three that had been analysed in report form) of 72, a score that was well above average for BBC drama series at the time.

Of course, aside from the very reasonable viewing figures and strong audience appreciation, the BBC also had to be sure that Gerard Glaister wanted to continue with his series. Given the sheer amount of time and effort that had gone into its realisation, it is unsurprising that Glaister was very keen for *Secret Army* to continue, but he had an important caveat, namely that if the second series went ahead there would have to be some changes. This particularly troubled John Brason and his concerns deepened when it became clear that Glaister was actually set on a total revamp of the series. However, when *Secret Army* returned to British television screens in a revised format in September 1978, Glaister's instinctive understanding of what made television drama appealing would, once again, be unequivocally demonstrated.

Episode 1: LISA – CODE NAME YVETTE

WRITTEN BY: Willis Hall   **DIRECTED BY:** Kenneth Ives

FIRST BROADCAST: BBC1, 8.05pm, Wednesday 7 September 1977

STUDIO RECORDING: 7 June 1977

VIEWING FIGURE: 6.7m

REGULAR CAST: Albert Foiret: BERNARD HEPTON; Lisa "Yvette" Colbert: JAN FRANCIS; Flt Lt John Curtis: CHRISTOPHER NEAME; Monique Duchamps: ANGELA RICHARDS; Major Erwin Brandt: MICHAEL CULVER; Sturmbannführer Ludwig Kessler: CLIFFORD ROSE; Natalie Chantrens: JULIET HAMMOND-HILL; Dr Pascal Keldermans: VALENTINE DYALL; Alain Muny: RON PEMBER; Gaston Colbert: JAMES BREE; Louise Colbert: MARIA CHARLES; Andrée Foiret: EILEEN PAGE

SUPPORTING CAST: Oberst Dieter Gundell: MARK BURNS; Farmer: HOWARD BELL; Farmer's Wife: CATHERINE BRANDON; Daughter: ABIGAIL BROWN; Son: DANIEL CHASIN; Luftwaffe Sgt: PETER HOLT; Sgt Thomas: JAMES LISTER; Sgt Mitchell: MICHAEL GRAVES; Sgt Howes: PETER QUINCE; Bertha: OLWEN GRIFFITH; Kurt: BILL ROURKE; Wehrmacht Corporal: ARNOLD WILLEMS; Taylor: KEITH ASHTON; Bartle: IAN LISTON; RASC Private: DAVID ENGLISH; Sgt Major: TIM BARLOW; Group Captain: VERNON JOYNER; Housewife: HERMIONE GREGORY; Husband: MICHAEL NAPIER BROWN; Belgian Policeman: RICHARD HOLDEN; Johnson: ANTHONY AINLEY; Brigadier: PETER CLAY; Luftwaffe Policeman: ANTHONY STAFFORD; Peasant: LUKE HANSON; Phillips: NEIL DICKSON

SYNOPSIS: Belgium 1941. Luftwaffe Major Erwin Brandt leads a troop of soldiers to a farmhouse where he believes an RAF evader is being harboured by a farmer and his family. Natalie Chantrens, a guide for a Belgian escape organisation called Lifeline, escapes detection by hiding on the farmhouse roof. After a fruitless search, Brandt takes the farmer and his wife away for further questioning. Meanwhile in Brussels, at the busy Restaurant Candide – the establishment from which Lifeline secretly operates – proprietor Albert Foiret is juggling the demands of his invalid wife Andrée and his mistress Monique Duchamps. Natalie returns to the Candide. She is concerned about the safety of Lifeline's founder Lisa Colbert – code name Yvette – and the three evaders in her charge, with whom Natalie had intended to rendezvous. In England, during an RAF escape and evasion training exercise, instructor Flt Lt John Curtis – a former downed pilot who was helped home by Lifeline – is sent for by the Air Ministry. Brandt learns that a Gestapo man named Kessler is on his way to Brussels to sort out the evasion line problem once and for all. Lisa, whose cover is to work as a nurse at Dr Keldermans's surgery, also learns of Kessler's imminent arrival. Oberst Gundell, who is due to leave Brussels, tells Brandt what he knows of Kessler. In London, Curtis is amazed to be asked if he would consider returning to Europe to help evaders out in the field. News reaches Lisa that one of the missing evaders has been found and she takes him to Dr Keldermans's surgery. Lisa's troubled Aunt Louise knows nothing of her niece's double life, nor the fact that her husband is also involved in resistance work. Curtis is briefed about his new posting, in which he is to act as a paymaster to Lifeline and work towards bringing all the evasion

101

lines together. Brandt crosses swords with the recently arrived Kessler when he learns that the entire family from the farm has been deported to a labour camp in Germany without his knowledge. Lisa and her Lifeline colleagues decide that Natalie should escort the three evaders currently in their care to Paris before stricter security measures are imposed by Kessler. Curtis arrives by Lysander and is met by a resistance group. The following day, while Natalie escorts the evaders to the station, Curtis surprises Lisa by turning up unannounced at the Candide. She and Albert are highly suspicious of his motives and interrogate him at gunpoint. Later that evening, while closing up the Candide, Albert is distracted by the air-raid siren and the noise of planes overhead.

REVIEW: The first episode of *Secret Army* is a hugely ambitious endeavour – not only does it attempt to introduce the major themes and dramatic context of the series, but all of the regular characters as well. Although this approach ensures plenty of hooks for returning viewers and a clear representation of the ground the series intends to cover, it does sometimes feel that rather too much is going on. Interestingly, this episode's writer, Willis Hall, shared this concern and felt that he was being expected to fit the equivalent of a feature film into this first 52-minute instalment.

When it was first broadcast, newspaper critics unsurprisingly drew comparisons with Gerry Glaister's previous World War Two drama *Colditz*, with particular reference made to the similarity of the signature tune and the inclusion of several of the same cast members. However, despite these elements, it is clear from this opening instalment that *Secret Army* has a different agenda altogether. In contrast to *Colditz*, here those evading capture are merely the supporting artistes – ciphers even – and it is the resistance workers and their oppressors who take centre stage instead. It is also readily apparent that *Secret Army* is not going to be a drama exclusively about British heroism and fortitude, but rather about the hugely courageous work of their Allies in Occupied Europe.

Given the time constraints of a single episode, the introductions to the series's main protagonists are necessarily brief. On the side of Lifeline, Hepton's Albert and Jan Francis's Lisa have the most material to work with and give believable and promising performances. Although the incredible bravery of all of the Lifeline operatives is engaging – especially the fact that unlike the men they are helping, they are facing death rather than imprisonment – an aspect of the series that is set to become just as interesting, if not more so, is the depiction of their personal lives. There is little indication here that Albert's relationship with Monique is a storyline that will span all forty-two episodes of *Secret Army*, but sufficient groundwork is laid all the same. We learn surprisingly little as to why each operative has decided to risk their life on a daily basis. Only Lisa's steely determination to fight back against the forces of the Third Reich is explained in terms of the devastating deaths, of not only her parents, but her fiancé as well. Despite the British Brigadier's assertion to Curtis that the evasion organisation in Brussels is an amateur outfit battling against a professional one, it is clear that all of the members of Lifeline are already well-versed in both keeping up the façade of relaxed normality (Natalie and Monique are more than adept at playing up to the Candide's customers before exchanging information) and the art of quick thinking (e.g. Lisa excusing the dirt on her clothes with the lie that she has been in attendance at the birth of a litter of pigs). It is also clear that Lifeline's network into France is well established, although they do seem to be short of safe-houses. Curtis's unexpected and unwanted arrival at the Candide towards the episode's close promises to upset both the security and efficacy of the evasion operations and, while Lifeline will undoubtedly take Curtis's money, it remains to be seen whether they will accept his expertise as well. What is certain is that they will not let the Flight Lieutenant attempt to fulfil his mission to "weld all the evasion lines together." It is a nice touch that the British appear totally unaware of the absolute necessity for Lifeline to remain entirely separate from other resistance and evasion groups in order to survive.

Despite the strength of the Lifeline regulars, it is their German counterparts who arguably steal the first episode. The introspective nature of Brandt, with his uncomplicated charm, signposts the fact that *Secret Army* is a series that will never choose to portray its German characters as black and white stereotypes. As a concerned Brandt discusses the arrival of the zealous Kessler with Oberst Gundell, we learn that they perceive a definite difference between their own standards and those of a man who once boasted that he personally executed eleven men on 'the Night of the Long Knives'. After a gradual build up to the eventual appearance of Kessler, the Sturmbannführer's opening scene is a superb introduction to the character, with Clifford Rose making certain that Kessler's arrival cannot be regarded as an anticlimax. Through his initial delay in volunteering his presence to Brandt, the revelation that he has ordered the deportation of an entire family to a labour camp, and the dressing down that follows – "You may not say so Major Brandt!" – we quickly learn that Kessler is a man to be reckoned with. As their first meeting strongly suggests will be the case, Kessler and Brandt will rarely see eye-to-eye and the differences in their methods and motivations will ensure a thorough and regular depiction of the well-documented rivalry between the Luftwaffe Polizei and the Gestapo. Brandt has more than met his match in Kessler, and although the former may cling to the clear-cut military regulations that state that captured enemy aircrew are the responsibility of the Luftwaffe and not the Gestapo, as Gundell warned him: "the blood purge at Lichterfelde Barracks could hardly come under the heading 'military regulations'." Kessler is a truly frightening and distasteful figure. The way in which he perceives Belgian civilians merely in terms of their usefulness to the Reich and the evasion line operatives as rats requiring extermination serves to emphasise the grim extremity of the Nazi value system and the character's fanatical devotion to the Fatherland. With Kessler running the show in Brussels, Lifeline's days seem severely numbered.

One of the few downsides of the episode, which would not have been apparent on first or repeat broadcast, is the presence of those elements spoofed so mercilessly by *'Allo! 'Allo!* In particular, this episode's occasional use of code-based dialogue ("The three puppies that escaped from your grandfather's place last night, they've caught another one – they're taking it back to the kennels now") could easily hail from an *'Allo! 'Allo!* script. Although *Secret Army* quickly transcends its spoof successor, simply by continually reminding us that it is such a damn good drama series in its own right, it certainly helps the modern viewer that silly code language such as this is ditched early on in series one.

A neat visual trick is employed in the first daytime sequence of the episode, in which two evaders are seen to be 'on the run'. There's a clever irony here in that the countryside looks unmistakably British, as it seems far too hilly and wooded for Belgium. The viewer therefore assumes that, due to budgetary restrictions, these scenes were filmed in England and that the narrative is asking them to believe that the two men are downed aircrew and this is Belgium. However, when the pair are finally cornered in a barn, the unexpected arrival of several British soldiers reveals that this is actually a training exercise in England after all! Although *Secret Army*'s production team carried out a substantial amount of location filming in Belgium – several scenes in this episode are from the Brussels filming block – it would have been far too costly to film all the exterior scenes there. In future episodes England would unashamedly double for Belgium, something which reportedly caused designer Austin Ruddy to cringe when he watched the show on its original broadcast, but which would rarely trouble the average viewer. Another notable recording decision was the employment of handheld camera sequences which add a definite realism to the proceedings, especially in the scene in which the camera follows Curtis into the back room of the Candide. It is a technique which is commonplace in modern drama but which seems somewhat adventurous and unusual for 1977.

One of the stars of this first episode is the Candide itself, which is unquestionably the most important – and certainly the largest – set of the first series. Ruddy's sidestreet establishment is an effective and atmospheric backdrop for the undercover action, and is especially believable in its first smoke-filled evening scene. Other than the three Candide sets (front of house, back room and Andrée's bedroom), for a single episode – albeit a series opener – a surprising number of additional studio sets were struck, including: offices at German Headquarters for both Brandt and Kessler; Dr Keldermans's surgery; Johnson's London-based office; and the Colbert family home. All of these sets are detailed and authentically realised, while costumes, hair and make-up are similarly in-keeping. The BBC has always excelled at faithful recreations of historical periods and *Secret Army* was to be no exception.

Despite a slightly over-crowded feel, there is more than enough interest in *Lisa – Code Name Yvette* to ensure that the viewer will return for the second instalment of the series: the dangers of Lifeline's work; the threat posed by Kessler – not only to Lifeline but also to his Luftwaffe colleague Brandt; the unresolved love triangle at the Candide; and the fate of Flt Lt Curtis. However, it is the planes flying above the Candide that fittingly have the last word: there will always be more work on the way for the courageous members of Lifeline.

HISTORICAL BACKGROUND

MI9

In 1939, the War Office engaged in a series of interviews with servicemen who had escaped during the First World War to decide how help could be given to prisoners during the new conflict. In December 1940, as a direct result of this consultation, MI9 formally came into existence as a department of the War Office, under Brigadier Norman Crockatt, with a view to training thousands of servicemen in the arts of escape and evasion. MI9 was under-resourced and under-staffed, largely due to its rivalry with MI6 and other outfits such as SOE. MI9's first major task was to assist soldiers who had been stranded after Dunkirk. However, over time, MI9 began to concentrate their efforts on the successful return of aircrew who had been shot down over enemy territory, termed 'evaders'. As key MI9 agent Airey Neave recounted: 'A newly returned evader, especially a trained pilot, was of far more operational value than a man who had spent several months 'behind the wire'.'[1] When Dédée, the leader of the Comète Line, sought assistance, it was MI9 who agreed to support their operations. In addition to Comète, MI9 also assisted the Pat O'Leary and Shelburne Lines.

The Night of the Long Knives

The blood purge at the Lichterfelde Barracks, referred to by Gundell, is otherwise known as 'The Night of the Long Knives'. This incident, ordered by Hitler, which took place between 30 June and 2 July 1934, involved the execution of at least 85 people whom he had come to consider as his enemies. Many of the operation's victims were executed at the Lichterfelde Barracks, which was at that time the headquarters of Hitler's bodyguard regiment, the 'Leibstandarte-SS Adolf Hitler', on 1 July 1934. The reference to Kessler's involvement in the blood purge (Oberst Gundell tells Brandt that Kessler claims to have personally executed eleven men) suggests that he was a member of the Leibstandarte at that time. This fits with Brason's comment in his novel that 'he was no longer a trooper, no longer part of the SS 'muscle'.'[2]

WHERE ELSE HAVE I SEEN..?

Anthony Ainley (Johnson)

Reverend Emilius, *The Pallisers*, 1974
Dietz, *The Land That Time Forgot*, 1975
Stephen Irving, *Anne of Avonlea*, 1975
Sir Mulberry Hawk, *Nicholas Nickleby*, 1977
The Master, *Doctor Who*, 1981-9

© John Vere Brown

Mark Burns (Gundell)

Captain William Morris, *The Charge of the Light Brigade*, 1968
Alfred, *Death in Venice*, 1971
Mad Scientist, *House of the Living Dead*, 1973
Captain Charles Pike, *By the Sword Divided*, 1983
General Pakenham, *Sharpe's Honour*, 1994

© Bob Carlos Clark

Episode 2: SERGEANT ON THE RUN

WRITTEN BY: John Brason   **DIRECTED BY:** Viktors Ritelis

FIRST BROADCAST: BBC1, 8.05pm, Wednesday 14 September 1977

STUDIO RECORDING: 17 June 1977

VIEWING FIGURE: 6.3m

REGULAR CAST: Albert Foiret: BERNARD HEPTON; Lisa Colbert: JAN FRANCIS; Flt Lt John Curtis: CHRISTOPHER NEAME; Monique Duchamps: ANGELA RICHARDS; Major Erwin Brandt: MICHAEL CULVER; Sturmbannführer Ludwig Kessler: CLIFFORD ROSE; Natalie Chantrens: JULIET HAMMOND-HILL; Dr Pascal Keldermans: VALENTINE DYALL; Alain Muny: RON PEMBER; Jacques Bol: TIMOTHY MORAND; Corporal Rennert: ROBIN LANGFORD

SUPPORTING CAST: Sgt Michael Walker: MARTIN BURROWS; Dr Bogaerde: NEVILLE BARBER; Claude: ANTHONY BLACKETT; Evaders: ANTHONY BARNETT, PERRY BEDDEN; Bistro Local: STEVE UBELS; Lalie: JEANNA L'ESTY; Sgt Donald Pickering: ROB EDWARDS; Sgt Child: IAN OLIVER; Guard: GEORGE MALLABY

SYNOPSIS: There is concern when Lifeline receives word that eight evaders are on their way, as they have no room for them. Lisa is also worried because they will not have had time to train them how to behave and asks Jacques Bol if he can make the evaders understand the dangers of their situation. Three of the airmen are directed to a bistro to eat a meal. While their guide goes to make a phone call, they are discovered. Two of the men are shot, while the third, Sgt Walker, escapes at first but is later apprehended. Albert and Lisa meet with Curtis at Jacques's cycle shop to discuss the matter of his assisting Lifeline. Lisa insists that they will only accept London's help if Lifeline retains its freedom of action and reminds him that they are not saboteurs who require explosives from him. Without Brandt's knowledge, Kessler interrogates Walker. While Kessler is distracted by his adjutant, the young sergeant makes a break for it and throws himself down a stairwell. Several weeks later, the injured Walker has recovered sufficiently to be moved to a ward with other British sergeants and begins to regularly visit a specialist called Dr Bogaerde. Bogaerde subtly encourages Walker to leave the surgery while the guards are distracted. The young sergeant subsequently takes his chance, setting off across Brussels on his crutches. News reaches Albert that Walker is on the loose and he gets out his gun. Kessler too is determined to track down the sergeant. Walker seeks help from a group of children in order to contact an old school friend who lives locally. After failing to remember his phone number he follows directions to his home, only to find that it has been destroyed in an air raid. While a distraught Walker is apprehended, on Albert's instructions the members of Lifeline gather at the Candide. He returns to tell them that the sergeant is no longer their problem as he is dead.

REVIEW: *Sergeant on the Run* – the first episode to be penned by the series's script editor, John Brason – has an entirely different look and feel to the series opener. This is partly due to the fact that it is far less studio-bound, boasting numerous Brussels-based film sequences, but mainly because a different director, with a very individual style, is at the helm: Viktors Ritelis.

Ritelis's typically adventurous approach to both the visuals and the soundtrack of his episodes works to great effect here, especially in the depiction of the fear and desperation of Sergeant Walker. The magnification of ticking clocks and whispered conversations, coupled with oppressive close-ups of the Belgian locals, generates an incredibly claustrophobic atmosphere. Latvian-born Ritelis is also keen to convey an accurate socio-cultural representation of the Occupied Belgium setting. His direction ensures that we can't ignore the way in which the locals eat, the sudden peals of hearty laughter, or passionate arguments in the street. He also makes sure that as the evaders make their way around the city, with the exception of their guide, Claude, they only hear Flemish or French, emphasising that Walker and his equally desperate colleagues are trapped in a very foreign land. This theme is also symbolically represented – imagery being another typical trademark of a Ritelis episode – in the form of the fly caught on fly-paper, which is observed by Walker in prolonged close-up in the bistro sequence. Later, when two of the men are shot dead and thrown unceremoniously into the back of a truck, the dying fly is briefly audible once again. Martin Burrows is engaging as the tragic Walker, whose attempts to find safety are imbued with a chilling sense of hopelessness, especially when he is reduced to seeking the assistance of a group of young children. Although the viewer wills him to have a happy ending, it never feels likely.

Great use is made of the allotted overseas location time, taking in such Brussels landmarks as the Place St Catherine for the scene in which Lisa passes the message to Alain and the statue-lined Place du Petit Sablon for the sequence in which Walker makes his bid for freedom. However, it is the local bistro scenes, filmed back in the UK in London's Covent Garden, which are easily the most resonant of the episode, bringing a heady and starkly realistic feel to proceedings. Unfortunately this carefully built atmosphere immediately and inevitably evaporates when the action switches back to the Candide which, although a superbly detailed and designed set, cannot help but suffer in comparison and remind the viewer that we are now back at BBC TV Centre.

Of the regulars, Brandt and Kessler are once again best served by the script. The ongoing antagonism between the pair is a joy to watch, especially as each exchange reveals that bit more about each character. When Brandt questions Kessler's decision to go out 'hunting' alone, asking "isn't there a saying about having a dog and barking oneself?" Clifford Rose gets to deliver the startling rejoinder "I do not bark, Major Brandt, I bite!" Kessler's later attempt to get answers out of Walker by hitting him about the face while he lies half-dead on the floor, more than proves that this statement was no idle claim. Unlike Brandt, who prevents Kessler from continuing with his attack, the Sturmbannführer will stop at nothing to get the results wanted by Berlin and in this sense Kessler is right to assert that in comparison with the Major his work matters to him far more. A further important insight into Kessler's disturbing psyche is provided via the scene in which he visits the shop of former athlete – and semi-regular character – Jacques Bol, where his admiration for the man's sporting accomplishments ("I just wanted to see the face of the man who won the 50 km race at Wuppertal") makes it clear that Kessler is a true Nazi who prizes highly the value of physical achievement and the ideal human form. Although Brandt certainly comes over as more human that Kessler, especially when he employs his disarming smile, we learn through the subterfuge carried out at the hospital – his assignment of the undercover German Leutnant in the same room as Walker – that he also has a cunning streak that should not be underestimated.

Walker's fall down the stairwell at German headquarters is utterly convincing. A freeze-frame reveals how the effect was achieved – with wires holding Burrows suspended in the air. The sequence is commendable and was presumably very time-consuming to achieve. Particularly well thought out is the reaction to the fall by the German personnel at different levels of the stairwell and the different perspectives of the witnesses.

Until the final scenes, the involvement of the Lifeline regulars is almost incidental to the central plot which motors along by itself. This is something of a strange scripting decision given their strong introduction in the opening episode. When they do briefly take centre-stage it is Bernard Hepton and Jan Francis who once again have the most material to work with. The resolution to the sub-plot involving the arrival of Curtis, last seen held at gunpoint towards the end of *Lisa – Code Name Yvette*, feels late in coming; it is fifteen minutes in before he is even mentioned. However, when it does, it allows for a useful and impassioned précis from Lisa as to what sort of work Lifeline will and will not become engaged in: "We are not a resistance organisation. We do not blow up bridges and kill Germans. That is not our purpose." In her other speech at the cycle shop (which begins with the exclamation "They are children!"), Lisa is equally fervent about the inexperience and idiocy of the British evaders, a view that is seen to be almost totally borne out by the actions of the terrified Walker and his short-lived companions, who could not look more out of place in Brussels if they tried. It is once again clear that, despite what London thinks, Lifeline do know what they are doing – although the fact that Walker apparently knows of a total of seventeen Lifeline people since his arrival, who he could feasibly name under interrogation, doesn't really tie up with this.

In a scene in the Candide's back room, Albert and Monique share a wonderfully tender moment in which he reveals that he remembers the first time Monique came into the café and ordered a cup of black coffee without sugar. Monique, who is regularly forced to play second fiddle to Andrée, the Candide and of course his work for Lifeline, is stunned but very pleased to learn that he remembers that. Monique obviously means a lot to Albert, a fact that the restaurant proprietor doesn't volunteer very often, even to her. Although this scene is important in fleshing out the pair, we learn a great deal more about Albert from his actions in the episode's final few scenes. With Walker once more 'on the run', Albert leaves the Candide to personally dispatch the young evader with his own gun in order to ensure the continued safety of the Line. That Albert is possessed of such strong conviction is a surprise, as is the fact that it is he who must dirty his hands to eliminate the security risk. His colleagues are shocked when they learn Walker is "no longer our problem" and appear to think less of Albert for his apparent callousness, especially as he adopts a front of false nonchalance, asking after Andrée and shrugging his shoulders – presumably in order to cope with what he has done. However, as the surviving members of Lifeline are to eventually discover during Albert's absence in the final series, 'grasping the nettle', even if it means killing someone, is absolutely vital if their work is to continue. When Natalie later comes to realise the necessity of such action, she asks: "How many times did we call him assassin in our hearts?" Nevertheless, as we have come to know Walker and identify with his increasingly desperate plight, this denouement is hard-hitting and very difficult to accept. Albert's closing comment that there are only thirty bottles left of his 'special' and he doesn't think they'll last out the war, implies that if they think that this particular situation has been bad, they should recognise that there is much worse to come.

Sergeant on the Run, from its very first handheld shots following Kessler's movement around headquarters, through to its final moments where Walker's prone body is seen dumped in the ruins of the bombed house, achieves a brooding and dark atmosphere. It is abundantly clear by now that *Secret Army*'s production team does not want the series to be a 'chocks away!' war drama but a grittily realised and authentic depiction of a terrible time in European history.

HISTORICAL BACKGROUND

Bill Randle in Brussels

Two of Bill Randle's memories of his time as an evader on the run in Brussels which found their way into this episode, are also recounted in his autobiography. The first took place when Randle was between safe-houses and had been left by a guide in the Notre Dame Du Sablon: 'I prayed earnestly for the safety of my crew. Almost as an answer from above, a portly, well-dressed man came to sit near me. I noticed that he was wearing the Belgian *boutonniere*. We sat alongside each other in silence for a minute or so, and then he got up and left. I counted off a minute, and followed him outside into the broad day-light, waiting at the top of the entrance steps and watching him cross to the other side of the road. When he got there, he turned and waved his hand in my direction, then walked off slowly to cross a busy main road and enter an ornamental garden shrouded with trees. I followed him into the garden, around a large stone pond in which goldfish were swimming, and up a semi-circular flight of steps at the back of which, in ivy-covered alcoves, stood statues of ancient notables. We left the garden...'[3]

The second concerned a time when he and his fellow evaders were left in a bistro to eat a meal while waiting for their next guide, Dédée: 'He seated us at the far end of the room, conveniently close to a fire exit. I noticed that the wall-clock was showing 12.45, giving us ample time to eat a leisurely meal. The restaurant was about half-filled and, not far from us, two German soldiers were already well into a meal.' When one of Randle's fellow evaders, American Dal Mounts, went to visit the toilet and inadvertently entered the Ladies rather than the Gents, the group were noticed by all about them: 'A hush had descended on the restaurant as attention was focused on the embarrassing scene.' After Mounts pretended that he was deaf and dumb, 'People were intrigued, many were laughing, including some German soldiers who had just arrived... we were the focus of all eyes as I led the crestfallen American back to our table. There was still time to be wasted before our rendezvous with Dédée but I decided it would be safer to do so downstairs and outside... The others went ahead and I paid the bill but, just as I was about to leave, a hand fell on my shoulder and someone behind me whispered in English "You really must try to do better or you will never get back to England."'[4] Randle and his colleagues were to fare much better than their counterparts in this episode.

WHERE ELSE HAVE I SEEN..?

Neville Barber (Dr Bogaerde)

Dr Cook, *Doctor Who: The Time Monster*, 1972
Sergei, *Anna Karenina*, 1977
Lt Col Brownlow, *The Lost Boys*, 1978
Howard Baker, *K9 and Company*, 1981
Mr Curtis, *Grange Hill (Series 3)*, 1981

Rob Edwards (Sgt Donald Pickering)

Chub, *Doctor Who: The Robots of Death*, 1977
Stephen 'Hibou' Lovell, *The Fourth Arm*, 1983
Gilbert Whippet, *Campion: The Case of the Late Pig*, 1989
Ben Edwards, *Dalziel and Pascoe: Guardian Angel*, 2006
Geoff Holhurst, *The Thick of It*, 2005, 2007

Episode 3: RADISHES WITH BUTTER

WRITTEN BY: John Brason   DIRECTED BY: Paul Annett

FIRST BROADCAST: BBC1, 8.05pm, Wednesday 21 September 1977

STUDIO RECORDING: 28 June 1977

VIEWING FIGURE: 5.8m

REGULAR CAST: Albert Foiret: BERNARD HEPTON; Lisa Colbert: JAN FRANCIS; Flt Lt John Curtis: CHRISTOPHER NEAME; Monique Duchamps: ANGELA RICHARDS; Major Erwin Brandt: MICHAEL CULVER; Sturmbannführer Ludwig Kessler: CLIFFORD ROSE; Gaston Colbert: JAMES BREE; Louise Colbert: MARIA CHARLES; Jacques Bol: TIMOTHY MORAND; Corporal Rennert: ROBIN LANGFORD

SUPPORTING CAST: Vidler: ANTHONY SMEE; Schliemann: MICHAEL BURRELL; Alma Schliemann: SHIRLEY JAFFE; Sarah Schliemann: HANNAH ISAACSON; Emile: DAVID HANSON; Boy: FRANCO MANZI; Stunt double for Lisa: VERONICA GRIFFITHS

SYNOPSIS: Curtis meets with Gaston at his place of work, the Bank of Brussels, to hand over the money he has brought from England to finance resistance activities. Gaston explains the coloured ration card system that is being used to deport Jews from Belgium. Curtis is followed to his next rendezvous. Kessler shares coffee and biscuits with Brandt and warns him that if he won't cooperate with him then he will report the matter to Berlin. At the Candide, Curtis finds himself at gunpoint again due to his suspicious meeting with an Abwehr man and the recent death of two Lifeline members, but manages to convince them of his innocence. Lisa accompanies Curtis as he carries out a favour for Gaston: taking new ration cards to a desperate Jewish family by the name of Schliemann. Curtis subsequently asks Lisa if Lifeline can help them, but she is not willing to take the risk. Gaston discovers that the notes brought by Curtis are obvious forgeries and, in order to ensure that they are not traced back to Lifeline, floods banks in Belgium and Holland with the counterfeit currency. Kessler is on to the forged currency and is certain that it can lead them back to the resistance. Louise Colbert pleads with her husband to take a break from his job. When he refuses she reveals that she knows what he and Lisa are up to and begs him to stop before things end in tragedy. During a night time visit to an evader, Curtis and Lisa are forced out on to a rooftop to avoid detection. Lisa falls but is rescued from certain death by Curtis. The pair kiss each other passionately. However, on their return to the Candide, she makes it clear that she can never have a relationship with him. Curtis visits the Schliemanns' again, bringing them food and the news that he may be able to get them out in six weeks time. Brandt advises Kessler to drop his strategy to locate resistance members via the forged notes and the Sturmbannführer reluctantly complies, but secretly orders that a Gestapo case file be opened on Brandt. While visiting Gaston at the bank, Curtis learns to his horror that the ration card colour which denotes Jewish deportation has been changed, meaning that the Schliemanns are now at risk. Curtis again asks Lisa for help to get the family out of Brussels. She reluctantly agrees after he reminds her that she owes him as much for saving her life. However, when Curtis returns to the Schliemanns' flat, he discovers that he is too late as they have already been taken.

REVIEW: John Brason's second script feels like the most solid and well-balanced episode of the series so far. For one thing the series regulars are more settled in their roles and several enjoy some significant character development, particularly Jan Francis's Lisa and Christopher Neame's Curtis. There is still an awful lot going on, almost as much as in *Lisa - Code Name Yvette*, but because the principal characters and the central premise are now familiar and in place, the overall feel is far less busy and more accomplished.

Radishes with Butter is the only episode of *Secret Army* to almost exclusively deal with the subject of the mass deportation of Jews from Belgium. The extreme hardship that Jews were subjected to prior to their fate under unconscionable Nazi policy is played out here through the desperate Schliemann family. Their poverty-stricken and fearful existence is well-realised and when Curtis foolishly asks "Is there anything you need?" the answer is, clearly, everything. We learn more about Curtis's character from this initial scene with the Schliemanns than in any other so far. His touching acceptance of the only thing that Schliemann can offer – a handful of radishes – shows the young Flight Sergeant to be both compassionate and sensitive, and is very nicely played by Neame. Unlike Lisa, Curtis recognises the need to play guest in order to ensure that the "last remnant of their pride" remains intact. The likely fate of the Schliemann family makes Curtis's ultimately futile attempts to help them all the more compelling and poignant. The Schliemann family is very believably portrayed, so much so that it is difficult to think of any of them as actors, an effect that is perhaps aided by the decision to make only the character of Schliemann – a particularly noteworthy performance from Michael Burrell – a speaking part. The silence of Alma and Sarah does not feel like an attempt to save on the casting budget, but rather an effective means of depicting the extent of the mother and daughter's suffering and hunger – their gaunt, blank faces tell the viewer far more about their desperate existence than dialogue could ever have conveyed. Whether the ultimate fate of Europe's Jews was at the time entirely comprehended by the Belgian people as clearly as Gaston's dialogue about labour camps implies ("That is what they say. That is what many pretend to themselves and to their wretched families") is debatable, but excusable in a narrative that seeks to inform about the evils of Nazism and the horror of the Jewish situation. Curtis's line, "They are all going to go," is particularly chilling and borne out by his own discovery at the end of the episode, with the only proof that they had ever been there being the remains of a simple meal – welcomed as "such riches" by the grateful Schliemann – of radishes with butter.

This episode allows for a very thorough and intelligent exploration of the character of Lisa Colbert. The viewer is initially made to feel that Lisa's refusal to put Lifeline at risk by helping the Schliemanns is unnecessarily harsh and that there is really no excuse for her dispassionate position. However, as the narrative continues, it becomes clear that it is precisely because of Lisa's strength of emotion – woefully misjudged by Curtis, leading her to indignantly exclaim "Of course I care!" – that she will not jeopardise all that she has built thus far. When Lisa eventually lets her guard down to Curtis after he saves her life, she reluctantly reveals just how emotionally scarred she is. Her dialogue describing how much her lost love, Pieter, meant to her ("He was all life to me. Laughter. Happiness. Hope. He had all the trust I could ever give to anyone") is beautifully delivered by Francis, and for the first time we have real empathy for the character. Lisa goes on to detail her numbing experiences back in 1940 – the loss, not only of Pieter, but also of her mother and father, somewhere under the rubble of her home town – to explain why she chose her new and dangerous existence: "My whole being revolted against these monsters who had destroyed everything dear in my life. That is why I came to Brussels. That is why I built Lifeline." However, the sad by-product of her intense desire to fight back against the Germans – also exemplified here by her plea to Vidler to "come back and bomb them again and again" – is an inability to permit herself any emotional life beyond her passionate resistance, which is why she feels she can only reject a romantic attachment with Curtis: "There can be nothing between us." It is this level of emotional complexity that gives *Secret Army* an added sophistication often lacking in other drama series.

The episode is also notable for the development of Lisa's aunt and uncle, who are both depicted as more capable and aware than their first appearance suggested. Judging by the fact that he has not taken a break from his position at the bank since the Occupation began, Gaston is seen to be thoroughly dedicated to his brave resistance work and dismisses Louise's idea of going to Liege on the grounds that "too many people's safety depends upon it." In his dealing with the crisis of the forged currency, he is also portrayed as quick-thinking and resourceful. It is interesting that, in contrast with his niece, Gaston does not limit his assistance to evaders but, through his contacts at the Hôtel de Ville, tries to help all those in need, including the Jews. Louise has up until now been depicted as a rather foolish, if care-worn, woman, who even the British seem to know has no clue about her husband's and her niece's secret work. However, here she is seen to finally reveal: "I may be nothing but a foolish housewife but I'm not completely stupid. You imagine I don't know what is going on?" She is understandably worried that she will lose both Gaston and Lisa and states: "I know it is dangerous and can only end in tragedy." While in retrospect this line seems rather prophetic, given the hugely perilous nature of their work it is perhaps more of an observation of an inevitable outcome.

As in the previous two episodes, the relentless sparring between Brandt and Kessler is eminently watchable. In scenes with absolutely sizzling dialogue, each character stands his ground and seeks to warn and put down the other. Early on in the action, Kessler demonstrates to Brandt his considerable influence in an attempt to intimidate him, by: offering real coffee from Brazil and English biscuits; warning him that "it would be unfortunate if I was obliged to report to Berlin that we were unable to work together"; and name-dropping Reichsführer Himmler into the conversation. He also demonstrates his power by making it clear to the Major that the ex-Kommandant of Brussels, Schalk, was replaced by the more hard-line General von Studendorff at his instigation: "He was unsuitable. I advised my superiors accordingly. They appear to have acted upon the advice." However, Brandt appears to be bravely oblivious to Kessler's show of strength and instead chooses to deliberately undermine him at every opportunity: sarcastically reassuring Kessler that his "ability was never in question"; professing relief that he has not yet met Himmler himself; and vocalising approval of Schalk's technique over that of Studendorff: "he understood when to be firm without seeming to be tyrannical" – a contrast of approach that could also be said to separate the Major and the Sturmbannführer. Kessler concludes their conversation with the loaded line: "I'm glad we now understand each other a little better," while Brandt is unable to resist mocking Kessler's obvious game-playing: "Thank you for the superb coffee and the English biscuit – I *am* impressed." Strained relations are further in evidence in later scenes when Kessler relishes taking his time in informing Brandt about his theories over the forged Belgian notes and even admits "I could not resist playing with you a little." However, Brandt once again holds his own, first by deliberately neglecting to toast the Führer and later, after Kessler's failure to trace the forged notes back to the source, by making it clear that he knows the resistance better than the recently arrived Sturmbannführer and suggesting that in future he should study his files a little more thoroughly! Brandt's jibe is finally too much for Kessler and he makes the significant decision to open a Gestapo case file on the Major, thus sowing the first seeds of the Luftwaffe Major's destruction. All of these scenes are not just brilliantly scripted by John Brason, but superbly acted too, with both Michael Culver and Clifford Rose on top form with an already intimate understanding of their respective characters.

Trust is unquestionably the central theme of the episode. Once again Curtis finds himself at the business end of a gun in the Candide's backroom, although when it is revealed that some Lifeline contacts have been killed and that the man he was meeting was a member of the Abwehr, Albert and Lisa's caution becomes understandable. As Albert states: "Trust works both ways." However, the scene is perhaps rather more worthy of note for its depiction of Monique than for the continuing mistrust of Curtis. Before now she has come over as rather biddable, but here she interjects to say of the Flight Lieutenant: "I may be stupid but I trust him and did from the beginning." She also deliberately delays in complying with Albert's instructions to return to the bar. Here are the first clues that, of all the characters, Monique is set to travel the longest journey. As they are here, Monique's reactions to people and situations throughout the series are invariably instinctive and rarely wrong and will ultimately prove vital to the continued existence of Lifeline in the later days of the war.

During this and the following scene, the inclusion of recorded music in several scenes in the Candide – snatches from 'J'attendrai' and 'Einmal wirst du wieder bei mir sein' – would be insignificant were it not for the fact that these songs would later become part of Monique's regular repertoire after her transformation into the new Candide's resident chanteuse from the start of the second series. These recordings continue to crop up regularly during the first series.

Although the streets and parks of Brussels – including the second appearance of Le Place du Petit Sablon, at which Curtis meets Albrecht Beerman – once again feature in several sequences, the humble room in which Curtis and Lisa meet Mr Schliemann and his family was actually filmed in a flat in Ealing, a location which Jan Francis remembers as particularly rundown and suitably dirty. The elaborate and enormous rooftop set designed by Austin Ruddy is totally believable as an exterior and must have cost a small fortune to build. The sights and sounds in the atmospheric scene in which Curtis and Lisa make their way across the roof, before they find a suitable hiding place amongst the chimney stacks, are reminiscent of the climactic sequence in *The Sound of Music* (1965) when the Von Trapps seek sanctuary in the abbey cloisters.

Radishes with Butter has an intricate and compelling plot which effortlessly adds dimension and depth to virtually all of the series's regular characters. From this episode on, *Secret Army* is firmly on its feet.

HISTORICAL BACKGROUND

The Persecution and Deportation of Belgium's Jews

In 1939, approximately 55,000 Jews lived in Belgium, of whom some were refugees who had fled from Germany and were hoping to reach the safety of the United States. For a short time after the German occupation of Belgium in May 1940, the Jews were left alone, however by October of that year, under orders from Berlin, the occupying powers inevitably began to persecute them. At first they were prevented from performing religious rites and barred from certain professions. However, the situation quickly escalated and, in 1942, Military Administrator Eggert Reeder set up the Bureau for Jewish Affairs, which was primarily intended to support the implementation of further unconscionable policies such as confiscation of property and enforced dismissal from employment. From May 1942, Jews were ordered to wear the yellow Star of David. Soon after, Reeder wrote to Berlin: 'The legislation dealing with the Jews in Belgium may be considered complete. The Jews have only extremely limited ways of earning a living. The next step now would be the evacuation from Belgium.' Evacuation was of course a euphemism for deportation to the death camps in the East, and from August 1942, fanatical anti-Semite Untersturmführer Kurt Asche arranged the first of these. In this month it was also decided by Adolf Eichmann that a quota of twenty thousand Jews should be

deported from Belgium. The Jews were summoned to report for evacuation (see photo on previous page of an 'evacuation' from Brussels), but of course many failed to register and so, because Eichmann's quota was out of reach, German police began to raid homes and make arrests. By the end of October 1942, a total of 17,000 Jews had been put on trains from Belgium to the East. A further 6,000 followed in 1943, while in the final year of the Occupation a further 3,000 were deported. Of the 26,366 Jews deported, 24,966 died, the vast majority in Auschwitz. A higher death toll was prevented by active Belgian resistance to the Nazi's 'evacuation' plans, as Jews were hidden, given new identities and forged ration tickets, and helped to safety along escape lines.[5]

Gestapo Headquarters, No. 453, Avenue Louise

During the scene on Kessler's office balcony, we learn from Brandt the reason why that building, No. 453 in the Avenue Louise, was requisitioned: "It's very convenient for our type of work. We can pounce quickly in most areas without having to go through the centre of Brussels." A tall Art Deco-inspired building of

concrete, steel and glass, No. 453 was built on the site of two old manor houses in 1939, towering over the surrounding structures. When the Germans invaded Belgium the following year, the Gestapo quickly seized upon the building as a headquarters for their operations. Despite a concentrated air attack in January 1943, reimagined by John Brason in *Day of Wrath*, the building was used by the Gestapo throughout the war and still stands today at the bottom of the Avenue Louise between the centre of Brussels and its outskirts; however, the buildings on its left have now risen to equal its impressive stature. (Above: A photo of the building during the Occupation. For photos of the building today, see the 'Location Guide'.)

SONGS IN THE CANDIDE

'Einmal wirst du wieder bei mir sein'

'Einmal wirst...' ('Once again you will be with me') was written by Willy Kollo and originally sung by Carl Raddatz in the 1939 German film *Wir Tanzen um die Welt* ('We are dancing around the world'), a musical about a troupe of dancers. A recording of the song is often heard during the first series, but it is not performed by Monique until the episode *Little Old Lady*.

Einmal wirst du wieder bei mir sein,
Einmal wirst du wieder treu mir sein.
Schenkst du mir auch heut' noch keinen Blick,
Einmal kommst du doch zu mir zurück.
Einmal wird es ganz bestimmt dir klar,
Daß ich doch der Allerbeste war.
Suchst du auch woanders noch dein Glück,
Einmal kommst du doch zurück.

'J'Attendrai'

Also heard for the first time here is a recording of the popular French song 'J'attendrai' ('I will wait'), originally a poem by Louis Poterat which was set to music by the Italian composer Dino Olivieri in 1939 (and retitled 'Tornerai'). Monique first sings this song in the new Candide in *The Hostage*. The song was a disco hit in France for Dalida in 1976 and featured prominently in Wolfgang Petersen's acclaimed film *Das Boot* in 1981.

J'attendrai, le jour et la nuit, j'attendrai toujours, ton retour
J'attendrai, car l'oiseau qui s'en fuit
Veint cher cher l'ou bli
Dans son nid, Le temps passé et court
En battant tristement, dans mon Coeur plus lourd
Et pourtant j'attendrai ton retour

Les fleurs palisent, Le feu s'e teint. L'ombre se glisse, Dans le jardin
L'horlo ge tisse, Des sons tres las
Je crois entendre ton pas, Le vent m'apporte
Des bruits lointains, Guettant ma porte
Je coute envain, Helas plus rien, plus rien ne vient

Au revoir, although we're apart, in the heart of me, here you are
Au revoir, as a song lingers on in the memory, so you are
Always dear to me, like a star from afar, you'll appear to me
So my sweet, till we meet, au revoir.

WHERE ELSE HAVE I SEEN..?

Michael Burrell (Schliemann)

Danny Steadman, *Spy Trap: With Friends Like You*, 1975
Waldo Winkler, *Wodehouse Playhouse: The Rise of Minna Nordstrom*, 1975
Alan Reeves, *The Professionals: The Female Factor*, 1978
Stationmaster Frost, *Swallows and Amazons Forever: Coot Club*, 1984
Pope Gregory, *Red Dwarf: Meltdown*, 1991

© Vince St Hilaire

Episode 4: CHILD'S PLAY

WRITTEN BY: Arden Winch   **DIRECTED BY:** Viktors Ritelis

FIRST BROADCAST: BBC1, 8.05pm, Wednesday 28 September 1977

STUDIO RECORDING: 23 August 1977

VIEWING FIGURE: 6.4m

REGULAR CAST: Albert Foiret: BERNARD HEPTON; Lisa Colbert: JAN FRANCIS; Monique Duchamps: ANGELA RICHARDS; Major Erwin Brandt: MICHAEL CULVER; Gaston Colbert: JAMES BREE; Louise Colbert: MARIA CHARLES

SUPPORTING CAST: Inspector Malaud: IAN McCULLOCH; Sophie Chantal: MARY BARCLAY; Madeleine Chantal: RUTH GOWER; Oberst Stoph: JEFFRY WICKHAM; Baroja: KEN STOTT; Maurice: JOHN BOWE; Sergeant Tommy Wright: JONATHAN COY; Pilot Officer Peter Daly: JONATHAN DARVILL; Sergeant Billy Hopkins: NIGEL GREAVES; Sergeant George 'Bert' Baker: RICHARD REEVES; Driver: LEONARD FENTON; Lacoste: PETER BIRCH; Old Man: ERNEST C. JENNINGS; Couple in Candide: DORIS KITTS, LEN MATHEWMAN

SYNOPSIS: A visitor from Berlin, Oberst Stoph, provides Brandt with an American evader's written account of his escape from Occupied Europe, which the British have prevented from being published in a US newspaper but has nevertheless ended up in the hands of German Intelligence. After studying the account, Brandt is confident that despite changes of names and places the writer has given away more than he knows, and so the Major is granted permission to go down to the Spanish border to investigate. Lisa is also on her way down to Spain, escorting several evaders down the Line and stopping off at the safe-house of Madeleine and Sophie Chantal en route. Brandt meets local policeman, the enigmatic Inspector Malaud, who agrees to help Brandt attempt to locate the safe-house described in the evader's account as long as he receives 1000 francs for each airman captured. Back in Brussels, during a visit to the Candide, Louise once more pleads with Gaston to stop his work with the resistance, while Monique, after enduring several cutting comments from Louise, tells Albert she is tired of their secretive relationship. Brandt and Malaud study the American's account in detail and after successfully homing in on a particular area, are initially confused that the safe-house is described as belonging to a doctor who keeps animals. Malaud reasons that the man must be a vet and after checking out his hunch informs Brandt that he has found the safe-house. After Brandt gives his word that the evaders will not fall into Gestapo hands, Malaud tells him where it is. Lisa arrives at the safe-house to provide the airmen with footwear and clothing for the trek over the mountains, but Brandt, a troop of German soldiers and Malaud and his men turn up soon after. Lisa is forced to abandon the evaders and hides in an underground tunnel with a smuggler called Baroja. After the airmen are rounded up by Brandt and Malaud, the Inspector locates the exit from the tunnel and covers it with a heavy barrel. Lisa and Baroja are forced to emerge back at the tunnel entrance where Malaud is waiting for them, but he surprises them both by letting Baroja go free and offering to take Lisa to the train station in Biarritz.

REVIEW: Arden Winch's single contribution to *Secret Army* is an interesting if dialogue-heavy episode, which is primarily set on the Franco-Spanish border, It is precisely because of the 'end of the line' location of *Child's Play* that it was decided to bring the episode forward from its original position later in the series in order to afford the viewer an earlier depiction of the sheer geographic scale of Lifeline's operations. That said, after the set-up of the first three episodes which have solely focused on the Brussels-set storyline, Winch's script somewhat inevitably feels like a trip up a blind alley and, interesting as it all is, something of a distraction from the main action. Perhaps it is just too early in the run to have such a linear and self-contained episode?

Child's Play is principally remembered for the presence of the series's first true – opening-credit securing – guest star: Scottish actor Ian McCulloch as Inspector Malaud. More familiar to viewers both now and then as Greg Preston in the BBC's *Survivors* (1975-77), McCulloch's performance here, as a grumpy, truculent French policeman, is very much in the same mould. The action of the episode in many ways hangs on the whims of this world-weary individual who neither Brandt – with whom he forms a temporary double act – nor the viewer can easily second guess. Malaud has been exiled to the border region from his beloved Paris for reasons that are not made entirely clear ("If they resent you, if they think you're too clever by half, they send you here to break you") and quickly makes it obvious to Brandt that even though he is willing to assist him, he is on nobody's side but his own. His passionate hatred of smugglers appears to arise from the fact that even though he believes himself to be a competent policemen (he is quite certain that it will be his detective work that will lead them to the safe-house) he knows that he has no chance of curbing their activities and that they therefore stand in the way of his return to Paris. However, this fact is only mentioned towards the end of the episode and is a revelation that is a little too long in coming for our interest in this complex character to be completely sustained.

One of the episode's problems is that it relies too heavily on repeatedly going over the American evader's overblown account of his escape experience. Although it is certainly a clever idea that Brandt thinks the airman may have "given away more than he knows" and that the route and safe-house he describes may actually be traced through investigation in the area, far too much time is spent in discussion rather than in physical detective work. There are also too many scenes in which Brandt and Malaud size each other up and negotiate terms, although both Culver and McCulloch work hard to make their wordy scenes interesting. Bizarrely, when they do finally make it out of the studio to the safe-house, Brandt receives no lines at all and only Malaud is present for the final denouement with Baroja and Lisa. Although it is understandable that, for Lisa to live to fight another day, Brandt cannot apprehend her at this stage in the series, it seems strange that given his prominence in this narrative Brandt gets so little to do or say in this final portion of the episode. Even when the evaders are caught it is from Malaud that they cower in fear rather than the uniformed Luftwaffe Major.

Child's Play bears surprisingly few hallmarks of its visually-ambitious director, Viktors Ritelis. The obvious exceptions are: the snatches of footage which suggest the train journey to Southern France; the sudden increase in volume of Sophie Chantal's bubbling cassoulet; and the movement of the camera down from the muddied soldier's boot to Baroja and Lisa hiding underground.

Of the rest of the team, designer Austin Ruddy does the best he can to disguise the fact that Brandt's apartment is studio-bound and that the entrance and exit to the underground tunnel are the same set redressed. The inclusion of stock footage is less adequate, but the effort to present an episode ostensibly set in Southern France is to be applauded and most successful is the scene in which the clean-shaven lorry driver – familiar as *Eastenders'* Dr Legg gives the four evaders directions to the safe-house. The Kent countryside doubled for France in the location sequences, a fact which Ian McCulloch found particularly amusing.

Unlike its immediate predecessor, there is little room here for character development, partly because very few regular characters get a look in. Natalie and Dr Keldermans are still enjoying extended leave from the action and are in danger of being forgotten altogether, while Andrée is reduced to being an invisible, if troublesome, invalid. Kessler and Curtis are also noticeably absent for the first time and it seems possible that Jeffry Wickham's Stoph may have been a last minute substitute for a certain unavailable Sturmbannführer. Monique's ongoing dissatisfaction with her role as Albert's 'second wife' is given some attention and it is interesting that she and Albert are seen to still be able to smile despite the fact that it seems impossible for the restaurant proprietor to extricate himself from his loveless marriage. Louise's fears over Gaston and Lisa's safety are aired for the second episode running and her response to her husband that she would rather have him just ignore their country's suffering and the invading barbarians is a surprising one and powerfully played.

Naturally, given their share of screen time, we learn more from this episode about Lisa and Brandt than anyone else. During her visit to the Chantal sisters in Senlis, Lisa's tiredness gets the better of her and out of exasperation at Sophie Chantal's thin grasp on reality she coldly tells her that the man with curly hair and the gap between his two front teeth was shot. It is an effective and chilling full stop to the scene. She is similarly short with the airmen before setting off from Brussels as they repeatedly question her instructions despite the fact that she has recently been instrumental in helping a total of fifty evaders home. Lisa's gender, age and stature all seem to diminish the level of respect she initially receives, a situation that was also reportedly true of her real-life counterpart Andrée De Jongh, and it seems only natural that this sort of reception coupled with the extreme nature of her work causes her to lose her cool occasionally. However, the most telling scene involving Lisa comes towards the episode's close when she is forced to leave the airmen to their fate and save her own neck by hiding with Baroja. It is the right decision given her role in Lifeline, but no less difficult for

Lisa, especially after she has just pleaded with the evaders to trust her. When interviewed about *Child's Play* in 2004, Jan Francis had few memories of the episode, but was delighted to hear that she had once acted alongside Ken Stott (Baroja) who is now perhaps best known for the role of Chief Inspector 'Red' Metcalfe in *Messiah* (2001) and its sequels.

Of Brandt, we discover that despite his obvious misgivings about the Führer and Nazism, he shares with Kessler a conviction that 'there's no question of who's going to win the war.' Unlike Malaud, he is also certain of the role France will play in the Thousand-Year-Reich. Through the Inspector's demand that Brandt does not hand over the evaders to the Gestapo, we also learn that the Major is, as Malaud suspects, a man of his word. However, it does seem a little odd that Brandt, although honourable enough not to involve the Gestapo, does not take the investigation in Southern France further than simply seizing the evaders. Not only does he fail to search for a guide, but there is no mention of his intention to interrogate the vet and his wife and children. Although the reason for this probably has more to do with the episode's time constraints, it is unsatisfactory nevertheless.

Based on two real-life charismatic and courageous ladies who operated a safe-house in Paris up until Autumn 1943 before escaping to England, the Senlis-based Chantal sisters are introduced here and are set to make irregular appearances in all three series of *Secret Army*. True to their historical counterparts, Sophie and Madeleine, played by Mary Barclay and Ruth Gower respectively, are seen to clearly revel in their hosting of the airmen in their care. It is a nice touch that the pair are characterised in such a contrast to each other: while one remembers Eastbourne as lovely, the other announces that she has always hated it. Sophie, set to appear again soon – without Madeleine – in *Too Near Home*, is clearly the more impractical of the two and as a result is saddened by the fact that the increased efficiency and speed of the evasion process means that she now hardly has a chance to get to know the airmen before they have to move on. The Chantal sisters are excellent creations who fully deserve their return appearances.

Although *Child's Play* – a title that presumably refers somewhat inaccurately to the task of locating the safe-house via the evader's written account – has a fairly linear structure, the overall feel is somewhat disjointed. Perhaps this is because of the imbalance between dialogue and action, or the regular interruption of the main safe-house plot with the short and obviously supplementary Candide-based scenes. While there are several elements of the episode which work well, such as the interplay between Brandt and Malaud and the Chantal sisters' double act, all in all (and in line with the episode's rather abrupt ending) *Child's Play* feels like a missed opportunity.

HISTORICAL BACKGROUND

Portrait in Brandt's Office

The portrait of a pilot seen hanging in Brandt's office at the start of the episode is 'Flugzeugführer einer JU-88' (right) by German illustrator Hans Liska, who while in the service of the Reich had his work published in neutral as well as German newspapers and magazines. In 1941 he was posted to the Russian Front and some of his best known pieces are from this time. After the war, Liska produced work for Mercedes Benz.

A Legendary Basque Smuggler

The most famous of all the Basque smugglers to assist the evasion lines was the legendary Florentino Goïcoechea (below). Bill Randle describes his first meeting with him in his autobiography: 'A tough strong-looking character with a deeply-lined sun-burnt face. He was suitably dressed in shepherd's clothes, a light sheepskin jacket over greasy denim overalls, rope sandals on his feet, and a wine sack over his shoulder.' He was described by another evader as 'tougher than any man he had ever come across, his huge body fortified by years of goat's cheese,

rough red wine and cognac' and that shaking his hand 'was like putting your fingers in a car-crusher!' Florentino knew every inch of the mountains, being as much at home there as the sheep, and led Dédée (and after her arrest, other agents) and a stream of evaders on the difficult journey across the Pyrenees until he himself was shot in the leg in 1944 and arrested by the Germans. After a daring rescue from hospital by Comète agents (see *Trapped*), the seriously injured Florentino recuperated in Biarritz, but due to damage to one of his legs was prevented from moving about his beloved mountains again. Randle met Florentino again in 1977 – while *Secret Army* was in production, as part of a feature for *Radio Times* – and found him to be an emotional and frail shadow of his former self who was nevertheless proud of the part he had played in the work of the evasion lines. Florentino passed away a few years later at the age of 82.

WHERE ELSE HAVE I SEEN..?

Ian McCulloch (Malaud)

Larry Page, *Colditz: Odd Man In*, 1974
Greg Preston, *Survivors*, 1975-7
Peter West, *Zombie Flesh Eaters*, 1979
Dr Peter Chandler, *Zombie Holocaust*, 1980
Nilson, *Doctor Who: Warriors of the Deep*, 1984

Ken Stott (Baroja)

Eddie, *Takin' Over the Asylum*, 1994
DI Pat Chappel, *The Vice*, 1999-2003
DCI Redfern 'Red' Metcalfe, *Messiah* (and sequels), 2001-5
DI John Rebus, *Rebus*, 2006-7
Tony Hancock, *Hancock and Joan*, 2008

John Bowe (Maurice)

Lt Col Ian Jennings, *Soldier, Soldier*, 1994
Jack Booker, *Class Act*, 1994-5
Duggie Ferguson, *Coronation Street*, 1999-2002
Derek Cotton, *Secret Smile*, 2005
Dr Morgan, *Cranford*, 2007

Episode 5: SECOND CHANCE

WRITTEN BY: James Andrew Hall   **DIRECTED BY:** Paul Annett

FIRST BROADCAST: BBC1, 8.05pm, Wednesday 5 October 1977

STUDIO RECORDING: 29 July 1977

VIEWING FIGURE: 7.8m

REGULAR CAST: Albert Foiret: BERNARD HEPTON; Lisa Colbert: JAN FRANCIS; Flt Lt John Curtis: CHRISTOPHER NEAME; Monique Duchamps: ANGELA RICHARDS; Sturmbannführer Ludwig Kessler: CLIFFORD ROSE; Natalie Chantrens: JULIET HAMMOND-HILL; Dr Pascal Keldermans: VALENTINE DYALL; Corporal Rennert: ROBIN LANGFORD; Yvonne: HENRIETTA BAYNES

SUPPORTING CAST: Eric Finch: PAUL COPLEY; Hans van Broecken: GUNNAR MÖLLER; Lena van Broecken: MARIANNE STONE; Alan: RICHARD AUSTIN; Michel Dupont: DAVID TREVENA; German Soldier: AL LAMPERT; Accordionist: GLADYS POWELL; Farmer: DAVID GOODEY; Bride: SALLY SINCLAIR; Groom: MIKE MUNGARVAN

SYNOPSIS: An injured and starving young airman by the name of Eric Finch is found by a Dutch bargee, Hans van Broecken. Monique is angry when Albert is late in coming to her flat. Albert explains that he was looking into the recent appearances at the Candide of a bespectacled man, Michel Dupont, who he refers to as the pimp from Pico's Bar. The next day Natalie tells Monique about her Aunt Lena and Uncle Hans who are due to visit Brussels. Lisa informs Dr Keldermans about the Candide being watched, but is unaware that the surgery is also under surveillance. Kessler is furious when he discovers that Rennert has shown a Gestapo file to Brandt before he himself has seen it. It transpires that Brandt's clerk is Michel Dupont. Finch tells Hans that he wants to get himself out of the war and go to Switzerland. Hans tries to convince him that he means to help, but Finch does not trust him. At the Candide, Lisa is angered by what she sees as Curtis ordering her around and reminds him that she runs Lifeline. Finch overhears Hans talking to his wife, Lena, in German and confronts him. Despite Lena's protests, Hans reveals to Finch that he is in fact a German called Hans Josef Fassler and that he deserted from the German army in 1916. The following day, while Lena and Finch are alone on the barge, Natalie calls and the airman attacks her. After he lets her go, Natalie tells him that she might be able to help. She brings Curtis to the barge and Finch explains to them that he is sick of killing and that before his mission he planned to desert in order to ensure that he can be a father to his unborn child after the war. Curtis tells him that they will help, but Hans is uneasy about the situation. Finch is brought into the Candide during a wedding celebration at which Monique is singing. Curtis alerts a German soldier to Finch's presence and as the airman attempts to flee, he is shot dead. The incident is observed by Dupont. Monique is horrified by Albert and Curtis's involvement in Finch's betrayal, but Albert is confident that they have done the right thing, especially as the Germans now believe them to be loyal collaborators. Natalie is particularly adamant that there was no alternative.

REVIEW: *Second Chance*, James Andrew Hall's first of three scripts for *Secret Army*, sees the series really hit its stride with a well-structured tale that presents two separate and engaging plots which converge in a truly shocking and memorable finale. The episode features terrific performances by all concerned, but especially Paul Copley as tragic Rear Gunner Eric Finch and German actor Gunnar Möller as 'Dutch' bargee Hans van Broecken. Paul Annett is in the director's chair and once again proves that he really does know what he is doing.

Although Lifeline is potentially under threat throughout the episode due to the unwanted attentions of the bespectacled 'pimp from Pico's bar', for the first time its personnel are not on 'red alert', allowing for a more relaxed insight into their everyday lives. While Natalie teaches a German officer how to say "rice pudding" and Lisa flirts playfully with an airman and shares jokes with Dr Keldermans, Monique and Albert finally receive the screen time these characters deserve to flesh out their relationship. Despite the fact that it is implied in *Child's Play* that Albert will never be able to leave the Candide to visit Monique at her flat, this is precisely what he does here and it sounds as though it is not the first time. However, as this first series is set over a period of two years (1942-43), it is entirely possible that this episode is set some months later and Monique's complaints have finally got him out of the Candide occasionally. Angela Richards and Bernard Hepton, who have been substantially under-used in the series thus far, succeed here in portraying an utterly believable relationship between Monique and Albert. Despite the multitude of pressures that threaten their commitment to each other, it is obvious they care about each other deeply. The fact that the incredibly thrifty Albert elects to give Monique what would have been a hugely expensive 'black market' Toblerone also speaks volumes about his feelings for her. However, chocolate is all well and good, but it is clear that what Monique really wants from Albert – marriage – remains impossible. It is perhaps significant that later in the episode, when Monique and Natalie discuss the latter's Aunt Lena and Uncle Hans and the fact that they may not actually be man and wife, Monique comments that marriage still matters to some people. Before the Manon wedding party, marital status is – somewhat inevitably – the topic of conversation once again, and when Monique tells the ghastly barmaid Yvonne, entertainingly played by Henrietta Baynes, that "When I get married sweetheart it won't be in the Restaurant Candide," Yvonne's cutting rejoinder is: "*If* you get married." As the series progresses it seems that Yvonne may just have hit the nail on the head.

Paul Copley is immediately convincing as the anxious Finch. The early scenes, filmed in the back lot of Shepperton Studios, showing his desperate struggles to open a milk churn and to see himself in a mirror shard – an effort which prompts a "bloody 'ell" in a broad Northern accent – are particularly effective. Neat plotting sees this would-be deserter quickly delivered into the arms of a former deserter: barge owner Hans van Broecken. In the lyrical and well-written scene in which the bargee decides to tell the airman the truth about his past in order to secure his trust, Gunnar Möller brings an outstanding emotional intensity to his character. His delivery of the line "I put my life in the palm of my hand and I give my life to you" being a particular highlight. The bringing together of these two characters is a masterstroke, not only because the revelation of their respective desertions cements a friendship and trust between them, but because, through the airman, Hans can look back at the decision he made in 1916 and, through the bargee, Finch can gain an insight into what his decision now might mean for himself in the future. The world-weary Lena, ably played by Marianne Stone, knows only too well that above all it will mean "a lifetime of running" and, as much as she loves Hans, she is aware that in many ways he wants Finch to desert "in order to justify himself" and urges the airman to reconsider: "Don't spend your life running from people, you'll end up running from yourself."

The arrival of Natalie, and later Curtis, puts a whole new complexion on Finch's plans. The members of Lifeline provide a stark contrast to Finch, in that they are risking their lives on a daily basis to bring the war to an end. It is therefore unsurprising that Finch's argument that he is "sick of killing people" falls on deaf ears and he is right to surmise that they believe that it his duty to go back whatever his feelings are. However, when Finch decides to reveal the main reason for his desertion; namely to survive the war in order to be "Eric Finch the Dad, not the Rear Gunner," it is difficult not to feel sympathy for the character, although both Curtis and Natalie appear notably unmoved.

Curtis and Albert's subsequent decision to sacrifice Finch (his death is not shown on screen, but Annett chooses to show the symbolic spilling of blood-red wine at the very same moment) to clear the Candide of suspicion is shocking enough, especially as we are party to Finch's background and know that his child will not have a father after all, but to subsequently discover that the majority of Lifeline agree that the right thing has been done is even more so. Natalie, who is actually seen handing a gun to one of the Germans pursuing Finch, is particularly vocal on the matter: "Why should we feel sorry for him? Every day we risk our lives to return airmen to Britain so that they can fight again and this one wanted to get out, to run away. I don't give a damn for his reasons." Only Monique is visibly shaken by what has happened. However, she isn't just shedding tears for the dead airman, rather she is far more distressed by Albert's complicity in the incident. She can only see the act as one of collaboration, asking him: "My God, did you see the way those people stared at you?" Albert is quick to defend himself on the grounds of expediency, and just as he was confident that killing Walker in *Sergeant on the Run* was the right thing to do, here too he is coldly practical about ensuring Lifeline's survival: "I know what we're doing. I thought you did... What do you want? Is it real help we're prepared to give, or just a rude gesture that earns us a sly pat on the back?" Both Richards and Hepton are again tremendous here and the scene acts as a startling counterpoint to their affectionate exchanges earlier in the episode.

Curtis and Lisa are at loggerheads throughout the narrative, with the latter feeling understandably threatened by the Englishman's tendency to take charge of situations and make decisions. When discussing the possibility of moving Lifeline's headquarters to Jacques Bol's cycle shop, Lisa snaps and reminds him: "You don't run Lifeline, nor does London. If there are any orders to be given I'll give them, not you!" Although Lisa does have a point, it seems fairly obvious that Curtis is a natural leader and is merely playing to his strengths. Nevertheless, his presence clearly has a negative effect on Lisa, who is horrified to realise that she argued against Curtis's idea, despite the fact that she knew it to be right, just because of his domineering attitude. The unpredictable dynamic between the pair is interesting, but events here do seem to suggest that Curtis's feelings for Lisa are not reciprocated; if anything, she seems to largely regard him as a thorn in her side. Like Curtis, Albert also demonstrates considerable leadership qualities here: it is he and Curtis who together engineer Finch's demise, and although Lisa approves of the decision, it is significant that she is not consulted about it beforehand. At this stage in its history Lifeline definitely could be said to have too many chiefs and not enough Indians.

Angela Richards sings for the first time in the series at the Manon wedding party. The ballad in question, 'Memories Come Gently', which Richards wrote herself, is so wonderfully in keeping with the period and adds so much atmosphere to the scene that it is no surprise that Gerry Glaister would later make the excellent decision to make Richards's songs and performances an integral part of the series. As in *Radishes with Butter*, two more musical recordings are heard during the episode – 'Je Suis Seul Ce Soir ('I'm so all alone') and 'Valentine' – both of which Richards would later perform herself in the series.

The episode's closing scene shows the Van Broeckens leaving Brussels in their barge, La Deuxieme Chance (Second Chance). Although Hans was given a second chance after his desertion all those years ago, Finch was not to be so fortunate. Once again, Lifeline has taken a life in order to stay in business, but it will not be for the last time.

HISTORICAL BACKGROUND

Dutch Bargees and the Second World War

In the early part of the 20th Century, Dutch bargees such as Hans van Broecken fulfilled a key role in the economy of the canal and river-rich Low Countries, delivering freight as diverse as potatoes, coal, peat bricks and gravel. Most bargees owned their own boats, often occupying them with their families and selling their goods wherever they could. They were often fiercely independent and enjoyed the flexibility and freedom of their chosen lifestyle. However, the Second World War threatened to drive these bargees from the water, simply because many boats were requisitioned by the German army, increasingly so as the war continued. Also, their boats were often tragically involved in Allied air attacks, leading many of them to elect to abandon their occupation as too hazardous.

SONGS IN THE CANDIDE

'Memories Come Gently' (Richards,Osborne, Warren)

Remember how it used to be when we were young
Younger than we are today and life had just begun
Dreams were full of hope, we held the master key
Memories come gently back to me.

If advice I give you, it's don't rush your youth
Lengthen every moment, never hide the truth
Wipe away the clouds, the gift of love is free
Memories come gently back to me.
Love is for the very young, let us raise our glass and say
Let them live, let them love
Let them have a future to be certain of.

Time goes very swiftly and for all the same
Those who've laughed at love have played a foolish game
Looking at you now at all the joy I see
Memories come gently back to me.

If I had the chance again
I would take you to my heart
And keep you safe, alone with me
Nothing then could reach us, even though apart

In these streets deserted now I search in vain
As I turn a corner in the pouring rain
Floating through a doorway comes a melody
Memories come gently back to me.

'Je Suis Seul Ce Soir'

Je suis seul ce soir, Avec mes rêves,
Je suis seul ce soir, Sans ton amour.
Le jour tombe, ma joie s'achève,
Tout se brise dans mon coeur lourd.
Je suis seul ce soir, Avec ma peine
J'ai perdu l'espoir, De ton retour,
Et pourtant je t'aime encore et pour toujours
Ne me laisse pas seul sans ton amour.

Je viens de fermer ma fenêtre,
Le brouillard qui tombe est glacé
Jusque dans ma chambre il pénètre,
Notre chambre où meurt le passé.

(Refrain)

Dans la cheminée, le vent pleure,
Les roses s'effeuillent sans bruit,
L'horloge, en marquant les quarts d'heure,
D'un son grêle berce l'ennui.

(Refrain)

Tout demeure ainsi que tu l'aimes,
Dans ce coin par toi dédaigné,
Mais si ton parfum flotte même,
Ton dernier bouquet s'est fané.

WHERE ELSE HAVE I SEEN..?

Paul Copley (Finch)

Jerry (Egg's Father), *This Life*, 1996
Peter Quinlan, *The Lakes*, 1997, 1999
Narrator, *How Clean is Your House*, 2003-6
Blind Man, *Dead Man Weds*, 2005
Ivor Priestley, *Coronation Street*, 2007

© K H Vogelman

Henrietta 'Hetty' Baynes (Yvonne)

Vera, *The Seven Dials Mystery*, 1982
Leila, *Running Scared*, 1986
Hilda, *Lady Chatterley*, 1993
Long Jane Silver, *Ken Russell's Treasure Island*, 1995
Tinker Haines, *Cutting It*, 2003

© Unknown

Episode 6: GROWING UP

WRITTEN BY: Willis Hall   **DIRECTED BY:** Kenneth Ives

FIRST BROADCAST: BBC1, 8.05pm, Wednesday 12 October 1977

STUDIO RECORDING: 8-9 July 1977

VIEWING FIGURE: 7.8m

REGULAR CAST: Albert Foiret: BERNARD HEPTON; Lisa Colbert: JAN FRANCIS; Flt Lt John Curtis: CHRISTOPHER NEAME; Monique Duchamps: ANGELA RICHARDS; Major Erwin Brandt: MICHAEL CULVER; Sturmbannführer Ludwig Kessler: CLIFFORD ROSE; Natalie Chantrens: JULIET HAMMOND-HILL; Dr Pascal Keldermans: VALENTINE DYALL

SUPPORTING CAST: Sergeant Clifford Howson: NORMAN ESHLEY; Jean-Paul Dornes: MAX HARRIS; Anna Dornes: SUSAN TRACY; Corporal Emil Schnorr: BRIAN GLOVER; Mademoiselle Gunet: VIVIEN MERCHANT; Pierre Bazin: STANLEY LEBOR; Navigator: DAVID McALISTER; Pilot: KEITH VARNIER; Wireless Operator: MICHAEL HALSEY; Bomb Aimer: MARTIN CONNOR; Luftwaffe Guard: PAUL RIDLEY; Luftwaffe Policemen: NORWICH DUFF, TONY MEYER; Sergeant Findlay: DAVID LYALL; Sergeant Hose: RICHARD HOPE; Sergeant Richards: DAVID LUDWIG; Neighbour: VILMA HOLLINGBERRY; Guide: ALEC WALLIS

SYNOPSIS: A Wellington crashes in the Belgian countryside near a mining village. Four of the crew are apprehended, but the fifth, who has a badly injured leg, is in hiding. A ten-year-old boy called Jean-Paul Dornes, who lost his father at the beginning of the war, finds the airman who introduces himself as Sergeant Clifford Howson. Jean-Paul promises to help Howson and to seek his mother's help. The airman gives the child his RAF badge. Jean-Paul returns home to find his mother entertaining a German Corporal called Schnorr and decides to keep quiet about Howson. Brandt and Kessler disagree about the best way of obtaining information from the captured airmen. Brandt has brought them together in a communal cell so that he can listen in on their conversation. When they learn that Howson is hiding in a barn, Kessler is keen to take some men to the area immediately, but Brandt insists that they begin 24-hour surveillance instead, with a view to following the man down an evasion line. Kessler reluctantly agrees. Jean-Paul helps Howson to a new hiding place in a cave near a disused quarry. The airman asks him if he can contact the resistance. During school, Jean-Paul's teacher confiscates the RAF badge and contacts Pierre Bazin, one of Lifeline's resistance contacts. News reaches Lifeline of Jean-Paul's assistance of the airman. Lisa decides that they will retrieve Howson from the caves in broad daylight and intends to take Albert horse-riding with her to achieve it. Jean-Paul says goodbye to the airman who lets him keep the RAF badge as a souvenir. Lisa and Albert stage a horse-riding accident, substituting Howson for Albert. After Lisa seeks help from Jean-Paul's mother and Corporal Schnorr who are out walking together, Albert and Natalie arrive in a van and take Howson to Dr Keldermans in Brussels. Anna Dornes finds the RAF badge and confronts her son with it. Despite his protestations, she decides to go and tell Schnorr at the barracks. Jean-Paul runs to tell Pierre what she plans to do and the shopkeeper intercepts her en route, running her over in his van. Curtis gives Howson a dressing down for giving Jean-Paul the RAF badge as it has caused the death of the boy's mother, before telling him that his leg will have to be amputated. While Howson is taken to Namur with some other evaders, Jean-Paul attends his mother's funeral. Schnorr is also present and, after the burial, comforts the orphaned boy as he cries.

REVIEW: *Growing Up* once again sees a Willis Hall script brought to life by Kenneth Ives. Although this tale of a young boy's discovery and assistance of an evader is affecting and well crafted, in some ways its linear content, which sees the Lifeline regulars mostly on the periphery of the action, feels less like an episode of *Secret Army* and more like a self-contained television play. Exhibiting shades of Hall's own *Whistle Down the Wind*, which he wrote with regular collaborator Keith Waterhouse, the narrative largely takes a child view of proceedings, the main difference being that this child, Jean-Paul Dornes, played remarkably well by Max Harris, is not labouring under any misapprehensions. Jean-Paul instinctively seems to know the right course of action to take, thus ensuring the safety of Sergeant Clifford Howson – a competent turn by Norman Eshley – until Lifeline make it on to the scene.

A real Belgian town was used for most of the location work (the exterior of the Dornes's house, cobbled streets, a local school, and a graveyard), while Belgian supporting artists were employed for the funeral procession and burial scenes. Both elements provide the episode with a commendably authentic continental feel, although the latter was not without its complications for Kenneth Ives, as the majority of the Belgians used did not speak a word of English. The only slight blunder in terms of visuals is the garish patterned wallpaper which is clearly visible in the entrance halls of the Dornes and Bazin homes – definitely more 1970s than 1940s! The remainder of the location work was filmed in the flat – and therefore feasibly Belgian – countryside near Peterborough.

The sequences with Jean-Paul and Howson – which incidentally were the very first to be shot for *Secret Army* – are sensitively realised, with Harris and Eshley working very well together. Jean-Paul's dialogue is particularly well-written and matter-of-fact, never once slipping into sentimentality. Although it is the boy who is assisting the RAF evader, Howson is nevertheless protective of his helper when the opportunity arises: for instance, putting his arm around the boy's shoulder when he sees a German patrol. He is genuinely grateful to the boy and seems to be as concerned for his safety as much as he is for his own. As with all child actors, a special licence had to be obtained in order to use 11-year-old Harris, who also had to be accompanied throughout the recording by his father. Harris was cast due to his performance opposite Alan Badel in Dennis Potter's BBC production of *Where Adam Stood* (1976).

The charge levelled at Jean-Paul by his mother, Anna, throughout the episode is that he's too young to understand war and that it is not a game. Although he is seen 'playing war' both in the schoolyard and before he finds Howson, the boy is depicted throughout as having a far more acceptable and understandable approach to war than she does. Jean-Paul and Anna have reacted very differently to the death of Henri Dornes at the start of the war ("one of the first to volunteer, one of the first to die.") While the boy now eagerly states "I hate the Germans," gives the thumbs up to the captured evaders and is clearly uncomfortable to have a German, Corporal Schnorr, in the family home, his mother has chosen to opt out of the war entirely: "We've had our share of the war, we don't take sides any longer, we just keep out of it." Schnorr immediately picks her up for her failure to understand that "we are none of us out of the war." She naïvely assumes that Jean-Paul will unquestioningly follow her lead, suggesting that since his father's death she has not taken the time to talk to, or understand, her son. That Anna also seems to be totally unaware of the fact that her relationship with Schnorr is likely to both upset her son and, more importantly, be viewed by outsiders as collaboration is also naïve in the extreme. Anna Dornes is such a deeply unsympathetic character – who you almost want to shake to get her to see her son's worth – that when her murder eventually comes it is difficult to feel sorry for her. It is terrible for Jean-Paul that he is now an orphan, but his mother's parenting certainly left something to be desired.

Brian Glover provides typically solid support as Emil Schnorr. Although first seen as a somewhat two-dimensional stock German who is not averse to frightening local school-children, his character is gradually revealed to be a victim of war himself. During his walk with Anna he tells her that after losing his wife Elsa in an Allied bombing raid, he "stared at a blank wall in the barracks" because he had nothing and no-one left. At the episode's close, it is Schnorr who repeatedly seeks to provide comfort to the orphaned Jean-Paul and although the boy resists at first, his arms are eventually accepted and the Corporal is clearly moved.

As the Lifeline regulars are effectively side-lined for the majority of the episode, there is no progression in their ongoing storylines, which after the excellent *Second Chance* feels like a step backwards. As interesting as 'the boy's war' is, at this point in the series it does feel as though the development and experiences of characters who viewers now know relatively well should really be the main focus of the action. As for the German regulars, as in the first two episodes of the series, Brandt and Kessler's involvement in proceedings is once again limited to their differences of approach. Brandt is disparaging about the Sturmbannführer's use of primitive rubber hose-pipes and bamboo canes which can sometimes result in a "pack of lies" rather than the truth and prefers to employ more considered methods. When they learn of Howson's location, Brandt once again opposes Kessler's desired course of action ("rushing in like a mad bull") and instead suggests that they combine forces and conduct surveillance on the area in order to capture far more than just one evader. This contrast between Brandt and Kessler is cleverly paralleled by the different approaches of the members of Lifeline to the same problem albeit from the opposite perspective. While Curtis's 'gung ho' mentality causes him to suggest that they go straight into the area, Albert and Lisa pragmatically think the situation through and recognise that they can't risk going near the place as it will be "swarming with police and military right now." Lisa's subsequent plan to get Howson out of the area is ingenious and an important reminder that she has both the brains and courage to run Lifeline.

Providing brief cameo appearances in the episode are: Vivien Merchant, as Mademoiselle Gunet, best known for her Oscar-nominated role in *Alfie* (1967), and for being the wife of acclaimed playwright Harold Pinter and taking lead roles – characters who she herself had inspired – in his plays; and Stanley Lebor, as Pierre Bazin (although only credited as 'shopkeeper' in the end credits), who will always be best remembered as the lovable but wet Howard Hughes in the BBC sitcom *Ever Decreasing Circles*. Incidentally, Pierre – presumably the same Pierre who Monique threatens Albert she will visit in the previous episode – was not originally intended to be the perpetrator of the 'hit-and-run'. Hall's original script had Natalie, who has very little to do here, kill Anna Dornes, but Bill Randle felt that this lacked credibility given that she wouldn't have had time to get there and suggested they use Pierre instead. Although he might have had a point, Natalie's involvement would have certainly added more shock value to the incident.

Several scenes towards the end of the episode don't really ring true or add anything to the episode. Curtis's dressing down of Howson seems oddly over the top: Howson couldn't have known that the boy would make his only real mistake with the RAF badge, by hiding it under his pillow, or that his mother – whose German sympathies Jean-Paul does not relate to Howson – would feel the need to immediately tell the Germans about him if she found it. Curtis is unsympathetic to the trauma undergone by the severely injured Howson and even elects to tell him about his impending amputation only after he has had the chance to berate him at length, just so he wouldn't miss the opportunity to vent his spleen! The scenes that follow, which show Howson's departure from Brussels, are interspersed with the excellent funeral footage, and seem oddly absent of significance, especially the confusing and superfluous business of the changeover of guides. The sole purpose of their inclusion is presumably to lead in to their cheerful rendition of 'Roll Out the Barrel', which provides a counterpoint to the solemn figures of Schnorr and Jean-Paul.

Growing Up is certainly a very watchable fifty minutes of television drama, but it too readily neglects the considerable talents of the resident cast in favour of its guest stars for it to be regarded as a classic slice of *Secret Army*.

HISTORICAL BACKGROUND

'Roll Out the Barrel'

The song 'Roll out the Barrel' (also known as 'The Beer Barrel Polka') which is heard towards the end of the episode, became well-known during World War II and was particularly popular with soldiers. It was originally composed by a Czech musician, Jaromír Vejvoda, in 1927. The English lyrics, written by Lew Brown and Vladimir Timm, are as follows:

Roll out the barrel
We'll have a barrel of fun
Roll out the barrel
We've got the blues on the run
Zing, boom, tararrel
Sing out a song of good cheer
Now's the time to roll out the barrel
For the gang's all here!

WHERE ELSE HAVE I SEEN..?

Norman Eshley (Howson)

Lt Last, *Warship*, 1973-4

Marcus, *I Claudius*, 1976

Baron Huon de Domville, *Cadfael: The Leper of St. Giles*, 1994

DCI Reed, *Murder Most Horrid: Whoopi Stone*, 1999

Billy Pierce, *New Tricks: God's Waiting Room*, 2007

© Unknown

Susan Tracy (Anna Dornes)

Crown Princess Stephanie of Austria, *Fall of Eagles*, 1974

Mrs Van Daan, *The Diary of Anne Frank*, 1987

Phyllida Campion, *Poirot: The Case of the Missing Will*, 1993

Felicity Gamelin, *Midsomer Murders: Death in Disguise*, 1999

Hilary King, *Midsomer Murders: King's Crystal*, 2007

© Peter Simpkin

Vivien Merchant (Mlle Gunet)

Sarah, *The Lover*, 1963

Lily, *Alfie*, 1967

Augusta Fullen, *Wicked Women: Augusta Fullen*, 1970

Ruth, *The Homecoming*, 1973

Queen Maria Theresa, *The Man in the Iron Mask*, 1977

© Unknown

Max Harris (Jean-Paul)

Truscott, *One of Our Dinosaurs is Missing*, 1976
Edmund Gosse, *Where Adam Stood*, 1976
Robert, *The Phoenix and the Carpet*, 1976
Colin Muirhead, *The Omega Factor: Child's Play*, 1979
Little Matt, *Love in a Cold Climate*, 1980

Brian Glover (Schnorr)

Heslop, *Porridge*, 1974
Magersfontein Lugg, *Campion*, 1989-90
Griffiths, *Doctor Who: Attack of the Cybermen*, 1985
Andrews, *Alien³*, 1992
Selwyn Price, *Anna Lee*, 1994

Stanley Lebor (Bazin)

Gaius, *The Tomorrow People: A Rift in Time*, 1974
Mongon Doctor, *Flash Gordon*, 1980
Inspector Lestrade, *The Baker Street Boys*, 1983
Howard Hughes, *Ever Decreasing Circles*, 1984-9
Uncle Hendreary, *The Borrowers*, 1992

Episode 7: LOST SHEEP

WRITTEN BY: N. J. Crisp   **DIRECTED BY:** Paul Annett

FIRST BROADCAST: BBC1, 8.05pm, Wednesday 19 October 1977

STUDIO RECORDING: 2 September 1977

VIEWING FIGURE: 9.5m

REGULAR CAST: Albert Foiret: BERNARD HEPTON; Lisa Colbert: JAN FRANCIS; Flt Lt John Curtis: CHRISTOPHER NEAME; Major Erwin Brandt: MICHAEL CULVER; Natalie Chantrens: JULIET HAMMOND-HILL; Alain Muny: RON PEMBER; Gaston Colbert: JAMES BREE

SUPPORTING CAST: Flt Lt Peter Romsey: CHRISTOPHER GUARD; Hugh Neville: PETER BARKWORTH; Dorothy Neville: JOANNA VAN GYSEGHEM; Inspector Pierre Dubois: BRUCE MONTAGUE; Victor: IVOR ROBERTS; Hunter: RAY ARMSTRONG; Don Fisher: ROGER DAVIDSON; Ken Jones: DOMINIC LETTS; Fisherman: JOHN MOORE; Fassbaender: MICHAEL ANTHONY; Oberst: WILLY BOWMAN

SYNOPSIS: Lifeline is suspicious when they come across Flight Lieutenant Peter Romsey, seemingly the only survivor of a plane crewed by just two men. However, London clear him and insist that he be taken down the Line as a matter of urgency. Curtis scolds him when he begins to speak openly about the new OBOE radio system, the results of which the British are very keen to learn. At the train station, Romsey loses his nerve when he comes across a German and consequently boards the wrong train. Alighting at a town fifty kilometres from Tours, Romsey seeks help from the locals. After a close call with a gendarme, he is directed to the home of English writer Hugh Neville. Meanwhile, Brandt learns that the shot down Mosquito was a very special plane. Neville and his wife Dorothy welcome Romsey into their home and get to know each other. Neville doubts the existence of the resistance, believing it to be British propaganda. He also questions the merits of Romsey's bombing raids and explains that living where they do, they are virtually unaffected by the war. A unit of German troops moves into the area, searching for Romsey. Dorothy suggests that Romsey can stay with them in hiding until a resistance contact comes for him. A Lifeline agent called Victor is sent to locate Romsey. Brandt also arrives in the area and impresses upon local Police Inspector, Pierre Dubois, the importance of finding him. Victor is invited to the Nevilles' and is introduced to Romsey, who he plans to come back for the following day. Dubois warns Neville that his house will be searched. During the search, Dubois makes it clear to Neville that he suspects he is harbouring the airman and that he should come clean before the Gestapo move in. The next day, Victor visits and tells Romsey how he plans to get him out of the area. Dorothy insists on accompanying Romsey to the rendezvous in the woods, where he is concealed in a part of Victor's vehicle. Soon after they depart, Victor is ambushed by a troop of Germans and shot dead. Romsey is discovered and taken prisoner. Dorothy returns home and tells Neville that the Germans were waiting for Victor and Romsey and therefore must have known about the arrangements. At the train station, Natalie observes that Romsey is now Brandt's prisoner. During their train journey, Romsey is conned by the charming Brandt into thinking that the Luftwaffe already know about OBOE and he unwittingly reveals its secrets.

REVIEW: Although on first viewing *Lost Sheep* appears to be a self-contained narrative, it is in fact the first part of *Secret Army*'s only two-part story. Both *Lost Sheep* and its immediate sequel, *Guilt*, were written by veteran television scriptwriter N J (Norman) Crisp. Like John Brason, Crisp seemed to have an instinctive understanding of what made the series work and as a result he was responsible for many of *Secret Army*'s finest hours. Although *Lost Sheep* is not among the best of these, it is nevertheless a good example of the high standard of characterisation and dialogue which typifies his episodes. As in *Growing Up*, the regulars largely play second fiddle to the episode's guest stars. However, the difference here is that *Lost Sheep* is building towards the events of *Guilt*, which will have far-reaching repercussions both for Lifeline and John Curtis in particular.

Peter Barkworth, the series's most prestigious guest star to date, brings a great deal of class to the episode as dogmatic English writer Hugh Neville. Neville is a well-drawn character who exudes arrogance and self-importance. His unerring belief in a blinkered and unrealistic worldview leads him to make some spectacularly incorrect assertions, particularly in respect of the war. For one thing he finds it very hard to believe that 'the Resistance' exists, stating: "personally I've always regarded the whole thing as British propaganda" and he also enjoys mocking what he terms "the current mythology" of the situation in France, which has "everyone alternately starving, terrified, being shot out of hand, knifing German soldiers on dark nights." Above all, he is supremely confident that the war will not touch him and, like Anna Dornes in *Growing Up*, believes he can choose to stay out of it. Besides, as he tells Romsey, he has "never seen any German soldiers around here." It is a great touch that the very next shot shows a troop of Germans searching a cornfield for the airman, demonstrating that Neville's confidence is misplaced and that whether he likes it or not the war will find him soon enough. Neville is not only presented as somewhat deluded, but also as incredibly selfish. While dealing with the life and death situation of hiding Romsey, he announces to his wife: "I'm getting tired of this. My concentration's gone. I'm not getting anything done" – a reference to his unfinished manuscript and the priority that his writing takes in his life. Neville's perspective on his own literary talents depicts him as immodest and pretentious. He is horrified when Romsey compares him to Joseph Conrad ("Simple soul, Conrad, I've always thought, far too one-dimensional for me") and summarises the content of his new book to Dubois as: "about a man questioning himself. What he is. The meaning of life. It's a theme I've touched on before." When asked if it is set during the war, Neville replies in the negative: "No. War has no meaning. It's an act of collective madness, collective lunacy." The writer is soon to find that war will have a very direct and personal meaning for him.

Although similarly upper class, Flight Lieutenant Peter Romsey is depicted as a wide-eyed innocent and therefore at the other end of the spectrum from Neville entirely. Romsey, with his incredible tally of 57 ops, believes in the war and his work ("someone has to do it") and is shocked to hear Neville question the integrity of the BBC, responding with the wonderful line: "I don't think the BBC would say anything if it wasn't true." While Neville is presented as too cynical, Romsey is clearly far too naïve and, as Curtis discovers, all too quick to reveal precious British secrets just because a man gains his confidence. Despite his considerable RAF experience, Romsey comes across as none too bright. He fails to grasp the reason why Albert asks him questions about his former occupation and his house at school and manages to immediately offend his new 'room-mates' with the ill-advised opening gambit: "Are you a driver or a brainy one like me?" for which he thoroughly deserves to hear the cutting reply: "No, I'm just a thick rear gunner." Showing a keen perception of a man he barely knows, Curtis correctly surmises that Romsey has 'the twitch', otherwise known as operational fatigue ("Great resolution one minute, indecision in an emergency the next"). This is an important rationalization for the young Flight Lieutenant's distinctly odd overreaction to the presence of a German officer in the station toilets and his hiding in a toilet cubicle before boarding the wrong train, and not just the obvious explanation of dramatic necessity.

Lost Sheep's other key characters are Neville's wife, Dorothy, played by Joanna van Gyseghem, and Bruce Montague's Inspector Pierre Dubois. The former is presented as a long-suffering victim of Neville's conceited behaviour who sees the arrival of young Romsey as a breath of fresh air. There is even a hint of an attraction between her and the airman. Dorothy is compassionate and open and immediately aware of her obligations to the evader. It is she who offers him the chance to stay there in hiding, while Neville himself remains distinctly silent. Dubois, who becomes a focal character towards the end of the narrative, openly collaborates with the Germans in the matter of the airman, but feels that he must excuse his actions under the guise of maintaining law and order in his district. In this regard he fools neither Neville nor himself, but he is nevertheless awake to the reality of war.

The episode's stand-out scene and turning point of the narrative is a conversation between Dubois and Neville which takes place during the search of the latter's house. Dubois begins the exchange by suggesting that Neville would have been the obvious person for Romsey to turn to, before pointedly observing that his cold (his excuse for his absence the previous evening) has got better and reminding him that he owes his special position in the area to his intercession. Dubois delivers these comments and observations with a considered false bonhomie, which becomes ever more insincere as the Inspector comes to the crux of the matter: "I mean, would you do anything so silly as to, well, assist an English airman to take an example? When you know you'd be arrested, charged and shot, and your wife would be put into a concentration camp?" Dubois spells out the reality of Neville's position, not only to make it clear that he already knows the truth, but also in order to save his own skin – Brandt has after all made it clear that if Romsey is not found, "it could go badly" for his district. Before closing the topic, to make sure his point has definitely hit home, Dubois even goes so far as to state that "Any information would be treated in the strictest confidence. Nobody would know, not even your wife," before levelling his final threat – that of the Gestapo. Bruce Montague is excellent as the manoeuvring Dubois, who may not profess to have the same intellectual persuasions as Neville, but certainly understands human behaviour well enough to obtain the results he needs.

Major Brandt is the only series regular with a direct role in the events down in France. His elation at finding Romsey is written all over his face and his good day continues when he finds the airman to be just as naïve and open as Curtis did. When Brandt adopts his charm offensive, he quickly tricks Romsey into revealing that the new OBOE radio system involves a beam that cannot be bent. Unfortunately, Curtis's warning about this very situation was not taken on board by the easily-led airman.

As the narrative of the episode chiefly moves among conversations between the four central guest characters, with carefully crafted dialogue that is consummately delivered by all concerned, *Lost Sheep* assumes an almost theatrical feel. The shifting tableau of the characters in the Nevilles' lounge – changes in who is sitting and who is standing – also suggest theatre, but this is no bad thing. The episode is not about adventure or spectacle, but about connection with the war, perspective and 'doing the right thing'. Although Neville ultimately does 'the wrong thing' by betraying Romsey – something which is not absolutely clear until the events of *Guilt* – it could be argued that it would have been difficult for him to do otherwise, given that Dubois all but states that he knows that the writer is hiding the airman,

Lost Sheep works well enough in its own right, but its themes and concerns lack resonance until the gripping events of the following episode unfold, events which would not have anything like the same impact without the accomplished groundwork that has been laid here.

HISTORICAL BACKGROUND

Oboe

The *Oboe* system, developed by Alec Reeves, was first introduced by the RAF in December 1942 and was to make no small contribution to the Allied victory: 'This was a blind-bombing device fitted into an aircraft but controlled from ground stations in England. Two stations transmitted pulses which were picked up by the aircraft and retransmitted to the ground stations again. The aircraft receiving the *Oboe* signals used the pulses to keep itself on the right track in order to pass over the target; the stations in England, by measuring the time taken to receive the pulses back again, calculated the aircraft's exact position and sent a short signal at the moment when its bombs should be released.' The system's limitations included: the fact that it was a 'line-of-sight device', which meant the signal could not be bent over the curvature of the Earth, thus limiting its operational range; each station in England could only control six aircraft and, as the maximum number of stations that could be used was three, only eighteen aircraft could use *Oboe* at the same time; the aircraft making the bombing run had to fly straight and level for a time, making an ideal target for night-fighters or flak. Nevertheless, the system was very successful and the Germans never managed to jam it. *Oboe* was quickly superseded by the *H2S* system which had fewer limitations.[7]

'Nuages'

Lost Sheep is one of many episodes in which a recording of Django Reinhardt's 'Nuages' ('Clouds') can be heard. Born in 1910, Jean-Baptiste (Django)

Reinhardt was a Belgian Gypsy who was to become one of the most famous jazz guitarists of all time. As with the Jews, Nazi policy was to exterminate all Gypsies by sending them to death camps, an act referred to by Romani people as the Porjamos ('the Devouring'), however Reinhardt fell under the protection of Dietrich Schulz-Köhn, nicknamed Doktor Jazz, a Luftwaffe Officer who deeply admired his music. Aside from 'Nuages', Reinhardt's other famous compositions include 'My Sweet', 'Minor Swing' and 'Tears'. He died in 1953.

WHERE ELSE HAVE I SEEN..?

Peter Barkworth (Hugh Neville)

Kenneth Bligh, *The Power Game*, 1965-6
Clent, *Doctor Who: The Ice Warriors*, 1967
Vincent, *Manhunt*, 1970
Mark Telford, *Telford's Change*, 1979
Edward Brett, *Late Starter*, 1985

© John Timbers

Joanna van Gyseghem (Dorothy Neville)

Det Sgt Hicks, *Fraud Squad*, 1969-70
Jean, *Play of the Month: The Linden Tree*, 1974
Marigold Featherstone, *Rumpole of the Bailey*, 1978-92
Susan Wade, *Pig in the Middle*, 1980-3
Linda Cochran, *Duty Free*, 1984-6

© Terry Hillyer

Christopher Guard (Romsey)

Marcellus, *I, Claudius*, 1976
Frodo (Voice), *The Lord of the Rings*, 1978
Wilfred Owen, *Wilfred and Eileen*, 1981
Philip Ashley, *My Cousin Rachel*, 1983
Bellboy, *Doctor Who: The Greatest Show in the Galaxy*, 1988

© George Wilkes

Episode 8: GUILT

WRITTEN BY: N. J. Crisp **DIRECTED BY:** Paul Annett

FIRST BROADCAST: BBC1, 8.05pm, Wednesday 26 October 1977

STUDIO RECORDING: 13 September 1977

VIEWING FIGURE: 7.5m

REGULAR CAST: Albert Foiret: BERNARD HEPTON; Lisa Colbert: JAN FRANCIS; Flt Lt John Curtis: CHRISTOPHER NEAME; Monique Duchamps: ANGELA RICHARDS; Major Erwin Brandt: MICHAEL CULVER; Natalie Chantrens: JULIET HAMMOND-HILL; Alain Muny: RON PEMBER

SUPPORTING CAST: Hugh Neville: PETER BARKWORTH; Dorothy Neville: JOANNA VAN GYSEGHEM; Inspector Pierre Dubois: BRUCE MONTAGUE; Madame Victor: VERA JAKOB; Patronne: PAULINE LETTS; German Officer: ROY PATTISON; Flt Lt Peter Romsey: CHRISTOPHER GUARD; Victor: IVOR ROBERTS

SYNOPSIS: Curtis goes to the Candide to tell Lisa and Albert that the Germans have published a newspaper article about the OBOE navigation system, containing information which the captured Flt Lt Romsey must have provided. They also discuss the betrayal of Victor. Curtis reveals that London are sending an agent to deal with the problem. However, the agent is killed by the Germans soon after his arrival. When Alain reports his death, Albert wonders if the agent could also have been betrayed. Curtis volunteers to investigate what happened near Tours, but Albert expresses doubts about his ability. Natalie visits Madame Victor to see if she can shed any light on her husband's death. After providing the widow with some money, she observes Dubois and Neville talking in the town square. Dubois is trying to convince Neville that neither of them should feel guilty for Victor's death. Neville begins to feel better about the situation, but his wife, Dorothy, remains withdrawn. Albert raises the possibility that Curtis might have been behind the agent's death, but Lisa is unconvinced. Nevertheless, Albert elects to send Monique to secretly follow Curtis, with orders to dispose of him should their worst fears be confirmed. Curtis checks in to a guest-house and hires a bicycle. Monique checks in to the same establishment and looks through Curtis's things while he is out. She also sees him talking with Inspector Dubois. The next morning, Curtis catches Monique in the act of searching his room. Monique, who arms herself with a gun, questions him about the dead agent and his recent movements. Curtis is furious both that he has been followed and that Lifeline still don't trust him. After opening a flick-knife, he manages to get Monique to drop her gun. Curtis visits Dubois, before arriving at the Nevilles' where he pretends to be Flt Lt Robert Green from Leeds. He learns that they hid Romsey and that Dorothy Neville is still distressed by Victor's death. After a heated discussion about the war and ideals, the Nevilles go to bed while Curtis elects to sleep downstairs. During the night, he reads Neville's manuscript which, due to it semi-autobiographical content, clearly points to his betrayal of Victor and Romsey. He confronts Neville the next morning, but Dorothy comes to his defence, recounting what happened. Neville draws a gun, admits to telling Dubois about Romsey and sends Dorothy off to fetch help. Curtis and Neville fight, but Curtis gains the upper hand and slits Neville's throat. Monique picks up Dorothy, and then Curtis, by car. After dropping Dorothy off some distance from the Neville home, they make their getaway. As they travel back to Brussels by train, Curtis tells Monique he has never killed a man before and that he lied to Neville about not feeling guilt.

REVIEW: *Guilt* is both a gripping and surprising conclusion to the Flt Lt Romsey saga. Picking up shortly after the events of *Lost Sheep*, the episode, as its title suggests, deals with the guilt associated with the betrayal of Romsey and the death of Lifeline agent Victor. The narrative benefits hugely from the screen time afforded Curtis and Monique, who take centre-stage alongside the guest characters who featured in the preceding instalment. Christopher Neame and Angela Richards rise to the occasion very well indeed, once again proving that the more material the regulars have to work with, the better *Secret Army* is. It is a simple formula that the series thankfully adopts without fail from now on.

Guilt immediately confounds expectations by continuing a storyline that had seemed to be very definitely over. This is nowhere more the case than in the early scene in which Natalie observes Dubois passing the time of day with Neville as if nothing has happened. The decision to go back not only allows N. J. Crisp to dig a little deeper – developing his characters further – but also to help us understand their motivations and even to care about their eventual fates. Crisp's rich dialogue is once again exquisitely delivered by all concerned and, if they hadn't done so already, the guest characters come across here as utterly believable three-dimensional people. Thankfully, continuity with *Lost Sheep*'s look and feel is maintained by Paul Annett's immediate return as director. Annett was not originally scheduled to direct both episodes, but he wisely insisted that he handle both given their shared content. His direction here is typically assured.

There are several genuine surprises in the narrative, not least the somewhat revelatory abilities and steel of Monique. Of all the female characters at the Candide, despite being Albert's mistress, Monique has been shown to be the least involved in the work of Lifeline thus far. And yet, here, when Albert seeks final, once-and-for-all proof of either Curtis's guilt or innocence, it is Monique he turns to. The reason Albert gives to her is that "you're the only one who can't be spared," but it later transpires that there is a little more to it than that. When Albert tells Lisa: "beneath that shapely exterior, Monique's as hard as they come," she still questions Monique's ability to carry out the mission, at which point he hints that he actually trusts Monique to do the job more than he does her: "She wants to believe in John Curtis, that's true, she has a soft spot for him, but if she finds out she's wrong she'll have even less compunction than you would, Yvette." Albert clearly has witnessed Monique in action before, and judging by the way she confidently loads the gun he gives her, she has plenty of experience behind her. Once 'in the field', Monique remains calm and considered and proves to be adept when it comes to trailing Curtis. When 'crunch-time' inevitably comes and she confronts Curtis about his movements, she initially manages to hold her own, boldly questioning him in her role as Lifeline's representative, despite the fact that she herself has always trusted him. The conclusion to this scene, in which Curtis produces a flick-knife and Monique levels her gun, is gripping stuff and, after she is overpowered, is cut in such a way that it is not at first entirely clear that she will survive the encounter. Later in the episode, Monique's presence allows Curtis a safe getaway and he gratefully acknowledges: "It's as well you were there." The last line of the episode belongs to Monique: "We all lie sometimes, at least to ourselves – it's necessary to makes things bearable." It is a line that is knowingly delivered by Richards, whose character we have come to know a great deal better through this storyline.

The episode's other surprising element is that, even after all this time, Curtis is still under suspicion from Lifeline. This scenario would seem far-fetched were it not for the inclusion of the death of a new agent and a particularly shifty look from Curtis as they discuss the man's death. Unlike the viewer, Lifeline's agents have not witnessed Curtis's initial recruitment in England, and are wise to be cautious – as Albert says, "We know very little about John Curtis." Nevertheless, Lisa is now confident that he is not playing a double game: "I just don't believe he would collaborate with the Germans." Curtis himself is both incredulous and furious when he discovers that he is still not trusted, spitting out: "You people give me a pain! You're the most miserable, cunning, suspicious shower I've ever come across." After Neville's death, when Curtis relates to Monique how Neville fought back, he is still mindful of Lifeline's distrust and sarcastically adds: "You've only got my word for it. You weren't there. You don't know." Monique effectively speaks for Lifeline when she firmly replies: "I believe you." Curtis's innocence is finally accepted.

Some much-needed humour occasionally alleviates the heavy mood of the episode. In response to Albert's question: "And suppose he comes back and says the culprit was Charlie Chaplin. Should we know any better?," Alain supplies the witty rejoinder "Only if Charlie made some new films," a line that is enjoyed by Natalie if not Albert! Monique also gets in on the act by exaggerating her mock sudden thought that, if Albert is going to miss her, "then why am I going?!" and through a dry comment about the time Albert can now spend with Andrée: "You can sit and hold hands and talk about old times. That should calm her down a bit."

Like Richards, Neame is given his most challenging episode to date and is especially superb in his scenes with the Nevilles, both during and after his adoption of his fake Yorkshire-born persona. The nine-minute scene in which 'Robert Green' inveigles his way into the Neville household is expertly handled and provides fascinating insights into all the characters present. Dorothy Neville, who interestingly appears to feel more guilt than her guilty husband, fails to see through Curtis's performance and is only too keen to make amends for the Romsey incident by helping another airman, offering both refreshments and their spare bed. Neville himself, who later states that he saw the truth of the situation as soon as Curtis arrived, takes the opportunity, just as he did with Romsey, to hold forth about his views on the war and ideals. The character's refusal to accept the reality of the war, as depicted in *Lost Sheep*, is somewhat explained by his horrific experiences on the Somme: "Should have been playing cricket for my school but I was fighting on the Somme instead. Mud, filth, corpses... I saw screaming men trying to hold in their own intestines." However, he also rejects the war on clearly erroneous grounds, saying of future historians: "I doubt if they'll regard it as being right against wrong." His eloquently scripted final word on the war is that: "The world is going through a period of insanity which it tries to camouflage by talk of ideals." Seeing the coinage of terms such as democracy and freedom as "too debased," instead Neville only believes in the human spirit. The writer's philosophy is so well expressed that it seems likely that it may have been, at least in part, shared by N. J. Crisp himself.

Although it is likely that Curtis would have uncovered Neville's guilt without the latter's semi-autobiographical book with its betrayed stranger is a clever plot device. When Neville first tells Curtis that his new book – an obvious catharsis for him – is about guilt and remorse and Curtis pointedly asks: "Is that a new theme?" we expect him to be tripped up by Neville's comment that he thought he knew his work. However, it transpires that Curtis is very familiar with Neville's output and can recognise that such a theme is firmly outside of "Neville country". As well as being well-read, Curtis is presented throughout the episode as an experienced and formidable agent: he volunteers his presence to Dubois to allay possible suspicion; realises that he is being tailed and catches Monique red-handed; drops his bike against Dubois's fence in order to learn that Victor never mended it (and therefore that he must have paid Madame Victor for the repair job out of guilt); convinces the Nevilles into letting him stay; and, during the night there, prepares for the following morning's showdown by cutting the telephone wires and locating and disarming Neville's gun. The final confrontation between Neville and Curtis is suitably dramatic. Neville responds to his wife's shocked exclamation of: "It was you!" by claiming that he had no choice, but shows his true colours when he tells Curtis: "I'm not fighting your war; France has signed an armistice. I'm here and if the French authorities demand my help I must abide by the law," retreating behind the very same excuse as Dubois. Interestingly, for Dorothy, in the end the matter comes down to her loyalty to their nationality: "We're not French, we're English!" It is a loyalty which her husband simply doesn't share. Curtis's final advance with his flick-knife on the unarmed Neville is chilling, proving that which Albert doubted – that he was "the right man to do it" after all.

Guilt maturely deals not only with those who are guilty, but with those who feel guilt and after Neville's death this almost certainly includes Curtis. Thanks to further exemplary plotting from N. J. Crisp, just as Neville believed that his betrayal of Romsey and the consequent death of Victor were "dead ashes," Curtis ends the episode believing that the writer's death is the end of the story. He could not be more wrong.

WHERE ELSE HAVE I SEEN..?

Bruce Montague (Inspector Dubois)

Det Sgt Harry Sutton, *The Link Men*, 1970
Charles Coghlan, *Lillie*, 1978
Leonard Dunn, *Butterflies*, 1978-83
Shah Mashiq Rassim, *Whoops Apocalypse*, 1982
Roland Beecroft, *Sharon and Elsie*, 1984-5

Episode 9: TOO NEAR HOME

WRITTEN BY: Robert Barr   DIRECTED BY: Viktors Ritelis

FIRST BROADCAST: BBC1, 8.05pm, Wednesday 2 November 1977

STUDIO RECORDING: 19 July 1977

VIEWING FIGURE: 6.1m

REGULAR CAST: Albert Foiret: BERNARD HEPTON; Lisa Colbert: JAN FRANCIS; Flt Lt John Curtis: CHRISTOPHER NEAME; Monique Duchamps: ANGELA RICHARDS;

Sturmbannführer Ludwig Kessler: CLIFFORD ROSE; Natalie Chantrens: JULIET HAMMOND-HILL; Gaston Colbert: JAMES BREE; Louise Colbert: MARIA CHARLES

SUPPORTING CAST: Sophie Chantal: MARY BARCLAY; Julius Laurent: SHAUN CURRY; Inspector Landre: GERALD JAMES; Jan: DAMIEN THOMAS; Denise: HELEN GILL; Maria Penargo: SOUAD FARESS; Wardress: BRENDA KEMPNER; Michel: JEFFREY HOLLAND; Gendarme: ANTHONY HOWDEN; Mac: JOHN ALKIN; Taff: DANIEL HILL

SYNOPSIS: In Senlis, Lisa tells Sophie Chantal about Lifeline's recent troubles and that she has three more 'customers' for her, who are waiting with Natalie elsewhere in the town. Lisa leaves to set off for Paris but decides to speak to Julius Laurent before she goes. Julius tells her about the grave situation in Paris and that two of her people, Jacques and Vincent, are in danger and therefore so is Lifeline. He urges her to leave, but she pushes for more information. Julius agrees to try to find out more, but their conversation is interrupted by the arrival of Inspector Landre and a group of German soldiers. Lisa tries to leave quietly but is prevented from doing so. Julius attacks the Germans who are tearing apart his workshop. As he is taken away, he manages to break free but is shot in the leg and recaptured. Landre does not accept Lisa's story that she had come to hire a bike, and sends her to the Pontoise prison. Back in Brussels, Louise pleads with Gaston to stop his resistance work. Natalie goes to see Sophie who tells her about Lisa's plans to see Julius. After she learns that Lisa has been arrested, Natalie returns to the Candide with the bad news. Albert sends Monique to warn their contacts north of Paris. Curtis arrives soon after and agrees to get word to the houses south of Paris. In the Pontoise prison, Lisa meets cellmates Denise and Maria and is questioned about her true identity. When the prisoners' leader Jan visits, Lisa learns that Julius has asked his 'reseau' to help her and reveals both her work and her codename. Jan tells Lisa that they are planning to escape from the prison and she agrees to go with them. In Brussels, Kessler brings Gaston in for questioning after he is observed throwing a bag into the river. He asks Gaston to write down all he knows about the people he socialises with, but considers the information he volunteers to be useless. Natalie tells Albert that Gaston is missing. Kessler presents Gaston with the retrieved bag which is full of stolen documents. Lisa learns more about the escape arrangements from Denise. Gaston claims that he will cooperate but Kessler refuses his request to call Louise. As Gaston is escorted out of the building to 'go visiting' with Kessler, he makes a run for it and is shot dead. Albert gives Louise the terrible news and she is inconsolable. Lisa manages to escape from the Pontoise prison, but Jan, Denise and Maria are not so lucky and are questioned by the wardress about Lisa. She demands to know why only Lisa's file was burnt and who she was. Denise is taken out to be shot and Maria is threatened with the same, but they don't give her away. Later that night, a devastated Louise daubs a 'Victory V' in red paint on a wall, before collapsing to the ground. Lisa finds her and takes her home.

REVIEW: Robert Barr's first script for the series, *Too Near Home,* presents a particularly desperate chapter in Lifeline's history, brutally re-emphasising the hugely dangerous nature of the work of its agents. Not only does Lisa's luck finally run out with the result that she is imprisoned in the Pontoise prison, but her uncle Gaston ends up being interrogated by Kessler himself. Faced with either betraying his niece and all her colleagues or death, Gaston makes the only choice he can and becomes the first series regular to be killed off. The episode's content is nail-biting and the pervading atmosphere is very emotionally-charged, all elements which will come to define the series more and more as it progresses.

There are several well-judged and distressing performances from the regular cast; James Bree and Maria Charles are especially believable as they play out their much-signposted tragedy. Over the course of the episode, Gaston is seen to degenerate from a happy husband to an utterly broken man. In their first scene together, Louise once again pleads for him to stop his resistance work ("Gaston, I want you to stop these other activities... if you care for me at all"), although for the first time she seems to have come round to the fact that preventing her niece's involvement is beyond her ("Lisa will do as she pleases, she is young.") That the pair obviously love each other dearly makes Gaston's eventual fate all the more tragic. The next time we see him he is sat in front of Kessler at Gestapo Headquarters. The scene is very well-placed in the narrative, as a sudden jolting low immediately after the plot's very first 'ray of hope': Lisa learning that her escape from the grim Pontoise prison may be imminent. Gaston's predicament quickly becomes very serious indeed and his desire to protect his niece – twice asking Kessler if there is anything in his file that implicates Lisa – almost makes matters a whole lot worse. For once, Kessler thankfully overlooks a possible lead. Nevertheless, when it is subsequently revealed that the Sturmbannführer is simply playing with Gaston and in fact already possesses his bag of stolen documents, it does almost feel likely that Lifeline is finished and that the entire series might just be wound up right there and then. However, Gaston's bravery and self-sacrifice stands between Kessler and the escape line, and despite the fact that when he returns to Kessler's office he claims to be ready to cooperate, this never seems like a betrayal of which this Belgian patriot is capable. One of the more distressing elements of Gaston's final few hours is his repeated request to call his wife. Initially, Gaston decides not to call her on the grounds that it may worry her more than reassure her (as Kessler cuttingly remarks: "very likely!"), but when it becomes clear that his position is completely hopeless, he requests to call her three more times. On each occasion he is clearly making the request because he knows his end is near and merely wants to call Louise just to hear her voice again and to say a final goodbye. Kessler's cool refusal each time paints him as very sadistic indeed. In fact, in his full Gestapo Death's Head regalia, pushing the defenceless Gaston along the corridor, we witness one of Kessler's darkest episodes in the entire series. When death comes, Gaston is both courageous and accepting.

During Gaston's 'disappearance', Louise's desperate worry, obvious disorientation and attempts to carry on as normal are all utterly convincing. Charles's performance is just as realistic when she finally hears the news she has dreaded being told for so long. Her grief which mixes utter despair with anger and disbelief is, as it should be, very difficult to watch.

Another actress who is particularly impressive here is Juliet Hammond-Hill. Other than her outburst at the conclusion to *Second Chance*, before now Natalie has been given very little to do. Although Natalie is still not pivotal to the plot here, it is clear that this is the first time that Hammond-Hill has really been stretched by the part. Natalie is an emotional and passionate character and although the actress has since gone on record to say that if she had her time on the series again that emotion-wise she'd cut her performance by half, in fact she judges it just right here. Natalie's fears about Lisa's safety as played out at Sophie's house and her subsequent delivery of the terrible news to Albert and Monique at the Candide are significant additions to the narrative, particularly as they serve to emphasise the gravity of Lisa's and therefore their own situation.

After some time 'in the wings', *Too Near Home* once again presents Lisa as the series's central character. Her arrest and imprisonment come as a complete surprise and for a time it looks as though her outlook is very bleak indeed. Unfortunately her amazingly short time as a prisoner and the subsequent prison break somehow just don't ring true and the constraint of needing to wrap up the story in fifty minutes is readily apparent. Lisa's no-nonsense cellmates, Denise (Helen Gill) and Maria (Souad Faress), although not wooden by any means are, perhaps partly due to time constraints, less believable and more two-dimensional than they could have been. Both of them tower over petite Jan Francis, making Lisa appear even less like the leader of Lifeline than she has done before now. It is a shame that both characters are suddenly seen to become squeamish and upset when they later witness a German guard being overpowered, especially as their subsequent refusal to cooperate with the formidable wardress – a template for *Prisoner Cell Block H*'s 'Freak' if ever there was one – is unbelievably brave. Although the ever-dependable Damien Thomas adds some class to the proceedings, the escape attempt demands considerable suspension of belief and, looking back at the episode today, the sudden appearance of *Hi-de-Hi!*'s Spike (Jeffrey Holland) doesn't help matters either. The undoubted highlight of the scenes in the Pontoise prison is Lisa's discovery that her friends know where she is and her pulling up of the covers as she dares to hope that she might soon be free.

Just as Albert relied on her in the preceding episode, here again Monique is sent out to deal with the highly dangerous business of informing their contacts north of Paris of the current troubles. That neither utter many words over this emergency scenario, particularly during her departure – all Monique needs to say is "I know" – suggests not only that, for the moment at least, their relationship is on firm ground, but also that they really do have an intimate understanding of how each other is feeling.

Once again Viktors Ritelis makes his mark with some effective directorial flourishes, including: Gaston's tinkling pocket-watch requiem; the wind blowing through Julius's ransacked workshop, the return of the loud ticking clocks (last heard in *Sergeant on the Run*); the transposition of Gaston's and Louise's faces as they sit lost in thought about each other; and – in what must have been a very time-consuming effect to achieve – the view of a troubled Louise through the Colbert fireplace. The only piece of direction in the episode which feels a little like 'over-egging the pudding' is the flashback shot to Gaston's bloodied hands sliding down the wall, as Louise's hands do the same over the red painted 'Victory V'. Nevertheless, the 'Victory V' scene is a fascinating conclusion to the episode, which shows that it has taken Gaston's death to spur Louise on to make her first show of defiant anti-German resistance. Although it is clear that she is not quite in her right mind here, further acts of resistance in later episodes prove that, like her husband before her, her strength of feeling has become stronger than her fear of being caught.

The episode also involves some very effective location sequences: as well as a return to Le Place du Petit Sablon in Brussels, Ritelis also took his team back to Covent Garden, which this time doubles for the Rue San Sebastian in Senlis.

Two scenes in the episode don't seem to have a great deal to do with the narrative and are somewhat baffling asides to the main action. The first is the inclusion of a disturbed woman who is taking a grubby doll out for a walk in a battered pram. Presumably she has lost her child due to the war and has since suffered a breakdown? The other is Natalie's observation of several rich 'party-people' getting into a car, which is contrasted with a poor elderly man chewing on a scrap of food. This possibly relates to the 'rich-poor divide' and alludes to the fact that despite the terrible events of war, with Lisa and Gaston both in Natalie's thoughts, life still goes on regardless.

Despite both Lisa's and Gaston's arrests, as the series continues it seems very surprising that there is no follow-up from either the Gestapo or the French police. Neither Louise nor Lisa are interrogated in respect of Gaston's activities, nor is Lisa's jailbreak investigated. She may have destroyed her prisoner file, but the jailers would surely remember her name, and if they did not, surely they could ask the fastidious Inspector Landre?

Robert Barr's first script for *Secret Army* is first and foremost an adventure yarn, a style which also characterises his later episodes. Its most memorable element is undoubtedly the haunting and desperately sad demise of Gaston Colbert, a death which reminds both the characters and the viewers that Lifeline's agents are by no means invincible and will not necessarily live to fight another day.

HISTORICAL BACKGROUND

'V' for Victory

In January 1941, Belgian refugee Victor De Lavelaye made a BBC radio broadcast in which he urged his countrymen to make a stand against the occupying Nazis:

> "I am proposing to you as a rallying emblem the letter V, because V is the first letter of the words 'Victoire' in French and 'Vrijheid' in Flemish: two things which go together, as Walloons and Flemings are at the moment

marching hand in hand, two things which are the consequence one of the other, the Victory which will give us back our freedom, the Victory of our good friends the English. Their word for Victory also begins with V."

De Lavelaye went on to encourage his countrymen to chalk or paint Vs on walls and make the sign wherever possible: "The occupier, by seeing this sign, always the same, infinitely repeated, will understand that he is surrounded, encircled by an immense crowd of citizens eagerly awaiting his first moment of weakness, watching for his first failure." The campaign was taken up enthusiastically and

became such a success that it prompted the Germans to institute a belated 'V for Viktoria' counter-campaign. However, this effort was in vain as the V sign was already regarded as definitively anti-Nazi throughout Europe. The sign was popularised by Winston Churchill, who regularly made the 'Victory V', as it became known, with his fingers whenever cameras were pointed at him. However, according to his private secretary John Colville, he often made the sign with his palm facing inwards "in spite of representations repeatedly made to him that this gesture had quite another significance."

Pontoise Prison

The Pontoise Prison was immortalised by French impressionist Camille Pissarro in his Spring 1881 painting 'View Towards Pontoise Prison'. In addition to Pissarro, fellow impressionists Van Gogh and Cezanne also spent time in the commune of Pontoise. In 1962, Pontoise, which is located in the north-western suburbs of Paris, became part of the new town of Cergy-Pontoise.

WHERE ELSE HAVE I SEEN..?

Gerald James (Inspector Landre)

Charles Caldwell, *Hadleigh*, 1976

Major Rice, *The Crezz*, 1976

George Tully, *Sapphire and Steel: Adventure Two (The Railway Station)*, 1979

Professor David Evans, *The Fourth Arm*, 1983

Dr Slammer, *The Pickwick Papers*, 1985

© Joe Cocks

Shaun Curry (Julius Laurent)

Rod, *Blake's 7: The Keeper*, 1979
Les Pinner, *Just Good Friends*, 1984-6
Sgt Maj McRuckus, *Then Churchill Said to Me*, 1993
Bosun, *Captain Butler*, 1997
Mr Jenson, *Waking the Dead: Mask of Sanity*, 2007

© Peter Willkinson

Damien Thomas (Jan)

Father Alvito, *Shogun*, 1980
Altan, *Blake's 7: Star Drive*, 1981
Jake Haulter, *Tenko/Tenko Reunion*, 1984-5
Colonel Max Dubois, *Wish Me Luck*, 1990
Paul Renauld, *Poirot: Murder on the Links*, 1996

© Unknown

Souad Faress (Maria Penargo)

Selma, *Blake's 7: Horizon*, 1979
Sera Kotwal, *Sixth Happiness*, 1997
Urmila Alahan, *Coronation Street*, 2001
Leela, *Being April*, 2002
Aamina Shafiq, *Family Affairs,* 2005

© Unknown

Episode 10: IDENTITY IN DOUBT

WRITTEN BY: Simon Masters   **DIRECTED BY:** Viktors Ritelis

FIRST BROADCAST: BBC1, 8.05pm, Wednesday 9 November 1977

STUDIO RECORDING: 23 September 1977

VIEWING FIGURE: 7.2m

REGULAR CAST: Albert Foiret: BERNARD HEPTON; Lisa Colbert: JAN FRANCIS; Flt Lt John Curtis: CHRISTOPHER NEAME; Monique Duchamps: ANGELA RICHARDS; Natalie Chantrens: JULIET HAMMOND-HILL; Dr Pascal Keldermans: VALENTINE DYALL; Alain Muny: RON PEMBER; Jacques Bol: TIMOTHY MORAND

SUPPORTING CAST: Noel Uys: CHRISTOPHER DOUGLAS; Lock-keeper: BARRY JACKSON; Teddy Marsh: EDMUND PEGGE; Farmer's Wife: SALLY SANDERS; Jean-Luc: JOHN CANNON; Hubert: ERNEST C. JENNINGS

SYNOPSIS: A lock-keeper comes across a young man who, despite his foreign accent, claims to be an RAF airman, so he takes him back to his barge. Lisa meets with Curtis who has been on the move and learns that he is working with a Communist, René Thierry. After much persuasion, she agrees to take four of his evaders. The lock-keeper's suspicions are aroused when the airman, who gives his name as Uys, says the word

149

'danke'. The lock-keeper decides to tie him up before seeking help at the Candide, where he hands over Uys' identity tags to Monique. Lisa listens while Albert asks the lock-keeper about the airman, who agrees to keep Uys for three days. Lisa seeks out Curtis again who is upset when he discovers that she only wants his help with another evader. Natalie and Jacques prepare to set off to interrogate Uys. Fearing he could be an infiltrator, Lisa has instructed them not to take any chances and to kill Uys if necessary. During his interrogation, Uys fails to confirm the clearance information from London and Natalie decides that they must dispose of him. The lock-keeper unties Uys and he and Jacques take him outside to be shot, while Natalie cycles up the path to keep look-out. Noel breaks free of his captors and shoots the lock-keeper. Jacques wounds Uys but is knocked unconscious. Uys takes Natalie prisoner and takes her to a deserted windmill. When they learn that Dr Keldermans could be in danger, Lisa, Albert and Alain leave the Candide unattended. Soon after, Monique is chased to the Candide by a group of people who believe her to be a collaborator. After she retreats inside, they attempt to break in and smash the windows. The mob is broken up when Albert and a German soldier arrive. Albert comforts a distraught Monique. Later that evening, Jacques returns with the news that Natalie has been taken. Lisa decides that the next day he should return to the lock area with Alain and Jean-Luc. Uys continues to protest to Natalie that he is not German. While Lisa is discussing Natalie's disappearance with Keldermans, Curtis arrives with more evaders. Uys tells Natalie about his home-life and how he lied to the Air Ministry about his age. She doesn't believe him, but Uys subsequently reveals that his gun is empty. Curtis confronts Lisa about her decision to have Uys killed. One of the evaders he has brought, Teddy Marsh, can positively identify Uys. At the windmill, an exhausted Natalie finally learns the truth from Uys. Alain, Jacques and Jean-Luc find Natalie's bicycle and are directed to the old windmill by a woman who has taken Natalie's shoes. Natalie helps Uys with his leg wound, but realises she must go and fetch help. She asks him to trust her and stay put. As Natalie leaves, the others arrive to kill Uys and the airman decides to make a break for it. Natalie explains that Uys is what he says he is. They run after him and save his life when he gets trapped on the mudflats. Natalie berates Uys for not trusting her.

REVIEW: Simon Masters's only script for the series centres around the problem of a South African evader called Noel Uys, who fails to correctly answer the all-important clearance questions set by London. Christopher Douglas gives a gutsy performance as Uys, and is joined at the forefront of the action by Juliet Hammond-Hill, who builds on her performance in *Too Near Home* and puts her all into an episode which, despite the inclusion of many other elements which compete for attention, is arguably most effective when it is pared down to simply being a two-hander between Natalie and Uys.

Uys initially comes over as an unsympathetic character, who in response to the lock-keeper's questions, and later those of Natalie and Jacques, is both surly and evasive. When he is unable to provide neither the correct address nor the names of his two character witnesses, it seems entirely plausible that he is, as Lifeline suspects, a German infiltrator. His subsequent actions – killing the lock-keeper, wounding Jacques and kidnapping Natalie at gunpoint – don't exactly suggest his innocence either, although, to be fair, if he hadn't reacted in this way they would have shot him. As the narrative relocates to the more intimate setting of the interior of the old windmill, Natalie's remains bravely defiant, despite the fact that she thinks Uys has a loaded gun and is most probably a German. After a frustrated Uys eventually manages to get Natalie to talk to him, even if it is just an ironic observation about his fear despite the fact that he is the one with the gun, he retreats to the memories of his home-life in South Africa. Douglas's delivery of this particularly expressive dialogue makes the young radio operator a thoroughly believable character and suggests an innocence and naïvety that will ultimately prove to be the key to solving the mess that he and Natalie find themselves in. It is the latter's presence that prompts Uys to think about his sister Tessa, which in turn causes her to ask how he could have joined the RAF when he is in fact too young to fly. It is his surprising answer to this pertinent question which turns out to be the unexpected twist in the tale: namely that he actually made up the information he gave to the Air Ministry in order to get away, both from the family farm and his mother. In her breathless responses to these revelations, Hammond-Hill ably depicts the combination of relief, exhaustion and frustration felt by Natalie as she slowly takes in not only Uys's incredible stupidity, but also the terrible and far-reaching repercussions of his lies. Before the episode moves to its action-packed, mud-soaked finale, we learn more about Natalie's intensely practical and detached take on war. When Uys reflects on the death of the lock-keeper (and the possible death of Jacques) and states: "I'm a murderer." Natalie quickly responds: "Some would say you were already that when you dropped your first bomb," but significantly adds: "I don't. It's war, it can't be helped." However, while Natalie may forgive him murder, judging by the very last line of the episode ("You stupid child. I trusted you!") she is seen to find it far harder to allow for the fact that Uys didn't stay put in the windmill as she requested. However, as the last words he hears before he legs it are "shoot him on sight," he can hardly be blamed for this!

Aside from the dramatic scenes between Douglas and Hammond-Hill, the bleak scenery – with its derelict windmill and desolate landscape – is another memorable feature of the episode. Director Viktors Ritelis decided to take full advantage of the area surrounding the chosen windmill and elected to incorporate some mudflats, which he had found while exploring the location, into the episode's finale. This sequence, which was not part of Masters's original script, took a considerable amount of time to film and saw both Ritelis and film cameraman David South join the actors waist-deep in mud in order to get the required shots in the can.

The events of this episode seem to be set some time after the tragic death of Gaston Colbert and the turbulent proceedings of *Too Near Home*. However, Lisa does briefly mention her uncle in connection with obtaining new papers for evaders: "It's not so easy at short notice. Not since Gaston died," and tells Curtis that she is "getting thinner," the implication being that the stress of their work is now really getting to her. The fact that Dr Keldermans's surgery is being watched does suggest that either Kessler or the French authorities might be on to Lisa, but she seems to be more worried about Keldermans's safety than her own. Although

Jacques Bol should really be in line for a severe reprimand from Lisa given his secret dual involvement in both Julius's resistance group and Lifeline, as referenced in *Too Near Home*, there is no indication that this has actually been followed up. It was presumably felt that viewers would have forgotten this minor plot point.

The unrequited love of Curtis for Lisa, a plotline that has not been much in evidence since *Radishes with Butter*, is once again given some attention here. When they first meet in this episode, a decidedly dishevelled and lonely Curtis clearly wants more from Lisa than just her word that she will take his four evaders, calling out her name expectantly as she leaves. On her return, when she needs his help with Uys, Curtis initially mistakes her intention, stating: "I just thought you might say something else," and thinking that she might be concerned that he looks too tired to travel. However, Lisa's matter-of-fact response – "Why should I?" – leaves him in no doubt that his feelings are not going to be reciprocated. When the pair meet up for a third time, Curtis is incredibly hard on her, ostensibly for making the decision that Uys should be killed. However the evidence against Uys is pretty compelling, and when Lisa asks: "He couldn't answer any of the questions London gave us and he killed the lock-keeper. What more do you need?" Curtis's response: "Well something just a little bit more conclusive" seems patently ridiculous. The truth of the situation is that Curtis's anger (which, after Teddy Marsh's revelation, even leads him to stick the knife in: "You've ordered an innocent man to be killed") clearly has more to do with the fact that she has rejected him than anything else. No wonder she's not interested!

The scenes in which Monique is accused of being a "Boche-lover!" and is forced to barricade herself into the Candide are very well handled. Richards succeeds in portraying real fear and distress as the angry mob smashes the front windows and tries to gain entry. Her desperation to get to Albert when he finally arrives on the scene, involving the quick removal of her hastily erected barricade, is particularly touching. In helping her to recover from her ordeal, Albert manages to do almost everything right – calling her "darling" and giving her some of his best brandy – but ultimately rather spoils these efforts by almost immediately expecting her help with the tidying up! Nevertheless, this is still far better than he manages in the final series when Monique finds herself in very similar danger. The charges of collaboration levelled here clearly depict the ironic paradox at the heart of Lifeline's chosen approach. As Albert explains to Monique here, they can't have anyone knowing what they are really doing and instead must suffer unsubstantiated claims of collaboration, especially as they help to put the Germans off the scent. It is a brilliant, if hugely dangerous, game.

One of the episode's most surprising scenes sees Lisa involved in one of its only light moments, when she finds herself unexpectedly sat opposite the German soldier who has come back to the Candide for his bottle of wine. In response to the soldier's playful wink, Lisa reacts in kind – Jan Francis showing a gift for comic timing that would later stand her in good stead as Penny in the BBC sitcom *Just Good Friends*.

Identity in Doubt is a tense episode which perhaps seeks to knit too many disparate elements together to form a coherent whole; however, there are no weak performances and the dramatisation of the central plot is impressive.

WHERE ELSE HAVE I SEEN..?

Christopher Douglas (Noel Uys)

© Catherine Shakespeare-Lane

Yan, *Arthur of the Britons: The Wood People*, 1973
Martin Bell, *Crossroads*, 1973-4
Honeybone, *Play for Today: Penda's Fen*, 1974
Samuel Onedin, *The Onedin Line*, 1977-80
Aleks Alexandrovich, *Reilly: Ace of Spies*, 1983

Barry Jackson (Lock-keeper)

John Cledge, *The New Avengers: To Catch a Rat*, 1976
Kendall, *Blake's 7: Mission to Destiny*, 1978
Drax, *Doctor Who: The Armageddon Factor*, 1979
McCann, *Fortunes of War*, 1987
Dr Bullard, *Midsomer Murders*, 1997-present

Episode 11: A QUESTION OF LOYALTY

WRITTEN BY: Willis Hall   **DIRECTED BY:** Kenneth Ives

FIRST BROADCAST: BBC1, 8.05pm, Wednesday 23 November 1977

STUDIO RECORDING: 4 October 1977

VIEWING FIGURE: 6.8m

REGULAR CAST: Albert Foiret: BERNARD HEPTON; Lisa Colbert: JAN FRANCIS; Monique Duchamps: ANGELA RICHARDS; Major Erwin Brandt: MICHAEL CULVER; Sturmbannführer Ludwig Kessler: CLIFFORD ROSE; Dr Pascal Keldermans: VALENTINE DYALL; Alain Muny: RON PEMBER

SUPPORTING CAST: Ernst Stoller: CLIVE ARRINDELL; Staff Officer: JON LAURIMORE; Oberleutnant: RICHARD WREN; Station Master: MALCOLM HAYES; Railway Worker: JAMES COYLE; Lebrun: WILLIAM SIMONS; Madame Lebrun: VALERIE SHUTE; Alec Lamb: RON FLANAGAN; Peasant: HUGH MARTIN; Sarah Lecartes: TINA JONES; German Private: PAUL RIDLEY

SYNOPSIS: Kessler visits the crash site of a downed Wellington Bomber and is informed that all five crew members are dead: just the scenario that he has been waiting for. After berating an Oberleutnant for his squeamishness, he departs with the identification tags of a Bomb Aimer named Maurice Clifton. At the Candide, after closing up, a tired Monique refuses to stay with Albert, telling him that their relationship is, in its current form, no longer enough for her. At Gestapo HQ, as Brandt is interrogating an SS officer called Ernst Stoller, Kessler arrives with the news that they will put their plan into action tonight. He reveals that Stoller's cover story – that of a man raised in England – is in fact his real background. Stoller memorises Clifton's name, rank and number and is taken out to the area near the crash site where he is briefed by Kessler. Before he goes, Kessler breaks Stoller's arm in order to add authenticity to his story that he is a British evader and the only survivor of the Wellington crash. Stoller is found by a Belgian in a railway building and Lifeline contacted. It is Monique who arrives to question Stoller and takes him back to a safe-house in Brussels. Monique leaves Stoller alone and goes to the Candide to tell Lisa what she has done. She also argues with Albert over Andrée's refusal to have an operation which could improve her health and tells him she cannot go on living this way. After Keldermans examines Stoller, Monique feeds him a meal. A sixth airman, Alec Lamb, is found by some locals near the crash site and given shelter, but he is in a very bad way and dies soon afterwards. Stoller asks Monique lots of questions about her personal situation. Initially she holds back, but soon she finds herself confiding in him about Albert and Andrée. She is angered by Stoller's simplistic take on life, but when he tries to kiss her she does not resist. After they make love, Stoller tries to persuade Monique to leave Brussels as he does not want her death on his conscience. Monique plays down the fact that they have slept with each other and tells him that he is unimportant to her. When she returns to the Candide, Albert is waiting for her. He reveals that Stoller is an SS officer and that he knows she has gone to bed with him. Lisa and Keldermans are also waiting for Monique and confront her with the news of the sixth airman and information received from London on Maurice Clifton's real background. Monique is shocked by the news but realises that he must be dealt with. Pretending to pass him on to another guide, she takes Stoller back to where she first found him. Albert is waiting there and kills him. Kessler is saddened by Stoller's death and decides to send his SS badge of kinship back to his English relatives. Monique and Albert resume their old life at the Candide.

REVIEW: Willis Hall's final contribution to *Secret Army* is arguably one of the highlights of the first series. The episode focuses upon Monique's thoughts and feelings as she finally runs out of patience with her deeply unsatisfactory existence at the Candide and a concurrent attempt by Kessler to infiltrate Lifeline with an undercover SS officer, Ernst Stoller. The two plots are weaved together ingeniously so that it is Monique who meets Stoller when she is at her most vulnerable and, as a result, acts in a way that may have terrible consequences for the Line. Aside from a superb script, the success of *A Question of Loyalty* is due in no small part to an absolutely mesmerising performance from Angela Richards, who deftly draws us into Monique's world and engenders understanding and sympathy for her character's impossible everyday life.

It is somewhat surprising to learn that in the episode's first drafts it was Natalie not Monique, who was intended to be the script's central protagonist. Fortunately, at some point during production of Series One it was recognised that, given Monique's stormy relationship with Albert (which was fast becoming one of the most fascinating and watchable elements of the series), having Monique, rather than Natalie, engage in a brief affair with an undercover SS officer would provide far more dramatic impact. As a result of this decision, the previous episode, *Identity in Doubt*, which was conceived well after *A Question of Loyalty,* came to feature Natalie in the central role.

As the episode begins, Monique is depicted as being far from happy with her lot as Albert's mistress. The presence of Sarah Lecartes, who is upset to have discovered that her soldier boyfriend has a wife in Leipzig, serves to throw Monique's own situation into sharp relief. She tells Sarah: "Forget his wife, Leipzig's a long way away," being all too aware that her own lover's wife, Andrée, actually lives above her head: "Half the time I actually think she's inside it!" Proving that she has finally run out of patience entirely, Monique goes on to confront Albert with terrible honesty: "Suddenly it's not enough having her asleep upstairs. I wish she wasn't asleep Albert, I wish she was dead." It is interesting that although Monique is not as trapped as Albert, who resigns himself to being a dutiful husband – at least outside of the bedroom – her feelings for him must be deep enough for her to find the idea of leaving the Candide behind very hard indeed. In one of the episode's stand-out scenes, which sees both Richards and Hepton on top form, a large part of Monique's frustration is seen to arise from Albert's refusal to push Andrée into having a life-changing operation: "Even if it's a chance in a million, surely it's worth taking!" Although Albert may see that Andrée's decision affects his and Monique's life as well as her own, he is adamant that she must be allowed to make her own choices: "She decides whether to have the operation. Not me. And not you!" Despite Albert's position on this matter, what is not at all obvious to Monique, or the viewer, is the surprising revelation that, despite her impatience, he is in fact very sympathetic to her views. He tells Lisa: "It is Monique who has no patience and I don't blame her!" That he believes this but is unable to tell her so himself is exactly the sort of complex characterisation which exemplifies *Secret Army*.

This episode sees the first of many attempts by Kessler and Brandt to infiltrate the evasion line. The infiltrator in question, Ernst Stoller, a British man turned Nazi, is an unusual and interesting guest character. Kessler's plan to use Stoller's real background is a clever idea that certainly allays Monique's suspicions, but which is ultimately flawed due to its failure to anticipate the inevitable clearance by London. Despite an engaging performance from Clive Arrindell, Stoller never really comes over as SS material, primarily because he is scripted with too much of a conscience, worrying more about Monique's life than the mission in hand. However, this is a minor quibble and takes little away from the narrative.

The episode's most accomplished and memorable scene sees Monique open up to Stoller (posing as Maurice Clifton) as she explains rather poetically that there are "no compartments" in her life. Richards's delivery is beguiling as the camera moves slowly towards her as she recounts what she is thinking when Albert makes love to her while Andrée is in the next room: "Asleep or awake I know she's there... sometimes I lie there and feel pity for this woman, but mostly it's hate, because she's no right to be there inside my head – not then." It is fascinating that despite the fact that the situation "sickens" her, she nevertheless believes that she belongs at the Candide and that she must return. However, when Stoller moves to kiss her she does not resist. That we next see Monique and Stoller in bed together after they have made love is something of a surprise, partly because we know that she loves Albert and has already intimated that she intends to return to him, but perhaps more simply because we have never even seen Monique in bed with Albert before, never mind with an undercover SS officer! Although Monique knows that this can only be a 'one night stand', it clearly has meant more to her than she pretends. Her telling pause halfway through the line "I'm unimportant to you and you are unimportant to me" speaks volumes. The way she delivers her subsequent line: "Tomorrow I'll be important to Albert," sounds like Monique has resigned herself to the fate of an unsatisfactory, and therefore unfulfilled, existence.

After Monique makes the painful discovery, not only that Stoller is an enemy agent, but that half her Lifeline colleagues, including Albert, know about her indiscretion, she has no choice but to cooperate in their plan to kill him. The chosen scenario finds Albert in the unique position of being able to take the ultimate revenge on the man who has slept with his lover without any repercussions whatsoever. Meanwhile, a visibly distressed Monique has the horrendous job of delivering Stoller to his execution, a task that is made all the more difficult by the man's show of affection for her. After the deed is done, Monique is shown back in the Candide again, even offering to take Andrée's tray upstairs. She is living once more in the same 'compartment' as Albert and his wife.

Although *A Question of Loyalty* predominantly sees Angela Richards centre-stage, she is not permitted to steal the show entirely, as Clifford Rose once again proves to be in sparklingly sinister form as Kessler. His scenes during this episode portray the character at his most ruthless and fanatical. His first appearance, which sees him loom out of the shadows in full Gestapo regalia staring straight into the camera, is particularly haunting. But even more so is his subsequent audience with a young Oberleutnant who fails to hide his discomfort at seeing the crashed Wellington's dead crew members. When the young officer proves unable to retrieve the identification tags from one of the corpses as ordered, Kessler impatiently snaps them off the body himself. Deciding that the green Oberleutant needs to be taught a lesson, he demands that the officer show him the body of a man whose flesh has been burnt to the bone. The Oberleutant's protest at this order only encourages Kessler, who ensures that the man looks into what he calls "the face of the enemy." Kessler continues with a speech that chillingly demonstrates his zealous belief in the Fatherland: "It is the face of defeat, it is the face of death. Isn't that what we all wish to see?" and remains totally impassive and unmoved as he is driven away from the site. The Sturmbannführer's loyalties are examined further in a scene in which he all but bursts with pride as he extols Stoller's virtues to Brandt. For Kessler, Stoller represents – despite his non-Aryan looks – the Nazi ideal and as a result his belief in him is absolute. However, this deep respect for Stoller does not get in the way of his overriding objective: to make sure that the SS man is accepted as a genuine evader. As a result, just before Stoller heads off into the night to begin his mission, Kessler quickly and without compunction breaks one of Stoller's arms, before saying: "Ernst, it's for your own good." This shocking scene, which demonstrates the lengths to which he is prepared to go for the greater glory of the Third Reich, is often regarded as *the* Kessler moment.

A Question of Loyalty is one of the most complete and well-rounded episodes of *Secret Army* which benefits from some excellent performances from the regulars and a solid script that seeks to emphasise the complexity of human existence, which is even further complicated at a time of war.

HISTORICAL BACKGROUND

A Very British Nazi

The real-life inspiration for the character of Englishman-turned-Nazi, Unterscharführer Ernst Stoller, was one Thomas Heller Cooper, who was born in 1919, the son of a British father and a German mother, and was brought up and educated in Chiswick, West London. In 1938, Cooper joined Oswald Mosley's British Union of Fascists. After being rejected by the RAF, the Royal Navy and the Police, Cooper went to Germany in 1939 just prior to the outbreak of war. Cooper worked as a private tutor until he met the Head of SS recruitment in 1940 and subsequently trained at the SS Leibstandarte before joining the Waffen SS. After he completed his training in Pomerania, he was posted to SS Topenkopf Wachbatallion Oranienburg stationed near Krakow. While there, he participated in the massacre of both Polish Jews and Russian prisoners of war. He would later boast how he had murdered over 200 Poles and 80 Jews in one day by lining them up against a wall and shooting them. By November 1941, he was promoted to Unterscharführer. In January 1943 he was transferred to the Transport unit of the SS Polizei Division and during this posting was seriously wounded and invalided out of action. He subsequently produced propaganda for the German Foreign Office, before becoming the NCO for a planned 'British SS' (Legion of Saint George) in Germany, for which he hoped to recruit British prisoners of war. He later formed the fascist British Free Corps, numbering less than thirty men, who unlike the SS were not required to take an oath to Hitler or subject to German Military Law, but nevertheless wore German uniforms. The BFC were regarded as incompetent and irrelevant by their Nazi masters and their numbers dwindled as the war progressed. At the end of the war, Cooper was taken to a British military prison in Brussels, and in 1945 faced trial for High Treason back in Britain. He was found guilty and sentenced to death, a sentence that was changed soon after to life imprisonment, before he was released altogether in 1953. Cooper is believed to have begun a new life in Japan.

The Wellington Bomber

First manufactured in 1936, the Vickers Wellington Bomber, popularly known as the Wimpey, was a twin-engine medium bomber that, from the outbreak of war, was initially used for day bombing raids. However, once it was recognised that they were vulnerable to attacking fighters because they did not possess self-

sealing fuel tanks or adequate defensive armaments, they were relegated to night bombing raids instead. A unique geodesic metal lattice framework, designed by Barnes Wallis, gave the Wellington tremendous strength, often allowing them to return home intact even if they had been badly hit by enemy aircraft. The Wellingtons were replaced by four-engined bombers as the war progressed, but they were still made up until 1945. Under RAF Bomber Command, Wellingtons flew 47,409 operations.

WHERE ELSE HAVE I SEEN..?

© Unknown

Clive Arrindell (Stoller)

Orsino, *BBC Shakespeare: Twelfth Night*, 1980
Ralph, *The Man Who Shot Christmas*, 1984
Cassius Charaea, *AD (Anno Domini)*, 1985
Lord Guarco, *Christopher Columbus: The Discovery*, 1992
Abbe de Frilair, *The Scarlet and the Black*, 1993

William Simons (Lebrun)

Mandrel, *Doctor Who: The Sunmakers*, 1977
Constable Thackeray, *Cribb*, 1980-1
Josef, *Wish Me Luck*, 1989
Inspector Fox, *Ngaio Marsh's Alleyn Mysteries*, 1990-4
PC Alf Ventress, *Heartbeat*, 1992-present

Episode 12: HYMN TO FREEDOM

WRITTEN BY: Michael Chapman   **DIRECTED BY:** Kenneth Ives

FIRST BROADCAST: BBC1, 8.05pm, Wednesday 30 November 1977

STUDIO RECORDING: 4 November 1977

VIEWING FIGURE: 7.3m

REGULAR CAST: Albert Foiret: BERNARD HEPTON; Lisa Colbert: JAN FRANCIS; Flt Lt John Curtis: CHRISTOPHER NEAME; Monique Duchamps: ANGELA RICHARDS; Major Erwin Brandt: MICHAEL CULVER; Sturmbannführer Ludwig Kessler: CLIFFORD ROSE; Alain Muny: RON PEMBER; Louise Colbert: MARIA CHARLES

SUPPORTING CAST: Hans van Reijn: JOHN CARSON; Achilles Becker: FRANK BARRIE; Flying Officer John Staples: PAUL GREGORY; Horst Schmidt: PAUL JERRICHO; Klaus Schoonheim: MICHAEL FORREST

SYNOPSIS: Brandt stakes out a safe-house in Bruges with a colleague called Schmidt. After arresting an evasion line guide, Schoonheim, Brandt visits the apartment in his place and interrogates a British officer, John Staples, who is in hiding there. Alain decodes an urgent message and arranges to meet up with Curtis. Albert becomes angry when he learns that Monique is due to carry out a pick-up at a safe-house in Bruges which has been under suspicion by the Germans in the past. After going through Staples's evasion kit, Brandt reveals his true identity and calls Schmidt into the room. Given Schmidt's uncanny resemblance to Staples, Brandt decides that he should take the Flying Officer's place in the safe-house and demands that Staples tell him everything about himself. Curtis follows instructions sent by London to make a rendezvous at Bruges railway station with Hans van Reijn, a minister of the puppet Belgian government, who has contacted the British to arrange his defection. Albert questions Lisa's decision to use the house in Bruges, but she explains her reasoning. Curtis arrives and asks Lisa if Lifeline can help Van Reijn. She reluctantly agrees to help the collaborator as long as his identity remains secret. Van Reijn suspects that his butler serves two masters and tells him as much. Plans are made to bring Van Reijn and Staples to Brussels where they are to be hidden in a disused mill. Brandt interrogates Schoonheim, but learns little. Kessler elects to take Schoonheim away for Gestapo questioning. Monique arrives in Bruges and takes Schmidt back with her to Brussels. Lisa is followed to the disused mill by her Aunt Louise, who offers to help her to look after the evaders. Kessler visits Van Reijn's home and talks to his butler about his master's recent behaviour and movements. While Curtis meets Van Reijn again, Monique brings Schmidt to the mill. Schmidt attempts to leave, but is stopped from doing so when Louise arrives to give him a gift of some sweets. Schmidt successfully alerts a German soldier to his presence there by throwing a package, containing a note, to the ground below. Louise observes the soldier go into the mill and goes to the Candide to tell Lisa. Kessler and Brandt discuss their suspicion that Van Reijn is planning to get out of Belgium via an evasion line. Brandt receives a message from Schmidt which suggests that Van Reijn is on the way. Lisa goes to the mill and, after ordering Van Reijn to go outside, kills Schmidt. Kessler and Brandt arrive and pick up Van Reijn. Under interrogation Van Reijn reveals that he only has six months to live and that he wants to be executed after he denounces National Socialism. Kessler tells Van Reijn that he will neither execute him nor allow his rejection of Nazism to become public knowledge. Van Reijn's butler arrives and takes him back home to live the remainder of his life under strict surveillance.

REVIEW: Michael Chapman's only script for *Secret Army* runs into exactly the same problems that plague the majority of the episodes of his ITV wartime drama *Enemy at the Door*: snail's-pace storytelling, dull characters and initially impenetrable plotlines. After the seemingly directionless first twenty minutes, things finally do get going plot-wise, but there is still not enough material for the regulars to get their teeth into. Thankfully the ever-reliable Clifford Rose comes to the rescue to ensure a terrific denouement, but this isn't quite enough to prevent *Hymn to Freedom* from being the least engaging episode of the first series.

Although the puppet minister Van Reijn is an interesting creation, John Carson fails to imbue him with enough spark or conviction to make the character memorable or to encourage the viewer to sympathise with his position. However, to be fair this is not entirely down to Carson. Far too often the narrative chooses to show Van Reijn deep in thought at his home, or at the railway station, without any indication of what the man is thinking or how he has come to this state of affairs. His excellent speech about his "political naïvety" and his belief that the Nazi victory "will be short-lived" is not delivered until the episode's penultimate scene and really is too little too late in terms of characterisation.

The episode's other guest characters are similarly two-dimensional for the majority of the piece, especially Van Reijn's butler, Frank Barrie's Achilles. Two notable exceptions are: Michael Forrest's Schoonheim, who is suitably shaken by his intimidating interrogation at the hands of Brandt; and Paul Gregory, who makes the most of the small role of indignant Flying Officer John Staples.

Given the tumultuous events of the preceding episode, *A Question of Loyalty*, it is a little surprising to witness Albert and Monique engaging in such obviously affectionate banter in the first Candide scene. Although Albert soon spoils the atmosphere by haranguing her when he hears about her forthcoming pick-up in the unsafe Maximillianstraat, it is clear that he only becomes so angry because of his love for her and his fears for her safety. For the second time in two episodes, Monique once again finds herself unwittingly acting as a guide to a German infiltrator, however she wastes little small talk on Schmidt.

Lisa, a character who has enjoyed very little screen time since her big moment in *Too Near Home*, is – with the exception of the horribly forced draughts game scene – portrayed as a particularly dour figure here. Given Gaston's death and the continued pressures of command this seems entirely fitting. Towards the end of the episode we finally have evidence that Lisa has no compunction about killing the enemy as she dispatches Schmidt with very little ceremony, albeit off-screen. There are also further indications of her intense practicality (her reasoning behind the use of Maximillianstraat) and her intimate understanding of Lifeline (her own acceptance of Van Reijn as a passenger, but her recognition that her colleagues may not be so willing). As such, in terms of character development, Lisa benefits more from the script than her resistance colleagues.

Brandt ably employs his disarming charm to put a British officer at his ease once again here. When it transpires that the Major intends to have Schmidt swap places with Staples – the resemblance between the two Pauls is pretty remarkable – it is abundantly clear that he loves his job and relishes this new plan. We can only assume that before he observed Staples's striking similarity to Schmidt, Brandt must simply have intended to take Staples away for interrogation? The false identity plot adds some much-needed suspense to the episode, but it is a shame that it leads to more screen time for Schmidt rather than Staples, as Paul Jerricho is easily the duller performer of the pair. It is also unfortunate that the connection between this identity plot and the Van Reijn storyline is too long in coming, thus contributing to a fragmentary and disorganised feel. The decision to use Bruges as the location for both Van Reijn's house and the safe-house was presumably employed by Chapman to suggest that the two plots are in some way connected, but the link is unnecessary and only promotes confusion. *Secret Army* never returns to Bruges for the remainder of its run, yet Alain, Curtis, Monique, Brandt and Kessler are all unable to keep away from the place here! Lisa's decision to take Schmidt and Van Reijn to the disused mill is similarly curious. We know from previous episodes that Lifeline maintains numerous safe-houses in Brussels and that some of them must be empty at the moment, as she explains to Albert that she has been forced to use Bruges as she couldn't get any evaders through to the capital recently. The mill, nevertheless, is an interesting location and, if nothing else, allows for a touching audio flashback, as Lisa thinks back to happier times there with Gaston and Louise.

There is some pleasing continuity with *Too Near Home* in respect of grieving widow, Louise Colbert. For the majority of the series, Lisa's Aunt Louise has been deliberately portrayed as an irritating character, but the fact that Gaston is now no longer with us, just as she feared would be the case, rather excuses her previous behaviour. The last time we saw Louise she was defiantly daubing a 'Victory V' on a suburban wall. Here, although still in mourning – a state she will presumably maintain until her death – we learn that this act of resistance has since translated into an admirable resolve to assist her niece in her dangerous work. This is a surprising and welcome development. As it turns out in this instance, her involvement in the action at the disused mill proves invaluable as it ensures the Line's survival. She will prove equally resourceful in her forthcoming final appearance.

The most memorable and atmospheric scenes in the episode are the separate interrogations of Klaus Schoonheim and Van Reijn. Brandt – who gives Kessler a run for his money in the nastiness stakes here – leads the former, initially appearing to be alone. Unfortunately, a brief long shot of the room gives the game away that Kessler is actually present too. This rather spoils what could have been an even more chilling moment as the Sturmbannführer suddenly intervenes and bellows the line "brave words!" at the terrified Belgian. Although Kessler is ultimately happy with their subsequent success in capturing "the big fish," it seems strange and unconvincing that nothing further is learned from Schoonheim about the evasion line after he is handed over to the Gestapo. Lifeline are perhaps a little too lucky in this regard.

Van Reijn's interrogation allows Clifford Rose to once again steal the acting honours, as Kessler berates the minister for his naïvety. While Van Reijn claims "political naïvety", excusing his choice of National Socialism as a way forward against the threat of Communism, and announcing that he now expects to be executed for switching sides, Kessler recognises that the man has actually been naïve in a far wider respect. That Van Reijn actually believes that the Nazis will first allow him to denounce them and then proceed to execute him, making him into a political martyr in the process, suggests that the politician is no great thinker. Conversely Kessler, who never misses a trick – except when he is blinded by his fanaticism – intends to make sure that Van Reijn will instead "die like a good National Socialist in harness" and, in what is easily the best line of the episode, reminds him: "You chose to ride on the back of a tiger, you cannot dismount when the fancy takes you!" The fact that Van Reijn seeks to make amends and die a martyr only after he learns that he has just six months to live, suggests that his motives may actually have far more to do with self-interest than being a sudden Saul-like revelation. It is expedient for Van Reijn to choose to side with the Anglo-Americans just prior to his death, so that he is not remembered as a traitor. That this motivation is neither explored nor intimated sufficiently is a missed opportunity. Nevertheless, this excellently scripted scene makes for a strong conclusion to an otherwise unsatisfactory episode.

HISTORICAL BACKGROUND

King Leopold and the Belgian Government

Although there was no 'puppet government' as such in Belgium during the Occupation – the senior members of the government having taken flight to Paris in the first week of the German invasion in May 1940 – there were of course many Belgians who remained in government service positions and ended up cooperating with the occupation regime. The Belgian 'government in exile', which eventually travelled on to London, was led by Prime Minister Hubert Pierlot. The fact that King Leopold III had not gone with Pierlot and the other ministers shocked them deeply. They wanted him to come to England and become a symbol of Belgian resistance. When the King instead declared that he had decided to share the same fate as his troops and stay with them in Belgium after capitulation, they took this to mean that he intended to form a new government and that he would reign as a sort of vassal of Hitler and described his actions as disgraceful and treasonable. Leopold subsequently agreed upon a complete surrender of the Belgian forces to avoid further bloodshed. Although this decision was heavily criticised at the time, historians have since mused that it probably saved the lives of around two million Belgians. Leopold went to Laeken Castle (where he lived in luxury) as a prisoner of war, but while there his actions were to prove controversial again when he married his second wife, Lillian, proving that he was not the grieving widower (his deceased first wife Astrid having been a favourite of the Belgian people) that his countrymen had imagined. The fact that Lillian was a commoner also provoked dismay. After a failed and misinterpreted meeting with Hitler in which Leopold actually hoped to win concessions for Belgium rather than show obedience, the King refrained from any further political involvement and the majority of the Belgian population gradually came to agree that he was more interested in his new wife than in the welfare of his country. The King and his family were deported to Austria in June 1944 and his brother Prince Charles was installed as regent. In 1950, Leopold finally returned to Belgium with Lillian, however, in protest against their return, workers went on strike and rioted. After a large-scale workers' march on Brussels was announced, Leopold was persuaded to abdicate in favour of his son Baudouin. The abdication papers were signed in 1951 and Leopold lived out his retirement with Lillian until his death in 1983.

Oscar Peterson's 'Hymn To Freedom'

As well as being the name of the piece that Hans Van Reijn was composing at the time of his attempted defection to Britain, 'Hymn to Freedom' is also the name of one of jazz pianist Oscar Peterson's most popular pieces. Peterson composed his 'Hymn to Freedom' in 1962, reportedly after being inspired to do so by Martin Luther King's fight for liberty and equality. The lyrics to the piece, written by Harriette Hamilton, are as follows:

When every heart joins every heart and together yearns for liberty,
That's when we'll be free.
When every hand joins every hand and together molds our destiny,
That's when we'll be free.
Any hour any day, the time soon will come when men will live in dignity,
That's when we'll be free, we will be
When every man joins in our song and together singing harmony,
That's when we'll be free.

Vidkun Quisling

Vidkun Quisling staged a *coup d'état* in 1940, as the Germans invaded Norway, and became its Prime Minister in February 1942. Quisling collaborated with the occupying German forces throughout the remainder of the war, encouraging his countrymen to serve in the SS, openly assisting with the deportation of Jews and

executing patriots who rebelled against the Nazi regime. Due to the extent of his collaboration, his surname became synonymous with the word traitor. It was first coined in this sense by *The Times* in an editorial on 15 April 1940, which read: 'To writers, the word Quisling is a gift from the gods. If they had been ordered to invent a new word for traitor... they could hardly have hit upon a more brilliant combination of letters. Actually it contrives to suggest something at once slippery and tortuous.' Quisling was convicted of high treason and executed by firing squad at Akershus Fortress on 24 October 1945 and his mansion home has been turned into a Holocaust Museum.

WHERE ELSE HAVE I SEEN..?

John Carson (Van Reijn)

James Langley, *The Troubleshooters*, 1971-2

Mr Knightley, *Emma*, 1972

Colonel Heatherstone, *The Children of the New Forest*, 1977

Ambril, *Doctor Who: Snakedance*, 1983

Richard Abernethie, *Poirot: After the Funeral*, 2005

Paul Jerricho (Schmidt)

Mr Hicks (P.E. Teacher), *Grange Hill: Slip on the Wet Floor Did You?*, 1981

Charles Woodhouse, *Triangle*, 1981-3

Castellan Spandrell, *Doctor Who: Arc of Infinity/ The Five Doctors*, 1983

Robert Hastings, *Howards' Way*, 1990

David Maybury, *The Ice House*, 1997

© Unknown

© Peter Simpkin

Episode 13: BAIT

WRITTEN BY: James Andrew Hall   **DIRECTED BY:** Viktors Ritelis

FIRST BROADCAST: BBC1, 8.05pm, Wednesday 7 December 1977

STUDIO RECORDING: 15 November 1977

VIEWING FIGURE: 6.3m

REGULAR CAST: Albert Foiret: BERNARD HEPTON; Lisa Colbert: JAN FRANCIS; Flt Lt John Curtis: CHRISTOPHER NEAME; Monique Duchamps: ANGELA RICHARDS; Major Erwin Brandt: MICHAEL CULVER; Sturmbannführer Ludwig Kessler:

CLIFFORD ROSE; Andrée Foiret: EILEEN PAGE; Corporal Rennert: ROBIN LANGFORD; Yvonne: HENRIETTA BAYNES

SUPPORTING CAST: Catherine Bidout: BARBARA COCHRAN; Leutnant Eric Schumacher/Pasco: MALCOLM BULLIVANT; Celeste Lekeu: KATHLEEN BYRON; Marcelle Gerome: SYLVA LANGOVA; German Officer: AL LAMPERT; Customer: LUCY GRIFFITHS

SYNOPSIS: In Brussels, a young man tries to make himself known to an Englishwoman named Catherine Bidout who has not yet been interned. Their meeting is observed by haberdasher Marcelle Gerome. Mme Bidout takes the man, who calls himself Pasco, back to her home. He tells her that he was put on to her by a woman in a market. She is very reluctant to hide him given the circumstances, but he browbeats her into letting him stay. Kessler is busy making preparations for the Führer's birthday when Rennert brings him information passed on from Mme Gerome. Albert returns home and asks a depressed Monique to sew the Nazi flag to the bunting for the birthday parade. She refuses at first but then relents. Mme Gerome tells Celeste Lekeu about Mme Bidout and a rumour that she is hiding an evader. Mme Bidout attempts to contact Major Brandt, whom she counts as a personal friend, but he is unavailable. Monique is having difficulty with occasional barmaid, Yvonne, when Mme Lekeu arrives to see Andrée. Before going upstairs, Mme Lekeu tells Monique about Mme Bidout and the evader. Albert decides to check the lead out. Andrée and Mme Lekeu discuss the Führer's birthday and the possibility of a relationship between Yvonne and Albert. Albert arrives at Mme Bidout's home, but she explains to him that she has called a German officer about her evader and he is on his way. Albert leaves just before Brandt arrives. A German officer bargains with Yvonne in order to retrieve his lost wedding ring. Yvonne asks Andrée to open the Candide cash box. After questioning Yvonne about Albert and retrieving the ring, Andrée discovers an envelope full of blank ration cards. Mme Bidout tells Brandt about the evader. After arresting him, the evader tells Brandt he is a German working for Kessler. Now that he realises that Mme Bidout has outlived her usefulness as a stooge with whom to trap the resistance, Brandt encourages her to contact the resistance and escape Belgium. After Albert is reprimanded by Curtis and Lisa for going to see Mme Bidout, Andrée accuses him of collaboration before showing him the ration cards. Albert succeeds in explaining them away. Kessler reproaches Brandt for keeping Pasco in his custody. Pasco subsequently tells Kessler that a picture of the Major is hanging in Mme Bidout's home. Mme Bidout packs her things and is about to leave her home when Curtis arrives. Curtis takes her back to the Candide during the birthday parade. When asked by Kessler, Brandt denies that he knew Mme Bidout's son and confirms Kessler's view that Pasco is unreliable. At the Candide, Lisa refuses to take Mme Bidout down the Line, but suggests that another organisation, which helps Jews, may be able to get her home. A brick wrapped in a Nazi flag is thrown into the Candide.

REVIEW: *Bait*, James Andrew Hall's second script for *Secret Army*, has a highly intelligent plot, boasting several surprising twists and excellent development for the regular characters. Nevertheless, for some reason, it remains one of the least memorable episodes of the first series.

Hall makes the interesting decision to centre his narrative around four mature women. The one thing that connects them is the fact that the war has affected them all dramatically, although their individual circumstances could not be more different. Catherine Bidout would be a rather ordinary old woman were it not for the fact that she is an enemy alien living in Occupied Belgium, who does not understand why she has not yet been interned. In contrast, haberdasher and Czech national, Marcelle Gerome, knows only too well why she has escaped internment because she has been acting as a collaborator. For Celeste Lekeu, the war has not only allowed her more opportunities to gossip, but also to lord her moral superiority over her fellow Belgians. She also acts as a window to the outside world for Andrée Foiret, who makes her first appearance in a long time here. Andrée is consumed by bitterness and suspicion, a situation caused by her physical disabilities which enforce her separation from a world that the war has changed beyond all recognition. There are also the first signs that Andrée's mental state may be deteriorating. Were it not for the threads that connect these four women, Lifeline would not become embroiled in what eventually transpires to be yet another infiltration plot (the third in three consecutive episodes!) which is specifically designed to trap them. With the possible exception of Sylva Langova's slightly OTT Marcelle Gerome – who is unfortunately also guilty of an '*Acorn Antiques* moment' when she answers the phone before putting the receiver to her ear – all four actresses rise to the occasion, including former film star Kathleen Byron (Lekeu). The addition of a number of significant guest characters does lead once again to some downsizing in terms of the Lifeline contingent. Natalie fails to appear for the third episode in a row (she is presumably 'down the Line'), while Curtis and Lisa are reduced to unsympathetic, and occasionally sanctimonious, ciphers when they do briefly appear. Curtis's attack on Albert's decision to visit Mme Bidout's home is particularly difficult to believe, especially given that he himself later endangers everyone at the Candide by recklessly deciding to take Mme Bidout there during the parade.

Albert and Monique fair much better as their characters and relationship once again take centre-stage. Monique is coping a little better with Andrée, but Albert's intention to further allay suspicions of their clandestine activities by flying the Nazi swastika outside the Candide to celebrate the Führer's birthday is almost enough to send her home. That she stays and agrees to sew the flag to the rest of the bunting as he requests, suggests that they are closer than they have been previously and that their unsatisfactory lifestyle is, for the moment at least, now enough for Monique.

Collaboration is one of the most prominent themes of the episode. In addition to the emotive matter of the celebration of the Führer's birthday and the idea of being, as Monique puts it, "willing collaborators" by flying the flag, Mme Gerome is guilty of direct collaboration in order to be given "a chance to survive," while Mme Bidout unwillingly collaborates by giving her evader up to her old friend Major Brandt. The episode ably demonstrates that there are different levels of collaboration and that while the acts presented here may not be excusable, all are, at the very least, understandable. However, as Andrée wisely and portentously observes, there will be a long-term price to pay ("What about after the war? What about reprisals then?")

The twist at the centre of the episode, that Pasco is in fact a German Leutnant who has been employed by Kessler to go to the Englishwoman, Catherine Bidout, in order to flush the resistance out, works brilliantly. However, Hall commendably adds further levels of complexity to the scenario. It is revealed that it is no mistake that Bidout has not yet been interned and that she has been left off the lists for this very plan, while the installation of Schumacher at her apartment actually succeeds not only in flushing out Albert but, by chance, Major Brandt too! When Brandt comprehends Kessler's strategy and the sudden worthlessness of his old friend, he is forced to suggest the only possible way out of the situation and encourages her to contact the resistance! That Brandt has firstly to make this out-of-character suggestion and then subsequently not imperil her by attempting to seek out these enemy contacts is ingenious scripting, especially as it could lead, via the presence of his photograph in Bidout's home, to a possible allegation of collaboration on his part! The ever-reliable Michael Culver sensitively brings out Brandt's genuine humanity here. Although Brandt's instinctive reaction is to push for information when she reveals that she knows the location of an evader, he is able to temporarily put aside his ambition to destroy the evasion lines, out of friendship and respect for Bidout. The fact that he seeks to secure her safety at the expense of his own is also a telling gesture.

When Kessler is tipped off by Schumacher about the photograph in Bidout's flat, it is lucky for the Major that the former has reservations about the Leutnant's tendency to "put emphasis on unimportant things." This allows Brandt to confirm Kessler's opinion that the Leutnant is unreliable thus getting himself off the hook. This whole conversation takes place while Kessler holds out of Brandt's view what could easily be the photograph in question, adding a significant degree of tension to the scene. However, Brandt is not drawn by Kessler's ploy and guesses that he is holding a different photograph entirely. Kessler and Brandt never seem to tire of playing these games of 'cat and mouse' and, as usual, this component of the episode is engaging and well-scripted.

Henrietta Baynes's return to the show is another welcome ingredient of *Bait*. Hall presumably decided to reintroduce the idle Yvonne, not only because he himself created her for *Second Chance*, but also because her presence is necessary to one of the episode's sub-plots. Yvonne's sexual presence, coupled with the idea of a possible liaison with Albert, are enough to send Andrée over the edge, while downstairs, she revels in getting under Monique's and Mme Lekeu's feet and flirts recklessly with anything in trousers. Thanks to Baynes's obvious enthusiasm for the role, she is both a funny and diverting creation who more than her earns her character's screen time.

Director, Viktors Ritelis, battles masterfully to make what is obviously a low-budget production appear believable. There is only one brief film insert in the

167

entire episode, a German flag flying above the (unseen) Avenue Louise HQ – everything else is entirely studio-bound. Although Ritelis should be commended for even trying to pull off the almost impossible task of staging the Führer's birthday parade in the studio, through the use of music, flags and as many of the episode's characters and supporting artists as he could lay his hands on, unfortunately he does not succeed and it is the weakest element of the episode. Perhaps it is this lack of location filming which more than any other factor causes *Bait* to be forgotten. If this episode's parade had received the same epic treatment as *Growing Up*'s funeral scene, perhaps its fortunes would have been different?

Ritelis's distinctive direction is once again obvious here, be it in the lingering close-ups on a brandy glass and a crucifix or, more noticeably, in the sequence in which Andrée has her first attack as Yvonne and Mme Lekeu swim into view. The latter is a successful effect that he would be set to take even further in the Series One finale.

The episode's concluding scene in the Candide once again concentrates on the well-developed premise that Lifeline cannot allow emotion to get in the way of their operations. However, in her coldness towards Mme Bidout, Lisa perhaps takes this tenet a little too far, prompting Monique to shout "Look at her!" in order to force her to make a final judgement while face-to-face with the innocent old woman. Through her decision to refuse to take the woman down the Line, Lisa seems to enjoy demonstrating to her colleagues, that she is harder than they imagine – perhaps in an attempt to reinforce her role as leader? – before revealing that she intends to seek the help of a specific evasion line for Jews in order to get Bidout home. Although the more powerful play-off between Brandt and Kessler would have arguably been a stronger concluding scene, the last few seconds of the Candide-set sequence provide a final reminder of the episode's overriding theme, as members of Lifeline are once again accused of collaboration via the arrival through the Candide's front window of a swastika flag wrapped around a brick. It is an effective reminder that both suspected and actual collaborators may ultimately have reprisals to face.

HISTORICAL BACKGROUND

Hitler's Birthday

Bait must take place on the eve and day of Hitler's 54th birthday, Monday 19 and Tuesday 20 April 1943. This is deduced from the fact that in 1943, Good Friday, the day on which the following episode is set, fell on 23 April, whereas in 1942 Easter was in early April. Every year, Nazi propaganda minister Josef Goebbels gave a speech on the eve of Hitler's birthday and up until 1942 the content had been uniformly upbeat and predominantly concentrated on Hitler's personal greatness. However, in 1943, Goebbels's speech made it clear that he now realised that the Nazis' position was precarious and the outcome of war less certain:

"The German people celebrate the Führer's birthday this year in a particularly sombre manner. This fourth year of the war has been the hardest yet, and an escape from its burdens and sorrows, or its end, is nowhere in sight. Its enormous political and military events span all five continents. Wherever one looks, peoples and nations are affected by its pains and sacrifices. Hardly a nation has been spared the grave political and economic impacts of this vast military drama… As a nation of 90 million, we lay before him our faith. We believe in a German victory because we believe in him. Our good wishes for him rise from the deepest depths of our heart. God grant him health and strength and his grace. Loyally and faithfully we want to follow him, wherever he may lead. He is our faith and our proud hope. We will walk firmly into the future his hand points toward…. We, the Führer's old fighting comrades gather around him now as always in the decisive moments of our struggle. We belong to him. We were the first he called. How often we walked with him through trials and dangers. At the end of the way was always the shining goal. So it is today. We never want to lose sight of it. With our gaze fixed on the goal we will fight and work on. We are the example of faith, of bravery, of unchanging conviction. We are the old guard of the party that never wavers. As the first soldiers of our people, our wish for the Führer on his birthday is the same one that has always moved our hearts. May he remain in the future what he is today and always will be: Our Hitler!"

WHERE ELSE HAVE I SEEN..?

Kathleen Byron (Celeste Lekeu)

Sister Ruth, *Black Narcissus*, 1947
Countess Gemini, *The Portrait of a Lady*, 1968
Fanny Assingham, *The Golden Bowl*, 1972
Clonemaster Fen, *Blake's 7: Weapon*, 1979
Edith, *Perfect Strangers*, 2001

Malcolm Bullivant (Pasco)

Cossack, *War and Peace: Austerlitz*, 1972
Cast Member, *Phoelix*, 1979
Bershar, *Blake's 7: Volcano*, 1980
Father, *Gathering Stones*, 1986
Swedish U.N. Guard, *Superman IV*, 1987

Episode 14: GOOD FRIDAY

WRITTEN BY: John Brason   **DIRECTED BY:** Paul Annett

FIRST BROADCAST: BBC1, 8.05pm, Wednesday 14 December 1977

STUDIO RECORDING: 6 December 1977

169

VIEWING FIGURE: 6.0m

REGULAR CAST: Albert Foiret: BERNARD HEPTON; Lisa Colbert: JAN FRANCIS; Flt Lt John Curtis: CHRISTOPHER NEAME; Monique Duchamps: ANGELA RICHARDS; Major Erwin Brandt: MICHAEL CULVER; Sturmbannführer Ludwig Kessler: CLIFFORD ROSE; Natalie Chantrens: JULIET HAMMOND-HILL; Andrée Foiret: EILEEN PAGE; Corporal Rennert: ROBIN LANGFORD

SUPPORTING CAST: Father Girard: MAURICE DENHAM; Father (Prior) Pierre Moussin: BREWSTER MASON; Father Anselm: RICHARD GALE; Brother Saul: BARTLETT MULLINS; Flt Lt John Henry Oliver: DAVID GRETTON; Celeste Lekeu: KATHLEEN BYRON; Brother Hugues: PETER GRAYER; German Sergeant: JURGEN ANDERSEN; Peasant in priory hospital: DENNIS BARRY

SYNOPSIS: Three evaders are guided out of the Candide's cellar, but there is not enough time to get the fourth and final man away. Monique takes Andrée's medicine up to her and prepares her for a visit from Mme Lekeu and Father Girard. Andrée opens her heart to Girard about Albert. After Brandt and Kessler watch a slideshow depicting the devastation caused by Allied bombing, the Major receives a report from the Abwehr about a British agent helping an evasion line. Lisa returns and Albert updates her on the evaders. Girard overhears them talking and offers to take the final evader, Oliver, to his priory. Back at the priory, Father Anselm observes Girard with Oliver. Girard informs the Father Prior, Pierre, about Oliver; Pierre approves of his decision to take the airmen in. Albert asks Andrée to try using her wheelchair again and loses his temper when she refuses. The next day, Kessler argues with Brandt about an informer called Bastian. Anselm asks Pierre about the airman and is angry when he learns that Pierre has agreed to his presence there, believing it to be against their vows. Albert and Curtis discuss Andrée, before Monique arrives to tell them that Bastian has been following Curtis. Albert leaves to get rid of Bastian before he can sell out to the Germans. He returns soon after, the job done. Anselm speaks out at the priory but his concerns are ignored. Lisa and Albert meet with Pierre to discuss the arrangements for Oliver's departure. Anselm makes a phonecall in secret. Before they set off to go to church, Curtis informs his Lifeline colleagues that he has heard that they have successfully guided 200 evaders home. At the priory, Kessler arrives with his men and pretends to kill Girard and some other monks in order to ensure cooperation. After revealing that they have not been killed, Kessler tries to bargain with Pierre but learns nothing. Kessler decides to take Girard and Oliver away for interrogation, but they make a run for it and are killed. Pierre continues to deny that he had anything to do with taking the evader in. Kessler and his men leave the priory. Pierre calls Lisa to tell her about the tragic events of the day. Anselm begs him for forgiveness and Pierre tells him his penance is to face his brothers for the rest of his life, knowing what he has done. Albert tells Andrée about Girard's death.

REVIEW: With *Good Friday*, another strong contender for best episode of the first series, John Brason proves once more that he has an intimate understanding of how to write for the *Secret Army*. The episode chiefly focuses on the involvement of a monastic order in the work of Lifeline, allowing not only for several hugely suspenseful scenes in which Kessler pays a terrifying visit to their priory, but also for an interesting examination of the perceived place of God in war. There are sterling performances from the hugely-experienced Maurice Denham and Brewster Mason as Fathers Girard and Pierre respectively, while amongst the regulars Bernard Hepton and Clifford Rose are both given the opportunity to shine.

Albert has a particularly rough ride in *Good Friday*. Despite the character's considerable reserves of patience and understanding, particularly in regard to his invalid wife, Andrée, he is finally seen to lose control here. Andrée's refusal to try to use the wheelchair is the catalyst for an outburst in which he observes that she doesn't want to help herself as that way she still has him "bound hand and foot," living an existence he describes as "crippled." In his next scene, after further musing on his lot, Albert feels moved to throw his wife's medicine against the wall in anger. However, rather than dissipating his frustration, the incident instead causes him to be consumed by disgust with himself, for descending into such self-pity. This is a particularly intriguing insight into this complex man, who feels everything far more than he is given credit for by either of the women in his life, although, to be fair, he does hide it very well indeed! The pace does not let up for Albert, as he subsequently learns that an agent called Bastian is about to betray Curtis and that he must kill him before the evening is out. His picking up and pocketing of the murder weapon – a flick-knife – on his way out, is shocking in its casualness. However, this is no easy task for the emotionally fraught Albert and upon his return, once the deed is done, the way he uncharacteristically falls into Monique's arms illustrates just how much the day's events have taken out of him. His lack of composure here could not contrast more strongly with his attitude after the dispatch of Walker in *Sergeant on the Run*. Hepton is in superb form here, especially in his portrayal of Albert's frustration and despair.

Brason ensures that the monks of San Raphael priory are wonderfully detailed three-dimensional characters, who Denham, Mason and Richard Gale must have enjoyed bringing to life. Father Girard is a refreshingly forthright man of God who believes that it is right for him and his beloved colleagues to take sides in the conflict against the Nazis: "God is on the side of the righteous and I have no doubt in my mind that for the first time in history the issues are clear for a man of faith." Girard proves to be incredibly brave and practical and, due to his faith, admirably steadfast when faced with the enemy. Girard's "oldest friend and much-loved colleague," the Father Prior, Pierre, also believes that faith and conscience demand that they become involved in the war, despite their cloistered existence. This he explains to a confused Albert with the terrific line: "My faith in the almighty has never precluded my giving him a helping hand when the opportunity arose. I suspect his hands were never fuller than now." Pierre is first described by Girard as "a deeply spiritual man but a very worldly one as well, if you can accept the paradox." It is a fact that Pierre himself puts down to having had a father who was a stonemason and therefore learning to use his hands in conjunction with his head at an early age. It is exactly this sort of complex and lyrical characterisation which makes this episode so good. It is a clever touch that on first meeting the Father Prior, a highly sceptical Albert confidently announces: "I have not always managed to retain my confidence in churchmen," only for him to be completely won over by the highly unusual religious man, so that at the episode's close he tells Lisa and Monique: "You know, I liked that monk better than I thought I could." Girard's and Pierre's views are seen to be entirely at odds with those expressed by the deeply unsympathetic character of Father Anselm, who cannot accept that God has anything to do with this conflict, therefore believing that as brethren in holy orders they should not be helping the RAF evader at all: "We cannot take sides and remain true to our vows, to our faith!" However, by subsequently inviting the outside world into the priory of San Raphael, in the hugely dangerous form of Kessler and his men, the incredibly naïve Anselm quickly realises that of all his brothers, ironically, he has become the least neutral and is ultimately responsible for the deaths of two men. The only monk who verges dangerously on stereotype is the gentle bespectacled Saul, who even gets to ape the car-tampering nuns from *The Sound of Music* by getting one over on the Germans ("It is a sin to permit such temptation to remain before such Philistines.")

For its second half, the episode is largely an examination of the effectiveness of the fear and intimidation techniques employed by the SS and the Gestapo – methods which are neatly signposted by Kessler when in conversation with Brandt near the start of the narrative. His cruel staging of the murder of Girard and two other monks is a chilling example of a typical Gestapo attempt to, as Kessler puts it; "obtain positive results with the minimum of persuasion." It is based on the premise that all their enemies are "conditioned by fear" due to their reputation. However, soon he is surprised to find himself frustrated in such an approach, perhaps for the first time in his career, because, with the exception of the weak Anselm, the monks do not fear him and his men. As Girard states: "I am contrite, but not afraid." For Kessler's purposes the men are far too accepting of the threat of death and he eventually realises that he has been rendered totally powerless in this respect and elects to take Girard and Oliver away for interrogation instead. Girard bravely decides to rob him of this option by effectively committing suicide.

Although earlier in the episode Kessler has fervently told Brandt: "I believe without reservation that Germany will not only win this war but that she has a divine directive to do so," this does not prevent him from showing complete contempt for the beliefs and chosen existence of the monks at the priory. He chides Father Pierre, when he requests that he be killed in the place of others: "Please no gestures, no martyrs. You can't resist it can you?" and later revels in "God-like powers" being responsible for bringing Girard and the other monks "miraculously back to life." He similarly enjoys the suggestion to Pierre that they are "both in the confession business." On meeting the worker with the gangrenous leg, he even makes the glorious, if heartless, quip: "I had no idea working in a priory could be so hazardous!" before unfairly berating Pierre for the monks' treatment of their workforce. However, he is seen to take the most satisfaction –

in a piece of both superb scripting and acting – from his last exchange with the Father Prior, in which he deliberately manoeuvres the man to deny three times that he knew about the evader's presence, just as his namesake disciple Simon Peter denied three times that he knew Christ. Kessler allows himself a smile after Pierre's third denial. He may not have the information he came for, but he has won a small victory over this man of God and that is clearly important to him. Incidentally, Pierre's denial, along with Anselm's Judas-like betrayal and Girard's Christ-like sacrifice, make it obvious that, among its other concerns, Brason also intends *Good Friday* to stand as a thinly-veiled re-telling of the Christian Passion.

Although Natalie, who appears here for the first time in weeks, is given very little to do plot-wise, other than remind us that it is Eastertide and notice that Bastian has been following Curtis (off-screen), we do learn some more about her character. The fact that she doesn't even look up from painting her eggs when as many as four RAF evaders emerge from the cellar into the Candide's back room, suggests that she is a seasoned member of Lifeline by now, who has seen it all before. This is also implied by her calmness as her colleagues flap around her – a state of affairs that she observes to be typical behaviour whenever Lisa is absent. It is interesting that Natalie suggests that Monique is only frustrated with Andrée because she feels guilt, as this seems very wide of the mark, as is suggested by Monique's reaction. The pair clearly do not yet enjoy the relationship of mutual understanding that they will both come to treasure in later series. In fact, what Monique is more obviously feeling is resentment and anger. This is demonstrated, during one of her visits upstairs, by her decision to play up to Andrée for a change and even to intimate that her suspicions about herself and Albert are correct!

Thanks to Eileen Page's sensitive portrayal, the scenes involving Andrée are well-handled here. The way she is seen to be suddenly reminded of the love they once shared as Albert moves her is particularly touching, as is her desperate attempt to keep him with her in the bedroom so she can receive the affection she craves. As she relates to Father Girard: "I don't want his kindness or his pity. I want his love and he has none to give." However, it is difficult to feel too much sympathy for the character, given that she does wilfully cripple Albert's existence and doesn't appear to be able to see very far past her own self-pity and distress.

It is rather sweet that Lifeline have chosen to attend church together, although an Easter Sunday service would seem a more likely choice than a mournful Good Friday one. The latter seems even less appropriate when Curtis tells his colleagues that they have cause for celebration, London having informed Alain that they have safely guided a total of 200 evaders home. Nevertheless, Good Friday is of course the perfect day to set such a tragic episode given Brason's storytelling objectives.

Although *Good Friday*'s central plot is not inherently complex, its characters and their reactions to the situation are, and this is what makes it such a strong and memorable episode. By its end, viewers have not only learned a great deal more about what makes the regular characters tick, but observed a highly literate examination of religion and faith in wartime.

HISTORICAL BACKGROUND

The Good Father Prior

The events of *Good Friday* are in part based on the experiences of Bill Randle, while evading capture in Belgium. In his autobiography, he recounts how he found himself at a monastery near the town of Namur and met one Father Marcel, who had been charged by the Father Abbott to look after him as he spoke English reasonably well. After enjoying a short period of safety within the monastery walls, Father Marcel came to Randle to exaplin the effect his presence there was having on the monks there: 'My arrival had been observed by others and the monastery was in ferment. A serious situation had arisen because although most of the monks were Belgian and in favour of helping me, there were also two Dutchmen, two Spaniards, an Irishman and even some Germans, who thought otherwise. All were aware that a British pilot was being hidden in the cells. The Father Prior had been petitioned either to have me leave the monastery at once, or to hand me over to the Belgian police which meant that the Germans would get me. All knew the penalties for helping a British flyer were ruthlessly applied. There was the very real possibility that everyone in the monastery would be put to death if I were discovered... Sensing my alarm, Father Marcel tried to reassure me that all would be well: "The Good Father Brocard, our Prior, has made the decision for you," he said, "He has admonished the reluctant brothers, reminding them that it is their bounden Christian duty to help those in distress... There are eleven who are more worried about their safety than yours, and they have been ordered to retire from the monastery for an indefinite period. This afternoon, they will leave for our sister monastery at Chevremont where the brethren are bound by a complete vow of silence."' Randle remained at the monastery for some time before an evasion line guide escorted him to a safe-house.[8]

WHERE ELSE HAVE I SEEN..?

Maurice Denham (Girard)

Nestor Turton, *The Lotus Eaters*, 1972-3

Rawley, *Porridge*, 1974

Azmael/Professor Edgeworth, *Doctor Who: The Twin Dilemma*, 1984

Luther Crackenthorpe, *Miss Marple: 4.50 from Paddington*, 1987

Reverend Lance Mandeville, *Inspector Morse: Fat Chance*, 1991

© John Vickers

Brewster Mason (Pierre)

Abel Wharton, *The Pallisers*, 1974
Bismarck, *Edward the Seventh*, 1975
Bismarck, *Disraeli*, 1978
Voysey, *Play of the Month: The Voysey Inheritance*, 1979
Gurov, *Quatermass*, 1979

Richard Gale (Anselm)

John Farrance, *The River Flows East*, 1962
Dr Gordon Faulkner, *Out of the Unknown: Some
    Lapse of Time*, 1965
Sir Peregrine Stilgoe, *The Flaxton Boys*, 1969
Dr Beard, *Wicked Women: Christiana Edmund*, 1970
Pelbright, *The New Avengers: Angels of Death*, 1977

Bartlett Mullins (Saul)

Second Elder, *Doctor Who: The Sensorites*, 1964
Carshott, *Half a Sixpence*, 1967
Committee Chairman, *The Prisoner: A Change of Mind*, 1967
Professor Farthing, *Bright's Boffins*, 1970
Old Man, *The Changes*, 1975

© Zoe Dominic

Episode 15: SUSPICIONS

WRITTEN BY: N. J. Crisp DIRECTED BY: Kenneth Ives

FIRST BROADCAST: BBC1, 8.05pm, Wednesday 21 December 1977

STUDIO RECORDING: 25 November 1977

VIEWING FIGURE: 6.5m

REGULAR CAST: Albert Foiret: BERNARD HEPTON; Lisa Colbert: JAN FRANCIS; Flt Lt John Curtis: CHRISTOPHER NEAME; Monique Duchamps: ANGELA RICHARDS; Major Erwin Brandt: MICHAEL CULVER; Sturmbannführer Ludwig Kessler: CLIFFORD ROSE; Natalie Chantrens: JULIET HAMMOND-HILL; Andrée Foiret: EILEEN PAGE; Louise Colbert: MARIA CHARLES; Alain Muny: RON PEMBER; Jacques Bol: TIMOTHY MORAND

SUPPORTING CAST: Flt Sgt Donald Frederick Simpson: ALBERT WELLING; Concierge: JOHN SCOTT MARTIN

SYNOPSIS: Kessler and Brandt have begun to investigate the death of Hugh Neville and their chief suspect is Monsieur Moreelse (Curtis). They go to his apartment but are told he is out and, on the advice of his concierge, elect to try the Candide. On finding him there,

175

they begin to interrogate him and discover that he is the same Moreelse who was in Tours at the time of Neville's murder. When Natalie arrives with an evader, Monique drops a tray of drinks as a diversion while Lisa greets the airman as an old friend. Kessler and Brandt decide to continue Curtis's interrogation back at his flat and he hands over the documentation which relates to his trip down to Tours. Lisa takes the airman, Donald Simpson, to her aunt's empty house, before returning to the Candide. She decides that, given Curtis's arrest, all members of Lifeline, including Albert, must be ready to disperse at a moment's notice. Kessler asks Curtis about a Mademoiselle Valois of Lyons – the false identity which Monique assumed when she followed him down to Tours. After explaining the details of Neville's death and questioning Curtis about his fertiliser sales, Brandt and Kessler decide to leave him be for now. Lisa tells her Lifeline colleagues that if the worst comes to the worst the airmen currently in their safe-houses are expendable. Albert telephones Curtis at his flat on the pretext that he did not pay his bill and therefore learns that he is not being held. Simpson makes a move on Lisa and she makes her rejection of him very clear. Andrée and Albert talk about the accident which crippled her and about her trying out her wheelchair again. Brandt reads the transcripts of the calls made to Curtis's tapped phone and pays a visit to the Candide, arriving just as he is paying his bill. Brandt asks Curtis about Mlle Valois again, before questioning Albert about Moreelse and telling him about Neville's murder. Brandt is satisfied that Albert is innocent, but subsequently arrests Curtis. Louise arrives back from her trip to Liege and encounters Simpson, who offers to give himself up. After she calls the Candide and Albert suggests a course of action, she visits Jacques Bol's cycle shop and buys a second-hand bicycle. After dressing Simpson in Gaston's clothes she sends him on to a rendezvous with Jacques. Lisa comes home and Louise tells her about her recent actions. Brandt and Kessler question Curtis at Gestapo Headquarters and focus on the car used by Neville's murderer. Curtis introduces a new element into his story – a pretty secretary called Jeanette whom he had romantic designs on. His revelation that she was married, hence his previous reticence to discuss the matter, convinces his interrogators that he is innocent. Curtis returns to the Candide and is reunited with Lisa. It appears that the Germans have given up watching the Candide and its most frequent customers, for the time being at least.

REVIEW: N. J. Crisp's final episode for the first series concludes the Hugh Neville storyline introduced in *Lost Sheep*, and continued in *Guilt*, with a gripping narrative which sees Curtis finally brought to account for the novelist's murder. The episode is perhaps best remembered for its intensely claustrophobic atmosphere, which is enhanced by an entirely studio-bound approach.

Suspicions is a particularly important episode due to the fact that it includes a scene which marks a significant turning point in the series. While on the trail of the elusive Monsieur Moreelse, Kessler and Brandt pay a visit to the Candide, having been sent there by Curtis's concierge. Their sudden presence in the café with the Lifeline characters, in what is effectively the evasion line's centre of operations, is quite a surprise. That this situation adds a considerable *frisson* of suspense and excitement to the narrative explains why, in future series, the production team would elect to have the opposing protagonists together in the same space for large portions of screen time, with the scenario even becoming one of *Secret Army*'s most defining and identifiable components. The scene is very well played by all concerned here. Kessler's show of impatience at Brandt's 'softly, softly' approach as he begins to interrogate Curtis is a joy to watch, as is Monique's first unflinching "Herr Major." Both she and Lisa find that they suddenly have an important role to play in maintaining Lifeline's safety when Natalie arrives at the Candide with Flt Sgt Simpson at the very worst moment possible. Both rise to the occasion admirably, with an upturned tray of beer and an enthusiastic lover's greeting respectively, proving once again that they don't need the men of Lifeline in order to get by.

The narrative also takes an interesting turn with respect to the relationship between Albert and his wife, Andrée, who barely featured in the first half of this series but has become a permanent feature of the last few episodes. Now that her story is almost over, we finally learn how she came to be crippled – a motor car accident – and why Albert maintains such a strong commitment to a woman he no longer loves. They spend more time together here than in any other episode and each is seen to demonstrate a genuine affection for the other. Albert carries Andrée to her bed after her bath, tenderly drying her as she wistfully recalls walking in the snow in the old days. There is also nostalgic talk of how they first met during his days as a taxi-driver and hers as a governess after the death of her first husband, and of a happy holiday in Le Touquet. However, for Albert, their connection no longer translates into love. As he observes, they are two different people now and the only comfort he can give her is that, as his wife, he will always try to do his best by her. This is not enough to dissuade Andrée from believing that there may be something more between them in the future: "Perhaps one day…" Monique also appears to be unconvinced that Albert's marriage is over, demanding that he must tell her if there is a chance he can work things out with Andrée. As Andrée suspects, there is some deterioration in her health. Her worsening eyesight and dizzy spills seem to prove that Dr Keldermans's knowledge of her condition is not as complete as Albert believes it to be. Although there is no reference in any episode to her having a specific illness, nor any indication that Albert is aware that Andrée's time is running short, John Brason's prequel novel conversely states that both he and Keldermans know that Andrée is suffering from GPI (General Paralysis of the Insane) caused by the effect of syphilis bacteria on the central nervous system, while the car accident is said to have 'advanced the final stage by providing a physical reason for a paralysis that would have come of its own volition anyway.' Whatever the exact nature of her on-screen condition, what is certain is that Andrée is convincingly played by Eileen Page, who even succeeds in eliciting some viewer sympathy here for one of the series's least sympathetic characters.

Excellent and pleasing continuity is maintained with events earlier in the series thanks to the employment of N. J. Crisp as this episode's script writer. However, the heavy concentration on the events of *Guilt* feels somewhat surprising given the fact that the events in question occurred seven episodes ago; a factor which is in the favour of the DVD viewer rather than the original 1977 audience. One of the episode's best constructed scenes only pays off if the

177

audience remembers the identity of Moreelse's accomplice at the village near Tours: a Mademoiselle Valois. The woman Brandt is seeking is actually Monique, who is right under his nose and in the process of serving him a drink while he is describing her! This enjoyable device is used regularly in later series, and in both *Trapped* and *Little Old Lady*, it is Monique again whose previous presence down the Line is under investigation back at the Candide.

Curtis's arrest and likely fate forces Lisa to honestly confront her feelings for the British agent for the first time since she closed down on him in *Radishes with Butter*. Although the revelation that she does actually hold a torch for him is an interesting development, it is not an entirely believable one. Lisa has appeared to barely give him the time of day in recent episodes, especially in *Identity in Doubt* in which she couldn't reject him more heartlessly. Yet Curtis shows no discernible surprise when she welcomes his release with a hitherto unseen show of affection. By rights he should be utterly amazed! Christopher Neame is in great form here, especially during Curtis's uncomfortable interrogation at the Avenue Louise. An interrogation also brings the best out of Bernard Hepton, as Albert hotly denies his involvement in any resistance activities to the inquisitive Brandt. Both Curtis's introduction of the delectable Jeanette into his complicated explanation and Albert's impression of a model Belgian collaborator are surprisingly plausible defences which are believably delivered as the pair separately fend off a barrage of difficult questions from their fearsome interrogators.

Despite his almost incidental significance to the narrative, Albert Welling makes sure that Donald Simpson is a memorable 'evader of the week'. This is partly because of the character's incredibly ill-advised attempt to make a move on Lisa, but also due to his surprising suggestion to a frightened Louise that he will give himself up to the Germans. It is arguable that because of her recent encounter with Simpson, Lisa is more ready to espouse the harsh view that, ultimately, their charges are expendable; however, it is more likely that this is just her intense practicality kicking in once again.

Lisa's Aunt Louise, who makes her final appearance in the series here, once again confounds both her niece's and the audience's expectations by proving for a second time to be invaluable to the evasion line effort. Lisa's departure at the start of the next series is undoubtedly the prime reason why Louise does not return as well. Although she has become a far more interesting character than her initial appearances suggested, after Lisa's death there would really be nowhere further for her character to go other than further into grief.

In terms of the threat to Lifeline, at several points in the narrative it feels like their organisation is about to come to an abrupt end – a feeling that is accentuated by doom-laden lines such as Albert's "Go home! Say your prayers." In line with this mood, the episode's visuals are suitably dark and funereal. Austin Ruddy designs a drab and claustrophobic apartment for Curtis, seen for the first and last time here, while his excellent Candide sets also add considerably to the atmosphere of the piece.

Suspicions works very well as the penultimate episode of the series, by cranking up the suspense in anticipation of the series's big finale. It is clear that Curtis's release is a false dawn and that it can only be a matter of time before Kessler and Brandt will identify him, either as Neville's murderer, or as the British agent who they know is aiding an evasion line, or both. Despite the episode's obviously low budget – there is no location filming, only one new set and two guest characters – it all works very well, once again confirming that the series's particular strength is undeniably its regular cast.

WHERE ELSE HAVE I SEEN..?

Albert Welling (Simpson)

The Rev. Kevin Bulstrode, *Paradise Postponed*, 1986
Metzhofen, *Wish Me Luck*, 1990
Graham Kavanagh, *Kavanagh QC*, 1995-6
Opposition Leader, *My Dad's the Prime Minister*, 2003-4
Denis Guest, *The Line of Beauty*, 2006

Episode 16:
BE THE FIRST KID IN YOUR BLOCK TO RULE THE WORLD

WRITTEN BY: John Brason   **DIRECTED BY:** Viktors Ritelis

FIRST BROADCAST: BBC1, 8.05pm, Wednesday 28 December 1977

STUDIO RECORDING: 16 December 1977

VIEWING FIGURE: 8.7m

REGULAR CAST: Albert Foiret: BERNARD HEPTON; Lisa Colbert: JAN FRANCIS; Flt Lt John Curtis: CHRISTOPHER NEAME; Monique Duchamps: ANGELA RICHARDS; Sturmbannführer Ludwig Kessler: CLIFFORD ROSE; Natalie Chantrens: JULIET HAMMOND-HILL; Andrée Foiret: EILEEN PAGE; Alain Muny: RON PEMBER; Corporal Rennert: ROBIN LANGFORD

SUPPORTING CAST: Sturmbannführer Reinecke: MICHAEL WYNNE; Marcel: MARK JONES; Emil Van Maas: JONATHAN SCOTT; Jean-Jacques Hatt: ADAM RICHENS; Louis Brusse: MARK FARMER; Belgian Doctor: ROBERT MacLEOD; Hubert: ERNEST C. JENNINGS; Brussels Checkpoint Leutnant: JOHN PEEL; German Officer: SIMON PAGE; French Border Sergeant: NICHOLAS GEAKE

SYNOPSIS: Kessler rewards a Brussels-based Hitler Youth unit with a scroll of honour and the promise of a trip to the submarine docks at St Nazaire. Sturmbannführer Reinecke brings him news that the British agent they are looking for has been narrowed down to one of three persons. A doctor visits Andrée about her dimmed vision. He thinks there is nothing to worry about but she is certain it is more serious. Jean-Jacques Hatt's Hitler Youth group visit the Candide to gather warm clothing for the German troops on the Eastern Front. After Hatt threatens Albert, he agrees to find some things for them by the following day. Alain arrives with the news that Curtis's cover is blown and that the Germans are searching for him. Curtis leaves to stay with a contact in Pelicanstraat and Lisa suggests that Albert rings the Gestapo to tell them that Moreelse has just left, to prove once more that he is a collaborator. Kessler is now convinced that Moreelse is the British agent and, together with Reinecke, interrogates Strebel chemical company's chief clerk, Emil Van Maas. Van Maas cracks under the pressure and confirms Kessler's suspicions. Kessler advances plans for a great troop encirclement of Brussels to flush him out. A Belgian policeman, Marcel, warns Lisa and Albert about these plans and the latter heads off to arrange for guides to take evaders out of Brussels that evening. Curtis returns to the Candide for help and Monique comes up with the suggestion that he escape by leaving with the Hitler Youth unit. When Jean-Jacques Hatt returns the next morning to collect the woollen goods, Monique manages to get more details out of him about their forthcoming trip. Later, Marcel brings a bus driver's uniform for Curtis and the news that the Germans have begun to search the city. Andrée is distressed when she observes Albert and Monique go into his bedroom together. Everyone says goodbye to Curtis, and he and Lisa share a kiss before he leaves. Curtis is accepted as the bus driver and the vehicle is cleared for exit at the city perimeter checkpoint. Hatt thinks that he has seen Curtis somewhere before and becomes more suspicious of him as the journey continues. Andrée tries out her wheelchair and attempts to get out of it just as troops arrive to search the Candide. Andrée falls down the stairs and breaks her neck. Curtis drives the bus to a checkpoint on the Swiss frontier. While Hatt demands that the border guard put a call through to Kessler, and the other boys get off the bus to stretch their legs, Curtis gets back on the bus and drives it through the checkpoint at high speed. Kessler and Reinecke learn about Curtis's escape. Alain brings news to the Candide that Curtis is in Switzerland. Lisa reminds them all that now that the search is over and the phones are back on, Lifeline is back in business.

REVIEW: John Brason brings the first series to an end with a gripping and ingenious storyline which is full of incident and intrigue. The episode brings several long-running plotlines to such a definite and satisfactory close that it is obvious that this instalment was scripted well before *Secret Army*'s future was assured.

The incredibly long episode title had been one that John Brason had always wanted to use. During the rehearsals for this episode, he explained to the cast – some of whom were confused by the meaning – that it referred to the kind of ideals and vision that the Nazis instilled into the boys of the Hitler Youth. Certainly Jean-Jacques Hatt has a manner that suggests that he is just such a kid. His motivation and activities for the new Europe are far more disturbing than they otherwise would be, because of his young age. As Albert states, Hatt and his unit are "bloody silly fools" but due to their affiliation to the German authorities he knows that they are bloody dangerous fools too, which is why they are given the run of the Candide when they first call for woollens for the Eastern Front.

180

Although the idea of this unit and its endeavours for the Third Reich certainly makes for uncomfortable viewing, the overall effect is somewhat diluted by the slightly wooden performance of Adam Richens, who gives the impression that he had such difficulty learning his lines that there was no time for him to be advised as to how to put some emotion behind them. At least Richens is far more imposing than his fellow young Nazis, who are wet and thin-legged weaklings to a man. The action even recognises this at one point, when Curtis has to advise one of the pathetic individuals to go to the toilet behind a tree! It is intelligent plotting which makes the Hitler Youth boys, of whom Kessler is so proud, the weak link in the chain. That Reinecke recalls the Führer's own (suddenly resonant) words at a youth rally – "Into the hands of our children we place the destiny of Germany" – is also a clever touch.

Just before this episode went into the studio Michael Culver had an attack of appendicitis, which is why Michael Wynne was drafted in to play Sturmbannführer Reinecke alongside Kessler. Unfortunately it is apparent that Reinecke is delivering dialogue that was originally intended for Major Brandt. His early line to Kessler: "It was our agreement was it not?" is particularly Brandt-like, as is his humanitarian assurance to Van Maas that his family will come to no harm: "I give you my word." Despite the fact that it is a shame that Brandt is not around to witness the denouement of the Moreelse storyline, it is a relief that the production team decided to make his replacement a member of the Gestapo rather than another Luftwaffe man. However, it seems surprising that no dialogue was inserted to explain the Major's absence, nor any change made to the line which incorrectly suggests that Reinecke has been on the trail of Moreelse, with Kessler, for some time. Despite his absence from the episode, Culver's name still appears in the opening credits.

Another notable absentee is Dr Keldermans, who also appears to have been replaced here by a nameless carbon copy when – presumably due to Valentine Dyall's unavailability – a Belgian doctor comes to the Candide to see Andrée. As we learned in *Suspicions* that Keldermans is supposed to know everything about Andrée's condition, that this new doctor has been called in at all and especially that he is going to arrange her overnight visit to St Xaviers is both odd and inconsistent.

The episode's chief highlight is the dramatisation of Monique's brilliant, if off-the-wall, plan to get Curtis out of Brussels via the Hitler Youth bus trip. Albert's awe-inspired reaction to her perilous idea is shared by the viewer. Yet, against the odds, Curtis of course makes it in the end and his action-packed exit over the Swiss border couldn't be a more fitting departure for the impulsive British agent. One obvious plot hole is the fact that it would have been far more sensible for Lifeline to just send Curtis down the Line once his cover was blown, rather than agreeing to his idea to initially hide elsewhere in Brussels. However, this approach would of course have made for a far duller exit for the character.

Although the way Curtis is written out is great, his final scene with Lisa is less effective than it might have been, primarily because it is difficult to believe in their relationship. The "I am part of you just as you are part of me" dialogue, in particular, does not quite ring true, especially as they have only recently reached a better understanding of each other. If anything, Curtis appears to have more of a genuine and knowing connection with Monique than he does Lisa. She certainly seems to understand him better and trusted him well before her colleagues started to follow her lead.

Several innovative and memorable visuals add both class and suspense to the proceedings. The shot in which a map of Brussels is shown superimposed with Curtis's hunted face is particularly effective, as is the repetition of Andrée's view in her wardrobe mirror of Albert and Monique as they go into his bedroom together. However, director Viktors Ritelis saves the best for last, as the picture moves out in stages from the forms of the perfectly still Monique and the despairing Albert as they sit at the foot of the stairs with Andrée's crumpled body between them (although it is arguable that the addition of a lightning strike to the scene is overdoing things a little). As usual, Ritelis is just as interested in the audio soundtrack as in the visuals and adds into the mix elements such as a beating drum and the distorted sound of a blaring radio at the city perimeter, both of which heighten the suspense considerably.

In what is to be her final episode, Eileen Page once again absolutely delivers as Andrée. Her reactions to the terrifying deterioration of her eyesight and the confirmation that Albert and Monique are definitely lovers are distressing to watch and cannot help but engender sympathy. Nevertheless, it is something of a relief to see Andrée killed off, mainly because it means that Albert and Monique are finally free of her crippling hold and may even have an opportunity of a future together.

One of the episode's guest characters, the Belgian police sergeant Marcel, played by Mark Jones, is an interesting addition to proceedings. He appears to be a person who Lifeline has counted on before, but this is his first appearance. From Series Two, almost exactly the same role would be taken by the character of Inspector Paul Delon, albeit irregularly, while Jones himself was cast in an entirely different role.

Now that he finally has the long sought-after British agent in his sights, Kessler clearly relishes the chase. He almost savours the inevitable outcome of the interrogation of Emil Van Maas, especially the opportunity to make him feel even more belittled and distraught by telling him to sit when there is no seat available. Unlike Reinecke, he also offers no guarantee that his family will remain safe if he cooperates. However, as is often the case with Kessler, it is his pride – this time in the rewarded Hitler Youth unit, whom he makes the only exception to his great search of Brussels – which ultimately causes his plan to fail. The news of Curtis's escape is seen to hit Kessler hard: first he removes his glasses and rubs his eyes and, after Reinecke's exit, he walks over to the map of Brussels, turns out the light and stands silently in the darkness. It is a compelling scene, cleverly enhanced by a pervasive air raid siren, which ably emphasises both Kessler's weariness and his dejection at his failure.

The episode's final scene serves as a coda to the first series and sees the principal members of Lifeline outside the Candide in the Rue Deschanel, which we see more of than usual, courtesy of an effective matte painting. Although the scene serves the purpose of wrapping up both the Curtis and Andrée storylines through the reactions of the regulars, its main aim is to remind the viewer that, despite all that has happened, the dangerous work of Lifeline must go on. As Lisa says: "We're back in business, don't let's forget that." Her final line before she retreats back inside the Candide: "I think we could have a busy night," is delivered heavenward and echoes the scene at the end of the very first episode, in which Albert also looks up to the night sky from the Candide's doorway. An awful lot has happened between these two moments, but only one thing has remained absolutely constant: the fact that as long as the war rages on, Allied airmen will continue to be shot down and they will continue to need Lifeline's help.

HISTORICAL BACKGROUND

Serments de la Jeunesse Rexiste

The youth movement which Jean-Jacques Hatt and his young Belgian friends are members of is not the Hitler Youth as such but an affiliated voluntary organisation called the *Serments de la Jeunesse Rexiste*, which was the youth branch of the Rexist Party. From 1941, the Rexist Party, founded by Catholic fascist Leon Degrelle, was one of just two Belgian political parties that were authorised by the Nazis. The *Serments* youth movement was open to boys and girls aged between six and eighteen, with the boys' uniform consisting of dark shorts and green shirts with a white Burgundian Cross on a green shield on the left breast-pocket.

Artur Axmann

Artur Axmann, who is referred to in this episode, was born in 1913 and joined the Hitler Youth movement in 1928, five years before Hitler came to power. Axmann impressed his Nazi superiors due to his notable recruitment efforts and by 1932 was called to Berlin to join the national leadership of the Hitler Youth. After serving on the Western Front at the start of the war, Hitler appointed him overall leader of the Hitler Youth in 1940. During a visit to the Eastern Front in 1942 he lost an arm, but this did not deter him from ordering his members into combat on behalf of the Reich. At the close of the war, Axmann was stationed in Hitler's  bunker in Berlin when Hitler and Eva Braun chose to commit suicide and in 1949 he testified that he was the last person to see the couple alive. As the Russians advanced on Berlin, Axmann, like many other survivors of the bunker, attempted to find a way through their lines, and claimed that he saw Martin Bormann's dead body en route and that, given his apparent lack of wounds, he must have taken a cyanide capsule. After the war, Axmann was sentenced to a three-year prison term but was judged to have served out his punishment during his detention prior to the 1949 trial. Axmann subsequently took up a career as a sales representative. He died aged 83 in 1996 and, to avoid his tomb becoming a Neo-Nazi shrine, was buried at a secret location.

WHERE ELSE HAVE I SEEN..?

© Michael Balfre

Michael Wynne (Reinecke)

Jacques, *Manhunt*, 1970
Fat Boy, *Ace of Wands: The Mind Robbers*, 1970
Gestapo Man, *Colditz: Missing, Presumed Dead*, 1972
Dieter Gisevius, *Cold Warrior: Bright Sting*, 1984
Mr Wishaw, *Doc Martin: Happily Ever After*, 2007

Mark Farmer (Brusse)

Gary Hargreaves, *Grange Hill*, 1979-81
Page Boy, *Partners in Crime: The Man in the Mist*, 1983
Eric, *Dramarama: Jack and the Computer*, 1983
Benjamin Partridge, *Mister Corbett's Ghost*, 1987
Justin James, *Minder*, 1989

'I think it stands up extraordinarily well today and I feel nostalgic for that quality of drama and for the passion with which it was made and played.'

JULIET HAMMOND-HILL

SERIES TWO
(1978)

REGULAR CAST

Albert Foiret
BERNARD HEPTON

Monique Duchamps
ANGELA RICHARDS

Sturmbannführer Ludwig Kessler
CLIFFORD ROSE

Major Erwin Brandt
MICHAEL CULVER

Natalie Chantrens
JULIET HAMMOND-HILL

Max Brocard
STEPHEN YARDLEY

Alain Muny
RON PEMBER

Madeleine Duclos
HAZEL McBRIDE

Dr Pascal Keldermans
VALENTINE DYALL

François
NIGEL WILLIAMS

Hans van Broecken
GUNNAR MÖLLER

Lena van Broecken
MARIANNE STONE

Inspector Paul Delon
JOHN D. COLLINS

Estelle Muny
JEAN RIMMER

Corporal Veit Rennert
ROBIN LANGFORD

CREW

Producer
GERARD GLAISTER

Script Editor
JOHN BRASON

Technical Advisor
GRP CPT WILLIAM RANDLE CBE AFC DFM

Writers
N. J. CRISP (1, 4, 8)
JOHN BRASON (2, 10, 13)
ROBERT BARR (3, 11)
DAVID CRANE (5, 9)
JAMES ANDREW HALL (6)
PAUL ANNETT (7)
GERARD GLAISTER (12)

Directors
TERENCE DUDLEY (1, 4, 9, 10, 13*)
PAUL ANNETT (2, 7)
VIKTORS RITELIS (3, 5)
ROGER JENKINS (6, 11)
MICHAEL E. BRIANT (8, 12)
[*Uncredited]

Designers
AUSTIN RUDDY (1, 6, 9, 11 studio)
RAY LONDON (2, 7, 13)
PAUL MUNTING (3, 5, 8, 12)
NIGEL CURZON (4),
MARJORIE PRATT (10, 11 film)

Production Assistants
JEAN ESSLEMONT (1, 4, 9)
TONY VIRGO (2, 7)
RONALD JONES (3, 5, 8, 12)
LIZ MACE (6, 11)
PHILLIP HILL (10, 13)

Production Unit Manager
JOHN FABIAN

Costume Designers
RICHARD WINTER (1-5, 7, 9)
PRUE HANDLEY (6, 8, 10-13)

Make-Up Artist
MARION RICHARDS

Film Cameramen
KEN WESTBURY (1-5, 7, 9)
JOHN SENNETT (7, 9)
GODFREY JOHNSON (6, 8, 11-13)

Film Recordist
BASIL HARRIS

Film Editors
M. A. C. ADAMS (1-5)
ALISTAIR MACKAY (6, 8, 11-13)
HOWARD BILLINGHAM (7)
LES FILBY (9)

Studio Lighting
PETER WINN (1-5, 7, 9)
ALAN HORNE (6, 8, 10-13)

Studio Sound
LAURIE TAYLOR (1)
FRANK RADCLIFFE (2, 5, 6-10, 12)
KEITH GUNN (3, 4, 11, 13)

Videotape Editor
STEVE MURRAY

Title Design
ALAN JEAPES

Theme Music
ROBERT FARNON

Original songs for series composed by
ANGELA RICHARDS
LESLIE OSBORNE
KEN MOULE

SERIES 2 - PRODUCTION

New Premise(s)

By the time that the final episode of the first series of *Secret Army* was transmitted (on 28 December 1977), its creator and producer, Gerard Glaister, and script editor and principal scriptwriter, John Brason, were already thoroughly immersed in the pre-production process for its second series – the BBC having given the green light some weeks earlier – in order that they would have time to produce the new series for broadcast from the following September.

As the first series aired, although Glaister was pleased with – and to a large extent proud of – his new creation, he was not entirely convinced that it was working as well as it could. Firstly, he harboured particular concerns about his cast of characters, feeling that some were in danger of becoming rather one-dimensional, while others had not worked out as he had envisaged. Secondly, he felt that the first run had not always achieved the levels of tension and suspense that he had sought to be an integral element of the series from the outset.

Bernard Hepton and Gerry Glaister
© Joan Glaister

Glaister believed that one particular first series episode provided a clue to the resolution of this latter problem. The episode in question was the N. J. Crispen-penned *Suspicions*, which had, for the first time, brought the leading German characters into direct contact with the agents of Lifeline, as the former investigated Curtis's involvement in the murder of Hugh Neville. The episode's extra level of danger and excitement arguably arose from the fact that Brandt and Kessler were closer than ever to uncovering the evasion line they were so

191

desperate to extinguish. This being the case, Glaister postulated that clearly the only way to maintain such levels of unbearable tension was to have the two opposing camps of characters cross each other's paths more regularly, and if at all possible, constantly. As there could be no justifiable reason in the second series for Brandt and Kessler to continue to pay frequent visits to what was essentially a working-class backstreet café, Glaister realised that the perfect solution was to have Albert and company open a new restaurant instead, specifically intended to cater for senior German officers, and thus the 'high-class Candide' was born. The new Candide would provide ample opportunity for all of the series's characters to interact and play off each other and, due to the fact that Lifeline would now be operating right under the noses of their enemies, for levels of suspense to be cranked up several further notches. Clifford Rose recalls the fact that the Germans did not know that the Candide staff were the enemy: "We thought they were just friendly Belgians – collaborators," but conversely "they knew we were the enemy and this added a huge *frisson* to the series."

Glaister's solution also made complete sense in terms of the ongoing narrative: Albert could afford to upgrade to new premises due to the monetary assistance he received from London for Lifeline's evasion work, a situation that also fitted neatly with the restaurateur's personal ambitions; while the move towards more open collaboration with the Germans, thereby providing better cover for their clandestine operations, was a natural evolution of the strategy that had already been adopted by Albert and his team at the old Candide (as first explored in *Second Chance*).

The new setup also provided several other highly successful payoffs, all of which would quickly come to define the revamped series: the chance to explore the black market activities necessary to keep a restaurant of this nature in business during the war; the need for a chanteuse to provide sophisticated entertainment to its clientele (a role for which there was already a very obvious candidate within the cast); but perhaps most importantly, the opportunity to get to know the German characters' off-duty personas. Indeed, as Clifford Rose recalls: "Kessler would sometimes appear in the restaurant in a suit rather than uniform, just like an ordinary private citizen." All in all, it was a decision that Bernard Hepton believes 'added immeasurably to the drama' and which, given its knock-on effect on all aspects of the series, could arguably be considered a stroke of genius on Glaister's part.

And it's goodbye from...

Although the new Candide was set to resolve one of the creator's major problems with the first series, his issues with the series's cast of characters would prove to be a more difficult prospect. One such issue had already led him, in consultation with Brason, to decide to have the character of John Curtis written out during the first series finale. Although Glaister had always admired Christopher Neame's work – after all, he had cast him in *Secret Army* due to his earlier performance in *Colditz* – during the course of the first series he had not always felt that the character of Curtis fitted entirely comfortably into the narrative. In some respects, as the audience now identified with the 'English-speaking' Lifeline regulars as closely as if they were British, a designated British character was surplus to requirements. Furthermore, Glaister had always considered Curtis to be inextricably linked with the central character of Lisa, seeing them as a pair (although they only finally declared their mutual feelings for each other in *Be The First Kid in Your Block to Rule the World*), and it so happened that Lisa was the other character with whom he was not entirely satisfied.

As with Christopher Neame, although Glaister considered Jan Francis to be a

good actress (having also cast her due to his familiarity with her work), he was not convinced that her character should continue into the second series with the same level of prominence. However, given that Lisa was inspired by Dédée and was therefore an entirely authentic creation, he was a little more reluctant to let her go. One obvious explanation for the need for her removal from the narrative is the way in which the distribution of power within Lifeline had been depicted thus far. The ostensible fact that Lisa is the head of the evasion organisation is increasingly undermined as the first series progresses, due to the emergence of Albert as the true wielder of power. It is Albert who takes the most important decisions and often overrules or ignores the 'nominal' leadership of Lisa, making her presence superfluous. Her role in the narrative aside, there is also the possibility that Glaister felt Francis was miscast in the part, something which he never went on record as saying (unlike director Viktors Ritelis, who ventured this opinion in his 2004 retrospective documentary on the series, *Remembering Secret Army)*.

Interestingly, there is divided opinion as to how Jan Francis actually came to be written out of the series. Before his death, Glaister recalled that it was always his plan to have Lisa exit the second series very early on, however Francis herself remembers the turn of events quite differently. As they had done on the first series, Glaister and Brason had prepared notes on the intended background storyline for the second series, including their plans for Lisa, and in late Autumn 1977 sent this document out to prospective writers. However, what they hadn't counted on was that one of the prospective writers was known to Jan Francis and decided to show her the document. Therein, Francis learnt that Glaister and Brason planned to have Lisa suffer a serious nervous breakdown, before being gradually withdrawn from the main action of the series (incidentally a fate that would befall Emily Richard's Clare Martel in LWT's wartime drama, *Enemy at the Door*, as it went into its second series). Francis decided that she had no intention of "spending a year of her life playing out a nervous breakdown," especially as she considered the development to be "at odds with the strong and independent Lisa." Francis sought a meeting with Glaister during which she requested that her character be granted a quick but dramatic exit from the series instead. Her wish was granted and Lisa's tragic death, during a bombing raid over Saint Nazaire, was written in to the opening episode of the second series – N. J. Crisp's *The Hostage* – providing arguably the most shocking finale to any episode thus far. Her ironic death, killed during an Allied air-raid, was entirely in keeping with Comète Line history, although this was not the end of Dédée but of one of her most trusted colleagues instead: Baron Jean 'Nemo' Griendl.

The Hostage was constructed in such a way as to confine Francis's involvement to telecine sequences only, filmed in April 1976, so that the actress would not have to return for the first rehearsal and studio recording block as well. Although Francis had very much enjoyed her time on the series, she was nevertheless quite happy to be moving on to new projects. In the years immediately after *Secret Army*, she would play Mina van Helsing in a new film version of *Dracula* (1979) and Susie Dean in the LWT musical drama series *The Good Companions* (1980). A few years later she would take on the role with which she will forever be associated: the snooty but lovable Penny Warrender, opposite Paul Nicholas's unreliable Vince Pinner, in John Sullivan's romantic situation comedy *Just Good Friends* (1983-6).

As Lisa would no longer be part of the series, the production team decided not to ask Maria Charles to return to play her Aunt Louise, despite the fact that Lisa's funeral would form part of the action of the second episode, *Russian Roulette* (albeit off screen). Charles's immediate post-*Secret Army* work included the role of Madge in the *Upstairs Downstairs* spin-off *Thomas and Sarah* (1979) and as interfering mother, Bea Fisher in the Maureen Lipman sitcom *Agony* (1979-81).

Another character who would not be returning was Timothy Morand's Jacques Bol, a rather ancillary character in the first series, who had played his most significant role in *Identity in Doubt* and had been seen little since. His sudden absence is never explained in the series, but John Brason took the opportunity to write him out of the action in his second *Secret Army* novel, *Secret Army Dossier*, in a between series-set chapter 'Pastures New', in which he is killed while assisting a British agent – who had agreed to help finance the new Candide – to escape by Lysander.

As they had also done with Curtis, Glaister and Brason had already elected to dispense with the character of Andrée Foiret at the end of the first series. The most significant knock-on effect of her death is that Albert and Monique are freed from the debilitating love triangle of which they have been a part since the series began. However, the production team felt that the idea that Albert would immediately marry Monique did not ring true and decided instead to present him inventing new reasons for not committing fully to his lover, a storyline that would ultimately run far longer than that of the initial love triangle.

Increased Prominence

Of all the returning Lifeline regulars, all of whom would enjoy increased prominence due to the absence of Curtis and Lisa, it was perhaps Angela Richards who would benefit the most from the significant changes that Glaister had wrought. However, as Richards recalls today, she was partly responsible for pushing this development herself. She remembers that she was, as she modestly puts it, "always fiddling with bits of paper and music and writing lyrics down," and after working on the first series for a short time it came to her that she could write a song for the series that would be in keeping with both the period setting and the series's atmosphere. As a result, she decided to go and see Glaister to tell him about her proposal for the inclusion of a song that was "very 'in the time',' having come up with 'Memories Come Gently (Back to  Me)'. After hearing Richards sing it, Glaister decided that it should definitely be included in the series and it eventually ended up being used for the wedding sequence towards the end of *Second Chance*, albeit with an accordion rather than

195

piano accompaniment. Richards subsequently told Glaister that she had several other ideas for some more original compositions that could feature in the series. By this time, she had teamed up with composer and jazz pianist Ken Moule, who she had first worked with on the musical *Cole* at the Mermaid Theatre in 1974, and together the pair came up with 'Velvet Blue' and 'Snow Time'. She would also write (with Leslie Osborne) 'I Bet You've Heard This One Before' and 'If This is the Last Time I See You', which along with 'Memories Come Gently' would become her most popular compositions. Although Glaister felt there was no room for any more songs in the first series, he was not about to let Richards's creativity go to waste – indeed, it is entirely possible that when he came to conceive of his new high-class Candide, he was partly encouraged in this direction by the availability in the cast of a chanteuse to sing in it, complete with her own collection of stunningly evocative compositions. Aside from her increased screen time as a vocalist, Glaister and Brason recognised that Richards's acting talents could also be better utilised – they had been particularly impressed with her performance in *A Question of Loyalty* – and as a result elected to put Monique in the centre of the action much more than she had been previously, going out 'into the field' in the episodes *Trapped* and *Little Old Lady*, and eventually making operational decisions about the Line (*Day of Wrath*).

Although Bernard Hepton had always been the series's ostensible lead, the absence of Lisa and Curtis would also give the character of Albert more room to develop. Method-actor Hepton was very keen to give a more detailed study of this complex restaurateur, and the new scripts, which brought Albert's motivations and moral code under the spotlight, would certainly allow him more opportunities to do this.

Natalie's role in proceedings would also be expanded. While Juliet Hammond-Hill had only been contracted for eleven of the sixteen episodes of the first series, she would appear in every episode of the second series and, due to her new status as Lifeline's principal guide, her character would regularly take centre-stage, most notably in *Lucky Piece* and *A Matter of Life and Death*. Although it was planned that Ron Pember's Alain would still only appear in just over half the episodes of the second series (just as he had done on the first series), he nevertheless would have far more to do when he was on screen, with his finest hours (thus far) coming in the penultimate episode *Prisoner of War* and the finale *Day of Wrath*.

New Characters

As well as giving more screen time to the regulars they had retained, Glaister and Brason also elected to write new characters into the series whose presence would offer a new angle on existing characters; specifically to combat Glaister's fears that several of them were in danger of becoming too stereotypical and limited in scope. It was a fear that was shared by several cast members, and none more so than Clifford Rose, who was keen that Kessler did not become just another "nasty Nazi" – something that he would have found "very boring" to portray. Partway

196

through recording of the first series, he had realised that "there was a need at some point to take this character further, by taking him into an area that had not yet been shown." As the first series was broadcast, Rose's wife, Celia, commented to her husband that if *Secret Army* returned she thought it would be dramatically interesting if Kessler was shown to have a relationship with a girlfriend or mistress. Funnily enough, Glaister and Brason were already on the same wavelength, writing just such a character into the series: Madeleine Duclos.

MADELEINE DUCLOS

Age: 31

- Slim, attractive and elegant Belgian woman.
- Lives in a one-bedroom apartment near the Gare du Midi.
- Her father was a well-to-do banker who after involvement in a fraud scandal committed suicide in 1934.
- The family home was sold to pay off his debts. Her mother died soon afterwards.
- She fell in love with the wealthy but married Baron Christian D'Aquise, and the pair were lovers for several years.
- The Baron planned to divorce and marry Madeleine but was prevented from doing so by his Catholic family. Even the Belgian royal family opposed the match.
- The affair was broken off and a condition of her receiving from his family a weekly allowance on which to live is that it stops if they ever meet.
- She has not yet recovered from losing the Baron and has become distraught, listless and even uninterested in her own future.
- When she meets Kessler she is a shadow of her former self and no longer worried about what people think of her.
- She has as little real contact with people as possible and lives inside her own head until events jolt her out of it.

Clifford Rose would later describe Madeleine's introduction as both "perfect" and "the making of the character," because it allowed him to show Kessler when he was off duty: "It brought out his private side. I think people exist as public personae and also as private individuals and what makes big powerful public figures interesting is how they are in their private life and that's what that did." Glaister and Brason hoped that this new angle might actually prompt the audience to consider the initially unthinkable: whether they could actually feel sympathy for the series's ostensible villain. Due to his previous research at the Imperial War Museum, Rose knew that, despite the fact that the Gestapo and SS officers were able to go out and do extraordinarily inhumane things in the name of their country, men such as Kessler were often purportedly warm and affectionate family men (which perhaps demonstrates just how disfigured they were as human beings). Kessler, therefore, would also be depicted as showing genuine affection and tenderness towards Madeleine.

Kessler would not be alone in gaining a partner – in fact, Glaister and Brason elected to give pretty much all of the regular characters someone to love and therefore potentially someone to lose as well, not only in order to flesh out their characters further, but also to heighten the series's dramatic stakes. Aside from Madeleine, Brandt's wife, Erika, would be introduced: a General's daughter, in whom the Major would notice a distinct change since they were last together, who wants to bring their two children to Brussels and live with him there. Natalie would gain a boyfriend: the naïve and bookish François, a student with little grasp of the huge dangers involved in the work that she undertakes. Natalie would also be reunited with her honorary Aunt and Uncle, Hans and Lena van Broecken, as the production team felt that their characters had worked very well when they first appeared in *Second Chance*. They would return on two further occasions in the second series, in *Scorpion* and *Weekend*. Alain, meanwhile, would gain a whole family: a wife Estelle, a younger brother Gil – who essentially runs the farm in order that Alain can carry out his work for Lifeline – and two children, an unnamed boy and girl (in the untransmitted *What Did You Do in the War, Daddy?* they would appear again as adults, named Etienne and Louise). In the series finale, a character is also introduced who Alain considers to be one of his best friends: André De Beers. We even learn that Dr Keldermans has a wife, although we are never introduced to her.

Brason and Glaister also decided to swell the ranks of the Lifeline regulars by creating one major new character, who was intended to have a significant impact on the events of the second series and specifically on the ongoing operation of the evasion line: Max Brocard.

MAX BROCARD

Age: 36

- An orphan.
- Max Brocard is not his real name but an assumed alias.
- Max's tough upbringing has made him quick-witted and well-versed in expedient action and self-preservation.
- Albert crossed paths with him before he was called Brocard.
- He is a talented forger and pianist.
- Before the war, he spent three years in a Belgian prison.
- He was called up on the outbreak of war and deserted four weeks later. He rejoined before the Germans invaded and promoted himself to Lieutenant.
- After being taken prisoner by the Germans at Fort Eben-Emael he was moved to a prisoner of war camp in Silesia. He escaped by forging his own set of release documents, and returned to Brussels.
- It is due to Inspector Delon's intercession that Max is first brought to the Candide.

- He has sworn allegiance to the Communist Party (a fact he will strive to keep from his new Lifeline colleagues) as he feels it gives him a purpose and a place in the world.
- His function within Lifeline is to forge documents. He is also employed as Monique's piano player.

Since the death of Gaston Colbert in *Too Near Home*, Lifeline had somehow gone without a forger (or at least we do not hear who is forging their documents during this period); Max, with his dubious criminal past, would now fulfil this function. Less significantly, he would also prove adept at 'tickling the ivories', so his cover for being at the new Candide was as Monique's piano player. His skills aside, Max would quickly be revealed to the viewer to be motivated by his fervently Communist beliefs, as he ultimately seeks a way to increase his standing in the Party by gaining a cell of his own, via total betrayal of his Lifeline colleagues. From this point on, the Communist threat to Lifeline would become a key component of *Secret Army*. That Albert and co. would now face threats on not just one, but two fronts, was once again down to Glaister's wish to considerably 'up the ante' in line with his view of the series, first and foremost, as a thriller. The surname Brocard was suggested by Bill Randle, after Father Brocard, the Prior who helped him while he was on the run in Belgium.

Another semi-regular new character would essentially fulfil the same role as did Mark Jones's Belgian Police Sergeant Marcel in the Series One finale: Inspector Paul Delon, a patriot whose information would occasionally prove vital in keeping Lifeline one step ahead of their enemies. Mark Jones, meanwhile, would return in a new role as Brandt's friend Oberst Manfred Neidlinger.

The Writers

When it came to commissioning scripts for the second series, Glaister and Brason principally turned to those writers who had already proved that they understood the nature and style of the show through their work on the first series. Glaister's long-term collaborator N. J. Crisp was invited to submit three scripts, including the crucial opening instalment, *The Hostage*. On the strength of *Too Near Home*, Robert Barr was approached to provide two more highly suspenseful scripts: *Lucky Piece* and *A Matter of Life and Death*, while James Andrew Hall was commissioned to script the return of the Van Broeckens, who he had created for his first series episode, *Second Chance*. The other Series Two script to feature these characters, *Weekend*, would be written by none other than director Paul Annett, who had directed their first series debut. Brason himself would script two instalments, including the jam-packed series finale, *Day of Wrath*, while Gerard Glaister would contribute the first of his two episodes for the series, scripting the penultimate episode, *Prisoner of War*.

David Crane

The only invited scriptwriter who had not already worked on the series, was David Crane, who would be commissioned to pen two episodes: *Not According to Plan* and *Little Old Lady*. Crane began his career working for Yorkshire Television, script editing: Gerald Harper drama *Hadleigh* (1969-76); *Castle Haven* (1969), a soap set on the Yorkshire coast which concerned the residents of two large Victorian houses which had been converted into flats; and the historical children's drama series *The Flaxton Boys* (1969-73) for which he also supplied scripts. He would later script edit and write for *Emmerdale Farm* which like *Castle Haven* had been created by Kevin Laffan. Just prior to working on *Secret Army*, he also wrote several episodes of another long-running soap, *Coronation Street*.

Directors

While the series's thirteen scripts – making a more typical quarter-year broadcast run than the previous series's sixteen – were being prepared, Glaister began to recruit directors for the new series. Both Paul Annett and Viktors Ritelis agreed to return albeit at a vastly reduced workload of two episodes each, although Annett would also be taking on the aforementioned scriptwriting duties for *Weekend*.

Terence Dudley

© Denis Lill

Approached to be the second series's 'lead' director, helming five episodes in total, including the important opening instalment as well as the finale, was the experienced Terence (Terry) Dudley. In accepting this role, Dudley (left) was casting aside his more familiar producer mantle. In the years immediately prior to *Secret Army*, he had produced all three series of the challenging post-apocalypse drama *Survivors* (1975-7) which had had more than its fair share of behind-the-scenes wrangling. As a result, it was quite possible that he was keen to take a much-needed break from shouldering a whole series almost alone (Dudley started out as a writer and therefore did not have a script editor on *Survivors* due to his insistence that he could rework the scripts himself).

Before Dudley began his long association with the BBC in the late Fifties, when his script for a comedy drama – *Song in a Strange Land* – was accepted, he had been Director of Production at the Grand Theatre Swansea.

Dudley's first BBC productions as a director were the police drama *Charlesworth* and the anthology series *The Nightwatchman's Stories* in 1959. His first producer credits were in the same year, on: *Break in Festivities*, a drama about a couple from the West Indies adjusting to life in England; and the second series of the Scotland Yard undercover drama *The Men from Room 13* (the first series having been produced by Glaister). Dudley went on to produce and direct the Francis Durbridge adventure series *The World of Tim Frazer* (1960-1) with Jack Hedley as the eponymous hero, and the popular six-part science fiction serial *The Big Pull* (1962). After scripting the well-received thriller *The River Flows East* (1962), Dudley worked for Glaister for the first time on the wartime series *Moonstrike*, directing several episodes in 1963. Further producer credits followed, on *Cluff* (1964-5), a drama about a plodding Yorkshire detective, for which he also regularly directed; *The Mask of Janus* (1965), a thriller set in the fictional European country of Amalia; and the second series of the drama *The First Lady* (1969) with Thora Hird. Dudley would subsequently score his biggest hits thus far, producing the ground-breaking science-fact drama *Doomwatch* (1970-2), on which he would also make many directorial and scriptwriting contributions; and the historical military series *The Regiment* (1972-3).

Before beginning work on *Survivors* in 1975, Dudley would direct for Glaister twice more: firstly on three episodes of the second series of *Colditz*, including the opening instalment, *Arrival of a Hero*, and the chilling *Odd Man In*, which guest starred Ian McCulloch (an assignment that led him to select McCulloch as one of the leads in *Survivors*); and secondly on two episodes of *Oil Strike North*. Given the frequency with which Glaister sought Dudley's direction in the mid-Seventies, coupled with the fact that he knew how reliable and adept he was at directing drama for him, it is likely that he would have asked him to direct on *Secret Army*'s first series had he not been busy producing the final series of *Survivors* at the time.

Film cameraman Godfrey Johnson recalls that, when it came to the location filming Dudley, who had a German wife and was therefore *au fait* with the language, would also often take an uncredited part in proceedings, providing voiceovers for German guards!

Roger Jenkins

Following on from the tradition of approaching former *Poldark* directors to work on the series (Ives and Annett had both worked on its first series), Glaister asked Roger Jenkins, who had worked on the successful second series of the Cornish-set drama, to direct two episodes.

Jenkins had begun his television career in the Fifties, joining Associated Rediffusion just three months before the launch of ITV in 1955, going on to put out three different programmes in its first week. As a staff director he worked on a variety of women's, children's and schools' programmes and for the drama department. For the latter he helmed episodes of the crime series *Murder Bag* (1957-8) and its successors, *Crime Sheet* (1959) and *No Hiding Place* (in 1960),

© David Clarke

all of which featured the character DCS Lockhart. In 1959 he also directed a notable version of *Twelfth Night* in the *For Schools* afternoon slot. After resigning from Associated Rediffusion, Jenkins had spells in theatre in Leatherhead and Coventry, and directed several episodes of *The Avengers* for ABC in 1961 (*Double Danger* and *Kill the King*) and his first series for the BBC – *Compact* and *Z Cars* – in 1962-3. Like Terence Dudley, Jenkins would also first work for Glaister on *Moonstrike*. As well as more theatre work at the Bristol Old Vic and RADA, the Sixties also saw television credits for Jenkins, which included Scottish drama *This Man Craig* (in 1966), the popular adventure serial *Adam Adamant Lives!* (1966-7), numerous episodes of the oil drama *Mogul/The Troubleshooters* (between 1965-71) which he worked on with his great friend Peter Graham Scott and enjoyed immensely, the BBC anthology series *Out of the Unknown* (in 1968), and drama series *The Borderers* (1969) which was produced by another personal friend, Anthony Coburn.

In the early Seventies, he directed episodes of *Softly, Softly* (in 1970), *The Onedin Line* (in 1972 and 1973) and episodes of the Thames daytime soap *Harriet's Back in Town* (in 1973). After directing several episodes of *Warship* (see Michael E. Briant section below) in 1974 and 1976, he would return to a maritime subject when he produced the anthology series *Sea Tales* (1977) for BBC Bristol. His work on *Poldark* was on four episodes of the hugely popular second series, which aired at the same time as the first series of *Secret Army*.

Michael E. Briant

Glaister's third and final new director was Michael E. Briant who had an incredibly varied and full CV and a reputation as an excellent 'action' director, capable of producing impressive action sequences on meagre budgets.

Briant had started out in front of the camera as a child actor, working extensively in theatre, film and television throughout the Fifties ultimately under the name Michael Tennant (so he would not be confused with actor Michael Bryant). Perhaps his most notable role was as Paul in the BAFTA-nominated film *True as a Turtle*, directed by Wendy Toye in 1957. Briant spent the money he earned from this feature on a Palliard Bolex 8mm cine camera, a purchase which contributed to his move behind the camera.[1]

Leaving acting behind, Briant joined the BBC drama department in 1962 as an Assistant Floor Manager. After progressing to Production Assistant in 1964, a post which incorporated a significant amount of time on early series of *Doctor*

Who, Briant took the BBC's directors' course in 1966 and was subsequently able to direct on a freelance basis, helming episodes of drama series such as *The Newcomers* (in 1967) and *The Doctors* (in 1968/9), while keeping his PA post. On his final return to *Doctor Who*, before becoming a director, he created the Doctor's legendary sonic screwdriver as a cost-cutting measure! Around this time, Briant started to use the initial letter of his middle name on his credits. He explains: 'The E in Michael E. Briant came about because of the same problem I had as a child actor and changed my name to Tennant, the actor Michael Bryant was much more famous than me. He started to get phone calls about his directing abilities and I started to get letters and calls from his fans! Michael Bryant's correspondence was much more interesting than mine but none the less I decided to insert my E initial, which stands for Edwin, into my credits.'[2]

With the support of the BBC Head of Drama, Ronnie Marsh, who gave him several directing engagements, Briant became a full-time freelance director in 1970. After directing several episodes of *Z Cars*, Briant renewed his acquaintance with *Doctor Who* by directing the six-part adventure *Colony in Space* (1971). Impressed by his abilities, producer Barry Letts invited Briant back to direct several more well-remembered *Doctor Who* adventures, including *The Sea Devils* ('the one with the creatures coming out of the water') in 1972 and *The Green Death* ('the one with the giant maggots') in 1973. In the same year as the latter Briant directed episodes of the new BBC series *Warship* (1973-7) which concentrated on the manoeuvres of the Royal Navy frigate HMS Hero – a series to which he would regularly return during its five-year run and which indulged and deepened his love of both the sea and sailing. Briant, who purchased his first boat in 1972, comments: "The sea and sailing have probably stopped me having a heart attack and dying young – directing can be quite stressful and I am pleased I had another great love, sailing, to change my lifestyle. Directing in television is the art of the possible... overrunning or overspending is not acceptable; sailing is totally dependent on wind, tide and the condition of your boat. You have to accept that the control of the situation is governed by forces far greater than anything mankind can produce. I have sailed around the world, been in some heavy weather, attacked by pirates, had an emergency operation in Thailand, been hit by lightning in the Chesapeake and had crew injured in heavy weather, but none of these are as stressful as getting into a serious over-run situation in the studio!'[3]

Over the next few years, as well as taking on the first series of *Z Cars* to be shot on Outside Broadcast, Briant directed episodes of the Iain Cuthbertson drama *Sutherland's Law*, two more *Doctor Who* adventures (this time featuring classic adversaries the Daleks (*Death to the Daleks* (1974)) and Cybermen (*Revenge of the Cybermen* (1975)), several episodes of another sea-related drama, *The Onedin Line*, and the very last series of *Dixon of Dock Green* (in 1976). In the years just prior to his time on *Secret Army*, Briant would helm a popular adaptation of *Treasure Island* (1977), direct what is regarded by Briant and fans alike as his best – and what would turn out to be his last – *Doctor Who*, the creepy

The Robots of Death (1977) before helping the BBC's new science-fiction drama *Blake's 7* (1978-81) get off the ground by directing the opening episode, *The Way Back*, as well as several other episodes of its first series. On *Secret Army*'s second series, Briant was recruited to direct *The Big One* and, due to its significant action components – some of which were sea-based – *Prisoner of War*.

Casting

When it came to casting, in contrast to his approach to the first series, Glaister decided that, with the exception of the pivotal Max Brocard (who would appear in every episode of the second series bar the finale), the directors he had assembled should cast the other new regulars as and when they were introduced into the narrative. The important characters of Madeleine Duclos and François would therefore be cast by Terence Dudley and Viktors Ritelis respectively, as they had been assigned their debut episodes.

Stephen Yardley (Max Brocard)

While making the first series, it had occurred to director Paul Annett that he could see Yorkshire-born actor Stephen Yardley working very well in the series. Clearly Glaister was of the same mind, as when Annett returned to direct his

© Unknown

Series Two episodes, to his surprise Yardley was there *in situ*, having been cast by the producer as Max.

At the time, Yardley was best known for the lead role of William 'Spider' Scott in the popular Granada TV series *The XYY Man* (1976-7), adapted from the novels by Kenneth Royce. The XYY of the title referred to the theory first expounded in defence of an American mass murderer – and since categorically disproved – that people with such a chromosomal variation have natural criminal tendencies. As such a person, cat-burglar Scott, who had been recruited by British Intelligence was presented as genetically incapable of going straight.

Yardley had left school at 16 and got a job in insurance, but quickly became bored and decided to work as a hod carrier on building sites instead. After a spell as trainee assistant stage manager at the Richmond Theatre, Stephen won a scholarship to RADA when he was 20. After RADA and a stint at the Dundee repertory theatre, Yardley won his first major television role: as womanising goalkeeper Kenny Craig in *United!* (1965-7), a soap made by BBC Birmingham centring on the fortunes of an ailing Second Division side, Brentwich United, that was produced for its first three months by none other than Bernard Hepton. Yardley would subsequently play PC May in almost 70 episodes of *Z Cars* (in 1968). He would go on to appear as Lieutenant Martin in the Spike Milligan film *Adolf Hitler – My Part in His Downfall*, Lannes in the mini-series *Napoleon and Love* and Captain Ramballe in the BBC epic *War and Peace*, all in 1972. His first work for Glaister came in a 1974 episode of *The Brothers*, in which he played Alan Dyter. Between this role and becoming *The XYY Man,* Yardley would appear in the 1974 pilot episode of *The Sweeney*, (entitled *Regan*) as Det Insp Laker, the classic *Doctor Who* story *Genesis of the Daleks* (1975) as Sevrin, episodes of the women's prison drama *Within These Walls* and the anthology series *Thriller*. Yardley had also maintained a connection with theatre through work for the Clwyd Theatre in North Wales, but had turned down the opportunity to work at the National Theatre, offered by prestigious director Christopher Morahan, in favour of the pursuit of more television roles.

Hazel McBride (Madeleine Duclos)

Terence Dudley cast Hazel McBride (who incidentally shares her birthday with Yardley – 24 March) in the role of Madeleine Duclos, following her performance in an episode of the final series of *Survivors* entitled *Bridgehead*, in which she had played Alice, a worried but headstrong survivor who had a young child.

McBride's earliest theatrical ambition was '…to take part in my older sister's puppet shows. I was paid threepence for winding up the gramophone, and was eventually allowed to work the caterpillar puppet!' She went to Bristol University to read History, where she 'did as much acting as possible, often taking shows to the Edinburgh Fringe.' After postgraduate training, she started to look for her first professional acting job: 'I got the equity card (essential in those days) by joining a children's theatre company travelling around the Glasgow area. That was followed by playing some exciting and demanding roles with repertory companies around the country. One of these was the Bristol Old Vic, from where I transferred to the West End with its production of *Tarantara*.'

By this time in her career, McBride had begun to take television roles, her first part being an episode of *Within These Walls* (*Labour of Love*) in 1974, directed by Paul Annett. In 1976 she would play Jean in the Children's Film Foundation film *One Hour to Zero*. In 1977, as well playing Alice in *Survivors*, McBride appeared in: a production of *Uncle Vanya* (as Yelena) at the Cambridge Arts Theatre; an episode of the Scottish drama *The Mackinnons*; the LWT *Sunday Drama*: *The*

© Jeremy Fletcher

Man Who Liked Elephants, co-starring Michael Gambon; and an episode of the Dutch detective drama *Van der Valk*, which also featured Michael Culver, entitled *Dead on Arrival*. Just before joining *Secret Army*, she appeared in the Shaun Usher-scripted *The Big H* (1978) and as a Medical Officer in an episode of the Gerry Anderson sci-fi series *Space:1999* (*The Dorcons*).

Nigel Williams (François)

© Stephen M. Prichard

Like Angela Richards, Nigel Williams, who was cast by Viktors Ritelis as François, was RADA-trained and had a CV that contained as much musical theatre as it did television. While at RADA, he had won the William Poel Shakespeare Prize and the Caryl Brahms Musical Award; however, he remembers finding it initially difficult to get work due to his height (6ft 2in).

His earliest television credit was as a Police Observer in the Glaister serial *The Long Chase*. Prior to *Secret Army* he had appeared in a musical version of Gaskell's *Cranford* for Thames Television, playing Jem Hearn, and as Percy Darling in Jerome Kern's *Very Good Eddie* in the West End, both in 1976. Just before taking the part of François, he took a role in an episode of the police series *Target* (in 1978).

John D. Collins (Inspector Delon)

Despite lazy journalism to the contrary, given the total number of actors who worked on *Secret Army*, only a handful – Richard Marner and Guy Siner in bit parts, and Hilary Minster and John D. Collins in semi-regular parts – went on to appear in *'Allo 'Allo*. Collins was contracted to appear in a total of four episodes of the second series of *Secret Army* as new character Inspector Paul Delon and was cast in the role by Terence Dudley. Collins had won the Ivor Novello and Robert Donat Scholarships to RADA, after which he spent several years in the theatre.

His early acting roles included the Hammer Horror film *Dracula Has Risen from The Grave* (1968) and the film versions of *Till Death us Do Part* (1969), in which he would play an RAF officer for the first time, and *Dad's Army* (1971), as a Naval Officer, which was to be the first of many roles for comedy writer David Croft. In the same year, he would take his first regular role, playing Peter Bryant in Granada's *A Family at War*. He would go on to play the doctor who delivers Frank and Betty Spencer's baby, Jessica, in sitcom *Some Mothers Do 'Ave 'Em* and Squadron Leader Baker in the Robert Lindsay vehicle, *Get Some In!* From 1978, the same year as he began to work on *Secret Army*, Collins started to appear in Spike Milligan's surreal *Q* (series 7, 8 and 9, 1978-80).

Jean Rimmer (Estelle Muny)

Paul Annett cast Jean Rimmer to play Alain's wife, Estelle, a character set to appear in two episodes of the second series: *Russian Roulette* and *Prisoner of War*. Annett had previously worked with Rimmer on an episode of *Within These Walls* (*Tea on St Pancras Station*). Before her time on *Secret Army*, Rimmer had had regular television roles as Sister Harrington in the British *General Hospital* (1973-9) and Betty in *Quiller* (1975).

Paul Shelley (Major Nicholas Bradley)

One further significant casting (by Viktors Ritelis) despite the fact that he would only appear in one episode of the second series, was that of Paul Shelley as Major

© Patrick Wiseman

Nicholas Bradley in *Lucky Piece*. At this point in his career, RADA-trained Shelley, the brother of actor Francis Matthews, had just completed two years with the RSC, playing Tybalt in the celebrated 1976 production of *Romeo and Juliet* (with Ian McKellen and Francesca Annis in the title roles) and Diomedes, and later Achilles, in *Troilus and Cressida* (1976-7).

His previous television and film credits included Frank Cheeryble in a 1968 adaptation of *Nicholas Nickleby*, Donalbain in Roman Polanski's *Macbeth* (1971), the RAF series *Pathfinders* (1972-3), and Richard Carmody in the James Herriot film: *It Shouldn't Happen to a Vet* (1975). Shelley's performance in *Lucky Piece* was to be so admired by the production team that they would later decide that Bradley should return in the final series as a regular.

A Question of Dates

Although both Glaister and Brason were very knowledgeable about the wartime period, especially due to the huge number of interviews they had conducted with war veterans about the adventures of Allied airmen in Occupied Europe, both men knew that in order to pull off a successful drama series, exact historical details and, more particularly, dates, had to come second to the ongoing fictional narrative they were crafting.

Over the course of the first series, they had remained deliberately vague about the dating of each episode, indeed, only the fact that the Führer's birthday is celebrated in *Bait* establishes that this and the following episode, *Good Friday*, must be taking place on Tuesday 20 and Friday 23 April 1943 respectively (a fact which is confirmed by Brason in *Secret Army Dossier*). Even the dating of *Secret*

Army's opening episode is a matter for debate: while the *Radio Times* episode listing clearly states 1941, production documentation (the Writers' Guide) cites 1942 instead ('Series One starts early in 1942 with the imminent dispatch of Curtis and Major Kessler of the Gestapo'). This latter dating also fits with the second episode, *Sergeant on the Run* – which must take place only a few days at most after *Lisa – Code Name Yvette*, as the matter of Curtis's return is still under discussion – in which Sergeant Walker makes his escape from Dr Bogaerde's surgery in a sequence which positively shouts springtime, with its trees in blossom and deafening birdsong. Of course, due to unavoidable production constraints, location filming would always take place over the Spring and Summer seasons, but the director, in this case Viktors Ritelis, would have been briefed as to the rough time of year of each episode and filmed scenes accordingly. It was actually originally intended that *Sergeant on the Run* would have an on-screen caption of 'Brussels 1941' at the start, but the fact that this plan was abandoned suggests that the production team were, at the very least, uncomfortable with being specific about dates. Further confusion was to arise when it came to dating the other end of the first series. Brason's *Secret Army Dossier* dates the finale (*Be the First Kid...*) as taking place in April 1943, which suggests he had forgotten that Easter occurred in late April 1943. It would be tight, if not impossible, for the passage of events of this and the preceding episode to occur in the week following *Good Friday*, a conclusion which can lead one to more properly date *Be the First Kid...* as happening in May 1943, or to instead drop any attempt at dating the episodes on the basis that this is only a television drama series! This latter option appears even more inviting when, during the third series, the subject of the dating of these events rears its head again, when Reinhardt looks back over Brandt's evasion line investigations and we are told that the events of *Be the First Kid*, and specifically Kessler's 'great encirclement' in order to flush out Curtis, occurred on 9 April 1943, some weeks before the events of *Bait*! This type of dating error is endemic to the third series, as the initial policy of vague dating comes back to haunt the production team as they seek to make the series more authentic – and arguably far more suspenseful – by having the series's narrative connect with real historical events, a move which requires the introduction of more specific on-screen dating via dialogue, plot or even the occasional calendar.

The action of the second series opens a few months after Curtis' departure and Andrée's death, just as Albert and Monique are preparing to open the new Candide for business, placing *The Hostage* circa late summer 1943. However, there are more definite staging posts as the series continues: the setting of *Guests at God's Table* over several days leading up to and including 6 December 1943 (St Nicholas Day); the calendar in Hervé's bakery placing *A Matter of Life and Death* in March 1944; and most notably, the revelation that *Day of Wrath* closes the second run of episodes on 6 June 1944 – D-Day. This definite historical backdrop makes it very clear that in late 1977/early 1978, when the second series's structure was being planned, either Glaister was confident that the BBC would soon give the go-ahead for a third series which would take place between 1944-5, or that the BBC had actually already given a green light to two further series after the broadcast of series one.

Actual Historical Events

Just as they had done for the first series, when coming up with plots for the second, Glaister and Brason (and their team of writers), drew upon actual historical events and people. Also, as before, the writers would essentially 'fill in the blanks' after the pair had already established the subject of each episode and overall structure of the series.

A good example of the way in which real historical events would be amalgamated into one coherent episode – with details such as dates and names necessarily changed – is second series opener *The Hostage*. The episode's central storyline follows the exploits of Brigadier General Markham, who is shot down over Belgium while en route to North Africa (and who is in possession of highly sensitive information relating to a forthcoming Allied offensive there) and subsequently becomes one of twenty hostages taken by Kessler who face being shot unless the identity of a man who is murdering German officers is discovered. The North African offensive is clearly Operation Torch, which was planned in mid-1942 and began with the invasion of Morocco and Algeria in November of that year, while Markham's story draws on two separate real-life incidents. One probable inspiration is the shooting down of one Air Marshal Sir John Whitley, albeit in a Halifax rather than a Dakota, over Belgium by a German night-fighter on 10 April 1943, and his subsequent evasion via Spain, while another is the experiences of Flying Officer Gouinlock, who was taken hostage along with 39 Belgian civilians in 1944 after two German soldiers went missing. Just as in *The Hostage*, Gouinlock was released after two hostages had been shot and his identity as an Allied evader was never discovered.

Every episode of the second series would follow a similar pattern of historical patchwork, as the narrative takes in historical elements such as: the secret work (development and manufacture of the V2 rockets) taking place in Peenemunde; British air raids on Frankfurt, Hamburg and Berlin; Nazi art theft; the severe disorientation of American aircrew who had never before left their home states; aircraft on the secret list; German fighter aces; and perhaps most memorably, the air attack on the German Headquarters on the Avenue Louise by Jean de Selys Longchamps, a Belgian patriot and Allied airman, who for the purpose of *Day of Wrath* becomes André De Beers. The Holocaust and the horrors taking place in the East are given scant coverage, largely because the last Jews have already been shipped out of Brussels, with the only reminder that they were there coming in the form of a haunting photograph of a Jewish girl left behind in Brandt's wardrobe. The news of the death camps themselves are set to shock the Major to his core, making his recovery from the news of his wife's death impossible as he now cannot believe that she died honourably. An overarching theme of the second series would be the idea that Hitler's vision of the thousand-year Reich was, during the period in which the series is set (August 1943 to June 1944), gradually becoming an increasingly unlikely conceit, a fact that is underscored by the rise of German plots against the Führer (led by senior officers who now regard him to be a "megalomaniac upstart") and ultimately confirmed by the news of the D-Day landings.

The series's storylines would also inevitably draw upon the history of the Comète Line. Just as Comète had to carry on after Dédée's imprisonment, Lifeline would also have to face up to life after the similarly indomitable Lisa. One particular episode, *Trapped*, which sees Monique shot and hospitalised would draw very directly upon Comète history, the only difference being that the real-life subject was not female but burly Basque guide Florentino. The second series would also see Lifeline having to deal with a deadly traitor in their midst. During Comète's years of operation, its members were betrayed by several double agents, amongst whom Jacques Desoubrie, an ardent Nazi who worked for the Line as Jean Masson from May 1943 to January 1944, is perhaps the most infamous; however, *Secret Army*'s particular twist would be that Max was an ardent Communist instead, who planned to take over Lifeline with a view to a post-war position of power for himself and his comrades.

The fact that the production team decided that the series's principal traitor would be a Communist rather than a Nazi double agent, with whom evasion line history is littered, is interesting. Is it possible that this particular piece of plotting, and the way that *Secret Army* continues to portray the Communists, perhaps owes more to the political biases of the production team than it does to history? Certainly the chief reason why the ill-conceived and untransmitted 'final' episode of *Secret Army* was pulled is likely to have been the feeling that its message (essentially that the Communists were responsible for far more deaths than the Nazis) was politically unacceptable. However, political bias or not, there is no denying that the addition of the threat of the Communists into the mix certainly makes the series more satisfyingly complex, as Lifeline seeks to defend itself against two sets of enemies.

Le Candide Mark II

One of the most important jobs facing those attending the overseas production recce for the second series in April 1978 was finding a suitable location for the new Candide, having decided that this time around they wanted to use exterior shots of the restaurant in the series. To this end, the team decided to pay a visit to one of Brussels's most famous landmarks: the resplendent Grand Place, the central market square with its mix of Gothic and Baroque architectural styles which date from the end of the 17th Century. During this visit, director Paul Annett remembers looking around the square and his eyes falling on a particular building (No. 28, known as La Chambrette de l'Amman (Amman's little bedroom)) that was "right in the centre of everything' and was a real restaurant. It was agreed that 'the new Candide" had been found. Austin Ruddy, who was also on the recce and had been recruited by Glaister to act as the series's lead designer

211

© Dave Hofstetter

once again, would have the task of realising the new Candide in the studio, and to this end set about taking details that would help him with this process when he returned to the UK. This principally involved photographing the building exterior, paying particularly close attention to the design and dimensions of the windows and the studded front and back doors (leading onto the Grand Place and the Rue des Harengs sidestreet, respectively), as he intended to reproduce them almost exactly in the studio. Measurement of the building's frontage was unnecessary, as the studio set would have to be at least double the size in order to fit in bulky television cameras. (Above left: No. 28 circa 1978.)

Another location scouted during this recce was the Galeries Royale St Hubert, one of Europe's largest and grandest shopping arcades, situated near to the Grand Place. Paul Annett, who was planning to use the location in *Russian Roulette* for the scene in which Claude Pelletain is shot dead, opted to use the Galerie de la Reine (there is also a Galerie du Roi) and the pillared intersection which leads out into the famous restaurant-crammed Rue des Bouchers, Andrew Morgan would

© Austin Ruddy

elect to use the same location when he came to direct the episode *Bridgehead* a year later.

Austin Ruddy also remembers a trip out to the top of the Avenue Louise to visit the building which had been the Gestapo Headquarters during the war (left), a very modern building for its time that had since been (and still is being) used as a block of flats. It was during this visit, that Brason and Ruddy saw the plaque commemorating the building's attack by a Hawker Typhoon in 1943, piloted by one Baron Jean de Selys Longchamps, prompting John Brason to choose this story as the principal inspiration for the second series finale *Day of Wrath*. Indeed, Ruddy remembers that Brason even started to write the script during the recce.

On his return to England, Ruddy set about creating his second Candide, for which he did not have a ready-made template for the interior as he had done on the first series. In contrast to the first rather down-market side-street Candide with its low-level lighting, dark colours (brown being the most prominent simply due to the amount of wood panelling and furniture) and overall impression of continental wartime frugality, the new classy restaurant would use a much brighter and far more colourful palette, in keeping with the opulent Grand Place. The new set would take in the deep turquoise blues of the velour furnishings, the rich creams of the ornamental statues and convincing marble-effect walls (actually made from fibreglass), and the crisp white of the floor tiles and the immaculate tablecloths. In order to match the look and feel of the new series, although not quite as grand as the front of house, the new Candide's back room would be just as brightly lit and dominated by rich walnut and mahogany furniture. Presiding over the clandestine meetings set to take place here was the portrait of a lady which had previously hung in Andrée's bedroom.

UK Location Filming

Production began on the second series in late Spring 1978 with the first of two periods of UK location filming. This time around, Peterborough's Nene Valley Railway and the surrounding countryside would be used a great deal more than in the first series, particularly Wansford Station, seen in *The Hostage* (as the location where Lisa meets Natalie and three evaders), *Trapped* (again featuring Natalie with several evaders) and *A Matter of Life and Death* (in which it becomes the train station at Marchienne where François meets his tragic end). Of

the former shoot, Jan Francis remembers that, during a filming break, she noticed some scribbled notes on the BBC photographer's pad: 'Not too many shots of her – she dies'! Several Series Two episodes also used the site of the Old Castor

Station (left), on the Nene line at the end of Station Road, Ailsworth, including *Trapped* (the checkpoint where Monique is shot), *Not According to Plan* (where the Communist saboteurs lay explosives), and *Little Old Lady* (where Natalie and Kelso first vacate the train at a checkpoint and later jump from it). *Little Old Lady* would also use nearby Castor Backwater (between the railway line and Waternewton Mill) as the river that Natalie and Kelso ford en route to Senlis and Willow Row field as the place where we first see the injured Kelso and where later the Dutch saboteur flees from the train and is shot by pursuing Germans.

Of the location filming for *Trapped*, Angela Richards remembers being carried around by a "wonderfully hefty chap – a grip – and it made me feel like a heroine." However, she also recalls that: "The scene required me to look into the sun, causing my eyes to pour with water." Nevertheless, Richards relished the experience, as she was always glad when she "got to go out into the field and have adventures." However, she also felt that: "They never gave me enough... I wanted to go out and fire guns!" One of the reasons why she enjoyed it so much was that there was so much studio work in those days that "location filming was like a gift," as it gave them the opportunity "...to go away, to stay overnight, and you played, you had nice meals out. There was a wonderful freedom to it, it was unconstrained," whereas, in contrast, in the studio "you've got to hit the mark, you've got to hit the lights, and you've got to know your lines."

Various buildings, farms and woods near the Nene Valley Railway would also be used. Natalie's walk up to the place where she first meets Bradley in *Lucky Piece* was filmed near Whitelands on the Old Sulehay Road, Yarwell (incidentally the same road on which Kessler's car and the ambulance pass each other in *Trapped*). For *Weekend*, Kessler's ambush by the American evaders, the subsequent hiding of the car and the scene in which Max and Monique locate it and switch the paintings, were filmed on the road near Top Lodge Farm, Upton and at Southey Wood respectively. The latter location would be used again for the scene in which Max and Alain move Hauptmann Braun from their van to a lorry in *Prisoner of War*. Salt Box Farm (Woodcroft Road, Marholm) would first be seen as the place where the injured Natalie, François and their charges hide after the train crash in *Not According to Plan*, and later as the location where Max and his comrades are killed in *Prisoner of War*. Abbots Barn Farm (right) at nearby Southorpe would also be seen in the same episode, doubling as Bertrand Lecau's farm. *Secret Army* would

return to both locations for the third series. Nigel Williams remembers that so many scenes were filmed in the Peterborough area at around the same time as each other that "it must have been a logistical nightmare" for the directors and their teams.

UK location filming would also once again take place in London. Lena van Broecken's suicide in *Weekend* would be filmed here, as would the sequence in *The Hostage* featuring the aftermath of the St Nazaire bombing and Lisa's lifeless body (shot on the South Bank of the Thames near the National Theatre). Other UK locations included the back-lot of Shepperton Studios, previously visited by Paul Annett for *Second Chance* and this time used by him for the chilling garden party sequence in *Russian Roulette*. Annett remembers that the sequence's supporting artists "were some of the best I've ever worked with."

Return to Brussels

Juliet Hammond-Hill remembers being the first cast member to return to Brussels in order to film scenes for *The Hostage*, flying out there with James Greene, who would be playing Natalie's charge, Brigadier General Markham. Meanwhile, Paul Annett recalls the huge operation of clearing the Grand Place – which is of an

equivalent size to Trafalgar Square – of thousands of tourists for *Russian Roulette*, so that the opening scenes featuring Alain could be recorded. He also recalls similar trouble to that which beset the cast and crew during the first series, when shooting the scenes involving Claude (Geoffrey Bateman) in the Galerie de la Reine (left). The arcade had been dressed on the

215

Saturday with Nazi flags and period posters ready for recording on the Sunday morning. As filming began, the supporting artists – who included local Belgians in German costumes – received torrents of abuse from the more elderly locals that were passing, who clearly believed that they were somehow back in Occupied Belgium. The scenes directed by Viktors Ritelis for *Lucky Piece*, featuring Juliet Hammond-Hill and Paul Shelley, also required filming around many of the capital's landmarks, such as the Au Cracheur fountain in the Rue des Pierres and the Cathedral of St Michael and St Gudula (below).

© Andy Priestner

Back to Acton and TV Centre

From 23 June 1978, after the first period of location filming had concluded, the series's cast were reunited and began the familiar pattern of rehearsals at the Acton Hilton followed by recording at BBC TV Centre, with the first episode, *The Hostage*, going in front of the cameras on 5 July.

Several members of the cast remember feeling more comfortable not only with their fellow actors, but also with their own characters. Juliet Hammond-Hill, for example, remembers that, on paper, when Natalie started out she "was very skeletal, very lightly drawn, so there were many decisions that any actress playing her could have made," and that over time "her reserve, her passion, her seductive quality, in a non-sexual way – because she was very intense... just evolved really." She also recalls putting more of herself into the role, as she felt it appropriate, and how she would withdraw aspects and approaches and rethink them if they didn't feel right. Director Viktors Ritelis believes that this kind of detailed character exploration and development was only possible because of the allotted rehearsal time, regarding it as "a time for exploration" that is not afforded actors and television productions today. Angela Richards sums up the difference between working on the first and second series by describing the former as "a getting to know you," whereas on the latter "we all knew what we were doing."

Corpsing and Laughter

Despite the fact that the Lifeline characters now shared more scenes with their German adversaries, Hammond-Hill remembers that "the two camps still rarely mixed during rehearsals." However, she also thinks that the fact that "they were very mature, the Germans, and Angela and myself were, I could say, immature!" may also have had something to do with it. As work on the second series progressed, she and Richards formed a closer bond than before: "From Series Two on, we were rather reprehensible in our behaviour. During rehearsals and filming we would spend an awful lot of time bantering and behaving badly." However, she qualifies this: "'Badly' in the sense that sometimes we would just giggle uncontrollably – I think that was part of our charm – but as soon as we went in front of the camera – we were terribly serious." Hammond-Hill does remember one particular occasion when this was not the case: during studio recording of the episode *Trapped* (on 6 September 1978). The scene in question involved Lifeline's rescue of Monique from the convent hospital. Hilarity was ensuing from the fact that Hammond-Hill was dressed as a nurse, and that Richards, whose facial expressions weren't on camera, was causing her to giggle: "I corpsed so badly and I think if they could have sacked me there and then they would have done. Gerry Glaister, who never, never did this, came down from the gallery to tell me off!"

Interestingly enough, the injection of more humour into the series was very much on Glaister's agenda for the new run, although this clearly did not extend to encouraging corpsing. Bernard Hepton remembers that some of the men and women who actually ran wartime evasion lines had been invited to the BBC to see several episodes from the first series and were asked for a reaction as to whether their efforts were acceptable: 'I'm glad to say that their verdict was "yes" and very positive, but they had one important caveat: we didn't laugh enough!' It was an observation that led Glaister to judge that a perceptible increase in humour, principally arising from the camaraderie of those Lifeline members based at the Candide, would be appropriate, which incidentally was now more naturally arising from this group anyway due to their increased familiarity with each other. The opening scenes of *Guests at God's Table* in which preparations are being made for St Nicholas's Day, are perhaps the best example of this.

Fresh challenges

The new Candide presented a fresh challenge for some of the series's regulars. Michael Culver, Clifford Rose and their new co-star Hazel McBride all had to learn to eat, drink and act at the same time. Rose recalls that: "The food in the Candide was real and you had to carefully work out when you were going to eat and when you had to be ready to speak. It was more difficult than you might think." The effort involved perhaps explains why McBride's chief memories of the second series are limited to "the amount of eating and drinking I either had to do or pretend to do!" McBride also had to contend with another new skill – smoking: "I have never smoked and could never quite get the hang of it. So after struggling through a cigarette during one of my first scenes and a few more attempts at rehearsals, I asked if maybe Madeleine could be someone who didn't smoke." Although the component was reduced, Madeleine would still smoke occasionally in the final series. Rose on the other hand was only too happy to smoke, as he saw a cigarette as a useful prop that could be incorporated into his acting arsenal (which is incidentally why the original plan to have Kessler abstain from smoking and alcohol was dropped, even though this fact is stated on screen in *Lisa – Code Name Yvette*).

Production Order

Several episodes went into the studio in a different order to that in which they would be transmitted. These notably included: *Little Old Lady*, which was transmitted ninth, but recorded fourth; *Trapped*, transmitted fourth, recorded seventh; and *Scorpion*, transmitted sixth, recorded eighth. This meant that Hazel McBride would end up recording Madeleine's first scenes a month after joining the series and that Marianne Stone would film Lena van Broecken's death scenes on location (in September 1978) before bringing her back to life in the studio the following month!

As the second series had three fewer episodes than the first, the episodes were rehearsed and recorded in two rather than three blocks. The first block of seven episodes ran from 23 June 1978 (first rehearsal day for *The Hostage*) to 6 September 1978 (studio recording of *Trapped*), while the second block of six episodes ran from the first week of October 1978 (the first rehearsal day for *Scorpion*) to 6 December 1978 (studio recording of *Day of Wrath*). Inbetween these blocks another period of location filming took place.

Studio-bound

As with the first series, due to budgetary constraints, several episodes would contain markedly fewer location sequences. It was decided that one in particular, *Guests at God's Table*, would be totally studio-bound, despite the fact that much of John Brason's script contained 'external' sequences on the streets of Brussels. The huge Rue des Ménages set, the work of designer Marjorie Pratt, would result from this decision. Other memorable sets included Barsacq's lounge (*Not According to Plan*), designed by Paul Munting and Hervé's bakery (*A Matter of Life and Death*), another Austin Ruddy creation.

Film and Music

A definite stylistic departure for the series was the post-production decision to incorporate a significant amount of authentic film material into the narrative, presumably in order to contextualise the drama. The most notable footage, included in *Weekend*, was from William Wyler's legendary documentary *Memphis Belle*, which had been filmed in colour in 1943 aboard B-17 bombers during actual raids over Germany. Another new stylistic decision was the use of incidental music in the series. Although a variation of Robert Farnon's *Secret Army* theme music (*Wall of Fear*) is regularly used to great effect, the addition of rousing war-movie style music, on *The Hostage*, *Trapped* and *Little Old Lady* in particular, arguably detracts from the action and tone of the series, as it has the unfortunate effect of emphasising unfolding events to be melodramatic and overblown, rather than gritty and suspenseful. The fact that this music only occurs on Terence Dudley-directed episodes suggests that this was a personal directorial decision rather than a policy assumed by the production as a whole.

Exhibition at Hendon

While the second block of studio recording was taking place, series technical advisor Bill Randle, designer Paul Munting and design assistant Les McCallum (uncredited on the series) collaborated on a project at the RAF Museum in Hendon: a *Secret Army* exhibition. The aim of the exhibition was to inform visitors about the evasion lines that operated in Occupied Belgium but also to

give them a behind-the-scenes insight into television production and the making of the series. A reporter related his experience of visiting the exhibition in the 16 October edition of *Broadcast* magazine: 'Visitors enter onto the drab set of a street in Occupied Belgium to follow the story of an RAF

SECRET ARMY

BBC tv
A Special Exhibition
now featuring new exhibits at

ROYAL AIR FORCE MUSEUM
Hendon, London NW9
(Nearest tube Colindale)

EXHIBITION OPEN UNTIL APRIL 1981
Weekdays: 10-5.30, Sundays: 2-5.30
Exhibition arranged by BBC Enterprises and the RAF Museum
CLOSED: Christmas Eve, Christmas Day, Boxing Day, New Year's Day, Good Friday

pilot who parachutes into enemy territory and is helped by the local resistance. Backed up by the Museum's collections of escaping aids, crashed aircraft and other displays for the connoisseur, the exhibition is half-fact, half-fiction with the

TV make-believe world balanced by the real thing. After exploring forger's den, Café Candide backroom, barn hide-out and Gestapo office lavishness, visitors leave by way of a German border post into neutral territory.' A reporter for *The Times* reviewed the exhibition as particularly exciting for younger viewers and was impressed with details such as 'the flashing of a searchlight and the playing of Dietrich records,' which added 'to the wartime atmosphere.' Admission was 40p for adults and 20p for children. The exhibition was originally set to run until July 1979, but eventually continued for a further two years.

Days of Wrath?

As *Day of Wrath* went into the studio on 5 and 6 December 1978 and recording on the second series drew to a close, tempers were becoming a little frayed on set. Assistant Studio Cameraman, Michael Minchin, who was working on his last of twenty-nine episodes of the show, remembers that "the studio atmosphere was not the happiest. I have no idea what was going on behind-the-scenes, but certain members of the cast were distinctly browned off." Minchin thinks that the episode's director, Terence Dudley, was also unhappy, possibly because Glaister had made some suggestions about his direction of the episode, and that "Terry, as an 'old-school' Producer/Director, resented such interference." Whatever really happened, the fact that Dudley left the show under a cloud (incidentally, just as so many directors had left his own *Survivors* series) is recorded for posterity by the absence of a director credit on the finished episode.

Transmission and Publicity

Secret Army's second series would be transmitted on Wednesday evenings on BBC1 as part of the BBC's new 'Autumn Season' from 27 September 1978. This was a little later in the year than the first series, but due to the reduced number of episodes (thirteen), broadcast was still scheduled to complete before Christmas.

Once again, Glaister would be denied a *Radio Times* cover for the series (which incidentally the publication was still calling by its original name in the 'Next Week' section of its 16-22 September edition: 'New recruits and a new battlefront for *The Secret Army*'), with that honour going to a new five-part dramatisation of *Wuthering Heights* starring Ken Hutchison and Kay Adshead. *Radio Times* coverage of the new series was limited to: a quarter-page photograph of Monique, Max, Natalie, Alain and Albert in the back room of the Candide, which was rather nonsensically captioned 'The Lifeline organisation plan another escape route,' a preview in the 'This Week' section ('An RAF transport plane is forced down over enemy-occupied territory. A Brigadier General is on board, with the Allied plans for the invasion of Mediterranean Europe. The *Secret Army* is remobilised'); and, most significantly, a one-page feature entitled 'Yardley's Dossier' which was essentially an interview with Stephen Yardley, carried out by Edward Neill outside Television Centre, about his new role. During the interview, Yardley described himself as "a director's dream, that is, if the director is dreaming of someone balding, thin as a whippet with the look of a failed rapist" and Max as "an expert forger" and a "two-faced"' four-letter word.[4] In the article, Neill mused that 'The appeal of the series seems to lie not with older people seeking to relive the past or monitor any apparent factual fussiness with pedantic relish, but with youngsters who find it suspenseful, a rattling good view, full of good, clean, slightly butch fun,' although he commented that Yardley 'himself seemed curiously unwilling to be drawn on what he feels to be the value of the series.'[5]

Meanwhile, *The Sun* newspaper published an article heralding the return of the series, written by Chris Kenworthy, which concentrated on Bernard Hepton's success playing foreigners entitled 'He's at home in foreign parts!' Hepton told Kenworthy: "I think it is because I look so ordinary that I try to make the characters I play a little out of the ordinary." Hepton went on to explain the new setup for the second series: "These days he has a restaurant... the Nazi officers – the very ones he has been hoodwinking – eat at his tables." The article also mentioned Angela Richards getting 'the chance to show off her singing talent as the restaurant's cabaret act,' before going on to mention that 'the only thing that has not changed is the irritating silliness of the RAF officers who pass through Brussels on their way to freedom, to which Hepton commented: "Sadly, we're assured they were really like that. They were all very young of course, but even so, they seem to have behaved very stupidly at times." The *Daily Mail* described 27 September as 'Belgium night', as the first episode followed the second international heat of a new series of *It's a Knockout (Jeux sans Frontieres)* from the Belgian market town of Rochefort, although it observed that the gamesmanship taking place in *Secret Army* had deadlier implications! Other papers concentrated on Jan Francis's return, unaware that she would only feature in one episode of the new series. In an interview with journalist Mary Malone, Francis explained that TV producers "find me useful... I look fragile, but really I'm as tough as nails. It keeps everybody guessing." She also commented that her *Secret Army* clothes, with their heavy square-shoulders, "make me waif-like and help disguise the fact there's a brain working away there."

Other new series starting in the same week were: the R. F. Delderfield period drama series about a country squire, *A Horseman Riding By*, starring Nigel Havers and Prunella Ransome: and veterinary drama *All Creatures Great and Small*, with Christopher Timothy and Robert Hardy – both of which had won the weekend slots that Glaister had hoped to secure for *Secret Army*.

On Wednesday 4 October, Bernard Hepton was the main guest on *Pebble Mill*, on which he was interviewed about the new series, the second of episode of which, *Russian Roulette*, was due to air that evening.

The most reviewed television dramas of Autumn 1978 were ITV's acclaimed *Edward and Mrs Simpson*, which later won the 1978 BAFTA awards for Best Drama Serial, Design and Actor (Edward Fox), and the infinitely more turgid *Lillie* starring Francesca Annis, for which Annis won the Best Actress BAFTA. It is baffling that a series of such high calibre as *Secret Army* did not get a look in at the BAFTAs, especially given its obvious superiority to *Lillie*, but its lack of newspaper reviews is perhaps more understandable given that it was now into its second series. However, the *Daily Telegraph*'s Ronald Hastings was a regular supporter of the second run, stating: 'It is good to see this series back... it has the same excellent theme music as before, but Albert's motives seem to have become less patriotic than mercenary.' As the series progressed, he asterisked the majority of episodes as his 'pick of the day'. However, his frequent comments about his frustration over where Max's loyalties lay (e.g. 'I wish they would clean up the ambiguity of the piano player' on 25th October), suggested that he did not understand narrative composition, particularly the need for the viewer to be privy to information that the characters are not, in order to instil a series with dramatic intrigue. Elsewhere, the *Observer*'s Jonathan Meades appeared to have paid very little attention to *Secret Army* and certainly had not watched the first series. His review of 1 October totally missed the reasoning behind the new Candide and inaccurately commented that 'last time out Albert owned a grubby authentic café frequented by top Nazis speaking at the top of their voices, now he owns a white tablecloth gaffe frequented by top Nazis speaking at the top of their voices'.

Despite the distinct lack of reviews, photographic publicity for the new series was prevalent on TV listings pages, for the first three episodes in particular, which were promoted with shots of Lisa, Von Elmendorff, and Bradley's first close encounter with Natalie, respectively.

Strike!

Some time into the period now known as the Winter of Discontent (due to the widespread number of industrial strikes in the UK), on Thursday 21 December, *Secret Army*'s popularity with the viewing public was confirmed when the *Daily Mail* chose to use a photo of Bernard Hepton and Angela Richards on its front cover above the legend 'It's a Black-Out' to cover the story of a sudden television strike.

The sudden pay strike, by all 5000 members of the Association of Broadcasting Staff, effectively pulled the plug on BBC broadcasts between Wednesday 20 and Saturday 23 December 1978, thus preventing the scheduled transmission of series finale *Day of Wrath*. The strike ended when the technicians concerned won a considerable pay rise and the episode eventually went out, some fifteen days after the penultimate episode (*Prisoner of War*), on Thursday 28 December in Christmas week 1978. The BBC were incredibly relieved at the relatively quick resolution to the strike as it had threatened to wipe out their Christmas schedule altogether.

Fanmail

During transmission of the second run, the series's actors noted a decided upturn in the quantity of fanmail they were now receiving, regardless it seems of their status as either Lifeline or German regular. Indeed, Clifford Rose recalls: "I got a tremendous amount of mail, a huge amount... which praised the series, were complimentary about the way it had been made, that they thought it was very true-to-life, and showed aspects of the war, particularly of the German side, that they were not aware of." He remembers that he also had "the odd occasional strange phonecall," and one German woman in particular "who rang up to say: 'You remind me of my husband who was in the SS during the war'" and wanted to meet up with him at the Ritz hotel! Similarly, Juliet Hammond-Hill recalls: "I received letters from men who lived in the war, who sent me photographs of themselves as they were then, pretending they were them now and would I meet them in Derry and Tom's for tea?"

Viewing Figures and Audience Reaction

The viewing figures for the second series were very respectable and a definite improvement on those received for the first series. The series opener, *The Hostage*, received 11.1 million viewers (over 20% of the UK population), beating the series's previous high of 9.5m for *Lost Sheep*, and scoring 3 million more viewers than its nearest competition in that time-slot, the musical *Must Wear Tights* starring Gemma Craven and Lionel Blair on ITV. For the next six episodes, *Secret Army*'s viewing figures settled around the 9-10 million mark and it continued to win its time-slot. A notable exception was the episode *Trapped* (5.8m), which had the misfortune of being broadcast opposite a Morecambe and Wise special on ITV, which won a colossal 20 million viewers. From 15 November, *Secret Army* met with new competition in the form of the popular ITV variety show *Wednesday at Eight*, which regularly received over 12 million viewers, with the effect of reducing *Secret Army*'s audience figure to around the 8 million mark. While on 28 December, it seems that only half of the series's audience (4.0m) caught up with the second series finale, presumably because it was a rescheduled programme and over two weeks since the previous episode had been transmitted. However, even taking this lowly figure into account, *Secret Army*'s second series averaged 8.3 million viewers, a marked improvement on its first run.

In line with the series's improved viewing figures, audience appreciation figures (as measured by the Audience Research Department) were also on the up. The average Reaction Index figure for the first series had been 72 and even the lowest-rated episode of Series Two, *Not According to Plan*, scored 73. *Little Old Lady*, which saw Monique take centre-stage opposite Andrew Robertson's Wing Commander Kelso, received the highest figure of the series, scoring an RI of 80, which in effect meant that the majority of those surveyed gave the episode either an 'A+' or an 'A'. Other high-scoring episodes were *Trapped*, *Guests at God's Table* and *Prisoner of War* (all with an RI of 79). The audience research reports regarded the scores for the series to be 'consistently impressive' and recorded an average RI of 77. Only the reactions to two episodes were examined in great detail: *The Hostage* and *The Big One. Day of Wrath* would also have been analysed had it not been for the industrial action. This factor led the department to produce a third report that summarised reaction to the whole of the second series instead. The report on *The Hostage* documented how 'a majority of viewers clearly welcomed the return of this popular series' and that 'the first episode did not disappoint them' although a handful found it 'difficult to adjust to the change of location for the organisation from a humble café to a sophisticated restaurant.' The story was described as 'exciting and full of suspense' and only a few lone critics stated that it was 'not as good as some of the previous episodes,' the vast majority having 'very much enjoyed the programme.' The whole cast was 'widely praised' for the 'standard of acting' with 'just occasionally Bernard Hepton as Albert being especially commended.' It was noted that most viewers, regardless of whether or not they were old enough to remember the war, were 'markedly impressed with the attention to detail and atmosphere conveyed.' *The Big One* was generally regarded as an 'exciting and believable story,' with many viewers feeling the need to defend the series by commenting that '*Secret Army* was not glamorising war but merely using it as a setting for gripping adventure stories,' which seems like rather an odd response to the episode out of the blue and suggests that the research department directly asked respondents whether *Secret Army* glamorised the war. Some viewers considered this episode to be 'the best' thus far, particularly as it depicted a 'German viewpoint on British bombing raids' and because the content 'moved' them. Among the cast, 'Michael Culver was singled out for his 'excellent and sensitive' performance and it was commented that 'the relationship between Brandt and Kessler as developed by him and Clifford Rose was the strongest feature of the series.' However, all of the regulars were praised because they had by now 'really "fleshed out"' their characters. In addition to the plot and the cast, the episode's 'standard of production' was also commended, 'especially in terms of reconstruction and atmosphere,' as was the inclusion of aerial footage. The third report on the second series recorded that 'the latest series of *Secret Army* had clearly been a great success with reporting viewers, who praised its exciting and compelling plots and regarded each episode as being very well written and full of suspense.' Furthermore, it noted that 'the variety of convincing and involving situations and characters and the bravery of the resistance workers all made the programme "a real highlight of the week."' The regular cast were again praised, with viewers feeling that they fitted 'exceptionally well into their respective parts.' The 'very authentic and realistic atmosphere of the time' was also commended and 'the sets, costumes and camera-work [were] so excellent that "the production was really alive."' In conclusion, 84% of those surveyed stated that they would very much like *Secret Army* to go into a third series, which is just as well as by the time this report was written, in February 1979, Brason and Glaister were already reviewing the first, and in some cases the second, drafts of scripts for Series Three.

Glaister's high-risk strategy of completely reworking the format of the series had paid off unequivocally. Finally its creator and producer felt the series was firing on all cylinders. He was not alone in this belief, for when it came to the Summer of 1979, when the programme schedulers met to decide when *Secret*

Army's third and final series should be broadcast, they unanimously agreed that it should move from Wednesdays to fill the channel's hottest prime-time slot on Saturday night.

Episode 1: THE HOSTAGE

WRITTEN BY: N. J. Crisp   DIRECTED BY: Terence Dudley

FIRST BROADCAST: BBC1, 8.05pm, Wednesday 27 September 1978

STUDIO RECORDING: 5 July 1978

VIEWING FIGURE: 11.1m

REGULAR CAST: Albert Foiret: BERNARD HEPTON; Lisa Colbert: JAN FRANCIS; Monique Duchamps: ANGELA RICHARDS; Max Brocard: STEPHEN YARDLEY; Major Erwin Brandt: MICHAEL CULVER; Sturmbannführer Ludwig Kessler: CLIFFORD ROSE; Natalie Chantrens: JULIET HAMMOND-HILL; Dr Pascal Keldermans: VALENTINE DYALL; Alain Muny: RON PEMBER; Inspector Paul Delon: JOHN D. COLLINS

SUPPORTING CAST: Paymaster: MICHAEL HAWKINS; Brigadier General R. G. Markham: JAMES GREENE; Duvivier: ALEX DAVION; Dakota Pilot: JASON KEMP; Navigator: ROBERT HOWIE; Wireless Operator: PETER TULLO; Farmer: TREVOR GRIFFITHS; Erich Devouglaar: PETER LAND; Hauptmann Schmidt: CRAWFORD LOGAN; Evader: TOM COTCHER; Rescue Worker: RICHARD HAMPTON

SYNOPSIS: During a bad storm, a Dakota plane, carrying a very important passenger, experiences difficulties due to an electrical storm in the night skies above Belgium. Matters are made worse when the port engine is hit by an anti-aircraft gun. The passenger bails out of the plane. Albert returns to the premises of the new Candide, in Brussels' Grand Place, which is due to have its grand opening night the following day, and gives a ring to Monique. Inspector Delon arrives and introduces Max Brocard to Albert as a possible forger for Lifeline and a pianist for his restaurant; Albert agrees to use Max's skills. Kessler and Brandt discuss Albert's invitation to the new Candide before receiving news about the Dakota passenger. Brandt has the Dakota crash-site searched and finds the tropical uniform of a Brigadier General in the British army. A British agent arrives by Lysander. Alain takes him to the Candide, where he provides Albert with money for Lifeline and tells him about the crashed Dakota and its passenger, a Brigadier General Markham, who knows all the details of a forthcoming major Allied offensive in North Africa. After securing more funds from the Englishman, Albert eventually agrees that Lifeline will help to find him. Down the Line, Lisa meets Natalie and tells her about an airman who a colleague is not sure about. Natalie goes to see the man and he turns out to be Markham. She returns to the Candide on its opening night and gives Albert the good news. After the murder of a German officer, Kessler gives Delon a few hours to find the culprit before he deals with the matter himself. Delon fails, so Kessler decides that twenty hostages will be taken and that one will be shot every day until the murderer is found. Natalie and Markham travel into Brussels and the latter has the misfortune of being taken as one of Kessler's hostages. Alain brings a message from London to the Candide instructing that Lifeline must secure Markham's release before he is interrogated. Albert asks Dr Keldermans for a dead body to present to the Germans as the murderer they seek. The first two hostages are shot and Markham, who attempts but fails to commit suicide, is set to be the third. Keldermans manages to provide the body of a man who died of a heart attack. He and Albert dress the body in the clothes described by the woman who witnessed the murder, and Max is called upon to modify his papers. Albert seeks the help of a man called Duvivier, who is regarded as a collaborator, to hand over the body to Kessler in order to convince him that the man is the murderer. The murder witness identifies the body and Kessler is satisfied that the matter has been resolved. Natalie meets Markham outside the prison after his release and they begin the journey down the Line. The next day, Keldermans comes to the Candide with the news that there has been a heavy Allied raid on St Nazaire. Knowing Lisa is there, he fears for her safety. Lisa has been killed in the raid.

REVIEW: In terms of establishing a new direction for the series, *The Hostage* has an awful lot of work to do. As well as offering a typically suspenseful evader plotline, the episode also has to incorporate the introduction of the new Candide, the recruitment of forger Max Brocard and the shock departure of Lisa. N. J. Crisp ably ticks all the boxes but, as in the very first episode, there is so much going on that the overall feel is somewhat disjointed. The most successful element of *The Hostage* is undoubtedly the presentation of the series's new central location: a high-class Candide restaurant which caters to senior German officers and therefore secures a safer cover for Lifeline's members by portraying them as willing collaborators. The dramatic opportunities provided by such a set-up make it an inspired way forward.

Although the episode suffers a little from the many disparate elements fighting for our attention, a far more serious problem is the inclusion of clichéd 'war movie-style' incidental music which pervades the proceedings. Whenever there is any dramatic sequence – and in certain places where there is not (the scene at the railway station, for instance) – this stock music kicks in. Rather than highlighting the tension, the music is so over-the-top that it actually makes the action feel less believable and, occasionally, even ridiculous, most notably when Markham attempts to sharpen the end of his shoelace. Unfortunately, its continual employment is made to sound even less appropriate by the occasional use of entirely suitable music elsewhere in the episode. The arrangement of the *Secret Army* theme tune which accompanies Albert's survey of the Grand Place, and the slowed-down version of Angela Richards's 'Memories Come Gently' which plays over the tragic discovery of Lisa's body, are both highly effective in underscoring the action. The only point in the episode at which the stock music seems almost bearable is during the opening – and arguably overlong – Dakota sequence, but only because it appears to be a knowing 'Chocks away!' homage to the war films of the Forties, with its archive footage and impossibly British aircrew.

Stephen Yardley makes a fine addition to the regular cast as the multi-skilled Max Brocard. His background is explored in such colourful detail that it is obvious that much thought has gone into his creation and that he is to become a key player in the new series. Max's views on the predicament of Markham's imprisonment ("Let the Germans shoot him") and the death of the hostages ("It can only strengthen the resistance") help to set out his stall as the most fiercely practical character yet to grace the series. His uncompromising views are difficult to accept as they show little compassion for human life, but their logic is difficult to fault. Any suspicions that Albert and his other new colleagues may harbour about his Communist sympathies ("You seem to approve of their methods") are deflected with the brilliant line: "How would I make a dishonest living if there was no private property?" The Communists, who have played no part in the series's narrative thus far, are to gradually emerge as just as serious a threat to Lifeline as the Germans, so this dialogue is important signposting.

Albert receives notable character development here with respect to his abilities as a businessman. He has always been portrayed as careful thus far, but in this episode the extent of his financial self-interest receives significant exploration. In his dealings with the man who is credited only as the 'Paymaster' – a solid performance from Michael Hawkins, whom director Terence Dudley had used the previous year in the BBC TV series *Survivors* – his monetary priorities are made abundantly clear: "My new restaurant first." As their conversation continues and the Paymaster suggests that Albert has already realised that the Candide will be his if the Germans win the war, his silence clearly betrays the fact that he has indeed thought the scenario through and has bought into the new restaurant thoroughly aware of the possible financial outcomes. His mercenary streak is further emphasised by his bold assertion that he will be able to move quicker, in terms of locating Markham, if he can have more of the Paymaster's money, and by his lack of hesitation in taking one more bundle of notes than he is first offered for his 'expenses'. Later in the episode, the fact that he is seen to be absolutely thrilled – even going so far as to abandon his usual reserve by kissing Natalie full on the lips! – when he learns that he will not have to spend any of this extra money is similarly illuminating. There is no sign as yet of the wedge that Albert's obsession with money will eventually drive between himself and Monique; the pair are portrayed here as particularly affectionate with each other. He even buys her flowers and a ring, although, significantly, he has no intention of marrying her yet, despite the fact that Andrée is now dead. Bernard Hepton takes centre-stage here with great panache, making Albert an even more intricately observed and interesting character than was already the case.

Monique is seen to have assumed a far more relaxed and radiant appearance than when we last saw her – a change which is presumably not only due to Albert's sudden freedom to commit to her, but also because of her new role as the Candide's resident chanteuse. The decision to have Angela Richards entertain both the restaurant clientele and the audience at home with her enchanting renditions of her effortlessly in-keeping self-penned songs, as well as French and German wartime favourites, is an excellent one. Here, 'J'attendrai', a recording of which is frequently heard to be played into the original Candide during the first series, finally receives the live treatment and adds both considerable interest and atmosphere to the sequence in question. Once again, Richards proves to be one of the series's greatest assets.

Natalie also returns looking more glamorous than before; however, far more significant is the fact that from this episode on she is set to become Lifeline's principal guide and therefore a key character rather than just a supporting one. It falls to Natalie to interrogate Brigadier General Markham and she proves herself to be a seasoned guide who has no need of Lisa's condescending advice to "double-check everything." She is also seen to play a more active part in the decision-making and discussion back at the Candide. However, one thing that remains unchanged is Natalie's passionate nature: she can't help but smile warmly at Markham on the tram as they travel across Brussels, nor can she stop herself from putting herself in danger by remonstrating with the Germans who subsequently take him hostage. Juliet Hammond-Hill puts her all into her scenes and is as a result completely believable as Natalie, so it is a real pleasure to see her receive increased screen-time here.

Of the other regular characters, Kessler and Brandt are less well served. Although Brandt characteristically deduces a great deal from very little (the purpose and destination of Markham's journey) and Kessler shows his cold-hearted mettle by refusing to give Delon more time to locate the murderer, neither is given enough material to really shine. However, given the amount of content in the episode, this is perhaps excusable.

Duvivier is an interesting addition to the plot, principally because of the way he is perceived, particularly by Monique. She twice calls him a Belgian Nazi and questions Albert's willingness to be seen publicly with him. However, the clever twist is that Duvivier is engaged in exactly the same sort of fake collaboration as Albert, a fact that only the latter knows. That Monique cannot tell that Duvivier is playing exactly the same game as Albert suggests that others will similarly not recognise that Albert is anything other than a Belgian Nazi himself.

One major inconsistency in the narrative is the fact that Markham is released without further interrogation, despite the fact that Kessler knows by his silence when he first tried to question him that the man must have something to hide. As Albert states when Markham's imprisonment is under discussion: "Well of course they'll question him, they always do, that's the way they are!" Two other scenes are worth noting, not so much for their inconsistency but for what is surprising to see in shot. During the first Candide scene, at the point at which Albert and Monique are talking to Delon, the end of the front wall of the Candide set is clearly visible together with what appears to be the studio wall beyond. While the location-shot Lysander arrival clearly takes place near to the visible wreck of the Dakota in the exact same spot where Brandt had his earlier location shot. Presumably Dudley decided to stay put to film this 'day-for-night' sequence there too.

Continuity with the first series is good in some places (e.g. the reminders of Albert's previous 'collaboration' with Kessler and Brandt (in *Second Chance* and *Be the First Kid in Your Block to Rule the World*)), but patchy in others – perhaps deliberately so, given Glaister's evident dissatisfaction with the format. Although Andrée does not warrant a mention, Curtis is referred to, but unfortunately it is

Brandt who recalls him and he, like Kessler, never did know that this was Monsieur Moreelse's real name. Lisa, meanwhile – who is kept very much on the periphery of the plot, presumably because screen time is being given to those characters that, unlike her, will be permanent fixtures of the second series – is only referred to as Yvette, a practice that will continue for the remainder of the series. This is very much out of keeping with the previous series, in which her Lifeline colleagues used her codename much less frequently than her real name, despite consistent use of the former in the end credits.

Lisa's tragic death is a shocking conclusion to the episode, especially as she only features in one other scene. To have her die in an Allied bombing raid like an ordinary civilian, rather than in an heroic fashion, is a brave, if surprising, move which somehow makes her death feel all the more realistic. The way in which she is uncovered by the rescue workers and left lying amongst the rubble as the camera zooms back out is particularly well done. It is an emotional goodbye to the series's female lead.

Despite its incredibly distracting incidental music, which is unfortunately set to return in Dudley's next episode, *Trapped*, *The Hostage* remains an intelligently written episode which successfully forges a promising new direction for the series.

HISTORICAL BACKGROUND

Operation Torch

November 1942's Operation Torch had several key objectives: establishing a foothold in the Mediterranean and North Africa; gaining complete control of French Morocco, Algeria and Tunisia; and destroying the opposition to Allied Forces in the Western Desert. The Operation allowed the Allies to test battlefield strategy, new equipment and amphibious techniques and was particularly significant as it saw the British and Americans join forces for the first time. Despite hard fighting against the Vichy French at Oran and Casablanca, the Allies won through and Winston Churchill

famously stated: "This is not the beginning of the end. It is the end of the beginning."

An Allied Hostage

Flying Officer Jack Gouinlock, a navigator with the Canadian Air Force, was shot down over Holland in 1944. After spending two months in hiding with the assistance of Belgian patriots, he was eventually taken hostage in Liege along with a group of 39 civilians after two German soldiers went missing. The Germans threatened that these hostages would be shot unless citizens came forward with information. After two of the hostages were shot, Gouinlock was released, his identity as an Allied evader never being discovered by the Germans.

WHERE ELSE HAVE I SEEN..?

Michael Hawkins (Paymaster)

Frank Walker, *The Brothers*, 1972
General Williams, *Doctor Who: Frontier in Space*, 1973
Inspector Jason, *The Duchess of Duke Street*, 1976-7
Colonel Clifford, *Survivors: Manhunt*, 1977
Richard de Lacy, *The Devil's Crown*, 1978

James Greene (Brigadier General Markham)

Mr Trimble, *Chocky*, 1984
Reverend Kenneth Bartlett, *Mapp and Lucia*, 1985-6
Comte de Vache, *Let Them Eat Cake*, 1999
Arnold, *William and Mary*, 2003-5
Narrowbolt, *The Colour of Magic*, 2008

Episode 2: RUSSIAN ROULETTE

WRITTEN BY: John Brason   **DIRECTED BY:** Paul Annett

FIRST BROADCAST: BBC1, 8.05pm, Wednesday 4 October 1978

STUDIO RECORDING: 15 July 1978

VIEWING FIGURE: 10.4m

REGULAR CAST: Albert Foiret: BERNARD HEPTON; Monique Duchamps: ANGELA RICHARDS; Max Brocard: STEPHEN YARDLEY; Major Erwin Brandt: MICHAEL CULVER; Sturmbannführer Ludwig Kessler: CLIFFORD ROSE; Natalie Chantrens: JULIET HAMMOND-HILL; Dr Pascal Keldermans: VALENTINE DYALL; Alain Muny: RON PEMBER; Corporal Rennert: ROBIN LANGFORD

SUPPORTING CAST: Oberst von Elmendorff: GUY ROLFE; Claude Pelletain: GEOFFREY BATEMAN; Ivan Ilyich Kusnetsov: CONSTANTIN DE GOGUEL; Alexei Alexeiyvich Lyublin: KAZIK MICHALSKI; Marin Marais: RICHARD MARNER; Estelle Muny: JEAN RIMMER; Gil Muny: DEREK BROOME; Gestapo Man: DOM DE GRUYTER; Corporal: CHARLES BRANKAERTS: Etienne Muny: DAVID PERKINS; Louise Muny: LOUISE HARDING

SYNOPSIS: Alain brings some black market vodka to the Candide. Dr Keldermans arrives soon after with the news that Lisa was killed during the recent raid on St Nazaire. Albert decides that he will take over Lifeline but that her codename Yvette should continue to be used. Brandt receives a call from Oberst von Elmendorff and they arrange to have dinner together at the Candide. Natalie meets fellow agent Claude Pelletain who has two Russians, Ivan and Alexei, to hand over to her. The pair have walked all the way across Germany to Belgium, neither speaks any French and they have a peculiar sense of humour. Albert tells Monique that the Line must continue, not just for Lisa's sake, but because he doesn't want to lose the new Candide. Natalie brings Russian-speaking Marin to the apartment where Ivan and Alexei are in hiding. When Marin asks them Natalie's questions they initially refuse to cooperate, but he is eventually convinced that they are genuine. Albert decides that they should be sent down the Line. Alain's wife, Estelle, and his brother, Gil, tell him that they think he should continue his resistance work. He in turn asks them if it is alright for an evader to be hidden at the farm. Estelle agrees, but it soon transpires that there are two men – the Russian pair – and that they may be staying longer than one night. At the Candide, Von Elmendorff shares his concerns about growth of Nazi power with Brandt and asks him if he will become involved in a plot to assassinate Hitler. Brandt agrees to think about his proposal. Kessler arrives and Albert overhears him tell Brandt that they are on to the Russians. Albert sends Natalie straight back to Alain's farm to get the Russians out of the area. She is upset when he instructs that she must take them down the Line the next morning, as this means she will miss Lisa's funeral. Alain and his family are enjoying traditional Russian dancing and music with their guests when Natalie returns to takes them away to hide in a railway carriage until morning. Kessler tells Brandt about his plans for a garden party to encourage their informers to cooperate more freely; he also quizzes him about his meal with Von Elmendorff, but learns nothing. In the morning, Natalie meets up with the Russians and they begin their journey down the Line. While Albert and Monique are at Lisa's funeral, Claude talks with Max and recalls that he saw him recently in Antwerp. Max shops Claude to the Germans by phone and, soon after, he is shot dead in a nearby shopping arcade. Some weeks later news reaches the Candide that the British sent the Russians back home and therefore to their deaths. Corporal Rennert arrives with an invitation for Albert to attend a garden party being thrown by Kessler. At the party, Albert and the other guests are forced to witness three men being killed by a firing squad. Albert returns to the Candide in a state of shock.

REVIEW: An excellent script from John Brason and solid direction from the ever-reliable Paul Annett make *Russian Roulette* one of the best-realised episodes of the second series. Unusually, rather than focusing on just a few characters, the script serves all of the regular characters well; however, it is Bernard Hepton who takes the acting honours this time around due to his utterly convincing reactions both to Lisa's death and Kessler's chilling garden party.

Russian Roulette marks a hugely important turning point in the ongoing narrative. Before this episode, it seems to be a given that the members of Lifeline are primarily motivated to risk their lives on a daily basis either because they are Belgian patriots (e.g. Natalie and Alain) or due to the fact that the Germans have caused the deaths of their loved ones and they are bravely trying to fight back (e.g. Lisa). However, when Albert declares here that he will assume command of Lifeline, the startling truth is that he is motivated less by bravery and patriotism than by the money received from London and the elevated position in society that the new Candide has given him: "We've got to keep it going for a very real reason: if we can't run it, London will soon find someone who can and they'll stop my money. I'm not going to risk losing this restaurant. I've waited too long to get where I am now." Monique is dumbstruck when she hears this explanation. It is obvious that she is seeing Albert in an entirely new light and, moreover, that she doesn't much like what she sees. As surprising as it is, Albert's disturbing revelation, which serves to colour his actions for the remainder of the series, is entirely characteristic of a drama, which as it progresses, increasingly revels in presenting uncomfortable truths. *Secret Army*, especially in its second and third series, is not simply about the goodies versus the baddies but the presence of both good and bad in all of the principal players. In lesser series, a character like Albert would be portrayed as a perfect selfless good guy, however *Secret Army* has the maturity of approach to occasionally present Lifeline's new leader as considerably less likeable than some of his German counterparts. Albert's dark and complex nature makes him a far more interesting lead than the departed Lisa who, despite the talents of Jan Francis, was just too nice a character to carry the series.

Although Albert's new motivation for continuing Lifeline may be self-serving, it is nevertheless clear that he held its former leader in great affection, something he makes overtly clear to Monique: "I loved that child you know, just like my own daughter" – a sentiment which is all the more powerful given that we know him to be a man who rarely shows emotion. However, on the evidence of the first series, it seems doubtful that Lisa herself would have realised the extent of his paternal feelings. On first hearing the news of her death, he appears to be more interested in how many bottles of vodka have been broken by Natalie – a reaction which is an obvious smokescreen for his true feelings. Once again both Hepton's performance and the writing for Albert are superb.

Unlike Albert, both Monique and Natalie are less able to control their emotions when they hear about Lisa. While Natalie immediately bursts into tears and rushes out, Monique attempts to close herself off from her grief, telling Albert: "Stop I don't want to think about it. She's just someone else we've lost and I don't want to think about it in any other way!" After returning from the funeral, Monique is seen to be completely silent and still, only coming out of her reverie to join in the toast to Lisa, at which point it seems that she may have emerged from her grief as a far more resilient and resolute person. On the other hand, the intensely passionate Natalie, who is always seen to feel everything very deeply, is not given the opportunity to process her feelings, as she immediately has to deal with the Russian evaders and even has to miss Lisa's funeral in order to get them out of Brussels. While protecting and guiding the pair, she proves to be patient, strong-willed and practical, an interesting contrast to her tender and emotional off-duty persona.

Given the grim subject matter of much of the episode, the occasional moments of light relief are very welcome. Aside from Ivan and Alexei, the cats and fish-obsessed Russian comedy duo (who even have their own catchphrase: "Russians!"), there is: Monique's cheerful singing practice with Max and her gleeful reaction to Alain's vodka; the joyful revelry at Alain's farm; the arrival of the wriggly eels; and the collective laughter after the po-faced Rennert has delivered Albert's invite. This increase in humour was, in part, an attempt to show that resistance workers couldn't possibly remain serious and afraid at all times, as the more sombre first series tended to suggest. The move to redress this balance not only serves to make the series's darker content more palatable, but also to make the principal resistance players appear far more human than was previously the case.

After a whole series spent very much as a background supporting player, farmer and wireless operator Alain Muny receives some welcome development here. Not only do we finally meet his wife Estelle – a solid performance from Jean Rimmer – but also their children and his brother Gil. However, given that there is so much going on elsewhere in the episode, we learn very little about them other than the fact that they are Belgian patriots who fully support Alain in his work. The narrative builds considerable expectation that their involvement in hiding the Russians will result in tragedy, especially given Estelle's line: "We'll just have to hope for the best," but this dramatic cliché is thankfully avoided.

It is unfortunate that the episode's title serves to remind the viewer only of the Russian component of the narrative, as in many ways it is its weakest link. This isn't to say that it is at all bad – De Goguel and Michalski make Ivan and Alexei entertaining and engaging and we do come to care about their fate – but when the episode also includes such consummate set pieces as Kessler's garden party, Von Elmendorff's attempt to recruit Brandt over dinner and Claude's death in the arcades, the Russian subplot does unfortunately suffer by comparison. It also doesn't help that Ivan's and Alexei's behaviour is so peculiar and unintelligible, something which the use of subtitles – certainly in the lengthy railway carriage scenes – could have avoided, although this would arguably have detracted from the emphasis on the language barrier which causes Natalie so much difficulty and frustration.

Brandt's meeting with Oberst von Elmendorff is an event which marks the beginning of the end for the Major. Brandt understandably greets Von Elmendorff's invitation to become involved in a military plot to assassinate Hitler (whom the Oberst memorably describes as a "megalomaniac upstart [who] is rapidly degenerating into a latter-day Caligula") with great caution. Although he clearly has misgivings about National Socialism – he is not a member of the party – there are his children to think of and moreover his loyalty to the Fatherland. The Oberst cleverly responds to this particular objection by telling the Major that it is exactly this loyalty that he is looking for: a loyalty to a different Germany to that which Hitler and his Nazis are currently fashioning. This scene's dialogue (with the exception of the rather too wordy sentence about "tacit industrial and municipal support") is well-crafted and proves to be an illuminating snapshot of the concerns of the German military high command. After Kessler finds Von Elmendorff and Brandt dining together – a scenario which is more than enough for him to suspect his sparring partner of treachery – he feels the need to remind the Major that, if divided, the Reich may still fail: "Not a comfortable thought for loyal Germans." This question of loyalty is an interesting and crucial one which directly connects the world of *Secret Army* with a specific historical event - the July 1944 bomb plot. As the series continues, such linkages with the actual timeline of the war become more frequent and, as here, serve to strengthen the dramatic context and lend the series a rewarding historical verisimilitude.

The theme of loyalty is further explored elsewhere in the narrative. It is Britain's new loyalty to "Uncle Joe Stalin" that causes Ivan and Alexei to be sent back to their homeland and certain death, while the main objective of Kessler's garden party is to inspire increased loyalty from its terrified attendees. The party, which incidentally Kessler elects to hold precisely because Lifeline's efficiency saves the Russians from his grasp, gives a chilling insight into the mind and methods of the Sturmbannführer. He shows no remorse for the victims of the firing squad and is seen to revel in the abject terror of his guests. When he turns to Albert and says: "You look pale, Monsieur. I do hope that this does not distress you," it is clear that the exact opposite is true. The whole scene, which was filmed in the grounds of Shepperton Studios, is incredibly well-realised and features not only an authentic setting but numerous well-coached supporting artists. Special mention must go to the actor playing the dishevelled, rain-soaked victim who was also seen in the Candide earlier. His desperation and fear as he waits for his execution makes for very uncomfortable viewing indeed. As the firing squad carry out their orders, Annett chooses to show Albert's reaction to the deaths, and it is obvious that the new leader of Lifeline is thinking just one thing: will this be his fate too? Equally well-directed is the sequence in which Claude Pelletain is shot dead in the arcades, filmed at the Galeries Royales St Huberts very near to the Grand Place in the heart of Brussels. The period flavour of the Galeries gives the sequence a great atmosphere, which is further enhanced by excellent set dressing, the use of barrel organ music and, as at the garden party, the judicious use of a large number of supporting artists. Aside from the latter, who are once again excellent, a particularly effective element is the deliberate exaggeration of the noise of the soldier's footsteps on the stone floor as they advance towards their prey. It is a clever touch that we later learn at the garden party that when Max betrayed Claude to Gestapo Headquarters, he gave Albert's name as the informant, something which has the effect of allaying any suspicions Kessler may have had about him at that point in time. Both location sequences are worthy of feature films and it seems nothing short of miraculous that both were achieved within the budget of a single episode of a BBC drama.

Other excellent moments in an episode which is jam-packed with notable content include: Monique incredulously reminding Albert that they have to ask Alain before they deposit the Russians at his farm ("He's got a family, Albert. We have to ask him!"); Natalie's emotional reaction to the news that she has to move the Russians again immediately after having left them with Alain; and the atmospheric shot as she later leads her charges to the safety of Molenbeek railway sidings, a scene which is underscored by beautifully melancholic concertina music. However, the episode's undoubted high point is the very last scene, in which Albert returns to the Candide after the garden party. Once he makes it into the back room we see him finally give way to his feelings of absolute revulsion and terror, as his hat falls off and he grabs the mantelpiece to stop himself from crumpling to the floor. Hepton's performance in this scene is startling and faultless. The sequence is further enhanced by the excellent decision to have the ever-sensitive Monique find Albert in this state and realise that the best thing she can do is to leave him to come to terms with his terrible ordeal alone. This episode ending, and indeed the whole episode, is arguably one of the best that *Secret Army* has to offer.

HISTORICAL BACKGROUND

Russian Deserters

During the war, but more significantly at its close, the two million or so Russians who now found themselves under the control of American and British forces, having reached Allied territory, or having been overrun by the advancing Allied lines, were repatriated back to the Soviet Union even though it was known that they were effectively being sent to their deaths. Stalin considered all of these Russians to be traitors regardless of whether they were deserters, unwilling or willing collaborators, Communist or anti-Communist, and had the majority swiftly and arbitrarily murdered. The remainder were sent to slave labour camps in Siberia.

RUSSIAN DIALOGUE

The scenes with Russian dialogue might have benefited from the addition of subtitles, especially as, just as Claude tells Natalie, they do indeed have "a sense of humour all of their own." The translated Russian is in italics.

Scene: A Brussels apartment (afternoon)

[Natalie has informed fellow agent Claude Pelletain that Lisa is dead. She wonders how she is going to deal with the two Russian men whom Claude is leaving in her care. She walks up to them]

NATALIE: Do you speak any French? [the Russians don't respond] German?

IVAN: *Ivan Iliyich Kuznetsov. This is my friend Alexei Alexeiyvich Lyublin. At your service, mademoiselle.*

[They take it in turn to kiss Natalie's hand]

ALEXEI [of Claude]: *I like her more than this bloke.*

IVAN: *She is pretty. Yes, I feel that we will like the West.*

ALEXEI: *What do you think, is it the same girl who helped us to come here?*

NATALIE: How does one communicate with them Claude? This is hopeless.

Scene: The same apartment (morning)

[Natalie arrives back at the apartment with Marin Marais who can speak Russian]

NATALIE [seeing they have drawn cats and fish all over the apartment walls]: IVAN, ALEXEI, WHAT ON EARTH ARE YOU DOING?!?

IVAN: *Our sweetheart!*

MARIN MARAIS: Who are you?

IVAN: *Pleased to meet you, sir* (shakes Marin's hand)

MARIN: *I have to ask you a few questions.*

IVAN/ALEXEI [shouting]: *WOW, YOU ARE RUSSIAN? YOU SPEAK RUSSIAN!*

[They jump around and hug Marin]

NATALIE [looking around the room]: Cats and fish, so that's what Claude meant. Marin, ask them how they got here.

[The Russians look at Natalie]

IVAN [telling Marin]: *What a sweetheart she is, but so skinny. Her eyes are so sparkling!*

ALEXEI: *Do you think she is a virgin?*

IVAN: *They say, in the West they sleep with anyone!*

NATALIE: For goodness sake, will you stop this incessant chatter? We must know about you, do you understand? We have to know!

IVAN [repeating her, not comprehending]: We have to know.

ALEXEI: *How I like her!*

NATALIE: Shall we get on with it Marin?

MARIN: How do we check their identity? London won't be able to help will they?

NATALIE: Ask them if they have some means of identification.

MARIN: *We need some ID. Do you have any form of ID?*

ALEXEI: *ID? Yes, we have an ID of the Air Forces of the Eastern Army.*

NATALIE [reaching out her hand]: Let me see. [She takes the ID from them] Ask them what their unit was and where they were stationed.

MARIN: *Tell us the number of your unit and where it is located.*

[The Russians look sternly at the pair and silently retrieve their ID from Natalie and walk away from them]

NATALIE [exasperated]: Now wait a minute!

[Natalie and Marin are at a loss as to what to do next.]

Scene: Alain's farmhouse (evening)

[Natalie has returned to Alain's farmhouse to take the Russian pair to hide them at a railway siding.]

NATALIE: Come on you two. You must be quick and careful.

IVAN: *I don't understand what you say, but I agree with everything!*

NATALIE: And quiet!

[The Russians kiss Estelle and Alain and leave with Natalie.]

Scene: A train carriage (evening)

[Natalie explains to the pair how the plan to keep them safe will work. It turns out that Ivan understands her completely this time and repeats the instructions back to her. Natalie leaves. The Russians turn to each other and smile.]

IVAN: *Let's draw something on the wall. I'll draw a fish.*

ALEXEI: *And I will draw a cat. Cat eats fish. So you start.*

IVAN: *How many matches do we have left?*

ALEXEI: *The whole box.*

Scene : A train carriage (morning)

[Natalie enters the carriage and is startled when Ivan jumps down to greet her]

IVAN: *Good morning. You are our rescuer! Today we will marry!*

[Ivan kisses Natalie's hand.]

ALEXEI: *No! **We** will marry.*

[Alexei shows Natalie the carriage ceiling which is covered in drawings of cats and fish.]

NATALIE: For goodness sake! Can't anyone leave you alone for a moment? You are supposed to be avoiding attention, not attracting it! Come on, out!

[Natalie leaves the carriage. Alexei climbs down to stand by Ivan]

IVAN: *Why has she gone? Maybe she didn't like our fishes and cats? We are real artists, aren't we?*

[Natalie returns.]

NATALIE: Will you COME! The train is being moved into the station.

IVAN: *Let's go.*

[Laughing, they follow Natalie out of the carriage.]

John Brason's original script included two further lines during the Russians' last scene, after Ivan's line: *We are real artists, aren't we?*, as follows:

ALEXEI: *After the war we will draw them on the walls of the Kremlin.*
IVAN: *No... the walls of Piccadilly Circus!*

WHERE ELSE HAVE I SEEN..?

Geoffrey Bateman (Claude Pelletain)

Simpson, *The New Avengers: Midas Touch*, 1976
Gawain, *The Legend of King Arthur*, 1979
Dymond, *Doctor Who: Nightmare of Eden*, 1979
Dandy Jack, *Lovejoy*, 1986
Hooperman, *This Life*, 1996-7

© Rick Cordell

Constantine De Goguel (Ivan)

Captain Nicholas Foxe, *Hannah*, 1980
Piernik, *The Fourth Arm*, 1983
Ardwyck Fenn, *The Mirror Crack'd*, 1992
Computer Store Manager, *Goldeneye*, 1995
Chris Feathers, *I'm Alan Partridge: Towering Alan*, 1997

© Charles Waite

Guy Rolfe (Von Elmendorff)

Travers, *The Avengers: Fog*, 1969
Dr Fedorov, *Nicholas and Alexandra*, 1971
Magus, *Space:1999: New Adam, New Eve*, 1976
Don Julian Yqueras, *Kessler*, 1981
Andre Toulon, *Puppet Master 3, 4* and *5*, 1991, 1993, 1994

239

Episode 3: LUCKY PIECE

WRITTEN BY: Robert Barr   **DIRECTED BY:** Viktors Ritelis

FIRST BROADCAST: BBC1, 8.05pm, Wednesday 11 October 1978

STUDIO RECORDING: 26 July 1978

VIEWING FIGURE: 9.2m

REGULAR CAST: Albert Foiret: BERNARD HEPTON; Monique Duchamps: ANGELA RICHARDS; Max Brocard: STEPHEN YARDLEY; Major Erwin Brandt: MICHAEL CULVER; Sturmbannführer Ludwig Kessler: CLIFFORD ROSE; Natalie Chantrens: JULIET HAMMOND-HILL; Dr Pascal Keldermans: VALENTINE DYALL; Alain Muny: RON PEMBER

SUPPORTING CAST: Major Nicholas Bradley: PAUL SHELLEY; Squadron Leader John 'Jack' Kennedy: PETER WIGHT; Dominique: PAUL SEED; Leutnant Rheinhardt: LOUIS SHELDON; Railway Worker: ERIC FRANCIS; Helmut Schultz: RUDI DELHEM; Stephan (Scientist): REG THOMASON

SYNOPSIS: After a heavy raid on Berlin, returning British bombers have run into a storm front and eight aircraft have been downed near Brussels. Kessler is unhappy to learn that only nine members of aircrew have been found so far. Three survivors of a crashed Lysander that was not part of the Berlin raid are hiding in a barn thirty miles east of Brussels, near a village called Jauche. One of the men is an injured Pole, the others are an RAF squadron leader and a plain-clothes British agent, who is determined to get the Pole back to England. Alain brings news that they have been sighted to Albert and it is agreed that Natalie will go and investigate. Arriving at the barn, Natalie is attacked by the agent. She explains that before the injured man can be attended to, she must check their identities with London. Kessler learns about the same three survivors and is intrigued as to the nature of their mission. Natalie is followed back to the Candide by the agent, who introduces himself as Major Nicholas Bradley. Bradley demands that help be given to his injured colleague, but is once again told that it will have to wait until London clears them. Kessler and Brandt interrogate a railway worker at the now empty barn near Jauche and are given a description of Natalie and find evidence that the men were there. Keldermans operates on the injured man. After escorting Bradley to a safe-house, Natalie makes her way back across Brussels, but is noticed by a Gestapo man who recognises her from a description that has been circulated. He begins to follow her, but Bradley is also on her tail and ensures that the man loses sight of her. Reporting back to Albert, Bradley insists that he stays at the Candide rather than the safe-house, believing that Lifeline needs his help. Leutnant Rheinhardt reports to Kessler that the Gestapo man, Helmut Schultz, has spotted a girl matching the railway worker's description. Kessler orders that Rheinhardt's office will be responsible for a special watch on the route she took and all railway stations. Bradley speaks to Natalie about the Gestapo tail and suggests that she should move to another part of the Line. When she refuses, he offers to protect her and get rid of Schultz. The next morning, Bradley and Natalie prepare to flush out Schultz and he tells her about his lucky piece (a Polish coin). Starting at the Cathedral, Natalie walks the same route as the previous day and is almost immediately spotted by Schultz who pursues her. The operation on the injured Pole, Stephan, has been a success, although Keldermans fears he will lose his leg. Natalie draws Schultz into an abandoned distillery where Bradley attacks and kills him. After disposing of the body, they return to the Candide and report back to Albert. A man called Dominique comes to the Candide to give Bradley the details of how he is to leave Belgium. Kessler and Brandt have intercepted the details of the pick-up and plan to locate them before they escape. In the event, Bradley and Stephan escape by Lysander but Dominique is killed. Back at the Candide, Natalie discovers that Bradley has left her his lucky piece.

REVIEW: *Lucky Piece* is an unusual *Secret Army* episode in that, more than anything else, it is a showcase for a guest character: the rogue-ish Nick Bradley, played with charismatic vigour by Paul Shelley. The episode is also unique because its writer, Robert Barr, who had previously penned the successful *Too Near Home*, chooses to follow one principal – and entirely linear – plotline to conclusion rather than adopt the more common multiple plot approach. Although there is enough to sustain interest, the result is that, the episode perhaps comes across as rather too straightforward, particularly in comparison with the preceding two instalments.

Shelley clearly relishes playing Bradley, especially his exchanges with the wary Albert. His flip explanation to Albert as to why he left the safe-house: "I didn't feel particularly safe," and his argument for staying at the Candide: "I'm useful about the house," are two comic gems from their discussions in the back room. The cavalier Bradley provides an interesting contrast to the dour and pragmatic Albert, and it is something of a shame that we don't get to see more 'cat and mouse' dialogue between them, although it is arguable that Max already winds Albert up in a similarly provocative role. After Bradley reveals that he is not from the Special Operations Executive (SOE), Albert appears to guess 'what' the Major is. This information is never given explicitly on screen, but the only possible explanation is that he is an MI9 agent. Certainly when Bradley returns in Series Three, presumably due to Paul Shelley's excellent portrayal here, his activities suggest that he is such, especially given their parity to the war work of MI9's agents.

From his encounters with Natalie in particular, it is obvious that Bradley is a red-blooded male. In fact, within seconds of him first coming into contact with her, he has her lying prone on her back with his body on top of hers. If he had been interrogating a man it seems likely that his approach would have been quite different! Before Natalie takes her leave of the barn, Bradley can't resist taking one more opportunity to manhandle her, on the pretext that he fears that she may still be an enemy Fraulein, grabbing her neck in an unashamedly physical manner. There is a palpable sexual tension between the pair from the outset and although this is mainly one-way traffic on the part of Bradley, it is possible that Natalie is protesting a little too much when she describes him as "an insufferable nuisance." Although Bradley's interest in Natalie may begin simply as a sexual attraction, as the narrative continues he seems to develop a real concern for her safety and well-being. After preventing Schultz from trailing her further he doesn't just criticise her for being followed but offers the explanation that she is making mistakes because she is tired. Although he comes across as slightly chauvinistic and patronising when offering advice to her in the Candide's back room, his suggestion that she should move to another part of the Line for her own safety is sensible and genuine. When Natalie refuses to leave, his offer to stay and protect her is further, evidence that he has begun to have feelings for her. When his work in Brussels is done, it is only Natalie who receives a goodbye in the form of the 'lucky piece' of the episode's title, another indication that she has made an impression upon him. Her reaction suggests that the feelings may have been more mutual than she let on. The interplay between Bradley and Natalie is by far the episode's most memorable focus and it is therefore pleasing that on the Major's return (in Series Three) the production team chose to explore their relationship further.

Although Monique and Bradley only share one scene in the whole episode, the battle-lines are immediately drawn between the pair, also setting the tone for their subsequent encounters. Apart from his reference to her as Albert's "assistant," quite why the pair manage to generate such open animosity so quickly is unclear, but it nevertheless makes for excellent viewing. Monique's thinly-veiled threat to Bradley once again proves that she is no push-over: "You know there are a lot of German soldiers out there. We welcome all sorts here: Luftwaffe, Wehrmacht, Abwehr, SS and sometimes... the Gestapo," but to the experienced Major it really is water off a duck's back.

One possible reason for Monique's antagonistic behaviour may be nothing to do with Bradley at all but much more about her increasing dissatisfaction with Albert and the revelation of his true motivation for running Lifeline, as detailed in *Russian Roulette*. Despite the fact that she is on Lifeline business at a convent as the episode opens, when she returns to the Candide, exhausted, Albert is clearly furious that she hasn't been around to help him in the restaurant. When it comes down to a choice between resistance work and the Candide, he makes it obvious that the latter is his top priority. Monique is also less than impressed by an incredible act of miserliness on Albert's part when Natalie asks him for her train fare to Jauche. After finding out that there won't be a train until the next day, he tells her: "I'll give it to you tomorrow"! Perhaps the suggestion of the episode's very opening shot, which sees Monique looking out of a window while it pours with rain outside, is that, despite Andrée's death, nothing has really changed for her and Albert since she last gazed mournfully out of a window at the rain in *A Question of Loyalty*?

Despite the promise of the opening two episodes, Max remains very much in the background here, although we do learn the importance and extent of his work for Lifeline and get to see where he works and sleeps for the first time. In Bradley he seems to recognise something of a kindred spirit, which is perhaps why he chooses to avoid him! Of the other regulars, both Brandt and Kessler are also given very little to do. Their scenes tell us nothing more about them and are sadly devoid of the sparring wordplay and games of oneupmanship that we expect from them. Only the interrogation scene at the barn, in which Kessler can barely conceal his contempt for the terrified railway worker who is trying to describe Natalie, affords them any truly memorable material. The man begins by moronically describing her as a bit like his daughter, to which Kessler swiftly replies: "I don't know your daughter." To the subsequent information that the girl he saw was wearing ordinary clothes, Kessler responds that: "There are no such garments as ordinary clothes!" When the Sturmbannführer finally loses his patience ("Oh, the man's an idiot. Take him away!"), Brandt can't help but see the funny side of the exchange.

Several visual effects betray the fact that director Viktors Ritelis is once again at the helm, including: the slat of light over Kessler's eyes during the climactic attempt to track the Lysander; the view through Schultz's broken glasses as Bradley finishes him off; and Stephan waking after his operation to see a sinister-looking Keldermans swim into view (a scene which immediately brings to mind Valentine Dyall's subsequent role as the Black Guardian in *Doctor Who*). Another Ritelis trademark is the employment of interesting supporting artists clearly engaged in stories and worlds of their own as the narrative passes them by. These include: the blind busker who Natalie stops beside; the distraught German soldier in the park with his Belgian girlfriend who looks like he is just heard that he has been posted to the Eastern Front; and the flirtatious young woman on the cathedral steps who has attracted a flock of German admirers. All add colour and reality to the proceedings, and are seen during the beautifully-shot Brussels location sequences in which Bradley and Schultz follow Natalie about the Belgian capital. As well as the aforementioned cathedral (the Cathedral of St Michael and St Gudula), Natalie's route also takes in the Cracheur (literally 'the Spitter') fountain not far from the Grand Place.

The weakest section of the episode is unfortunately its last ten minutes which are taken up with Bradley's and Stephan's escape by Lysander, which Brandt and Kessler attempt to prevent with just one transport lorry and a kubelwagen. Although the scenes are accomplished enough, they add little of value or note to the episode. Unfortunately, Dominique, the resistance agent who is leading the operation, is as two-dimensional and under-written as Kennedy and Stephan. Perhaps these characters wouldn't be quite so forgettable if Paul Shelley wasn't so damn good?

Although the central storyline of *Lucky Piece* is involving and appealing, particularly due to the performances of both Paul Shelley and Juliet Hammond-Hill, it doesn't quite make the grade due its failure to furnish the regulars with enough material and its overly simplistic content and structure.

HISTORICAL BACKGROUND

Organisation Todt

Organisation Todt was the Third Reich's civil and military engineering group and was named after its engineer and senior Nazi, Fritz Todt. After Todt's death in a plane crash, it was headed up by Albert Speer. Military projects in which Organisation Todt were engaged during the war included: the Westwall (the Siegfried Line), which was built opposite the Maginot Line; and an Atlantic Wall to be built on the coastline of German-occupied countries in  mainland Europe, which included the fortification of the Channel Islands. Later in the war, the organisation also constructed V1 and V2 launch platforms in Northern France, air-raid shelters back in Germany, and underground refineries and armament factories. By 1944, Organisation Todt employed some 1,400,000 people, including over a million foreign workers and prisoners of war. Its forced labour workers were treated as nothing more than slaves and often lived in conditions that were no better than those in the concentration camps. Thousands died in the service of the Third Reich.

WHERE ELSE HAVE I SEEN..?

Paul Seed (Dominique)

Michael, *Doomwatch: Say Knife, Fat Man*, 1972
Frank Orchard, *The Double Dealers*, 1974
Grant, *Survivors: The Peacemaker*, 1977
Graff Vynda-K, *Doctor Who: The Ribos Operation*, 1978
Father Harris, *Coronation Street*, 1979

Episode 4: TRAPPED

WRITTEN BY: N. J. Crisp   DIRECTED BY: Terence Dudley

FIRST BROADCAST: BBC1, 8.05pm, Wednesday 18 October 1978

STUDIO RECORDING: 6 September 1978

VIEWING FIGURE: 5.8m

REGULAR CAST: Albert Foiret: BERNARD HEPTON; Monique Duchamps: ANGELA RICHARDS; Max Brocard: STEPHEN YARDLEY; Major Erwin Brandt: MICHAEL CULVER; Sturmbannführer Ludwig Kessler: CLIFFORD ROSE; Natalie Chantrens: JULIET HAMMOND-HILL; Dr Pascal Keldermans: VALENTINE DYALL; Alain Muny: RON PEMBER; Madeleine* Duclos: HAZEL McBRIDE; Corporal Rennert: ROBIN LANGFORD

(*Although spelt Madelaine in all her on-screen credits for Series Two, in the final series this credit changes to 'Madeleine' - the spelling remembered by both Hazel McBride and Clifford Rose and used throughout this book.)

SUPPORTING CAST: Hauptmann Neumann: JOHN STONE; Sister Louise: PEGGY SINCLAIR; Miles Coubet: JOHN REES; Police Inspector: EDWARD ARTHUR; RAF Evader: WILLIAM RELTON; French Railwayman: ROBERT VAHEY; German Officer: DEREK LAMDEN; German Guard: FRED TARTTELIN; French Police Inspector: FRANK VINCENT

SYNOPSIS: Monique is guiding three evaders down the Line when the train they are travelling on is stopped and searched at the French border. A smuggler called Miles Coubet tries to take Monique's suitcase when it becomes clear that the diamonds in his own case have been discovered. When Coubet tries to make a break for it, both he and Monique are shot. Coubet is dead, while Monique – travelling under the name Marie Chardin – is seriously wounded and taken to a nearby hospital attached to a convent. Monique is interrogated by Hauptmann Neumann, who initially suspects her to be Coubet's accomplice. The three evaders meet Natalie and tell her what happened to Monique. At the Candide, Kessler meets a Belgian called Madeleine Duclos who agrees to dine with him. Kessler is intrigued by the enigmatic Madeleine, who seems to have withdrawn from life and has very little to say. Monique fears that Neumann will find out that she is an evasion line guide due to the four rail tickets concealed in her handbag. Natalie informs Albert of Monique's predicament. Kessler escorts Madeleine home and discovers that she is living very modestly indeed. Neumann tells Monique that he is satisfied that she is telling the truth about Coubet, but a French police inspector finds the tickets in Monique's handbag and tells Neumann. Rennert reports to Kessler on Madeleine's background, specifically about her affair with an aristocrat – the Baron D'Aquise. Kessler learns about Marie Chardin and reprimands Rennert for missing the possibility that she might be an agent for an evasion line. He plans to visit her at the hospital the following day. Fearing that Kessler will soon discover that Marie is none other then Monique, Albert decides that she must be rescued. Monique begs Sister Louise to be discharged, but her request is denied. Disguised as medical personnel, Max, Alain and Natalie make their way into France by ambulance. Once at the hospital, Natalie presents a forged order authorising Marie Chardin's transfer to Brussels. Sister Louise refuses to accept that the papers are genuine, but when Natalie explains that her patient will be tortured and killed if she doesn't let them take her away now, they are permitted to leave the hospital with Monique. En route they almost run into Kessler, who is travelling in the other direction, at a checkpoint. To Albert's great relief, Monique is escorted safely back to Brussels. That evening, Madeleine once again dines at the Candide with Kessler and learns that he is a member of the Gestapo. When Kessler asks Albert if Monique will be singing it is decided that, due to her recent absence and the fear that he may suspect her to be Marie Chardin, she will perform despite her leg injury. Monique gives a stirring rendition of the song 'I Bet You've Heard This One Before', the lyrics of which remind Madeleine of her love affair with the Baron D'Aquise. Distracted by his interest in Madeleine, Kessler fails to realise that anything is wrong with Monique as she is assisted to the back room.

REVIEW: *Trapped* is arguably one of the most entertaining and well-constructed episodes of *Secret Army*. A characteristically cracking script from N. J. Crisp puts Angela Richards firmly centre-stage as Monique suffers being shot, hospitalised and interrogated, before she is whisked back to the Candide to give the performance of her life. The 'perils of Monique' aside, *Trapped* also marks an important turning point for Kessler due to the introduction of Madeleine Duclos, played by Hazel McBride, a character who is set to bring out a previously unseen side of the formidable Sturmbannführer.

Crisp's main idea for the episode, to have Monique (while travelling under the assumed name of Marie Chardin) injured and subsequently trapped in a hospital, with Kessler on his way to identify her as none other than the Candide's chanteuse, is both involving and exciting. Although Lifeline has regularly faced equally grave situations in the past, because this particular threat is presented as very real throughout – just as it was when Curtis was pulled in for questioning in *Suspicions* – with the unthinkable consequences spelt out ("Once they identify Monique, we'll all find out what the inside of Gestapo Headquarters is like!"), the levels of suspense are gratifyingly high. The fact that a phenomenally dangerous rescue mission is the only way to ensure Monique's, and therefore Lifeline's, safety also raises the stakes considerably, as does the fact that Kessler can't wait to get to the bedside of the woman who he suspects to be an evasion line guide: "I'm very much looking forward to meeting Marie Chardin!" The final ingredient which ensures that this episode makes for compelling viewing is the audience's 'insider' knowledge that, at the episode's conclusion, Kessler's intended prey is singing her heart out right in front of him. Before one even considers the weaving in of the expertly-written Madeleine subplot as well, the above elements come together to make *Trapped* very rewarding viewing indeed and something of a plotting master-class for the series's other writers.

In narrative terms, due to the now permanent absence of Lisa it makes perfect sense that Monique has also started to work as a guide, as well as at the Candide, otherwise poor old Natalie would be doing it all! The fact that Monique has made the mistake of keeping all of the evaders' train tickets in her handbag is in keeping with her inexperience, although she is unlucky to become entangled with diamond smuggler Coubet. On first viewing, the moment when Monique and Coubet are shot down comes as a huge shock. The incident succeeds in making more impact than it otherwise might due to the fact that Lisa's tragic death took place only a few episodes ago and as a result it seems entirely possible that Monique could be dead too. Unfortunately, as was also the case in the previous episode that Terence Dudley directed (*The Hostage*), the stock music used to underscore Coubet's and Monique's flight is far too melodramatic to be taken seriously and robs what could have been an absolutely breathtaking scene of some of its reality. Later on, the music also plagues the ambulance get-away scene; thankfully, however, from the checkpoint sequence on, Dudley switches to an atmospheric arrangement of the *Secret Army* signature tune, which serves as a very appropriate theme for the Lifeline regulars as they succeed in evading Kessler and make their way home.

Almost as shocking as Monique's actual shooting is the subsequent scene at the railway station during which Natalie first hears about the incident, almost casually, from one of the three evaders. She is understandably horrified by the news. Her reaction, coupled with her subsequent daring efforts to secure Monique's transfer from the hospital, during which she has to use all her guile, suggests that Monique has become very important to Natalie and much more than just a colleague. Although there were moments in previous episodes when they got along well, from here on in they are increasingly seen to rely on and comfort each other; indeed, by the time they reach the events of Series Three, the pair are almost inseparable. While the production team were always keen that their closeness should be played down, presumably for fear of unintentional lesbian overtones, Richards and Hammond-Hill felt it important that Monique and Natalie should be shown to care about each other very deeply and acted accordingly. This development was due in no small part to the fact that the two actors enjoyed an equally strong off-screen friendship, which is no doubt why the closeness of their on-screen characters comes across as so believable and genuine.

While Monique's predicament causes Natalie to display the depth of her feeling and a desire to help her friend against all odds, the situation is seen to have a quite opposite effect on Max. In direct contrast, Max's reactions instead emphasise his preoccupation with self-preservation. He as good as announces to the others that his only motivation for getting Monique out is in order to secure his own survival. It is a position that infuriates Albert, whose subsequent use of the phrases "If we didn't need you..." and "One day..." serve to foreshadow the events of *Prisoner of War*.

Albert's acute distress over the danger Monique is in is obvious. The fact that he is actually prepared to leave his beloved restaurant behind to rescue her – something that, crucially, he is not willing to do in the final series – certainly suggests that she is, at this point in time at least, very important to him. His outburst when Dr Keldermans continues to be unhelpfully negative about their chances of rescuing her – "For God's sake, what else can we do but try?" – also confirms his strength of feeling. His palpable joy at Monique's safe return becomes coupled with a feeling of immense pride when she manages to get through her song in front of Kessler, gripping on to her as he tells her: "I'll give you another medal." The final shot of the episode sees Albert look thoughtfully into the middle-distance, presumably thinking that he nearly lost Monique this time around and that recent events, as Monique has just suggested in the back room, really have been too close for comfort.

John Stone gives a favourable performance here as Hauptmann Neumann of the Feldpolizei, a character who follows in the great *Secret Army* tradition of being a German but nevertheless a human being. However, it is only after he is satisfied of Monique's innocence of the charge of diamond smuggling that he shows his softer side, firstly by telling her that she should just concentrate on getting better, and then revealing that he has a wife, was a teacher before the war; and that he is relieved not to be fighting in the front line. He later seems a little disappointed to learn that Monique may be involved in something more serious than smuggling, but his sense of duty prevails and he immediately puts in a call to the military police in Brussels. (Although, when Kessler gets to hear about Marie Chardin's escape, Neumann's quick action may actually not be enough to prevent him from being sent to fight at the front line after all.)

Peggy Sinclair's Sister Louise is another strong, if infuriating, supporting character. Through her, the vexed issue of religious neutrality, already examined in some detail through the experiences of the monks in *Good Friday*, is revisited. Sister Louise eventually comes to realise – thanks to a very persuasive argument from an incredibly level-headed Natalie ("She'll be tortured, horribly and then killed... Many others will die in the same way, not only her. Those are the consequences unless you let me take her now!") – that on humanitarian grounds she should not continue with the phone call checks on Marie Chardin. After all Sister Louise is showing more than just a concern with nursing the sick, but is actively interfering in the affairs of man, something which she earlier told Neumann that she would not and could not do.

Unlike the singular and linear narrative of *Lucky Piece*, *Trapped* follows two parallel and contrasting plotlines and as a result the episode achieves a more balanced feel. The secondary plot concentrates on the introduction of a new regular character who is set to become Kessler's mistress: Madeleine Duclos. From the outset, the young Belgian woman is presented as particularly unusual and intriguing. In her opening scene alone she is portrayed as: utterly detached from her surroundings; very direct in her response to a polite enquiry from Kessler ("I don't believe I have seen you here before." "I haven't *been* here before"); and incredibly difficult to read – when she moves to stand up it is because she is taking up Kessler's offer of dinner, not, as he assumes, because she is about to leave. During their subsequent meal together, her refreshingly matter-of-fact approach and disinterest in both what Kessler is ("I don't mind anything very much") and the war itself ("It's happened, all kinds of things happen. There's nothing I can do about it") fascinates him. By the end of the meal, the Sturmbannführer's interest in Madeleine is self-evident and any possibility of an homosexual persuasion, as suggested in his initial character brief, is definitively ignored by the production team as he appears set to pursue a relationship with her. As he later states during their second date: "I am also a man, Mademoiselle."

The intriguing Madeleine subplot is constructed in such a way that the explanation for her curious detachment from the world is not revealed until half-way through the episode. When Kessler escorts Madeleine back to her humble apartment – which is made to feel even more grim and claustrophobic than it actually appears due to the strains of a crying baby – it becomes clear that her private means are very modest indeed. Her apartment contains the one and only clue to her behaviour: a photograph of "someone I used to know." The man turns out to be the Baron D'Aquise, Madeleine's former lover who was forced to break off their engagement. That his absence from her life has caused her to not care about anything or anyone is an indication of how deeply she must have loved him. Interestingly, it is because she is in just such a state that her unlikely relationship with Kessler – a man she would have presumably avoided had she been in a different frame of mind – is given the opportunity to begin. Hazel McBride, who naturally thought a great deal about Madeleine's motivation, reasons that by the time Madeleine came out of her grief over the loss of the Baron – later in the Series Two narrative – and had become more like her old self again, it was too late for her to reject Kessler on the grounds of who and what he was, as by then she had found herself in love with him and couldn't face losing him as well as the Baron. That Kessler and Madeleine's relationship arises so naturally out of such complex emotions and comes to feel so believable is a credit not only to the series's writers but to the performances of Rose and McBride who, as the series progresses, judge their scenes together so perfectly that we actually want them to find happiness together despite Kessler's primary role as the series's villain. Gerry Glaister's intention to introduce Madeleine in order to make Kessler a more fully-rounded character is therefore an unqualified success.

Given the excellence of Angela Richards's performance in *A Question of Loyalty*, it is somewhat bewildering that the production team decided to wait so long before they gave her another starring episode; however, what we have here almost makes up for the wait. Richards is seen to be particularly adept at portraying Monique's understandable feelings of helplessness and fear throughout, but especially in the scene in which she pleads desperately with Sister Louise, ending with the memorable line: "I shall need rather more than your prayers Sister." However, Richards's finest moment in the episode is unquestionably her mesmerising delivery of her own song, 'I Bet You've Heard This One Before.' Monique's performance of the song (written by Richards especially for the finale of *Trapped*) not only demonstrates the character's immense resilience and bravery, but also underscores, through its emotional and poignant lyrics, Madeleine's deep sorrow over the end of love affair. In this way, the scene serves to showcase the dramatic efficacy of the marriage of song and plot that uniquely characterises *Secret Army*'s second and third series. Her accomplished acting aside, it is for this reason that Richards's creative contribution to the series should not be underestimated.

HISTORICAL BACKGROUND

The Rescue of Florentino

The luck of Florentino, the great Basque guide who, initially with Dédée, had helped to bring over two hundred airmen safely over the Franco-Spanish border, eventually ran out in July 1944, while returning to France after the delivery of some crucial Allied intelligence. After crossing the Bidassoa river and while descending to a safe-house regularly used by the Comète Line in Urrugne, Florentino was suddenly shot in the leg by a troop of patrolling Germans.

Although he tried to conceal himself, he was discovered and shortly after transferred to the civilian hospital in Bayonne. The news of his arrest reached regular Comète agent Elvire de Greef (alias Tante Go) who, after learning where he was being held, became determined to rescue Florentino. While pretending to visit a young Frenchman in the bed next to Florentino, she made it known to him that they would attempt to return for him at two o'clock:

'At two o'clock there was a noise and commotion at the far end of his ward. Loud voices in German frightened the patients. Three stern-looking men stood arguing with the Sisters of Mercy. "He cannot be moved, it would be dangerous!" cried the nuns. The men brushed aside these protests. One of them waved a paper. The others rudely pushed past the nuns.'[1]

The men informed Florentino that he was going to be transferred to another hospital. As he was carried out on a stretcher, the nuns' protests grew louder, but they were unable to stop their patient being driven away in an ambulance:

'Despite the jolting of the ambulance as it sped along the road to Anglet, Florentino was grinning broadly. The 'Gestapo' had now removed their hats, and shook each other by the hand... They no longer spoke German, and the scowl had disappeared from their faces. Florentino had easily recognised their leader. It was the gallant l'Oncle, the husband of Tante Go, and two of his friends.'[2]

SONGS IN THE CANDIDE

'I Bet You've Heard This One Before' (Richards, Osborne)

So you ask why I'm looking lonely
Cigarette ash upon the floor
Listen mister, it's an old old story
I bet you've heard this one before.

Saw him first at the club I sang in
When he smiled and he called for more
I went back to his place that evening
I bet you've heard this one before

He was young, he was strong, I loved him
I gave all that I had and more
And he swore that he'd never leave me
I bet you've heard this one before

So don't smile, don't be kind
Leave me now, I won't mind
Take your drink, time to think, move away.
Don't be warm, touch my cheek
Hold my hand, no don't speak
Take your glove, keep your love, move away.

And then I awoke one morning
Found a note underneath the door
And it said that he didn't need me

I bet you've heard this one before.

Since that day all the good times left me
Now I don't even keep the score
Of the men that I've warmed on cold nights
I bet you've heard this one before.

So don't smile, don't be kind
Leave me now, I won't mind
Take your drink, time to think, move away.
Don't be warm, touch my cheek
Hold my hand, no don't speak
Take your glove, keep your love, move away.

WHERE ELSE HAVE I SEEN..?

John Stone (Hauptmann Neumann)

Captain John Dillon, *Quatermas II*, 1955
Submarine Captain, *You Only Live Twice*, 1967
Major George Fancy, *The Avengers: The Joker*, 1967
Max Brassington, *Flesh and Blood*, 1980
Jack Kingsley, *Strike it Rich*, 1986-7

Peggy Sinclair (Sister Louise)

Jane Redvers, *The Power Game*, 1965
Det Sgt Allin, *Softly, Softly*, 1967-9
Miss King, *Angels*, 1975
Mrs Preston, *Grange Hill*, 1978-9
Louise, *Don't Wait Up*, 1983

Episode 5: NOT ACCORDING TO PLAN

WRITTEN BY: David Crane   **DIRECTED BY:** Viktors Ritelis

FIRST BROADCAST: BBC1, 8.05pm, Wednesday 25 October 1978

STUDIO RECORDING: 26 August 1978

VIEWING FIGURE: 9.4m

REGULAR CAST: Albert Foiret: BERNARD HEPTON; Monique Duchamps: ANGELA RICHARDS; Max Brocard: STEPHEN YARDLEY; Major Erwin Brandt: MICHAEL CULVER; Sturmbannführer Ludwig Kessler: CLIFFORD ROSE; Natalie Chantrens: JULIET HAMMOND-HILL; Dr Pascal Keldermans: VALENTINE DYALL; François: NIGEL WILLIAMS

SUPPORTING CAST: Danielle: EMMA WILLIAMS; Paul Vercors: MICHAEL BYRNE; Jean Barsacq: JONATHAN NEWTH; Oberst Bruch: LEON EAGLES; Jean-Louis: RICHARD CORNISH; Bluebeard: FRANK JARVIS

SYNOPSIS: François, Natalie's new boyfriend, discovers Max going through Albert's desk drawers. Meanwhile, a Communist called Paul Vercors tells a fellow comrade, Jean-Louis, that Max must come to their next meeting and that he intends that they take over Lifeline. Vercors's girlfriend, Danielle, leaves the house of a blind music instructor by the name of Barsacq for whom she does the housekeeping. Barsacq is part of Lifeline and informs Albert that he is hiding two evaders. Albert is worried about Natalie's next trip down the Line, as the inexperienced François is going with her. Vercors holds a meeting with the local Communist cell, which Max attends. Vercors thinks it is time that their resistance efforts changed tack and proposes that they take over Lifeline immediately. Max thinks a takeover can only be done gradually and Vercors loses his temper. Before the Candide opens for business, Albert gives Monique some expensive perfume and Natalie and François set off down the Line. Kessler dines with Oberst Bruch, from Berlin who enjoys Monique's rendition of a German lullaby but is furious about the ongoing operation of the evasion lines and threatens Kessler with a posting in the East. The train on which Natalie and François are travelling is derailed by the Communists and many passengers are killed. After receiving goods from a black marketeer known as Bluebeard, Albert hears about the train crash from Alain. Jean-Louis is one of twenty Communists arrested and taken before Kessler for interrogation. As Kessler is not getting anywhere with them, Brandt suggests that he asks the Communists not in their custody to identify Lifeline members in exchange for the release of their comrades. Max informs Albert that Bluebeard has been taken in for questioning and Monique tells him to dump all the goods he obtained from him. Monique and Dr Keldermans set of to the countryside near the site of the train crash in order to find Natalie, François and the evaders in their charge. François returns to the barn where Natalie and the evaders have been hiding, having contacted Albert by phone. Natalie is injured but not as badly as the evaders, one of whom has already died, while another is close to death. Vercors visits Danielle at her father's shop with news of the arrests. She tells him that Monique and Keldermans were there asking for directions to Barsacq's house. Vercors leaves after a heated argument with Danielle about her feelings for Barsacq. Keldermans and Monique are directed from Barsacq's to a barn where they are reunited with Natalie and François, just after François has revealed his suspicions about Max to Natalie. Before they leave, they have to bury one of the evaders. That evening, Kessler and Brandt pay a visit to Barsacq's house, as Vercors has identified him as a Lifeline agent. Vercors tells Danielle about his deal with Kessler and she hurries to Barsacq's house to see if he is alright. Once there, she wrestles Kessler's gun from him; he then orders a soldier to shoot her. At the Candide, Kessler discusses the girl's elimination with Brandt and it is clear it does not matter to him whether she was a Lifeline agent or not. Natalie guides the only evader to have survived the train crash down the Line.

REVIEW: *Not According to Plan* marks another important turning point in the series as the nature of the Communist threat to Lifeline, which will be the subject of this and many future episodes, is properly established, specifically through the revelation of Max's true colour(s) and the introduction of local cell leader, Paul

Vercors. However, the episode seeks to cover an awful lot of ground, and despite several outstanding sequences (including: the train crash and its aftermath; some terrific Candide-set interplay between Monique and Albert; and best of all, Oberst Bruch's dinner with Kessler), the episode feels overloaded and occasionally disjointed.

That *Secret Army* is now headed in a new direction is clearly signposted by Albert's comment to Monique: "We've got into the habit of thinking that the war begins and ends with the escape line. We've had to learn to be ruthless in our business; the Communists have always been ruthless in theirs." The new Communist threat promises to increase the level of intrigue and to add another layer of complexity to a series which Monique neatly summarises as so far consisting of an unending cycle of foreign airmen: "We pass them down the Line. They get back to England. They fly out again. They get shot down again. It all starts again." Although this will continue to be the series's *raison d'etre* for as long as the evaders can be guided down the Line, the Communist subplot, and in particular Max's treachery, is a welcome and diverting addition to the ongoing narrative.

The members of the Communist cell, to which Max belongs and which Vercors appears to head up are presented as an over-emotional and idealistic bunch who have long-term objectives – they are preoccupied with their post-war dominance – but no clue how to organise themselves to achieve them. As such they provide a marked contrast with the capable members of Lifeline, whose operations Vercors naïvely imagines they can assume control of overnight. The way in which Max's insider knowledge and expertise is ignored amidst a cloud of rhetoric, despite the fact that his is the only voice of reason, makes it surprising that the forger will have anything to do with this sorry group. Although we are given clues later in the second series as to the reason for his socio-political affiliation, Max's Communist leanings somehow never seem to quite ring true, simply because he appears to fit into the Lifeline group so much better. They, like Max, are all pragmatic individuals who seem far more likely to command his respect than his flaky Communist colleagues. However, it is perhaps this factor which makes Max's terrible betrayals so much more shocking.

It has to be said that, in its portrayal of Communists, *Secret Army* regularly finds itself severely lacking. The stereotypes start here and get no better; worse still, in future, they are not only presented as clueless and vindictive, but as possessing no honest objectives whatsoever. No attempt is made to draw out nuances in their characters and in many respects they resemble little more than moustache-twirling pantomime villains. Although John Brason did not write this episode, his aggressive treatise on the Communist 'canker' in *What Did you Do in the War, Daddy?* makes it clear that he for one was a capitalist through and through, while Glaister's political credentials are nowhere more obviously presented than through the 'Thatcherite wet dream' that is his Eighties super-soap *Howards' Way*. Although it does not excuse their approach, it is arguable that it can largely be explained by the time in which *Secret Army was* made, when the

253

Cold War was still very much raging and, in the case of this second series, when distrust of, and disgust at, the Left was at an all-time high as the UK entered the infamous 'Winter of Discontent'.

Although reported action is a necessary ingredient of any drama series, this episode includes too many narrative-jarring examples. The absence of Monique's and Dr Keldermans's visit to Danielle's shop and François's post-crash mission to contact Albert seem odd, while the decision not to include a scene in which Barsacq, Monique and Dr Keldermans meet for the first time is just plain confusing. With this latter instance the result is that we have to assume that the vital information – that François and Natalie are alive and at a nearby barn – has already been exchanged from just one line: "As soon as George gets back he'll take you straight out to the barn." The obvious explanation for the episode's resultant edited feel would be that David Crane's script was overlong, however director Viktors Ritelis does find time to include several lengthy and atmospheric film sequences which don't necessarily serve to advance the plot. Several directorial touches make it obvious that Ritelis is back at the helm: the presence of rowdy and authentically European extras in the railway carriages; the slow pan out from the iron *fleur-de-lys* fence post in Barsacq's garden; and a rather strange (and arguably pointless) cross-fade between the barn and Barsacq's purring black cat.

This is Nigel Williams's first episode as Natalie's ill-fated love interest, François. Although the character works well enough, he comes across as a little too wet and naïve to be a good match for his battle-hardened new lover. This is especially true in the sequence in which Natalie just cannot understand why he is still thinking about an evader who is already dead ("Forget about him... he's dead") and worrying about another who is about to die ("Well, *what* about him?") However, Natalie's passion for him appears to be genuine, perhaps because he is able to display the sensitivity that she cannot always show or feel herself. Although two faceless evaders – *Secret Army*'s equivalent of *Star Trek*'s 'redshirts' – die in the train crash, François, and to a lesser extent Natalie, escape relatively unscathed. Nevertheless, the signs are all here that François's time with his new girlfriend may be short; indeed, Monique's stunned reaction to the news that he is set to travel down the Line initially suggests that he may not even make it through his first episode.

Of the other key supporting cast members, Jonathan Newth – still a couple of years away from playing his career-defining role as Colonel Clifford Jefferson in *Tenko* – impresses as the sympathetic and wise Barsacq; however, both Michael Byrne (perhaps now best known for *Sharpe*) and Emma Williams feel like theatre actors moonlighting in the wrong medium. Throughout the episode, Byrne sounds as though he is recovering from major root canal treatment (perhaps he was?) and on the strength of this performance it's not all that surprising that he was not invited to return to reprise the role of Vercors in the final series. In fact, by casting Ralph Bates (of Poldark fame), in the role, the production team showed no interest in securing a Byrne-lookalike. Unfortunately, they were similarly uninterested in maintaining continuity with the events of *Not According to Plan*, electing to make Albert's betrayal of Max and the other members of his cell in *Prisoner of War*, an episode in which Vercors neither appears nor is mentioned, as the reason why he is bent on vengeance. Given Max's lack of cooperation with Vercors here, it seems very unlikely that Vercors would later seek to avenge the forger's death so readily. However, it is easy to see why Albert's betrayal of Max was chosen to be Vercors's principal motivation for his actions in the final series, as it stands as one of the most memorable incidents of the second series.

The episode's most accomplished sequence takes place in the Candide and features a tremendous performance from Leon Eagles as Oberst Bruch, whose comment about Monique – "she could almost be German" – tells us everything we need to know about this particularly unpleasant and thoroughly believable Nazi. The action of the scene appears to come together effortlessly despite the complexity of the required interplay between Bruch, Kessler, Albert and Monique, in one continuous – and therefore very impressive – take. Monique's major contribution to the scene is to sing, by special request, 'Mozart's Lullaby' (Schlafe Mein Prinzchen). The song, as is often the case, acts as a backdrop to conversations taking place in the foreground, and frames the sequence beautifully. The scene is another great example of the *frisson* of excitement that is derived from the audience's knowledge that Lifeline's centre of operations is the very place that the high-ranking Germans most commonly frequent. Here this is emphasised by Monique's knowing comment: "In our own way we try to do what is right," and by Bruch's statement that an evasion line is operating right under Kessler's nose, just as Albert finishes pouring the Sturmbannführer's drink from precisely that position. The employment of such narrative devices may be becoming more frequent in the series, but they are never anything less than pleasing to observe.

Perhaps the most memorable element of this scene is Kessler's shell-shocked reaction, superbly played by Rose, to Bruch's observation that he has been sent "too far from Berlin" and his threat of a posting on the Eastern Front. That this is one of the only times that we see Kessler so utterly dejected and distraught is quite right, as here he is being criticised for failing to carry out his duty to the Fatherland, a duty that is – with the possible exception of his relationship with Madeleine – the be all and end all of his existence. Although this incident reveals Kessler's vulnerable side, equally as interesting in terms of character development is the later scene, also in the Candide, in which he openly acknowledges the expediency of having Danielle shot, regardless of whether or not she was actually a member of Lifeline, in order to convince his Berlin-based superiors of his efficiency and therefore save his own skin. Kessler may be a devoted member of the Reich but he is also a survivor.

Although they add detail to the continued operation of the Candide, the scenes relating to the black market are perhaps the most unnecessary ingredient of the episode. The inclusion of black marketeer Bluebeard, in particular, contributes little to the narrative other than to remind the viewer that, Lifeline activities aside, running the restaurant through the use of black market contacts is a dangerous game in itself. Another unnecessary element is the unfortunate reversion to the dreadful code language of Series One for the evaders, who are described here variously as children and sacks of potatoes!

The dynamics of Albert's and Monique's relationship remains as interesting as ever, particularly in the scene before the Candide opens for business. When talking about Max's absence due to a possible girlfriend, Monique doesn't miss the opportunity to remind Albert that he still hasn't asked her to marry him: "I hope she has a better time than me and if she's lucky he might even marry her." Although Albert's gift to Monique of a box of expensive perfume may not be the wedding ring she desires, it is a show of true affection nevertheless and one that she clearly appreciates. However, she is understandably less appreciative of Albert's comment about Natalie and François falling in love at such a perilous time, which clearly implies that he perceives that they themselves have not. Although Albert states: "I want us both to survive" and therefore sees his relationship with Monique as a permanent commitment he nevertheless seems unable to offer her marriage, believing that the war means that "there's no time for anything else." This suggests that he sees marriage as demanding more of him than their relationship currently involves, ignoring the fact that he already worries for her safety and would be just as devastated if he was to lose her due to their evasion work, regardless of their marital status. His reaction to Monique's capture in the previous episode couldn't illustrate this fact more strongly. It thus seems more and more likely that the war is a convenient excuse for Albert.

Like Natalie and François, the aforementioned box of perfume endures a perilous journey of its own throughout the episode. After travelling halfway across Belgium, it eventually ends up, more or less intact, in the hands of Kessler. Unfortunately the reason for its recurrent appearances is mystifying. It is distinctly odd that Monique took the empty perfume box with her on her mission in the first place. Equally strange is that Danielle has it with her when she goes to check on Barsacq. When Kessler eventually sniffs the box it seems possible that its relevance will become clear: that he will smell the same perfume on Monique when he next visits the Candide, perhaps? However, this avenue remains unexplored. Its presence at Danielle's shop is presumably meant to emphasise Vercors's boorishness and also to confirm that it definitely was Monique and Keldermans whom Danielle met off-screen; however, on both counts it seems like a clumsy device to choose. One last word on the perfume box: it appears to have supernatural powers of regeneration. Either the scenes were filmed out of order or the box had a stunt double!

Although *Not According to Plan* has much to recommend it, its lack of discernible focus and disparate content has the effect of making the episode far less memorable than it otherwise might have been. The unfortunate result is that it is often simplistically referred to as 'the episode with the blind man.'

HISTORICAL BACKGROUND

Communist Resistance

Communist Party followers began to engage in radical resistance against the Occupiers after the German invasion of the Soviet Union in 1941. On formal instruction from 'the Komintern', the Belgian Communist Party organised a resistance coalition of social and political forces and a partisan force to engage in guerrilla warfare. The main target for the first generation of these militant partisans, which in Brussels were largely made up of engineers and scientists, was German transportation. At first there was an attempt to avoid human targets, but after the Germans responded more harshly to sabotage, which had tripled on a daily basis since the Communists mobilised their forces, they abandoned this policy. When, in December 1941, Communist leader and Belgian MP Georges Cordier was tortured to death and seventeen Communists were executed, and another thirty were sentenced to death or deported to Germany, the nature of Party resistance changed markedly. In particular, they began to show their hatred for those Belgians who they believed to be collaborating with the Occupiers. In April 1942, the Communist underground press announced that all collaborators would 'perish as dogs' and partisans began to murder those who they suspected had informed on their colleagues. In the latter half of 1942, they executed a total of sixty Belgians – many of them dignitaries and police officers – who they considered to be collaborators and, most infamously, three Rexist (a Belgian Fascist party) Mayors. Between December 1942 and January 1943, the Germans responded by executing a further 68 militant Communists, which in turn led to Communist attacks on German military personnel. As a result, over 800 Party members and partisans were arrested in early 1943. In July, the Germans also succeeded in rounding up the Party and partisan leaders. By this time, the militant Communists in Belgium were in a very poor state indeed and in order to continue the partisan action they had to begin to recruit more members. It is at this stage, in the latter half of 1943, that *Secret Army* chooses to pick up the Communist story. It is possible that, in part, Vercors and his heavies were based upon a group (or cell) of militant Communists around Leuven, who led a very violent campaign of sabotage and execution of collaborators. By the end of the war, surviving partisans claimed to have executed some 1,100 'traitors' during the Occupation.[3]

The Belgian Black Market

Throughout the war in Occupied Europe, German authorities fluctuated between working with the black market or trying to suppress it. Attempts to do the latter in Northern Russia reportedly had very negative results, as goods disappeared and the urban population consequently lacked basic foodstuffs to live on. To resolve the problem, the Germans had no choice but to 're-admit' these markets. According to German secret military police records, in Belgium, the incidence of strikes and anti-German sentiment rose when food was scarce, particularly in the Spring of 1941. In the following year, by which time the black market had been permitted to become fully established, these same records showed that the Germans largely regarded the populace to be passive and believed that the two factors were inextricably linked. However, by 1943, black market or no, food shortage was a day-to-day reality.

SONGS IN THE CANDIDE

'Schlafe Mein Prinzchen'

Once attributed to Mozart because of its originality, naïvety and playfulness, the German lullaby 'Schlafe Mein Prinzchen' ('Sleep my little prince') – more properly titled 'Wiegenlied' ('Lullaby') – was actually composed by Bernard Flies, with lyrics by Friedrich Wilhelm Gotter, in the 18th Century. The version which Monique sings here varies from the standard lyrics.

WHERE ELSE HAVE I SEEN..?

Jonathan Newth (Barsacq)

Nicholas Fox, *The Brothers*, 1973-4
Captain Blamey, *Poldark*, 1975
Orfe, *Doctor Who: Underworld*, 1978
Colonel Clifford Jefferson, *Tenko*, 1981, 1984
Russell Bryant, *After Henry*, 1988-92

Michael Byrne (Vercors)

Fritz, *Edward the Seventh*, 1975
Peter Guillam, *Smiley's People*, 1982
Colonel Patrick Ansell, *Saracen*, 1989
Major Nairn, *Sharpe*, 1994
Ted Page, *Coronation Street*, 2008

Leon Eagles (Bruch)

Colonel Van Deken, *The Black Tulip*, 1970
Jabel, *Doctor Who: The Face of Evil*, 1977
Terry Kane, *The Famous Five: Five Have a Wonderful Time*, 1978
Major Hughes, *The Tomorrow People: Hitler's Last Secret*, 1978
Seddon, *The Fourth Arm*, 1983

Episode 6: SCORPION

WRITTEN BY: James Andrew Hall   **DIRECTED BY:** Roger Jenkins

FIRST BROADCAST: BBC1, 8.05pm, Wednesday 1 November 1978

STUDIO RECORDING: 14 October 1978

VIEWING FIGURE: 8.9m

REGULAR CAST: Albert Foiret: BERNARD HEPTON; Monique Duchamps: ANGELA RICHARDS; Max Brocard: STEPHEN YARDLEY; Major Erwin Brandt: MICHAEL CULVER; Sturmbannführer Ludwig Kessler: CLIFFORD ROSE; Natalie Chantrens: JULIET HAMMOND-HILL; Dr Pascal Keldermans: VALENTINE DYALL; Madeleine Duclos: HAZEL McBRIDE; François: NIGEL WILLIAMS; Hans van Broecken: GUNNAR MÖLLER; Lena van Broecken: MARIANNE STONE

SUPPORTING CAST: Erika Brandt: BRIGITTE KAHN; Madame Louise Van Artevelde: MARGERY WITHERS; Vic Hutton: WILLIAM BOYDE; Roger Parker: JAMES WYNN; Geoff Lloyd: CHARLES ROGERS; Bill Godley: JULIAN ASHTON; Peter Bridge: DAVID TAYLOR; Billy Boyce: STEPHEN REYNOLDS; Tim Woodridge: HARRY H. FIELDER; Piano Tuner: ALBERT WELCH

SYNOPSIS: At Albert's request, Dr Keldermans calls in at the Candide and is told about a downed airman whose arm he must amputate. Natalie has persuaded her uncle, Hans van Broecken, to bring the man to Brussels by barge, despite the fact that he is still angry with Albert for causing the death of Finch. Before he leaves, Keldermans tells Albert that Brandt is due for a visit from his wife. Erika Brandt sees her husband's apartment for the first time. After Brandt leaves for work, Erika discovers a photograph of a young woman in the wardrobe. Brandt's cleaning lady, Mme Van Artevelde, arrives and allays her fears by telling her that her husband never entertains. Monique and Max brief a new group of evaders. Erika confronts Brandt about the photo, but he denies knowing the girl. She asks if she and their children can come and live with him in Brussels. After his successful operation on the injured evader, Keldermans returns to the Candide and learns how the man received his terrible injuries. On the Van Broeckens' barge, Lena and Hans receive a visit from Natalie and François. Natalie thanks her uncle for helping the evader, but he warns her that she must not ask for his help again. Mme Van Artevelde overhears Brandt tell Erika that he may be close to leaving Brussels and smashing the evasion line, as an infiltration attempt has been successful. She hurries to the Candide and tells a stunned Albert the news. Albert discusses the matter with Keldermans and Max and tells them that he thinks they may have to shoot all of the evaders that they are currently hiding. Max suggests that they should seek Hans van Broecken's assistance (because he is German) to flush out the infiltrator instead, while Keldermans advises medical examinations that might reveal the infiltrator if he is an SS man. Albert makes an unexpected visit to the barge and insists on a private audience with Hans. The bargee is very reluctant to help Albert, but eventually agrees on the understanding that he will not have to kill anyone. Hans enters the safe-houses in turn and manages to eliminate some suspects, but Albert still fears that they may have to close the Line all the way to the Spanish border. That evening, Brandt and Erika dine at the Candide; Kessler and Madeleine are also there at a separate table. Erika asks a second time about leaving Berlin, but Brandt again refuses.

Back at Brandt's apartment, Erika muses about the fate of the girl in the photograph, before raising the matter of leaving Berlin once more. Brandt reveals that he does not want her to be involved in his work in Brussels and agrees to a compromise instead. Hans tells Albert that he has done all he can. Max suggests another approach which should reveal which of the remaining three suspects is a professionally trained killer. Max leads the men from the barge, where they have been temporarily incarcerated, into an ambush. During the struggle it is obvious that 'Vic Hutton' is the trained man. In order to make him reveal what, if any information he has aleady passed on, Hans ties an anchor to him, throws him into a lock and begins to fill it. Max informs a relieved Monique that they have got the infiltrator and she relays the news to the others. As the lock fills, Hutton confesses. Hans wants to set him free, but Max prevents this and the man drowns.

REVIEW: *Scorpion* contains the sort of rewarding and believable character development that is typical of the series. It is an episode that is also notable for the quality of its guest cast, with both Brigitte Kahn – making her first and only appearance as Erika Brandt – and the returning Gunnar Möller providing mesmerising performances.

Scriptwriter James Andrew Hall elected to bring back the characters of Natalie's honorary Aunt and Uncle, Lena and Hans van Broecken, because they had worked so well in his first script for the series, *Second Chance*. Despite the fact that those events occurred some seventeen episodes ago, continuity is bravely maintained through dialogue that reminds viewers of the death of Paul Copley's Finch who, as a fellow deserter, Hans had promised to assist, only to have Lifeline take him off his hands and murder him. Although killing Finch out of expediency (in order to avert suspicion from the Candide) had been Curtis's idea, here Albert has to take the blame for an act that he sanctioned rather than planned. It is a detail which Albert does not choose to raise in his defence, perhaps because he is now living with the guilt of many more deaths arranged for similarly expedient reasons? The 'Finch incident' has affected Hans deeply and, as Max observes, he really does mean it when he tells Albert that he will not kill for him. As in *Second Chance*, the bargee is still insistent that he and Lena will not become involved in the war and their nomadic existence on the edge of society demonstrates this clearly. However, this and the subsequent episode will prove that, like novelist Hugh Neville, Hans is naïve to think that he can continue to stay out of it, whatever his views on governments not caring "when they send you out to be blown to pieces." His naïvety also extends to his failure to realise that Lifeline have no choice but to kill the German infiltrator when he is finally identified. There is no denying that the man's death is disturbing and distasteful, but Lifeline's members have long since accepted the occasional fatality as essential to their ongoing operations. Hans, however, will never be able to condone such actions and will always view Albert and his colleagues as "heartless vicious murderers." Of course, it doesn't help at the episode's conclusion that Max clearly relishes Hutton's death; nevertheless, the forger's argument that otherwise more people would be tortured and killed is a convincing one and it still feels as though Hans needs, as Max says, to "get his priorities right." Möller is superb throughout, but especially in the scene in which Hans realises, to his great frustration, that he has no alternative but to help Albert.

When she heard that the part of Brandt's wife was being cast, Juliet Hammond-Hill immediately thought her friend and fellow actor Brigitte Kahn would be perfect for the role. She couldn't have been more right. The elegant and striking Kahn effortlessly inhabits a role which not only helps us to better understand Brandt, but also the historical context from a German civilian's point of view. Erika's repeated pleas to her husband that she and their children be allowed to leave the intensively bombed Berlin to come and live with him in Brussels provides a grim picture of an increasingly desperate existence. As Erika recounts: "Every night now we have to sleep in the shelters. Buildings burn and fall down all around; not one here and another there, it's every other building!" To British viewers, this dialogue immediately conjures up images from newsreel footage of the devastation of the London Blitz of 1940, an episode of the war which incidentally the series's German characters conveniently – and perhaps authentically – forget whenever the British bombing of German cities is mentioned. Erika's understandable reaction to her newly endangered existence is to now consider the war to be "a ghastly mistake." Brandt's response ("This time last year neither you nor anyone else thought it was such a ghastly mistake. Was that because it seemed to be going well then?") proves that he is unafraid to call out his fellow countrymen for their capriciousness, even when that includes his wife, and perhaps also suggests that he has become frustrated with hearing the same assessment from his demoralised fellow officers. It is a response that cannot help but make us like Brandt for his startling honesty. Throughout the course of the episode, Erika asks Brandt three times if she and the children can leave Berlin, before he finally provides a decent explanation for his refusal. However, Brandt's reason is a good one and proves very illuminating in terms of his views on his wartime duties: "I don't want you involved in the work I have to do in this city – I'm not proud of some of the things I have to do and I don't want my children to grow up not understanding." When Erika claims not to understand either, Brandt asks her: "Who do you imagine performs all of the disgusting tasks of an occupation force? Who do you think takes women and children hostage and shoots them?" His answer to his question: "the Nazis," is delivered in such a way that he makes it plain that he desperately wants to distance himself from their actions. However, Brandt is no fool and has already realised that history will not make fine distinctions between the Nazis and the Luftwaffe Polizei: "We are Germans, that's all." However, this excellent scene proves that *Secret Army* thankfully does recognise the difference, and is an all the more intelligent drama for it.

The recognition of the existence of firm divisions between the two groups is also explored elsewhere in *Scorpion*; not, as is so often the case in the programme, in terms of their differences of approach, but this time in terms of class. Erika's arrival makes obvious the – previously ignored – detail that she and Brandt are of upper-class military stock. As Monique observes after first meeting

261

her in the Candide: "His wife's a bit grand isn't she?" an observation to which Albert responds with the shrewd explanation: "It's the way they've been brought up." As the daughter of a General, Erika is mortified by the idea of having to acknowledge Kessler and is totally unable to comprehend why her husband, as a Luftwaffe officer, has to associate with such "riff-raff." It is telling that only when Erika learns that Madeleine was once the mistress of Baron Christian D'Aquise – a man of similar status to herself – can she permit herself a glance across at Kessler and his dining partner. In stark contrast to his wife, Brandt considers their respective class statuses to be irrelevant, therefore coming over as far less of a snob than his wife. These social dynamics are made more interesting by the fact that Kessler knows all too well that Erika thinks of him as beneath her dignity. However, even more fascinating is Kessler's explanation to Madeleine that he is only ignoring Erika's "idiotic pretensions" because he quite likes Brandt and considers him to be "a most reliable officer and colleague"! Although Kessler and Brandt have been seen to enjoy a much more civil and cooperative working relationship thus far in the second series, it is still a huge surprise to hear Kessler speak of Brandt with such obvious affection and respect. The suggestion is that the pair have finally put their respective affiliations aside in order to work together, presumably for the greater good of the Reich, even though its future is depicted as increasingly uncertain.

Almost as surprising as Kessler's current take on Brandt is his growing devotion to Madeleine. Here he openly bares his soul to her, explaining that: "I sometimes feel lonely, but it doesn't bother me – I can exist cocooned within myself quite happily; but I sense in you a kindred spirit." This speech is beautifully written and delivered and gives us a real insight into the character of the socially awkward Sturmbannführer. Her response ("I feel quite happy this evening, something I haven't experienced for a long time") is practically effusive by Madeleine's standards and suggests that she believes that she may have found a kindred spirit in him as well. Given that Madeleine has the effect of making Kessler a truly three-dimensional character, her continued presence in the series can only be a good thing.

Although Brandt's character is perhaps always in less danger of slipping into stereotype than Kessler's, simply because he is presented as a more likeable and human character with whom the audience can more readily identify, it is nevertheless a shame that this is the one and only opportunity where we get to learn more about him through his wife. For one thing, Erika's arrival means that we get to see his Art Deco-styled apartment, albeit, for the first and last time. It is as neat and ordered as we imagined it would be, although Erika insists that its orderly state suggests he must have changed. Although the pair are slightly stilted with each other to begin with, the love that exists between them is quickly obvious ("You are exactly as beautiful as I remember") and it is not long before they retire to bed. However, both are keenly aware that "everything has changed" since they were last together. In particular, the last few months have caused Erika to become far more independent and outspoken; a far cry from the submissive general's daughter he married. It is a transformation which Brandt finds difficult to accept and views as a loss of dignity. Erika's heartfelt riposte: "Dignity will not save my life Erwin, nor the lives of our children," suggests that she may simply have a better handle on the dangers that the Brandt family's life in Berlin currently involves, and heavily signposts the tragedy that is to follow. The choice of a piano solo of 'If This Is the Last Time I See You' to underscore this scene is also deliberately prophetic. Brandt's repeated refusal to agree to Erika's request that she and the children come to live with him in Brussels ensures that when the terrible news inevitably reaches him (in *The Big One*) he will feel as much guilt as he does grief and the Major will never be the same again.

A theme which is expertly threaded through both the Erika and the infiltrator plotlines is that of 'the invader' and 'the invaded'. The first example of this is Erika's discovery of the photograph of Rachel, a Jewess who probably lived in Brandt's apartment before him, and who is now almost certainly dead. Although Brandt is presented as a humane German, the photograph is a stark and important reminder that he is nevertheless part of an occupying force that has coordinated the deportation of an entire race with a view to their extermination. He may argue that the Luftwaffe does not have anything to do with the deportation of Jews, but he and his colleagues have nevertheless stood by and let it happen. Just as Rachel reminds us that Brandt is an invader, his cleaner, Mme Van Artevelde, has a similar dramatic function with respect to Erika. Although the two women initially exchange pleasantries about Brandt's habits, the subject of the lack of goods in the shops leads Mme Van Artevelde to briefly forget herself and complain about "the wretched war." It is a comment which prompts a severe look from Erika and immediately redefines them both as invader and invaded. The injured man whom the Van Broeckens' take in is another example of an invader, albeit on a different side. We eventually learn that he was caught in Germany by a group of locals and viciously attacked as a 'terrorflieger' by a woman with a hatchet. However, this woman is not the only invadee in the narrative who has chosen to fight back. Mme Van Artevelde is a real surprise package, whose actions undoubtedly save the lives of all the men and women of Lifeline. The scene in which she excitedly tells Albert what she has learnt is a joy, partly because of how the dawning realisation of what she is saying is played out on Albert's face, but also because she delivers the news as if she is just recounting the latest gossip from the fish market. This character provides a sobering reminder to Albert of just how tenuous Lifeline's continued operation actually is and how it sometimes relies on the patriotism and bravery of the most unlikely people.

Secret Army's ever-present conflict between expediency and morality is examined again here through Albert's reactions to the infiltrator problem. His natural tendency, as in previous episodes, is towards expediency first ("Shoot all nineteen of them if you have to") to ensure the continued safety of the Line. However, he is soon talked around by Max and Keldermans to a less drastic solution which requires the assistance of Van Broecken. Brilliant scripting subsequently has Van Broecken, on first hearing about the infiltrator, sarcastically suggesting: "Why not shoot them all – you have had a lot of experience in that!" unaware that he has actually correctly guessed Albert's first solution to the problem. Albert's quick-fire response ("All nineteen of them?") hides this fact very well, although the bargee's words and his subsequent outburst ("To me you are a murderer and I don't like you Albert Foiret!") cannot fail but to have a profound effect on him. Sure enough, later on when there are only three suspects left and Max suggests killing them, Albert decides upon a quite out-of-character course of action, ordering: "Not yet, but it may come to that." Albert may still have the bigger picture at the forefront of his mind, but the events of *Scorpion* have forced him to question the moral code that the war has caused him to adopt.

Although by no means the focus of the episode, when Monique does appear her confidence and practicality are brought to the fore. She is seen to be both commanding and scolding with the clueless evaders, intelligent in her reasoning (it is her deduction that, if Brandt is behind the plot, then the infiltrator is more likely to be a Luftwaffe man than SS) and, in contrast to the worried Albert, more than capable of keeping it together in the face of Lifeline's imminent collapse. Although they may have to leave the Candide to go into hiding, she realises that she cannot neglect the possibility that their current existence may not change after all and therefore the restaurant will continue to open as usual and so she checks with Albert if his suit needs cleaning and views the hiring of a piano tuner as a necessity. This is not to say that she isn't fearful about what the future holds ("I'm really scared this time, Albert") but she seems to have the resources to deal with the desperate uncertainty all the same, signposting the fact that, later in the war, she will become a worthy successor to Albert. The scene in which she and Albert set up the Candide for business is later mirrored in the Series Three episode *Collaborator*. Both are highly effective scenes and the contrast between the two is fascinating, principally because they take place a year apart and so, due to the characters' respective intervening experiences, the alteration to their respective outlooks on life is enormous.

Max, who thanks to Stephen Yardley's charisma is always interesting to watch, also receives some welcome development here. His criminal past plays an important part in both coming up with the suggestion of involving Van Broecken ("You set a thief to catch a thief") and in finally identifying the infiltrator by virtue of the fact that he will be unsentimental about hurting anyone. Max not only calls on his past experience to solve this problem, but also the actual criminals who he used to be inside with! Interestingly, when faced with the prospect of soiling his hands, Max is not troubled by his conscience at all, replying to Albert in a matter-of-fact voice: "Oh yes."

In retrospect, infiltrator Vic Hutton, played by a young William Boyde – who is still best remembered as Willmott-Brown, the proprietor of the Dagmar pub in *Eastenders* – is perhaps the most obvious suspect due to the fact that he has the most archetypally English things to say. He asks for "grub," calls himself a "nuisance" and even dubs the safe-house Pooh Corner! However, before the reveal, both ubiquitous extra Harry H. Fielder (who is unfortunate not to receive an on-screen credit given his role here) and James Wynn (*Grange Hill*'s Mr Sutcliffe) seem just as likely to be the man that Lifeline is after.

One of *Scorpion*'s very few downsides is that some of the incidental music in the latter half of the episode is very off-putting as it sounds uncannily like the opening bars of the Star Trek theme and so one half expects to hear William Shatner saying: "These are the voyages of the Starship Enterprise." Another is the episode title – which Glaister would re-use as a series title, albeit with a 'k', for a 1983 thriller series starring Terrence Hardiman – which presumably refers to the infiltrator, but fails to sum up the episode effectively. However, these are both very minor criticisms of an episode crammed full with intriguing character development and incident, that reminds the viewer that *Secret Army* is a complex and deeply satisfying drama.

HISTORICAL BACKGROUND

Junkers

In German, Junker literally means 'young lord'. The nearest English equivalent is 'country squire'. In the Middle Ages, a Junker was a lesser noble and, as such, considered relatively insignificant; however, over the centuries Junkers rose up the social hierarchy and by the 19th Century had become rich landowners and influential commanders, especially in Prussia. The Junkers controlled the Prussian Army, occupying all the high offices, and as Prussia controlled Germany and the Junkers ruled Prussia, the Junkers effectively ruled Germany. Their influence was at its height during the German Empire and the later Weimar

Republic, holding sway over the industrial classes and the government from 1871 to 1933. Hitler blamed the Junkers for the failure of the Beer Hall Putsch in 1923, due to the involvement of a Junker named Otto von Lossow (right). Although Hitler was occasionally outspoken about his disdain for the Junkers, when he came to power he was nevertheless supported by them and, it is said, that while they hated him, they hated democracy more. Hitler certainly took no specific actions against them and permitted them to retain their extensive estates. Many Junkers held high-level military positions in the Reich, including Gerd von Rundstedt and Erwin Rommel. The abortive 20 July 1944 bomb plot was set to dent Junker power in Germany considerably, hundreds of the 5000 men identified as conspirators were of this aristocratic stock. Hitler may have left their land alone, but after the war the Communists stripped them of their estates in line with their land redistribution policies. While many Junkers fled to the West, many others were killed. Since the reunification of Germany, some of the old Junker families are seeking to reclaim their pre-Communist estates.

Bombing of Hamburg

The raid against Hamburg, which Keldermans describes as "pretty indefensible," must refer to one of a series of heavy raids in late July/early August 1943, otherwise known as 'The Battle of Hamburg'. The operation, codenamed

Operation Gomorrah, was a joint effort between the RAF and the USAAF, planned by Winston Churchill and Air Chief Marshal Arthur 'Bomber' Harris, and consisted of continued bombing of the city over 8 days and 7 nights. The night of 27 July saw such concentrated bombing that a firestorm was spawned which incinerated large parts of the city. Over 50,000 civilians were killed during Operation Gomorrah, the majority during the night of 27 July. (Above: Hamburg after the devastasting bombing.)

WHERE ELSE HAVE I SEEN..?

Brigitte Kahn (Erika Brandt)

Rebel Officer, *The Empire Strikes Back*, 1980
Maria Lang, *Nanny*, 1982
Dagmar, *Auf Wiedersehen, Pet*, 1983-84
Baroness, *The Remains of the Day*, 1993
Ruth, *Unfinished Business*, 1999

William Boyde (Vic Hutton)

Dr Crick, *The Nation's Health*, 1983
James Wilmott-Brown, *Eastenders*, 1986-87, 1992
Edward VIII, *A Dance to the Music of Time*, 1997
Lord Ravenswood, *Lucia*, 1998
Tim, *'Orrible*, 2001

Episode 7: WEEKEND

WRITTEN and DIRECTED BY: Paul Annett

FIRST BROADCAST: BBC1, 8.05pm, Wednesday 8 November 1978

STUDIO RECORDING: 16 August 1978

VIEWING FIGURE: 9.0m

REGULAR CAST: Albert Foiret: BERNARD HEPTON; Monique Duchamps: ANGELA RICHARDS; Max Brocard: STEPHEN YARDLEY; Sturmbannführer Ludwig Kessler: CLIFFORD ROSE; Natalie Chantrens: JULIET HAMMOND-HILL; Corporal Rennert: ROBIN LANGFORD; Hans van Broecken: GUNNAR MÖLLER; Lena van Broecken: MARIANNE STONE

SUPPORTING CAST: Oberleutnant Horst: CHRISTIAN ROBERTS; Peter Harris: PAUL WAGAR; Charles McGee: VINCENT MARZELLO; Madame Desmarts: DOREEN MANTLE; Mother Superior: SYLVIA BARTER; Yvonne: HENRIETTA BAYNES; Pilot: GILBERT O'BRIEN; Jacques: JOHN WALDON; Claudette: SUSAN DADY; German Officer: MISHA BERGESE

SYNOPSIS: Two American airmen arrive at an airbase in England and board a plane bound for a raid over Europe. An art-loving Oberleutnant by the name of Horst informs Kessler that the three Rubens paintings, of which he has photographs on his desk, are hanging in a convent near Amsterdam. Kessler declares that he is indebted to Horst for this information and invites him as his guest to a Bach recital. The next day, Albert and Monique meet with the Mother Superior of the same convent that Horst described, in order to discuss a plan to replace the three Rubens with copies and sell the originals with a view to generating some money for Lifeline. After arrangements for the paintings' collection are made, Albert and Monique travel back to Brussels by train. En route, they discuss Lifeline's current cash flow problem and Albert reveals that he thinks the British have stopped sending money due to their fears that their organisation might be spreading Communist doctrine. By pawning the paintings to a Swiss speculator, Albert hopes to buy Lifeline some independence. The bomber in which the Americans – McGee and Harris – are flying is hit while over Belgium and they bail out. News of their escape reaches Lifeline via a Madame Desmarts, who has taken the pair in. Natalie has promised her that they will be collected the next day, but McGee and Harris are nervous about staying there. Kessler and Horst visit the convent and remove the paintings. However, on their way back to Brussels their car is ambushed by McGee and Harris who have struck out on their own. They order Horst to drive on while holding him and Kessler hostage, before hiding the car and continuing on foot. The party reaches a river where Hans van Broecken's barge is moored. News reaches Albert that the paintings have been confiscated. On the barge, while holding Kessler and Horst at gunpoint, McGee tells Hans that he wants him to take him and Harris all the way to Switzerland. Horst reveals Kessler's identity to Hans. Lena persuades Hans that they should contact Lifeline in order for them to take the airmen off their hands. She subsequently calls the Candide and tells Natalie about their current situation. On returning to the barge, she confides in Hans that she is worried about the possibility of being questioned. McGee decides that the time has come to kill Kessler, but is prevented from doing so by Harris who tells him about Lena contacting Lifeline. Hans tells McGee about the massacres that followed Heydrich's murder and the American agrees to being handed over to Lifeline. Max and Monique, disguised as medical personnel and driving an ambulance, pick up the Rubens copies from the convent and, after locating Kessler's abandoned car, switch them with the originals. Hans releases Kessler and Horst. Max and Monique rendezvous with Natalie and the airmen, who begin their journey down the Line. Lena returns to the barge and discovers that Kessler has also come back. Kessler escorts Hans and Lena to Gestapo HQ. Once there, Lena throws herself in front of a passing vehicle – committing suicide rather than facing questioning.

Kessler lets Hans go and the bargee tells Albert what has happened by phone. Max suggests that Kessler be told the lie that the paintings hanging in the convent were always forgeries.

REVIEW: *Weekend* holds the unique distinction of being the only episode of *Secret Army* to be written and directed by the same person: Paul Annett. Annett, who was very keen to write for a series which he very much enjoyed directing, came up with a script that reflected both his fascination with what he had read about the severe disorientation experienced by young American airmen who had never before left their home state, never mind their country, and his interest in news stories breaking in the Seventies concerning the recovery of several significant paintings which had become 'lost' during the war. Although these ideas, together with a particularly central and meaty role in the proceedings for Kessler, should add up to success, unfortunately, looking back at it today, *Weekend* – more than any other episode of *Secret Army* – is afflicted by the fact that it conjures up too many images of the BBC comedy series *'Allo! 'Allo!* to be taken seriously.

There can be no doubt that when Jimmy Perry and David Croft were scripting *'Allo! 'Allo!* in the early Eighties, one of the episodes they watched to refresh their memory of *Secret Army* was *Weekend*. The relentless pursuit of Van Clomp's 'The Fallen Madonna with the Big Boobies' and the alarming frequency with which the characters disguised themselves as nurses and nuns are perhaps the most memorable elements of that show, and both can be traced back to here (and to a lesser extent, to *Trapped*). For the 'Fallen Madonna' read the Rubens paintings, while donning the disguises here are Max and Monique. Although *'Allo! 'Allo!* flagrantly takes off many other elements of *Secret Army*, nowhere is it more obvious and harder to forget than in this one episode. However, this is not the fault of the scriptwriter, but is rather just unfortunate circumstance.

Nevertheless, a criticism that can be more squarely levelled at Annett is that the episode arguably contains too many dramatic contrivances. Not only does Kessler happen to find out about the Rubens paintings from a visiting Oberleutant who happens to know exactly where they are hanging, coincidentally just as Lifeline happen to be after them as well, but he also ends up at Van Broecken's barge which just happens to be moored in the area. Although all drama series require such narrative devices in order to move the plot along, there are really too many for comfort here.

Thankfully, however, *Weekend* still has a great deal to recommend it. One idea that the narrative emphatically reinforces is a theme also touched upon in the preceding episode: that no-one can opt out of the war. In fact, Van Broecken, who only became involved in the events of *Scorpion* due to Natalie's direct request that he help a wounded evader, finds here that the war will as good as seek him out, even when his niece does not. In response to Van Broecken's statement: "My Lena and I, we just want a simple life, we don't take sides," Kessler insists: "That's a state you can maintain no longer. You must commit yourself." This is something Van Broecken finally appears to have accepted by the time the end credits roll.

Another element of this episode that was also examined in *Scorpion* is the effect that the ever-rising death toll is now having upon Albert. As he and Monique involve the Mother Superior, and therefore her Sisters as well, in their plan to sell on the paintings, he is reminded of the tragic events of *Good Friday* and is keen to warn the woman of the dangers of assisting them. When he says: "We don't want anything more on our conscience than we have already," it is obvious that what he really means is that he does not want to have to feel responsible for any more deaths.

Lifeline's difficult relationship with its London paymasters is given some rare illumination through discussion of the recent drying up of funds. The always distrustful Albert views this as "a show of strength" on London's part that is tied up with their fears over the emerging political situation after the war and specifically that Lifeline is spreading Communist doctrine. This serves not only as a reminder of Max's treachery, but also to depict Albert as being uninterested as to who funds Lifeline as long as one power does, be that Russia or the Western Allies. However, in contrast to the startling revelation in *Russian Roulette* that Albert is in Lifeline just for the money, he is merely presented here as intensely practical and only willing to continue the business of evasion while they have the funds to do so.

One of *Weekend*'s greatest strengths is its tangible climate of fear. Fear permeates the majority of the scenes, prompting Horst's sycophancy, Lena's startling choice and the American evaders to cause all the trouble in the first place. It is Kessler and what he and his fellow high-ranking Nazis represent (and the horrors of which they are capable) which is the focus of all this fear, and the Sturmbannführer is seen to positively revel in this. His calm reaction to the danger he faces allows for a chilling reminder as to why his safety is assured: because of the fear of terrible reprisals akin to those meted out to the people of Lidice, Czechoslovakia, after the murder of Heydrich. Such a threat effectively makes Kessler unassailable. Nevertheless, Hans underestimates Kessler's personal awareness of the terror he and his kind inspire. His simple reply to Hans: "Oh, I do bargee, I do," makes it patently clear just how aware he is. Clifford Rose is in excellent form throughout as a more sinister and brooding Kessler than we have seen of late, primarily due to the effect of Madeleine's inclusion in the series. The look of absolute fury on the Sturmbannführer's face immediately after Hans releases him makes it apparent that, despite his new-found romance, he remains a very dangerous man indeed.

Several wonderfully natural scenes, which serve as much-needed breathers from the main plot, are devoted to the relationship between Albert and Monique. The best of these takes place in their little-seen bedroom, during which Monique tries to ascertain whether Albert thinks she can get away with a purple feather boa or not. This beautifully observed scene adds little to the plot but adds further colour and depth to both characters, as well as realistically playing out the difficulty women have getting a firm opinion out of their partners about the clothes they are wearing! The later scene in which Monique expectantly waits up in bed for Albert, only for him to ignore her intentions, fulfils a similar function and, thanks to Richards's comic timing, is very funny. Although she is amused by the fact that her mother has told the Mother Superior that she and Albert are married, presumably in order to save face, Albert is much less so. Such humourless responses from Albert come to preoccupy Monique for the duration of the episode, although to call this a subplot would overstate its importance. When Max talks about appealing to Albert's sense of humour, she dryly remarks that: "He hasn't smiled at me in weeks." In fact, she is so concerned about this that she looks daggers at Max when he himself finds this amusing. This sub-subplot finds resolution when Albert finally laughs at one of her jokes and all is right between them again, for the time being at least. The chemistry between Richards and Hepton is as engaging and believable as ever and one of the highlights of the episode.

Despite the overtones of unreality forced upon *Weekend* by the unfortunate legacy of *'Allo! 'Allo!*, one element of the episode that conversely brings home the reality of the subject matter is the inclusion of actual colour footage of B-17 bombers on missions over Occupied Europe from William Wyler's acclaimed *Memphis Belle.* Clips from the film are cleverly interspersed with the newly recorded footage and the overall effect is admirable. The glass painting used at the airbase to make up for the lack of available bombers for the shoot is similarly effective and easy to miss if you're not looking out for it.

Paul Wagar and Vincent Marzello are well cast as the sensitive and sensible Peter Harris and the thoughtless Charles McGee respectively. Although Harris has the wide-eyed innocence of a disorientated soul and therefore engenders some sympathy, McGee is so thoughtless and objectionable that, when Natalie and Monique finally berate him for his recent actions, it is difficult not to want the latter to follow up on her threat and shoot him. That Natalie and Monique get to lay into McGee in such unbridled fashion is immensely satisfying, especially as he initially underestimates them both and has the idiocy to try to come on to them!

The scene which is undoubtedly the most memorable in *Weekend* is that in which Kessler arrives back at Gestapo Headquarters with Hans and a terrified Lena who, knowing that she cannot face being questioned, elects to commit suicide by throwing herself in front of a passing vehicle. Although Lena's fear of divulging information about Lifeline under questioning has already been revealed through earlier conversation with her husband, this tragic turn of events still remains totally unexpected. Its impact is perhaps made more shocking by the fact that she decides upon her course of action in an instant. Worse still, it subsequently proves to be a pointless sacrifice as Kessler informs Hans that he did not suspect either of them anyway, letting the latter go there and then. As affecting as it is, it is difficult to understand why Hans silently and dejectedly walks away from the scene of the tragedy rather than going to the body of his dead wife and holding her. The implication seems to be that either he has not got the reserves to face up to the sudden death of his wife or that he is simply still in a state of shock. The scene is desperately sad to watch, as by now we have come to care about the fate of the Van Broeckens, due to consistently superb performances from both Gunnar Möller and Marianne Stone.

Unfortunately, *Weekend* doesn't end there and then, and a full five minutes of relatively inconsequential action follows which feels like rather desperate padding, that was presumably recorded in order to get the episode up to the required 52 minutes. Both the scene in which Monique bitches with Yvonne, and that in which Max tells Albert how they should proceed with the paintings, would have worked fine earlier in the episode, but here they just have the effect of dulling the impact and significance of Lena's death. There are other problems with the scenes too. Yvonne's return after ten episodes seems plain odd, especially given her previous track record as a waitress. The chances of either Monique or Albert re-hiring her for the new restaurant seem pretty remote (although clumsy Claudette does rather suggest that there is a dearth of good waitresses in Brussels!) From a casting point of view, there is no denying that Hetty Baynes (who Annett cast in *Second Chance* in the first place and was obviously keen to reintroduce here) is always good value, but she is simply given nothing to work with here. The one-sided phone conversation between Albert and Hans is the other main failing of the episode's final minutes. The idea that Hans would be in a fit state to make a coherent call immediately after the death of his wife is unlikely in itself, but the chances of him choosing to call Albert, a man whom he has frequently said he despises, seem even more so. Similarly, as much as it neatly ties up the theme that no-one can opt out of the war, having Hans choosing to take sides, by offering Albert his assistance in the future, doesn't ring true either. Given what we know of Hans, it seems far more likely that, as a result of losing Lena, he would become more bitter and reclusive instead. This assessment is arguably borne out by the fact that Hans never does help Lifeline again, although he does supply information about Kessler to the Allies.

Although it is not without its problems, particularly from a post-*'Allo! 'Allo!* perspective, *Weekend* nevertheless stands as an effective and emotional conclusion to the loose Van Broecken trilogy, which Paul Annett saw in as director and here sees out as both director and writer.

HISTORICAL BACKGROUND

The Assassination of Heydrich and the Rape of Lidice

Reinhard Heydrich, the executive Head of the Gestapo and the man infamously responsible for organising the *Einsatzgruppen* (extermination squads) as the engines of genocide, had been appointed Acting Reich Protector in September 1941 of the German-occupied Czech Protectorate of Bohemia-Moravia. As the Protectorate was the core of the German armament industry and the Czech workers had taken to rioting, sabotage and strikes, Heydrich was charged with the task of implementing conciliatory measures (e.g. increasing worker food allowances) with a view to increasing production, in order to oil the German war machine. Alongside this seemingly humanitarian policy, Heydrich (right) oversaw the continued executions of traitors and resistants and set up another Jewish ghetto, Theresienstadt, which would become a transit station to the death camps. The London-based Czech government in exile were deeply concerned about Heydrich's conciliatory overtures to the workers, fearing that they might believe that German protection was not as oppressive as they had thought. As a result, a plan was formed whereby several Czech agents trained by the SOE would fly to Prague and assassinate Heydrich. Although

reprisals were feared, it was judged that the risks were nevertheless worthwhile. At 10.30am on 27 May 1942, the Czech agents attacked Heydrich as he was driven through the streets of Prague in a Mercedes, firstly with a malfunctioning sten gun and then with a bomb. Heydrich was badly wounded and died a week later due to wound infection. On hearing this news, Hitler was apparently incandescent with rage and commanded that Heydrich's murder would be paid for in 'oceans of blood'. Initially, random shootings took place and 3000 Jews were deported from Theresienstadt to the death camps. However, the most unspeakable act of vengeance was still to come. Although no connection has ever been proved between the assassination of Heydrich and the mining village of Lidice (in the district of Kladno to the northwest of Prague) the Germans

nevertheless decided to retaliate by murdering the majority of its inhabitants and razing it to the ground. On 10 June 1942, a German squad moved in and 199 men were executed, and 195 women were arrested and, after having their babies and younger children taken away, sent to Ravensbruck concentration camp. Of Lidice's 95 children, 9 were considered worthy of Germanisation and sent to SS families in the Reich, while the remainder were either murdered or sent to Ravensbruck. Only 16 of the children are believed to have survived the war. Of the village of

Lidice no trace remained, while Heydrich's assassins were subsequently betrayed and died fighting for their lives. The destruction of Lidice, which had been recorded by the Reich film unit and showed laughing and joking German troops, was used in evidence at the Nuremberg trials after the war.[4]

SONGS IN THE CANDIDE

'When We Can Live in Peace Once More' (Richards, Osborne)

Evening shadows while I'm in your arms
Closer to you than before
We'll have memories to talk about
When we can live in peace once more

Fragrant breezes of a summer night
Moonlight walks along the shore
We'll hold hands the way we used to do
When we can live in peace once more

We'll have perfumed gardens after the summer's rain
We'll have children who will teach us to laugh again
We'll believe again that promises can come true
And darling now I promise you

Warm Septembers and a misty moon
This I promise you and more
All the ordinary things we'll do
When we can live in peace once more

'Oh I'll Wait Laddie' (Richards, Osborne)

I remember it was late
Standing by the garden gate
And Theresa wore an apron that was red
She was little and petite
Had a smile so truly sweet
And when I held her tenderly she said

Oh I'll wait laddie, Oh I'll wait laddie
So be sure and come back safely to my side
Don't be late laddie, Don't be late laddie
For in a month or two I'll be your bride

But then I was called to war
So I kissed her just once more
And I left her on the platform in the rain
As the train was pulling out
Well I heard her give a shout
And she ran toward me saying once again

(Refrain)

Well now that was long ago
What Theresa didn't know
Was that I had been a man already wed
But lads every now and then
Well I think of her again
And I still recall the tender words she said

(Refrain)

WHERE ELSE HAVE I SEEN..?

Christian Roberts (Horst)

Denham, *To Sir with Love*, 1967
Huxton, *The Avengers: Invasion of the Earthmen*, 1968
Foncimagne, *Clochmerle*, 1972
Tim Redman, *UFO: The Long Sleep*, 1973
Renor, *Blake's 7: Breakdown*, 1978

Vincent Marzello (McGee)

Culpepper, *Never Say Never Again*, 1983
Luke's Father, *The Witches*, 1990
Scott Williams, *The House of Eliott*, 1992
Hank, *Ted and Alice*, 2002
US Ambassador Joseph Kennedy, *When Hitler Invaded Britain*, 2004

Doreen Mantle (Madame Desmarts)

Mrs Catchpole, *The Duchess of Duke Street*, 1976
Mrs Reynolds, *Pride and Prejudice*, 1980
Jean Warboys, *One Foot in the Grave*, 1990-2000
Mrs Randall, *The Sarah Jane Adventures*, 2007
Queenie, *Jam and Jerusalem*, 2006-8

Episode 8: THE BIG ONE

WRITTEN BY: N. J. Crisp   **DIRECTED BY:** Michael E. Briant

FIRST BROADCAST: BBC1, 8.05pm, Wednesday 15 November 1978

STUDIO RECORDING: 25 October 1978

VIEWING FIGURE: 7.8m

REGULAR CAST: Albert Foiret: BERNARD HEPTON; Monique Duchamps: ANGELA RICHARDS; Max Brocard: STEPHEN YARDLEY; Major Erwin Brandt: MICHAEL CULVER; Sturmbannführer Ludwig Kessler: CLIFFORD ROSE; Natalie Chantrens:

JULIET HAMMOND-HILL; Alain Muny: RON PEMBER; Madeleine Duclos: HAZEL McBRIDE; Corporal Rennert: ROBIN LANGFORD

SUPPORTING CAST: Albert 'Bert' Lewis: DANIEL HILL; Michael 'Mick' Murray: DANIEL ABINERI; Oberst Manfred Neidlinger: MARK JONES; Wing Commander: NIGEL LAMBERT; Farmer: ROY EVANS; Air Raid Warden: ROYSTON TICKNER; Navigator: DAVID SEAGER; Rear Gunner: DAVID LUDWIG

SYNOPSIS: In England, a large group of airmen are briefed prior to a large-scale raid on Berlin, a target they know as 'The Big One'. Meanwhile, in Brussels, Brandt is dining at the Candide with an old friend, Oberst Manfred Neidlinger. They discuss the recent air attacks on Berlin and Brandt's impending visit there to move his family to safety. Kessler and Madeleine arrive and Brandt introduces Neidlinger. After Brandt and Neidlinger have gone, Kessler and Madeleine talk about the Oberst and the Baron D'Aquise. At his office, Brandt is pressed by Neidlinger to join him in a conspiracy against the Führer, but the Major has several reservations, including the distinct possibility of the Allies refusing a conditional surrender. Kessler and Madeleine discuss the illusions they have – and how they are coming to care – about each other. An aircrew drop their bombs over Berlin, short of their intended city centre target. As they return home the plane is hit and the two surviving crew members, pilot Mick Murray and bomb aimer, Bert Lewis, bail out. The next morning, Brandt arrives in Berlin and learns that his wife, Erika, and son, Kurt, died in the previous night's raid. Murray is captured and Kessler interrogates him, while Lewis is discovered by a farmer, hiding in a barn. Alain brings news of Lewis to the Candide, and he and Monique subsequently question him. After they learn that Lewis can speak German, they suspect he may be an infiltrator and grill him about his identity. Kessler commiserates with the returned Brandt and informs him of Murray's capture and interrogation. Kessler tells Madeleine of Brandt's loss and also talks about his late father. Alain informs Albert and Monique that Lewis has been checked out with London, but on their return to the farm they discover that the airmen has run away and they regret having frightened him so much. Kessler dines with a surprisingly matter-of-fact Brandt at the Candide. The superficially cheerful Major, who has already been drinking, teases Kessler about Madeleine, before telling him that he has nothing to say about his recent loss as he regards that part of his life as being in the past. Kessler tells him that Lewis has been captured. The next day, Brandt begins his interrogation of Bert in his usual charming and friendly manner, but his manner quickly changes when he presses him about the location of the farm. Losing his temper, he tells Lewis how he and his colleagues bombed a Berlin suburb and that they may be responsible for the death of his wife and son. After asking again about the people who interrogated him at the farm and its location, he completely loses control and begins to physically beat the man with his bare hands. Kessler intervenes and orders that Lewis be taken away.

REVIEW: N. J. Crisp's sixth script for the series focuses attention almost entirely on the series's German characters and proves once again that he is one of *Secret Army*'s most significant contributors. The episode is chiefly, and quite rightly, remembered for the superb performance of Michael Culver, as Brandt reacts to the devastating news that his wife and son have been killed and, when faced with a man who could be the very Bomb Aimer responsible, eventually spirals out of control. It is also notable for the development afforded to both Kessler and Madeleine through several well-handled scenes which serve to examine further their unlikely relationship and their respective characters.

Michael E. Briant, in the director's chair for the first time here, makes sure that the overall feel is very bleak and dark. This is of course automatically achieved to a large degree through the tragic subject matter, but the deliberate decision to go with very low-level lighting throughout ensures that considerable atmosphere is added to proceedings, making the episode's many soul-bearing conversations feel much more private and intimate than they otherwise might. Equally commendable for the way they are lit and filmed are the Lancaster Bomber-set scenes, which give a real insight into just how terrifying and confusing such missions must have been. As in previous episodes, this newly shot live action is successfully inter-cut with archive footage, but here the achievement is greater as, for the first time, the viewer gets to follow the mission from take-off, to target, to bailing out.

The episode's most prominent guest character, Oberst Manfred Neidlinger is a sympathetic Brandt-a-like who fulfils several important functions in the narrative. As a representative of the aristocratic Junkers, his presence allows exploration of the class divisions still extant in the Reich, and particularly Kessler's fervent Nazi ideal that such divisions will in time be removed from the Fatherland for good; while as a colleague of Admiral Canaris and Von Elmendorff, Neidlinger also represents the conspirators who want Brandt to join them in their plot to remove the Führer. Thanks to a sensitive portrayal from Mark Jones (previously seen in *Secret Army* as Belgian policeman Marcel) and the inclusion of some stirring classical music on Brandt's office radio, Neidlinger's closing gambit ("Think of the Germany you want your children to grow up in. Are they to be free to think for themselves? Or are they to live in fear of Kessler and his kind?") is certainly persuasive on an emotive level, but Brandt is seen to view the situation more realistically and practically. His certainty that the Allies will demand unconditional surrender and will seize the chance to "crush Germany yet again" (a reference to the destructive reparations agreed at the Treaty of Versailles) regardless of whether they clear out their "own stable first" is just as compelling. This scene is a perfect example of what *Secret Army* does best: presenting all sides of a dilemma without ever resorting to stereotype or simple generalisation. The series often reminds the viewer that not all Germans were card-carrying Nazis, but here it also reminds us, through Brandt's protestations to Neidlinger, that it is a distinction that the Allies would have neither recognised nor cared about at the time. Brandt ultimately finds himself unable to join the conspirators because of what he sees as his duty to his country and because of his poetic, if practical, take on the reality of war as being a choice between evils. As the Hitler bomb plot ultimately failed, we will of course never know for sure whether the Allies would have agreed to a conditional surrender brokered by non-Nazi Germans, but it seems far more likely, as Brandt states here, that they would not have done so.

From the moment we learn that Brandt, like the British aircrews, is on his way to Berlin, in his case to get his family out of the city to safety, it is clear that tragedy will swiftly follow. Although his initial reaction to the news of Erika's and Kurt's deaths is one of utter desolation – expertly played by Culver through a series of close-ups – his subsequent matter-of-fact attitude to this loss is far more difficult to watch and has the effect of making the episode darker still. One of the reasons why the devastated Major's brave face and false jollity make for such uncomfortable viewing is that they point to the inevitability of his painful unravelling before the episode's close. The moment in which Brandt finally loses control during the final minute and attacks Lewis in a fit of rage and despair is unquestionably one of the most powerful moments of all three series. To see the charming and likeable character in this state is shocking and Culver's performance ensures that we utterly believe both in Brandt and his pain. In terms of the series's ongoing narrative, the events of *The Big One* mark a significant turning point for the Major, as from this point on he is never quite the same again.

Another regular character whose personality has changed due to the loss of a loved one, albeit not during this episode, is Madeleine Duclos. Crisp, who created this unashamedly complex character for *Trapped*, sensitively handles here her realisation that she is now on the road to recovery, having finally come out of a period during which she "guarded her own wretchedness," keeping herself separate from life and, more specifically, love, and therefore safe. Her initial exchange with Kessler in the Candide shows how far she has come since she met him. Firstly she actually notices that Kessler is being quiet – which comes as something of a surprise to him ("That's strange coming from you, someone who always seems to say as little as possible") – secondly she wants to know who the man with Brandt is, when previously she would not have been interested, and thirdly, and most importantly, she appears to have finally accepted what happened with the Baron D'Aquise ("I think he really did love me… but the pressures were too great"), someone who she could not previously bring herself to talk about.

The scene which follows in Madeleine's flat, one of the most accomplished that Rose and McBride share in the second series, sees them deliver some eloquent dialogue from Crisp around the plausible and interesting idea that their relationship works because they "both need illusions." Kessler's view that she is not quite right about his kindness is painfully obvious to any viewer of the series, but nevertheless is soon visually borne out by his subsequent scene with the tortured Murray. However, just because he is quite willing to terrorise an evader does not mean that he cannot be kind to her, and as the series progresses the almost schizophrenic contrast between how Kessler behaves with Madeleine and how he is 'at work' is increasingly well-developed and always interesting to watch. As regards Kessler's take on Madeleine, at this point in the series we really have to take her word for it that she is not as gentle as he assumes, although her initial sharpness in *Trapped* and the way she confidently disagrees with Kessler about the removal of the aristocracy here certainly hints at the fact that we still have a lot more to learn about Mademoiselle Duclos. Whatever the truth of

Kessler's view that they both need "to be blind to what someone else is really like," in terms of their relationship it is significant that Madeleine is seen to finally turn over the picture of her beloved Baron. However, although she confides in Kessler that she could come to care for him and therefore face what he emphatically describes as becoming "truly alive again," the fact that she turns the picture back over after he has gone suggests that she is still not quite ready to face this. That Kessler also has fears about the progression of their relationship is not only suggested by his profession to Madeleine that it could be dangerous for him too, presumably in terms of his feelings clouding his judgement, but also by his incredibly defensive response to Brandt's later line of questioning about what Madeleine means to him.

While his relationship with Madeleine reveals one side to Kessler, Brandt's loss, which causes him to think of his late father, prompts revelation of another: the basis for his adherence to the Führer's ambition to forge a new Germany. It is immediately evident from the way that Kessler talks passionately about his father that it was his fate and that which befell "thousands like him" – having to endure the inflation, depression and unemployment of the Thirties despite their war records and hard-working natures – that not only turned the young Kessler against the aristocracy, but more significantly motivated him to join the National Socialist party. Given Kessler's background, it is not difficult to understand why Nazi ideals became so compelling to him and why he is so disparaging about Junkers like Neidlinger. When it comes to the series's regulars, through carefully written exposition such as this, Crisp demonstrates an unerring ability to believably fill in the blanks. The rewarding result here is that Kessler comes across as more complete and three-dimensional than ever.

However, it is unavoidable that not all of the series's characters can receive the same amount of attention from the scriptwriter. In respect of the Lifeline characters, Crisp appears to be almost revelling in ignoring them here, not only by deliberately placing them on the fringes of the action – only Monique is really given anything to do – but by even choosing to poke fun at this fact, as when she and Albert attempt to listen in to Kessler and Brandt and are unable to overhear anything. This is an amusing touch which is made even more so by the fact that, after they have moved away from the oficers' table, they are still obviously debating in the background what the pair are saying in the foreground!

The Big One boasts strong and pleasing continuity with previous events and characters. As well as references to Von Elmendorff's attempt to recruit Brandt in *Russian Roulette* and Erika's request to leave Berlin in *Scorpion*, we learn that the report on Madeleine which Kessler requested in *Trapped* also detailed her – previously undisclosed – brief liaisons with a series of men after the collapse of her love affair with Baron D'Aquise. Both John Curtis and Yvette are also referred to for the first time in ages, although neither has any direct bearing on the narrative.

The two Daniels, Hill and Abineri, provide solid support as the evaders of the week. Abineri is particularly impressive when making his childlike pleas for his prisoner-of-war status to be recognised by an impassive Kessler, while Hill, who had previously evaded in Series One's *Too Near Home*, is believable throughout as an unusually quick-witted airman. Although Bert's evasion experience is vital in setting up the all-important final interrogation, there is a sense that, this far into the series, we've seen all this 'hiding in barns' business too many times before and so, as a result, these scenes are the least significant element of the episode. One scene involving both Hill and Abineri right at the start of the episode is particularly odd, as it actually made the final edit despite being out of sequence. After seeing the pair sat waiting for their briefing, the next shot shows them finding the same seats and sitting down! Incidentally Daniel Hill makes an uncredited third contribution to the series as the BBC announcer heard on the Candide's radio.

The Big One's tight focus on the series's central German characters (if one considers Madeleine as an honorary German) allows for an admirably sensitive exploration of their motivation, hopes and fears. By now, Culver, Rose and McBride effortlessly inhabit their roles and, despite the fact that their characters are officially the series's oppressors, the narrative engenders considerable empathy and understanding for all of them from the viewer. This is no mean feat and a reminder that *Secret Army*'s sophistication should not be underestimated.

HISTORICAL BACKGROUND

Allied Raid on Berlin

Despite his reputation, RAF Bomber Command's Air Marshal 'Bomber' Harris refused to condone attacks on Berlin throughout 1942 due to the fact that there would be too many civilian casualties. However, his other reason was that it was difficult to mount successful and accurate attacks on the city until the development of the OBOE system. In the late summer of 1943, by which time OBOE had been superseded by the even more useful H_2S, Bomber Command prepared itself for a series of very heavy raids on Berlin which would begin in earnest in November. However, before then, several smaller scale raids took place, one of these was on the night/morning of 31 August/1 September. The raid was not at all successful in terms of hitting intended industrial targets, with the markers being dropped well away from the target areas due to cloud cover, problems with the H_2S equipment  and the ferocity of the German defences. As a result, 85 dwellings were destroyed and a total of 66 civilians killed. After the raid, Goebbels ordered the evacuation from Berlin of all children and adults not engaged in war work. It is likely therefore that it is this very raid which is dramatised in *The Big One*, causing the deaths of Erika and Kurt Brandt.

The Lancaster Bomber

The four-engined Avro Lancaster, which effectively replaced two-engined medium bombers such as the Wellington, was capable of carrying heavy bombs and bomb-loads. It was popular with aircrew as it was highly manoeuvrable, well armoured and capable of sustaining heavy damage. Affectionately known as the 'Lanc' or 'Lankie', this aircraft arguably became the most famous and successful of the Second World War night bombers, dropping over 600,000 tons of bombs. The Lancaster is most famous for being the aircraft flown by squadron 617 during their famous 'Dam Busting' raid ('Operation Chastise').

WHERE ELSE HAVE I SEEN..?

Daniel Hill (Bert Lewis)

Chris Parsons, *Doctor Who: Shada*, 1979
Chasgo, *Blake's 7: Sand*, 1981
Tom Redburn, *Tenko*, 1981
Harvey Bains, *Waiting for God*, 1990-4
Simon Norwalk, *Judge John Deed*, 2003-7

Mark Jones (Manfred Neidlinger)

Michael Armstrong, *A Family at War*, 1970-2
Arnold Keeler, *Doctor Who: The Seeds of Doom*, 1976
Chuck, *The New Avengers: Sleeper*, 1976
Ray Mason, *Buccaneer*, 1980
Major Templeton, *Blott on the Landscape*, 1985

Daniel Abineri (Mick Murray)

Lacey, *King Cinder*, 1977
Wilson, *International Velvet*, 1978
Father Neil Boyd, *Bless Me Father*, 1978-81
Jake Sanders, *Return to Eden*, 1986
Bruce, *Bring Me the Head of Mavis Davis*, 1997

Episode 9: LITTLE OLD LADY

WRITTEN BY: David Crane   DIRECTED BY: Terence Dudley

FIRST BROADCAST: BBC1, 8.05pm, Wednesday 22 November 1978

STUDIO RECORDING: 5 August 1978

VIEWING FIGURE: 8.1m

REGULAR CAST: Albert Foiret: BERNARD HEPTON; Monique Duchamps: ANGELA RICHARDS; Max Brocard: STEPHEN YARDLEY; Major Erwin Brandt: MICHAEL CULVER; Sturmbannführer Ludwig Kessler: CLIFFORD ROSE; Natalie Chantrens: JULIET HAMMOND-HILL; Madeleine Duclos: HAZEL McBRIDE; François: NIGEL WILLIAMS

SUPPORTING CAST: Wing Commander Kelso: ANDREW ROBERTSON; Sophie Chantal: MARY BARCLAY; Madeleine Chantal: RUTH GOWER; Louis-Victor Condé: DAVID KING; Shepley: JASON KEMP; Felicien: JOHN HERRINGTON; Else Lambrichts: JENNY LAIRD; U-Boat Commander: RICHARD HAMPTON; Dutch Saboteur: MICHAEL MUNDELL; German Soldier: STEPHEN HATTON; SS Officer: RENNY KRUPINSKI; Henri Lambrichts: DONALD GROVES

SYNOPSIS: A downed British airman, Wing Commander Kelso, is discovered in the Belgian countryside by some elderly locals. At the Candide, Albert bids goodbye to Madeleine, who has been dining there alone. Another patron, Madame Lambrichts, passes comment on her and tells Albert that he is considered to be "too well in with the authorities." Natalie tells Albert that London regard Wing Commander Kelso, who is now safely in Lifeline's hands, as 'special' and that they want him back urgently. Albert visits a safe-house, where the badly-scarred Kelso is also confined, to instruct two young airmen that it is time for them to go down the Line. Albert tells Kelso that he will not leave yet. At Madeleine's flat, Kessler leaves Madeleine behind in bed, telling her about the RAF ace that is believed to be hiding in the area. At the Candide, Albert learns that the Luftwaffe know about Kelso and he and Monique argue about whether he should go down the Line. A stick grenade is thrown into the Candide and the restaurant is evacuated. The next day, Monique tells Kelso that he can only make the journey through France if he agrees to go dressed as a woman – his scar disguised with heavy make-up. Kelso refuses and tells her that he intends to go without a disguise. To Monique's chagrin, Albert agrees to this to keep London happy and assigns Natalie to guide him. The train is stopped at a checkpoint and Kelso runs through the carriages to masquerade as a railway worker at its other end. Albert asks Monique to take over from Natalie who has called to tell him that she is at the end of her tether with Kelso. Madeleine is dining alone again and is in a bad way, so Monique accompanies her back to her flat. After exchanging confidences, Madeleine gives Monique a Balenciaga fur coat. Kelso and Natalie are lost in the countryside until the former finds and starts a train; however, they soon have to abandon it when they reach a rail checkpoint. Monique arrives at the home of the Chantal sisters in Senlis where she is to rendezvous with Natalie and Kelso. When she learns of Monique's plan to disguise Kelso as a woman for the remainder of his journey, Sophie Chantal decides to enlist the help of an actor friend called Louis-Victor Condé. After meeting Kelso, Louis-Victor agrees to help by showing him how "to believe." Natalie is reunited with François. Kelso begins his journey with Monique disguised as a Comtesse. That evening, Kelso apologises to Monique for being pig-headed and she suggests that he share her bed. Albert is arrested by the Gestapo and Natalie threatens Max in order to keep him at the Candide. Monique and 'the Comtesse' continue their journey to the Pyrenees. En route a Dutch saboteur is shot. Having ditched the disguise, Kelso, who is unwell, and Monique arrive at the farm of Felicien, one of Lifeline's Basque guides. Albert is released without charge. Monique sees Kelso off and gives him her fur coat for the trek. Back at the Candide, Monique sings while Brandt tells Kessler about his colleague's discovery of a Balenciaga coat at the Spanish border.

REVIEW: David Crane's second and final script for *Secret Army*, which is a far more complete tale than his previous effort (*Not According to Plan*), is in some ways a retread of the equally enjoyable first series episode *A Question of Loyalty*. Once again Monique is the main focus of attention as her dissatisfaction with her lot is examined. This time around though, her distraction comes in the form of 'RAF hero' Wing Commander Kelso, who although a complex character is considerably less dangerous than an SS infiltrator! However, this is not Monique's story alone, something which reflects the fact that by this stage in its life *Secret Army* is far more of an ensemble drama than it was in its first series, and so both Albert and Madeleine also enjoy some welcome development here. Surprisingly it transpires that both share common attributes, most notably the way they are perceived by others and, more personally, in terms of their desperate need for their respective partners.

Angela Richards once again succeeds in drawing us in to care about Monique's difficult existence. Although it is not immediately clear that Monique's anger early in the narrative – particularly her initial outburst at Kelso – is due to the fact that her relationship with Albert is still going nowhere, her emphatic response to his question as to what is wrong with her – "Nothing very different from before!" – settles it. It has become increasingly obvious throughout the second series that although Monique is now in a far more bearable situation than she was at the old Candide, what she currently has with Albert is still not enough for her. She details what she wants in her heart-to-heart with Madeleine: "The man I live with wants to wait until the war ends for marriage, security, children. Trouble is by that time I could be a very old, old woman… like Madame Lambrichts!" However, as the narrative progresses, it turns out that what she told Madeleine may no longer be a realistic picture of how she really feels. When she is asked a second time for her thoughts, this time by Kelso, she tells him: "I had plans once but they got left behind somewhere. I don't know what I want anymore." Her subsequent decision to sleep with Kelso is just as telling. Although she is not ready to leave Albert, the suggestion is here that she has now come to realise that he may never offer her what she wants and so she may just have to find it elsewhere.

Typically neat plotting sees Monique effectively give up on Albert at a point when he is portrayed as needing her more than ever. However, this need is not obvious, until – as usual – situations of grave danger arise. In *Trapped*, the possibility that he might lose Monique filled him with terror and his huge relief at her safe return was self-evident. Here, having been faced with the collapse of Lifeline and his restaurant business due to his interrogation at the hands of the Gestapo, on his release the only word he can find the breath to say, twice, is "Monique!" When all is said and done, it transpires that it is Monique that matters most to him. Unfortunately she is not there to witness this fact.

Rarely do we find out as much about an evader as we do about Wing Commander Kelso. Kelso, who is nicely underplayed by Andrew Robertson, initially comes across as an arrogant chauvinist. Although he openly tells Albert: "I couldn't do what you're doing," he does not possess enough respect for Lifeline's experienced agents to actually go along with their plans, especially when they are suggested by a woman. However, after it is proved to him – through his misadventures north of Paris with Natalie – that his way will not work, he has the good grace to admit that he may have been wrong. Once he is en route to the Pyrenees with Monique, he tells her why he did not think her plan would work and explains: "I made a success of my squadron by being arrogant and pig-headed." He also freely admits that he is "ignorant about women," a fact which is quickly borne out by his failure to deduce that Monique will ask him to bed. The way Kelso talks to Monique about what she has done for him: "Without you I wouldn't have made the first 100 yards of this operation," his reflection on the fact that, after they reach the Pyrenees, they won't see each other again, and his direct question about her future plans, all suggest that he has really fallen for her. However, Monique is unable to respond other than by telling him, for the final time: "You're a fool," and kissing his scar, which is clearly her way of telling him that she has come to care for him. His final retort: "I was born lucky," is certainly supported by his recent journey – and also by the 51 operations under his belt! – but he is also presented as unlucky in having found Monique in the wrong place and at the wrong time in terms of a lasting relationship.

Although the fact that Kelso brings Natalie to the end of her tether during the first half of the episode suggests that she may be losing her usual strength, her reaction to Albert's arrest confirms that she has lost none of her resolve, and that Kelso must simply have been impossible to control. Her immediate response to the arrest is to rein Max in, barking at him to join her in the backroom. There she proves that she knows him all too well and threatens: "If you go Max and they pick me up, I'll talk and the first name I'll give them will be yours!" Natalie is still saddled with the puppy-eyed François here, but the pair still clearly adore each other despite their apparent incompatibility. Perhaps François appeals to her due to the fact that she can tell him to shut up and call him an idiot when he worries about her. What is certain is that he is not going to stop her carrying out her work for Lifeline.

Collaboration, and specifically the threat of reprisal for such activity, is an important element of the narrative. Both Albert and Madeleine are presented as obvious targets and both are seen to suffer for their respective connections with the German authorities. Albert almost sees the Candide blown up before his very eyes, while Madeleine suffers at the hands of the lipstick-wielding Madame Lambrichts. Both get off lightly here, but the implication is that they will not be so lucky in future. Madeleine, who has now consummated her relationship with Kessler, appears to have already faced up to the inevitability of punishment for such a liaison, rather morbidly offering several different scenarios for her death: "A knife, one night in a dark street, or another bomb;" or "A brave resistance hero will shoot me as a traitor." However, what seems to terrify her more is that she may die alone, as she says to Albert: "I can die, Monsieur, a little thing, but please God not alone." Albert, on the other hand, has not yet accepted the possibility that he may face such an end, presumably because his undercover Lifeline work for the Allies makes the idea seem so unthinkable. He is visibly shaken by the stick grenade incident, so much so that when Brandt comes to his aid, he utterly convinces as a collaborating restaurauteur, a man whom the Major would never in a million years suspect of running Lifeline!

Although Brandt does not play a huge part in the narrative, it is obvious from those moments when he does appear that his recent loss has damaged him. When Albert seeks his support after the bomb incident, when once he would have no doubt uttered some words of sympathy, here the Major retorts: "What do you expect of me?" in a way that suggests that he has nothing to give . He also seems to enjoy the allusion that Albert makes about the red wine on Madame Lambrichts's dress, finishing Albert's: "Next time…" with the remark "…it could be blood?" delivered with a definite smile. His determination to track down Kelso also suggests that he has elected to decline once-and-for-all the invitation to join the Hitler bomb plot conspirators.

In David Crane's original script, Madame Lambrichts does not only serve the function of making accusations of collaboration. In a scene that did not make it to the final cut, Monique helps her to recover from the stick-grenade incident in the ladies' room. During their conversation, Lambrichts reapplies her make-up and warns Monique that when she gets old she too will have to put on as much make-up as she does. Monique was to have been seen reacting to this comment with a look of dawning realisation that this is precisely the way they can get Kelso down the Line. Without this scene there is no explanation as to where Monique gets the idea, which is a bit of a shame as it is a piece of very tidy plotting. Another more minor cut was Kelso's incredibly direct first line, when he sees the Belgian farmers coming towards him: "All right, you bastards. Whose side are you on?", a line which was presumably a victim of the series's time-slot.

Significant interest is added to the narrative through two distinctly unlikely scenarios, which add the usual *frisson* of excitement to the episode of the 'if only they knew' variety. The aforementioned failed bombing leads to Brandt taking charge and finding himself in the backroom of the Candide for the first time, from where he actually makes a call on the very phone which is used for all of Lifeline's business! Monique, meanwhile, finds herself exchanging confidences with Madeleine Duclos in her flat. Madeleine has no idea just how close she gets to the truth when she sarcastically remarks that Monique could be "the Queen Bee of Belgian resistance" and she still wouldn't tell Kessler. This scene is arguably one of the most enjoyable of the entire episode, primarily because it connects two characters who have barely spoken two words to each other before and in such a way – a woman-to-woman chat – that we learn more about them as a result. As well as learning about Monique's hopes, the scene reveals that Madeleine does not love Kessler in the same way as she did the Baron D'Aquise ("Lightning doesn't strike in the same place twice") and, by way of the superb line: "Or Kessler will take me back in triumph to Berlin and marry me. I honestly don't think that possibility is anything more than a possibility," that she is also uncertain of Kessler's feelings for her. Unlike Max, Albert wisely recognises that Monique and Madeleine's friendship can only be a good thing in terms of further cover for their operations: "I'd be a fool to discourage any friendship." However, their new friendship – by way of the gift of Madeleine's Balenciaga fur coat which Monique in turn gives to Kelso for his mountain trek – unbeknownst to everyone but the viewer, does almost blow the whole gaffe on Lifeline, due to its discovery on the Spanish border and Brandt's relation of this fact just seconds before Madeleine returns from powdering her nose! This conversation leads skilfully into the last line of the episode, spoken by Madeleine: "Doesn't she sing beautifully, my friend Monique," to which the obvious rejoinder is 'That's not all she does!' Thankfully Monique will not have to put to the test Madeleine's claim that she would keep all of her secrets from Kessler!

The Senlis-based Chantal sisters make a welcome return to the series here, still retaining their status as the only evasion line workers who we know and care about outside of Brussels. Although both are as matter-of-fact as ever about the terrifically dangerous work in which they are embroiled, we see a different side to the ditzy Sophie as she speaks her mind about the likely problems extant between Monique and Kelso. Sophie is also responsible for bringing Louis-Victor Condé into the fray as a distinctly unlikely saviour for Kelso. Louis-Victor's performance with the 'napkin-baby' is as mesmerising as it is uncomfortable to watch. Whatever your view of it, one thing is definitely clear: David King only manages 'insane old woman with a baby', not 'insane young woman!' Kelso's Comtesse Henriette almost convinces, which is no doubt why the slight Robertson was cast in the role. It would, of course, have been quite wrong to have Kelso as an especially convincing woman, as the point, as made by Louis-Victor, is more about Kelso believing and therefore others believing that he is the *Little Old Lady* of the episode's title. *Little Old Lady* was presumably chosen because *Middle-Aged Haughty Comtesse* doesn't quite have the same ring! One thing about Kelso that does not convince (nothing to do with his female disguise), is his scar, which starts off looking a great deal better than it does by the time we see him in the first safe-house, before ultimately improving far too dramatically in time for his role as the Comtesse.

This episode, as with all those directed by Terence Dudley in this second series, is unfortunately plagued by snatches of horribly melodramatic stock music, most notably in the opening scene in which the Belgian peasants first discover Kelso. Although the music played towards the episode's close at Felicien's farm to suggest that 'we are in the mountains' is far more pleasant, it is still fairly invasive and one half expects a Basque musical troupe to follow Monique and Kelso in through the open doorway! The undoubted musical highlight of the episode is Angela Richards's first slow performance of her emotional show-stopper 'If This is the Last Time I See You' (first heard sung in a jazzy style back in *Lucky Piece*), which is also destined to close the entire series. Here, the song is used to great effect in the very last scene – in much in the same way as 'I Bet You've Heard This One Before' closed *Trapped* – to reflect and emphasise the feelings of the characters present in the Candide. Monique herself has clearly chosen to sing the song as a goodbye to the recently departed Kelso, though her words certainly hit home with the grieving Brandt who is obviously lost in thoughts of his late wife. The fact that Richards's compositions have by now effectively become the soundtrack to the series is the basis for an amusing in-joke as an irritated Kessler asks Madeleine – who is playing 'I Bet You've Heard This One Before' on her record player – "Is that the only record you've got?" Kessler subsequently redresses the situation by buying her some 'Nazi-friendly' Wagner and Strauss records!

Despite some questionable incidental music choices, Terence Dudley's direction is strong throughout. One directorial touch which really stands out as inspired is the cross-fade from Monique in the mountains to Monique in the Candide as she turns to sing. Another, which comes at the very end of the same scene, is the hugely effective frozen tableau as Monique holds the last note of the song while Kessler gazes adoringly at Madeleine and Brandt stares mournfully into space. It is a superb ending to an accomplished episode.

HISTORICAL BACKGROUND

The Rhine Maiden

While working on *Colditz*, Glaister and Brason had chosen not to dramatise a famous attempt by a Frenchmen named Lieutenant Bouley to escape while disguised as a woman, an incident dubbed as that of 'The Rhine Maiden' by P. R. Reid in his book *The Colditz Story*. Although the actual scenario is quite different, it is likely that this was nevertheless the inspiration for *Little Old Lady*'s audacious evasion plot. Reid recounts how Bouley, who had been sent the disguise by his wife, was almost successful in his bid for freedom after donning the outfit while out on a march: 'The majority had just wheeled right down the ramp roadway, when a gorgeous-looking German girl passed by. She haughtily disdained to look at the prisoners, and walked primly past.' Unfortunately Bouley was found out when the watch that was part of his disguise fell off and a prisoner called Paddon chivalrously alerted a German guard to the fact and made him run after 'her' and return the object. When the guard caught up with Bouley, he quickly realised that he was no maiden. Given that the only photograph that was taken of Bouley in his disguise shows him to be more of a hatchet-faced spinster rather than 'a gorgeous-looking German girl,' Reid's account must be a rather playful and fanciful exaggeration.[5]

Cristobal Balenciaga

Cristobal Balenciaga (the man responsible for Madeleine's well-travelled fur-coat) was a Spanish fashion designer who first found success after opening boutiques in Madrid, Barcelona and San Sebastian. The Spanish Civil War caused the closure of these boutiques and Balenciaga moved his operation to Paris, where he joined the ranks of fashion icons such as Coco Chanel and Elsa Schiaparelli. His first runway show took place in 1937, with a collection influenced by the Spanish Renaissance. By the outbreak of World War II, Balenciaga was considered a revolutionising force in fashion and his creations were so highly sought after that some clients even risked travel to Occupied Europe in order to purchase his latest designs. His trademark was to create garments which were said to accentuate fluidity and grace and he remained at the 'top

of his game' for many years after the war. Balenciaga died in 1972, but there are still new Balenciaga collections every season and stores in New York, London, Hong Kong, Milan, Cannes and, of course, Paris. (The other fashion designers Madeleine name-checks are Fath, Chanel and Balmain.)

WHERE ELSE HAVE I SEEN..?

Andrew Robertson (Kelso)

© Charlie Waite

Andrew Randle, *Far From the Madding Crowd*, 1967
Donald Cameron, *Oil Strike North*, 1975
Mr Fibuli, *Doctor Who: The Pirate Planet*, 1978
Jock Drummond, *One By One*, 1987
Hodson, *Little Lord Fauntleroy*, 1995

David King (Louis-Victor Condé)

Burdett, *A for Andromeda/The Andromeda Breakthrough*, 1961-2
Sagamore, *The Last of the Mohicans*, 1971
Mr Barnard, *The Changes*, 1975
Barnaby, *To Serve Them All My Days*, 1980
Viney, *Shine*, 1996

© Geoff Shields

Episode 10: GUESTS AT GOD'S TABLE

WRITTEN BY: John Brason   **DIRECTED BY:** Terence Dudley

FIRST BROADCAST: BBC1, 8.05pm, Wednesday 29 November 1978

STUDIO RECORDING: 4 November 1978

VIEWING FIGURE: 8.7m

REGULAR CAST: Albert Foiret: BERNARD HEPTON; Monique Duchamps: ANGELA RICHARDS; Max Brocard: STEPHEN YARDLEY; Major Erwin Brandt: MICHAEL CULVER; Sturmbannführer Ludwig Kessler: CLIFFORD ROSE; Natalie Chantrens: JULIET HAMMOND-HILL; Inspector Paul Delon: JOHN D. COLLINS

SUPPORTING CAST: Maurice Tourtellat: JOHN LINE; Wim: KEITH JAYNE; Marie-Claire: RACHEL BEASLEY; Bobo: JOHN NANI; Gaby: NATASHA GREEN; Roland Huys: MICHAEL REMICK; German Corporal: BILL ROURKE; Group Captain R S Holbrook: MARK TAYLOR; German Trooper: STEPHEN PHILLIPS

SYNOPSIS: At the Candide, Natalie, Monique and Max are preparing for St Nicholas's Day. Albert arrives with the news that the airmen of a Lancaster have bailed out over the city, but a Group Captain who was part of the crew is missing. Brandt brings news of the Lancaster crew to Kessler, before the latter receives news by phone about the one missing airman. The badly wounded Group Captain is being looked after by a group of orphans who are living in an abandoned house in the city. Natalie returns to the Candide with no news of the airman. Albert muses as to where Max gets to when he is not working. Wim, the eldest of the children, decides to sell the Group Captain so that the four of them can celebrate St Nicholas's Day in three days' time. Max arrives at the Candide with the airman's name tags and a letter from Wim demanding food, clothes, toys and money. Albert is wary that it might be an elaborate hoax to entrap Lifeline, but agrees to strike a bargain with the children. Brandt brings news to Kessler that the airman's parachute has been found and begins a house-to-house search in the Molenbeek area. Tourtellat is brought to see the Group Captain who is now very ill. Wim insists that they must receive their demands before he is taken otherwise he will tell the Germans. Natalie, Monique and Max pack up a box with all the things on the list. After Monique adds more money from the till, Albert adds even more from his wallet. At dinner, Kessler and Brandt discuss the black market and the fact that the Major hasn't taken leave since his wife was killed. Wim collects the box from Tourtellat's house. Back at the Candide, Brandt relates to Kessler what an old friend told him was happening in Poland. The pair argue and Kessler leaves. Brandt invites Monique to join him. The children's contact with Tourtellat, Huys, tells them that the Group Captain will be picked up on St Nicholas's Day. Wim is arrested by the police for stealing schnapps from the Germans. Max brings Tourtellat to the Candide to tell them about Wim's arrest and the German house-to-house search which will prevent them from picking up the Group Captain. Max brings in Delon, who suggests giving Wim a false criminal record in order to have his case dealt with by the civil authorities. Wim is released and he and the other children dress the airman as St Nicholas in order to get him past the Germans and deliver him. Tourtellat returns to the Candide to explain that the kids will deliver the airman in broad daylight in a hand cart. Albert and Monique are doubtful that the plan will work but Max is not so sure. Despite Albert's protestations, Monique and Max decide to go and see how they get on. The children manage to deliver the Group Captain to the rendezvous. Monique returns to the Candide and questions whether they have their priorities twisted looking after airmen rather than homeless children. Max stays in the streets watching the children as he is an orphan too.

REVIEW: *Guests at God's Table* is the closest *Secret Army* gets to having a Christmas Special. As well as all the festive ingredients of St Nicholas, a carol, decorations, presents and Dickensian urchins, it even has a moral Christmas message, delivered not by the Queen, but by Monique (her "Haven't we got our priorities a bit twisted" speech). The Lifeline regulars are in party spirits too, larking about with each other in a way that we have not seen previously. However, the viewer is not allowed to forget that this is the realistically bleak *Secret Army* they are watching and, in stark contrast to these cheerful hijinks, screen time is also given over for the first time to discussion of the abominable atrocities taking place in Eastern Europe.

Unfortunately, *Guests at God's Table* is often simply dismissed as the episode with the annoying children, but, whatever your take on this part of the story, there is a lot else here to enjoy. Arguably the most accomplished element of the narrative is the scene in which Brandt and Kessler dine together at the Candide. Kessler invites Brandt to dinner, as the Major rightly surmises, in order to stop him from drinking alone. Kessler has previously admitted that he quite likes Brandt and here calls him "a valued colleague," and therefore his motivation does seem to be to help him through a difficult time by ensuring that he remains the good soldier he believes him to be. However, Brandt himself is not sure if this will be possible, especially as he finds himself diametrically opposed to Kessler on several counts and, moreover, no longer sure that the Fatherland is honourable. One subject they disagree on is the necessity for a black market. On this matter, Kessler is presented as more realistic than Brandt, acknowledging it as "a fact of life" and defending its continued existence on the grounds that without it "Occupied Europe would be more explosive than it need be." Although it seems unlikely that Brandt would not have thought this through himself before now, the point of placing the conversation here seems to be to suggest that Brandt, in his new-found state of grief, may no longer be able to face the realities of war. Another reality he is certainly not up to facing is the revelation that the Jews are being systematically exterminated by his fellow countrymen in Eastern Europe. As Brandt tells Kessler, he can only come to terms with the death of his wife if he can believe that "she died with dignity and honour." News of this "almost unbelievable" horror would therefore appear to make his recovery impossible. Although Brandt and Kessler have always had their differences of opinion, against all the odds they had begun to work together in the name of the Third Reich; however, the way that their communication breaks down here – so badly that Kessler feels he must leave – suggests that the professional relationship may not recover either. The dramatic conclusion to their bristling exchange is reached through some incredibly intense and powerful dialogue ("A soldier does not confuse political necessity with extermination!") which demonstrates not only the calibre of Culver's and Rose's performances, but also that of Brason's writing.

Despite this extremely dark subject matter at the heart of the episode, the majority of the narrative has a light-hearted feel, courtesy of some amusing and refreshingly 'up' sequences in the Candide. The very first scene sets the tone, with Natalie all smiles as Monique prats about vocally and possibly even ad-libs ("Pass me that fern thing") before enjoying banter with Max about his cowardice. From this cheerful scene it is impossible not to get the sense that the actors are not merely playing at enjoying each other's company, but do actually all get on very well, and having been given full rein to mess about are gladly doing just that. Other fun scenes include: Max pretending that he failed to find a jumper for the children's present box; Monique giddily running in with a plate of fake marzipan; and the subsequent game of five card stud for it. However, the episode's most enjoyable and memorable sequence sees Monique, with a decided twinkle in her eye, deciding to add more money to the children's envelope from the till, before Albert returns and, after making a public show of removing a bottle of cognac from the box, secretly adds some notes from his wallet too! This is a lovely bit of characterisation which rather belies the impossibly mean Albert who Monique has come to know and despair of! Earlier in the episode, when Albert muses that the children may have taken the name-tags from the airman's dead body, she exclaims: "And you don't want to fork out for no reason! Is that it? My God you're mean!" Although Albert defends himself by claiming that he is concerned that it may be an elaborate trick ("Christmas games with the Gestapo") and that the Germans might have invented the children due to their capacity for sentimentality, the extra francs he places in the envelope imply that he too has his softer side and is not entirely the miserly stick-in-the-mud he appears to be.

Rather neatly, in the scene immediately after Albert first suggests that this might be a sentimental German plot, we witness Kessler in his office nostalgically listening to a piece of music – the highly-appropriate 'Scenes from childhood' (Kinderszenen) by Schumann – that his mother used to play on the piano (excellent continuity with this memory is maintained in *Kessler* when we actually see both his mother, in a flashback sequence, and finally Kessler himself, playing the piece on a piano). He even apologises to Brandt for being sentimental;

however, as we have already seen the children, we know that their list of demands is genuine.

As the episode features Monique singing the line "Christmas is for children…" added to the fact that the plight of four young orphans forms a significant portion of this Christmas-themed narrative, we can assume that this lyric is something John Brason believes too. For the eldest child, Wim, Terence Dudley cast Keith Jayne, who he had previously worked with three years earlier on the *Survivors* episode *Corn Dolly* and who would later impress in the title role in *Stig of the Dump*. Jayne, who was 24 at the time but looks much younger, is entirely believable as the group's father figure. Although Wim's list of demands presents him as rather naïve, to his credit he does come up with the idea of selling the airman to an evasion line in the first place. He is unswerving in his aim to ensure that his younger charges can enjoy St Nicholas's Day, and when Tourtellat attempts to take the airman before keeping his side of the bargain, Wim demonstrates this avowed intent by calmly telling him: "You take him and I'll tell the Germans… We're going to have a Saint Nicholas!" Rachel Beasley (the actresses's name appears incorrectly as Rachelle Beasly in the end credits) as gaunt and ghostly Marie-Claire is the female equivalent of Wim, who has taken to mothering the children in her care. She too has learned to be tough: shouting at Roland for getting Wim involved in theft and, when it appears the latter has gone for good, determined to continue in her role, declaring: "I'll look after them – there isn't anyone else." Wim and Marie-Claire's attempts to build an existence as pseudo-man-and-wife suggest that Brason may have been inspired by Jill Paton Walsh's acclaimed children's novel *Fireweed* (1969), in which a very similar boy and girl have to face up to the grim realities of war as they squat in an unoccupied house in London during the Blitz, but end up looking after a baby rather than an airman. Of the episode's remaining children, Gaby is the baby of the group and as a result thankfully doesn't say a great deal; unfortunately the same is not true of John Nani's irritating Bobo. Given the amount of repetitive dialogue Bobo is given, it seems likely that Brason had originally intended him to be played by a younger (or at least a more endearing!) child. As it is, Bobo grates in every scene he is in, mainly because Nani overacts, particularly when pestering Marie-Claire or when he has to drop the wood and exclaim: "What about the man?!" His performance would probably not matter so much were it not for the fact that *Secret Army* so rarely contains any poor acting. Beasley remembers that Nani was a handful during both the rehearsals and the filming ("He was a little terror!") and had a great deal of trouble with his lines, while Natasha Green (Gaby) was "in awe of everything and everyone throughout the whole experience." She recalls that Terence Dudley was incredibly patient with her and the rest of the child actors, gently suggesting how the children could get into their characters, deliver their lines and react to situations, and she also remembers that, of the regular cast, both Angela Richards and Stephen Yardley made a particular effort to welcome the youngsters to the show and make them feel at ease. Not as bad as Bobo, but still rather wooden, is Michael Remick's Roland Huys, the children's mysterious older friend who is introduced clumsily and whose function in the narrative as their go-between is initially unclear as a result. The St Nicholas song, which is sung almost continuously during the episode's closing minutes, becomes very wearing and the fact that you can sing every word yourself after the credits roll suggests that it is used too much. That said, it is a nice touch that they cannily sing the song in German in order to get a contribution from the German soldiers and their voices arguably underscore the closing moments, as Max leaves the area, very effectively. Interestingly, the song does not feature in Brason's original script. One problem with the children's scenes, which has nothing to do with the child actors, is that there are too many scenes in their den with not enough going on. The sequence in which the set is introduced, which is accompanied by an extended version of the *Secret Army* theme, is interminable. However, along with the children, the den set is suitably grimy and therefore believable. Another set which deserves mention is the mammoth Rue des Menages exterior, given its size and the expense involved in its construction, must have been agreed on the basis that the episode was entirely studio-bound. There is no question that these scenes would have been far more effective if they had been filmed on location.

Max is given more to do than usual here. As the last time we were reminded of his double-game was way back in *Not According to Plan*, Kessler and Brandt's discussion about the Communists gaining control of resistance groups in France, including the Sturmbannführer's assertion that: "One day soon the local reds will attempt to take over the evasion lines," is a timely reminder of the forger's intended treachery. However, the episode plays with our perception of Max, as he is presented throughout as affectionate and endearing, therefore lulling us into a false sense of security. Monique, who as Albert puts it, always "thinks from her gut," appears to have his measure: "Max never gives anything away. He's one of the world's takers," but the way he subsequently behaves with Natalie and Monique, along with his efforts for the children's box of presents, suggests that she may have got him wrong. The revelation that he too is an orphan also engenders sympathy for the character, especially given the fact that he has to come to terms with the reality that he can't really do anything for his fellow orphans in Molenbeek (as Natalie says, in the best line of the episode: "Well, give him half an hour and he will have worked that out for himself.") That *Guests at God's Table* makes us feel that we now understand and even care about Max just prior to the unfolding of the surprisingly sinister events of *A Matter of Life and Death*, demonstrates script editor John Brason's skilful plotting of the series's over-arching narrative. Stephen Yardley is excellent as always as the shady Max, imbuing the character with just the right amount of likeability without overdoing it.

Due to a number of line fluffs, pauses and occasionally even some incomprehensible action – the barely audible whispering and what sounds like instructions from the studio gallery after the red blanket is placed on the Group Captain – *Guests at God's Table* does feel as though it was recorded in something of a rush. This is especially suggested by the fact that the ever-reliable Bernard

Hepton needs Stephen Yardley to help him complete his sentence about the Liege Network. Part of the problem may be that some of the dialogue, especially in the Candide, seems very awkward to deliver. The script itself – perhaps late interpolations agreed at the rehearsal stage – almost acknowledges and pokes fun at this fact, with Max delivering two similar punchlines after some difficult lines: "Is that clear?" and "Do you mind saying that again?"

Maurice Tourtellat, like Roland Huys, is a surprisingly redundant character. Dudley presumably cast John Line in the role after his moving performance in the 1976 *Survivors* episode, *Face of the Tiger*, in which he played a convicted child-killer. However, Line is given surprisingly little to work with here. However, another supporting character, John D. Collins's unassuming Inspector Delon (last seen in *The Hostage*), is vital to the plot and his "second nature to a copper" solution to the problem of getting Wim released is a clever touch.

After Brandt and Kessler's spat in the Candide, the foundations are laid for a new and interesting subplot involving Monique. The devastated and lonely Brandt is depicted for the first time as being attracted to the Candide's resident chanteuse and with Albert's permission, she joins him in a glass of wine. Although Monique complies, it is clear from her eye contact with Albert as he pours out the Burgundy that she is wondering just how far he is willing to let this go. Albert, however, seems blissfully unaware of this subtext or of the possible repercussions and is ostensibly excited by the prospect of Monique gaining the confidence of the Major. Once again, this can only signpost trouble ahead for their relationship!

Although it is by no means an unqualified success, even if you cannot cope with the children (and the fact that the St Nicholas song is almost burnt on to your memory!), there is more than enough of interest in *Guests at God's Table* to make it an enjoyable and refreshingly different episode.

HISTORICAL BACKGROUND

St Nicholas – Belgian Tradition

In Belgium, Saint Nicholas (Sinterklaas in Dutch), the children's saint, is quite different to the British and American Santa Claus (although the derivation is the same). He dresses like a bishop, wears white and red robes and a mitre, and carries a crook. He also carries a big book in which it is recorded whether children have been good or bad during the year. He is not a jolly fellow, but tall and dignified. He is considered to be all-knowing and strict, but fair. His servant is called Black Pete (Zwarte Piet in Dutch), a black

© Beckman

servant wearing a velvet suit and ruff collar with a feather in his floppy cap. Black Pete (or Peter) is a joker and carries a large sack that contains presents and, it is said, space for a naughty child. Up until World War II, Saint Nicholas was only accompanied by one Black Pete, but the tradition was modified as a result of Canadian servicemen who dressed up as numerous Black Petes and helped organise the first post-war Sinterklaas celebrations. Saint Nicholas arrives in Belgium in November, having travelled from Spain. On 5 December, the eve of St Nicholas Day, children put their shoes by the fireplace (in which little presents are to be placed), with a letter for Saint Nicholas and a carrot or turnip and sugar for his horse. That night he rides over the rooftops, climbing up and down chimneys leaving toys and sweets. The Belgian 6 December is much like the British and American 25 December, with children, and therefore parents, waking early to open their presents. There are many traditional songs sung by Belgian children around St Nicholas day. The song sung here is in a similar vein – a request for gifts because they have been good children:

Nicholas please come home to us,
We've been good, bring gifts to us,
Happy, joyful we will be then,
Now St Nick has come again,
Now St Nick has come again.

SONGS IN THE CANDIDE

'Snow Time' (Richards, Moule)

Monique's seasonal song, which begins 'Christmas is for children and that means you and me' was, like *Velvet Blue*, written by Richards in collaboration with Ken Moule; however, Richards has little memory of it and the lyrics are 'lost'.

WHERE ELSE HAVE I SEEN..?

John Line (Tourtellat)

Captain Alan Marshall, *Colditz: Murder*, 1973
Atkins, *Oil Strike North*, 1975
Alistair McFadden, *Survivors: The Face of the Tiger*, 1976
Garside, *To Serve Them All My Days*, 1980
Wilkins, *Blood Money*, 1981

© David Hart

Keith Jayne (Wim)

Mick, *Survivors: Corn Dolly*, 1975
Tom Arnold, *The Onedin Line*, 1979-80
Stig, *Stig of the Dump*, 1981
Will Chandler, *Doctor Who: The Awakening*, 1984
Boxer, *Murphy's Mob*, 1986

Episode 11: A MATTER OF LIFE AND DEATH

WRITTEN BY: Robert Barr   **DIRECTED BY:** Roger Jenkins

FIRST BROADCAST: BBC1, 8.05pm, Wednesday 6 December 1978

STUDIO RECORDING: 15 November 1978

VIEWING FIGURE: 7.9m

REGULAR CAST: Albert Foiret: BERNARD HEPTON; Monique Duchamps: ANGELA RICHARDS; Max Brocard: STEPHEN YARDLEY; Major Erwin Brandt: MICHAEL CULVER; Sturmbannführer Ludwig Kessler: CLIFFORD ROSE; Natalie Chantrens: JULIET HAMMOND-HILL; François: NIGEL WILLIAMS

SUPPORTING CAST: Victor Hervé: DUNCAN LAMONT; Flying Officer Thomas 'Tommy' Miller: JOHN FLANAGAN; Flight Sergeant Joseph 'Joe' Waldon: LEONARD PRESTON; Philippe: MICHAEL GRAHAM COX; René: MICHAEL GOLDIE; Priest: JAMES OTTOWAY; Pilot: MARTIN SMITH; Paul Mitchell: RICHARD ALBRECHT

SYNOPSIS: March 1944. Two evaders, who came down in a Lancaster near Charleroi, decide to make for the French border. Kessler receives news that the pilot has been caught and that a search of the area is taking place. After narrowly avoiding a German patrol, the evaders decide to find a priest instead. Kessler thinks that these men are responsible for the death of an SS sentry and for sabotaging the railway line, and that they have joined up with the Communists. When Max meets a friend called Philippe, the latter asks him for papers for two different airmen. Max tells him that he is ready to take over Lifeline. A priest, worried for the safety of the people of his village, refuses to help the innocent evaders. Kessler interrogates the remaining member of the Lancaster crew and accuses him of the murder of the SS sentry. The evaders find a bakery at Marchienne and meet a man called Hervé who agrees to help them. François questions them and learns about the SS sentry and another two airmen who are now with the Communists. He reports back to Albert, who warns him off approaching the Communists. Max meets Philippe again and he is asked to stay for a meeting with a man called René. François returns to the bakery to tell the evaders they have been cleared by London. He asks Hervé about the Communists and is warned off a second time. However, he relents and gives him Philippe's contact details with the proviso that he must seek permission from Albert first. Max tells René his plan to take over Lifeline and that he is prepared to kill Albert, and Monique if necessary. After the meeting, François, who has disobeyed Hervé, happens upon Max. Philippe offers him one of the airmen they are hiding, then subsequently tells Max that he must dispose of François before he gets back to Brussels as he has seen too much. Natalie arrives at the bakery and Hervé tells her that François is following up on the other airmen. François returns and tells Natalie about the airman who who he will be picking up from Marchienne in the morning, who has his own papers provided by Max. Max anonymously calls Kessler and gives him details of the pick-up and a description of François. Natalie wants to go with François to the station, but he refuses on the basis that he wants to prove to her that he can do what she does. The next morning, Natalie and Hervé wait in his van by the train station while François waits for the evader. The Germans are waiting for him and when he tries to make a run for it down the tracks he is shot dead. Hervé and a horrified Natalie witness the shooting. After checking that François has been killed, Hervé drives away while his distraught passenger cries.

REVIEW: Robert Barr's gripping third script for the series finally sees Max reveal his hand as his inevitable betrayal of Lifeline takes shape, while, due to his dogged determination to prove himself, naïve François meets his end. Thanks to a beautifully-judged performance from Juliet Hammond-Hill as his beloved Natalie, the young student's death makes for one of the most heart-rending finales of the entire series.

The opening shot of a steam train shrouded in darkness sets up the shadowy mood of the story, much of which takes place in dark and grubby corridors and rooms. Although the first section of the episode's plot involving the two evaders includes several twists, such as the fact that they have been wrongly accused of murdering an SS officer and that for once the church refuses to get involved, it really is too derivative to be involving. However, the narrative really begins to get going when Max first meets with Philippe in Thuin (pronounced 'Twan').

When Max was first urged by Paul Vercors in *Not According to Plan* to rush through the Communist takeover of Lifeline, he refused on the grounds that a far better approach would be to remove and replace its personnel one by one. The fact that he has not followed through on this implies either that he did not want Vercors's cell – who were admittedly a pretty useless bunch – to get their hands on Lifeline, or that he has since had second thoughts about betraying his colleagues; his recent camaraderie with Monique and Natalie certainly suggests this. This latter state of affairs in particular makes his revelation to Philippe that the takeover of the Candide is still on the cards come as a real surprise. However, there is something about Max's bravado ("It gets easier every day. It could almost be any time") that doesn't quite ring true, especially given his difficult-to-read response to Philippe's observation that he could have a cell of his own soon ("Yes, that's right.") Max's reaction aside, it is still just as difficult as it was before to imagine how he actually hopes to go about 'taking over', particularly as Lifeline is not as much about just the Candide as their discussion suggests. Whatever Max's intentions are towards his 'friends' at the Candide, we know that he was quite happy to betray Claude Pelletain (in *Russian Roulette*) and see here that he has no scruples about suggesting that Philippe should shop the airmen at Marchienne to the Germans and therefore implicate Hervé into the bargain. A clearer picture eventually emerges when René arrives on the scene; a 'senior Communist' whom Max is visibly eager to impress. When René asks about his Candide scheme, stating: "I'm told Foiret has a mistress," Max's chillingly unexpected answer ("If there's trouble they'll fall together") seems to confirm that he has finally crossed the line. However, once again he seems to backtrack when he is subsequently put on the spot about killing Albert, by failing to answer in the affirmative immediately. But there appears to be no stopping him as he details what taking over Lifeline could mean to the Communists, prompting Philippe to give Max the recognition and approval he seems to crave by stating:

"We'll make you a hero!" The details Max provides are not entirely accurate. He is not, for instance, the most experienced member of Lifeline after Albert, nor is it likely that he is "known and trusted by London" so, to an extent Max appears to be blagging his way in order to impress these senior comrades. However, he still does not have to put his words into actions just yet; until, that is, poor François blunders into him in Thuin. From this point on, as Philippe makes abundantly clear to him ("This one must be dealt with before he gets back to Brussels, and that is your job!"), there is no turning back – a fact which is written all over Max's face as he contemplates what he must do next. The way the complexity of this situation is conveyed is laudable, especially as it adheres to *Secret Army*'s admirable code of never portraying things as black and white. Max may end up betraying Lifeline terribly, but his journey to this decision appears to be a result of his background, his beliefs and, most importantly, his apparent lack of self-worth. Stephen Yardley is in fine form throughout as he finally gets to portray all the different elements that go to make up his complex character in the space of one episode.

Nigel Williams's final appearance in the series demonstrates how well cast he is as the unfortunate and eager-to-please François. Unlike Natalie, François has not yet learnt that he simply cannot trust everyone he meets, primarily because, compared to his partner, he is vastly inexperienced when it comes to evasion work. That his efforts on this occasion will lead to tragedy is not initially obvious, especially given his status as a regular character. However, as the narrative progresses and he continues to ignore clear warnings – first from Albert ("We make no approaches to Communists!") and then from Hervé ("These are not your pale pink University reds. The men of Thuin are hardcore activitsts, revolutionaries!") – his fate is set. Another clue that this is his last episode is Monique's performance of 'If This is the Last Time I See You', which had previously serenaded Brandt and Erika in *Scorpion* as they shared their last meal together. And as if this isn't a big enough hint in itself, Natalie even joins in, singing the words directly to her ill-fated lover! Although François is a bit of a drip, the character eventually engages our sympathy when he reveals the reason for his stubbornness to Natalie: "I've got to prove to myself that I can do what you do – get them safely home." The sad fact is that in his eagerness to prove himself to his lover he overreaches himself and only succeeds in demonstrating that he was never up to the job. However, one thing to be said in his favour, in a manner of speaking, is that if it hadn't been for his naïvety then Max's affiliation may not have been revealed before it was too late for Lifeline.

A Matter of Life and Death includes several well-rounded and charismatic supporting characters, brought to life by actors whom Roger Jenkins had previously worked with on *Poldark*. Duncan Lamont, in particular, is a joy to watch as genial baker Victor Hervé. Lamont imbues Hervé with continental warmth as he heartily throws himself into helping the evaders. Despite the considerable risks he is taking, he still manages to retain an optimistic outlook and a wicked sense of humour; he even winds up the evaders by pretending that he will hand them over to the SS! When Natalie arrives on the scene, he greets her almost as if she was his own daughter. He maintains this paternal status through his warnings to her about François's stubborn character and his decision to accompany her the next morning on "station business." Given that Hervé is one of the few non-Candide Lifeline characters to have any sort of impact – the Chantal sisters are two other obvious candidates – it is a great shame that the affable baker could not make a return appearance in the series. However, even if it had been considered, sadly this would turn out to be Duncan Lamont's last ever television performance (although he did subsequently complete all of the location filming on the *Blake's 7* episode *Hostage*, he died before the studio recording and a remount saw John Abineri play his character, Ushton, instead).

Another totally believable character is Michael Graham Cox's gruff, no-nonsense Philippe, a Communist who would have proved to be a far more likely match for Lifeline in the final series than the unstable and inconsistent Vercors. Coincidentally, in *Poldark*, Cox played Sid Rowse, the violent henchman of the scheming Sir George Warleggan, who was in turn played by Ralph Bates who would be cast as none other than Vercors Mk II the following year. Almost as convincing as Cox is Michael Goldie's René, although the character's name is unfortunate for obvious reasons. Their solid performances aside, to learn that these two straight-talking men are prepared to back Max to the extent of removing Albert by murdering him makes the Communist threat to Lifeline seem more real than ever before.

Unusually, Kessler and Brandt barely get a look in here. Nevertheless, continuity is maintained with their falling out in *Guests at God's Table*, as it appears that they are once more at 'daggers drawn' as they fight over the custody of an enemy airman just like they used to. Albert and Monique also take more of a back seat than usual, although there is a nice bit of playfulness on Monique's part (her amusing salute to Albert, accompanied by a "Yes Sir!", is one of the episode's few lighter moments), as well as further proof that she is a good judge of character (when she recognises François's need to prove himself, before he himself reveals this to Natalie). Meanwhile, Albert's observation that what Max gets up to *is* "Lifeline's business" is more spot on than he knows!

If the dates on Hervé's calendar are to be believed, the events of this episode can be pinpointed as taking place four months after those of *Guests at God's Table*, on 13 and 14 March 1944. Assuming this is the case, Kessler's claim that the Allies are now only engaged in 'terror raids' is actually a reasonable one, as between November and March 1944 Sir Arthur 'Bomber' Harris was given a completely free hand to order saturation bombing raids over German cities. However, the pilot may of course still be telling the truth when he reveals to Kessler that their mission was to destroy a factory in Leipzig.

The episode's final tragic scenes at Marchienne train station were filmed at Wansford station on the Nene Valley Railway, a location previously used in the opening episode of the second series (*The Hostage*). The fact that director Roger Jenkins wanted to capture François's flight along the platform and onto the tracks in a particularly complicated way (a way that was ultimately not achieved) led to problems for both Nigel Williams and Juliet Hammond-Hill: for Williams, it was because he found himself running all afternoon on a sweltering July day; and for Hammond-Hill, because Jenkins had spent so long on that scene that he decided that the shots of Natalie's reaction to François's death would have to be 'picked up' cold the following morning. Although Hammond-Hill remembers finding this extremely difficult, it doesn't show; in fact, her heart-felt scream and subsequent devastation are believably performed. Barr's decision to have Natalie witness François's death is an excellent one, especially as we quite naturally, after some twenty-seven episodes, care more for her than we do for him. Although his shooting would have been just as shocking had Natalie not been there, arguably it would not have had the same emotional impact. That Natalie is forced to hold the tears back until she and Hervé have driven away – a feat which we know by now must be almost impossible for someone as passionate as her – is also very powerful dramatically, while choosing to end the episode by cross-fading Natalie's tear-stained face with the closing credits is inspired, as it has the effect of enhancing the gravity of what has just occurred.

The events of *A Matter of Life and Death*, and specifically the fact that Natalie now definitively knows that Max has been meeting with the Communists, make it clear that, from here on in, things will never be quite the same again for any of the Lifeline characters. This fact inevitably heightens expectation of the content of the remaining two instalments of the second series.

HISTORICAL BACKGROUND

Betrayal of the Comète Line

The worst betrayal in the history of the Comète Line (the line on which Lifeline was based) occurred in the Summer of 1943. In April of that year, Jean Masson, a 21-year-old blue-eyed, blond-haired Belgian, joined the Line as a guide for the route from Brussels to Paris. It wasn't until June that it was discovered that he was a traitor working for the Gestapo. Masson, whose real name was Jacques Desoubrie, was responsible for the betrayal and death of Dédée's father, Frédéric De Jongh, and as many as fifty others, his actions almost bringing down the Line completely. After the war, he was tried and executed for his crimes.

WHERE ELSE HAVE I SEEN..?

Michael Graham Cox (Philippe)

© Unknown

Sid Rowse, *Poldark*, 1976
Bigwig (voice), *Watership Down*, 1978
Boromir (voice), *The Lord of the Rings*, 1978
DI Jack Slater, *The Gentle Touch*, 1984
General Platek, *The Deliberate Death of a Polish Priest*, 1986

Duncan Lamont (Hervé)

David MacMorris, *The Texan*, 1959-60
Station Sgt Cooper, *Dixon of Dock Green*, 1964-8
Wilks, *The Avengers: Stay Tuned*, 1969
Dan Galloway, *Doctor Who: Death to the Daleks*, 1974
Bartholomew 'Tholly' Tregirls, *Poldark*, 1975

Episode 12: PRISONER OF WAR

WRITTEN BY: Gerard Glaister   **DIRECTED BY:** Michael E. Briant

FIRST BROADCAST: BBC1, 8.05pm, Wednesday 13 December 1978

STUDIO RECORDING: 25 November 1978

VIEWING FIGURE: 8.2m

REGULAR CAST: Albert Foiret: BERNARD HEPTON; Monique Duchamps: ANGELA RICHARDS; Max Brocard: STEPHEN YARDLEY; Major Erwin Brandt: MICHAEL CULVER; Sturmbannführer Ludwig Kessler: CLIFFORD ROSE; Natalie Chantrens: JULIET HAMMOND-HILL; Dr Pascal Keldermans: VALENTINE DYALL; Alain Muny: RON PEMBER; Inspector Paul Delon: JOHN D. COLLINS

SUPPORTING CAST: Betrand Lecau: JOHN ABINERI; Jones: SEBASTIAN ABINERI; Mike Rogers: EDWARD HAMMOND; Estelle Muny: JEAN RIMMER; Jacques Lamboit: JOHN BAKER; Rear Gunner: NICK JOSEPH; Hauptmann Braun: GUS ROY

SYNOPSIS: While on its way back home, an Allied plane is hit by flak from a German night flyer and the crew bail out. A farmer called Bertrand Lecau delivers some dead livestock to Alain and Estelle at their farmhouse. Alain notices that a plane is in trouble over Lecau's farmhouse; Lecau goes home. At the Candide, Albert offers the company of Monique to a lonely Brandt. Brandt flirts with Monique and asks her whether she plans to marry Albert. Natalie loses her composure over Max's continued presence in the Candide as she is convinced that he is responsible for François's death. Albert asks Inspector Delon to investigate. Lecau comes across two British evaders and decides to help them. After kissing Brandt goodnight, Monique confronts Albert as to whether he expects her to have an affair with the Major. Lecau brings the evaders to Alain rather than hiding them himself, as his daughter, Cosette, has taken in a seriously wounded German flying ace.

Estelle offers to look after them until Alain can arrange to have them moved on. Kessler interrogates Lamboit, a man arrested with an evader at the French border. Brandt tells Kessler about the disappearance of the German ace, Hauptmann Braun, and his plane which is still on the secret list. Lecau tells Alain and the evaders that he has found the German's plane near his farm and takes them to see it. Alain tells Albert and Monique about the German. After interrogating an air gunner, Brandt believes that Braun and his plane came down nearby. Natalie brings the evaders to the Candide while Alain tells Albert that London have instructed that they want Braun sent to them together with details of his aircraft. It is agreed that Braun will be held at the Candide with the airmen and that Max will sketch his aircraft. Max's sketching is interrupted by a German patrol. Lecau and Cosette are arrested and taken to Gestapo HQ. Alain makes it back to the Candide with Braun. After some time, Max returns with the sketches. Alain receives news from London that they intend to pick up Braun by launch from the Cherbourg peninsula in twelve days time. Max suggests that his 'friends' may be able to help with the operation and subsequently confirms that they will do so in return for arms and explosives. Albert asks Natalie to take the evaders to Senlis. While he is looking for Monique, a drunken Brandt stumbles across one of the evaders talking with Albert in the backroom, but suspects nothing. The deal with Max and his friends is agreed and Alain delivers Braun to them in the Ardennes. Delon visits the Candide and confirms that it was Max who betrayed François, that Albert was next on his list and that he intended to take over both the Candide and Lifeline. Max and the Communists exchange a drugged Braun for arms at Carteret. Returning to their base, they are wiped out by a squad of German soldiers and French policemen who have been lying in wait for them. Albert tells Monique and Natalie that Max has been killed.

REVIEW: Producer Gerry Glaister's first of two scripts for the series places an incredibly strained Albert centre-stage as he deals with both ordinary and extraordinary airmen, encourages relations between Monique and Brandt, and finally faces up to the terrible reality of Max's betrayal. Although *Prisoner of War* definitely succeeds in being both engaging and suspenseful it does not (unlike the episodes that surround it) have a specific tone or feel, perhaps because it is packed with such a variety of content.

Given the tragic climax to *A Matter of Life and Death*, it is something of a surprise to find that nothing seems to have changed at the Candide as the episode opens. However, Natalie's sudden outburst and Albert's subsequent call to Inspector Delon suggest that this is merely the calm before the storm. Although this is indeed gradually revealed to be the case, surprisingly Max still spends the first half of the narrative very much in the background as another subplot takes precedence over the issue of his betrayal.

This subplot takes us back to Alain's farmhouse which, together with his wife Estelle, we have not seen since *Russian Roulette*. In fact, with the exception of *The Big One* we haven't seen that much of Alain recently either. Although their children are mentioned, Alain's younger brother Gil, who runs the farm, appears to have been forgotten altogether. Alain is joined here by a similar salt-of-the-earth type who is also a farmer in the area, Bertrand Lecau, played by the versatile John Abineri. John, who was best known at the time for playing the even grubbier and gruffer Hubert Goss in *Survivors* (in 1976-77), is the second member of the Abineri acting clan to appear in the series, the first being his son Daniel in *The Big One*. A third Abineri, his other son Sebastian, appears just a few scenes later here as the evader Jones. Lecau seems slightly less intelligent than Alain and a little more unreconstructed ("I wanted to finish him off but you know what women are!"); however, he appears to be an old hand when it comes to evaders and makes several wise decisions as the airmen situation gets out of control. Incidentally, this 'too many airmen' storyline, which proves headache enough here, will become an even more serious problem in the final series, when the evasion line becomes inoperative due to the Allied advance.

Although the idea of Lifeline having to deal with a German flying ace, Hauptmann Braun, is refreshingly original, a decision seems to have been made not to make him a character in his own right, and instead much of what happens to him is either reported through lengthy exposition or witnessed when he is either seriously wounded or drugged up to the eyeballs (the actor doesn't even warrant an on-screen credit for his efforts!). This would not be a problem were it not for the fact that several of the reported off-screen incidents involving Braun, sound as though they would have made for interesting viewing, such as Lecau's reaction to Cosette taking the flyer in, and Jones's and Rogers's attempts to keep the man at bay with a chair leg in one of the Candide's upper rooms. Braun is presumably based on the likes of Colonel Hans Rudel, who by the war's end had flown 2,350 missions against the Allies and was considered to be the Luftwaffe's 'ace of aces.' John Brason would later use Rudel as the inspiration for a more pivotal character, Colonel Hans Ruckert, in *Kessler*.

Another subplot which diverts our attention from Max's betrayal involves the development of a surprising relationship between Brandt and Monique, the possibility of which was first suggested in *Guests at God's Table*, shortly after Brandt lost his wife. Here, however, after Albert engineers that Monique join the Major at his table, there is suddenly far more going on than simply the sharing of a bottle of Burgundy. Brandt now claims to consider Erika to be "forgotten" and puts her loss down to merely "the fortunes of war." Now he wants to toast the future and the way he looks at Monique, and then touches her, suggests that he actually wants her to be a part of it, for a time at least. At first Monique seems much less enthusiastic at the prospect, partly because she is furious that Albert is wilfully using her for Lifeline's ends, but also presumably due to both the fear that she might be accused of collaboration and the fact that he is, after all, 'the enemy'. But perhaps most of all, it is because, as she told Kelso in *Little Old Lady*, she doesn't know what she wants anymore. Her lack of response to Brandt's question as to whether she will marry Albert is likely to be as much to do with the fact that she really does not know the answer as it is to do with her keeping up her guard. However, Brandt certainly knows how to turn on the charm, and a compliment ("You'd have no difficulty in finding someone else"), followed by several sensuous kisses on Monique's wrist (together with perhaps the most suggestive look in the series so far!), prompts her to throw caution to the wind. Their tender parting at the end of the evening, witnessed by a silent Albert, is one of the dramatic high points of the episode and is beautifully played by all concerned. Although the passionate kiss which precedes Brandt's cheerful, but frustrated, parting cry ("Oh Monique, Monique, come home with me!") suggests that she be falling for him, the way she pauses, lost in thought, as she bolts the door after him and breathes in deeply as she moves away, seems to confirm it. Although she is initially defensive to (the suddenly present) Albert, and despite the fact that she has clearly enjoyed her evening with Brandt, it does not take long for Monique to remember that she is angry that Albert has used her in this way. As Albert fields her direct questions about his intentions, the fact that his defence – that he merely thinks Brandt would be a very useful contact – is peppered with use of the exclamation "Ha!" suggests that either he is uncomfortable or he is not admitting the whole truth, or both. Monique seems certain that Albert is intent on her prostituting herself for Lifeline ("And I'm the woman you say you're going to marry?!)" and his response, when pushed, about Lifeline needing to "use all available means" would certainly seem to suggest that she might well be right. Interestingly, the repercussions of this realisation are diverted by an accusation of collaboration ("First collaboration, now me!") and the riveting scene reaches its climax as Albert grabs Monique by the shoulders and insists "I am not a collaborator!" Her shrewd retort: "Well, let's hope you can convince everyone of that after the war," foreshadows the problems they are set to experience in the final series. After all, if he cannot even completely convince his lover that he is not a collaborator, what chance does he have of persuading others of his innocence? Hepton and Richards are both first-rate here, making us believe in the feelings and fears of their respective characters totally.

Although Brandt and Monique share a rather risqué kiss later in the episode in full view of everyone in the Candide, this is as far as the relationship goes. That there wasn't the opportunity to take this storyline further is something that Angela Richards regrets, believing that it would have been an interesting avenue to explore. However, the fact that Michael Culver's time on the show was almost up, save for one last episode, dictated otherwise.

Culver's imminent departure also seems to influence the episode's attempt to suggest that Brandt's professional relationship with Kessler is repaired, and that he has a renewed commitment to the Fatherland. Where this subplot does not convince is in Monique's comments that Brandt "is becoming a real fanatic like Kessler in a way" and has uncharacteristically begun to call British airmen 'terror-flyers'. Similarly unlikely is Brandt's relation to a pleased Kessler of how he chose to interrogate an air gunner before he was allowed medical attention for his broken ankle. This is not the humane Brandt we know and is in marked contrast to the previous episode, in which Kessler actually complains to the Major about his consistent fairness towards enemy airmen. Even when Brandt was at his lowest point in *The Big One*, he still resisted calling Mick Murray a 'terror-flyer' and it is still almost impossible to imagine him using the term. We might have an easier time accepting this suggested change in Brandt had he reacted to his wife's and son's deaths differently. Up until now his loss has always prompted him to question the validity of the Third Reich and of his role in the war, but here he suddenly appears resolute enough to promise Kessler that he will do "anything that is necessary" to break the evasion lines. Their subsequent joint interrogation of Lecau confirms that the pair are once again working with each other effectively, even though it leads them nowhere.

Thankfully there is no attempt, other than the above 'ankle incident', to portray Brandt as a real fanatic, although Kessler himself is given ample opportunity to behave like one. When Brandt relates the hard facts about how the evasion lines have survived for years now and that those who operate them have become battle-hardened, as usual Kessler retreats behind rhetoric – his defence when he does not have the answers. As well as dismissing Brandt's view as "Defeatism!" he pronounces that "In the end the Führer will succeed and then no sacrifice will have been too great," a statement that owes more to his beliefs than to a realistic assessment of the situation.

It is in this episode that Kessler is seen for the first time to wash his hands thoroughly immediately after an interrogation. This is an activity, with obvious overtones, which will become a trademark of the character in the rest of the series. Also debuting in *Prisoner of War* is an extended set for Gestapo Headquarters. As well as Kessler's bathroom, there is a new corridor and stairway. As *Secret Army* moved into its third series, the same set would be extended even further; as Clifford Rose remembers: "It just kept on growing!"

As the episode presses on towards its final set piece, Albert, like Natalie, Victor and Alain, finally appreciates the inexorable truth of Max's betrayal of François. The problem he has with accepting this fact is not so much bound up with his personal feelings about Max, but moreover with what this will mean for Lifeline. His initial standpoint ("Just because he's a Communist doesn't make him responsible for François' death") is entirely borne out of his recognition that Max is the best forger in the country. He knows that Max is vital to Lifeline's continued operation and that without him they, like Jacques Lamboit with his "obviously fake papers," could very easily find themselves being interrogated by Kessler at Gestapo Headquarters. For this reason, Albert refuses to rely on his instincts until he has concrete proof from Inspector Delon, despite the trouble this causes him, particularly with Natalie. Understandably this situation is extremely stressful for Albert to bear, especially as he knows full well that he could be endangering Lifeline's existence by choosing to coming down on either side, which is why his exclamation of "Damn Max!" is so heart-felt. Although the scene in which Max offers the help of his 'friends' is, from her face, the clincher for Monique, Albert still stubbornly refuses to accept this and continues to combat Natalie's complaints with the explanation: "Not while we need him. Not until I'm sure." However, after their exchange during which she calls Max a murderer, the way he downs his drink suggests that he knows that her instincts are spot on. When Albert finally receives confirmation of Max's guilt, and he tells Delon that it would not upset his conscience if Max and his Communist friends were all killed, he refuses to accept Monique's observation that he is a vicious and ruthless man. Instead he counters with the certain and solid response: "No I'm not." This self-perception, together with his explicit announcement that their deaths will not trouble him, suggests a return to the more steadfast and expedience-driven Albert of old, rather than the more introspective man who was visibly shaken by Van Broecken's accurate assessment of his callousness in *Scorpion* and worried by the prospect of having the deaths of the Sisters on his conscience in *Weekend*. Perhaps Max's out-and-out treachery makes this brutal course of action an easy decision for Albert; after all it is not on a par with murdering innocent evaders for the sake of the Line. However, it may also be a reaction to the fact that he now realises that he may have been a little more even-handed of late, something which he now sees as a weakness following the shock revelation that Max has pulled the wool over his eyes for so long. Whatever the explanation for Albert's murderous decision, it is certainly one that will come back to haunt him.

As the revelation of Max's guilt is no surprise to regular viewers, Glaister and director Michael E. Briant clearly elect to up the suspense levels in other areas. When Alain goes to pick up Braun, we are made to think that the Germans are just behind him and that he will be arrested. Brandt's dangerous wandering into the backroom of the Candide brings him closer to the truth of its dual function than ever before, but thankfully he is too drunk to comprehend it. Suspense is also conveyed through the more-dramatic-than-usual reactions of the Lifeline characters. When they receive news of Lecau's arrest, Monique's heightened emotion as she takes the call and Albert's subsequent inability to take the strain, holding his head in his hands, effectively emphasises the danger they are facing. The addition of portentous drumming to certain scenes also contributes considerably to the disconcerting atmosphere of the episode.

By his own admission, Briant was often chosen to helm the more action-packed episodes of *Secret Army*, and *Prisoner of War* is certainly no exception, especially in its final ten minutes. Both the scenes at Carteret, featuring the British launch and the climactic ambush of the Communists, are arguably of feature film standard. However, the latter is the more carefully crafted and memorable. The opening shot, which focuses on plants in the foreground before refocusing on the Communists' truck coming down the road in the background, is particularly effective. Another inspired choice is the piano music – this is Max's swansong after all – which accompanies the entire sequence. This gentle – if unsettling – music (the melody to the song 'That Lovely Weekend' which Monique later sings in *Ambush*) which stops and starts at irregular intervals, underscores the action perfectly, building the tension far more effectively than the more typical 'suspense tracks' that have at times dogged rather than complemented the action of the second series. The gun-battle itself is very believable and pulls no punches in terms of brutality. Especially unforgettable is the way in which Max, who has always been adept at covering his back, notices the danger before his comrades and is the first to turn to face the Germans with

305

his gun blazing. Max may have said previously that he was a coward, but this sequence suggests otherwise. There is a tragic air of futility to Max's last few minutes. Although he desperately fights for his life – as we would expect him to – as his comrades are gradually and grimly despatched, it seems increasingly certain that he will not live to fight another day. The gripping conclusion to the sequence sees Max finally cornered, looking bewildered, perhaps even surprised that it has come to this. To emphasise his final moment of life, the noise of the cocking of the weapon trained on him is enhanced so that it echoes ominously before he is mercilessly mown down.

Although it's difficult to feel much pity for Max, it's a great shame to be saying goodbye to Stephen Yardley, as over the space of twelve episodes he has very much become a defining element of the 'new look' series and always succeeded in making the character interesting to watch. Given the inscrutable forger's complexity, it is perhaps no surprise that Max Brocard is still one of his all-time favourite roles.

SONGS IN THE CANDIDE

'Auprès de ma Blonde'

A popular French song, the title of which translates as 'Next to my Girlfriend', which after its first appearance in the 17th Century gained widespread popularity due to its lively pace and memorable melody.

Chorus: Auprès de ma blonde, Qu'il fait bon, fait bon, fait bon
Auprès de ma blonde, Qu'il fait bon dormer

WHERE ELSE HAVE I SEEN..?

John Abineri (Lecau)

General Carrington, *Doctor Who: The Ambassadors of Death*, 1970
Chingachgook, *The Last of the Mohicans*, 1971
Hubert Goss, *Survivors*, 1976-7
Ushton, *Blake's 7: Hostage*, 1979
Herne the Hunter, *Robin of Sherwood*, 1984-6

Sebastian Abineri (Jones)

Big Bill, *The Queen Street Gang*, 1968
Dick Wright, *Flambards*, 1979
DS Dick Maltby, *Juliet Bravo*, 1983-5
Major Ron Williams, *Coronation Street*, 1994
Godfrey Fuller, *Cadfael: The Rose Rent*, 1997

© Unknown

© Frazer Wood

Episode 13: DAY OF WRATH

WRITTEN BY: John Brason   DIRECTED BY: Uncredited*

FIRST BROADCAST: BBC1, 7.40pm, Thursday 28 December 1978

STUDIO RECORDING: 6 December 1978

VIEWING FIGURE: 4.0m

REGULAR CAST: Albert Foiret: BERNARD HEPTON; Monique Duchamps: ANGELA RICHARDS; Major Erwin Brandt: MICHAEL CULVER; Sturmbannführer Ludwig Kessler: CLIFFORD ROSE; Natalie Chantrens: JULIET HAMMOND-HILL; Dr Pascal Keldermans: VALENTINE DYALL; Alain Muny: RON PEMBER

SUPPORTING CAST: André De Beers: JOHN ALKIN; Jelinek: DAVID NEILSON; Wullner: NEIL DAGLISH; Weikmann: JOHN ROLFE; Jacques: IAN RUSKIN; Guard: DAVID BECKETT

*Terence Dudley was the director assigned to the episode but he is not credited.

SYNOPSIS: Belgian RAF man, André De Beers, witnesses the death of his brother Dirk under torture at Gestapo Headquarters. De Beers manages to escape, while his guards are distracted by a new listing of officers being posted to the Russian Front, and goes to Alain's farmhouse. Alain tells Albert and Monique about De Beers. After a discussion about whether he can be trusted, Albert agrees to think about getting him down the Line. Monique and Natalie accompany Alain back to the farm, where Dr Keldermans has not been able to locate De Beers. Back in Brussels, De Beers slits the throat of a German officer. While Kessler outlines his plans to test television surveillance with Brandt, he is interrupted by Jellinek who has news of the murder. Kessler orders that twenty civilian hostages be taken. Alain believes that De Beers, who has returned to his farmhouse, is responsible for the killing. Albert refuses to let Alain take him down the Line himself. When Alain reveals that De Beers may have killed more than one German, Albert thinks he should be stopped permanently; Alain initially refuses to accept this view. Monique and Natalie decide that they will take De Beers down the Line without Albert's knowledge. When De Beers tries to leave the farmhouse again, Alain attempts to stop him and the pair brawl. Alain convinces him that he must stop the killing. Natalie arrives with news of their plan to take him down the Line. Kessler provides Brandt with information about a failed assassination plot in which Von Elmendorff and Neidlinger were involved and reveals that he knew that they had approached the Major. Nevertheless, he states his loyalty to Brandt and leaves him in charge while he goes to Berlin for a top-level security conference. Six weeks later, Monique is forced to reveal to Albert that they took De Beers down the Line. Albert reprimands Monique severely, telling her that he will kill her if she ever tries anything like that again. Kessler returns to Brussels. The next day, Alain tells Albert that the German radio stations are silent, while Brandt informs Kessler that there is another rumour of an Allied landing in France. While Kessler and Brandt are given a demonstration of the television monitoring equipment, a Mosquito piloted by De Beers arrives over Brussels and attacks Gestapo Headquarters. Brandt and Kessler survive the attack but the building is badly shot up. At the Candide, Albert, Monique, Natalie, Alain and Keldermans receive confirmation of the target from Paul Delon, who also advises that they tune their radio to the BBC. They listen to an announcement about the Normandy landings. Kessler and Brandt also hear the bulletin. Kessler subsequently opens a letter, delivered by courier, which reveals that, before he died, Neidlinger implicated Brandt in the plot against the Führer and instructs that the Major is to be relieved of command and delivered into custody. After writing a letter to his daughter, Brandt commits suicide. In the Candide, an emotional Monique and Albert consider the day's news and their future. Albert removes his wedding ring. A desk calendar shows that it is 6 June 1944.

REVIEW: *Day of Wrath* brings the second series to a close in gripping style as Brandt finally pays the ultimate price for his contact with Von Elmendorff and Neidlinger. Although Brandt's exit from the series – which is shocking and moving in equal measure – is perhaps the most memorable element of the narrative, the episode is also notable for the superb performance given by Ron Pember, as Alain takes a far meatier role in proceedings than usual.

Like Daniel Hill before him, John Alkin first appeared in *Secret Army* as an evader in the first series episode *Too Near Home*, and just as it was a good idea to bring back Hill to give him more to do in *The Big One*, so too it proves with Alkin here. His character, André De Beers, is one of the most interesting evaders yet to grace the series, partly because of his Belgian nationality, partly because he is so desperate to exact his revenge on the Germans, but mainly because he is the very first evader that we see again after seeing him go down the Line. Given the death of his brother under torture at the episode's opening, the close-up of De Beers's eyes, filled with hate, which accompanies the title caption, strongly suggests that if anyone is going to be visiting wrath upon someone it will be him. As Monique later states: "No-one's going to stop him getting his revenge." However, what is not immediately obvious is that the title also applies to the fact that the action of the episode concludes on D-Day. Alkin gives a sensitive portrayal throughout, although he has far more reaction shots than actual lines with which to build up the character. His desolation at the loss of his brother and his subsequent aimless – and literal – first stabs at revenge are convincingly portrayed. The slow shake of his head in response to Alain's question, "There's more isn't there?", is a particularly effective moment, as is his release of emotion after he accepts that he must stop the killings and he and Alain hold each other, united as friends once more. This contact between them deliberately parallels the earlier scene in which De Beers held his dead brother; however, this time the suggestion is that young evader is able to see past his grief. Because we are party to his tragic experiences in Gestapo Headquarters, when he later mounts his one-man air attack on the building (based on the real-life attack by Baron Jean de Selys Longchamps in April 1943 - see below) we don't merely empathise with his actions but also, like the man himself, find them immensely satisfying! Although Albert observed that De Beers had more than enough hate in him to make it home, he would probably be surprised to discover that he actually had enough hate in him to come all the way back to Brussels again, this time armed with far more than just a cut-throat razor! But although the attack on Gestapo HQ clearly gives De Beers the catharsis he sorely needs, presumably the over-zealous torturer whose actions actually prompted the Belgian's fury in the first place has long since been posted to the Russian Front.

Given the fact that neither the Mosquito nor the Gestapo building could actually be filmed in or above Brussels's Avenue Louise due to wholly insurmountable logistical and budgetary constraints, the supremely challenging attack sequence is still very well realised. The television monitoring room receives a very convincing battering in some excellent film sequences, while Kessler's and Brandt's offices also meet with suitable devastation in the studio. Although the pair narrowly avoid being shot during the attack, symbolically the Hitler bust is less fortunate and is glimpsed in the aftermath, sat at the foot of the stairwell. After two long series comprising of some twenty-nine episodes, seeing the German characters amidst the ruins of their Headquarters, together with the aforementioned decapitated Adolf, suggests that the tide is finally turning in the Allies' favour. So much so in fact that it is something of a surprise to discover at the start of the third series that the building has not only been repaired, but also seems to have actually grown in size! It is probably churlish to mention that Albert's observation during the attack ("It sounds like the Avenue Louise") and the subsequent scene in which the Candide staff 'watch' the action are both geographically ridiculous given that the Grand Place is several miles away from Gestapo Headquarters.

Although the television monitoring project is largely incidental to the main plot, nevertheless it is neatly slotted into the narrative as an intelligent, if hugely optimistic, given that this is 1944, response to Kessler and Brandt's problem of dwindling personnel. The project also serves to illustrate the extent of Kessler's blind pride in the Fatherland. He believes that television was invented in 1834 by a German called Paul Nipkopf and delights in correcting Brandt's assertion it is a British invention. However, in a priceless later scene, he too is corrected by the television expert himself, Weikmann, who explains that the equipment they are using was actually developed from the iconoscope which was created by a Russian, Vladimir Zworykin! It is a correction which Brandt greets with smiling eyes. The television subplot also allows for very effective visual framing of the HQ attack sequence, as the single Mosquito is seen both arriving and leaving on the surveillance monitors.

We learn more about Alain's character in *Day of Wrath* than in any preceding episode. Although he is usually one to follow orders, here Alain finds the response of Albert and Monique to the news that De Beers has escaped from Gestapo Headquarters both patronising and unpalatable. Their advice that De Beers could be a plant and that he should get rid of him fails to acknowledge not only that Alain has already stated that he counts the man as a friend, but moreover the honed instincts that his experience as a Lifeline agent has afforded him. Alain, quite understandably, pulls them both up short, reminding them that he started radio work for them in 1941: "And I'm still alive and still operating it. Now show me another one that is. Then you tell me I'm not careful." It is a good point, well made, that, together with his assurances that he would not put his family at risk unduly, or say he trusts De Beers lightly, makes us believe that Alain really does know what he's doing. Thankfully Albert has the good grace to make a rare apology to Alain; however, the new information that De Beers has been on a killing spree soon prompts Albert to propose, yet again, his most frequent solution to any problem: permanent removal! Although Alain eventually relents and promises to "do what has to be done," it seems likely that he only agrees to this because he is convinced that he can dissuade De Beers from continuing his murderous activities. The moving argument he later makes to De Beers, lyrically scripted by John Brason, is not only important in terms of its effect on his listening subject, but also because it eloquently describes why he and his colleagues in Lifeline put their lives at risk for RAF evaders like him ("Because of you, me and thousands more do what we do. You're our backbone!"). The final line of his speech ("But it's not your own personal war out there. It's ours. It's all the people that stayed at home because we couldn't leave... you're not going to destroy all the people who stayed at home to fight") is delivered in heart-felt fashion by Pember and, given its emotive resonance, is unsurprisingly more than enough to stop De Beers in his tracks.

Interestingly, Brason chooses to use the same two-hander format, in which one person reprimands a silent other, twice more in the episode. One of these scenes sees Kessler rebuke Brandt for not revealing what he knew about the plot against Hitler, while the other sees Monique brought to book for her decision to take De Beers down the Line without Albert's knowledge. Although we can understand why she took the decision (essentially on compassionate grounds in order to prevent Alain from having to kill his friend), we can also appreciate Albert's argument that Lifeline can only have one leader: "And there can only be one captain in a ship. It's nothing to do with egos, it's nothing to do with pride or protocol, it's to do with survival." What is less easy to comprehend is Albert's apparently deadly serious subsequent promise: "God knows I love you, but if you threaten those people again, I will kill you!" While Albert arguably needs to impress upon Monique the seriousness of what she has done, the idea that he would actually murder her if she went against his orders ever again seems unthinkable, especially given that, paradoxically, in the same breath, he declares his love for her! Nevertheless, Monique seems to accept the terms of his reprimand and meekly replies: "I said I'm sorry and it won't happen again." Despite the fact that it is difficult to accept either that Albert would actually kill Monique, or the idea that such an act could be justified under the terms of his leadership role, the scene still makes for convincing viewing.

The relationship between Kessler and Brandt comes under the microscope in the aforementioned scene in which the Sturmbannführer not only reveals that he always suspected the now-exposed anti-Hitler plotters of attempting to recruit Brandt, but also that he still regards the Major as more than just a colleague despite this fact. Rather than forcing Brandt to explain why he didn't come to him about their approaches, Kessler elects to give him an easy way out by providing him with a reason: "You kept silent out of loyalty to your friends, but you should have spoken out of loyalty to your country!" He even goes on to volunteer why he thinks Brandt did not do this (due to the death of his wife), before telling him that he is effectively 'letting him off the hook': "I have come to respect you as a good soldier and colleague and that is why you have not been charged and shot." In conclusion, he refers to the Gestapo case file that he first opened on the Major way back in *Radishes with Butter*, affirming that the loyalty testified to within it has been "rightly and properly placed." Although we were already aware of Kessler's respect and affection for his colleague, to learn that he has decided not to report him and has even maintained paperwork as a form of character reference rather than to discredit him (he certainly opened the file for that latter purpose in the first place) is surprising. The implication is that Kessler has come to regard Brandt as a friend as much as a colleague and that, when all is said and done, the loyalty he feels towards his friend even allows him to ignore the differences of opinion and approach that have always had the effect of dividing them. There is no question that this regard and loyalty is more than a little one-sided; after all, it was Neidlinger's argument about removing the likes of Kessler from Germany that seemed to have the most impact upon Brandt. That Kessler has reprimanded him for disloyalty to his country is ironic, as from Brandt's perspective that is exactly why he did not speak to him: out of loyalty to the old Germany, rather than to Hitler's new Fatherland. Kessler knows that Brandt did not become involved in the plot against the Führer, but he fails to realise that the only reason why he didn't throw in his lot with them was because he felt sure that their belief in the brokering of a conditional surrender with the Allies was naïve in the extreme. Although a great deal remains unsaid about the matter, particularly by Brandt, the Major is undoubtedly grateful to Kessler for his loyalty and when he thanks him for being left in charge he is really thanking the Sturmbannführer for his life.

However, it later transpires that what he has done for Brandt is merely a stay of execution. Kessler may have just affirmed his loyalty to Brandt, but the Fatherland is about to disown him as a traitor (due to Neidlinger's confession). Following the raid on Headquarters and the dispiriting (for the Germans) BBC broadcast, Brandt, with his shoulders drooped and arms hanging by his side, looks like a defeated man even before Kessler reads the new instruction from Berlin for his arrest. Kessler is genuinely upset at the news ("I am sorry Brandt. Truly I am."), but realises that the situation is now beyond his control and that all he can offer his friend is the assurance that his last communication will be delivered and the privacy of an empty office in which to write it. Aside from his daughter, to whom his letter was presumably addressed, we have now seen Brandt lose everything: first his faith in Germany, then his wife and son, and finally his position in the Luftwaffe. It is no wonder, therefore, that he chooses to end his own life by calmly putting a gun in his mouth and pulling the trigger. It is a fitting, if shocking, end for the increasingly disillusioned Brandt. The importance of Michael Culver's contribution to *Secret Army*, particularly its second series, which required the actor to make Brandt an even more multi-faceted character, cannot be overstated and, as a result, his departure is perhaps the most significant since the series began.

Day of Wrath has a very specific time frame. The first half of the episode take place in mid-April 1944, while the second half is set some six weeks later on 5 and 6 June 1944. Plot-wise this not only allows for De Beers to go down the Line, get back to England and return by air to take his revenge, but also to tie the series into a specific historical event: D-Day. This makes for a fitting end to the second series, especially as it means we get to witness the elation and relief of all the surviving Brussels-based members of Lifeline as they hear the news of the Allied landings and realise that their efforts have been worthwhile and that the end of the war is finally in sight. However, anyone who knows their Second World War history will also know that this means that there are still three long months left before the liberation of Brussels in September 1944, so in this way the tight time frame of the final series is also duly established.

It seems appropriate that the very last scene of the second series is given over to Albert and Monique as they reflect in private on the news of the Allied invasion. Monique's relief ("I didn't believe it would ever really happen!") is tempered by Albert's astute assessment that "it isn't over yet." However, more significant is that Albert finally removes his old wedding ring, suggesting a renewed commitment to Monique and an improved prospect of the pair finally becoming man and wife.

Day of Wrath is a stirring and memorable finale which successfully incorporates all the familiar hallmarks of the series: an intelligent script, brilliant performances, action and adventure and, most importantly, three-dimensional characters who we have come to care about deeply.

HISTORICAL BACKGROUND

Attack on Gestapo HQ in January 1943

Born in Brussels on 31 May 1912, Jean-Michel De Selys Longchamps, was a Belgian cavalry officer when the Germans invaded in May 1940. After the Belgian surrender he travelled to England, as part of the evacuation of Dunkirk.

He returned almost immediately to France to continue the fight, but was soon forced to flee again, this time via Gibraltar. After his arrest in Morocco by the Vichy authorities, he was imprisoned in Marseilles, but later escaped and crossed the Pyrenees into Spain before returning to England. He was subsequently accepted as an RAF pilot and joined 609 Squadron in Kent. By 1943, 609 Squadron were being sent on ground attack missions in Hawker Typhoons, destroying transportation and communication infrastructure. Longchamps had long begged his superiors that he be allowed to attack the Gestapo HQ in Brussels's

Avenue Louise, particularly as his father and several other friends and relatives had previously been taken there and tortured, but he was turned down each time. (Below: Longchamps stands against the propeller of a Hawker Typhoon, together with fellow 609'ers and Belgian minister Camille Gutt, at Duxford in 1942.)

However, on the morning of 20 January 1943, when he and another Belgian RAF pilot, André Blanco, flew from England to Belgium in order to destroy some locomotives near Ghent, after completing the mission, unlike Blanco who returned to England, Longchamps chose to fly his Typhoon south to the Belgian capital, determinedly making for the Avenue Louise and the hated HQ. Herman Bodson relates the attack in his book, *A Belgian Saboteur in World War II*, as follows:

> 'Coming from the west, the pilot was able to see the building from quite a distance as it faced the wide Avenue de Mot and the adjacent Parc de la Cambre. Approaching over the suburban community of Ixelles and flying at rooftop level to avoid early detection, the pilot could easily aim at the building and direct the fire of his wing guns at its base. Continuing his fire while pulling up on the joystick, he sprayed the complex from basement to roof with a murderous hail of (20mm) explosive bullets... The attack had taken place around ten in the morning while the building was fully lit by the rising spring sun... The morale boost for us was immense, for the pilot had demonstrated that the Germans were vulnerable and unable to exercise complete control of their air space. They could also be victims.'[6]

After the attack, Longchamps reportedly threw both a Belgian and a UK flag out of his plane to the street below before leaving the area and safely returning to base. A total of four Germans were killed in the raid, including a high-ranking officer by the name of Müller. News of the attack swept across the city and, after

secretly listening to BBC radio broadcasts detailing what had happened, some of the oppressed citizens of Brussels visited the Avenue Louise in order to see the damage for themselves. Afterwards, Longchamps was simultaneously demoted and awarded the DFC for his bravado, but died later that year, on 16 August, while

LES GLOIRES DE L'AVIATION MILITAIRE BELGE
5. — Jean-Michel de Selys-Longchamps
PRODUITS LIEBIG ... BIEN MEILLEURS!

returning from a mission to Ostend. Today, a stone memorial with a golden bust of Longchamps stands on a grass verge in front of the former Gestapo HQ

313

building and a plaque on the building façade commemorates his actions – see the 'Location Guide'.

WHERE ELSE HAVE I SEEN..?

John Alkin (André De Beers)

Young Frank Skinner, *Timeslip: The Wrong End of Time*, 1970
Frank Cox, *A Family at War*, 1970-1
Barry Deeley, *Crown Court*, 1972-4
DS Tom Daniels, *The Sweeney*, 1975-8
Lomand, *Doctor Who: Planet of Fire*, 1984

© Peter Espe

Neil Daglish (Wullner)

Cliff Lewis, *Play of the Month: Look Back in Anger*, 1976
Damon, *Doctor Who: Arc of Infinity*, 1983
Michael Barnabas, *Campion: Flowers for the Judge*, 1990
Arthur Mace, *Egypt: The Curse of Tutankhamun*, 2005
Dr Prescott, *Eastenders,* 2006

© Jan Gay

David Neilson (Jelinek)

Mike, *Survivors: The Chosen*, 1976
Lawton, *Boys from the Blackstuff*, 1982
Desmond Gaskell, *Chimera*, 1991
DS Graham Millington, *Resnick*, 1992-3
Roy Cropper, *Coronation Street*, 1995-2008

'It's not sentimentalised, it's not romanticised and the characters are complex and believable human beings.'

CLIFFORD ROSE

SERIES THREE
(1979)

REGULAR CAST

Albert Foiret
BERNARD HEPTON

Monique Duchamps
ANGELA RICHARDS

Sturmbannführer Ludwig Kessler
CLIFFORD ROSE

Natalie Chantrens
JULIET HAMMOND-HILL

Major Hans Dietrich Reinhardt
TERRENCE HARDIMAN

Alain Muny
RON PEMBER

Madeleine Duclos
HAZEL McBRIDE

Major Nicholas Bradley
PAUL SHELLEY

Dr Pascal Keldermans
VALENTINE DYALL

Captain Stephen Durnford
STEPHAN CHASE

Paul Vercors
RALPH BATES

Hans van Broecken
GUNNAR MÖLLER

Major Turner
JACK McKENZIE

Hauptmann Müller
HILARY MINSTER

Inspector Paul Delon
JOHN D. COLLINS

Reichskommissar Glaub
ROGER BOOTH

Wullner
NEIL DAGLISH

Colonel von Schalk
PETER ARNE

Inspector Benet
RICHARD BEALE

Maitre Guissard
MORRIS PERRY

Eugene Zander
ROBERT GILLESPIE

Jacques Gavain
DUNCAN PRESTON

Geneviève
TRISHA CLARKE

Paul (Candide pianist)
KEN MOULE

CREW

Producer
GERARD GLAISTER

Script Editor
JOHN BRASON

Technical Advisor
GRP CPT WILLIAM RANDLE CBE AFC DFM

Writers
N. J. CRISP (1, 3, 7)
LLOYD HUMPHREYS[†] (2)
ALLAN PRIOR (4)
JOHN BRASON (5, 8, 13, 14*)
ROBERT BARR (6)
ERIC PAICE (9, 11)

GERARD GLAISTER (10)
MICHAEL J. BIRD (12)

Directors
MICHAEL E. BRIANT (1, 5, 7, 8, 10)
VIKTORS RITELIS (2, 11, 14*)
ROGER CHEVELEY (3, 13)
TRISTAN DE VERE COLE (4, 6, 9)
ANDREW MORGAN (12)

Designers
RICHARD MORRIS (1, 4, 7, 10, 13)
GRAHAM LOUGH (1, 3, 13)
RAYMOND LONDON (2, 6, 8)
MARJORIE PRATT (3, 5, 9, 12)
ERIC WALMSLEY (11)
JOHN HURST (14*)

Production Assistants
RONALD JONES (1, 5, 7, 8, 10)
ROBERT ASHBURN (2, 11, 14*)
GEOFFREY MANTON (3, 13)
CHRIS GREEN (4, 6, 9)
CATHERINE PAGE (12)

Production Unit Manager
JOHN FABIAN

Directors' Assistants
JANET WRAY (1, 5, 7, 8, 10)
WENDY PLOWRIGHT (2, 11, 14*)
FRANCES GRAHAM (3, 13)
JEAN DAVIS (4, 6, 9)
MICHELLE M. MENDOZA (12)

Assistant Floor Managers
JENI TYRRIL (1, 8, 10, 12)
PENNY WILLIAMS (2, 11)
JEREMY WOOLF (3, 4, 6, 9, 13)
MAGGY CAMPBELL (5, 7)
MATTHEW KUIPERS (11, 14*)

Costume Designers
ANNA DOWNEY (1-13, 14*)
CAROLINE MAXWELL (8)

Make-Up
MARION RICHARDS (1, 2, 4-13, 14*)
MAGGIE WEBB (3)
CAROLYN PERRY (14*)

Film Cameramen
GODFREY JOHNSON (1-8, 10-13, 14*)
JOHN TILEY (9)
LEX TUDHOPE (11, 12)
FINTAN SHEEHAN (13)

Film Recordist
TERRY ELMS

Film Editors
ROBIN SALES (1-13, 14*)
SUE WYATT (12, 14*)

Studio Lighting
PETER SMEE (1)
BRIAN CLEMETT (2)
BERT POSTLETHWAITE (3-13, 14*)

Studio Sound
MARTIN RIDOUT (1-4, 6, 10, 11, 14*)
FRANK RADCLIFFE (5, 7-9)
JAMES CADMAN (12, 13)

Vision Mixers
JAMES GOULD (1, 5-8, 12)
SHIRLEY COWARD (2, 11, 13)
FRED LAW (3, 10)
JIM STEPHENS (4, 9, 14*)

Videotape Editors
ALAN GODDARD (1, 4, 6, 8)
SAM UPTON (2, 3, 5, 9)
ROSS ARCHER (7, 14*)

MALCOLM BANTHORPE (8, 10, 13)
PETER BIRD (11, 12)

Property Buyer
BOB SUTTON

Title Sequence
ALAN JEAPES

Theme Music
ROBERT FARNON

Music Arranger
KEN MOULE

Original Songs for series composed by
ANGELA RICHARDS, KEN MOULE and LESLIE OSBORNE

The BBC would like to thank the RAF Museum Hendon,
the RAF Regiment and the Belgian Air Force for their
cooperation in the making of this series

A BBC TV Production in association with BRT (Belgium)

† Lloyd Humphreys was the pen name of Kenneth Ware
*Episode 14 was made but not broadcast

SERIES 3 – PRODUCTION

Leaving the Best 'Til Last

The final series of a television drama is often greeted with a lukewarm reception, as viewers and critics hark back to the glory days of a first series when the premise was still fresh and dynamic. However, *Secret Army* is a unique and obvious exception to this rule, as it arguably leaves its finest acting, plotting and production to its last thirteen episodes. The final series, for which an appropriate metaphor might be a quietly ticking time-bomb, also sees the tension and suspense (which were already becoming draining in Series Two) reach almost unbearable new levels, as it becomes inevitable that the identities of Lifeline's leaders will finally be uncovered by their German enemies. Throw in the additional threats of the vengeful Communists and the locals, who believe those at the Candide to be murderers and filthy collaborators respectively, and the fates of characters who we have come to know and love become gut-wrenchingly unclear, after all this is a series which thinks nothing of killing off its regular cast. To cap it all the series even manages to end on a high, leaving viewers on the one hand gasping for more, but on the other completely satisfied that their loyalty to all 42 episodes has been thoroughly worthwhile.

Given that the third series is regarded as such an unequivocal success, with startling first transmission viewing figures (even for those episodes unaffected by the ITV strike), it is fascinating to discover just how much of that which made it on screen had been shaped by circumstance rather than as a result of Glaister and Brason's original plans, and how their crucial decisions, some of which were made very late in the day, ensured that it would be a series that would come to be regarded as one of the best BBC dramas of all time.

Just as they had done while working on series one, Glaister and Brason began to discuss and draft their ideas for the next series long before production had finished on Series Two. Both agreed that the move to the new Candide, something which Brason had been much less certain of than his producer, had given the series a compelling new direction and energy. Glaister was particularly pleased that the series's levels of suspense now emulated those fashioned by

© Joan Glaister

323

his beloved Hitchcock. However, he believed that even more could be done to crank up the tension, especially given the timeframe of the final series, which was somewhat dictated by their decision to end Series Two on D-Day. The obvious strategy was to cover the final year of the war (1944-5) with the series ending on VE Day, but to set the majority of the action between June and early-September 1944, given that Brussels was liberated only three months after D-Day.

Absent Albert

© Peggy Leder

This timeframe agreed, the pair now began to discuss how the stories of their principal characters would be developed and ultimately concluded; however, they had not got far with this when one of their lead cast members delivered them a bombshell. Bernard Hepton had accepted the roles of Jacques in *As You Like It*, Richard in *Richard II* (left) and Caesar in *Julius Caesar* by acclaimed theatre director George Murcell, over a five-month Shakespeare season at his theatre (a church that had been converted into an Elizabethan-style theatre in 1975) in Tufnell Park, which was set to begin in March 1979. This would mean that Hepton would be unavailable for the first four months of production on the new series, in other words almost half of the total production time. Upon hearing this news, Glaister did not for one minute consider losing Hepton from the series and, together with Brason, began to explore both the way in which Albert could be written out of the series for a period of episodes and how the series's production order could be constructed in order to address his absence. They quickly hit upon the idea of having Albert arrested by the civil police, charged with the murder of Andrée and incarcerated in Brussels's Havenlaan prison while helping them with their investigations. Furthermore, they decided that Hepton could still feature in most episodes via pre-recorded film inserts, filmed in one block before beginning his stint at Tufnell Park. Hepton, who was keen not to give up on the part of Albert, readily agreed to the proposition. Now Glaister and Brason had to work out how to deal with the knock-on effect of Albert's absence on the series's ongoing narrative.

On hearing of Hepton's period of absence from the new series, Angela Richards went to see Glaister with a simple solution to the problem: "I said to him that Monique should take over the Line." This was a scenario that would have the potential to go some way towards addressing Richards's only real dissatisfaction with the series, which was consistently "feeling overwhelmed by the male aspect," not only in terms of the series's cast and crew, but also in terms of its plotting, which she felt was at odds with historical evidence: "In actual fact, it would have been the women who would have taken the most responsibility for the Resistance, because there weren't too many men around." Furthermore, she thought it would be very interesting to explore how Monique would cope with the responsibility, not by presenting her as a heroine, but as an ordinary human being who was capable of making mistakes, just like their real-life counterparts: "I wasn't into heroes, as such. I thought they should show that the people who were left behind, who were mostly women, would not nec-

© Unknown

essarily be amazingly good at it, but would have to learn on their feet and that would have been an interesting process to watch, because that would have happened."

Basic Format

Glaister agreed that Monique should indeed take over Lifeline for a time and initially liked the idea of observing her making serious mistakes, so much so that he and Brason wrote into an early overview of the narrative of the third series (which must date from around October/November 1978) entitled 'Basic Format', a significant storyline whereby 'Monique takes over the Line but an early decision... an emotional one... causes the death of Dr Keldermans.' However, Richards's happiness with the new setup was to be short-lived, as Glaister and Brason almost simultaneously decided, for a number of narrative reasons, to bring

325

a character back into the fray who would actually be reintroduced to the series in order to vie with Monique for control of the Line: Major Bradley. Paul Shelley, who agreed to return as Bradley, remembers that the production team "felt the character had worked" during his initial outing. Shelley too recalls being happy with his first episode: "It was such a meaty piece of writing and a good role and therefore really enjoyable to work on." Other than bringing Bradley back in order to put him into direct conflict with Monique for dramatic purposes, Glaister and Brason saw a role for him that was directly inspired by historical events.

The pair had already decided that the third series should open with the severance of the evasion line due to the Allied invasion. Their Basic Format document read as follows: 'We open with the evasion line (to the Pyrenees) being strained and under threat as German security and the Allied thrust into France from the Normandy beach heads make it almost impossible to continue. Certain sections of the Line are severed, blown, and generally out into turmoil.' The document goes on to relate that: 'At the same time as the escape route is severed the numbers of evaders increase (due to the increased air activity) and the problem of what to do with them grows daily,' and that to deal with it, immediately after Monique's 'emotional decision' causes the death of Dr Keldermans: 'London sends in Bradley to take over and cope with the worsening situation of 'stacking' evaders. Attempts to get them to Switzerland are only partially successful.' Finally, the document details how: 'Such numbers of unreturnable evaders exist that Bradley commences his own private army working with the Resistance.' All of these ideas, and Bradley's coordinating role, have their roots in London's real-life attempts to address the problem of 'stacked evaders.' This work had fallen to MI9's Airey Neave – who by this point in the war headed up Room 900 (the headquarters of the MI9 division dedicated to the recovery of Allied servicemen downed in occupied territories) – who devised 'Operation Marathon', which instigated the removal of the growing number of trapped evaders from cities and towns into wooded areas where they would live bivouac-style until the Allies reached them. 'Marathon' was intended to take place throughout France and Belgium. Neave decided to send a shrewd agent called Ancia to Belgium in May 1944 to set up such a camp in the Ardennes. Three months later, when Neave finally reached Brussels during its liberation, he discovered that Comète had actually been so suspicious of Ancia and unenthusiastic about Marathon that the majority of 'their' airmen had remained hidden in safe-houses. Glaister and Brason – who were fully aware of Neave's wartime activities and the full history of Comète – considered the idea of the evaders' camp in the Ardennes to have great dramatic potential so, despite the failure of Marathon's execution in Belgium, Neave's vision of such a camp would finally became a reality in *Secret Army* (although Neave – then Shadow Secretary of State for Northern Ireland – did not live to see it, as he was killed by an INLA car bomb in late March 1979, just a few months after Glaister and Brason decided to write it in to the series). A significant difference to the historical scenario would be that in *Secret Army*, Lifeline, not MI9, would have already decided to move the airmen out to the Ardennes. As a result, Bradley, who was loosely based on Ancia, comes to Brussels not to organise the camp but instead to ensure its arming and protection. The *Basic Format* document also confirms that Glaister and Brason always planned to kill Bradley off: 'Bradley is killed on a military mission'; however, there is no mention anywhere of the rekindling of his attraction to Natalie.

What is particularly striking about the Series Three *Basic Format* document is how closely the central narrative it details – the gradual uncovering of a trail that ultimately leads to the discovery that the Candide staff were behind Lifeline all along – would eventually be followed in the final transmitted episodes, even down to the Major refusing to leave Brussels at the same time as Kessler and deciding, after he confronts Albert, that it no longer matters that he was the leader of Lifeline. However, the crucial difference in this initial draft is that the Major referred to throughout is Brandt rather than Reinhardt! This fact suggests that Michael Culver made his decision to leave the series very late in the day, perhaps even less than a month before production on the second series reached completion. Further confirmation of this fact is offered by Brason's *Secret Army Dossier* novel, in which his adaptation of *Day of Wrath* includes the death of Corporal Rennert instead of Brandt, presumably matching his original script for the Series Two finale. Following Culver's revelation that he did not want to continue in the role, Brason hurriedly rewrote *Day of Wrath* to bring forward the

© Unknown

discovery of an invitation extended to Brandt to join in on an assassination attempt on Hitler which, despite the fact that he actually declined to be involved, due to Neidlinger's naming of Brandt under torture, left him with no option but to commit suicide. Glaister and Brason had originally intended for the conspiracy against the Führer in which Brandt was implicated to have been the infamous 20 July 1944 bomb plot and to have Brandt face interrogation from Kessler over his involvement during an early episode of the third series set soon after this failed assassination in late July 1944. This meant that not only did Glaister and Brason need to find a replacement Luftwaffe officer to fill Brandt's shoes, but that the implication of involvement in the Hitler bomb plot would have to be transferred to this new character if it was to remain in the series at all. The fact that a decision was made to do exactly that suggests that that by this time N. J. Crisp had already started writing the third series episode in which it would feature (*Revenge*).

Another interesting feature of the *Basic Format* document is that the Communist threat to Lifeline is not mentioned in it at all; indeed, when Albert is attacked in the Candide, it is only stated that this act is perpetrated by his fellow countrymen who believe him to be a collaborator. Furthermore, it is stated that he is not the only member of Lifeline who is treated in this way: 'He is saved from being strung up, but the hunt is on for the Candide people. Some are captured and degraded, others manage to stay free.'

Perhaps the most interesting storyline in the document that did not make it to the screen is the idea that Lifeline would be remobilised some time after the liberation of Brussels in order to 'assist in the recovery of as many paratroopers as possible' after the Arnhem debacle. This idea would be further refined in later pre-production documents, to be limited to efforts made by only Natalie and her uncle Hans van Broecken, who are approached to do this by Allied forces, before this plot was as good as abandoned.

Kessler and Madeleine's storyline survives almost completely intact from the *Basic Format* document to the transmitted episodes, and even includes: his attempts to persuade her to leave Brussels for the relative safety of Germany, to stay with his mother not his brother; Kessler's flight and capture (although without Madeleine in tow); and Madeleine's final bribing of the guards before the pair 'disappear in the direction of Germany.'

The document's penultimate paragraph details the (original) fate of Major Brandt, which follows exactly the same pattern of events as those that would instead befall Reinhardt: 'Brandt is eventually stuck in with the other officers and Kessler accuses him of cowardice and desertion. A German court martial is held in their confines and Brandt convicted. When their Canadian captors are approached to provide four rifles and four bullets for a firing squad they agree.' However, the conclusion of his story is utterly different: 'But Brandt is saved from death at the hands of his own kind by intervention from Albert... a small return for his own safety (Brandt's case file on the Candide having previously exonerated Albert).' This ultimately abandoned eleventh-hour rescue, as well as being rather out of keeping with *Secret Army*'s grimly realistic pretensions, would also have diverged from the real-life incident on which it was based: the execution of a German officer at an Allied prison camp at Schellingwoude, North of Amsterdam, five days after the end of the war, for whom there was no such saviour. This startling situation would also end up being dramatised in Paul Verhoeven's acclaimed 2006 film *Black Book*, although it is unknown whether the director got the idea from *Secret Army* or because he, like John Brason (right), was also aware of the original incident.

© Jan Olav Flatmark

The remaining elements of Glaister's and Brason's first attempt to get their ideas for the third series down on paper were the comments that: it 'will, inevitably, be more closely linked with historical happenings than was desirable in the preceding series'; that 'The episode storylines will, of course, be the province of the individual writers, but will incorporate a fairly tight running story development of our main characters and their situations'; and finally the flagging up of the fact that 'One interesting aspect [of the new series] is how the Germans, once the 'hunters', find that, with the approach of the Allies, they are becoming the 'hunted'. Resistance is more overt... repression greater... yet at the same time many more Germans are sweetening the pills for after the war.'

Hartmann and Bradley

A few weeks later, a new pre-production document was drafted which incorporated information about Brandt's replacement and sought to detail the basic background to each of the series's intended fourteen episodes The new character, who would effectively fulfil exactly the same function in the narrative as Brandt, was originally named Major Hans Dietrich Hartmann (presumably after decorated Luftwaffe ace Erich Hartmann).

MAJOR HANS DIETRICH HARTMANN

- Known as Dieter.
- Knight's Cross with Oak Leaves.
- Seconded from Flying Duties with Luftwaffe Bomber Squadron (well established and war scarred bunch of Heinkel 111's) after seriously wounded in abdomen.
- A conscripted (1939) airman, he has seen service over Britain, Greece (Crete), the Balkans and Russia.
- A master printer in civvy street, he is neat, tidy, dogged, efficient by nature. The war has made him worldly-wise, cynical and weary.
- He is not overtly anti-war or anti-Nazi, merely aware.

- He is not frightened of Kessler or the Gestapo and is impossible to intimidate.
- Neither is he wedded to Nazi ideology.
- He is a native of Stuttgart (therefore a Swabian).
- He regularly suffers from his abdominal wounds (described by him as acute indigestion).

Although Hartmann was clearly based in part on Brandt, it seems likely that Glaister was also thinking back to his time on *Colditz*, as the character bears more than a passing resemblance to SS Security officer Horst Mohn (played by Anthony Valentine), who also had a Knight's Cross with Oak Leaves, was fastidious and impossible to intimidate, and suffered from serious abdominal wounds. However, it is significant that Hartmann, unlike Mohn, is not a member of the Nazi party and no sadist. Perhaps the characteristic that is most unique to Hartmann is his overt cynicism and weariness of the war. A later pre-production document would see the new Luftwaffe Major's surname change from Hartmann to Reinhardt, while retaining the same Christian names.

In their second pre-production document, Brason and Glaister also elected to provide background details on SOE agent Major Bradley. Interestingly, however, they temporarily decided that he should be revealed to be a native Belgian and his real name to be Luc De Vriendt, information that is not shared in *Lucky Piece*.

MAJOR BRADLEY

- Real name: LUC DE VRIENDT
- Native of Antwerp.
- Escaped with Belgian forces in 1940.
- Has worked on special operations since 1942. Expert on the Peenemunde (V-weapons) operation and retains contacts with the organisation.
- Has posed as, and carries papers of, a Todt Organisation Engineer.
- Speaks fluent English and German as well as his natural Flemish and French.
- Unmarried.
- Parents both dead, a sister 'somewhere in Europe'.
- University trained in electronic engineering, but too young to have 'outside' experience in that field.

This description confirms Bradley's involvement in V-weapons operations at Peenemunde that were only hinted at during his first appearance in the series, when he was returning from there with a Polish scientist in tow. A later pre-production document (the same which renames Hartmann as Reinhardt) has reference to his real name as Luc De Vriendt struck out. Instead this name would merely become his alias. The idea that he was a native Belgian who had escaped back in 1940 was also abandoned, although his character description is not revised to state that he is an Englishman or any other nationality for that matter.

His cover as a member of Organisation Todt and the De Vriendt alias would eventually be used in the transmitted series when Bradley dines with Kessler in *Just Light the Blue Touch-Paper*.

Before Glaister and Brason's second pre-production document detailed their vision for the series (on an episode-by-episode basis), the series's 'running characters' were listed. Several notable absentees from this list include supporting characters such as Captain Durnford, Major Turner and Hauptmann Müller, which suggests that they had not yet been conceived. However, what is more surprising is that, as in the *Basic Format* document, the return of Paul Vercors is still not mentioned. Furthermore, the Communists only warrant two brief mentions in the subsequent episode breakdown (references that do not suggest the inclusion of Vercors and his heavies), so the resumption of his threat to Lifeline (and specifically Albert) must have been a rather late addition to the series's running storyline.

Episode-by-Episode Breakdown

For each episode, the document's remaining six pages detail the general wartime context, as well as the current situations for the Lifeline and German characters.

EPISODE 1

WARTIME SITUATION: Tightening up by Germans culminating in Keitel's directive. The Allied advance across Normandy is almost cutting the evasion line route to the Pyrenees.

LIFELINE: Last Pyrenees run. Possibly show difficulties of tight checks, disruption, loss of safe-houses etc. Albert making plans for new route to Switzerland (Brussels – Namur – Dinant – Luxembourg – Metz – Nancy – Epinal – Belfort – Audincourt – Switzerland). Sudden retreat of Germans in Northern France has exposed three safe-houses and operators have been 'roped in'.

GERMANS: Arrival of Hartmann [Reinhardt], Brandt's replacement. Opening of relationship with Kessler. Reintroduce Madeleine (just to keep her in mind).

In this way, the information acts as a list of suggestions for the writer, in this case N. J. Crisp, as well as a sort of check list. The main differences to the episode it would eventually become (*The Last Run*) are that the last evasion run is not actually completed and that Albert makes no efforts to seek out new routes to Switzerland. Ultimately Crisp would of course further bulk out the episode by also incorporating: Kessler's raid on a Brussels safe-house; the return of Vercors and the revelation of his vengeful intentions towards Albert; Reinhardt and Kessler arguing over Tucker (in the episode-by-episode breakdown it is suggested that the first time they cross swords is not until episode four!); and the start of the trail that will lead Reinhardt to Lifeline. This neatly illustrates the way in which writers would build and develop their episodes from the broad structural guidelines suggested by Glaister and Brason. As the document states: 'These are not intended to be fixed story requirements. They merely indicate in very general terms the running storyline as it affects the regulars. It is NOT intended to lay down any confines to the episode story, merely to guide what we would like to happen as background to that storyline.'

EPISODE 2

WARTIME SITUATION: Escape route now totally severed. Pyrenees route finished. Allies continuing to advance towards Paris with northern thrust towards Belgium.

LIFELINE: Safe-house losses have repercussions, but unable to trace back very far, 'next' operatives warned. Natalie given job of seeking out possible route across Holland to Denmark (sea escape).

GERMANS: Hartmann's thorough search of Brandt's files (recently not pursued) reveals Brandt not far off truth and Hartmann follows up leads one by one.

This breakdown barely resembles *Invasions* at all, apart from Reinhardt's use of Brandt's files and the fact that it concentrates on the loss of safe-houses. What is most interesting about this summary is the idea of a new evasion storyline for Natalie which never materialised.

EPISODE 3

WARTIME SITUATION: Attitudes of Occupied to Occupier slowly changing. Resistance more overt. Hitler plot (Stauffenburg) almost succeeds. Repercussions – vicious.

LIFELINE: Liege safe-house blown and Kessler rounds up operatives, they do not talk, but Resistance more incriminated than Lifeline and big round-up occurs. First successful Swiss escape. Albert suddenly arrested by Civil Police on charge of murder of his wife (1943).

GERMANS: Kessler succeeds with Resistance. Promoted to Standartenführer (full Colonel). Hartmann still following up leads.

The resistance activity and 'big round-up' mentioned here do not make it into the third series at all, while Kessler's promotion comes much later in the finished series: concurrent to the events of *Prisoner*, an episode for which he is absent. A handwritten arrow on the page brings forward Albert's arrest from its original home as part of episode four, while the year of Andrée's death was incorrectly ascribed to 1942 but typed over to become 1943, hinting at the inconsistency towards, and confusion over, dates that would occasionally dog this final series.

EPISODE 4

WARTIME SITUATION: Paris liberated. Northern thrust given new impetus. Last deportation of Jews and forced labourers.

LIFELINE: Safe-houses now becoming very full with RAF and American bombing activity. Escape route limited and bottleneck building. Monique takes over the Line. Albert in prison.

GERMANS: Hartmann has first cross-swords with Kessler. Kessler knows he will not be able to intimidate Hartmann. Hartmann makes first arrest of Lifeline operator.

Of the above content, only the start of Albert's prison term and Monique's leadership of the Line are identifiable elements of the eventual fourth episode (*A Safe Place*), and both of these were originally listed as taking place in the fifth episode instead (an arrow in pen once again moving them to their new position).

EPISODE 5

WARTIME SITUATION: Advance continues, but slower. Resistance now in the open and trying to disrupt Germans.

LIFELINE: Decide impossibility of springing Albert despite help of friendly Delon. Natalie has explored Dutch outlet and finds negative answers. Constant build up of evaders now critical.

GERMANS: Kessler advises Madeleine to leave for Germany. She refuses.

Once again this breakdown bears little resemblance to its ultimate counterpart. The idea of a plot to rescue Albert from prison is somewhat surprising, as is the suggestion that Natalie has been continuing to investigate the possibility of evasion by sea via Holland. Although the number of evaders on Lifeline's hands is recognised as a problem, none of these alternative evasion route ideas are ever given serious consideration, or indeed much airtime in the broadcast versions of any Series Three episodes.

EPISODE 6

WARTIME SITUATION: V1 attacks on UK about to be superseded by V2 rockets. Allies approach Belgian border.

LIFELINE: Albert still in prison awaiting trial. London sends Bradley (De Vriendt) on triple mission: a) to cope with evaders (not return them) and help – or take over – Lifeline, b) to attend to V2 situation, he has previous knowledge of Peenemunde, c) undisclosed. Immediate aggro between Monique and Bradley.

GERMANS: Kessler pelted with stones and rubbish. Resistance now explosive. Communists highly active and determined to take control. Germans just as determined to see they don't.

This breakdown is more on track with the series, as it details the arrival of Bradley and the immediate hostility he receives from Monique. By this time in their planning, Glaister and Brason had clearly decided that Bradley's mission would also encompass the gathering of intelligence about V2 rocket sites and attempts to destroy them, a mission that tied in more directly with his *Lucky Piece* back story and was masterminded in reality by MI9's Airey Neave. The V2 rockets were, of course, the Third Reich's last desperate hope for victory and as a result, by August 1944 (when this episode is set), rocket sites were springing up all over Belgium and Holland. Also here is one of the two brief mentions of the Communists in the entire document.

EPISODE 7

WARTIME SITUATION: Allies in Belgium. Local loyalists determined to overthrow Communist bid for power, London even more determined to see to it. V2 attacks on increase. Patton thrusting out towards German border.

LIFELINE: Bradley collects evaders into small 'private' army of Resistance to join locals where possible. Bivouaced in Ardennes. Swiss Escape route is now finally closed. Lifeline's job is really over as an evasion line. They decide to assist Resistance. Monique works with Bradley in uneasy dual command. Monique makes sentimental or emotional decision causing the death of Dr Keldermans.

GERMANS: Overt hatred of Germans now apparent in streets. Kessler quite ruthless in restoring order. Hartmann now with last piece of Lifeline puzzle. Knows it is too late anyway, but cannot resist the finale.

Especially in its concentration on Bradley's 'private' army, this summary reflects *Ambush* pretty well, the main difference being that Monique makes a practical (rather than an emotional) decision that leads to a man's death, the death: not of Dr Keldermans, but of one Flt Lt Cox instead. Also, the idea that Lifeline's job is 'over as an evasion line' would be confirmed as early as the opening episode of this series. In terms of Kessler, *Ambush* would actually concentrate more on his relationship with Madeleine than his meting out reprisals for anti-German activity.

EPISODE 8

WARTIME SITUATION: Allies advancing towards Brussels. German garrison withdraws leaving only token force to control civilians and disrupt and destroy.

LIFELINE: Bradley instrumental in destroying V2 installations, but evader 'army' depleted. Albert still in prison, but case is proving thin. Court asks for German report on death of Mme Foiret (during German search).

GERMANS: German report awakens thought in Hartmann who is beginning to find the old Candide more than interesting. Now the link is with Foiret. Kessler considering his next move, again approaches Madeleine to leave for Germany. The Germans are rapidly becoming the 'hunted' in the partisan war.

Again this episode summary directly mirrors the events of its final counterpart: *Just Light the Blue Touch-Paper*, with the exception of Natalie's crucial involvement in the narrative, both in terms of the V2 rocket site attack and Reinhardt's interest in her.

EPISODE 9

WARTIME SITUATION: The Allies reach Brussels. Though ostensibly an undeclared 'open city', there is still token resistance from the remaining troops.

LIFELINE: Albert is released – insufficient evidence coupled with the German report. Finds Lifeline quite different – objects to Bradley but recognises necessity of aiding. Bradley killed in escapade with Lifeline members trying to save installation (or whatever) in the city. The Allies enter the city, resistance fighting with them, everybody hastily and tardily becoming a patriot.

GERMANS: Hartmann has the last piece of his puzzle – it *is* Foiret and the Candide. He informs Kessler, but the Allies are moving through the city and Kessler is concerned with getting out 'to fight another day' (Madeleine goes with him). Hartmann refuses to go. Kessler is livid and orders him – he refuses. Kessler goes.

Ultimately, Kessler and Madeleine would not leave, and the Allies would not arrive, until episode ten. Albert's release would also be delayed to the following episode, a factor which meant that he would not meet up with Bradley again before the Major's death. It is clear that the production team are leaving the exact means of Bradley's demise to the episode's writer by merely suggesting one possible exit for the character.

EPISODE 10

WARTIME SITUATION: Allies take over Brussels. Germans fall back towards Germany. Allied thrust into Low Countries.

LIFELINE: Hartmann confronts Albert with his knowledge, brings out gun only to hand himself over and they drink together. British lieutenant comes in and takes Hartmann prisoner. Patriots arrive to attend to Albert as a collaborator.

GERMANS: Hartmann taken into custody as Allied prisoner.

The main difference here is that Reinhardt's confrontation would fall at the end of this episode and the arrival of Allied assistance at the Candide would not occur until the start of the next. Additionally, Albert, Reinhardt and Monique would, of course, all be taken away by Vercors and his Communist friends rather than by other parties.

EPISODE 11

WARTIME SITUATION: Germans mopped up. Advance into Holland bogged down slightly.

LIFELINE: Albert strung up. Natalie brings Brits in time to stop it. It is Hartmann's evidence that finally convinces patriots of Albert's participation. Monique is missing – presumed taken by patriots 'out for blood'.

GERMANS: Hartmann taken prisoner. Kessler caught near border with other fleeing Germans. Manages to convince that Madeleine is a hostage and she is released. Returned with other officers to Brussels.

In the end, Reinhardt's evidence proves irrelevant, as Vercors knows that Albert is a patriot and just doesn't care, as he is hell-bent on avenging the death of Max. Monique, who is not taken from the Candide in the breakdown for episode 10 is, as in the final series, in the hands of a group of patriots here. Once again, the Kessler and Madeleine narrative would translate to screen almost exactly, with the exception that this summary suggests they are fleeing in a group with other Germans rather than alone.

EPISODE 12

WARTIME SITUATION: Allies try to shorten fight by drop at Arnhem. A debacle.

LIFELINE: All personnel exonerated. Brits ask them to 'come out of retirement' and assist with extricating as many Arnhem paratroopers as possible. Natalie is especially helpful in this. Monique rescue by Brit.

GERMANS: Hartmann interrogated, but held for 'war crimes' commission. Kessler in custody.

As mentioned previously, the content of this episode twelve diverges wildly from the final version. Ultimately, the Battle of Arnhem (Operation Market Garden) is merely a distant historical backdrop against which Hans van Broecken's tragic end is played out. Furthermore, Lifeline would take no part at all in the operation, being far too busy licking their wounds after recent traumatic events. There is a suggestion here that little thought has been put into Monique's rescuer thus far.

He is not even afforded a name – a situation which is little improved by subsequent references to him simply as a British Lieutenant or Monique's husband.

EPISODE 13

WARTIME SITUATION: War in Europe moving towards its end. Battle of the Bulge has failed. General feeling of rounding up the bits and pieces before trials etc. Allies into Germany.

LIFELINE: Aftermath. Still repercussions but now insignificant. Monique marries British Lieutenant who saved her. Goes to England.

GERMANS: Hartmann sent to join other officers held in clearing house in Brussels. Kessler there with other SS and officers. Kessler accuses him of treason and cowardice. Decide to hold court-martial. Canadians (who have replaced Brits) don't give a damn. Hartmann tried and condemned to death. Germany surrenders. Hitler dead. War over. Canadians give Kessler four rifles and four bullets. Hartmann shot by firing squad AFTER war over. Germans to be transported to Nuremberg for trials. Madeleine bribes guards and she and Kessler melt into the night.

By this time in their planning, Glaister and Brason had clearly decided to abandon Hartmann's rescue by Albert, judging it to be out-of-keeping. The amount of detail under the 'Germans' section suggests that the pair were much more definite about how this section of the narrative would be realised on screen than they were with the Lifeline side of things. Most significantly, there is no reference to Albert's ownership of the Candide or to how he feels about Monique's choices, both of which are crucial elements of the transmitted final episodes. Additionally, a very minor point is that Monique's husband-to-be would be promoted to the rank of Captain.

EPISODE 14

WARTIME SITUATION: Twenty-fifth anniversary of end of hostilities. Celebration in Brussels attended by everybody in forces, evasion, resistance etc. BBC doing a 'Panorama-like' coverage of the event and 'what happened to the people'.

LIFELINE: Albert, Alain and Natalie still alive. Monique comes over from England with husband and meets Albert again. Evaders interviewed (possibly with clips of film). All are exaggerating or lying.

GERMANS: Kessler trying not to be interviewed. Now a prosperous industrialist who denies all knowledge of his Belgian operations.

The ill-fated episode fourteen would be scripted and made pretty much in line with this summary. An important difference is that the anniversary being celebrated would be that of the liberation of Brussels, not the 'end of hostilities' (thus setting the episode in September 1969). Another change made would be that Monique would return to Brussels alone. Significantly, no reference is made to the exploration of the worth of Lifeline's work and the relative evils of the Nazis and the Communists – the very elements that would contribute to this ill-conceived episode finally being abandoned. The reference to Kessler's role in the narrative as a successful industrialist is the earliest indication that Brason and Glaister had clear ideas about Kessler's post-war life, and is the first seed sown of an idea that would eventually become the spin-off series *Kessler* (1981), a project that incidentally might not have gone ahead at all had episode fourteen hung together satisfactorily and been broadcast.

Writers

Now that they had a clear episode-by-episode breakdown in place, Glaister and Brason began to recruit writers to develop their summaries into full-blown episodes. Brason himself would elect to tackle the final wartime episode and the anniversary reunion, as well as the second and seventh episode (the latter being the one which originally contained Keldermans's death). Glaister would once again pen a single episode, deciding to tackle the crucial tenth episode in which Hartmann (Reinhardt) finally confronts Albert in the Candide. N. J. Crisp, who had previously contributed six well-received episodes to the show (three for each series), was approached to pen a further three, including the series opener, episode five – which had by this stage been developed further to chiefly focus on Natalie and her uncle Hans following Monique's instructions to explore possible North Sea escape routes from Holland and Denmark – and the V2 rocket attack episode (eight). Robert Barr would be approached to provide his fourth script for the series, in which he would reintroduce Bradley, a character he himself had created for *Lucky Piece*. On the strength of his excellent scripts for the second series, David Crane was also asked to write for the series again, being assigned the instalment in which Monique takes over the Line (episode four). Willis Hall, who had not written for *Secret Army* since the first series, and who had written for *Hazell* and a play (*Mr and Mrs Bureaucrat*) for BBC2's *Play of the Week* in between, was also approached to pen a script: the episode featuring Lifeline's remobilisation at Arnhem.

Michael J. Bird

One accomplished writer who was new to the series but an old hand when it came to scripting television drama was Michael J. Bird. By 1979, Bird had two successful Mediterranean-set drama serials, *The Lotus Eaters* (1972-3) and *Who Pays the Ferryman?* (1977), under his belt, and had completed work on a third: *The Aphrodite Inheritance*, which was due to start broadcast in the early part of 1979. Bird had created and written all three (of these, only *The Lotus Eaters* contained scripts penned by other writers), and along the way struck up a friendship with Viktors Ritelis, who had directed episodes of both *The Lotus Eaters* and *The Aphrodite Inheritance* (the latter series being a contributing factor to Ritelis not directing more episodes of *Secret Army*'s second series). Gerry Glaister knew Bird because he had scripted an episode of the final 1976 series of *The Expert* (*A Family Affair*), but also because Bird had previously submitted several unsuccessful scripts for both *Colditz* and *The Brothers*. After completing all the scripts for *The Aphrodite Inheritance*, in mid-1978 Bird began to put together a new television series, which would again be set in the Mediterranean, entitled *Hotel Armageddon*, about the terrorist infiltration of a luxurious Greek hotel.

The BBC's Head of Series, Ronnie Marsh, felt that the writing credits should be shared, and as a result John Brason also came on board as Bird's co-writer. Brason, of course, had to juggle his involvement with the production of *Secret Army*'s second series; nevertheless, by October 1978 he had completed work on two episodes. For a number of reasons *Hotel Armageddon* was never made by the BBC, and as Bird had some time on his hands as a result, Brason approached him to write for *Secret Army*, initially commissioning him to pen the third episode which was to deal with the Hitler bomb plot.

Eric Paice

Eric Paice was another writer new to the series. Paice's most recent television work had been on the risible science fiction series *Star Maidens* (1976) – which could not have been further away from the subject matter of *Secret Army* – and N. J. Crisp-created drama series *A Family Affair* (which aired from May 1979). However, the reason for Paice's commissioning was his previous scripting of a huge number of scripts for the first five series of Glaister's *The Brothers* (between 1972 and 1975). Paice's first television credit was for ABC's *Armchair Theatre* in the late Fifties, after which he moved on to the popular *Pathfinders* (1960-1) space serial for children, which he co-wrote with Malcolm Hulke, early episodes of *The Avengers* (between 1961 and 1964); and writing and script editing many episodes of *Dixon of Dock Green* between 1963 and 1974. Initially Paice was commissioned to script just one episode for *Secret Army*'s third series, the instalment in which Bradley would die (episode nine) which, incidentally, Brason had noted in pre-production documentation should, if possible, be entirely studio-bound due to budgetary constraints.

Switching Episodes

Some time after the series's episodes were initially matched to their writers, several changes were made. Firstly, Norman Crisp was given episode eleven (Kessler and Madeleine's flight across Belgium) instead of five, which in turn was taken on by Brason himself. However, Brason subsequently decided that Crisp should pen episode seven instead, and so gave episode eleven to Eric Paice who as a result was now working on two episodes. Secondly, both David Crane's and Willis Hall's involvement ceased, either due to other work commitments or unsuitable first drafts of their scripts. In the case of Hall, it is entirely possible that he did not have time due to his work with long-term collaborator Keith Waterhouse on the scripting and development of their new *Worzel Gummidge* series, which was also due for its first transmission in 1979. As a result of Hall's departure, Michael J. Bird was switched from episode three to episode twelve, leading to Crisp taking over three in his stead. Crisp did not want to tackle as many as four scripts, so Brason took over episode eight as well. Crane's episode (four) was subsequently assigned to another writer who was new to the series: Allan Prior.

Allan Prior

© Unknown

Prior, like Paice, had started out in television on *Armchair Theatre*, in 1954. He had worked with Gerry Glaister as far back as 1958, when he wrote twenty episodes of the soap *Starr and Company* which Glaister had produced and directed, and would work with him again on eight episodes of *Moonstrike* (in 1963) and three of *Dr Finlay's Casebook* (in 1965). Prior's most significant work was on *Z Cars*, writing a total of 86 episodes between 1962 and 1978, before going on to pen a further 44 episodes of its spin-off series – *Softly, Softly, Softly, Softly: Taskforce* and *Barlow at Large* – between 1966 and 1976. During the Seventies, Prior also penned the adventure serial *Hawkeye the Pathfinder* featuring Jan Francis (1973), and episodes of *The Onedin Line*, *Warship*, *The Sweeney* and, in 1976, like Michael J. Bird, the final series of Glaister's *The Expert*.

Kenneth Ware (Lloyd Humphreys)

The new series's second episode had (like many others!) been originally assigned to John Brason, however ultimately it would be penned by Kenneth Ware. Ware's most recent television work at the time had been as script editor on the 1978 series of *The Professionals*. Ware's earliest writing credits were on the soap *Compact* and *The Troubleshooters,* while his first script editing credits were on

Catch Hand (1964), a series about two builders, and *Z Cars* (between 1964 and 1965). Subsequent writing credits included *Softly, Softly* (in 1966), the screenplay for the Stanley Baker war film *The Last Grenade* (1970), and the Wilfred Greatorex-created *Hine* (1971), a drama series about an arms dealer for ATV. Although the exact details are not known, the fact that Ware's episode ultimately went out under the pseudonym Lloyd Humphreys suggests that the writer was unhappy with the finished episode, or more specifically with Brason's script editing rewrites.

Changes

By the time that all the writers on the series were confirmed, in early Spring 1979, Glaister and Brason had also worked out which episodes of the final run would not feature certain regular characters. It had been decided that, aside from film inserts featuring the character in prison, Albert would not be required for episodes four through nine, which because of Hepton's absence would therefore be studio recorded first. Glaister and Brason had also been informed by now of another significant absentee from the action, Clifford Rose having decided to take a family holiday to the USA. Originally it was planned that Rose would miss episodes five and six, but he would eventually only miss the latter. A brief sojourn in Berlin would explain Kessler's brief absence from the series. Around this time, it was also decided that Natalie was not required in episode thirteen, however, this was soon changed to episode two. It was also agreed that Hans would not be needed for episode five as was originally planned, the sea escape investigation storyline having been dropped, and would instead feature in episode seven, before it was decided that he was not required there either and would

© Unknown

better serve the plot of episode eleven! By now, Glaister and Brason had also changed their minds about Keldermans's death, agreeing that the character should be allowed to survive to the end of the series instead.

As the early scripts reached the second draft stage, several new storylines emerged while others were abandoned altogether. The most significant in the latter category was episode twelve which, despite the fact that it continued to be titled *Bridgehead* in deference to the battle of Arnhem, would focus instead on the fate of Monique and the start of her new life away from the Candide. Allan Prior's episode four meanwhile would gain a brand new direction: Kessler's implementation of a bogus escape line and the reappearance of a previously returned evader, both of which would put considerable strain on Monique's leadership of Lifeline, a mantle she has only just taken on. Following the abandonment of the 'evasion by sea' storyline, for episode five, John Brason was inspired by an incident that occurred in Northern France in October 1944: an outbreak of bubonic plague.

The Final Pre-Production Document

The final extant pre-production documentation volunteers some fascinating information about the influence of the audience research department's reports on the content and style of the third series adopted by the production team. The document starts by stating: 'With the experience of two series and a close study of viewers reaction to those series, two conclusions may be drawn: 1) That the viewing public like to identify as much as possible happenings in the story episodes to actual historical events; 2) That their main interest centres around the running story of the lead characters. The third series will home-in on these aspects even more than hitherto.' As the last of the second series's two audience research reports would not have been available until February 1979, the document dates from this month at the earliest. The document goes on to detail how the storyline of the third series would be matched against the actual historical timeline of the war: 'Our intention is that the series will follow in general terms a tight adherence to the events leading to the termination of hostilities, as these events are, in fact, our main storyline.' It goes on to outline a list of problems and threats that Lifeline were set to face (refined from previous documentation): the curtailment of their evasion activities due to the Allied advance (and 'whether or not any attempts at evasion lines is worth considering at this late juncture'); the V2 rockets 'operating from mobile sites in the Low Countries'; the 'whole aspect of more overt resistance (though only in so far as it effects our regulars)'; 'the use of Ardennes-based evaders who join in resistance activity', and 'the aftermath of liberation… including: the suspicions of the local populace against the Lifeline personnel, who seem to have been collaborating; the settling of old scores; the mistakes and personal vendetta that come to light; and not least the attitudes and happenings that affect our German regulars.' The document concludes that 'the end of the war in Europe will round off the series where it should legitimately end' and that, as before, 'in all cases, storylines will follow actual documented happenings… but always letting the closing days of the Second World War be told through the lives and experiences of our regular characters.'

The document still makes no direct reference to the Vercors revenge plotline, but it is likely that 'the settling of old scores' and 'personal vendetta' refers in part to him. However, they also definitely refer to the role of Celeste Lekeu (last seen in *Good Friday*) who, despite the fact that the audience would probably not remember her, was originally the only agent responsible for Albert's prison term, as an expanded summary for episode nine states: 'The German report seems to exonerate a case largely built upon the malice and envy of Mme Lekeu (Andrée's friend).' The confusion over how and why Albert is imprisoned is one of the few elements in the third series that reveals the piecemeal way in which the narrative evolved.

Although a few previous episodes in the series had taken place on specific days, and very occasionally on historically significant dates (*Bait, Day of Wrath*), the episodes of the third series would be very definitely dated in order to match the series's fictional narrative with its historical counterpart. This is most important for episodes eight through twelve, in which the action takes place on consecutive days, a decision that allows an in-depth retelling of the liberation of Brussels from the perspective of the regular characters. Interestingly, the timing of the action was ultimately far tighter than was originally planned, as documentation originally lists episode eleven as taking place three days after ten, but in the event, its storyline starts minutes after that of ten has finished (as Natalie and Alain make it back to the Candide with Major Turner, just after Albert, Reinhardt and Monique have been taken by the Communists). Similarly, episode twelve was originally intended (at a point when it was only going to cover Arnhem) to start on 25 September, but would eventually follow on directly from eleven. Conversely, the original dating of episodes nine and ten suggests an intention to dramatise an even tighter timeline, with the former taking place on the morning of 3 September and the latter in the afternoon! In the event, episode nine would be set on 2 September with episode ten beginning the morning after.

Directors

By early Spring 1979, Glaister set about recruiting directors for the final series. By accepting the invitation to direct a further three episodes, Viktors Ritelis became the only director to work on all three series. However, it would be Michael E. Briant who would return as principal director, helming five episodes in total. Glaister allocated these episodes to him largely on the basis of their inclusion of extensive action sequences (as Briant notes: 'This was what I was known for') – a train bombing; a machine gun ambush of a convoy; an assault on a V2 rocket site; the siege of a German-held farmhouse by Allied troops – all of which he felt sure Briant could handle well. The remaining six instalments would all be directed by newcomers to the series.

Roger Cheveley

Glaister assigned the third and crucial thirteenth episodes (of which the latter would ultimately become the series finale) to Roger Cheveley. It is possible that N. J. Crisp suggested Cheveley to Glaister, as the director had recently completed work on several episodes of the Crisp-created drama series *A Family Affair* (1979). Cheveley had started his television career as a designer in 1964. His early design work was for the BBC and took in comedy such as *Scott on Birds* (1964) and drama series like *Softly, Softly* (in 1966). Perhaps his most demanding work

343

in this period was on the epic ten-part *Doctor Who* story *The War Games* (1969) which required Cheveley to come up with both futuristic and historical settings for the serial's action. Cheveley moved on to Yorkshire Television in 1969 and continued as a designer on programmes such as *The Main Chance* (in 1970) and Les Dawson's *Sez Les* (1971-2). Still with Yorkshire Television, Cheveley first tried his hand at direction in 1973, on the Diana Dors vehicle: *All Our Saturdays*, and *Hey Brian!*, which showcased the talents of Brian Marshall. More directing work followed on children's storytelling series *The Witches Brew* (1973) and *Animal Kwackers* (1975), which was essentially Britain's answer to *The Banana Splits*. Cheveley left Yorkshire Television behind in 1977 after a stint on *Emmerdale Farm*, moving on to Granada for several episodes of *Coronation Street* and the second series of sitcom *Yanks Go Home!* (1976-7), which concerned the arrival of the US air force in Lancashire, during World War Two. Before returning to the BBC in 1979 for the Su Pollard and Paul Nicholas sitcom *Two Up, Two Down* (and subsequently *A Family Affair*), he also directed the children's series *The Paper Lads* for Tyne Tees Television in 1978.

Tristan de Vere Cole

Glaister approached seasoned director Tristan de Vere Cole to helm a total of three episodes. De Vere Cole's recent work included episodes of Terence Dudley's *Survivors* in 1977 (including the chilling rabies episode *Mad Dog*), *Coronation Street* (also in 1977), and drama series *Fallen Hero* (1977-8) which concerned a Welsh former Rugby Union player played by Del Henney. De Vere Cole, who incidentally is one of the many illegitimate children fathered by the

De Vere Cole directing on location for the TV series *Survivors* in 1977

infamous gypsy painter Augustus John, began directing in the Sixties. His early credits included *Z Cars* (35 episodes between 1967 and 1971), *United!* (in 1965), the four-part Elizabeth drama *Kenilworth* (1967), a six-part *Doctor Who* adventure (*The Wheel in Space*) featuring the Cybermen (in 1968), and comedy drama *Take Three Girls* (in 1969), all for the BBC. In 1972 he worked on the Robert Barr-created *Spy Trap* and was the very first director of *Emmerdale Farm*. He subsequently returned to the BBC to work on *Owen MD* (1974) with Nigel Stock and *Trinity Tales* (1975), a series of modernised versions of *The Can-*

terbury Tales scripted by Alan Plater, as well as episodes of *Warship* (in 1974/6) and nursing drama *Angels* (in 1976/8).

344

Andrew Morgan

Andrew Morgan, who had only just started out as a freelance director was assigned the remaining episode, Michael J. Bird's *Bridgehead*, and was grateful to Glaister for the opportunity. The previous year, Morgan had gained some useful directorial skills while working as a production assistant on *Who Pays the Ferryman?* which was also scripted by Bird. It had been intended that the series would be produced and directed by William (Bill) Slater, but when the role became too much for Slater, especially after he put his back out, Morgan stepped in to handle a lot of the location filming. The situation was all the more ironic because Slater's back injury had been caused by lifting up Morgan's ten-year-old son. Morgan remembers the shoot as "a tremendous experience [that] helped set me off as a freelance director." Morgan was even more pleased with his new assignment when it became clear that the film and studio schedule allowed him to concurrently work on an episode of the third series of *Blake's 7*: *Children of Auron*.

New Supporting Characters

By this point in the pre-production process, several new supporting characters were being shaped and fitted into the second and third drafts of the new scripts, including an adjutant for Reinhardt (as the character was by now called) named Hauptmann Müller, who the Major could use as a 'sounding board'. Other new characters included: the odious Reichskommissar Glaub, created by Allan Prior (although he would first appear in N. J. Crisp's *Revenge*); Major Turner, created by Glaister, and the dashing Captain Stephen Durnford (Monique's future husband) and the war-weary Colonel von Schalk, both created by Michael J. Bird for *Bridgehead*.

Casting

Terrence Hardiman (Major Hans Dietrich Reinhardt)

Gerry Glaister was understandably anxious to hire the right actor to play the series's new Luftwaffe Major, especially as they would have the unenviable task of following in Michael Culver's footsteps. Ultimately the solution was provided by none other than Clifford Rose, who thought that his friend and fellow actor Terrence Hardiman would be perfect in the role: "I had worked with Terry Hardiman at the Royal Shakespeare Company and I knew him quite well – we were quite good friends – and I suggested to Gerry Glaister that he might be interested in doing it, because I thought he'd be very good casting." After seeing Glaister, Hardiman accepted the part, much to the delight of Rose.

London-born Hardiman began his acting career while at Cambridge University in the late Fifties, acting with the Amateur Dramatic Club (ADC). He also turned his hand to some directing with the ADC, and in 1958 directed Ian McKellen in a production of George Bernard Shaw's *The Applecart*. In 1960 he

© Nobby Clarke

took the title role in *Dr Faustus*, a production that played in Cambridge, Stratford and London, which also featured McKellen, Derek Jacobi and Trevor Nunn among the cast. Hardiman subsequently joined the Old Vic theatre company in Bristol, and between 1962 and 1965 played Roderigo in *Othello*, Cicero in *Julius Caesar*, Boyet in *Love's Labours Lost* and the Dauphin in *Henry V*. After a period in repertory at Bristol, he went on to join the RSC, where he would meet Clifford Rose. His RSC roles over the next five years included Ambitioso in *The Revenger's Tragedy* (which also featured Rose), Gremio in *The Taming of the Shrew*, Albany in *King Lear*, Don John in *Much Ado About Nothing* (Rose would take over the part from Hardiman), John Littlewit in Ben Jonson's Bartholomew Fair, Lucio in *Measure for Measure* and Clarence in *Richard III*. In a recent interview, Hardiman modestly stated of this time that "Looking back, I feel sorry for the audiences because I must have been pretty awful. But that's how we got our chance to learn." Like Rose, Hardiman decided to break into television in the early Seventies and almost immediately landed the regular role of Inspector Armstrong in the 1971 series of *Softly, Softly*. Hardiman remembers that this casting "was a little ironic as my father was a policeman. He gave me a few tips on things like how to hold a truncheon. He was a bit upset that I went straight in and played an inspector, which he never became." Roles followed in *A Family at War* (Tim Bernard), *Crown Court* (Stephen Hardesty QC) and as a Gestapo Officer in the third episode of *Colditz*. Hardiman's first film role came in 1972 as Cardinal Anastasius in *Pope Joan*. Further TV roles followed in *The Caucasian Chalk Circle* (a *Play of the Month*) (1973), *The Carnforth Practice* (1974), *Edward the Seventh* (1975) and *When the Boat Comes In* (in 1976). Hardiman made a notable return to the theatre in 1977 to play Peter Mortensgaard in Ibsen's *Rosmersholm* in London's West End. Two wartime TV roles followed in *Wings* (Major Lanchester) in 1977 and *Enemy at the Door* (Hauptmann von Bulow in the episode *The Prussian Officer*). Hardiman's role in the latter is particularly reminiscent of Reinhardt. Just prior to joining *Secret Army*, Hardiman played Frank Crawley in a new adaptation of *Rebecca*, Aegisthus in *The Serpent Son* and

346

the lead role of Charles Pooter in *The Diary of a Nobody*, all of which would air in 1979.

Ralph Bates (Paul Vercors)

The second actor to be cast as the vengeful Paul Vercors (it is unknown whether Michael Byrne was approached to reprise the role) was Ralph Bates. At that time, Bates was best known for playing the scheming George Warleggan over two series of *Poldark*. Bates's first significant television role was as Caligula in Granada's acclaimed *The Caesars* in 1968. Roles followed in several Hammer Horror films: *Taste the Blood of Dracula* (1969), *The Horror of Frankenstein* (1970), *Lust for a Vampire* (1970) and *Dr Jekyll and Sister Hyde* (1971). Meanwhile, further television work included *The Six Wives of Henry VIII*, *The Woodlanders* (both in 1970) and episodes of adventures series such as *Jason King, The Persuaders!* and *The Protectors* between 1972 and 1973. In 1973 he also took the lead role of Michael Lebrun in BBC sci-fi series *Moonbase 3*, which had been partly scripted by John Brason. Further horror film roles followed, when he appeared opposite Lana Turner in *Persecution* (1974) and Joan Collins in *I Don't Want to be Born* (1975). After *Poldark*, Bates guest-starred in *Softly, Softly* and *Crown Court*. During 1979 he would juggle his *Secret Army* commitments with the role of Laurence Castallack in *Penmarric*.

© Unknown

Stephan Chase (Captain Stephen Durnford)

Bryan Drew, agent to both Bernard Hepton and Angela Richards, who had suggested to Glaister that he should see Richards back in 1977, now contacted him to see if another actor on his books would be suitable for a key part in the final series. The actor in question was Stephan Chase; the role that of Monique's husband-to-be Captain Stephen Durnford. Chase had a varied career which took off in the early Seventies, playing Sean Whitman in the horror film *Cry of the Banshee* (1970) and Malcolm in Roman Polanski's *Macbeth* (1971). Early

television roles included Osborne Hamley in a BBC adaptation of *Wives and Daughters* (1971), Horgren in HTV's *Arthur of the Britons* (1972) and Gerald Loughlan in an episode of the acclaimed *Country Matters* (1973). In 1975, Chase played Hamlet at the Theatre Royal in Bath, a production which, after playing around England, went on a *Shakespeare Wallah*-esque tour of India. The following year he played Cucrovitz in the Tennessee Williams play *Suddenly Last Summer* opposite Hetty Baynes. The year before *Secret Army*, Chase played a villain in *Five Get Into Trouble* (part of the second series of Southern TV's *Famous Five* series) and, in stark contrast, Max Rowlands in the feature film *The Golden Lady*, which is perhaps best described as a female version of James Bond.

Into Production

The third series went into production in Spring 1979, beginning with a few days of filming, between 19 and 23 March, with some of the cast and crew back in the Belgian capital, and others filming sequences in the UK featuring Albert in Brussels's Havenlaan prison. Despite the fact that Tristan de Vere Cole would direct half of the episodes incorporating these prison sequences, he had no involvement in their realisation, with Michael E. Briant directing them all instead. De Vere Cole remembers being unhappy with the finished scenes: "I was concerned that they were very indiscreet – shouting out information about their [Lifeline's] setup!" Once the prison sequences were in the can, Hepton was free to concentrate on his theatrical endeavours at Tufnell Park and would not return to the series until the Summer.

The familiar pattern of rehearsals at Acton followed by recording at TV Centre began again on Monday 26 March as the regular cast, minus Hepton, assembled with Glaister, Brason and Briant for a read-through of N. J. Crisp's *Ambush*. Although *Ambush* would be transmitted seventh, it was one of six episodes that did not require Hepton and would therefore form part of the first rehearsal/recording block, which ran from March to June. During rehearsals it quickly became apparent to Paul Shelley that the return of Major Bradley to the narrative was not at all popular with Angela Richards. Richards recalls: "That to

348

me spoilt it, because we didn't need another character, especially one as excessively chauvinistic as Bradley." The effect of Bradley's arrival on Richards may have been exacerbated by the fact that she had not yet recorded the episodes in which Monique was in sole charge of the Line prior to Bradley's arrival, perhaps making her feel as though the Major had been brought into the narrative more immediately after Albert's departure than was actually the case. Shelley remembers: "There was some feeling, which I didn't take personally, that Nick Bradley didn't need to be there and that they could have run the Line themselves and strangely I was kind of sympathetic to that and yet at the same time, wearing my other hat as an actor, it was a lovely part, so if I was offered it I was going to do it!" Unlike Richards, Juliet Hammond-Hill was more receptive to Bradley's return due to the dividends it paid in terms of atmosphere and characterisation: "Natalie had that quite interesting *frisson* with him [in *Lucky Piece*], that was partly built on a heroic and sensitive sense of compatibility. I quite liked the idea of him coming back in terms of adding heightened tension. I thought it was good from her perspective and in a way from the viewers', otherwise you are just seeing these incredibly heroic people that don't have needs and wants and desires." She also muses that: "Although we never really articulate our desire for one another in any very real sense, I think there is a strong pull between Bradley and Natalie," and as the series continued, "it was also better in a way underplayed than them having a fully-fledged affair." Although Richards still felt that Bradley's drafting from England was "condescending" to the characters of Monique and Natalie, and that there was a definite element of chauvinism extant in this decision, upon revisiting the third series for the first time in over twenty years in 2004, she commented that, Paul Shelley's performance was "absolutely excellent" and brought "a very valuable colour" to the series, in fact she even admitted to not only being surprised when Bradley was killed but "quite sad" too.

In addition to Paul Shelley, the rehearsal and recording of *Ambush* also saw the return of Hazel McBride as Madeleine, whose last appearance had been in the ninth episode of Series Two: *Little Old Lady*. In the second series, McBride had featured in a total of four episodes, but in the final run she was set to feature far more regularly, in over two-thirds of the series's episodes. McBride recalls: "I was very pleased. Madeleine was obviously introduced into the second series to allow for an extra dimension to the character of Kessler, but by the third series I felt that Madeleine became an interesting character in her own right." She remembers that, particularly during the third series, as an actor she thought hard about why someone like Madeleine had fallen for a man who was Head of the Gestapo: "You have to try and humanise and understand how that character came to be in that situation." She concluded that: "It was very much there in the writing, she's had this failed love affair with the Baron and when she first meets Kessler she's in a very bad emotional state... and doesn't actually care what happens to her... and lets herself therefore get into that relationship, and by the time she begins to heal emotionally, which paradoxically is through the relationship with Kessler, it's too late, because she's in love with him." As in the second series, McBride would once again find herself in a unique position as a regular on the series, as she had scenes with both the German and Lifeline characters. She thinks that the two camps that her fellow actors have described as existing during production arose logistically, rather than for any other reason: "We were called to rehearse certain scenes… in my case I'd have been called for my 'Nazi scenes' and the others would have finished theirs and gone off for a coffee break, or they weren't necessarily around, so you didn't have perhaps as much 'hanging out' time together, but because I did have these scenes with Monique, I did get to hang out with them, so I did have a foot in both camps. I was in a very privileged position!"

© Anthony Gardner

After *Ambush* came rehearsals and recording of *Prisoner*, Tristan de Vere Cole's first episode as director, which narrative-wise was the instalment in which Bradley actually returned (chronologically, *Ambush* is Bradley's second episode in the final series) and also featured Eric Deacon as Klein, who effectively took Kessler's role in the episode, due to Rose's concurrent absence in the US. Rose returned in time for the recording of *Ring of Rosies* which for both director Michael E. Briant and those actors involved in the bubonic plague component of the plot, was not an altogether satisfactory experience. Despite the fact that Brason's script was based on historical reality, Angela Richards felt that there was something lacking in the way it was executed: "I thought it was too far-fetched – I mean, sticking a hanky over your face! It just didn't ring true and it

350

wasn't done well enough. It should have been worked harder." Briant was similarly unhappy with the end result: "There's nothing wrong with any of the acting, it was just a very difficult idea to sell and lacked a certain reality." The action required make-up artist Marion Richards to work hard due to the number of plague victims at various stages of sickness, indicated on the camera script as 'slight spots', 'spots', 'bad spots' or 'dead'! The studio recording of *Ring of Rosies* would also include the only reference to the Candide's kitchen staff: Jean-Pierre and Gaby. Unfortunately their inclusion only serves to highlight the absurdity of the fact that they have never been seen or heard of before (nor would they be again).

A Safe Place was the fourth episode to go into production (in May), again with De Vere Cole at the helm. He was particularly pleased with the cast he secured for the episode, which included Struan Rodger ('Mad' Mike Miller), who had previously worked with him on *Warship* and Anthony Head (Hanslick), who would later work with him again on *Howards' Way*. He was also pleased with the decadent club scene in which Kessler lets rip at Reichskommissar Glaub. Clifford Rose himself counts the scene as one of his favourites of the entire series.

By now, Terrence Hardiman had fully settled into playing Reinhardt, a role which he felt had been expertly conceived: "The character was laid out for me so clearly that I felt that most of the work was done for me. I didn't have to invent, I didn't have to think what kind of character is this. It was there." He recalls that, from the rest of the established cast, there "was a wonderfully generous greeting" which meant it was both comfortable and easy for him to get into the series. He was also delighted that Reinhardt, like Brandt, proved not to be a stereotypical Nazi from the old war movie mould: "Here was a character that was complex and not a 'Nasty'. He had his tough side, he had his warm side… and he had a history that was immediately attractive to me as an actor to delve into." He also recalls that, as he and Rose "were great buddies, it was fun to play hating each other's guts." Rose too was equally

© Unknown

pleased to be acting alongside Hardiman: "As with Michael Culver, we worked together in great harmony." By now, Rose regarded the role of Kessler almost as a 'second skin': "When you live with a character for two years and the part has been well-written and conceived, you are at the stage when you know everything about that character. You will know how he will react in any given situation. You will know what he will say in any given situation, which with the best will in the world, individual writers and directors didn't know quite as well and so therefore one did feel that you knew better than them how he would react and behave."

Angela Richards concurs that "by that time we knew what we were doing and also what would work." Richards also remembers that the third series gave her

and Juliet Hammond-Hill the opportunity to develop a closer relationship between Monique and Natalie, in part because of Albert's absence, and muses that: "It might have been the first time that it was shown that women could cope on their own, but more importantly that women could have friendships… they hadn't seen before the closeness that you had with a woman friend." Furthermore, she recalls that it was something that "very much came naturally in the series" because of the bond the pair had formed over the previous two years and because of their respective personalities: "I adore Juliet and she does me and she's very, very tactile and emotional and it was Juliet who *felt* so. She has a really great heart and whenever anything happened to Monique it happened to her – she would have killed somebody to save Monique." Interestingly, she recalls that there may have been some fears from the production team that their relationship occasionally appeared too intense, too close: "There were sometimes worries in the studio that it was a little too much, but what's too much if you love people?" Neither Richards nor Hammond-Hill were prepared to play down or back away from this development, especially as it arose from the situation and their respective characters.

Just Light the Blue Touch-Paper was the fifth episode to go into production, in late May. This was the only episode to have two costume designers, with Caroline Maxwell joining Anna Downey who otherwise tackled the remaining twelve episodes alone. Hazel McBride particularly remembers the blue-green evening dress that was made for her to wear in this episode, and which she would

352

later wear again when Invasions was recorded in August; however, she comments that: "In reality, having new clothes made for you in wartime must have been very difficult, but I suppose it made sense if you assume that Kessler gave Madeleine a clothes allowance." McBride also recalls that, as well as preferring the clothes that she was given in the third series – the pale linen suit which she would wear in *The Last Run* being another favourite – it "also made a nice change to wear my hair down sometimes."

Back to Brussels

Paul Shelley's final studio work for the series followed, for *Sound of Thunder*, which was the sixth episode to be rehearsed and recorded, in early to mid-June, and completed the first block of studio recording. However, there was to be no break for the cast and crew, as they then made their way back to Brussels. Glaister and Brason had been keen for there to be more foreign location film content in the final series than had previously been the case, so this was one of several trips made to Belgium during production in 1979; however, this particular summer trip was to have by far the longest and most demanding schedule. Nevertheless, Production Unit Manager John Fabian recalls that the regular cast loved being over in Belgium, and that "one of the great joys was the Belgian

© Terrence Hardiman

beer" and he would "sometimes meet Bernard Hepton and Clifford Rose at the airport and go off to a bar where they have incredible fruit beers called Gueuze and Kriek."

On 16 June, a key sequence was filmed requiring Angela Richards, Stephan Chase (his first work on the series) and Juliet Hammond-Hill, dealing with Monique's rescue from punishment as a collaborator, which would feature at the start of the penultimate episode, *Bridgehead*. The experience was not one that the regular cast were to ever forget, principally due to the highly charged

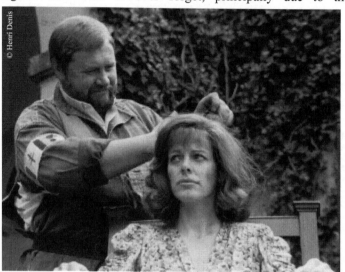

performances of the Belgians cast to play the angry mob who were demanding that Monique be shaved for her 'crimes'. Richards recalls that: "It felt like more than just a piece of filming. It was like a time-warp. The crowd of extras impetuously and instinctively acted as if it was yesterday." Cameraman Lex Tudhope remembers that, as a result, Hammond-Hill was particularly caught up in the moment and deeply distressed by the apparent reality of the scene unfolding before her. Director Andrew Morgan recalls that he found the bespectacled girl who was to have all her hair shaved off, by having BRT place an advertisement in a newspaper. He was subsequently introduced to three or four applicants: "This particular girl struck me as being very good for the part – she was an art student and desperately keen to buy some more paints and brushes and was prepared for her art to have her head shaved. As it was a worthy cause, I thought 'Why not?'" Although Angela Richards found these emotive sequences challenging, she regretted that when it came to Monique's turn in the chair, Morgan instructed the actor playing the 'barber' (Werner Van De Sarren) to gently snip off, rather than hack off, a lock of her hair, an action which she felt lacked reality. However, given that the sequence that was initially submitted for approval to the BBC Head of Series was rejected on the grounds that it was felt to be too harrowing for an early Saturday evening audience, it is perhaps just as well that Morgan took this decision.

The day after the hair-cutting scenes were filmed, Morgan brought *Secret Army* back to the Galeries Royale St Hubert, last used as a location in *Russian Roulette*, for another sequence in *Bridgehead* in which the courting Monique and

354

Durnford stroll through the Galeries and stop to listen to a barrel organ, before the Captain gives out chocolate to the assembled children and a less-than-impressed monkey. The barrel organ still does the rounds of the Galeries today, but one imagines the monkey has long since passed on. Also filmed on that day were the sequences from the same episode set in the Rue Therese near the Gare Du Midi, where Natalie's apartment is located and which Durnford and Albert both visit. The street chosen was actually the opposite side of Brussels to the Gare du Midi: Rue Arthur Roland in the Scharbeek district. As well as several exterior scenes, an interior lobby and stairwell would also be used.

Between 18 and 20 June, much of the filming activity centred on Rue des Minimens, a typical cobble-stoned street below the Palais de Justice, leading back to Brussels's historic centre. The imposing St Jean et Etienne aux Minimens church, situated two-thirds of the way along this street, had been chosen as the exterior location for Monique and Durnford's wedding. The location would be seen before the service when Natalie buys some flowers and then enters, and afterwards as the happy couple and their guests mill about in the street with a large cast of Belgian supporting artists celebrating the news that the war has ended. The sequences, which were directed by Roger Cheveley, had been carefully storyboarded in order that they evoked the right look and feel. Also in attendance for this important piece of filming were Glaister and his wife Joan. Richards and Chase would have to go through it all again a few weeks later when their characters got married for a second time back in the UK! Another scene filmed near the Palais de Justice, directed by Michael E. Briant, involved Kessler being pelted with rotten fruit and vegetables by a group of Belgian boys, for

Juliet and Angela between takes in the Rue des Minimens

the episode *Just Light the Blue Touch-Paper*. Beyond the Palais de Justice, towards the Gare du Midi, Briant also directed a sequence in the Rue des Fleuristes involving a sizeable crowd of Belgian supporting artists ransacking Madeleine's apartment and burning her possessions in the street for the episode *Collaborator*.

Roger Cheveley would also film the opening sequence of the episode *Revenge* around this time, in which Kessler is driven up to the grand building in which he has his frosty meeting with Reichskommissar Glaub. This building, which is situated immediately behind the Place du Petit Sablon (used elsewhere in the series) is the Palais d'Egmont, which is used today by the Belgian Ministry of Foreign Affairs for meetings and receptions. The interior scenes would be filmed in two separate locations back in the UK (see later).

A large amount of the summer filming in Brussels would, as before, centre on the Grand Place and specifically around the exterior of 'Le Candide' as characters returned to or left the restaurant, including the scenes directed by Michael E. Briant in which: Natalie and Geneviève switch places in *Just Light the Blue Touch-Paper*; Albert returns from prison and attempts to scrub the graffiti off the Candide wall in the Rue des Harengs (in *Collaborator*); and Reinhardt's arrival at the Candide to finally confront Lifeline (also from *Collaborator*). Andrew Morgan would briefly visit the square to film Albert buying some flowers outside the Residences of the Dukes of Brabant, and also to take a shot of the clock on the Hôtel de Ville's left wing (almost opposite 'the Candide'), both for *Bridgehead*. On another day, Tristan de Vere Cole directed various scenes from *Sound of Thunder* around the square, featuring: German soldiers posting bills and laying explosives; Kessler ordering that a prematurely displayed Belgian flag be taken down and Bradley setting off to meet his resistance contacts. This episode would also see the only scenes filmed inside No. 28 (the Candide), as Bradley observes from an upper floor 'Mansard' window, the goings-on in the square below.

© Dave Hofstetter

The final exterior scenes to feature the Grand Place and the Candide would be seen in *Days of Judgement*. Handled by Viktors Ritelis, these scenes required Juliet Hammond-Hill, Ron Pember, Jack McKenzie (Major Turner) and Trisha Clarke (Geneviève). For the subsequent mercy dash by Jeep across Brussels, impeded by crowds of celebrating Belgians, Ritelis chose narrow roads such as the Rue des Pigeons and the Rue de la Samaritaine near the Place du Grand Sablon. The journey, however, would end back in the UK.

London Again

In early July, a period of UK location filming began in and around London. On 4 July, the first of two interior sequences from *Revenge*, which would immediately follow Kessler's arrival at the exterior of Glaub's HQ (filmed several weeks earlier at the Palais d'Egmont), was tackled at the Orleans House Gallery in Twickenham. These scenes, involving Clifford Rose and Roger Booth, were filmed in the famous Octagon Room designed by the Scottish architect James Gibbs. Rose would return to the Octagon Room in 1981 when making *Kessler*. The second interior location was the staircase inside Westminster Central Hall,

Storey's Gate, near the Houses of Parliament, which we see Kessler making his way up before registering his arrival with a soldier at a desk.

The next day, Cheveley and his team remobilised across London in Kensington Gore at Holy Trinity Church on Prince Consort Road, behind the Royal Albert Hall. It was here that the interiors for Monique and Durnford's wedding would be shot. The church had been chosen

© Andy Priestner

357

due to its continental (Dutch) interior, which was in keeping with the exterior of the church in the Rue des Minimens in Brussels. The sequences would be enhanced by an ad hoc arrangement of the Hornpipe from Handel's 'Water Music' by Richard Pilliner (an accomplished musician who had won all the prizes at the Royal Academy of Music for organ playing, accompaniment and improvisation) and sections of 'Pieces de Fantasie Op.53' by Louis Vierne ('Clair de Lune') and Widor's 'Symphony No. 5 (Toccata)'. Joining Richards and Chase for the wedding were Hammond-Hill, Pember, Valentine Dyall and Michael Leader playing the uncredited part of Durnford's Best Man.

London, more specifically the Borough of Southwark, would also be the location used for the remaining telecine sequences from *Sound of Thunder* directed by Tristan de Vere Cole, which chiefly featured Major Bradley (Paul Shelley) and Lamotte (Davyd Harries). All of the sequences at the closed fruit and vegetable market, which both Bradley and Lamotte walk around, were filmed in Southwark Borough Market (London's oldest food market), most notably in Cathedral Street (the lane next to Southwark Cathedral). The ambush of a German patrol and Bradley's subsequent flight were also filmed here. The scene from later in the episode when Bradley carries the dying Lamotte onto the streets in order to dump his body as a looter, were filmed just off London Bridge by the steps leading down from Borough High Street to Green Dragon Court and then through the archway into Montague Close. Bradley stops with Lamotte at Montague Chambers further down Montague Close, before releasing Lamotte into the street to be fired at by German soldiers (a street which has now changed beyond all

recognition). Bradley's sudden and unexpected death was filmed around the corner at the flight of steps that lead down from London Bridge itself, which incidentally are inextricably linked with the death of another fictional character. Known as 'Nancy's Steps', the steps feature in Dickens's *Oliver Twist*, as the location where Nancy meets Rose and Mr Brownlow in order to save Oliver, but is overheard by a concealed Noah Claypole, leading to her subsequent murder by Bill Sykes. In the 1968 musical *Oliver!*, Nancy is killed at the foot of the steps, although the film recreated the steps on a soundstage rather than actually filming in Southwark. When it came to filming the scene, Shelley informed de Vere Cole that he was, quite understandably, concerned at the prospect of having to fall backwards down a flight of steps as specified in the script. In the event, Bradley's fall took place in stages to prevent injury to the actor.

De Vere Cole selected several more London locations for his remaining two episodes. *A Safe Place* saw him use a popular television drama location, Southall

Juliet Hammond-Hill during the London filming block in July 1979

Gas Works, for the climactic scenes in which Alain kills 'Mad' Mike Miller. The following year, the location would also be used in the *Blake's 7* episode *Death-Watch*. Meanwhile, *Prisoner* would use the derelict East India Docks, where De Vere Cole remembers he 'retrieved' two 8-foot garden seats, a table and other items from the rubble! He also recalls that, at that location, "We were not going to complete in the scheduled time the sequence where Reisener and Bonnier were flung against the wall by the Resistance. I had planned at least six setups, so I said we'll have to cover it all in one shot hand-held with my hand gently guiding Godfrey [Johnson], the cameraman. We had a quick rehearsal and then did it in one take." He also remembers that the supporting artists playing the Resistance men were excellent, "particularly John Cannon – flinging Reisener to the floor, dragging him up etc… not only did the extras do it for real (without harming the actors), they knew when we closed in how to move with the camera. Good extras make a big difference." Michael E. Briant would also use the East India Docks as the location for the safe-house in *Ring of Rosies*; in fact, the chase sequence in which Natalie and Alain chase the plague victim includes the very same room in which Bradley is first introduced to Reisener in *Prisoner*.

Two further London locations would be used by Roger Cheveley for two significant sequences in what would turn out to be the final episode, *The Execution*: Major Reinhardt's execution, and Kessler and Madeleine's riverside rendezvous. The former was filmed on 20-21 July at New Crane Wharf, a set of warehouses that have since been converted into luxury flats in a cul-de-sac at the Corner of Garnet Street and Wapping High Street (it would also be seen briefly near the start of *Bridgehead*). The latter was filmed 'day for night' on 11 September at the back of a warehouse on the bank of the Thames, just off Wapping High Street, not far from the execution location. The original intention was to have Madeleine row up to the warehouse and take Kessler away by boat,

Clifford Rose and Hazel McBride film Kessler and Madeleine's final scenes by the Thames in July 1979

but in the event the pair steal away on foot along the pebble shore.

Final Location Filming

The summer filming period would also see *Secret Army* return to the Nene Valley Railway for the last time, specifically to record sequences featuring Natalie attempting to make one last trip down to the Pyrenees with a group of evaders in *The Last Run*. Juliet Hammond-Hill remembers: "We had to go up and down on the train endlessly and we were filming for several days. Because we couldn't get off the train, and it was in Summer, I did almost feel incarcerated. It was quite a difficult episode to shoot." The episode's director, Michael E. Briant, has strong memories of the sequences involving the train fire: "The one carriage, which the railway company didn't mind if it was damaged, really did catch fire and at some point it started to spread to the two other carriages either side of it and we had to stop shooting. The fire brigade came in, but they hadn't recced the place properly and they only had one tender of water. Once they had used it up they had to drive away to get some more and by the time they got back the entire train was very nearly on fire!" *The Last Run* not only saw the use of Wansford Station once again (last seen in *A Matter of Life and Death*), but also a return both to Abbots Barn Farm – last seen as Lecau's farm in *Prisoner of War*, this time it would be the French farm where Natalie leaves the surviving evader before making the trip back up to Brussels – and to Waternewton Mill (last seen in *Lisa – Code Name Yvette*), the interior of which was used as the chosen rendezvous for Vercors and Inspector Benet, for the scene in which the Communist relates his intention to take his revenge on Albert for the death of Max. Later that Summer, the mill would be used for a third and final time as a backdrop for an idyllic day out in the country, featuring Juliet Hammond-Hill, Ron Pember, Angela Richards and Stephan Chase, for inclusion in *Bridgehead*. Chase recalls that, due to the hot summer weather, he prevented the physical discomfort caused by his battle-dress trousers by wearing pyjama bottoms underneath!

Following his rather too successful train fire in *The Last Run*, Briant went on to direct two of the most action-oriented and explosive sequences yet seen in the series, for *Ambush* and *Just Light the Blue Touch-Paper*. For the former, which saw Bradley and his private army of evaders attack a convoy of vehicles, Briant recalls: "We could have done with about half a dozen stuntmen, but we couldn't afford that. Instead we had Stuart Fell, who's been a stuntman mate of mine for years and years. He was the guy who came out of the lorry in flames, he was the guy

who crashed the motorcycle, he was the guy who fell backwards down the cliff... I think anybody who died in that ambush was Stuart!" The convoy sequences were filmed in the UK, as was the V2 rocket site attack for *Just Light the Blue Touch-Paper*. The location for the latter was a Ministry of Defence military training camp. Although one of the missiles was real, a glass painting was used for the scene in which a pile of warheads are shown together. Briant recalls that the scene in which Bradley guns down the German troops in the canteen was

heavily re-edited, by order of the BBC's Head of Series, to remove shots of bullets flying all over the table, crockery smashing and extras falling backwards in their chairs, as the overall effect was considered far too gruesome. Brason's 'tail' plotline in the same episode presented Briant with a particularly difficult

361

problem relating to the geography of the Grand Place. The script demands that, during the course of the episode, Natalie and other characters look out through the Candide windows at the Gestapo tail sat outside the Café du Breste opposite the restaurant. Anyone who has been to the Grand Place will know that it is a huge square – one of the largest in Europe – and that you would have to be possessed of incredible eyesight to be able to identify someone sat at a café at the other side of it. A further problem was that Briant did not have the time in Brussels to film any café exteriors. His ingenious solution was to film these scenes during the UK filming block by constructing the Café du Breste in the same woods as the airmen's bivouac! Although a tight frame is kept on these café scenes, evidence of the woodland setting is provided by a few tell-tale tree branches at the top of the screen and occasional shadows on the customers. And while Briant solved his problem, geographical purists may be troubled by the fact that the café is effectively sat in the middle of the Grand Place!

Juliet Hammond-Hill, who once again found herself taking part in more location filming than any other actor on the series, continued to earn her reputation as the series's 'action-girl'. She recalls that the location filming "was a great joy to me as it suited my temperament. I was not a primadonna and totally without vanity, and I was prepared to go into the fray alongside the boys and therefore got treated accordingly." However, she thinks that: "Occasionally the male directors could have taken a little more care with me. They got a bit carried away with having a young pretty girl that they could maul around the place!" This situation was nowhere more true than during filming of the battle sequences in *Collaborator*, for which, via Bill Randle, Michael E. Briant had secured the services of the RAF Regiment. Hammond-Hill remembers hating using the machine gun in these sequences and how on her first attempt to fire it no-one had prepared her for the sound that

© Unknown

would come out of it: "I was knocked flat. The sound completely took me off balance. And I said '[Why didn't you warn me about this, why didn't you tell me I'd have to wear ear-plugs?!'" She completed the filming with ear-plugs but still found it "terrifying to wield that gun and to have no control over your body." Briant recalls that Hammond-Hill was also 'in the wars' during the shooting of the checkpoint scene (at Southey Wood): "I said to the [RAF] men before the take: 'Juliet and Ron are actors, be very careful with them, please don't hurt them.' Well when we rehearsed it these guys hauled Juliet and Ron out of the van, slammed them down on the bonnet and kicked their ankles apart with their boots... I remember that Juliet ended up just covered in bruises, and this had been done at what they considered to be 'half-throttle'!" Film cameraman Lex Tudhope also recalls the 'enthusiasm' of the RAF soldiers during the *Collaborator* battle sequences: "These guys really took it seriously and were absolutely cracking. As far as they were concerned it was like a real exercise. The difference between them and the chaps we usually had was just amazing." On this occasion, Group Captain Bill Randle's involvement in the episode was to extend beyond the checking of the script for period accuracy, to actually appearing in the episode. When asked if he would like to play the German officer in charge of the troops occupying the besieged building, Randle was thrilled and jumped at the chance. According to Glaister's script, Randle's character, unnamed on screen but remembered by Randle to be called Oberleutnant Helmut Rath, was supposed to fall forwards out of a farmhouse loft to the ground below. Randle recalls: 'I managed to avoid this dangerous manoeuvre for an almost-sixty year-old by convincing the director that half a dozen bullets from a Sten gun would knock me backwards... in the event, the demise of Rath was filmed downstairs!' So taken was Randle with his brief role in the series that when he wrote his first work of fiction, *Kondor* (1999), he elected to include Oberleutnant Rath as a central character and give him a full life-story.

Film cameraman Godfrey Johnson (who also took the role of 'unofficial language consultant': "Because I could speak German, I spent a lot of time with the actors playing soldiers, correcting their German and getting their pronunciation right.") remembers the great time constraints that he and the rest of the crew worked under when filming, and that on average eight minutes of material was shot per day, a very tough proposition indeed. Hammond-Hill recognises that this was one of the reasons why directors perhaps took less care over her safety than they otherwise might: "They had so much to shoot in such a short amount of time. Once the filming slot was over, there was very rarely the opportunity to go back and pick up shots." On a more emotional level, the actress remembers that playing Natalie on location and in the studio had become a complete way of life: "There was no other life for me at that time but her." Furthermore she recalls that: "I spent a lot of time on the road in the knowledge that, as we were coming to the end of the war, I was coming to the end of her [Natalie's] life as a resistance worker, and also as an actress I was coming to the end of my life with the series. There was a dual experience going on for us all as actors and as characters which increased the tension and accelerated the sense of engagement, anticipation and commitment."

A key location shoot on the final series was that of Kessler's and Madeleine's flight in *Days of Judgement*, directed by Viktors Ritelis. Hazel McBride was thrilled to have more to do for a change, but one of her overriding memories of the shoot is of stinging nettles: "When Madeleine falls over in the ditch and sprains her ankle, the ditch was full of stinging nettles... the production team beat them down so that they were flat, and said 'They're fine, they won't sting you now. They don't sting when they're flat,' but they do. I was in a short-sleeved

summer dress, and as we had to do so many takes, I got very badly stung and someone had to go and get some antihistamine cream." She adds: "I don't think Clifford was affected too much because he was well protected by the German uniform." She also remembers very much enjoying the fact that Madeleine featured in so many scenes in the episode and was so much more central to the plot and that, stinging nettles aside, "it was great fun to be out on location."

After the episode aired, McBride recalls receiving a letter from a viewer commending the fact that Madeleine kept her handbag with her at all times while she and Kessler were on the run, as a touch that was in keeping with her character. Although this might be the case, McBride remembers that the real reason for this was entirely pragmatic – in order to explain how she still had the diamond necklace with her with which she would later buy Kessler's life. McBride notes that, ultimately, "Madeleine produced the necklace from her bra in

© Hazel McBride

episode thirteen," thus rendering the carefully thought out handbag plotline redundant! Rose recalls that Madeleine was originally supposed to slap Kessler after his arrest at the farmstead, but when it came to filming the scene it was felt by all concerned that it would work far better if she spat at him instead. (Above: A series of continuity polaroids of Hazel McBride for the filming of *Days of Judgement*.)

For the same episode, Ritelis would use Bushey Park, near Hampton Court, for the scenes involving Hans van Broecken and an evader taking refuge in a river, his sighting of Kessler and Madeleine and subsequent meeting with some Allied troops. Ritelis and his team drew on all their ingenuity to achieve the river-based scenes: "You have to bear in mind that we were working on small budgets, which precluded special effects equipment such as underwater housing. But I wanted the camera to be in the water with Gunnar Möller and Kevin O'Shea, so Tex, our grip, devised a waterproof plywood box which held our camera. It was primitive but it did the job (see below). As for the water being strafed with machine gun fire, that was all of the crew with improvised sling shots firing

© Viktors Ritelis

365

During filming at Bushey Park for *Days of Judgement*, directed by Viktors Ritelis

More filming at Bushey Park for *Days of Judgement*

Viktors's team between takes at Bushey Park

© Viktors Ritelis

pebbles!" Gunnar Möller's final scenes for the series, which would form part of *Bridgehead*, were directed by Andrew Morgan on the Kennet and Avon canal, intended to represent a canal near Arnhem.

Location filming for *What Did You Do in the War, Daddy?* also took place during the summer shoot, taking in locations in Belgium (the Grand Place, Brussels airport and Brussels town cemetery) and in the UK (principally RAF Northolt in Ruislip, Middlesex, which was used for the scenes set at a Belgian airbase where Albert receives honours on behalf of Lifeline during a liberation anniversary ceremony). Joining Bernard Hepton on this shoot were Ron Pember and Juliet Hammond-Hill, while the TV crews seen covering the event included several actual *Secret Army* crew members, including cameraman Godfrey Johnson. Of the Belgian filming, Richards recalls the shoot at Brussels town cemetery, in the Evere district of the city, in which Monique visits Lisa's grave which contained a cameo picture of Lisa as part of the headstone. Richards took a photo of the prop and sent a copy to Jan Francis so that she could see 'her own grave'!

Recording Resumes

In late July, the familiar rehearsal and studio recording process resumed for the remaining seven episodes. As *The Last Run* was the first episode to be tackled in this block, for Terrence Hardiman this meant that he would end up rehearsing Reinhardt's very first scenes the day after filming his final death scene by the Thames! *The Last Run* also saw Bernard Hepton 'return to the fold', back from his theatrical interlude, his performances as Julius Caesar ('Bernard Hepton was a Caesar to justify the title: long after death, the man governed the play') and

Richard II ('He dominated Richard II with a close examination of the man's mind') being deemed particularly successful.

Although it would be in *The Last Run* that the extravagant new German Headquarters set would be seen for the first time on screen, it had already been used extensively during the first block of studio recording, for *Just Light the Blue Touch-Paper*. Clifford Rose recalls: "They kept building more on, adding an interrogation room here and a bathroom there, and a huge hallway. I remember that finally it was an enormous set which took up almost the entire studio floor!" Rose was very pleased with the sequences in which the elegant drinks reception was juxtaposed with the interrogations in the cells below: "For my character that was absolutely wonderful, as it pinpointed the dichotomy that was in his nature... the difference between his public face and his private life." More trivially, he also remembers that the reference that Reinhardt makes in his first episode to his accommodation at the Hotel Arenberg was actually an in-joke, as it was the name of the hotel the cast and crew stayed at in Brussels.

The Last Run went into the studio for recording during the last few days of July and would be followed chronologically (in a recording and narrative sense) by episodes two (*Invasions*) and three (*Revenge*), in early- to mid-August.

© Henri Denis

Invasions would see the final contribution of Mary Barclay and Ruth Gower to the series as the Senlis-based Chantal sisters. Angela Richards recalls that: "As they really were like your favourite aunts, they played it beautifully." This episode would conversely see the first chronological appearance of the musician and composer, Ken Moule, who co-wrote with Richards some of the songs in the series, as the Candide's new pianist. He is referred to as Paul in the series, but as Victor in John Brason's final *Secret Army* novel: *The End of the Line*.

As episodes four to nine had already formed the first recording block, *Revenge* was followed into production by *Collaborator*, with the final climactic scenes, in which Vercors and his cronies storm the Candide, being filmed on the evening of Friday 31 August. Angela Richards remembers that, despite his on-screen nastiness, Ralph Bates was a great actor to be around: "He was delightful and funny and made us laugh an awful lot!" Bates was also required for the following episode's (*Days of Judgement*) studio recording on 10 September, on the 'old works' set where Vercors seeks to hang Albert. Once again, the BBC's drama executives scrutinised the scene in some detail, but ultimately only shaved off shots here and there. However, when the episode came to be transmitted on UK Gold over twenty years later, this episode would suffer the largest cuts of any episode in the series due to these sequences. Indeed, so extensive were the cuts that a new title caption had to be added.

Days of Judgement was the first episode since *Lost Sheep* for which Angela Richards was not required in the studio; however, she did not enjoy a complete ten-day break, as she was required for the recording of several studio sequences for the ill-fated fourteenth and final episode, *What Did You Do in the War, Daddy?*, that Viktors Ritelis, the director of both episodes, had decided to record in advance. The reason for this was two-fold: firstly, Richards featured in the most scenes in this final episode; and secondly, the large number of location sequences in *Days of Judgement* meant that Ritelis had more studio time to play with than usual.

The Finishing Post

By this point in the production, with the finishing post in sight, the cast began to contemplate the fact that they would soon have to say goodbye to their fellow actors and their own characters. Angela Richards in particular felt that the end had come too soon: "It was as if we'd skipped a year somehow. I think there should have been a series before that third series and that should have then driven it to the conclusions that a fourth series would have made. That could have made it stronger and possibly even have changed it?" Looking back now at the developing storyline for her character, which became one of the most prominent of the last few episodes, particularly in *Bridgehead* (which went into the studio on 20 September 1979), Richards feels: "It was too rushed. Leaving Albert, the end of the Occupation, meeting some chap on a tank and then getting married. I wasn't convinced, I have to say... I think that semi-fairytale ending was a little too glib." As to what she would have preferred for Monique, she is not entirely sure: "I would have liked something perhaps more interesting, another road she might have taken, totally independently." Hazel McBride also would have liked the opportunity to explore her character further as, despite her faults, she "quite liked Madeleine." She adds: "It's quite sad when something that you've enjoyed doing comes to an end. As an actor it happens all the time though, so you do get used to it, but I had enjoyed *Secret Army* very much, so in that respect it was sadder than most." However, she feels that "It did seem right that it ended when it did – often series are tempted to go on too long and go into another series and then they're not as good as they had been." Clifford Rose also felt that the time was right ("I think it was best for it to go out on a high") although he does recall that it was "very sad" as it had been "a great time… It was a long period of my life, overall three years, a great group of people to work with and a lot of us had become great friends."

© Angela Richards

Angela and Juliet in costume in *Blue Peter*'s Italian Sunken Garden during studio recording at BBC TV Centre in the Autumn of 1979

The eventual final episode, *The Execution*, began rehearsals on 24 September and, in line with all of the episodes in the last studio production block from *Collaborator* onwards, went into the studio just seven days later rather than the more typical ten. The main recording took place as usual, after supper in the BBC Canteen, at 7.30pm and continued until 10pm that evening, with the main sets being the Candide, Natalie's apartment and the interiors of the Canadian-run cantonment. Recording was set to conclude with the VE Night scenes in the 'party dressed' Candide, with the very last sequence to go before the camera being Monique's final emotional rendition of 'If This is the Last Time I See You'. Juliet Hammond-Hill remembers: "The last day was absolutely impossible, it was just heartbreaking, absolutely heartbreaking. Because I cry quite easily, the camera goes on me every time I fill up with tears. I was in character, I was out of character, I don't know what I was. I was on another planet! I was so grief-stricken." Angela Richards adds: "We all knew we were being a little indulgent, with looks one to another. But then it was very genuine. We also knew underneath it all that there was something quite true."

371

Myths and Rumours

Although the regular cast, without exception, recall *The Execution* as their very last work on the programme, in actual fact all of them, bar Terrence Hardiman and Hazel McBride, would come together once again on Thursday 4 October to start rehearsals for the abortive episode fourteen, set some 25 years later in September 1969: *What Did You Do in the War, Daddy?* From the outset, the cast felt that the episode was poorly conceived and executed, something which is all the more surprising when one considers that it was penned and directed by two of the series's stalwarts: John Brason and Viktors Ritelis respectively. Since 1979, various myths and rumours have been widely circulated as to why Gerry Glaister decided, as late as December 1979, to pull it from the broadcast schedule. The BBC Written Archives hold a copy of a memorandum sent to all the cast by Glaister, which suggests that it was in fact an industrial strike that put paid to the episode's broadcast: 'Owing to the difficulties caused by the industrial dispute it was not possible to complete the editing required on this very complicated programme. As a result the programme has been withdrawn for the time being. The approaching Christmas holiday put a very heavy strain on the editing facilities and a number of programmes had to be remounted after the strike and edited before the Christmas holidays. In the New Year I will let you know if there is a new transmission date on completion of the programme.' However, after viewing the episode again for the first time in 25 years in 2004, Viktors Ritelis asserts that the episode held in the BBC archives is the final completed version, believing that no more editing or dubbing would have been needed. Why then was the production abandoned? The late John Brason always maintained that the episode was as good as banned due to its strong anti-Communist message. The fact that Juliet Hammond-Hill was given controversial dialogue to deliver (such as: "We talk of the horror of the Final Solution... What was it? Eight million people... Jews, gypsies, minorities... yes it is terrible. But the Communists have liquidated one hundred and thirty million so far... it makes the Nazis look like amateurs") suggests that this explanation is the most likely. The other most popularly cited explanations – that the make-up for the aged regular characters was too poorly realised, and that the decision to make *Kessler* caused it to be shelved – are both highly unlikely. The former because there is nothing wrong with it (in fact this is the least of the episode's problems!) and the latter because the decision to make *Kessler* was not made until well into 1980, after Glaister's new drama series *Buccaneer* (also featuring Clifford Rose) floundered. Brason admitted that the episode "was one of my few things that looked better on paper than on screen" and it is difficult to disagree with him. It is Juliet Hammond-Hill who best sums up the episode's problem: "It was totally out of sync with the rest of the show – it was quite arty and it had a lot of symbolism in it, and they didn't feel it had any marriage with what had gone before." She also believes, its anti-Communist message aside, that its cancellation was: "Above all else, a decision based on comparison with the rest of the final series." Indeed, after viewing it for the first time in 2004, she, Richards and Rose agreed that they were very relieved that it had never been aired, believing it may have even tarnished the series's reputation if it had been and that *The Execution* was a far more fitting end to the series. After seeing it again, its director Viktors Ritelis was more interested in its stance on the rights and wrongs of war, feeling that: "It was not the most definitive statement about wars, quite the opposite in fact – the script has a naïveté about it which speaks so eloquently about the Seventies, when we must have thought the worst we can do to each other was behind us." While this book was being written, yet more reasons for the pulling of the episode were provided to the author by the episode's designer, John Hurst, and Series Three's lead director, Michael E. Briant. Hurst recalls that there was a dispute over the inclusion of the black-and-white footage for the documentary and dream sequences as they showed prisoners of war – content that BBC policy of the time would not allow to be broadcast. Apparently Ritelis point-blank refused to remove the material in question, hence the episode's subsequent cancellation. Ritelis himself has not confirmed or denied this. Although this BBC 'point of principle' sounds unlikely, it is the self-same policy that forced the makers of *Dad's Army* to abandon their original title sequence, which featured black-and-white footage of the war, in favour of the now immortal animated sequence in which British flags and swastikas move around a map of Europe. Briant, on the other hand, simply remembers that: "Gerry looked at it, decided it was not of sufficient quality and insisted the BBC pull it, never transmit it. They wrote it off together with all its costs."

Post-Production

Each of the third series's episodes were edited and dubbed in the two to three weeks following studio recording, with work on *The Execution* completing on Saturday 20 October, the same day that *Ring of Rosies* first aired. Once again, during editing, various pieces of authentic wartime stock footage – that did not offend BBC senior management – would be added, such as the lengthy scene-setting sequence that starts *The Last Run* (featuring Allied troops fighting their way through Normandy), and a newsreel showing VE Night in Brussels that was incorporated into *The Execution* (obtained from EMI for the sum of £40). Perhaps the most interesting interpolation was made by Andrew Morgan who, rather than using stock footage to represent Arnhem in the episode *Bridgehead*, instead wrote a 'sob story' letter to Sir Richard Attenborough, whose epic film about Arnhem, *A Bridge Too Far*, had come out in 1977. Morgan recalls that in this letter he explained that this *Secret Army* episode was his "first ever job as a freelance, and asked if he'd be prepared to give me some offcuts that he hadn't wanted for the film. He was very sweet and said 'Go and see my editor at Pinewood', and I went down and chose some fantastic footage. I was charged £100 for charity!" During the sypher dub, the episodes were enhanced by the addition of incidental music, with many pieces this time around being instrumental arrangements of the songs sung by Monique, such as 'Lili Marlene'. Militaristic drum beats would also be heavily used in order to underscore the action (e.g. in *Revenge*), while great synthesiser-created crashes were experimented with on *Days of Judgement*, with a view to heightening the tension.

Scheduling and Publicity

For its third and final run, *Secret Army* received the scheduling that Glaister had always hoped for: a prime-time slot on Saturday evenings, starting on 22 September 1979. The new series would air as part of a classic Saturday line-up that began with magazine show *Junior That's Life* at 5.35pm, replaced from 13 October by *The Basil Brush Show*, continuing with *Doctor Who* (with Tom Baker as the Doctor and Lalla Ward as his current companion) at 6.15pm, *Larry Grayson's Generation Game* at 6.40pm (in which the camp comic was joined by "the lovely Isla St Clair"), followed by *Secret Army* at 7.35pm, then impressionist Mike Yarwood at 8.30pm and a new series of the hit US police show *Starsky and Hutch* at 9pm (and from 17 November the series of *Dallas* which ended with the 'Who Shot J.R.?' cliffhanger).

Strangely there was very little publicity about *Secret Army*'s return, other than a handful of newspaper previews. Indeed, *Radio Times* offered nothing more than a listing accompanied by a photo of Reinhardt. The compilers of *Radio Times* may well have been reticent to cover the series's return as elsewhere in their 22-28 September 1979 issue they concentrated heavily on another wartime drama: a celebrated play featuring Timothy West entitled *Churchill and the Generals*. Other new series that week included chat show *Parkinson*, the drama *The Camerons* with Morag Hood, and a new Richard Beckinsale comedy entitled *Bloomers*. Bernard Hepton and Terrence Hardiman could also be seen in two quite different roles over on BBC2 at the time, as Toby Esterhase in *Tinker, Tailor, Solider, Spy* and Charles Pooter in *The Diary of a Nobody* respectively. In the same week that *Invasions* aired, two new BBC series were broadcast for the first time: detective drama *Shoestring* with Trevor Eve, and *To the Manor Born*, a new comedy vehicle for Penelope Keith, both of which would be broadcast on Sunday evenings and consistently top the ratings.

Viewing Figures and Audience Reaction

The viewing figures for the first five episodes of the new series would be considerably enhanced by an ITV strike. Due to instructions from ACTT (Association of Cine and Television Technicians) to its members, the strike, which had started at Thames Television, went national from 10 August. From this date until 24 October, ITV were unable to broadcast anything but a message apologising for the loss of service. What was very bad news for ITV was great news for the BBC, who continued to operate as normal without any competition. As a result, *Secret Army*'s third series debuted (with *The Last Run*) with its highest viewing figure yet of 16.8 million viewers. It was a figure that would rise even higher as the series progressed, with a further million watching both *Invasions* and *Revenge*, before *A Safe Place* was seen by a huge 19.5 million. However, the best was yet to come, as viewing figures peaked at an incredible 21.3 million for *Ring of Rosies*, meaning that 42% of the UK population had watched the episode. The return of ITV dented viewing figures for the next episode, *Prisoner*, considerably, as it lost over ten million viewers. However, viewers would pick up again week on week from this point, despite the fact that it was now facing competition from the very popular US show *The Incredible Hulk* on ITV. *Collaborator* was seen by 14.4 million viewers, while the following episode, *Days of Judgement*, was watched by 16.2 million viewers, a huge audience given that the strike was long since over. The remaining two episodes, *Bridgehead* and *The Execution*, received a very respectable 14.3 and 15.1 million viewers respectively. These figures suggest that the third and final series was certainly striking the right chords with the British public. All told, *Secret Army* was the eighth most popular programme to be broadcast in 1979.

In addition to the final series's exceptionally high viewing figures, the BBC's Audience Research Department's reports once again revealed a very satisfied and loyal viewing public; indeed, of those respondents specifically commenting on episode one (*The Last Run*), 81% said they would be watching the remainder of the series. While the second series had received an average Reaction Index of 77 (which meant that the majority of viewers had awarded the episodes either an 'A' or an 'A+') the third series topped this by managing an even more impressive average of 79. In fact, all the episodes from *Prisoner* onwards scored 80 or over, with *Just Light the Blue Touch-Paper*, *Collaborator* and *The Execution* recording the joint highest figure of the entire series of 82. The regular cast were widely agreed to be 'outstanding' and the standard of acting in general to be 'very high.' The locations used were considered 'most appropriate' and it was thought that the wartime atmosphere had been 'well conveyed.' All in all, respondents reacted to the final series 'with a great deal of enthusiasm' and considered it to be both 'appealing and exciting.'

One problem with the new series which was not mentioned in the BBC's audience research reports was raised instead in the letters pages of the *Radio Times* over October and November. The letters in question concerned the order of the Saturday night schedule. Ms E. M. Siber from Oxford complained: 'On Fridays and Saturdays most small children are allowed to stay up later than usual – so why has BBC1 scheduled *Secret Army* for 7.25pm? This is one of my favourite programmes, but as I spend most of the time explaining the plot to my two small children, I miss most of it. As the children would love to see *Starsky and Hutch* (but are not allowed, due to its lateness) would it not have been better planning to have put the more adult programme on later, and the childish rubbish earlier?' She also felt that the time-slot was too early given the question of its violent content: 'I know that there is not much actual violence in *Secret Army*, but even children understand menacing threats and implied violence.' Another mother, Mrs P. Wood of Hitchin, agreed: '*Secret Army* is a programme that requires total concentration and really is only suitable for adults or older children who can absorb the main points of the story,' while Mrs D. Lane of Great Yarmouth felt that Mike Yarwood was 'far more suitable material for young people' than *Secret Army*. The debate continued a few weeks later when Mrs June Bucknell of London wrote in to say: 'I find the present format for Saturdays most satisfactory. *Secret Army* is a very good drama but it is heavy and often very involved, and as such, does demand concentration. Its present slot on Saturday is, therefore, perfect since it follows the very light-hearted *Generation Game* which is always easily understood and enjoyed.' Sally Thompson of Weybridge was to have the last word on the subject, stating: 'What a pity your correspondents are unwilling to help their children understand the courage, suffering and incredible selflessness of so many brave people, which lie behind *Secret Army*. I much prefer my children to watch this programme than to be mesmerised by the stultifying stupidity of *Starsky and Hutch*.' Interestingly, those viewers who complained about the new time-slot were completely ignored, in fact by the time the series neared the end of its run, it began to air even earlier, just after 7pm!

Critical Reception

British newspaper and magazine television critics, who had not always been as fulsome in their praise as the series's viewers, now unanimously expressed their support for the show by penning very favourable reviews. The most notable of these was written by Bernard Davies in *Broadcast*, on 19 November 1979, who when reviewing the first series back in 1977 had felt compelled to suggest that television should leave the subject of World War II well enough alone, but was now much less reluctant to argue such a position because he had come to regard *Secret Army* to be 'a very distinguished series, with good storylines, superb acting, and a growing sense of tension week by week.' Furthermore, he admitted that the black and white goodies and baddies that he had feared would be depicted were not identifiable in a series that instead always offered complex characters that were not 'neatly polarised'. Among the German characters he noted that 'Kessler is a hard-line Nazi with an almost mystical loyalty to the Führer, but Reinhardt is a much more sympathetic figure. He has doubts and uncertainties, but he is still loyal and obedient to duty,' while on the Belgian side 'different attitudes, different motives, different loyalties are clearly defined.' He concluded his review by stating that the series succeeds because it 'is less... a them-and-us situation than a human situation.' Hazel Holt, who had conversely supported the show since its inception, wrote a detailed review in *Stage and Television Today* in the week following the broadcast of *Invasions*. Holt observed that: 'Consistently strong, intelligent acting in demanding roles is provided by Bernard Hepton as Albert, the tired and frightened organiser, and Clifford Rose as his Gestapo opponent, who manages to convey the grotesque combination of ruthless brutality and formal good manners of the Nazi officer.' She also noted that: 'Both the

© Henri Denis

Invasions was a hit with
TV critic Hazel Holt

appearance and characterisation of Angela Richards as Monique (whose singing deserves a mention of its own) conveys the perpetual alertness combined with physical exhaustion of someone permanently living on her nerves,' while she felt that Terrence Hardiman, in a role that could be made ludicrous by a lesser actor, was 'credible, his sharp, melancholy face conveying both the cunning of a hunter and the guilt of a soldier who finds himself terrorising old women and children.' Holt also praised the episode's location filming, the writing and the camerawork, and the 'strong direction by Viktors Ritelis,' believing the end result to be 'exciting and gripping.' Her only concern was that, although the clichés of the wartime thriller were absent, the tone of the piece was 'inescapably melodramatic,' however she ended her review by asserting that: 'If we feel the situations are sometimes overtly melodramatic, we need only consider just how melodramatic was reality.' On 20 October 1979, it was reported in the *Sunday*

Telegraph that: 'Thanks to the BBC's *Secret Army*, many more now know of the wartime activities of the Belgian Resistance fighters and in particular of their highly successful efforts to rescue British and Commonwealth aircrew shot down over their country.' The article was written on the occasion of a memorial service in Brussels attended by 30 members of the RAF Escaping Society. Air Chief Marshall Sir Alasdair Steedman of NATO, who was leading the group, told the reporter from Brussels that: 'British television viewers have been well-informed by *Secret Army*; though the characters are fictitious the facts are true.' Ronald Hastings of the *Daily Telegraph* awarded the series a 'recommended star' throughout the run, particularly commending Robert Barr's *Prisoner* ('a real nail-biter') and describing the series overall as 'consistently worthwhile.' In the *Daily Mail*, Elizabeth Cowley gave the series a rather back-handed compliment: 'The spirit of the Lifeline resistance men and women has remained credible and intact throughout despite the recent barrage of plotlines,' while Peter Lavalle of the *Times*, described the series as both 'a fictional thriller with a touch of class' and 'a wartime adventure that rings true' Guest contributor Barry Took commended *Secret Army* highly in the 'Preview' section of *Radio Times* in the 24-30 November issue, describing it as 'frequently outstanding' and 'absorbing... being, as far as it's possible to judge, both accurate and truthful.' He also reserved particular praise for several leading players: 'Bernard Hepton as Albert, Angela Richards as Monique and Juliet Hammond-Hill as Natalie, deserve nothing but praise.' He concluded his preview by lauding series producer and creator Gerry Glaister 'for the consistent excellence of *Secret Army*.' A memorable review of the series penned by novelist Fay Weldon, appeared in *The Times* on Monday 26 November, in which she extolled the virtues of the series and expressed the view that 'in the making of dramas like *Secret Army*, there is a level of professionalism, and sheer patient, largely unacclaimed, hard work from producer to script editor to writer to designer to vision mixer to editor by way of sound and lighting engineers that is probably equalled only in a heart transplant theatre.' She also described the series as 'craft bordering on art,' 'taut, exciting and subtly written' and specifically commended the fact that its 'pretty girls turned out to be real people' and that 'everyone behaved, as people observably do in the real world, when under stress – that is, not very well at all.' On 6 December, in the week following the transmission of *Days of Judgement*, Peter Buckman wrote in the *Listener* that the final series had been 'consistently well-acted, well-directed and well-written,' and that 'No-nonsense realism in characters and background produced a series (or two) in which you knew where your sympathies lay, a far from common thing in these equivocal times.'

Given this level of critical acclaim, it is hard to understand why neither the series, nor indeed its leading actors, were even nominated for BAFTAs. The only nod to the series was a long overdue award for Alan Jeapes's superb title sequence. One can only assume that *Secret Army* was regarded as too popularist, unworthy as it was not an adaptation, or that it simply wasn't considered because it was now into its third series. In the event, *Testament of Youth* and *Tinker,*

Tailor, Soldier, Spy swept the board. Although BAFTA all but ignored the series, thankfully due recognition was received at the Radio and Television Industry Awards in April 1980, which celebrated the most popular and successful TV programmes and personalities of 1979, with *Secret Army* beating both *Testament of Youth* and *Tinker, Tailor, Soldier, Spy* to the award for Best BBC Television Programme of the Year.

The End of the Line?

During broadcast of the final series, the series's regulars received an unprecedented amount of fan-mail. Despite the character he was playing, the actor who was receiving the most was Clifford Rose: "I've never had such fan-mail in my life! I was with a large agency called ICM and while Series Three was going out they told me that I had more fan-mail than any other client they had at the time." This fact did not go unnoticed by Gerard Glaister and John Brason, who began to realise that there was sufficient interest in Kessler that a sequel series might be a feasible proposition. As Brason would later write in the foreword to his novelisation of the sequel, which would eventually be titled simply *Kessler*, the way in which *Secret Army* left his story, with the former Standartenführer and his mistress Madeleine making for the ruins of Germany, left matters unresolved. He noted that this was 'an attitude clearly felt by viewers so that the necessity of creating a follow-up short series of 'What happened to Kessler?' became incumbent upon us.' However, before the sequel became a reality, both Glaister and Brason elected to take a 'break from the war', respectively producing and script editing/writing contemporary air freight drama *Buccaneer*, created by *Secret Army* writers N. J. Crisp and Eric Paice and which featured none other than Clifford Rose as one of the leading players. For the time being, the *Secret Army* story was over.

Episode 1: THE LAST RUN

WRITTEN BY: N. J. Crisp   DIRECTED BY: Michael E. Briant

FIRST BROADCAST: 7.35pm, Saturday 22 September 1979

STUDIO RECORDING: 30 July 1979

VIEWING FIGURE: 16.8m

REGULAR CAST: Albert Foiret: BERNARD HEPTON; Monique Duchamps: ANGELA RICHARDS; Sturmbannführer Ludwig Kessler: CLIFFORD ROSE; Natalie Chantrens: JULIET HAMMOND-HILL; Major Hans Dietrich Reinhardt: TERRENCE HARDIMAN; Dr Pascal Keldermans: VALENTINE DYALL; Alain Muny: RON PEMBER; Madeleine Duclos: HAZEL McBRIDE; Paul Vercors: RALPH BATES; Inspector Benet: RICHARD BEALE; Wullner: NEIL DAGLISH

SUPPORTING CAST: Flt Sgt Tucker: CHRISTOPHER GOOD; Flt Sgt Wally Bond: PETER DAHLSEN; Flt Sgt Graham Sharp: STEWART BEVAN; Hauptsturmführer Kupper: ANTHONY GARDNER; Farmer: ALEC WALLIS; Train Guard: CLAUDE LE SACHE; Station Official: NORMAN ATKYNS; Feldwebel: DAVID ROY-PAUL; German Soldier: TONY BROOKS

SYNOPSIS: June 1944. While the Allies slowly push out from Normandy, in Brussels Kessler is coordinating house-to-house searches with the help of Inspector Benet. Dr Keldermans comes to the Candide to tell Albert which evaders are fit to travel down the Line. Alain arrives to warn them about the searches. He leaves to clear one safe-house while Albert goes to clear another. In the Avenue de la Couronne, three evaders called Tucker, Bond and Sharp see that the Germans are about to search the house they are hiding in. Albert leads two of them to safety across the roof, but Tucker is taken prisoner. Natalie sets off from the Candide to take Bond and Sharp down the Line. Kessler alternates between interrogating Tucker and attending a drinks reception in the officers' mess with Madeleine. Brandt's replacement, Major Reinhardt, arrives and Kessler immediately takes against him. Reinhardt insists that he takes over Tucker's interrogation. Natalie finds that the usual train journey through France is becoming impossible due to diversions and sudden timetable changes. Reinhardt begins to interrogate Tucker in his office. The train on which Natalie and the evaders are travelling is bombed by an Allied plane. Sharp is killed, but Natalie and Bond escape the wreckage unharmed. Reinhardt decides to continue Tucker's interrogation over dinner in the Candide. Monique learns that Reinhardt is Brandt's replacement. Albert is concerned that the late Brandt may have had suspicions about the Candide which may have appeared in files that Reinhardt now has access to. A further interruption to their journey prompts Natalie to decide to leave Bond at the next available safe-house. Having been plied with drink by Reinhardt, Tucker reveals that an American evader he met in England got back home thanks to the help of two old ladies living in a place beginning 'Sen'. Tucker doesn't complete the name as he realises he has said too much. Reinhardt asks Hauptmann Müller to make a list for him of all places in Belgium and Northern France beginning 'Sen'. Communist Paul Vercors meets with Benet, whom he has a hold over due to his 'red' past, to ask him to find out who betrayed Max Brocard and the rest of his reseau. Natalie leaves Bond with a farmer at St Aubin, where he will have to wait until the Allies arrive. Kessler demands that

Reinhardt hand Tucker over due to a new directive which states that all captured aircrew are now Gestapo prisoners. Kessler is infuriated to learn that Tucker has already been sent to a POW camp. Natalie eventually makes it back to the Candide and tells Albert and Monique that they will not be able to get any more airmen down the Line to Spain. Vercors learns from Benet that it was Albert who tipped off Delon about Max, and is determined to exact his revenge.

REVIEW: The ever-reliable N. J. Crisp opens the third series in style with an action-packed and engaging episode which introduces a whole new set of problems for Lifeline, the most momentous of which is the end that is put to their long established evasion route due to the Allied advance. Elsewhere, Terrence Hardiman makes an effortless debut as Major Hans Dietrich Reinhardt, while Ralph Bates makes his first appearance as the new face of the vengeance-set Paul Vercors.

We return to Brussels just a few weeks after the D-Day-set finale to Series Two at a hugely significant turning point in Lifeline's history. One of the narrative's main aims is to illustrate clearly that this is the last time that they will attempt to guide airmen down the Line. Thankfully this is achieved through a large number of filmed location sequences rather than via dry exposition, so that when Natalie eventually makes it back to the Candide we, like her, are absolutely convinced that they cannot get any more men down to Spain. However, as Monique points out: "Airmen will go on being shot down and if we can't get them down the Line what do we do with them?" It is a good question and just one of the many dangerous dilemmas to face the Lifeline operatives during the final series. Although this enforced change of direction for Lifeline is historically informed, it is nevertheless timely, ensuring as it does that the storylines of the third series will be markedly different to those presented in earlier series.

Although they don't know it yet, another major threat to Lifeline is the arrival of Brandt's replacement, the assured Major Hans Dietrich Reinhardt. Given the brilliance of Michael Culver's contribution, it would have been fair to expect that during the third series we would find ourselves missing Brandt; however, Terrence Hardiman's immediately engaging and charismatic performance ensures that this never turns out to be the case. From the moment he arrives at Gestapo Headquarters, dressed in his leather flying jacket and white scarf, we know that Reinhardt is no ordinary Luftwaffe Major and moreover that Kessler will not like him one little bit.

We learn a great deal about Reinhardt from his initial uneasy audience with Kessler. From the outset, it is clear that the new Major is not in the least bit interested in making a good impression on the Sturmbannführer. Even in his first words to him ("Yes, I know who you are") he barely conceals his resentment for the man and his kind. He goes on to waste no time in reminding Kessler that, despite the fact that they supposedly worked together "cordially," Brandt shot himself, and awkwardly presses for clarification when Kessler intimates that he had a good reason for doing so. Reinhardt's 'flying dress' uniform is the next point of contention and the Major is quite insistent that he has no intention of changing it, firmly and cheerfully stating: "Well we'll have to disagree about that." Even when Kessler tries to make small talk about the aircraft his new colleague has been flying, Reinhardt cannot resist contradicting his opinion that Heinkel 111s and Junker 88s are "fine aircraft," conversely stating that "they're out of date." But he is still not finished with the increasingly rattled Kessler and ends his first meeting with him by insisting that it is his right to take Flight Sergeant Tucker off his hands! That Reinhardt appears to enjoy his first run-in with Kessler, and keeps his cool throughout it, makes the character very appealing, while his lack of deference to Kessler's authority is incredibly refreshing. Indeed, compared to the careful and considered Brandt, Reinhardt – whose every response to Kessler is intended to wind him up – is an outspoken maverick. This sequence suggests not only that Kessler may have met his match in Reinhardt, but also that their warring relationship, which is expertly pitched by Hardiman and Rose here, will be a joy to watch.

Reinhardt may not be as immaculately dressed as Brandt always was, but *The Last Run* does suggest that he may well be more intelligent than his predecessor, or at least more thorough at any rate. Although his interrogation of the gullible Tucker ("This is it?") at the Candide puts us in mind of the charm offensives used by Brandt in order to obtain information (most memorably employed to target Romsey in *Lost Sheep*), Reinhardt is seen to extrapolate from what he learns, taking it to the next level. Because of this, even though all that he knows by the end of this episode is that two old ladies, living in a place beginning 'Sen', in either Northern France or Belgium, have helped evaders before, by the next episode the Senlis-based Chantal sisters are in grave danger of being arrested. Similarly, although Brandt's investigations, particularly in May 1943, took him to the Candide, earning the restaurant a mention in his files, he did not follow up on any suspicions he might have had, whereas Reinhardt's surprise visit to the Candide with Tucker already suggests that the Major is checking the restaurant out, having read about it in said files. His enigmatic statement: "My predecessor used to come here quite often... I believe," infers that Albert's concern that Reinhardt's visit may not just be pure chance, but could "be something else," may be justified. We are certainly made to think that Albert and Monique are right to look worried.

Reinhardt's second run-in with Kessler, after Tucker is already on his way to a POW camp – a situation which the Sturmbannführer interprets as deliberate defiance, especially given Field Marshal Keitel's new orders – sees Kessler accuse the Major of being a Communist, clearly something he considers to be the worst crime imaginable. Reinhardt responds not with defence but attack, by asking Kessler: "How many campaigns have you taken part in? How much fighting have you done for Germany?" no doubt having previously noted the effect of his Knight's Cross on his new colleague. Although Reinhardt definitely wins this round, the signs are that he may be made to care and "give a damn," as

Kessler's threat – "You'd be wise to change your attitude, otherwise the consequences could be very unpleasant, Herr Major!" – is no idle one.

Despite De Beers's best efforts, Gestapo HQ looks in remarkably good nick here. And if the bountiful reception in the officer's mess is anything to go by, the Germans are in far better shape than when we last saw them too. The reception scenes serve not only as an important reminder of the fact that the German defeat is still some months away and that therefore the series is far from over, but also to bring Kessler's mistress, Madeleine Duclos, back into the fray. Before this episode, Madeleine's last appearance was in *Little Old Lady*, so it is high time we were reacquainted with her. Judging by the way they behave around each other here, Kessler and Madeleine's relationship appears more stable than ever; in fact, the pair act like they are a married couple: talking about the latest war news with one breath and complimenting each other with the next ("You look nice"). Kessler revels in showing Madeleine off, which is presumably the main reason why he invited her to the event, and the attention she receives makes him positively swell with pride. In fact, before Reinhardt arrives to spoil his evening, we have rarely seen him looking so happy. However, these cheerful civilised scenes also have a darker purpose. Their deliberate juxtaposition with the grim intercut cell scenes, in which Kessler callously interrogates the badly beaten Flight Sergeant Tucker, emphasises the Sturmbannführer's almost schizophrenic personality. Although Kessler does need to make a transition between the two duties by thoroughly washing his hands, disturbingly his general mood does not appear unduly affected.

As always, Kessler appears certain that Germany will not be defeated by the Allies, but the fact that he concedes that a "remarkable number of men" have landed in Normandy and that he considers a "stalemate" to be the worst-case scenario suggests a definite shift in his thinking. That Madeleine asks Kessler about the possibility of the Germans losing the war suggests that she is all too aware of the danger that such a situation would place her in as a known collaborator. She has already told Monique that she is aware that if the war goes the Allies' way then a brave resistance hero may shoot her as a traitor. However, the gaiety and civility of the reception makes it very difficult to believe that the Allies are really on their way.

This episode's evaders are a mixed bag. Christopher Good gets the most to do as Tucker and, although he is very susceptible to drink as well as to Reinhardt's charm and ends up saying too much, he is much less irritating than Peter Dahlsen's Aussie evader, Wally Bond. We've seen some idiots in the series, but Bond takes the biscuit and eats it too! As well as impatiently walking right up to Natalie on their first delayed train and asking her what is going on (thus blowing their cover), he even has the cheek to observe that they are running late. On the next train, he once again endangers their evasion when he fails to understand the guard's message in French – that the train is not going any further – and, rather than keeping quiet, says "Eh?" out loud. Unfortunately for the long-suffering Natalie it is, of course, the more two-dimensional Sharp rather than Bond who buys it when the train is bombed. Although he now seems to accept that she knows what she is doing ("Whatever you say, lady"), his subsequent attempt to come on to her by fondling her hair is remarkably ill-advised, as is his ungrateful whining about being left at the farm ("Where does that leave me, mate? What am I supposed to do?") and having to wait for the Allies ("Oh, when's that going to be?"). That Natalie responds to him with just a slight reprimand ("You're alive and you're safe. Think yourself lucky") demonstrates just how inured to the idiocy of her charges she must have become. This being the case, when it becomes apparent to her that this will have to be her last run, we can only assume that a part of her must be very relieved indeed. The prominence afforded in this episode to Natalie's various train journeys in the narrative, successfully conveys the incredible stamina and tolerance required of an evasion courier, although this demanding trip is of course clearly her worst yet. There is a suggestion in an early scene in the Candide's backroom that Natalie's experiences may well be making her too hardened. Albert's face when Natalie coldly responds to his statement that there will only be two in her next party with the line "Well, that's better for me," suggests that he is genuinely concerned about her and given her horrendous experiences in the past few months he has good reason to be. Unfortunately there is no room, in what is a very tightly-packed episode, to explore this any further.

As noted previously, the return of Paul Vercors as another threat to Lifeline, and specifically to Albert, some eight episodes after his last appearance in *Not According to Plan*, is not without its problems. Even today's DVD audience might have trouble remembering who he is – especially as he is now played by a new actor – never mind the audience of 1979 who would have waited a year between series! However, the main continuity error is that Vercors has not been referred to as the leader of Max's reseau since his debut episode. In fact, in *A Matter of Life and Death*, Max reports to Philippe instead, so to have Vercors return here with no mention of that character is confusing to say the least. A further problem is that there is no explanation as to why he was not with Max and the rest of 'his' ill-fated reseau in *Prisoner of War* (although Brason explains in his novel, *The End of the Line*, that he was not present as he was injured two days before when he and his comrades blew up a railway track). Yet another problem is that although his desire to seek revenge for the deaths of his comrades is understandable, his motivation to specifically avenge Max does not tie up with the portrayal of their decidedly uneasy relationship in *Not According to Plan*. The production team decided to cast 'baddie specialist' Ralph Bates, best known at the time for playing the villainous Sir George Warleggan in *Poldark*, as the new incarnation of Vercors. Although on the surface this would seem to be a good choice, unfortunately the character comes over as quite two-dimensional here, although this is arguably due to the fact that Bates is given little to work with in the two scenes in which he appears.

Angela Richards is in fine voice as usual as she belts out German favourite 'Lili Marlene' to an appreciative audience in the Candide. For the first time (with the exception of *Second Chance*) she is not accompanied by Max at the piano, and the mood of her performance – and the atmosphere in the restaurant – is enhanced by a manually-operated spotlight. Although the new pianist is glimpsed briefly during a subsequent scene, he is not introduced as a character or even referred to by name (although he does eventually get the name Paul). The man playing him is Ken Moule, the jazz musician who has actually played the piano in the Candide all along, a fact hidden during the second series by some convincing 'piano-mime' on the part of Stephen Yardley. Moule is credited as 'Music Arranger' on this episode, but not as the Candide's 'new' pianist. Although Albert has clearly recognised the wisdom of Monique's request in *Day of Wrath* for someone to replace Max, on the basis that their customers can "listen to the radio at home," there is nothing stated in the episode to suggest that the far more urgent priority to find a new forger has been addressed, although we do witness Natalie dishing out new papers for this episode's evaders, so someone has been busy on Lifeline's behalf. This question joins the other most frequently asked question about the series: Who actually cooks the food in the Candide?

The strains of 'Lili Marlene' are not only confined to Monique's performance, in fact Michael E. Briant chooses to use the melody to great effect throughout the episode, both to highlight moments of suspense and danger and, in a slowed down form, to accentuate the weary nature of Natalie's stop-start train journey through France. In this way it almost becomes the soundtrack to the episode. It is even sung, very badly, by the drunk Tucker and (playing drunk) Reinhardt on their return to Headquarters!

The episode's extensive location filming, the majority of which took place, once again, on the Nene Valley Railway and specifically at Wansford station, is beautifully shot. Many of these sequences with their huge number of supporting artistes and props would not look out of place in a feature film, particularly the slow pan back from Natalie and the other passengers as they wake up on the station platform and the shot filmed from the tracks looking across to Natalie and Bond just before the train pulls away to obscure them from view. The sequence in which the train is bombed is also superb and looks as though it must have been a logistical nightmare to shoot, especially as it involves a real train, huge explosions, heaps of supporting artistes and a real carriage fire. The establishing aerial shot of the train in motion, filmed as if from the plane's perspective, is also worthy of note. Briant also proves that he *is Secret Army*'s 'action' director (Viktors Ritelis being the only other rival for the crown) through the Brussels-shot house-to-house search sequences, which memorably end with Tucker falling down a tall flight of stairs and Albert (or at least 'stunt Albert') making his escape with Bond and Sharp across a rooftop. These scenes also benefit from a large number of civilians, soldiers and vehicles, all of which accentuate the episode's admirably authentic atmosphere.

If only one word could be used to sum up the final series of *Secret Army*, then either 'gripping' or 'nail-biting' would undoubtedly be the chosen candidate. Although less is at stake here than further down the line in the enthralling *Collaborator* and *Days of Judgement*, *The Last Run* still contains a high quotient of suspense. This is partly down to the incident and threat contained in Crisp's excellent script, but also due to Briant's directorial decisions. Aside from his impressive realisation of the aforementioned train bombing and house-to-house search sequences, he also uses some very noticeable, but nevertheless effective, extreme close-ups to enhance the tension. The close-up of Kessler's lips as he threatens Tucker in the cells makes him seem even more intimidating than usual; those of Natalie and the evaders on the packed trains emphasise the claustrophobic and harrowing nature of their journey; while in the episode's closing moments the forbidding new face of Vercors fill the screen as he insists that he will get Albert.

All opening instalments have a difficult job, for as well as setting the tone and scene for the series that follows and launching its key storylines, ideally they should also be involving in their own right. Thankfully *The Last Run* succeeds in ticking all these boxes and furthermore suggests that *Secret Army*'s final series will be its best yet.

HISTORICAL BACKGROUND

Belgium in June 1944

Communique N1: "Under the command of General Eisenhower, Allied Naval Forces supported by strong air forces began landing Allied armies this morning on the northern coast of France." The news, heard by thousands of Belgians on the BBC European Service, that the Allies had landed in Normandy and were

seeking to advance, was initially met with jubilation. However, in the subsequent days and weeks (the time between the episodes *Day of Wrath* and *The Last Run*) speculation soon mounted about the possible failure of the Allies, especially when it became clear that fierce fighting was being reported in order for the Allies to merely consolidate their positions on the Normandy coast. Matters were made worse by the fact that in reaction to the news, the Germans tightened their grip on the country by imposing stricter curfews and threatening severe punishments for anyone caught listening to enemy broadcasts or simply for the spreading of news heard over the radio. After about a week, the majority of Belgians were convinced that the spectacular Allied advance that they were hoping for was now very doubtful indeed.

SONGS IN THE CANDIDE

'Lili Marlene'

'Lili Marlene' started life as a poem, entitled *The Song of a Young Soldier on Watch*, which was penned by a German soldier serving in the First World War named Hans Leip. Leip reportedly took the name from his girlfriend and another female friend. It wasn't until just before the outbreak of the Second World War that Norbert Schultze set the words of Leip's poem to music, calling it 'Das Madchen unter der Laterne' ('The Girl Under the Lantern'). It was subsequently recorded by Lale Andersen, but did not become popular until Radio Belgrade began to play the song and eventually became so inundated with requests (from Erwin Rommel among others!) that it ended up having to play it every evening at 9.55pm. After the war, Marlene Dietrich recorded the song in both English and German.

Underneath the lantern by the barrack gate
Darling I remember the way you used to wait
T'was there that you whispered tenderly
That you loved me, you'd always be
My lily of the lamplight, my own Lili Marlene

Time would come for roll call, time for us to part
Darling I caress you and press you to my heart
And there 'neath that far off lantern light
I'd hold you tight, we'd kiss goodnight
My lily of the lamplight, my own Lili Marlene

When we are marching in the mud and cold
And when my pack seems more than I can hold
My love for you renews my might
I'm warm again, my pack is light
It's you Lili Marlene, it's you Lili Marlene

Resting in a billet just behind the line
Even tho' we're parted your lips are close to mine
You wait where that lantern softly gleams
Your sweet face seems to haunt my dreams
My lily of the lamplight, my own Lili Marlene

Ken Moule

Ken Moule makes his first on-screen appearance here as Candide pianist Paul. A celebrated pianist, composer and arranger, Moule had been a member of several British dance bands, including the John Dankworth Quartet, Oscar Rabin's band and Bobby Kevin's band, before forming his own jazz septet in 1954 and a trio in 1955. In the late Fifties he worked as a staff arranger for Ted Heath and, in 1959, wrote and recorded the suite 'Jazz at Toad Hall'. In the Sixties he worked as musical director on two of Lionel Bart's musicals – *Fings Ain't What They Used To Be* and *Twang* – and regularly featured in *Melody Maker* polls as one of the UK's best composers and arrangers. 1970 saw the recording of his *Adam's Rib*

Suite, by the London Jazz Chamber Group. This suite was later turned into a jazz ballet for television, starring Wayne Sleep, which was broadcast on BBC2 in November 1979 (incidentally on the same evening as *Sound of Thunder*). Moule scored several other musicals during the Seventies, most notably *Cole* (1974), a celebration of the work of Cole Porter, which featured Angela Richards as one of the main performers. After his time on *Secret Army*, and the recording of the *Au Café Candide* soundtrack album, Moule retired to Spain. He died in 1986.

WHERE ELSE HAVE I SEEN..?

Christopher Good (Tucker)

Phillip Hanning, *Upstairs Downstairs*, 1974

Lt Majoribanks, *The Duchess of Duke Street: The Passing Show*, 1977

Major West, *Danger UXB*, 1979

Christopher Hawes, *Miss Marple: The Murder at the Vicarage*, 1986

Uncle Quentin, *The Famous Five*, 1996-7

© John Vere Brown

Peter Dahlsen (Bond)

Richie Bates, *Bellbird*, 1967

Stanley Morton, *Bergerac: Campaign for Silence*, 1981

Horton, *Doctor Who: Time Flight*, 1982

Frank Hurley, *Shackleton*, 1982

Bill Ashley, *Sons and Daughters*, 1985

© Geof Shields

Stewart Bevan (Sharp)

Professor Clifford Jones, *Doctor Who: The Green Death*, 1973

Ray Oswell, *Emmerdale Farm*, 1977

Paul (DJ), *Shoestring*, 1979

Max, *Blake's 7: Death-Watch*, 1980

Dr Brogan, *Nanny: The Sault*, 1983

© Unknown

Richard Beale (Benet)

Bat Masterson, *Doctor Who: The Gunfighters*, 1966

Saymon, *Blake's 7: The Web*, 1978

Edward Derwent, *A Horseman Riding By*, 1978

Ulf, *The Tripods*, 1985

Mr Proctor, *A Touch of Frost: Widows and Orphans*, 1994

© Unknown

Episode 2: INVASIONS

WRITTEN BY: Lloyd Humphreys **DIRECTED BY:** Viktors Ritelis

FIRST BROADCAST: 7.25pm, Saturday 29 September 1979

STUDIO RECORDING: 10 August 1979

VIEWING FIGURE: 17.7m

REGULAR CAST: Albert Foiret: BERNARD HEPTON; Monique Duchamps: ANGELA RICHARDS; Sturmbannführer Ludwig Kessler: CLIFFORD ROSE; Major Hans Dietrich Reinhardt: TERRENCE HARDIMAN; Madeleine Duclos: HAZEL McBRIDE; Hauptmann Müller: HILARY MINSTER

SUPPORTING CAST: Louis Bastiat: ARTHUR WHITE; Simone Borel: HELEN BLATCH; Jacques Borel: RAY ROBERTS; Jean-Paul: STEPHEN NOVAK; Sophie Chantal: MARY BARCLAY; Madeleine Chantal: RUTH GOWER; Mother: JUDY WILSON; Child: BART VANHECKE; Policeman: JEREMY ANTHONY

SYNOPSIS: Mid-July 1944. Kessler and Reinhardt discuss Brandt and the huge number of files he left behind, which his replacement is now working his way through. Reinhardt receives a tip-off by phone and sets off with a kubelwagen and a support unit for Keerbergen. Jacques and Simone Borel, the victims of the informant, have been taking in evaders for Lifeline for years and when Reinhardt and his men arrive at their farmhouse they know that the game is finally up. After a brief interrogation Reinhardt starts the journey back to Brussels with the Borels and a young man called Jean-Paul who is staying with them. En route, the Borels commit suicide. Louis Bastiat, a man who witnessed the arrests at Keerbergen and is currently hiding two airmen, comes to the Candide to tell Albert about the situation. Reinhardt begins the interrogation of the silent Jean-Paul at Gestapo Headquarters. Albert and Monique hear from Willi, their contact at Headquarters, that the Borels are dead. Kessler learns that Reinhardt has interrogated Jean-Paul and demands that he be handed over to him. Before the Major does so, he speaks to Jean-Paul one last time, but he refuses to cooperate. Albert and Monique learn, again from Willi, that Jean-Paul is in the custody of the Gestapo. Reinhardt's adjutant, Hauptmann Müller, visits the Candide to consult their books and specifically to ask where they obtain their eggs from. Kessler brokers an uneasy peace with Reinhardt and invites him to dine with him at the Candide. Kessler and Reinhardt are joined at the restaurant by Madeleine Duclos. Monique sings to the customers while Jean-Paul suffers water torture at Headquarters. Kessler is called away and Reinhardt and Madeleine remain at the Candide and get to know each other better. Albert tells Monique about Jean-Paul's background and his belief that they won't break him. The next morning, Kessler tells Reinhardt that Jean-Paul died during questioning and that the only things he spoke about that made sense were a woman named Sophie and a town called Senlis. Reinhardt deduces that this is the same place that Tucker was referring to and was mentioned in Brandt's files, and that there must be a safe-house there. Willi tells Albert about the death of Jean-Paul and Reinhardt's imminent trip to Senlis. Monique sets off by train to try to get Madeleine and Sophie Chantal away from their house before Reinhardt finds them. Reinhardt arrives in their street just as they are leaving with Monique, but luckily a mother and her son distract him. After threatening to take her son away, the woman reveals the location of the Chantal home. A search of the property reveals nothing of value. On his return to Brussels, Reinhardt tells Müller about the raid in Senlis and muses that Brandt was closer to the truth than he knew.

REVIEW: *Invasions* is easily the darkest and most harrowing episode of *Secret Army* thus far. As well as its scenes of torture and suicide, the plot emphasises just how precarious Lifeline's position actually is, suggesting a very bleak future if the Allies don't push on through France soon. As the new high-tension series progresses, it is becoming increasingly easy to imagine the Lifeline regulars – represented solely by Albert and Monique here – meeting the same tragic end as the Borels and Jean-Paul.

The direction of the episode is taut, terrifying and incredibly atmospheric, making this Viktors Ritelis's strongest and most complete contribution to the series thus far. Apart from the outstanding sequence which juxtaposes Monique's song with Jean-Paul's torture, discussed in some depth below, Ritelis employs a variety of techniques which make this episode particularly special. One of the most striking effects is the slow fade on Monique, Reinhardt and Madeleine and the other dancing couples in the Candide, who are all still seen to be dancing away long after the restaurant has closed. Another is the slow pan on Kessler standing alone outside Reinhardt's office while contemplating his next move, which, thanks to a snatch of incidental music, comes across as very creepy indeed. Similarly sinister is the intensely claustrophobic direction of Reinhardt's interrogation of Jean-Paul with its close-ups, intermittent bright lighting and enhanced sound of dripping water, all of which make the cell seem like the crowded "box" that the Major refers to. Overall, the episode has a definite 'after hours' mood, which in some ways makes it feel very much like *The Big One*, although somehow it has the impression of containing far less daylight-set sequences than it actually does.

Invasions features a smaller regular cast than usual. Although Keldermans and Alain frequently miss the odd episode, Natalie is absent from proceedings for the first time since the episode *Bait*. Although the resultant focus on Albert and Monique alone adds to the claustrophobic feel of the episode, their Lifeline colleagues are very noticeably absent. The episode does feature one new regular character, albeit on the German side: Hilary Minster as Reinhardt's adjutant, Hauptmann Müller. Minster, like John D. Collins (Delon), would later become a regular on *'Allo! 'Allo!*, playing General von Klinkerhoffen. Unlike Kessler's rather two-dimensional adjutants Rennert and Wullner, Müller gets rather more to do and, although he may not receive character development as such, more time is spent on his characterisation and his relationship with his superior.

The fall of the Borels' safe-house and their subsequent suicide is engaging and desperately sad. This is partly down to the considerable talent of Helen Blatch and Ray Roberts, who are utterly convincing in their roles as the ordinary, but courageous, Simone and Jacques. They make far more of their roles than is on the page and by the time they meet their end we have come to care about them.

The situation they face also naturally encourages the viewer to empathise with them, especially as their work for Lifeline has been discovered, as Simone says: "After all this time, and with the Allies already in France." Their bravery, and immediate acceptance of the fact that their lives are over as soon as Reinhardt and his men arrive, is awe-inspiring. Neither of them resorts to overt histrionics, nor do they hesitate over their suicide pact ("We knew the risks"); in fact, they are almost merely rueful that the inevitable has finally occurred.

One of the most disturbing sequences yet seen in the series comes halfway through the episode, beginning in the Candide soon after Monique and Albert have received the news of the deaths of Jacques and Simon Borel and experienced an unsettling visit from Hauptmann Müller. Quite understandably, Monique is in no mood to play up to the Candide's German customers and elects to sing them an "appropriate" song. However, instead of actually singing 'You've Been Good to Me' (the song she chooses), Monique recites the first three verses while the action switches between the Candide and Jean-Paul's cell at Gestapo Headquarters, where he is suffering horrendously under a form of water torture. Monique has evidently chosen the song due to the irony of its sentiment when applied to her German audience, as 'good' is of course the last thing they have been to the peoples of Occupied Europe. However, Ritelis's decision to combine it with the footage of Jean-Paul's torture makes the message even more powerful, especially the words from the second verse: "But you've never, never failed to understand. And you've always been there with a helping hand. Oh yes, you've been good to me." And reciprocally, the torture itself somehow seems more horrific when underscored by Monique's voice. After Monique has sung the last verse, Reinhardt, Madeleine and Kessler appear too thick-skinned to have realised the song's irony and heartily applaud her vocals. This inspired sequence makes for incredibly distressing viewing and, as a result, it stays with you long after the episode has finished. Although we have seen bruised and battered evaders before, this is the first time we witness torture in progress and it is startling in its brutality and an important reminder not only of how other members of Lifeline may end their lives, but also more generally as to what lengths the Nazis were prepared to go, to, in order to obtain information. The horror of this sequence is later exacerbated by the news that Jean-Paul died that night and, moreover, that the cheerful Kessler is not even particularly interested in the information they did manage to get out of him before his death. This has the effect of inferring that Jean-Paul was being tortured for the sake of it, simply because that is what they do to civilian prisoners at Gestapo Headquarters.

As in *The Last Run*, there is a marked contrast between the methods of interrogation chosen by Reinhardt and Kessler. Compared to his wining and dining of Tucker, Reinhardt appears to change tack completely with Jean-Paul – and we see a surprisingly dark side to his character as a result – however, his approach is still psychological rather than physical. Kessler's approach to Jean-Paul's interrogation once again involves the authorisation of violence, proving that Reinhardt's assessment of his colleague in the previous episode – that he is not happy unless he is inflicting pain on a prisoner – is an entirely accurate one. It is an interesting paradox that, although we know that first and foremost Kessler is a quick-witted strategist, he can never see the virtue of approaching interrogation psychologically, despite the results that both Brandt and Reinhardt have yielded with such an approach. The suggestion of those scenes in which Kessler does meet with his prisoners, who incidentally he never touches himself despite his subsequent hand-washing, is that he always appears so outraged that they have defied the Third Reich that he simply cannot conceive of not resorting to violence. It is important to note that although Jean-Paul does finally yield the names 'Sophie' and 'Senlis' under the torture authorised by Kessler, these names are useless as they mean nothing to him, whereas to the more laterally-minded Major they are the final piece in the puzzle that began with Tucker's tale of an evader helped by some old women.

The relationship between Kessler and Reinhardt takes an interesting turn here. It is the former who is the first to proffer an olive branch, by stating: "Knowing the man I'm to work with is, in my experience, being halfway to making the relationship work." His motivation is presumably not only to keep Reinhardt under control but also, given his statement about Brandt ("...we became, I like to think, friends"), to attempt to befriend his new colleague. Although Reinhardt's secret interrogation of Jean-Paul rather throws Kessler's new open approach, the Sturmbannführer, after calming down, still tries again, observing: "To know each other socially might obviate the kind of misunderstanding we have had." As well as inviting him out to dinner, he even magnanimously offers Reinhardt an opportunity to speak to Jean-Paul again (something that the Major has already done, again in secret!) Kessler makes further attempts to butter his new colleague up over dinner, telling Madeleine that he is being modest about his heroism and that "he flew many long and dangerous missions." Although civil, Reinhardt refuses to return the compliment when prompted by Madeleine, who describes her lover as "a most conscientious and remarkable man," responding to her cheerful insistence that he must take her word for it with the polite but firm: "No Mademoiselle, I must be allowed to make my own judgement." Although Kessler is delighted that Reinhardt offers to stay with Madeleine and escort her home after he is called away, thanking him profusely the following morning, it is obvious that the Major has not and will not take to Kessler and that his guard is still decidedly up.

There is an unfortunate problem with the dating of this episode due to the explicit reference (on the Borels' radio) to the wounding of Erwin Rommel by Allied aircraft as having occurred three days ago. Rommel was attacked on 17 July 1944, so this means the first day of *Invasions* takes place on 20 July 1944, the very day of the Hitler bomb plot. If this is the case, it is strange – especially as the episode takes place over three days, concluding on the evening of 22 July – that neither Kessler nor Reinhardt refer to this hugely significant event and instead continue with business as usual. It seems even odder that this mistake is made as the subsequent episode, *Revenge*, actually revolves around the repercussions of the bomb plot. The episode also includes some other, admittedly rather insignificant, oddities. One is Reinhardt's sudden and mystifying interest in the Borels' ID cards after their deaths (which in the script he merely hands over to an infantryman in order that they can be taken to the Civilian authorities and the necessary arrangements made). The other is Albert and Monique's apparent confusion ("What was all that about?") after Müller's visit to the Candide to ask where they source their eggs from, when it has already been stated that they get their eggs from Jean-Paul and they know that he is in Gestapo custody. The connection between the two seems glaringly obvious.

Although there is little space in the narrative for the stormy relationship between Albert and Monique to be examined further, for the most part, their hopes and fears seem to be uniting them, temporarily at least, as they spend the episode waiting for news, first of the Borels, then of Jean-Paul. However, the news of Reinhardt's trip to Senlis significantly sees Albert fail once again to offer the woman he supposedly loves the support and affection she needs as she prepares to set off on an incredibly dangerous mission. That Albert is merely puzzled by Monique's bowed head and thinks that he might have forgotten something practical is very telling, as is the fact that when Monique spells it out to him ("I just thought you might want to say… 'Take care,' 'I love you,' 'See you after the war'") he finds himself unable to show that he loves her, either through words or affection, and simply gives her the coldest of pecks on her head before she leaves the Candide for what could easily be the very last time. Interestingly, the camera script has the direction 'They kiss', but by the time it was recorded either Hepton and Richards or Ritelis, or all three, decided on this alternative conclusion to the scene.

This is the last appearance of Madeleine and Sophie Chantal, who we first met way back in *Child's Play*. The need for Monique to make a mercy dash to Senlis in order to save their lives injects some real suspense into the episode's closing minutes. Monique's interruption of their babbling about how good it is to see her is particularly well done, as are the characteristic reactions of the sentimental Sophie ("You will surely understand, my dear, that we couldn't leave") and the no-nonsense Madeleine ("This is only bricks and mortar") to the news that they must leave their home immediately. Given that the Germans are only two streets away, the provision of a small suitcase each seems rather too generous, especially as they only just make it out of the area in time, but that of course notches up the tension. The fact that the viewer can see Monique and the Chantals leaving the street in the background while Reinhardt is in the foreground makes for a tremendously exciting scene, especially given the repercussions if Reinhardt was to see the Candide's chanteuse in Senlis.

Reinhardt's encounter with the unnamed mother and her child, which could easily have just been a run-of-the-mill distraction from the departure of his prey, is elevated by the passionate performance of Judy Wilson, whose terror at the thought of harm coming to her child and her pleading to the Major is as moving as it is believable. Wilson, like the other supporting actors in *Invasions*, makes what is a very small role surprisingly memorable.

More than any other character this is Reinhardt's episode. Throughout the narrative we see many different aspects of his complex character. While several scenes strongly reinforce the fact that Reinhardt is working towards the victory of the Third Reich, others see him appear to reflect, like Brandt before him, on the validity of this objective. On the one hand, during the raid at Keerbergen, the Major is sensitive to the fact that he has invaded the Borels' home ("I understand. Believe me, I do understand. It is a matter of your privacy. I apologise") and orders his men to search the house carefully. Furthermore, he appears to understand that the Borels' resistance work is: "No more than we should have expected of you. You resent our occupation of your country, and have done what you can to get rid of us." However, his apparent empathy with their situation does not translate into a belief that the German occupation is wrong; indeed, his subsequent actions, particularly the harrowing start to his interrogation of Jean-Paul in which he fixates on the guilt of his subject, suggest the opposite. Later in the episode, both his blunt interest in whether Jean-Paul talked before he died and his treatment of the mother he encounters in Senlis suggest that he is far more heartless than he first appeared to be. However, the very last scene depicts the Major to be ashamed of his actions: "This isn't the life for a Luftwaffe officer. I have distinguished myself today by threatening a child and his mother and chasing two old women, and what is more to the point I came off worse," and to pointedly reflect that: "It isn't the Allies who are at war with us, its the human race." However, his final words (which are also the last line of the episode) about Brandt being "nearer than he knew" suggest that he is still just as determined to uncover the evasion line.

Invasions is a stylish and deadly serious episode, which contains some excellent performances from both its regular and supporting cast and proves that, although Michael E. Briant may be *Secret Army*'s best action director, Viktors Ritelis is arguably the series's most visual director.

HISTORICAL BACKGROUND

Air Attack on Rommel

On the afternoon of 17 July 1944, while driving back to his HQ from the Normandy front, Field Marshal Erwin Rommel (left), known as the 'Desert Fox' due to his exploits on behalf of the Reich in North Africa, was seriously wounded when his staff car was shot up by several low-flying Allied fighter planes. Rommel had recently failed to persuade Hitler to end the war while Germany still had an army, and as a result had decided that his rule must end; however, unlike the 20 July bomb plot conspirators, he was opposed to his assassination.

Although it was feared that he would not survive his injuries, Rommel lived on for a further four months until October 1944 when he was charged with high treason for suspected involvement in the bomb plot. As Rommel was a national hero, Hitler promised him his family's safety and a state funeral if he agreed to take poison rather than go on trial. The German people were told that he died after suffering a brain seizure as a result of the injuries he received back in July.

Spinster Agents

In Autumn 1943, the work of two elderly spinster ladies, who had been hiding evaders in their Paris flat, came to an end. Luckily they escaped to England before they were caught. On their arrival in England, both complained of toothache and about the lodgings that had been found for them, by MI9 agent Airey Neave, in Kensington. Neave agreed that MI9 would pay for new dentures for them both. The MI9 chief, Colonel Normal Crockatt, was furious when he received a cheque for £70 for the new teeth and refused to pay it. However, Neave, who was due to go on a mission when this news reached him via a go-between, passed the following message back: "You tell Crockatt that these women risked their lives to save airmen and he should pay. I'll take all the responsibility. After all, they might have been sent to a concentration camp where the Nazis would have stolen all their teeth!"[1]

SONGS IN THE CANDIDE

'You've Been Good to Me' (Richards, Osborne)

First heard at the conclusion of *Not According to Plan*, this Angela Richards composition receives a full airing here as Monique performs it ironically in the direction of Kessler, Reinhardt and Madeleine.

When we reach the sweet September of our days
I shall stop and think of all our yesterdays
Of our love and kindness, the many, many ways
That you've been good to me
So very good to me

Things have seldom seemed to go just as we planned
But you've never, never failed to understand
And you've always been there with that helping hand
Yes you've been good to me

I remember too the happy times we shared
I remember too when all in life seemed fair
With you by my side, life has been beyond compare
While you were there, while you were there

If I had to live this life all through again
With its happiness, its sorrow and its pain
I should worship you and love you just the same
For you've been good to me
So very good to me, So very good to me

WHERE ELSE HAVE I SEEN..?

Helen Blatch (Simone Borel)

Receptionist, *Blake's 7: Powerplay*, 1980
Helen, *A Doll's House*, 1983
Fabian, *Doctor Who: The Twin Dilemma*, 1984
Mrs Briggs, *Tenko*, 1984
Pyke's Maid, *The Buddha of Suburbia*, 1993

Ray Roberts (Jacques Borel)

Fred Chambers, *Doomwatch: Tomorrow, the Rat*, 1970
Master Mariner, *Oil Strike North: Quiet Day*, 1975
Captain, *Lillie*, 1978
Doctor, *The Fourth Arm*, 1983
Second Citizen, *BBC Shakespeare: Coriolanus*, 1984

Hilary Minster (Müller)

Fritz, *Timeslip: The Wrong End of Time*, 1970
Marat, *Doctor Who: Planet of the Daleks*, 1973
Thal Soldier, *Doctor Who: Genesis of the Daleks*, 1975
Yagon, *The Tomorrow People: Achilles Heel*, 1978
General Erich von Klinkerhoffen, *'Allo!, 'Allo!*, 1984-92

Episode 3: REVENGE

WRITTEN BY: N. J. Crisp   **DIRECTED BY:** Roger Cheveley

FIRST BROADCAST: 7.35pm, Saturday 6 October 1979

STUDIO RECORDING: 20 August 1979

VIEWING FIGURE: 17.9m

REGULAR CAST: Albert Foiret: BERNARD HEPTON; Monique Duchamps: ANGELA RICHARDS; Sturmbannführer Ludwig Kessler: CLIFFORD ROSE; Natalie Chantrens: JULIET HAMMOND-HILL; Major Hans Dietrich Reinhardt: TERRENCE HARDIMAN; Alain Muny: RON PEMBER; Madeleine Duclos: HAZEL McBRIDE; Paul Vercors: RALPH BATES; Inspector Benet: RICHARD BEALE; Wullner: NEIL DAGLISH

SUPPORTING CAST: Reichskommissar Glaub: ROGER BOOTH; Gestapo Man: IAIN RATTRAY; Customers in Candide: PETER DAVIDSON, STEVEN CROSSLEY, ROBERT CAVENDISH; Waiter: REGINALD STEWART

SYNOPSIS: 29 July 1944. At his headquarters, Reichskommissar Glaub discusses the aftermath of the 20 July Hitler bomb plot with Kessler and charges him with the task of flushing out the remaining guilty men working in Brussels. Kessler begins to investigate files and service records on his suspects, who include Major Reinhardt. Alain brings news to the Candide that the Communists know that Albert was responsible for the death of Max and his comrades and that they intend to kill him. Inspector Benet persuades Kessler to hand over a Communist called Brouillet to him, then meets Vercors to give him this news. Much to Benet's chagrin, Vercors wants his help in respect of Albert too. He wants Albert alive, believing a quick death to be too good for him. Monique warns a worried Madeleine that she should leave Brussels and forget about Kessler. Kessler arrives and Madeleine suggests that they should end their relationship. They each relate how much they mean to one another, before Kessler surprises her by asking if she would consider marrying him. At the Candide, Albert, Monique and Natalie prepare for the worst, arming themselves before the restaurant opens for business. Alain arrives to confirm that the Communists will come for Albert that night. Kessler brings evidence to Glaub that suggests Reinhardt's guilt. However, as the Major is regarded as a war hero and enjoys the protection of Goering, Glaub demands further proof. Kessler tells Reinhardt he wishes to speak to him, but invites him to dine at the Candide first. After the Candide opens, Benet arrives and Albert, who recognises him as a policeman, offers him a meal 'on the house'. Three businessmen enter and make a fuss, first about which table they want, then about Monique's singing. It seems likely that they are the ones who have come for Albert. Kessler reveals to Reinhardt that he wants to speak to him about the attempt on the Führer's life and that he knows of his friendships with the men involved. Back at Gestapo Headquarters, Kessler continues what has become an interrogation. At the Candide, the three men refuse to pay their bill until Benet intervenes. After they leave, it is noticed that one of the men has left behind a briefcase and it is feared that it may be a bomb, but it is a false alarm. Kessler turns up the heat on Reinhardt by questioning him about his attendance at a conference on 20 July. Reinhardt denies that traitors were present at the meeting and when Kessler tries to leaves him his gun, indicating that he should take his own life, the Major hands it back to him and leaves. While locking up the Candide, Albert is forcibly arrested by Benet and taken away by his men. A distressed Monique and Natalie realise what has happened. Glaub tells Kessler that he has failed to prove Reinhardt's guilt and that he must learn to work with him.

REVIEW: Although it contains several engaging plotlines, most notably Kessler's doggedly determined attempt to prove Reinhardt's complicity in the 20 July attempt on the Führer's life, *Revenge* is markedly less dynamic than the preceding episodes of the third series. This is perhaps largely due to the fact that the episode is almost entirely studio-bound and rather dialogue-heavy.

This episode was initially written with Brandt as the subject of Kessler's investigations into the bomb plot before Michael Culver's decision to leave at the end of the second series prompted Brason and Glaister to rethink their plans for the third. Seeing no alternative to writing Culver out other than to kill Brandt off, they decided to have him implicated by Neidlinger in a lesser plot against the Führer than was originally intended, and elected to have the new character of Reinhardt suspected of involvement in the infamous bomb plot instead. Perhaps the biggest clue to this reworking of the narrative is the fact that Reinhardt is given exactly the same friends (Von Elmendorff, Neidlinger) and acquaintances

(Admiral Canaris) as Brandt. If this really was the case, then it seems implausible that Brandt and Reinhardt would not themselves have known each other.

Despite the fact that Vercors has already told Inspector Benet that he expects his help in exacting his revenge on Albert for the deaths of Max and his other comrades, he repeats the information here as if for the first time, albeit in a different setting, presumably for the benefit of the inattentive or casual viewer. Once again, Bates is given little screen time to develop Vercors and, for the time being at least, he remains a stereotype. When Albert learns that the Communists know that he was responsible for the tip-off and that they intend to kill him for it, he is surprisingly matter-of-fact. However, what is perhaps more unexpected is that he immediately thinks about the safety of Monique, Natalie and Alain before himself and is very relieved when he hears that the Communists just blame him: "Well they're right there, that's something." It is an instinctive reaction which suggests that he cares about them all more than he can typically show. Unfortunately, the scenes in which Albert and the others prepare for the eventuality of his assassination in the Candide do not feel entirely credible, despite the fact that the characters have all wielded guns before. This is partly because Natalie and Monique wave their loaded guns about every which way and therefore appear dangerously incapable of protecting Albert, while the camp image of Monique potentially having to whip a gun out of the top of the piano mid-song doesn't help matters much either.

After her relative stability in *The Last Run* and *Invasions*, here, initially at least, we see an insecure Madeleine who no longer seems to understand her relationship with Kessler. Given the state she is in, it is a nice touch that it is Monique who comes to her aid, just as she did in *Little Old Lady*. However, this time around, out of genuine concern for her welfare, Monique elects to give Madeleine a wake-up call by reminding her in no uncertain terms that "every day that passes the Allied tanks are nearer to Brussels" and that she "must get out while there's still time." Despite the strength of Monique's argument, Madeleine finds herself unable to give up on Kessler or her life in Brussels so easily. However, when Kessler finally does arrive, she is totally unprepared to discover that, just as she regards him as all she has, he views her in the same way and, furthermore, wants to know whether she would consider marrying him. His proposal is too much for her to take in, especially as she has only just dismissed their relationship as nothing more than a "little escapade." Although her stilted response is that she does not know what to say as she had never thought about it before, her physical reaction suggests that she considers the idea out of the question, particularly given her current state of confusion. Madeleine's hopes and fears and Kessler's sensitive support for the woman he so obviously loves are beautifully portrayed by McBride and Rose who by this point in the series share a real chemistry. Despite what Kessler is and the fact that the complicated Madeleine is by no means one of the series's more likeable characters, it is nevertheless difficult after all this time, especially after seeing them bare their souls to each other, not to root for their relationship to work out in the end.

The episode's limited location filming, apart from an insignificant scene in which Benet makes his way to a rendezvous with Vercors, consists entirely of scenes set at Reichskommissar Glaub's Headquarters, represented by the Palais D'Egmont, Brussels (for the outside) and Central Hall, Storey's Gate, Westminster and the Octagon Room at the Orleans House Gallery, Riverside, Twickenham (for the inside), respectively. Director Roger Cheveley wisely chose to use one of these location sequences, featuring Kessler's arrival, to open the episode in a stylish and dramatic fashion, thanks to low camera angles and the now familiar militaristic drum soundtrack. The opulent Octagon Room is an excellent choice of location, which lends real gravitas to Glaub's orders, making what could have been a run-of-the-mill studio scene into something rather special. Clifford Rose would return there two years later to film a black-and-white flashback scene for *Kessler* depicting his induction into the SS.

Roger Booth is thoroughly believable as the unpleasant Glaub, who is all too aware of his own importance and gives Kessler a taste of his own medicine by making him wait before acknowledging his presence. In his dealings with Kessler, throughout this episode, there is the underlying suggestion that, although the Reichskommissar is keen to bring the bomb plot conspirators to justice, he is rather less fanatical than the Sturmbannführer. What is merely an impression here is given full expression in the next episode, when Kessler encounters Glaub again, albeit in markedly different surroundings.

The episode's two plots are cleverly, if briefly, linked through what for several gripping moments seems like a direct re-enactment of the method by which the conspirators intended to kill the Führer: a bomb in a briefcase. The briefcase in question is left behind in the Candide by one of three strange businessmen (they are so objectionable that they don't even enjoy Monique's singing!) and with Kessler's dialogue about the plot fresh in our minds, together with the fact that Alain has vocalised his concern about the possible contents of the briefcases the men are carrying, we are conditioned to believe, as Albert clearly does ("Alain! Don't touch it!"), that the abandoned object is indeed a bomb. Given that good plotting is partly about confounding viewer expectations, it turns out, of course, to be simply a harmless briefcase.

Anticipation of both the expected attempt on Albert's life and Kessler's inevitable interrogation of Reinhardt builds steadily throughout the episode, so that our expectations of these narrative pay-offs are heightened. Although Benet's arrest of Albert is something of an anticlimax, especially given the promise of a possible shoot-out, the conclusion to Kessler's investigations are anything but disappointing, thanks to sparkling dialogue by Crisp and typically brilliant performances from Rose and Hardiman. From the moment that he discovers that Reinhardt is suspected of complicity in the bomb plot, Kessler works long into the night in order to prove it, having no intention of passing up this opportunity to discredit a man to whom he took an instant dislike. It is an approach that suggests that there was very little substance to Kessler's recent attempts to make amends with Reinhardt for their shaky start in *The Last Run*. However, before going in for the kill, Kessler decides to display more false bonhomie, softening the Major up at what he hopes will be his very last meal with his colleague. This is a sharp reminder of just how cool and calculating Kessler can be when in pursuit of an objective. Even the quick-witted and perceptive Reinhardt can have little idea that Kessler's toast – "Well, here's to a very pleasant evening, Reinhardt, and a happy outcome for both of us" – is, at the very least, a toast to his forthcoming downfall. During the interrogation back at headquarters, despite Reinhardt's seemingly perilous situation, the last thing he does is play dead – much to Kessler's frustration. Instead he remains as entertainingly provocative ("I'm sure I'm not as clever as the Führer, and he didn't suspect Colonel von Stauffenburg") and cutting ("Are you planning to write my biography, Kessler?") as ever. Kessler, meanwhile, is at his threatening best: "You flying men. You have a strange sense of humour. I used to find the same with Major Brandt... before he killed himself." Kessler waits some time before electing to play his trump card: his knowledge that Reinhardt attended a conference at Abwehr HQ on the day of the bomb plot (a conference which, incidentally, if we are to believe the dates given in *Invasions*, Reinhardt would have to have attended after returning from the Borels' farm at Keerbergen and before interrogating Jean-Paul, making for a very full day indeed!). Kessler's desperation for Reinhardt to slip up and reveal his guilt is especially obvious from the way he positively pounces on Reinhardt's comment that the SS were not excluded from the conference – a fact that suggests to Kessler that several SS personnel may have been in attendance who have subsequently been found guilty. When this line of questioning gets him nowhere ("Draw whatever conclusions you like!"), Kessler seizes upon the only option he has left: to suggest that Reinhardt should take his own life in order to meet with an honourable end. It seems likely that this is a suggestion that the Sturmbannführer may have always intended to make. However, in presuming that he will take this way out, Kessler woefully misjudges Reinhardt, for this is a man who is not afraid of Kessler's threats and, more importantly, is rather uninterested in whether he lives or dies: "We all die sooner or later – even you, Kessler. I just don't care all that much." Kessler's fury both at having his own gun pointed at him and at Reinhardt's flip dismissal of his accusations is tangible, and by the episode's close it is more certain than ever that he will not rest until he has proved the Major's guilt, even if, as he tells Glaub, he has to wait.

What seems to infuriate Kessler about Reinhardt more than anything else is that, despite the fact that he regards him to be a thoroughly dishonourable person, the Major nevertheless has an exemplary military record and wears the highest honour of the Fatherland: the Knight's Cross. Ever since he first clapped eyes on the medal, Kessler has obviously coveted it: indeed, in *Invasions* he is even seen to be openly distracted by it while talking to the Major. Here though, the Knight's Cross does not only represent something that, from Kessler's perspective, does not match Reinhardt's attitude, but moreover, as Glaub's warning reminds him ("But he *does* have a Knight's Cross – awarded him by the Führer himself"), it gives the Major a hero status and actually serves to protect him from those high-ranking Germans who are bringing the bomb plot conspirators to a swift and merciless justice. It is a situation which makes Kessler even more resentful that the medal hangs around his colleague's neck.

Although *Revenge* is a solid enough episode, which is particularly notable for the excellent performances of the 'German' regulars, it nevertheless fails to match the exceedingly high standards of the instalments that both precede and follow it.

HISTORICAL BACKGROUND

The 20 July Bomb Plot

At 12.42pm on 20 July 1944, Hitler was meeting with two dozen generals and staff officers in a briefing hut at the Wolf's Lair (Hitler's HQ in Rastenburg, East Prussia) to discuss the latest developments in Russia, when a bomb, concealed in a briefcase that had been left there moments earlier by Colonel Claus van Stauffenburg (right), exploded: "A deafening crack shattered the midday quiet, and a bluish-yellow flame rocketed skyward... shards of glass, wood and fibreboard swirled about and scorched pieces of paper and insulation rained down... a body covered by Hitler's cloak was carried from the barracks on a stretcher, leading them [the conspirators] to conclude that the Führer was dead." After a failed takeover of the government of the Reich in Berlin, the conspirators, who were stunned to discover that Hitler had survived after all, were put to death. The fact that the Führer had survived the blast led him to believe he was divinely protected.[2]

The Reichskommissar

A factor that is not made at all clear in *Revenge* is that, in terms of the actual timeline of the war, Kessler is visiting the Reichskommissar at the earliest possible opportunity, as his position, and the civilian administration (or Reichskommissariat) he controls, only came into existence in mid-July 1944 – just before this episode is set. In reality, the Reichskommissar was called Grohe, in *Secret Army* he is called Glaub. Hitler had wanted to install a civilian administration run by a senior party official from the outset in 1940, but due to several initially insurmountable complications (the relationship with King Leopold – especially the fact that he was a relative by marriage to a member of the Italian monarchy which was allied with Germany; Belgium's strategic location with a view to the invasion of Britain; and the aim to cloak ultimate German intentions to annex Belgium completely), he had no choice but to rubber stamp the presence of a Military Command, under General von Falkenhausen, instead. However, by December 1943, distrust of Von Falkenhausen, a deteriorating security system and thriving resistance activity, as well as the increasing irrelevance of previous obstacles, eventually led Hitler to approve the establishment of a Reichskommissariat. However, further bureaucratic delays

meant that the final decision on the matter did not take place until June 1944. On 12 July 1944, Hitler, Bormann, Himmler and several advisors met Grohe. As the newly-appointed Reichskommissar, Grohe (left) was instructed by Hitler to begin the work of dividing Belgium into two new provinces (*Reichsgaus*) in the greater German Reich – a Flemish and a Walloon *Reichsgau* – and to implement German national interests, in Hitler's (translated) words: "ice-cold… and totally ruthlessly and selfishly." In the event, the new regime was no harsher than the Military Administration that preceded it, partly because Grohe was unexpectedly moderate, but also because he elected to retain many of the same staff that had been used by the previous administration. Hitler's new Reichskommissariat lasted just over six weeks in total before the September 1944 arrival of the Allies.[3]

SONGS IN THE CANDIDE

'Boom, Why Does my Heart Go Boom?'

This song was first popularised by Charles Trenet as 'Boum!' in the Thirties. The English version with lyrics by Roma Campbell Hunter, which incidentally does not have Trenet's quacking ducks and gobbling turkeys, became a well-known song during the war.

Boom, Why does my heart go boom
Me and my heart go boom
Boom-pety boom
'Cause I found you

Boom, When I'm with you it's boom
I can see love in bloom
Boom-pety boom
All around you

Was it at seven or half-past eleven
Or floating around the Pacific
I only know that I can't let you go
Your effect upon me is t-errific

Boom, When we are a bride and groom
Then my heart will go boom
Boom-pety boom
'Cause I love you

WHERE ELSE HAVE I SEEN..?

Roger Booth (Reichskommissar Glaub)

Tubby Vincent, *The Avengers: Escape in Time*, 1967
Rabowski, *The Tomorrow People: The Medusa Strain*, 1973
Plomacy, *The Barchester Chronicles*, 1982
Mr Pelham, *Miss Marple: Nemesis*, 1987
Baldwin Peche, *Cadfael: The Sanctuary Sparrow*, 1994

© Unknown

Episode 4: A SAFE PLACE

WRITTEN BY: Allan Prior   **DIRECTED BY:** Tristan de Vere Cole

FIRST BROADCAST: 7.20pm, Saturday 13 October 1979

STUDIO RECORDING: 18 May 1979

VIEWING FIGURE: 19.5m

REGULAR CAST: Albert Foiret: BERNARD HEPTON; Monique Duchamps: ANGELA RICHARDS; Sturmbannführer Ludwig Kessler: CLIFFORD ROSE; Natalie Chantrens: JULIET HAMMOND-HILL; Major Hans Dietrich Reinhardt: TERRENCE HARDIMAN; Alain Muny: RON PEMBER; Inspector Paul Delon: JOHN D. COLLINS

SUPPORTING CAST: Reichskommissar Glaub: ROGER BOOTH; Squadron Leader 'Mad' Mike Miller: STRUAN RODGER; Alec Ashton: STEVE GARDNER; Sydney Oliphant: GORDON KANE; Ronnie Whale: ROBIN DAVIES; Hanslick: ANTHONY HEAD; Josef Marek: ALFRED HOFFMAN; Gavain: DUNCAN PRESTON; Zander: ROBERT GILLESPIE; Guide: JON CROFT; First German: GUY SINER; Second German: PETER RICHARDS; Stripper: BUNNY LANE; Paul: KEN MOULE

SYNOPSIS: Early August 1944. Albert is taken to his prison cell. Alain spots two evaders, Miller and Ashton, travelling with a guide who he doesn't know. After following them for a time, he witnesses them escape a faked German ambush. Reinhardt tells Kessler about a bogus escape line for which Brandt laid the foundations and which he has now put into operation. Kessler is impressed by the information that the Major has obtained through it so far. At the Candide, Natalie urges Monique to take over Lifeline. Alain arrives and they tell him that Albert was arrested last night. He too thinks Monique must take over the Line and she agrees. Reinhardt introduces Kessler to a Jew called Marek who he has employed to send radio messages to London, masquerading as Alain. Alain tells Monique and Natalie about the bogus line. Two more evaders, Whale and Oliphant, join Miller and Ashton in the bogus safe-house. Their conversation is being monitored by two Germans in the room below. Monique seeks help from Inspector Delon about what has happened to Albert. Whale and Oliphant learn that Miller is the infamous 'Mad' Mike Miller and are deeply impressed. Due to a slip up from the monitoring Germans, Miller realises that the room is wired and that they have been picked up by a bogus line. Alain tells Monique that he has discovered that the Germans are transmitting to London on his wavelength. From the information received in London's reply, they learn that one of the men is Miller. They remember him and worry about the fact that he has been down the Line before. At the bogus safe-house, the evaders overpower the monitoring staff and Miller kills them. A notary, called Zander tells an astonished Albert that he has been accused of the murder of his late wife, Andrée, and that the Public Prosecutor has evidence to prove it. Delon tells Monique the same news, but also that Vercors is involved. At the Candide, Kessler tells Reinhardt that he has learnt he has been promoted to Standartenführer, and also that Glaub is the new Military Kommandant of Brussels and he has invited them both to an informal party. They ask Monique the whereabouts of Albert; she explains that he has been called away. Kessler and Reinhardt go to Glaub's party but are unprepared for the hedonistic scene they find there. Kessler makes a stand, telling the party-goers that he is disgusted by what he beholds. Glaub makes his presence known and invites Kessler to join them. Kessler declines, and before he leaves, warns Glaub not to cross swords with him. Monique visits Albert in prison and confirms that she has taken over Lifeline. Reinhardt learns that Miller is amongst their captured evaders and orders that they all be brought to Headquarters, unaware that they are now 'on the run'. Alain tells Monique that Miller and the others have escaped and she orders him to find them and kill Miller. Reinhardt learns that they are hiding at the old gasworks. Natalie also receives this news and Alain sets off there. At the gasworks, Reinhardt tries to persuade Miller to give himself up. As Miller does so, Alain shoots him dead from his vantage point above them. Later that evening, Alain tells Monique that he won't kill anyone else for Lifeline. Natalie rounds on him, reminding him of the dirty work they must do in order to survive.

REVIEW: Originally entitled *A Safe Harbour*, Allan Prior's *A Safe Place* is unquestionably the most accomplished episode of the final run so far. Not only does it have pace and excellent characterisation, but a number of memorable set pieces, such as: Kessler's stand in the bierkeller; Alain's murder of Miller at the gasworks; and Natalie's impassioned speech about survival.

A fair summary of *A Safe Place* would be to describe it as the episode in which Monique finally comes into her own. For some time now, it has been inferred that Monique is capable of running the Line herself; indeed, her actions in *Day of Wrath*, which are only condemned because she is not in charge, could be viewed as something of a 'dry run'. However, her considerable nerve and strength of character were first flagged up as far back as the first series episode *Guilt*, when Albert told Lisa: "Beneath that shapely exterior, Monique's as hard as they come." Although Monique shows some initial reluctance to take over when Natalie first asks her, once she agrees her transformation is immediate and she is issuing clear-minded instructions in no time. Interestingly, although Allan Prior's script notes suggest that, after assuming control of Lifeline, Monique is rattled by her first contact with Kessler and Reinhardt, Angela Richards quite rightly plays these scenes with the self-assurance and quick wit we have come to expect of her character. Richards is in fact uniformly superb throughout and, as she has proved time and again in the series, always interesting to watch. When Monique visits Albert, although the meaning of his pronouncement that only she can 'keep the Candide going' is clear, the fact that she dismisses out-of-hand his impractical idea that he advise her from prison prompts a wounded Albert to say:

"I think I've underestimated you, Monique." Her cool response (which incidentally does not appear in the original script): "That's the way men are," not only affirms this fact, but suggests that she is going to relish the opportunity she now has to prove that a woman can do as good a job as a man. Her putdown is in part fuelled by her frustration at Albert's inability to ask after her, as well as after the restaurant. She is by now used to such omissions, which ironically over time have had the cumulative effect of bolstering her independence, preparing her for just such a time as this. It is lonely at the top but this is something that her predecessor has inadvertently trained her to deal with.

Although Lifeline was originally said to be run by Lisa, it was always apparent that the real power lay with Albert, a fact which made his transition after her death to the role of leader little more than a formality. So it is only here then that a woman is independently making all the decisions and giving all the orders for the first time. This fact, together with Natalie's increased prominence as Monique's capable second, gives the series a more female dynamic. Thankfully this does not precipitate an overtly feminist 'sisters are doin' it for themselves' feel – *Secret Army* is never that glib. That they are women undeniably adds an extra dimension to the narrative, but this is always secondary to the fact that they are strong characters who are more than capable of dealing with the task in hand.

Monique's first formal order, in which she commands Alain to kill Miller, is a hugely significant turning point for her character: assuming control is one thing, but taking responsibility for the expedient deaths of innocent people is quite another. The fact that she can countenance this suggests that she has come a very long way since her abject disgust at Finch's murder back in *Second Chance*. Quite rightly she is seen not to take the decision to remove Miller lightly and is clearly distressed at the thought but, like Albert before her, she now appears to accept that it has to be done to ensure Lifeline's safety. Moreover, you can well believe that she would have shot Miller herself if Alain had continued to refuse to go through with it. After Alain has killed Miller and he tells Monique that he will not kill again ("Not for you, not for Lifeline, not for anybody"), appropriately enough it falls to Natalie (who, if anything, is now even harder than she was when – unlike Monique – she accepted that Finch had to die back in 1942) to pull him up short. While we can sympathise with Alain for feeling like this, Natalie's fiercely practical take on the situation, which reminds him of the many times that they have called Albert an assassin in their hearts and how they have to accept the necessity of killing in cold blood if they are to survive, is compelling enough to be met with cowed silence by the farmer. Her short speech, which ends with the line "Next time you visit Albert, Monique, tell him two more have joined the club," reminds us just how good an actress Juliet Hammond-Hill actually is and serves as a hugely effective conclusion to the episode.

Kessler's stand in the seedy bierkeller in the Bouchers district is undoubtedly one of the finest moments of the entire series. Clifford Rose gives his all as the furious Sturmbannführer vents his spleen over the depravity and degradation he witnesses there: "You are a disgrace to the uniforms you wear. I am ashamed…

We are Germans! It is our destiny to shape and rule the world and *this* is what I find. It disgusts me!" Although this is a Nazi holding forth about moral codes, one cannot help but empathise with his reaction. However, after Kessler's speech is slow-clapped in a sarcastic manner by the previously hidden Glaub, we expect that in the face of a superior officer he may have to back down. Kessler's initial shock at seeing the Reichskommissar certainly suggests this outcome; however, when Glaub refuses him permission to leave, it becomes obvious that he has badly misjudged Kessler. In a glorious display of might and self-confidence, the fearless Sturmbannführer proceeds to tell Glaub that he will go without his permission and furthermore that he should "consider well" before crossing swords with him again given that they are a long way from Berlin and that it is he who holds the true power in Belgium! Although it is the series's ostensible villain who delivers this chilling threat, it is once again difficult not to get behind him here; indeed even Reinhardt seems impressed by the courageous performance of his sparring partner. There is little room here, or in the rest of the series, for further exploration of Kessler's disappointment in fellow party members, however, it does become an engaging central theme in *Kessler*.

Josef Marek, Sudeten-German Jew, is an interesting and unusual supporting character, played well by Alfred Hoffman, who serves several important functions in the episode. In straightforward plot terms, Marek's technical expertise assures the initial success of the bogus evasion line. However, his presence also allows Reinhardt to voice his opinion on the Nazi treatment of the Jewish people. In explaining why Marek is cooperating with him on the project, the Major sarcastically details how the man has been "kicked, starved and beaten in the Sunshine Homes of the Third Reich" and that "he now works for whoever is not going to kick him." Unlike Kessler, Reinhardt can see past Marek's race and recognises him as one of the finest radio technicians and operators in the "civilised world." Kessler is clearly uncomfortable in Marek's presence as it is, but the fact that this 'sub-human' Jew is the first man to crack Lifeline's code must be even more difficult for him to swallow. Although Marek is a broken man, who Prior notes as walking 'with a touch of the automaton of the camps' and is understandably eager to impress Reinhardt in order to prevent his return to them, in his evocative description of the individual radio operators ("the second, a plodding Richard Strauss, the third made Strauss sound like Biergarten musik") we receive a significant hint of Marek's pre-war existence as a colourful and opinionated classical pianist – a reminder of the Third Reich's dehumanisation of the Jewish people.

There are several reminders throughout this episode that the series has now reached the last days of the German occupation of Belgium. This is a reality that Kessler, in particular, does not yet seem to have grasped. The Sturmbannführer is delighted to receive confirmation that his promotion to Standartenführer is imminent, but seems to display no awareness of the fact that he is not likely to enjoy this 'exalted' status for very long. Reinhardt, on the other hand, is all too aware of the limited time they have left, as illustrated by his exasperated response to Kessler's idea of taking Miller to Berlin for the purpose of propaganda: "Sturmbannführer, the Allies are fast approaching our front door. We don't need propaganda... we need victories!" The bierkeller scene, which in itself can be viewed as the occupying forces indulging in one last fling of debauchery, prompts Kessler to inform Berlin about the sort of man he believes Glaub to be. As a result of this action he considers the Reichskommissar's days in Brussels to be numbered, without any apparent perception that this is likely to be the case for them all anyway; as Reinhardt reminds him: "Days in Brussels are numbered for us all Sturmbannführer. We might as well realise that." Kessler considers such talk to be defeatism, and despite news of the ever-advancing Allies, who he himself has recognised as being "less than a hundred miles from here," he still appears to believe wholeheartedly that it is the Third Reich's destiny to rule the world. It is a belief that never quite deserts him until the final few hours of his life, some thirty years later.

Given that the German operation of a bogus line seems like such an obvious plotline for *Secret Army*, it is somewhat surprising that it is not until *A Safe Place* that an episode chooses to explore the dramatic potential of such a scenario. Director Tristan de Vere Cole (who actually began his association with the series with *Prisoner* – the first episode to be recorded in 1979) certainly makes the most of Prior's script and, on the evidence of the gasworks and bierkeller sequences in particular, seems to be a very capable director indeed. The suspense-filled scenes filmed at the disused Southall Gasworks are particularly memorable, especially Miller's death and the poignant reactions to this tragedy on the parts of both Reinhardt and Miller's comrades. Although Prior's script notes suggest that he hoped for the antics in the bierkeller to be more debauched, particularly in respect of Glaub's state of undress and how far the stripper gets before Kessler brings the proceedings to a halt, De Vere Cole does as much as he can to suggest a Bacchanalian scene within the constraints naturally imposed by *Secret Army*'s pre-watershed timeslot. Right at the start of the episode, he also adds significant interest to Miller and Ashton's first scenes by selecting a country estate over a more typical farmyard location, as indicated in the script, for the sequences in which Alain witnesses the fake attack by Hanslick – Anthony Head getting far too little to do – and his men.

Through Alain and Monique's discussion of 'Mad' Mike Miller as a second-time evader, one of the biggest paradoxes at the heart of the series is brought to light more conspicuously than ever before. Monique's summary of the evasion cycle in *Not According to Plan* – "We pass them down the Line. They get back to England. They fly out again. They get shot down again. It all starts again" – suggests that on their return to England, evaders are once again sent out on air missions over Occupied Europe. Lisa's plea to an evader in *Radishes with Butter* to "come back and bomb them again and again" similarly suggests this to be the case. However, here we suddenly have Alain saying: "What do the British think they're up to? He's been shot down once and they send him out here again!" While we can immediately appreciate the danger of Miller, or indeed any other

407

airman, being shot down again, when they have already been down the Line and could therefore identify Lifeline agents, the fact that this is an explicit policy that has been agreed with London in order to ensure their continued operation has not been made clear before now. Presumably the reason why this historical fact has not yet been addressed in the series is that if the airmen they save are not going to fly out over Europe again then it rather robs Lifeline of its *raison d'etre*. Yes, these men will still be able to assist in the war effort in different regions or in new roles, but the poetically neat cycle as previously outlined by Monique is revealed here to be an entirely false picture.

Prior's episode title is well chosen as it has several meanings. As well as Albert referring to it directly as both an appropriate description for his prison cell and as something "we are all looking for," it also points up that the bogus 'safe'-house is anything but safe; although, given the fate that subsequently befalls Miller at the hands of Lifeline, rather ironically it *was* safer for him!

A Safe Place draws together several disparate threads of the ongoing narrative into an incredibly coherent and pleasing episode which provides significant development for all the major characters, but especially for Monique and Kessler, whose lives are about to become a great deal more complicated and dangerous as the series begins to gain some real momentum on the way towards its conclusion.

HISTORICAL BACKGROUND

Impersonating a Fist

The patterns, pauses and relative lengths of dots and dashes as radio operators sent messages were collectively known as an operator's distinctive 'fist'. Once identified, this fist could in theory be mimicked in order for fake messages to be sent. This technique, although often used by the Germans in an attempt to send fake messages back to the Allies, was also employed extensively by Allied troops, notably by a US tactical deception unit known as the 'Ghost Army', operating after D-Day in Northern France in order to mimic operators on their own side with a view to confusing the enemy who were listening in.

Dummy Lines

The 'Dummy Line' dramatised here was a more sophisticated approach to the evasion line problem than had been previously tried by the Occupiers, especially as the principle behind the idea was that intelligence about the lines was more valuable than their elimination. However, there are few records as to where this scheme actually operated and on how many occasions, although historians M. R. D. Foot and J. M. Langley reports that rumours suggest either Brussels or Antwerp.[4]

SONGS IN THE CANDIDE

'I'll Never Know' (Richards, Osborne)

I'll never know what made him love me
I'll never know just why he's here
I only know that he's my world

What is the reason for his staying
Sometimes I treat him like a child
I only know he's all I love
Sometimes there'll be misunderstanding
When I can't say the words I feel
I hear his footsteps on the landing
Then my life begins again

I'll never know why he adores me
I'll never know just why he cares
I only know my life's all wrong when he's gone
I only know he's all I need

WHERE ELSE HAVE I SEEN..?

Struan Rodger ('Mad' Mike Miller)

David Tate, *Chandler and Co*, 1994

Mr Richardson, *The Fortunes and Misfortunes of Moll Flanders*, 1996

Det Chief Supt Fergusson, *An Unsuitable Job for a Woman*, 1997, 2001

Gideon, *Distant Shores*, 2005

The Face of Boe (voice), *Doctor Who*, 2006-7

© Charles Waite

Anthony Head (Hanslick)

Rupert Giles, *Buffy the Vampire Slayer*, 1997-2003
James, *Manchild*, 2002-3
The Prime Minister, *Little Britain*, 2003-6
Mr Finch, *Doctor Who: School Reunion*, 2006
Uther Pendragon, *Merlin*, 2008

© Chris Coughlan

Steve Gardner (Alec Ashton)

Willy Campbell, *Sutherland's Law*, 1972-3

AB Grogan, *Warship*, 1973-6

Alexander Fleming, *Microbes and Men: The Search for the Magic Bullet*, 1974

Billy Martin, *The Sweeney: Ringer*, 1975

Philip, *Jesus of Nazareth*, 1977

Episode 5: RING OF ROSIES

WRITTEN BY: John Brason   **DIRECTED BY:** Michael E. Briant

FIRST BROADCAST: 7.35pm, Saturday 20 October 1979

STUDIO RECORDING: 4 May 1979

VIEWING FIGURE: 21.3m

REGULAR CAST: Albert Foiret: BERNARD HEPTON; Monique Duchamps: ANGELA RICHARDS; Sturmbannführer Ludwig Kessler: CLIFFORD ROSE; Natalie Chantrens: JULIET HAMMOND-HILL; Major Hans Dietrich Reinhardt: TERRENCE HARDIMAN; Alain Muny: RON PEMBER; Dr Pascal Keldermans: VALENTINE DYALL; Inspector Paul Delon: JOHN D. COLLINS

SUPPORTING CAST: Maitre Guissard: MORRIS PERRY; Zander: ROBERT GILLESPIE; Adam Girton: ROB EDWARDS; Shaw: TIM PEARCE; Jerry Wade: JOHN CASSADY; Gavain: DUNCAN PRESTON; McQuaig: GARETH MILNE; Clint: NICK WILKINSON; Geneviève: TRISHA CLARKE; German Officer: ALAN BUTLER; Jones: MARK ALLINGTON; Wray: CHRISTOPHER HOLMES; Campbell: PETER JESSUP

SYNOPSIS: Early August 1944. A B-17 bomber is in trouble in the skies above Belgium. One of its survivors, McQuaig, is located and whisked away by some local patriots. At the Candide, Monique is up late making arrangements for the movements of more airmen and the delivery of food to those evaders now camping out in the Ardennes. Natalie visits a safe-house that is popularly known as 'the Ritz'. She talks to McQuaig, who has become ill since his arrival and is complaining about a swelling. In prison, Albert meets his advocate, Maitre Guissard. Delon tells Albert that Vercors is behind his arrest and the 'trumped-up' charge of murder. Monique and Keldermans arrive at 'the Ritz'. After examining McQuaig, Keldermans discovers that a few of the other men there are feeling ill and have swellings too. Kessler and Reinhardt argue over their limited resources. After locking the door and appropriating a gun, Keldermans reveals that McQuaig has bubonic plague and that therefore everyone must stay there to stop it from spreading. A man called Shaw makes a break for it and Keldermans shoots him in the leg. Without medicines, all they can do is sit and wait it out, preventing further pneumonic infection by wearing face masks. Monique tells Keldermans that she must be allowed to go in order to run Lifeline, but he threatens to shoot her if she tries to leave. Reinhardt returns from a scouting trip and argues with Kessler once again. Albert fills Alain in on Vercors, while Alain explains that London are sending an SOE man over as liaison while he is in prison. At 'the Ritz', several men have died and many more have become ill. Natalie is worried about Monique's whereabouts but keeps the Candide open for business. Keldermans reveals that he too has now caught the plague. Alain and Natalie arrive and Keldermans tells them, through the door, about the situation and asks Alain to burn the place down, if no-one is left alive, in a week's time. Before leaving for Berlin, Kessler asks Reinhardt if he had any success with breaking Lifeline and berates him for not having progressed any further. Reinhardt asks after Monique at the Candide, and is told that she is visiting her mother who is ill. While Alain and Natalie are bringing provisions to 'the Ritz', one of the infected men, Clint, escapes. They give chase and Natalie shoots him dead and Alain burns the body with a Molotov cocktail. Some time later, Monique, who has escaped the infection, is back at the Candide, entertaining the troops. Reinhardt asks after her mother and about events involving Albert at the old Candide. It is clear that the Major is beginning to suspect their involvement in resistance work. Monique visits Albert in prison and brushes off the terrible events of the past few days as "nothing to worry about."

REVIEW: *Ring of Rosies* is regarded by its cast and crew alike as one of the weakest episodes of the third series. Perhaps its single biggest problem is that its bubonic plague storyline just seems too far-fetched to be believable. However, similarly unfortunate is the confusing – and occasionally inaccurate – exposition delivered in the episode's prison sequences which make the circumstances of Albert's arrest unnecessarily convoluted. Despite these major stumbling blocks there is still much to enjoy here, including a breathtaking action sequence featuring Alain and Natalie and, in the final five minutes, a bravura performance from Angela Richards ending the episode on a high.

In his preface to his novelisation of *Secret Army*'s third series, *The End of the Line*, John Brason reveals that his inspiration for *Ring of Rosies* was a real-life outbreak of bubonic plague which occurred in Northern France in October 1944. That the episode's audience was not privy to this startling fact is a great shame as it is information that, once known, lends the piece some much-needed credibility. Aside from the feeling, as director Michael E. Briant put it, that the episode "lacked a certain reality," other elements of the action at 'the Ritz' are relatively successful. The initial 'all lads together' humour of the evaders, especially of the more ribald American pilots, feels genuine, especially their reaction to Natalie. Given how far they push it, for a time it seems likely that several evaders are going to receive something far more violent from her than a sharp retort; however, Wade's sarcastic but affectionate patter ("Four years! Can you beat that? Why, you must have been all of, what, twelve years old when you started?") eventually melts Natalie's 'ice maiden' act and it is pleasing to see the character break into a radiant smile for the first time in ages.

The development afforded to both Keldermans and Monique during their grim stay at the safe-house is also well-judged. Up until now, Keldermans has rarely functioned as a three-dimensional character in his own right, often being reduced to the thankless role of messenger, but here we get a glimpse of the grit which has spurred him on to work for Lifeline for all these years. Upon discovering what they are up against, he is admirably decisive and quick-witted: taking Monique's gun and locking the door and disposing of the key under it. Similarly, when Shaw makes a break for it, he does not hesitate to shoot him in the leg. Indeed, his determination to keep the outbreak contained even prompts him to threaten Monique: "I'll use that gun, even on you if I have to." We receive further insights into Keldermans's considerable strength of character when he dispassionately reveals that he too has become infected, even finding it possible to make the ironic comment that the immunity of doctors is "a myth fostered by the American cinema." His subsequent clear-headed decision to establish Girton as his 'successor' (thoughtfully sparing Monique the dirty work), and his aim of ensuring that the plague does not spread and thus will not be instantly identified as "deliberate germ warfare," are similarly selfless. For the most part, Valentine Dyall rises to the challenge of a more prominent role for his character, although it is probably fair to say that he is not quite in the same league as the series's other principal actors.

In respect of Monique, Brason commendably does not take the obvious route of transforming her – as the only female present – into a 'Florence Nightingale' character for the period of her incarceration in the safe-house. Instead, far more interestingly, she proves to be of little help to Keldermans, explaining: "I'm no good around sickness... never have been." She is simply concerned, as most of us would be, with her self-preservation. Monique is understandably devastated, and not a little bitter, to be suddenly facing death at this stage of the war, after all she has been through, especially as she has only just won her independence from Albert and begun to prove herself by running Lifeline. Furthermore, she has no difficulty in recognising the irony of the fact that her death will be down to "a filthy disease" and not, as she had expected, due to be being found out by the Germans: "I never thought that we would die like this." This is possibly another factor which contributes significantly to the episode's failure, as after all this time, like Monique, the audience does not want to be cheated of Lifeline's final confrontation with the Germans, nor have the series diverted from its journey towards this inevitable destination into what is effectively a narrative cul-de-sac.

A definite highlight of the episode is Alain and Natalie's location-filmed pursuit of one of the diseased evaders through the derelict rooms below 'the Ritz'. This well-directed sequence concludes in exciting fashion with Natalie showing her mettle by racing after the man and, after his impressive leap to the ground below, filling him full of bullets, before Alain makes sure that the plague dies with him by throwing a Molotov cocktail over his body.

Also enjoyable, albeit for very different reasons, is Monique's performance of the Marlene Dietrich number 'Boys in the Backroom' after her return to the Candide. While Angela's vocals are always worth listening to, this sequence deserves special mention due to the poignant section in which Monique is clearly reflecting on her horrendous experiences at the safe-house – the lighter flame reminding her of the recent (off-screen) burning of the dead bodies – before she recovers from her reverie and belts out the last few lines to her appreciative public. Her demeanour after the song, particularly once she lets her guard down in the Candide's backroom and the fact that, rather uncharacteristically, she seems to have had rather a lot to drink, suggest a woman who is understandably at the end of her tether. Although she is clearly in no fit state to put the inquisitive Reinhardt off the scent in her usual blasé fashion, she nevertheless displays a remarkable fortitude when responding to his questions and manages to keep his suspicions at bay, for the time being at least. In the episode's subsequent and final scene, the fact that Monique elects not to tell Albert the true extent of the danger she has been in may not just be about preventing him from worrying, but rather a sign that she no longer needs, or indeed expects, his support. By keeping the details of the incident to herself she can maintain her hard-won independence, proving that she is now more than capable of coping with whatever life throws at her.

Perhaps the weakest element of an otherwise uniformly superb final series is the convoluted 'Albert in prison' subplot, which becomes even more complex here. That it is Paul Vercors who wants revenge on Albert is strange enough (see episode analysis for *The Last Run*), but quite why he has had him removed from the Candide and sent to prison is even more confusing. Why didn't he just kidnap Albert himself at the end of *Revenge*, or have Benet deliver the restaurateur to him? Although Delon suggests that the reason for Albert's imprisonment is that Vercors may want to try to take over Lifeline while he is out of the way, this does not fit with what the Communist has told Benet. All Vercors has been seen to specify is that he wants Albert to die slowly for what he has done, so the question remains why has he engineered him to be in prison on a charge of murder? The situation is made even more baffling here due to the inclusion of several continuity-ridden conversations which require an encyclopaedic knowledge of *Secret Army* to be understood. Not only are we asked to remember the events of *Not According to Plan*, and specifically Vercors's deal with Kessler which saw him betray Barsacq the cellist, but also Andrée's friend, Mme Celeste Lekeu, a very minor character from the first series who even the most attentive DVD viewer would do well to remember! Furthermore, quite why Mme Lekeu's circumstantial evidence has been gathered now and how Vercors knew of her, or indeed of Andrée's death, is not revealed. Why should he think that Albert will be convicted of Andrée's death when he wasn't there and doesn't know the circumstances? And, moreover, why would he attempt to have Albert legally charged and executed for her murder, when not only is it not his style, but also there is a good chance that Albert might get off? Unfortunately the waters are muddied even further by several related inaccuracies and problems. When referring to the events of *Not According to Plan*, Delon says that they took place "last spring" but does not specify whether he means 1943 or 1944. Either way, both dates are wrong as the events of the episode definitely took place in the autumn of 1943. When Albert talks to Alain during visiting hours, he mentions how a man called Marc tipped Alain off before about the Communists' plans and that they will have to rely upon him to do the same again. He is presumably referring to the tip-off about their plans to kill him in *Revenge*. However, on that occasion the man who passed the information on to Alain was named Dirk, not Marc. Perhaps the biggest inconsistency of all, though, is the fact that in *A Safe Place*, when Delon asks Monique about Paul Vercors, she immediately knows who he is talking about, but when Albert is asked the same question in this episode, he replies that he only knows him vaguely. What is more, Albert and Alain are seen here to learn for the first time that Vercors is behind the former's imprisonment, even though Monique has seen them both several times since meeting with Delon and so for some reason she has not told them despite having no discernible reason for withholding this information. The most obvious explanation for these latter slip-ups and for the confusion surrounding Vercors's intentions is simply the fact that the episodes of the final series were filmed wildly out of order and so errors, particularly chronological ones, crept in as a result. The fact that all the prison scenes were filmed in one block to later be divided up between episodes four to nine as appropriate may also have contributed to the regrettable confusion which surrounds this sub plot.

Throughout *Ring of Rosies* there appears to be a serious and illuminating disparity between Albert's and Monique's views on who is in control of Lifeline. Monique is now indisputably running the Line on a day-to-day basis, as evidenced by her first scenes in the Candide. Indeed, while trying to convince Keldermans that she must be allowed to leave 'the Ritz', she tells him in no uncertain terms: "I am Lifeline now." However, the fact that Albert has gone so far as to actually deny Monique access to the 'London money' along with his reference to her only having "power of attorney" until he comes back, suggests that he sees her role quite differently. The obvious corollary of this scenario is that if, and when, Albert finally does get out of prison, it will be very unlikely that the newly-empowered Monique will be satisfied with a return to her former existence.

Much is also made here of the contrasting views of two other principal characters, Kessler and Reinhardt, over three scenes which are distinctly separate to the main narrative. Once again Kessler refuses to listen to what he regards as defeatist talk, while his colleague is presented as all too aware of the desperate situation the Germans now face. The Major finds not only Kessler's blind optimism difficult to stomach but also his unwillingness to admit to the enemy's obvious successes. Upon hearing Kessler talk of mere "attempts" to get airmen out of the country, Reinhardt's response is a 'no-holds-barred' reality check: "Their 'attempts' have been eighty or ninety percent successful! They're not sending them back, Sturmbannführer, because they don't need them back. They have petrol to burn and they have trained flyers to abandon. They are knocking at our door, man!" He goes on to respond to Kessler's subsequent order – that he should scour the countryside for terrorflieger – with a tart observation about his difficulty in obeying him due to their lack of both petrol and men, thus reinforcing his keen grasp of reality: "Belgium may not be a very big country, Sturmbannführer, but it does take ten men a very long time to cover it on foot!" Although Reinhardt appears to be unafraid of Kessler and even says as much to him, when he responds to the Sturmbannführer's threat to have him "skinned alive" with the line: "I know those powers, Kessler. Europe is littered with such obscenities," he looks as though he realises that he may have finally taken things too far. Kessler's furious expression as he stalks out of the room certainly suggests that he will make him pay for these words.

When compared to the episodes that surround it, *Ring of Rosies* certainly suffers in comparison, especially in respect of its believability and continuity problems; however, it does contain some moments of brilliance, although admittedly these are few and far between.

HISTORICAL BACKGROUND

Bubonic Plague

John Brason cites the real-life outbreak of bubonic plague in Northern France during October 1944 as the inspiration for *Ring of Rosies*, scripting the airman who has come back from a mission to North Africa as its carrier – a plotline which fits with the fact that there were some 95 cases of plague in North Africa (Algeria) in 1944. The episode shares themes with Albert Camus's classic existential novel *The Plague* (1947), generally regarded as an allegory of the German occupation of France, in which the central character is a world-weary doctor, Bernard Rieux, who fights to stop a bubonic plague epidemic in the sealed-off Algerian town of Oran.

SONGS IN THE CANDIDE

'The Boys in the Backroom'

This song was written for Marlene Dietrich for the film *Destry Rides Again* (1939) which concerned a lawman, played by James Stewart, who resolves problems without resorting to violence. Dietrich played saloon singer Frenchy.

See what the boys in the backroom will have
And tell them I'm having the same
Go see what the boys in the backroom will have
And give them the poison they name

And when I die don't spend my money
On flowers and my picture in a frame
Just see what the boys in the backroom will have
And tell them I sighed
And tell them I cried
And tell them I died of the same

And when I die, don't buy a coffin
Of silver with the candles all aflame
Just see what the boys in the backroom will have
And tell them I sighed
And tell them I cried
And tell them I died of the same

And when I die don't pay the preacher
For speaking of my glory and my fame
Just see what the boys in the backroom will have
And tell them I sighed
And tell them I cried
And tell them I died of the same

WHERE ELSE HAVE I SEEN..?

Morris Perry (Guissard)

Charles Moxon, *Special Branch*, 1969-70

Captain Dent, *Doctor Who: Colony in Space*, 1971

Det Chief Supt Maynon, *The Sweeney*, 1975-6

Richard Fenton, *Survivors: Mad Dog*, 1977

Mr Wells, *Agatha Christie's Poirot: The Mysterious Affair at Styles*, 1990

© Peter Berggren

Gareth Milne (McQuaig)

Müller, *Kessler*, 1981

George Cranleigh, *Doctor Who: Black Orchid*, 1982

Tony Bragg, *Bergerac: Treasure Hunt*, 1987

Bryant, *The Inspector Alleyn Mysteries: A Man Lay Dead*, 1993

Edward, *Death at a Funeral*, 2007

© Chris Arthur

Episode 6: PRISONER

WRITTEN BY: Robert Barr   **DIRECTED BY:** Tristan de Vere Cole

FIRST BROADCAST: 7.20pm, Saturday 27 October 1979

STUDIO RECORDING: 20 April 1979

VIEWING FIGURE: 10.7m

REGULAR CAST: Albert Foiret: BERNARD HEPTON; Monique Duchamps: ANGELA RICHARDS; Natalie Chantrens: JULIET HAMMOND-HILL; Major Hans Dietrich Reinhardt: TERRENCE HARDIMAN; Major Nick Bradley: PAUL SHELLEY; Alain Muny: RON PEMBER; Dr Pascal Keldermans: VALENTINE DYALL

SUPPORTING CAST: Hauptsturmführer Klein: ERIC DEACON; Jacot: PRENTIS HANCOCK; Reisener: MICHAEL WYNNE; Paul Frenay: DENIS HOLMES; Bonnier: PAUL ANTRIM; Klaus: BUNNY REED; Postman: RIK BRAVENBOER

SYNOPSIS: 23 August 1944. Alain saves Natalie from being taken for 'service in the Fatherland', but is arrested himself and taken to the Gestapo prison on the Avenue Louise. Major Bradley arrives at the Candide and receives a frosty reception from Monique, who fears he has come to take over Lifeline. He tells her about the situation in Paris and that he has come to help the airmen hiding out in the Ardennes. Dr Keldermans arrives and tells them about Alain's arrest and that there is no sign of Natalie. Monique sends Bradley to Alain's farm to tell Estelle the news and instruct her to leave for Namur with the children. Keldermans introduces Bradley to resistance leader Jacot, who tells him that he has no hope of rescuing Alain. Alain is brought before Hauptsturmführer Klein for questioning.

Klein does not believe that Alain is Jacques Durand of Laeken, as his ID card claims, as none of the people living in Laeken recognised his photograph, so he begins to have him tortured. To Monique and Bradley's relief, Natalie returns to the Candide. She has been in hiding and fearful to come back in case she was being followed. She is pleased that Bradley has returned. Jacot tells Bradley that they may be able to get Alain out by giving the German who takes prisoners for interrogation a bribe of a million francs. Bradley asks Monique if this can be paid using the money sent by London, but she doesn't know. Bradley and Jacot meet the German in question, Reisener, who in addition to the money also demands a letter detailing how he saved the life of a member of the resistance. Bradley agrees to his terms. Monique tells Albert about Alain and asks him if she can have access to the million francs required. Soon after, Bradley discovers for himself that there is not enough money at the Candide for the deal. Reinhardt seeks an audience with Alain as he thinks he may work for an escape line, but he is denied this opportunity by Klein. The Hauptsturmführer subsequently subjects Alain to further torture using an electric shock device. Jacot introduces a rich patriot called Paul Frenay to Bradley, with a view to him putting up the money for their deal with Reisener. In order to make Frenay trust him, Bradley has arranged for a specific radio message to be broadcast by the BBC. Reinhardt tells Klein that his men recognise Alain and that Brandt would have known him, but the relevant file is missing. Bradley tells Natalie about the situation in Paris before they listen to the radio message for Paul. Natalie returns Bradley's 'lucky piece' to him. After receiving the money from Frenay, Bradley and Jacot meet with Reisener, who is now accompanied by Alain's guard, Bonnier, who also wants in on the deal. After agreeing to his price and another letter, Bradley returns to the Candide for this extra money. Natalie wishes him "Good luck." Reisener is unable to get hold of Alain and tries to trick Bradley by handing over another man instead. Bradley threatens Reisener and gives him a second chance to produce Alain. Despite the added complication of an extra guard, who Bradley knocks unconscious, Reisener delivers Alain as promised. While they check their money, Reisener and Bonnier are shot dead by Jacot and Bradley.

REVIEW: *Prisoner* is Robert Barr's last and possibly best script for the series, which is chiefly notable for the rewarding return of the character he created for *Lucky Piece*, Major Nick Bradley. Bradley is once again played with suave and charismatic assurance by Paul Shelley, who clearly 'has a ball' in the role. Plot-wise, Bradley appears just in time as Alain becomes the first regular character to be interrogated at Gestapo Headquarters since Curtis back in *Suspicions*.

There is a decidedly mixed reaction from the Lifeline characters to Bradley's return. Monique's behaviour towards the Major is nothing short of hostile and there is a strong implication that this is not only due to her fears that he has returned to take over Lifeline, but also because, regardless of his intentions, she just doesn't like the man. Admittedly Bradley doesn't make it easy for Monique to like him, particularly in their wittily scripted first scene together, in which his smart comments and wide smiles suggest that he is deliberately goading her. However, perhaps what most infuriates Monique about Bradley is the fact that he has actually come to provide genuine assistance and has a tendency to continually confound her preconceptions. She assumes that he has come to take over and moreover that he will assume that she is not capable of being in charge. However,

417

she is wrong on both counts; in fact his straight reply about her leadership ("I'm sure you're very good at it") suggests that, unlike Albert, he does not underestimate her abilities in the slightest. Their verbal sparring is great fun to watch and at times highly amusing, especially Monique's dry response when Bradley tells her he can pass for a German: "That doesn't surprise me." Perhaps one of the reasons why Monique's barely concealed loathing of Bradley is so convincing is the fact that at the time Angela Richards herself was not altogether pleased that the decision had been taken to bring back Bradley to assist Monique.

In sharp contrast to Monique, Natalie welcomes Bradley's return and even tells him as much ("I'm glad you're back"); however, this is hardly surprising considering she has just learned from Monique that: "This man wanted to blow up trains for you!" The *frisson* between them, which was suggested from their very first meeting in *Lucky Piece*, is once again sensitively handled and continues to be nicely underplayed for the duration of Bradley's return to the series. In a pleasing piece of continuity which suggests that Natalie has never forgotten the Major, we learn that she is still actually carrying his 'lucky piece' around with her. The fact that she gives it back to him, before he carries out the dangerous deal with the Germans also implies that she cares very much what happens to him. Nevertheless, Natalie remains characteristically guarded with Bradley, particularly in those scenes in which he searches for and locates Albert's preciously guarded funds and later returns for this money when the deal changes. However, when he reminds Natalie that Alain's life is more important to her than Albert's money and also that she is free to use his first name, her intonation of the line "Good luck, Nick" suggests a thawing of her ice-cool persona and that, for the first since the tragic death of François, she may come to have feelings for another man. Juliet Hammond-Hill is in sparkling form here and incidentally also at her most glamorous. It is little wonder that Bradley can't keep his eyes off Natalie!

Money, and specifically the relative value that different characters place upon it, is a key aspect of the narrative. Bradley sees it as no more than a means to an end and has no interest in it himself. Meanwhile, Albert is seen – not for the first or last time – to value it more highly than his closest friends. There is even a dark suggestion that, although Monique pleads with him for the million francs needed to save Alain's life, he actually has more money put by than the notes Bradley finds in his second safe. Although both Monique and Natalie defend Albert's use of the regular supply of money from London to Bradley, it was only in the preceding episode that Monique vented her fury over the fact that Albert was going to have Zander give her the money she needed, rather than just granting her full access to the 'London money' – a situation which prompted her to tell Natalie: "He just doesn't want anyone to know how much he's tucking away for himself." If Albert is withholding money here – and there is every indication that he is – this is a terrible indictment on his character. In stark contrast to Albert, wealthy Paul Frenay appears very willing to use his money in order to help others, even though he doesn't know Alain. In fact, if anything, Albert shares more similarities with the greedy Reisener and Bonnier, who at the episode's close give the money a higher priority than their own safety and pay the ultimate price as a result. Will Albert do the same?

Prisoner continues the final series's trend of having each episode crank up the danger level a notch higher. Alain finds himself in a situation which appears very grave indeed and, as a result, Monique's and Natalie's lives are also seen to be at great risk. Bradley is given some incredibly sobering dialogue to emphasise this, advising them: that they may have to "run for the hills"; that if Natalie had been arrested as well as Alain that the Germans "would have had Lifeline by the end of the day"; and in respect of the money, that "an hour's delay could put you all in Dachau." Barr also increases the tension by cleverly using Bradley's recent experiences in Paris – this episode closes the day before it was finally liberated on 25 August 1944 – to preview the chaos that will also characterise Brussels in its last few occupied days. Unlike Klein's report, Bradley relays an accurate picture of the situation there, of: infighting between Communist and moderate resistance groups; public executions; the fate of collaborators; and the laying of explosive charges in principal buildings – all of which suggest that the members of Lifeline are in for a very rough ride in the remaining episodes.

Barr's script originally featured Kessler interrogating Alain, but when it became clear that Clifford Rose would be unavailable for recording, due to a holiday with his family in America, it was decided to send Kessler off to Berlin for his promotion and to introduce a new SS character, Hauptsturmführer Klein, instead. Although Klein is well played by Eric Deacon, he is, and was always going to be, a poor second to Rose. Nevertheless, like many of the new supporting players in *Prisoner*, he is given a distinct and three-dimensional character of his own. Unlike the Sturmbannführer, he is vain (we observe him admiring himself in his hat in the mirror) and sadistic (although Kessler is quite happy to have his prisoners beaten up, he is never seen to take pleasure in their pain). However, while meeting with Reinhardt (who unfortunately has very little to do here), Klein proves that, like Kessler, he is a fervent Nazi who will not question "a Führer Order" or consider its consequences – in this case the destruction of a beautiful city like Paris. Incidentally, Klein responds to a characteristic and entertaining dig from the Major about whether it will become a rule that the Gestapo is always the first to leave, by mentioning the Führer's reprisal weapons. One of these weapons, the Vergeltungswaffe 2, will become central to the plot of the following two episodes.

Prisoner's other deeply unpleasant German is Michael Wynne's Reisener, who unfortunately pays more than a passing resemblance to Steve Pemberton's Herr Lipp character from *The League of Gentlemen*. Nevertheless Wynne, who had previously appeared as Reinecke in first series finale *Be the First Kid in Your Block to Rule the World*, is thoroughly convincing in the role. His initial appearance in a smart business suit and flamboyant hat, for his meeting with Jacot and Bradley suggests that he has a higher status and power than his work uniform and trouble in actually keeping his side of the bargain later reveal. Along with the sadistic Bonnier, there is no chance of his eventual death eliciting any sympathy whatsoever. Interestingly though, Barr's original script does attempt to achieve just that in respect of the guard, Sturmann, who Bradley eventually dispatches by breaking his neck. Barr had intended there to be several scenes en route to the rendezvous which suggested that Sturmann was pleasantly sympathetic to Alain's predicament and showed him giving the prisoner a cigarette. Just before his death, he even details 'a young innocent face, a pity – but it is war.'

Other elements of Barr's script which did not make it into the final episode were: a larger role for Bonnier; far more threats from Bradley and Jacot to ensure that he and Reisener eventually go through with the deal as planned ("Between your home and the prison you will die if you trick us again"); and more detail about how exactly Alain would be collected and delivered, with Bonnier even drawing a diagram in a grimy window to show Bradley and Jacot where Gestapo Headquarters and the Avenue Louise are in relation to the location of their rendezvous.

As resistance leader Jacot, Prentis Hancock gives a far less wooden performance than he usually delivers. He is another character who Barr has put some thought into creating, carving him very much from the same mould as Bradley. He too is intensely practical and possesses an unflinchingly direct manner, thereby ensuring that the pair will automatically understand each other and, during the course of the episode, even become friends.

Ron Pember gives a terrific performance as Alain, who once again proves to be incredibly brave in the face of danger. Not only does he selflessly save Natalie's life in the atmospherically-directed opening scene, but despite horrendous torture – the breaking of his fingers with a truncheon – he does not give away his true identity or the nature of his resistance work, as Monique knew he would not. Although he does not have a huge number of lines, Pember imbues Alain's reactions to his terrifying situation with true emotion and pathos. The only criticism that can be reasonably levelled in respect of Alain's part in the storyline is that, considering his wife's long-trailed fear that he may be arrested, it would have paid dramatic dividends to witness her reaction to the news here. For the same reason, it is also something of a shame that we do not get to see Alain reunited with his Lifeline comrades after his ordeal.

The same derelict house in which Alain and Natalie chased the infected evader in *Ring of Rosies* is used here as the location for Bradley and Jacot's first meeting with Reisener. In the studio, rather than creating a brand new set for Hauptsturmführer Klein, Kessler's office set was redressed instead, a cost-saving measure which Barr himself had suggested. The most elaborate new studio set is the garage with its adjoining office where Jacot works. The set, designed by Raymond London, is surprisingly large and incredibly intricate, boasting stained glass, huge windows, a vintage car and even a spiral staircase. It also features what may be the largest 'No Smoking' sign (Defense De Fumer) in a drama series ever; however we still see one of Jacot's employees walking around with a gitane in their mouth!

Prisoner is quite simply one of the most accomplished and exciting episodes of *Secret Army* thus far. Paul Shelley is an integral part of its success, proving that the decision to bring Bradley back into the fray to drive this and subsequent episodes was an inspired one. This is also a very strong episode for both Monique and Natalie, whose very different respective reactions to Bradley's return also make for compelling viewing.

HISTORICAL BACKGROUND

The Liberation of Paris

From 19 August 1944, the resistance movement sprang into action around Paris. Both Gaullist and Communist groups were expecting the Allies to arrive shortly and built barricades throughout the city. However, as well as fighting the Germans, some also fought each other with a view to post-war political control. A few days later, General Leclerc's French 2nd Armoured Division arrived in the capital, closely followed by the US 4th Division, and seized control. As well as forcing the German surrender, Leclerc's arrival also prevented the Communist takeover that was feared by De Gaulle. As the fighting in Paris began to subside, Howard Marshall, a BBC correspondent, described how: "All along the French advance route soldiers and people are embracing one another, women and children wave French and Allied flags, shouting 'Vive la France! Vive De Gaulle!'"

Ancia and Operation Marathon

When SOE agent Ancia arrived in Brussels in May 1944, he 'experienced great difficulties with the Comète organisation.' Ancia had been tasked with encouraging the Comète evasion line agents to move airmen out of their increasingly overcrowded safe-houses in Brussels and into bivouacs in the Ardennes. Comète were unenthusiastic about 'Operation Marathon', as it was known, and as a result Ancia 'was unable to do much useful work.' As Airey Neave recounts: 'Comète retained the fierce spirit of Belgian independence and the majority of airmen hidden in Brussels remained there.'[5]

WHERE ELSE HAVE I SEEN..?

Eric Deacon (Klein)

Steve Walter, *Survivors*, 1977
Jan-Yves, *Penmarric*, 1979
Mykros, *Doctor Who: Timelash*, 1985
Peter Tranter, *Casualty*, 1987
DC Dennis Hardwick, *Lovejoy*, 1991-4

© Carole Latimer

Prentis Hancock (Jacot)

Vaber, *Doctor Who: Planet of the Daleks*, 1973
Salamar, *Doctor Who: Planet of Evil*, 1975
Paul Morrow, *Space:1999*, 1975-6
McIntosh, *Survivors: A Little Learning*, 1977
Arnold Meyer, *Chocky's Children*, 1985

© Peter Cartwright

Denis Holmes (Paul Frenay)

Major Williams, *The Dark Island*, 1962
Captain Bray, *Poldark*, 1975
Albert Banks, *Survivors: Long Live the King*, 1977
Admiral Fisher, *Reilly:Ace of Spies*, 1983
Colonel Foster-Biggs, *Bergerac: Roots of Evil*, 1990

Episode 7: AMBUSH

WRITTEN BY: N. J. Crisp   **DIRECTED BY:** Michael E. Briant

FIRST BROADCAST: 7.25pm, Saturday 3 November 1979

STUDIO RECORDING: 6 April 1979

VIEWING FIGURE: 12.1m

REGULAR CAST: Albert Foiret: BERNARD HEPTON; Monique Duchamps: ANGELA RICHARDS; Standartenführer Ludwig Kessler: CLIFFORD ROSE; Natalie Chantrens: JULIET HAMMOND-HILL; Major Hans Dietrich Reinhardt: TERRENCE HARDIMAN; Major Nick Bradley: PAUL SHELLEY; Madeleine Duclos: HAZEL McBRIDE; Dr Pascal Keldermans: VALENTINE DYALL; Hauptmann Müller: HILARY MINSTER; Wullner: NEIL DAGLISH

SUPPORTING CAST: Flight Lieutenant Alan Cox: DAVID YELLAND; Henri: BRIAN COBURN; Maître Guissard: MORRIS PERRY; Flight Sergeant Burton: RICHARD SEAGER; Flight Sergeant Watson: DAVID LUDWIG

SYNOPSIS: 26 August 1944. Bradley goes to meet the airmen hiding out in the Ardennes and asks if any of them are air-gunners. None of them are but he recruits two men, Watson and Burton, who have had some military experience. Kessler returns from Berlin as a Standartenführer. Wullner asks him about the state of both Berlin and the Führer. Bradley takes Watson and Burton to meet a Belgian resistance man called Henri at a mine. Henri is trying to repair a Hotchkiss machine gun. Bradley tells the airmen that they need the gun, for some planned attacks on the new V2 weapons, but unfortunately they don't know how to fix it either. Reinhardt is still working through Brandt's files and thinks that the Candide may have something to do with the evasion lines, so he takes another look at everything they have on Albert. At the prison, Albert is attacked as a collaborator. Elsewhere in Brussels, Madeleine is in similar trouble and races back to her flat to hide. Bradley comes to the Candide to ask if there any air-gunners in their safe-houses and is told about a Gunnery Leader called Cox. Bradley explains that he needs Cox to repair a broken machine gun which will be vital to an attack on a convoy of lorries containing parts for V2s. After initially refusing to get involved, Monique agrees to ask Cox if he is prepared to help. Cox is reluctant to do so, especially as he had thought his war was over, but after Monique explains the situation fully he agrees. Kessler is reunited with Madeleine and comforts her when he learns that she has been attacked. Monique tells Bradley that Cox has agreed. Bradley asks for the assistance of Dr Keldermans as he knows there will be casualties after the attack. Cox is taken to the mine and strips the gun down. Meanwhile, a suspicious Reinhardt observes the comings and goings at the Candide. Monique meets Keldermans and they discuss Bradley and his request for the doctor's medical assistance. Kessler urges Madeleine to leave Brussels for Berlin to stay with his brother and later, when they are alone, tells her about the Germans' contingency plans to evacuate the Belgian capital. Madeleine tells him that she is reluctant to leave 'her Belgium'. Cox fixes the gun but warns Bradley that it might jam again, leading the Major to insist that he joins them on the operation. During the ambush, the gun jams and while Cox is repairing it he is shot. Bradley and Henri subsequently discover that the lorries they attacked were empty. Cox is brought to Dr Keldermans at the mine but it is too late to save him. Reinhardt orders Müller to have Monique, Natalie and Keldermans followed day and night with immediate effect. At the restaurant, Monique berates Bradley for Cox's death, especially when she learns that they hit the wrong convoy. A guilt-ridden Monique visits Albert in prison and tells him what has happened.

REVIEW: N. J. Crisp's last contribution to *Secret Army* – which, although broadcast seventh, was actually the first episode of the final run to be recorded – takes the series closer to the liberation of Brussels and Reinhardt ever nearer to learning the truth about the Candide. The episode deals almost exclusively with Bradley's first attempts to curb the burgeoning V2 threat, allowing for some exciting and explosive action. However, it also boasts plentiful character development too, as we see Kessler and Madeleine at their most intimate thus far and Monique continuing to grapple with the responsibilities of leadership.

One way in which we are drawn into the narrative is through the tragic story of young Gunnery Leader Alan Cox, who pays the ultimate price for agreeing to repair a damaged machine gun. Although David Yelland is perfectly acceptable, if a little uncharismatic, as Cox, it is difficult to have that much sympathy for a character who is so unwilling to risk his life for others, especially at such a crucial point in the war. The fact that he has a wife and is the father of a three-month-old child does go some way to explaining his reluctance, as does the fact that psychologically – as he tells Monique – he had begun to think that his war was over; however, neither is enough of an excuse when one considers that all the other characters in the episode, particularly Bradley and the Lifeline regulars, are still risking their lives on a daily basis. Although Bradley comments that "aircrew don't understand personal warfare" and that "they don't like it and they'd only get in the way," given that Cox is an air-gunner, the Flight Sergeant's extreme reaction to the later gun battle seems somewhat over the top. Maybe he has been an air-gunner for too long? After Cox is shot while trying to repair the gun, quite why the decision was taken to append a scene back at the mine, where his death is confirmed by Dr Keldermans, is unclear. Perhaps this is just to show that Keldermans was involved in the aftermath of the operation as arranged?

Monique's overt sensitivity to Cox's reluctance to agree to assist in the operation seems a little out of character, especially as she is now more regularly depicted as hardened to the expedient realities of war. Similarly, her emotional outburst, after Cox's death, in the final prison-visiting scenes does not ring true. Compare this reaction with the concluding moments of *Ring of Rosies*, in which she puts an incredibly brave face on the fact that many men have died and chooses not to tell Albert about the horrendous life-threatening experience she has just endured. Elsewhere in the episode, Monique spends most of her time opposing Bradley on just about anything and everything. She is determined to make him understand that she is in charge and that she doesn't like his attitude: "You're in my country now; we've lived under German occupation for four years. Don't walk in here and try and give orders to me. I'm not your subordinate!" The power-play between the pair is believably performed and very entertaining. This is especially true of their final scene together in which she lets Bradley know just how furious she is about Cox's pointless death. When Monique responds to Bradley's admission that he is to blame for Cox's death, she ends the line: "Oh I do. I do blame you. And now I would like you to leave, Major Bradley," by literally spitting out his name, as if it offends her to use it. She is of course not only angry with the Major, but also with herself for agreeing, against her better judgement, to ask Cox to become involved in the first place.

As well as the rather obvious and unfortunate effect that Bradley's presence has on Monique, the Major's return has also prompted an interesting new dynamic to develop between her and Natalie. Although they are still close, there is a definite sense that Natalie is increasingly finding that she has divided loyalties. Her first scene with Bradley in this episode is played to suggest that if Monique had not appeared to intervene in their conversation then he could well have talked her into providing him access to Cox, and when Monique subsequently refuses to listen to Bradley's demands, Natalie mediates between the pair: "Come on, Monique. It never does any harm to listen." However, when it comes to the crunch, after Monique has made her feelings on the matter known and the Major turns to Natalie for support ("If you can just take me there now, Natalie"), she remains loyal to Monique, agreeing that they cannot help him. However, in the episode's final scenes, after Cox's death, Natalie finds herself once more defending Bradley to Monique: "It's not his fault... he only did what he thought was right." Although Monique does not vocalise her concerns over the way Natalie reacts to Bradley, her facial expressions often suggest disapproval and possibly even a hint of jealousy.

The ambush sequence is very effective, and despite the fact that director Michael E. Briant remembers with some amusement that everyone you see die during it was in every case the same stuntman, Stuart Fell, it doesn't feel cheap, especially as it involves a long gun battle and several very healthy explosions.

However, the episode's other film sequences are unfortunately rather limited and it is a particular shame that rather than seeing Madeleine escape from a mob, this is merely reported action. The nearest we get to witnessing this incident is seeing her desperately trying to open her apartment door while one stray vegetable is limply thrown into shot.

The establishing scenes in which Bradley arrives at the bivouac in the Ardennes and the ambush itself are particularly important for his character, as they successfully establish him as a believable and fearless leader of men who is more than willing to get his hands dirty to achieve his objectives. One side effect of this courageous depiction is that it makes us far less sympathetic than we otherwise might be to Monique's consistent hectoring of the man. Just because she learns that the information the resistance received about the convoy was incorrect, this is by no means reasonable justification for the way she subsequently treats him. As he calmly states: "The resistance had every reason to believe their information was correct. They acted in good faith and so did I." Given how ungrateful Monique always appears to be towards him, and remembering that this is only a few days since he risked his life to get Alain out of the Gestapo prison, it is somewhat miraculous that he is still willing to assist Lifeline.

Now that he has been inside for nearly a month, Albert appears to have finally accepted that he must leave the Line and all its attendant responsibilities to Monique. However, she is not prepared for the fact that Albert views the inevitable feelings of isolation and guilt, that she now has (and that he himself has experienced) as part-and-parcel of leading Lifeline, and is therefore unwilling to offer her the comfort she is clearly seeking: "You're making the decisions now. You don't ask me. You don't apologise to me. You just live with them." Although Albert, once again, only appears in the episode's film inserts, at least one of these provides more interest than the usual prison visit sequences by virtue of the fact that it takes place outside the prison building. The scene in question, which sees Albert receiving a beating from his fellow prisoners due to their belief that he is a collaborator, is deliberately juxtaposed with the scene in which Madeleine escapes from a similar fate. By choosing to include this latter scene immediately after the one featuring Albert, Crisp makes the point that, regardless of their respective guilt, anyone who is believed to be a collaborator is at risk from reprisal, particularly as every Belgian is suddenly a patriot now that the Allies on their way!

Although the fact that Reinhardt is getting closer and closer to uncovering the truth about the Candide ably builds the narrative's momentum, the idea that Brandt kept records of every single visit he ever made to the Candide ("Why did he painstakingly record every visit, even make notes of conversations?") does not ring true. He was certainly suspicious of the original Candide in the aptly named *Suspicions* (due to Curtis's activities and connection with the establishment), but the idea that he strongly suspected the new Candide isn't ever really borne out by the narrative of the second series. In fact, his lack of suspicion of the restaurant

425

was arguably illustrated by the fact that he often chose to use the Candide for clandestine meetings. Furthermore, although it is understandable that Reinhardt would be interested in his predecessor's files, especially as they have already yielded some results, there is no decent explanation as to why he suddenly seems so certain that the Candide is a front for an evasion line. However, it feels a little churlish to criticise a plotline which, after all this time, finally sees the staff of the Candide fall under suspicion, and when we see their files and photos held aloft in Reinhardt's office it is startlingly clear that this is the beginning of the end.

Just as he did in *The Last Run*, Briant decides to utilise one of Monique's songs as the equivalent of a soundtrack to the episode. On this occasion the song is 'That Lovely Weekend' which, given that the episode must take place (although this is not stated or shown on-screen) on Saturday 26 and Sunday 27 August 1944, the last full weekend of the German occupation of Brussels, is an interesting choice.

As we have had the opportunity to follow their relationship from its inception in *Trapped* through to its current state of uncertainty, almost in spite of ourselves we have come to care about what happens to Kessler and Madeleine. As this episode is penned by N. J. Crisp, the creator of Madeleine and most regular contributor to the development of her relationship with Kessler, we are once again treated to several very true and illuminating scenes between the pair. It is readily apparent that Kessler is determined not only to come out of the war alive, but also to have her by his side when it is over: "I intend to survive this war, Madeleine, and I want to ensure your safety." To this end, he hopes to arrange for either his brother in Berlin or his mother in Augsburg to take her in on a temporary basis. Madeleine's evident doubts about the idea, together with the fact that she presumably still has not answered Kessler's sort-of-proposal of marriage in *Revenge*, would seem to suggest that she is unwilling to commit to him. However, after Kessler bares his soul by describing what her presence in his life has done for him ("For my part, I found kindness, consideration, someone who would treat me as a human being in difficult circumstances in a foreign country"), she responds in kind. It is pleasing that she chooses to do so by touchingly referring directly to Kessler's dialogue in *The Big One* about taking the risk of embarking on a relationship with him in order to be "truly alive again," confirming that doing just that, had the very effect he promised her: "You made me realise all myself." This being the case, it subsequently transpires that the main reason why she does not want to take him up on the offer of a haven in Germany is simply that she does not want to leave the country she was born and brought up in: "This is where I belong." This revelation suggests that Madeleine may actually have more in common with Kessler than we previously thought. Her connection with her native country may not be so fierce or all-consuming as Kessler's national pride, but is nevertheless strong enough to prompt her to want to stay in Belgium despite the potential wrath of her fellow countrymen and the related possibility of her making, as Kessler describes it, "a pointless sacrifice." Although he is adamant that she should begin a new life in the Fatherland, when she asks him how he would feel if he was asked to flee Germany and deny his nationality, his thoughtful reaction to her question, suggests that he would find such a prospect almost impossible to bear. It was Briant's brave and inspired decision to enhance the excellent dialogue between the two characters here by electing to have them deliver it while in bed together. Although 'bed scenes' more usually offer sensuality rather than sensitivity, this scene is definitely more about love than lust. In fact, the way the pair touch and kiss each other here is so genuinely affectionate and natural that they come across like a happily married couple and, if anything, rather than suggesting sexuality, their semi-nudity – especially in Kessler's case – suggests vulnerability and honesty instead.

Although *Ambush* contains many individual scenes of merit and highly creditable performances from the regulars, it has neither a complete nor a cohesive feel. Nevertheless, it makes an important contribution to the ongoing narrative by setting the scene for the stunning conclusion to the series that is played out in the uniformly brilliant episodes that follow.

SONGS IN THE CANDIDE

'That Lovely Weekend' (Moira and Ted Heath)

I haven't said thanks for that lovely weekend
Those two days of heaven you helped me to spend
Keep smiling my darling and some day we'll spend
A lifetime as sweet as that lovely weekend

WHERE ELSE HAVE I SEEN..?

David Yelland (Cox)

David Copperfield, *David Copperfield*, 1974
Nick Rumpole, *Rumpole of the Bailey*, 1975, 1978-9
Prince of Wales, *Chariots of Fire*, 1981
Captain Jenkins, *A Dance to the Music of Time*, 1997
George (Poirot's valet), *Poirot: Third Girl*, 2008

© Pat Ward

Brian Coburn (Henri)

Marshall Howe, *The Roses of Eyam*, 1973
Vektaan, *The Tomorrow People: Into the Unknown*, 1976
Uther Pendragon, *The Legend of King Arthur*, 1979
Stanley, *Forever Green*, 1989
Thomas Beverbridge, *Campion: Police at the Funeral*, 1989

Episode 8: JUST LIGHT THE BLUE TOUCH-PAPER

WRITTEN BY: John Brason   DIRECTED BY: Michael E. Briant

FIRST BROADCAST: 7.20pm, Saturday 10 November 1979

STUDIO RECORDING: 1 June 1979

VIEWING FIGURE: 11.9m

REGULAR CAST: Albert Foiret: BERNARD HEPTON; Monique Duchamps: ANGELA RICHARDS; Standartenführer Ludwig Kessler: CLIFFORD ROSE; Natalie Chantrens: JULIET HAMMOND-HILL; Major Hans Dietrich Reinhardt: TERRENCE HARDIMAN; Major Nick Bradley: PAUL SHELLEY; Alain Muny: RON PEMBER; Madeleine Duclos: HAZEL McBRIDE; Dr Pascal Keldermans: VALENTINE DYALL; Hauptmann Müller: HILARY MINSTER; Wullner: NEIL DAGLISH

SUPPORTING CAST: Maître Guissard: MORRIS PERRY; Obersturmbannführer Stroem: BUNNY MAY; Tony Newman: NIGEL LAMBERT; Jerry Wade: JOHN CASSADY; Willi De Hooch: DERRICK SLATER; Geneviève: TRISHA CLARKE; Gestapo Tail: REG WOODS; German Officer: MAX FAULKNER; Paul: KEN MOULE

SYNOPSIS: 29 August 1944. Natalie realises that she is being followed. It transpires that Keldermans also has a 'tail'. Natalie provides Bradley with information on a permanent V2 rocket site at Zandvliet near Antwerp. Bradley intends to do something about it with the help of some airmen. Guissard meets with Albert and tells him that he wants to see the report submitted by the German soldiers who were at the Candide on the night of Andrée's death back in 1943. Much to Monique's annoyance, Bradley engineers dinner with Kessler by posing as a member of Organisation Todt. He manages to learn from Kessler that Obersturmbannführer Stroem has the details of Zandvliet's firing days. Monique berates Bradley for his audacity before he requests her help in obtaining the schedule from Stroem's office. Monique arranges for their regular contact, Willi De Hooch, to get it for him. Bradley and Natalie arrive at a woodland bivouac near Zandvliet and meet the airmen hiding there. The Major explains about the V2 rocket site and his intention to knock it out with their assistance. Meanwhile, De Hooch successfully obtains the rocket schedule. While walking along the Avenue Louise, a group of boys throw rubbish at Kessler. The furious Standartenführer arrives at Headquarters for a meeting with senior officers, including Reinhardt, at which he gives the latest military information in his possession. After quarelling with Reinhardt, Kessler agrees that instead of trying to fight the Allies, they should institute delaying tactics to slow down their advance. After the meeting, Reinhardt tells Kessler that he thinks he will soon know who is running Lifeline. Guissard rouses Reinhardt's interest by asking him for a 1943 report on the Candide, and orders Müller to find it for him to examine first. Geneviève poses as Natalie so that the real Natalie and Bradley can leave the Candide for the attack on Zandvliet without being followed. After collecting the airmen from the bivouac, Bradley and Natalie reach the rocket site area and, utilising a variety of tricks, the Major and an airman called Newman appropriate a staff car which they drive into the compound. While they kill all the German soldiers in the Mess Hall, Natalie, Alain and the other airmen lead a ground assault on the site. After hearing about the ongoing attack Kessler sends Reinhardt there to assess the situation. Soon after, Wullner informs Kessler that the Reichskommissar has withdrawn from Brussels. Before they leave Zandvliet, Bradley and his forces blow up all the V2s as well. On his return, Reinhardt is told by Müller about a message from an informant advising the Major to check on Natalie's whereabouts. At the Candide, Madeleine tells Kessler that she wants to stay with him in Brussels. Kessler tells her that "the war is lost to Germany." Reinhardt arrives and asks Monique if he can see Natalie. Natalie, who has only just arrived back, volunteers her presence to the dismayed Major. He leaves as Bradley arrives. While Monique sings, Bradley dances with Natalie.

REVIEW: John Brason's action-packed *Just Light the Blue Touch-Paper* is a hugely entertaining episode which is characterised by its pace and wit. On the side of Lifeline, Bradley and Natalie take centre-stage as they target a V2 rocket site and each other, while the Germans assess their current position and Kessler finally faces up to the fact that they are losing the war. Although the episode is very much an ensemble piece, both Paul Shelley and Clifford Rose in particular are given the opportunity to shine and neither disappoints.

Secret Army's 'action director', Michael E. Briant, once again achieves the impossible on a BBC budget, making many of the episode's location sequences feel like excerpts from an expensive feature film. The British military base which doubles for the permanent V2 site at Zandvliet is a superb choice of location, not only due to its atmospheric setting on a plain surrounded by brooding foothills and woodland, but also because of its sheer size – an attribute which Briant takes full advantage of through several long-distance shots. As in *Ambush*, Briant does not hold back when it comes to the battle sequences and explosions, and they are once again satisfyingly heavy-duty and realistic. Bradley and Newman's brutal massacre of the soldiers in the Mess Hall, which concludes with another huge explosion and an impressive dive through a serving hatch by a stuntman, is particularly well done and chillingly realised. Due to the understandable absence of an available stockpile of V2 weapons, Briant decided to commission a matte painting instead, which is seen briefly in the foreground when Wade shouts to Bradley: "Hey Major. We gonna blow these too?" And when in pursuit of a suitable finale for the action sequence, he chose to enhance the final explosion with stock footage, rather than resorting to blowing up the British army's base!

Aside from the principal action sequence, several location filmed scenes elsewhere in the episode are worthy of note. Briant elects to present the opening sequence, which features a resistance man observing the arrival of a German officer at Zandvliet, in black and white in order to tie in the newly-filmed action more seamlessly with the available archive footage of a V2 rocket launch. The brief scene which immediately follows, which sees Natalie pursued by a Gestapo 'tail' down a Brussels street, could so easily have been inconsequential but is instead perhaps one of the most beautifully-shot of the entire series, standing out due to the care taken over the relative positions of the subjects to the camera, the use of the sunlight and the switching of focus between the two characters.

One brief scene, viewed from the vantage point of this Café, has Geneviève supposedly disguised as Natalie seeing off Monique, Bradley and the real Natalie. However, for some odd reason, instead we see Juliet Hammond-Hill playing Geneviève pretending to be Natalie, while, even more bizarrely, Trisha Clarke (Geneviève) is playing Natalie who is pretending to be someone else entirely. Confused?!

Throughout the episode there is a real sense that the Lifeline regulars are in very serious danger. This is partly due to the increased threat posed by Reinhardt's investigations, which prompt Bradley to spell out their possible fate ("swinging at the end of a rope") and Monique to stubbornly stand her ground as she declares that she can "handle it enough to keep Lifeline in operation." There is also terrible danger inherent in the V2 operation, as both Natalie and Alain appear more than willing to join Bradley in risking their lives. Fittingly, however, the most suspenseful scene is left until last, as Reinhardt's information about Natalie's absence leads him to go to the Candide just before her return from Zandvliet. Juliet Hammond-Hill conveys Natalie's relief with a huge sigh and an impression that she is still overcome with this emotion when Bradley sweeps her off her feet for the final Viennese waltz. The way things are going, there is an underlying suggestion that not all of them will make it through to the end of the war.

Although, in their first scene here together, Bradley and Monique appear to be sat together rather civilly with Alain and Keldermans, they once again remain at 'daggers drawn' for much of the episode. For instance, it is only minutes before he is questioning her decision not to tell Albert about the Gestapo tails: "You mean you don't want him to think you can't handle it?" Brason subsequently chooses to play their continued conflict to humorous effect, particularly in an immensely enjoyable scene in which Bradley infuriates Monique by choosing to dine at the Candide. We have to admire Bradley's front as he chooses to sit at a table reserved for German officers and quips: "I don't mind if they join me. I don't like them much, but their table manners are faultless," before proceeding to ingratiate himself with Kessler, inviting him to be his dinner guest! Monique's attempt to control her fury is amusing and, although we can appreciate her concerns, our sympathies are very much with Bradley as he enjoys winding her up further by ordering an expensive bottle of Montrachet. Bradley is of course more than capable of dealing with the situation, and Natalie's remark ("He certainly has a lot of cheek. Maybe that's why he's survived all that he has") seems well-observed. It is interesting that, the following day, Monique chooses to reacts to Bradley's antics with a flatly delivered reprimand, presumably so that she does not give him the satisfaction of seeing her lose her temper yet again. Although it doesn't feel much like one, this scene nevertheless marks a turning point in their working relationship as she agrees to cooperate over the rocket schedule and, more significantly – and in stark contrast to *Ambush* – as she permits him access to Lifeline's airmen. Bradley cannot resist commenting on the change in her attitude, with the line: "You see? It can be relatively painless."

Monique may not be able to hide the fact that she dislikes the Major (he only asks her to call him Nick precisely because he knows she never will!), but she is seen to be learning to adjust to both his presence and his demands.

Bradley finds much more favour with Natalie who, now that her Lifeline work is effectively over, is eager to throw herself into the missions he devises. Unlike Monique she appears to enjoy his game-playing and although she is shocked when he enters the Candide on the night he dines with Kessler, she observes him with smiling eyes and later defends his actions, receiving a flat rebuke from Monique for her interference: "This is between Bradley and me." We already know that, on his return to Brussels, Bradley was quite prepared to blow up trains for Natalie, and here we receive further proof of his intentions towards her. As well as openly flirting with her ("They'll watch you. Well, I would!"), when he and Natalie arrive at Zandvliet he finally gets the opportunity to kiss her and not just on the cheek. Their first kiss is for the benefit of the passing Germans, but Bradley takes advantage of their close proximity for a second, far more urgent and passionate, kiss after they have gone. Natalie is clearly surprised by his ardour and although she instinctively attempts to resist him, she doesn't find the experience altogether disagreeable, merely responding with the line: "I must go." Before she does, he invades her personal space again by suggestively holding her blouse between his fingers, telling her: "Be careful." Given the context of their connection here, it seems entirely possible that the sexual attraction between the pair is heightened by the dangerous nature of the task ahead of them and the associated flow of adrenalin. As the subsequent action sequence bears out, both are as brave and heroic as the other; indeed, Natalie actually gives the signal for the attack to begin, before fearlessly running forward with the airmen, and there is a sense that this common bond might be a part of the reason for their attraction to one another. However, whether there is anything more substantial to their feelings than this mutual attraction is for the moment left unsaid. The success of the 'Bradley and Natalie' subplot is in no small part due to the obvious chemistry between Shelley and Hammond-Hill, which makes the relationship between their characters thoroughly believable.

The Security Headquarters conference, which begins with Kessler and Reinhardt trading sarcastic jibes (Kessler: "Is it the habit of the Luftwaffe to hold back in the office as it does in the air?"; Reinhardt: "I am trying to adjust to a front line desk in Brussels... it is such a shock after the nursery slopes of the Russian Front"), is brilliantly scripted. As the meeting progresses, Stroem ("Is it not possible to make a stand?") and the surprisingly 'gung-ho' Müller ("Surely there will be superior forces retreating to add to the complement?") are presented in stark contrast to the brutally realistic Reinhardt, who revels in putting them right. His response to Müller that "If they were superior forces they would not be retreating!" is particularly amusing. Although Kessler pulls him up for what he considers to be a defeatist attitude, he does at least appear to finally recognise that Reinhardt is being realistic.

The conference scene also offers another illuminating perspective on the Standartenführer (on a matter which even affords him a specific mention in John Ramsden's recent non-fiction work *Don't Mention the War*, which examines British attitudes to Germany), namely Kessler's order that the paperwork they have produced since their occupation of Brussels began in 1940 should be: "...accorded priority in vehicle transport from the city," and the additional directive that: "Nothing is to be omitted... the structure of the Reich is founded upon thorough and accurate records. No personnel are to have priority over records – is that clear?" Whether this is too much of a German stereotype is a debate beyond the scope of this book, but it is fair to say that these orders fit with the mentality of the person we have come to know over the course of the series.

The title of the episode refers just as much to preparations for an explosive finale for the series as a whole, as it does to the attack on the Zandvliet V2 rocket site. Reinhardt, more than any other character, is the catalyst for the former, due to his motivation to complete the mission with which he has been charged: to eliminate the evasion lines. However, it transpires that he views the task in a very different way to his SS colleague. When referring to the identity of Lifeline's leader, Reinhardt remarks: "It's academic now of course, but I could never resist a puzzle." It is an attitude for which Kessler immediately rebukes him: "It's not academic, I want their leader. I want to see him and I want to see him dead!" Despite Kessler's anger, their difference of opinion does not seem wildly significant; however, it will ultimately lead to the Major's downfall.

Kessler's final scene of the episode, which he shares with Madeleine at the Candide, is notable not only for the latter's new-found commitment to him ("I don't want to leave you"), but also due to his revelation that, because of his recent visit to Berlin, he is now resigned to the fact that "the war is lost to Germany." Although this fact wounds him deeply – his pronunciation of the word "lost" emphasising just how much – it seems entirely fitting that he is, nevertheless, far more distressed about the state of mind of his Führer. For the duration of the series, it has been clear that, to Kessler, Hitler *is* Germany. Given this fact, when he learned in Berlin that his glorious leader was "no longer himself," an obvious consequence was for him to finally come to terms with the fact that Germany would not win the war. Due to the many evils that Hitler perpetrated we cannot help but find Kessler's heartfelt tribute ("I would have given my life for him, willingly, and with pride") disturbing, but it is nevertheless a historically faithful, and therefore important, reflection of the awe he inspired in his followers. As Brason noted in his original script: 'I think this point is important and should be made for what it is, not fatuous or funny, but very genuine to those who followed him.' Rose invests his dialogue with just the right amount of emotion and gravitas, making the scene both captivating and memorable.

The only element that really mars an otherwise perfect episode is the 'Albert in prison' subplot, which continues to be as convoluted as it is confusing. While Guissard's new aim – to obtain the report lodged with the German authorities about the night Andrée died – is understandable, why he repeatedly asks Albert if there could be anything in the report that could be incriminating is not immediately obvious. It can only be clear to the most attentive viewer that Guissard already knows about Lifeline and so is not in fact pushing for any sort of revelation and instead is just trying to ascertain if any Lifeline-related activities occurred that evening which might give Albert away in the report in question. Regardless of what Albert can remember, Guissard does not appear to realise that just the simple act of asking for the report from the very German who has been charged with wiping out Lifeline might prompt him to consider Albert and the Candide in a new light. Unfortunately, this subplot is once again left hanging in an unresolved and unsatisfactory manner.

Angela Richards remembers that Michael E. Briant "always wanted me to sing all the time" and, on the evidence of this episode at least, this certainly seems to be the case. Here Monique sings no less than three (very different) numbers: the upbeat 'Valentina' is followed later by a sultry rendition of Richards's own 'Velvet Blue', while the episode closes with a rousing version of 'Under the Bridges of Paris'. Spaced out as they are across the narrative, all three help to vary the mood and pace of the episode. The fast-paced waltz time signature of the final number is particularly effective in the way that it echoes the momentum of the series itself as it moves at a relentless pace towards its finale.

The idea that these are the last few days of the German Occupation is successfully conveyed throughout the episode, giving the proceedings a tangible air of nervous expectancy. However, nowhere is this achieved more effectively than in the episode's final moments, via Bradley's loaded response to Kessler: "It is late for us all," and the subsequent sweep back to show the Candide full of dancing couples and carousing diners, all apparently oblivious to the chaos and danger ahead of them.

Through its inventive plotting and vivid characterisation, *Just Light the Blue Touch-Paper* proves to be an almost perfect distillation of *Secret Army*'s defining elements, and is therefore undoubtedly one of its finest hours.

HISTORICAL BACKGROUND

The V-Weapons

From mid-1944, Hitler's last hopes of victory rested almost entirely on the Vergeltungswaffe (Reprisal Weapon) programme, which saw the development of the V1 pilotless aircraft (nicknamed 'doodlebugs') and the devastating V2 rockets, which were developed at a research base in Peenemunde on the Baltic coast. The V1s first landed in England in June 1944, while the V2s followed in September, the first hitting streets in Chiswick and Epping on 8 September 1944, a full five days after the liberation of Brussels. The V2s, which had an operational range of

234 miles caused greater destruction than the V1s because of the high-pressure shockwave produced by its speed of arrival – three times the speed of sound, a fact that meant that, unlike with the V1, there was no audible warning of its arrival.

SONGS IN THE CANDIDE

'Under the Bridges of Paris'

A popular French song written in 1931 by prolific French composer Vincent Scotto and lyricist Jean Rodor. The original French title is 'Sous les ponts de Paris'. The English lyrics were written by Dorcas Cochran. The song was popularised in the Fifties by both Dean Martin and Eartha Kitt.

How would you like to be
Down by the Seine with me
Oh what I'd give for a moment or two
Under the bridges of Paris with you

Darling I'd hold you tight
Far from the eyes of night
Under the bridges of Paris with you
I'd make your dreams come true

'Velvet Blue' (Richards, Moule)

Velvet blue,
the way I feel about you
Can't go on if living is without you
Won't you stay a little longer tonight
And I'll pray that we can make it alright again
Velvet blue,
this feeling that I'm lonely
Without you to be the one and only
Won't you hear my plea
And stay with me
And make my wish come true
If you do I'll no longer be
Velvet blue

WHERE ELSE HAVE I SEEN..?

Bunny May (Stroem)

Hermes the Messenger, *Up Pompeii*, 1970
Various, *Rutland Weekend Television*, 1976
Bostock, *The Bounder*, 1983
Assistant Manager, *Duty Free*, 1984
Big Ron, *London's Burning*, 1989

© Unknown

434

Trisha Clarke (Geneviève)

Customer, *Secret Army: Radishes with Butter*, 1977
Mutoid, *Blake's 7: Games*, 1981

© Unknown

Derrick Slater (Willi De Hooch)

Security Guard, *Doctor Who: The Seeds of Death*, 1969
Charlie, *The Brothers: The Party*, 1972
Mr Ford, *Take an Easy Ride*, 1976
Tom, *Treasure Island*, 1977
Joe, *A Tale of Two Cities*, 1980

Episode 9: SOUND OF THUNDER

WRITTEN BY: Eric Paice   **DIRECTED BY:** Tristan de Vere Cole

FIRST BROADCAST: 7.20pm, Saturday 17 November 1979

STUDIO RECORDING: 15 June 1979

VIEWING FIGURE: 12.9m

REGULAR CAST: Albert Foiret: BERNARD HEPTON; Monique Duchamps: ANGELA RICHARDS; Standartenführer Ludwig Kessler: CLIFFORD ROSE; Natalie Chantrens: JULIET HAMMOND-HILL; Major Hans Dietrich Reinhardt: TERRENCE HARDIMAN; Major Nick Bradley: PAUL SHELLEY; Alain Muny: RON PEMBER; Madeleine Duclos: HAZEL McBRIDE; Wullner: NEIL DAGLISH

SUPPORTING CAST: Maitre Guissard: MORRIS PERRY; Jean Lamotte: DAVYD HARRIES; Jacques: GRAHAM WESTON; Marie: MAUREEN MORRIS; Farrier: JOHN WHITE; Van Hoyt: PAUL SEED; German Corporal: HAROLD SAKS; Jacques Gavain: DUNCAN PRESTON; Geneviève: TRISHA CLARKE

SYNOPSIS: 2 September 1944. The Allies are now in Belgium and the Germans are making final preparations to withdraw from Brussels. A group of Belgian workers accuse Monique and Natalie of collaboration and openly threaten them. Kessler and Reinhardt discuss the current situation. The Major is still intending to uncover Lifeline in the time he has left in the city. Alain arrives at the Candide and Natalie tells him about what happened earlier. He offers her and Monique temporary lodgings at his cousin's farm. Bradley observes the Germans planting explosive charges under the Hôtel de Ville and discusses with Monique whether they are dummies or not. Monique and Natalie discuss Alain's offer and elect to stay together at the Candide. Bradley questions Natalie's decision, but she is adamant. Guissard tells Albert, who is now desperate to be released, that a hearing of his case has been called for 3 o'clock that afternoon. Reinhardt and Kessler lunch together at the Candide. Meanwhile, Alain returns to the restaurant and tells Monique that the work of Lifeline is officially over and that a Special British Intelligence unit will contact her when the Allies' spearhead force arrives. The Major tests Monique by suggesting that she set up a new restaurant for them behind enemy lines. She declines his offer. Gavain tells Albert that he thinks he would be attacked as a collaborator if he were released. Bradley meets a group of resistance leaders in a bar to discuss where the Germans have been laying explosives. Jean Lamotte, one of the men who threatened Monique and Natalie earlier, is present and questions Bradley's credentials. Monique and Natalie discuss the liberation and Reinhardt's suspicions. After leaving the meeting, Bradley has to elude a German soldier who believes him to be responsible for an ambush on a motorbike and sidecar. Reinhardt tells Kessler that he suspects that Albert is Lifeline's leader. Guissard calls Monique to tell her that Albert's release papers are due to be signed and she sets off for the prison. Wullner informs Kessler that Madeleine has been attacked and has been calling for him. He tells her he will see her shortly. Lamotte breaks into the Candide and Natalie confronts him with a meat knife. He tries to extract information from her about Bradley and Lifeline, but she will not be drawn. Bradley returns to the Candide and Lamotte tells him about an evader hiding out at a bus depot, who needs their assistance. Albert's release is delayed. When Guissard finally arrives, he tells him that he will not be released until the following morning. Kessler finds Madeleine in a bad way and tries to comfort her. They discuss their relationship and do not agree on what matters in life. Natalie has dressed as a nurse in order to carry out the mission detailed by Lamotte and leaves the Candide. Bradley realises that Lamotte is Reinhardt's agent and shoots him. Monique returns from the prison and Bradley tells her that Natalie is walking into a trap. Bradley sets off to find her, taking the half-dead Lamotte with him. After dumping his body, Bradley finds himself cornered by a German soldier and is shot dead. Natalie returns to the Candide having decided not to go through with the plan. Reinhardt believes he now has all the information he needs.

REVIEW: Eric Paice's first of two contributions to the series is a terrifically suspenseful episode, which is perhaps best remembered for the sudden and unexpected death of Major Bradley. However, it is also notable for particularly engaging and thoughtful performances from Juliet Hammond-Hill and Clifford Rose, as the plot focuses on the respective challenges faced by Natalie and Kessler as the Germans make their final preparations to leave Brussels.

This is the first of only three episodes in the entire series to concentrate on events which take place over a single day. Although this does not exactly make the series feel like *24*, it is nevertheless a highly effective way of cranking up the narrative tension and tying events in with the series's rich historical setting – in this case, the last full day of the German Occupation of the city: 2 September 1944. The same dramatic dividends are assured in the following two episodes as they too adopt this storytelling structure, portraying the day on which the Allies arrive (*Collaborator*) and the first full day of Brussels as an 'open city' (*Days of Judgement*), respectively. The passage of time is also a key component of the narrative. The Germans now have very little time left in the city and it is stated that Reinhardt only has 24 hours left to crack Lifeline. Elsewhere, Albert is naturally obsessed with the time of his release from prison, while the imposition of strict curfew hours also informs the action.

The choice of episode title is highly appropriate, not only as it emphasises the fact that the Allies are now close enough to Brussels so as to be heard, but also because it aptly describes the episode's soundtrack, which is constantly peppered by the noise of distant barrage and gunfire. That the artillery sounds like thunder is specifically referred to by factory worker Marie, who relates how her little girl mistakenly thought that a storm was coming, an observation which is not literally accurate, but nevertheless a fair description of the upheavals they are all about to experience.

The first few Candide-set scenes are intended as a timely reminder that, as has been previously hinted, the locals may well seek to punish Monique and Natalie as collaborators once the Germans withdraw from the city despite their innocence. Unfortunately, these scenes don't quite work, mainly because the scenario feels so artificially engineered. For one thing, it seems strange that a high-class restaurant like the Candide is open to factory workers so early in the morning (scripted as 8am), especially as this is something we have never witnessed in the series before now. For another, it doesn't seem at all likely that such a group would actually choose to drink there rather than at the sort of bar that Bradley later visits. It is possible that the factory workers only elected to pay the Candide a visit in order to threaten its staff, although they do not round on Monique and Natalie from the outset. The other possibility, given the episode's later revelation, is that Lamotte persuaded the others to accompany him there so that he could pursue his undercover investigation for Reinhardt. Such issues aside, these scenes also fail to convince due to poor performances from the supporting cast. Maureen Morris as the aforementioned Marie, and Graham Weston as Jacques, are unfortunately as wooden as the bar they are standing at. Marie's overtly sentimental soliloquy about her little girl and the 'black ghosts' is especially dire, although to be fair it is difficult to tell whether this is down to Morris or the script.

Paice chooses to give Natalie the majority of the Lifeline dialogue and action, and throughout the episode we witness her display a variety of emotions as she reacts to the events unfolding around her. Given all that she has done for her country, it is easy to empathise both with Natalie's outrage over the accusation, made by the "one-day patriots" in the Candide, that she has been sleeping with the Germans, and with the temptation she feels to tell them the truth. The fact that Natalie, like her Lifeline colleagues, cannot prove her patriotism without compromising the security of their operation – which has always sought to outwardly appear to be a venture run by collaborators – is a well-developed paradox that has been at the heart of the series since its earliest episodes. When Alain suggests that she leave Brussels with him, Natalie initially objects on the grounds that she must stay behind for Monique's sake. She realises that this decision invites danger, and admits to Bradley that she knows it does not make much sense, but that her loyalty to a woman who has become her closest friend is more important than her own safety. However, when Bradley pushes her further on the matter ("You're a clever girl, but you're not being particularly clever at the moment!") it becomes clear that her loyalty to Monique is only part of the reason, and that another is that she simply cannot contemplate missing out on witnessing the liberation of Brussels: "I want to see the Germans run! And I want to see your troops arrive. And I've waited too long for that day. No-one is going to cheat me of it!" It is clear that she is not after glory, but that she needs this final payoff in order for all her efforts and all the sacrifices she has endured to have been worthwhile. This desire seems especially reasonable as this is the dramatic ending which viewers also crave given their long-term commitment to the series.

Following their passionate kiss in *Just Light the Blue Touch-Paper*, little time is given over to further development of the romantic attachment between Natalie and Bradley. Although the Major is clearly very keen to get Natalie to safety, he makes no further advances towards her. Natalie herself is very practical about the place she may hold in Bradley's affections, having clearly prepared herself for his presence in her life to be merely temporary: "Your job is nearly over. You'll be moving on." However, her tone hints that she may well be searching for confirmation of this fact from him. As in the last episode, in their final scene together it is once again suggested that the attraction they share relates in some way to their recognition of, and respect for, each other's heroic qualities. Despite the terrible risks, Natalie is going out on to the streets of Brussels to carry out her very last job, and Bradley realises all too clearly that it may also be her very last act. In her refusal to lie low as instructed, it seems as though Bradley sees in Natalie something of himself and is impressed by her bravery. His last words to her, which are rendered more significant and portentous by the fact that they are delivered in the past tense – "The bravest girl I ever knew" – make the extent of his affection and respect for her readily apparent. Although they only kiss each other's cheeks before they part, their goodbye remains intensely passionate. The episode's closing shot, of Natalie's reaction to the news that Bradley has not returned from looking for her, also confirms her feelings for him.

Natalie's involvement in the Lamotte subplot also deserves a mention, particularly her choice of a huge meat knife with which to defend herself from him, which neatly echoes Monique's comment that this will be Lifeline's 'Night of the Long Knives'; while her hostile instruction after providing him with a drink – "Drink that up quickly, please" – is priceless and arguably the best delivered line of the episode.

Although the close bond between Natalie and Monique is strongly emphasised by their decision to stay with each other at the Candide, thankfully this element is not overplayed. However, Paice's directions in the camera script suggest that the scene in which the pair tidy the Candide together was originally intended to be handled in a more overtly sentimental manner: 'In the sudden release of tension they each embrace each other. Tears in Natalie's eyes. Monique pulls herself together.' Whether the decision to keep the characters' emotions more 'in check' on this occasion was that of the actors or the director, it is a very good one and inkeeping with the fact that the pair have learnt – particularly while Albert has been in prison – to control their emotions and get on with the task in hand. It is also possible that this element was played down at the behest of the production team, as Richards remembers that they were always wary of portraying their relationship as too close for fear of lesbian overtones.

Once again, the differences of approach favoured by Kessler and Reinhardt are examined in some detail. Although we know from the previous episode that Kessler is all too aware that Hitler is no longer himself and that therefore he believes that the war is effectively over, he still refuses to use the word 'defeat' and continues to extol his Führer's infallible nature: "We see only a part of the picture here. The Führer sees it all!" The Major is far less convinced of this: "He sees only what he's told by his acolytes. And maybe what his stars foretell – disaster!" Although Kessler has more information than Reinhardt does on the situation in Berlin, he is presented as dangerously ignorant of what is actually going on around him in Brussels: while he is still relying on second-hand reports and phone-calls to ascertain the current picture, a fact which leads him to comment that "one hardly knows who to believe," Reinhardt, in stark contrast, has actually gone out on to the Ghent road to see for himself and is incredulous that Kessler is still so blinkered: "Open your eyes and ears, man!"

Despite the bleak outlook for the German forces, neither Kessler nor Reinhardt seem unduly distressed by the situation. In fact, Reinhardt is seen to almost thrive on the uncertainty, particularly enjoying the reactions of the locals to his presence in the Candide – quipping that his quiet fellow diners must be "mourning the lack of vegetables" – and more broadly to the prospect of a German withdrawal. His playfulness even seems to extend to making what Kessler describes as a "stupid promise" to Monique: offering to set her up in business behind the new German lines. However, this being Reinhardt, there is more to his proposal than first meets the eye – presumably he wants to see how she reacts now that he is almost certain that she is a Lifeline agent.

While Reinhardt remains determined to solve the Lifeline puzzle before he leaves Brussels, Kessler too is, as Bradley observes, "Game to the last!" – doggedly reminding Belgian citizens in no uncertain terms that the Germans are still in command, by ordering both the burning of a Belgian flag in the Grand Place and a house-to-house search after his men are attacked. However, just as he always feared it might, for the first time Kessler's work-life is set to face disruption due to his relationship with Madeleine Duclos. Initially he attempts to juggle these conflicting demands, as demonstrated by the scene in which he manages two phone-calls – one from a distressed Madeleine and the other from one of his subordinates – however, he quickly, if unwillingly, recognises that the former requires his full attention. Despite the fact that Madeleine has just been attacked, after he arrives at her apartment Kessler behaves in a distinctly unsympathetic manner. When she clings on to him as he first attempts to leave, it does seem that he agrees entirely with her observation that "there's nothing more irritating than a weeping woman." However, his cold response is proved to have far less to do with his feelings for Madeleine and far more to do with the fact that, against his better judgement, he has finally had to neglect his duties for her sake.

The internal conflict this causes him is brilliantly demonstrated by the passionate kiss he shares with her before he pulls away, guilt-ridden.

Unlike Madeleine, Kessler has never feared that their relationship might be untenable, only that it might cause his judgement to become clouded. However, Madeleine once again expresses further misgivings about it here. On the subject of their respective nationalities, she recognises that Kessler has no comprehension of the idea that she could regard being his mistress as betraying her birthright, assuming instead that she will happily become his wife and therefore take on full German citizenship and nationality. As she pointedly observes: "Nothing would convince YOU to betray Germany, nothing would make you change your allegiance. But you expect it of me." Kessler neatly sidesteps this accusation by concentrating on the fact that he has never asked anything of her previously and by ignoring the fact that he is actually asking her to leave Belgium with him now. However, he singularly fails to convince her that her views are "nothing more than sentimentality." Furthermore she finds his opinion that: "there are no longer absolutes... only expedients," to be entirely abhorrent, advising him: "Then I am not sure I want to go with you, my darling. There are such things as right and wrong." This speech, beautifully delivered by McBride, suggests that Madeleine may have finally realised that she has previously misjudged the extent of Kessler's zeal and glimpsed her lover's true colours for the first time. His insistence that: "The only thing that matters is to survive," and his startling belief that: "Germany will rise again, never fear. We will rise with the Fatherland when it does... there is nothing else," are disturbing to say the least. This speech, more than any other in the series, lays the groundwork for *Kessler* – Brason and Glaister's spin-off from *Secret Army* – perfectly, centring as it does around the theme of survival ("I am a natural survivor, Madeleine") and the terrifying prospect of *Der Tag*: the revival of the Nazi Fatherland through the work of the Kameradenwerk. Remarkably, Paice manages to give Kessler an even harder and more fanatical edge here, primarily because he chooses to directly juxtapose his totally unpalatable beliefs with his love and affection for Madeleine. This contrast, coupled with a tremendous performance from Rose which just exudes menace, reminds us that Kessler is a truly warped human being.

Although location filming is fairly limited as usual, there are a pleasing amount of scenes filmed in the Grand Place itself. Bradley passes the reliefs of Charles Buls and Everard 't Serclaes in the passageway opposite the Candide, while Kessler is seen in the square for the first time as his vehicle is parked up outside the Hôtel de Ville. Another first is the view down into the Grand Place from a floor above the Candide (the script specifies the 'mansard' window). Given the sense of reality that such location work lends the episode, it is unfortunate that the scenes set at the Candide's side door, in the Rue des Harengs, had to be recorded later in the studio. Paice's script also suggests that several location scenes should be filmed in a suitably industrial district of Brussels, but director De Vere Cole opted for a (presumably cheaper) UK-based alternative: the

London Borough of Southwark by the Thames. Most notable of these sequences was Bradley's final scene, which was filmed on the steps of London Bridge.

Throughout the episode, there is repeated signposting that not only may Monique and Natalie ultimately have to face the judgement of the mob after the German withdrawal, but that, together with Bradley, their lives are in very real danger during these last desperate hours of the Occupation. Lamotte, who is incidentally one of the episode's few three-dimensional supporting characters, rather poetically describes the Germans' new 'shoot first, ask questions later' approach as: "The final snarl of the wounded tiger, before he turns tail and runs." In line with this, Paice's script unashamedly plays with the viewers' expectations as to which of the series's regulars will become the victim of this wounded tiger by periodically placing each character in potentially fatal situations throughout. Bradley is first in the firing line, quite literally, when he becomes caught up in a motorcycle ambush after his meeting with Brussels's resistance leaders. However, he escapes this close confrontation with a trigger-happy German unscathed. Next up, we have the news that Albert's release is due to be signed, which prompts Monique to impulsively leave the relative safety of the Candide to make her way to the Havenlaan prison, despite the fact that she might not make it back before the curfew. The danger this puts her in is emphasised by Natalie's obvious concern at this decision: "You're surely not going to the prison now?!" A little later, Natalie's decision to take on the mission outlined by Lamotte is presented as a similarly perilous risk, especially as the script rather ominously has Natalie describing the job as the last she'll have to do and Bradley providing a past-tense eulogy about her bravery. After she has gone, the revelation that Lamotte is a double agent appears to confirm that we may well be losing Natalie. However, in the last few minutes, Paice once again subverts our expectations by having Bradley go out onto the streets of Brussels again to look for her. It is at this climactic point in the narrative that he, rather than Natalie or Monique (both of whom return to the Candide unharmed) becomes the unexpected victim of German gunfire. Bradley's death is sudden as well as unforeseen, and the decision to not have him die as heroically as he lived, in line with *Secret Army*'s admirable determination to avoid clichés, is an important one. Although he is out looking for Natalie and pays the ultimate price because of this, he does not die as a direct result of saving her life, but is instead dispatched effortlessly and unceremoniously for no other reason that being in the wrong place at the wrong time.

Although Bradley has been crucial to the plot of this and the three preceding episodes, it is surprising that there is no mention of him whatsoever in the subsequent episode, especially as it starts the very next morning. Even Natalie, who was affected by his presence more than anyone, is not given the opportunity of a scene in which to mourn his loss. However, this presumably has more to do with the fact that there is already so much going on in *Collaborator*, rather than being a deliberate decision to ignore the considerable contribution that Bradley has made to the third series. Once again, Paul Shelley gives a thoroughly engaging and charismatic performance, ensuring that we are suitably saddened by his character's sudden and shocking demise.

A far less difficult goodbye is said to the irritatingly fastidious Maitre Guissard, whose unending exposition relating to the chances, and later the terms, of Albert's release is torturous in the extreme. When it is finally confirmed that Albert's stay in prison is indeed almost over, it is perhaps as much a relief to the viewer as it is to Albert! Throughout its duration, this prison plot strand has remained inconsistent, unnecessarily confusing and surprisingly poorly executed. Another weak, if minor, element of the prison scenario has been the horribly miscast – and therefore distinctly odd – prison guard, Gavain, played by Duncan Preston, who would later prove himself far more suited to comedy when he became one of Victoria Wood's repertory of actors.

Arguably, the most important knock-on effect of Albert's enforced absence from the Candide, and therefore from the work of Lifeline, has been the elevation of Monique to the positions of restaurateur and leader respectively, a development that has principally forced her to become considerably more independent. It is interesting therefore that she reacts to the news of Albert's release with such unbridled enthusiasm ("That is wonderful! Thank God!"), especially as his return inevitably threatens to put her back where she was when the final series started: unfulfilled, underestimated and frustrated with her lot in life. Thankfully the series's remaining scripts address this situation sensitively and intelligently, and although Monique's reaction here suggests that she still seeks a happy ending with Albert, the reality is that the challenges she has faced over the last long month have changed her in such a way that it will be impossible for the pair to simply take up where they left off.

Although *Sound of Thunder* boasts perhaps the weakest supporting cast in the entire series – with the obvious exceptions of the dependable Davyd Harries and Morris Perry – thankfully the regulars are in immaculate form and for the most part it stands as an engrossing episode which marks the beginning of the end for *Secret Army* in some style.

HISTORICAL BACKGROUND

Laying Charges

In late August 1944, Germans laid charges under a selection of prominent buildings in Brussels, including the Palais de Justice (left), the Military Academy and the Theatre Royal, with a view to the arrival of the Allies. On the eve of the city's liberation, in early September 1944, the retreating Germans elected to start a fire in the Palais de Justice. As a result, the cupola collapsed and part of the building was heavily damaged. The charges in the Palais and the other buildings were all successfully cleared by British sappers later that same month.

Sepp Dietrich

Senior SS figure Sepp Dietrich, whom Reinhardt describes here as the Führer's blue-eyed boy who probably doesn't know where half his tanks are, had been given command of the SS First Panzer Division by Hitler for the Normandy campaign in June 1944. During the campaign, Hitler rejected Dietrich's plan to withdraw to territory that was easier to defend as cowardly, despite the fact that Dietrich had previously made several skilful tactical withdrawals in Russia. When news of the 20 July bomb plot broke, Dietrich volubly expressed his outrage, however it is widely asserted that Dietrich had sworn loyalty to Rommel over the Führer. Hitler never learned of this, or at least did not believe it, and later entrusted Dietrich with the success  of the Ardennes Offensive, giving him command of the Sixth Panzer Army. Although initially successful, the offensive (which is more commonly known as the Battle of the Bulge – the bulge being the initial incursion made by German forces into Allied lines) was ultimately won by the Allies. Dietrich was subsequently sent to fend off the Red Army in Vienna but failed to stop them taking the city. He eventually surrendered to the Americans on 8 May 1945.

Von Runstedt

General Feldmarschall Gerd von Rundstedt, whom Reinhardt describes as the one man who can save the German Army's reputation because he is a "real solider", and who was previously referred to in *Russian Roulette*, was 69 years old in 1944. In fact, at the start of the Second World War he was called out of retirement by Hitler in order to take Poland. After succeeding in this mission, he further proved himself to Hitler on the Western Front and was promoted to Feldmarschall. Von Rundstedt later resigned his commission in 1941 due to Hitler's meddling with the Eastern Campaign, but was recalled in 1942 to become Commander-in-Chief of the West and made plans  to defend France against the Allies. In this posting he disagreed with Rommel over strategies for coastal defences, but Rommel's plans to disperse troops widely was approved (as he was the one who had Hitler's ear), a decision that would ultimately have disastrous consequences for the Germans. In June 1944 when Von Rundstedt suggested Hitler seek peace with the Allies, he reacted by replacing him with Gunther von Kluge. In mid-August 1944, Von Rundstedt returned to the Front and was Commander-in-Chief of German forces during the victory at Arnhem. He retained this position for the Battle of the Bulge but was opposed to this offensive. He was relieved of command for the final time in March 1945, again for suggesting that Hitler sue for peace. Von Rundstedt was captured by the Allies on 1 May 1945.

WHERE ELSE HAVE I SEEN..?

Davyd Harries (Lamotte)

Victorin, *Cousin Bette*, 1971

Jack Dutton, *Accident*, 1978-9

Shapp, *Doctor Who: The Armageddon Factor*, 1979

Det Sgt Hammond, *The Charmer*, 1989

DI Spalding, *Emmerdale*, 1998-9

© Unknown

Maureen Morris (Marie)

The Great One/Giant Spiders (voices), *Doctor Who: Planet of the Spiders*, 1974

Lizaveta, *Anna Karenina*, 1977

Karen Muirhead, *The Omega Factor: Child's Play*, 1979

Petra, *The Tripods*, 1985

Mrs Macready, *The Lion, the Witch and the Wardrobe*, 1988

© Frazer Ashford

Episode 10: COLLABORATOR

WRITTEN BY: Gerard Glaister   **DIRECTED BY:** Michael E. Briant

FIRST BROADCAST: 7.20pm, Saturday 24 November 1979, BBC1

STUDIO RECORDING: 30 August 1979

VIEWING FIGURE: 14.4m

REGULAR CAST: Albert Foiret: BERNARD HEPTON; Monique Duchamps: ANGELA RICHARDS; Sturmbannführer Ludwig Kessler: CLIFFORD ROSE; Natalie Chantrens: JULIET HAMMOND-HILL; Major Hans Dietrich Reinhardt: TERRENCE HARDIMAN; Alain Muny: RON PEMBER; Madeleine Duclos: HAZEL McBRIDE; Dr Pascal Keldermans: VALENTINE DYALL; Paul Vercors: RALPH BATES; Hauptmann Müller: HILARY MINSTER; Wullner: NEIL DAGLISH

SUPPORTING CAST: Flight Lieutenant Dean: RALPH ARLISS; Major Turner: JACK McKENZIE; Squadron Leader Bain: MICHAEL OSBORNE; Pierre: FRANK JARVIS; Marc: KEVIN FLOOD; Jean: HUGH FUTCHER; Madame Faucad: YVONNE MERTENS; Woman Patient: EILEEN WAY; Geneviève: TRISHA CLARKE; Gestapo Tail: REG WOODS; Hauptmann: JULIAN FOX; German Soldier: DEREK CREWE; Candide Customers: MARGARET JOHN; SHEELAGH WILCOCKS, ARNOLD PETERS, ESMOND WEBB; Voice of Newscaster: KEVIN FLOOD

SYNOPSIS: 3 September 1944. As the Germans begin their withdrawal from Brussels, Albert returns to the Candide. After a brief reunion with Monique and Natalie, he immediately sets to work removing the graffiti that has been daubed on the restaurant's exterior. Aware that Albert has been released, Paul Vercors is determined to take revenge on him personally for the death of Max and the rest of his *reseau*. While Kessler burns secret Gestapo papers and worries about Madeleine's whereabouts, Reinhardt is still set on uncovering Lifeline. Alain arrives at the Candide with the news that a unit of Allied troops is due to rendezvous with them at 5pm. A patriot called Marc arrives soon after and tells them of Vercors's intentions. Despite this threat, Albert refuses to leave the Candide for fear that it will be vandalised. Wullner is sent to Madeleine's flat, only to find it being looted by civilians. Albert wonders if the special unit could get to them quicker, prompting Alain and Natalie to volunteer to make contact with them, taking an evader with them in order to prove their identity. A Gestapo 'tail' observes Natalie collecting an evader called Bain from a safe-house run by Madame Faucad and forces entry after they have left. Monique tells Albert that she wants to lead a separate life from him from now on. He asks her if she would consider marrying him, but she replies that she needs time to think. Keldermans arrives and offers to act as the Candide's barman for the afternoon. Reinhardt interrogates Dean, an evader picked up at Mme Faucad's safe-house. A preoccupied Kessler tells Reinhardt that there is no time left to take action against Lifeline. A terrified Madeleine arrives at the Candide. Kessler rings her there and promises to send a car to collect her. Alain, Natalie and Bain, who are now travelling by van, are stopped at a German roadblock, but are permitted to continue their journey via another route. Madeleine is reunited with Kessler. Reinhardt takes Dean and Faucad with him to the Candide, from where he lets the latter go free. The other customers are stunned to see him there, but he takes a table with Dean as if nothing is amiss. Later, when Reinhardt and Dean are the only remaining customers, the Major reveals that Dean is an evader and that he now knows that Albert is the leader of Lifeline. Reinhardt allows Dean to leave the Candide. Alain and Natalie meet Major Turner, a British officer who will accompany them back to Brussels. Reinhardt invites Monique and Keldermans, to join Albert before surrendering himself to them. At that moment, Vercors and his men arrive and attack Reinhardt and Albert. Natalie, Alain and Turner are attacked by some Germans hiding at a farmhouse and they become embroiled in the combat. Meanwhile, Vercors and his mob take everyone except Keldermans prisoner and leave the Candide.

REVIEW: Gerry Glaister's accomplished second script for the series is chiefly remembered for the momentous Candide-set scene in which, after some thirty-nine episodes, Lifeline's cover is finally and comprehensively blown by the dogged Major Reinhardt. Appropriately enough, given its title, *Collaborator* is also the first of a trilogy of unbelievably tense episodes to deal with the heavily signposted repercussions of both founded and unfounded suspicions of collaboration. The addition of a healthy dose of action sequences involving the RAF regiment completes the mix, and the overall result is one of the most polished episodes of the entire series.

Monique's reaction to the event which opens this episode – Albert's return to the Candide from prison – throws up some interesting questions. Albert's arrest and subsequent incarceration affected no-one more than Monique, as it gave her no choice but to face up to the challenge of keeping both Lifeline and the restaurant in business. Although she has always been presented as strong, the impression we have been given during the third series is that her new responsibilities have changed her, making her not only more objective and cynical, but also far more independent. This being the case, when she first hears of Albert's impending release in the previous episode, her state of obvious joy and relief ("That is wonderful! Thank God!") comes as something of a surprise. Her enthusiastic reaction to his actual return to the Candide feels similarly out of keeping and further suggests that either Monique is going to attempt to subjugate her new-found independence with a view to slotting back into her old life with Albert or that, rather disappointingly, the production team have decided to dispense with her empowerment storyline altogether now that he is back on the scene. Thankfully, however, neither is the case, and when the pair first find themselves alone together she immediately tells him that she thinks it will be impossible for them to simply take up where they left off: "We'll lead separate lives from now on." Not only is it obvious from his manner that Albert has failed to anticipate just how much her recent experiences will have changed her, but once her cards are on the table ("I've just found out that I'm capable of living as a solitary human being without relying on anyone"), he underestimates how serious the problem is, believing he can solve it by finally offering to marry her. Although she is clearly surprised to hear the words that she has previously longed for him to say, she declines because her perspective on life has altered so dramatically that she is not sure she wants him anymore and, moreover, because she recognises that despite his recent experiences he doesn't appear to have changed at all. One of her main problems with his outlook on life is that money still appears to rule it. She even goes so far as to suggest that he has avoided marriage to her in order to duck out of legal obligations to share his wealth! Although this assessment seems harsh, subsequent events will prove demonstrably that it is startlingly true that money – and specifically the Candide – is more precious to him than anything or anyone else. Although by the close of this scene Monique only agrees to stay at the Candide if in her own room, Albert's reaction seems to suggest that he is still not taking her particularly seriously and that he believes all will be well between them eventually. The scene, which is as engaging as it is emotional, is cited by director Michael E. Briant as one of his favourites due to the performances of Richards and Hepton. It also sticks in Richards's mind as one of the scenes that she is most proud of, particularly due to the complexity of delivering important dialogue while simultaneously laying the Candide's tables during one continuous take. Incidentally, this scene acts as a direct counterpoint to a sequence in the second series episode *Scorpion* which also features Albert and Monique in discussion while they set tables in the Candide. Whereas their activity is identical, because so much water has gone under the bridge in between, the dynamic between them is markedly different here.

During this episode, Madeleine is set to pay a far more significant price for her relationship with Kessler than merely being chased back to her flat and having her face scratched. In *Sound of Thunder*, she was startled to discover that Kessler's moral code was very different to her own, prompting her to announce that she might not leave Brussels with him. However, the chain of events here, which start with a guard being withdrawn from outside her flat, leading her to seek out the safety of the Candide and be located there by Kessler, ultimately dictate that she no longer has the luxury of the moral high ground and must leave Brussels with him, regardless of what she thinks of his worldview. When she takes Kessler's call and is subsequently reunited with him at the deserted Headquarters building, she is clearly relieved to be back at his side. However, the lengths to which Kessler is prepared go in order to survive will soon prompt her to question again how she feels about his values, and to consider more broadly whether she really can have a future with this man.

Just as Madeleine caused Kessler to neglect his duties in the previous episode, there is a suggestion here that one of the contributing factors to his decision not to assist Reinhardt with his final investigations into Lifeline is the Standartenführer's preoccupation with her whereabouts. Of course, the excuses he gives to Reinhardt are that they haven't got enough time left in the city to follow this lead up and that they must destroy any remaining secret papers before they leave. On the subject of the outcome of the war, he seems similarly intent on withholding his true feelings and continues to feed Reinhardt the party line: "We have not lost the war... merely the battle for France. We are to withdraw into the Fortress Germany to regroup under the Führer." Although Reinhardt responds with the line: "Oh, you cannot seriously believe that," it is unclear whether he is really aware that Kessler has actually accepted for some time, as he has already confided in Madeleine, that "the war is lost to Germany."

The scene in which Dr Keldermans is harassed by one of his patients is presumably included not only to demonstrate that, like his Lifeline colleagues, he too is in danger of being regarded as a collaborator by his fellow countrymen, but also to explain the reason for his subsequent visit to the Candide. Although this is convincing, the idea that he is suddenly keen to play barman during the afternoon is less so. By the time we reach the next episode it becomes apparent that the main reason why he has been employed in this way is one of dramatic necessity: so that he can be left behind by Vercors and therefore able to tell Natalie and Alain what took place there.

One of the series's final two evaders, Ralph Arliss's Flight Lieutenant Dean shares the majority of his scenes with Reinhardt. The idea that the pair hold a sneaking respect for each other, despite the fact that they are on opposite sides, is gradually developed throughout the episode and appears to be principally founded on the fact that both are experienced and, as the Major puts it, "battle-hardened" flyers. However, as they trade information about their war records, both are still keen to score points off each other – while Reinhardt enjoys recounting just how much he thinks he knows about the exact circumstances of Dean's arrival in Belgium via Mosquito, the young Flight Lieutenant revels in pointing out that: "There are a lot of aircraft in the sky at the moment. Ours!" The Major's initial attempt to wind Dean up by implying that liberators are the same as occupiers reminds us that, although he is more humane than Kessler, he is nevertheless unrepentant about Germany's warmongering and therefore more of an unknown quantity than he often appears. When Reinhardt subsequently takes the airman to the Candide and lets Madame Faucad go, Dean is impressed ("That was generous"). The Major's decision to also release him in order that he can "enjoy the fruits of victory" prompts Dean to even wish him, rather than Albert, luck. While this mutual admiration is all well and good, the fact that Dean does not think to help defend a man who has just been revealed to be the leader of an Allied resistance organisation that has been helping flyers, and instead just walks out the door, is odd to say the least!

The slow manner in which Reinhardt chooses to reveal his hand to Albert and his colleagues during his visit to the Candide maximises the dramatic potential of these scenes brilliantly. We are already aware that the Major effectively knows that Albert runs Lifeline, but we are very much in the dark as to what he intends to do about it. The shock of his unexpected arrival at the restaurant, despite the fact that all of his compatriots have now left Brussels, is emphasised by the sudden break in Monique's cheery rendition of 'Pack Up Your Troubles' and the exclamation "Look at that!" from a customer. The fact that the Major is accompanied by an unknown guest and proceeds to order lunch, and even a bottle of champagne, because he views his visit as "a special occasion," adds to the mystery further. After the Candide empties, Reinhardt's revelation that Dean is a British airman makes it clear that, despite Albert's and Monique's protestations, the game is finally up. However, the Major has one last surprise up his sleeve, as – in a superb moment – he hands over his unloaded gun and voluntarily places himself in their custody. Terrence Hardiman's portrayal of Reinhardt's obvious marvel at their admirable nerve – "The Candide. It was always the Candide" – is perfect and, despite the fact that he is a German officer, it feels highly appropriate that the Major is shown to have great respect for the opponents he has so persistently tracked down over the past few months. It is interesting that, as we expected (and like Brandt before him), Reinhardt is uneasy about what Germany has become and replies to Albert's question as to why he is not running back there with: "There's nothing for me there." Reinhardt has clearly reached a point in his life where he is accepting of whatever lies in store for him, and it is interesting to note in retrospect that it is the act he has just committed of surrendering to Albert which ultimately seals his fate. The way Glaister expertly handles this hugely climactic confrontation makes it abundantly clear that he is keenly aware that the series's viewers have waited a long time for this moment, and the payoff certainly does not disappoint.

Although Natalie and Alain's mercy dash towards the ever-advancing Allied lines, in order to get the Special Intelligence Unit to Brussels more quickly, certainly makes for exciting viewing, the logic behind the plan does not stand up to much scrutiny. Given the chaotic situation in Belgium their journey is inevitably going to be an insanely dangerous one and the chances of them successfully rendezvous-ing with the right unit are slim to say the least, never mind the issue of whether they will actually be able to hurry them up! Although dramatic convenience has clearly won out, the quality of the action on offer makes this very easy to forgive.

The farmhouse battle sequence is particularly well executed, standing out chiefly because Briant made the excellent decision to employ a real RAF regiment to supplement the actors on location, thus providing a more realistic edge. These scenes are also notable for the fact that, as in *Just Light the Blue Touch-Paper*, Natalie is once again presented as being just as capable as the men she is fighting alongside. She even gets to kill the senior German officer!

It is rather ironic that, given the continuous signposting of the inevitable judgement day on which Albert and his colleagues will finally have to pay for being suspected collaborators, all that they actually suffer here from the handful of accusing locals is some graffiti and a slow hand-clap. Instead, the real threat to their safety is in fact levelled by a man – zealous Communist Paul Vercors – who knows full well that they are patriots! When Vercors outlines to his heavies the reason for his determination to kill Albert, crucially he chooses neither to disclose his knowledge of the work of Lifeline nor the details of the Communist plan to take it over via the late Max. As these new cronies all appear to be in the dark about Lifeline's existence and the betrayal of the *reseau*, we can only assume that they are recently-recruited comrades. Further to the rather confused account of events previously presented in this series of Vercors's connection to Max and the *reseau* who perished alongside him, which Vercors regards as 'his', we hear for the first time that he apparently learnt about the massacre from a man who survived it – a fact which given the thoroughness of the ambush in *Prisoner of War*, seems rather unlikely. However, the reason for Vercors's non-participation in this tragic mission is still not disclosed on screen.

Collaborator's gripping final scenes, in which Vercors and his heavies revel in taunting and abusing their prey, strongly suggest that Albert's and Monique's lives are in more danger than ever before and, given *Secret Army*'s dark track record, that it is by no means certain that they will survive their coming ordeal. It is a clever touch that when Reinhardt attempts to defend the pair – something which was unthinkable just five minutes previously – it actually has the opposite effect from that which he intends, as it plays right into Vercors's hands, suggesting as it does that they are in with the Germans. Somewhat fittingly, it is Monique rather than Albert who is the most vocal about their wrongful treatment, reminding us just how strong she has become during the last difficult and dangerous month of the Occupation, astutely summing up the reason for their attackers' unashamedly brutal behaviour: "It's easy to be brave now, isn't it? Now the Germans have all left!" She is also portrayed as far less prepared to go down without a fight, shouting expletives and openly threatening their leader: "You'll get yours, Vercors!"

After all that they have been through, the injustice of this terrible scenario is almost unbearable, and the idea that the characters – who are dragged out of the

449

Candide as the episode ends – may actually suffer the fates that Vercors intends is even more so. The decision to end *Collaborator* with this riveting cliffhanger is a excellent one. The episode's very last shot of the deserted Candide, which contrasts sharply with the preceding scenes of violence and high emotion, also begs the question: will Albert and Monique ever see it again?

It is arguably during this skilfully-scripted and frenetically-paced episode that *Secret Army* becomes utterly compulsive viewing, a fact which, given that it was scripted by series creator and producer Gerry Glaister, is entirely fitting. After the first series, Glaister always knew where he wanted to take *Secret Army* and, as its grand finale gets ever nearer, there can be little doubt that there could not have been a better man at its helm.

HISTORICAL BACKGROUND

Madame Fourcade

It is likely that Gerry Glaister chose Madame Faucad as the name of the safe-house owner here after one Madame Marie-Madeleine Fourcade, who became the head of the Alliance Reseau in Vichy France. Fourcade was eventually captured but escaped by squeezing through the bars of her prison cell window. She subsequently joined the Maquis, working with British SOE agents during the last days of the Occupation, and survived the war.

WHERE ELSE HAVE I SEEN..?

Jack McKenzie (Major Turner)

Det Insp Perry, *Blood Money*, 1981
Chief Insp Perry, *Skorpion*, 1983
Fergus, *The Mad Death*, 1983
'Ram' Ramsey, *Piece of Cake*, 1988
Mr Parker, *Sharpe's Rifles*, 1993

© Jan Gray

Ralph Arliss (Dean)

Tuar, *Doctor Who: Planet of the Spiders*, 1974
Jim, *Survivors: Mad Dog*, 1977
Geoffrey Bastard, *The Devil's Crown*, 1978
Kickalong, *Quatermass*, 1979
Captain Samuels, *The Jewel in the Crown*, 1984

Episode 11: DAYS OF JUDGEMENT

WRITTEN BY: Eric Paice **DIRECTED BY:** Viktors Ritelis

FIRST BROADCAST: 7.20pm, Saturday 1 December 1979

STUDIO RECORDING: 10 September 1979

VIEWING FIGURE: 16.2m

REGULAR CAST: Albert Foiret: BERNARD HEPTON; Monique Duchamps: ANGELA RICHARDS; Sturmbannführer Ludwig Kessler: CLIFFORD ROSE; Natalie Chantrens: JULIET HAMMOND-HILL; Major Hans Dietrich Reinhardt: TERRENCE HARDIMAN; Alain Muny: RON PEMBER; Madeleine Duclos: HAZEL McBRIDE; Dr Pascal Keldermans: VALENTINE DYALL; Paul Vercors: RALPH BATES; Hans van Broecken: GUNNAR MÖLLER

SUPPORTING CAST: Major Turner: JACK McKENZIE; Spaatz: ROY BOYD; Corporal: SIMON NEEDS; Dunlop: JAMES SMITH; Sergeant: BRIAN OSBORNE; Evader: KEVIN O'SHEA; Sergeant Major at farm: MICHAEL CASSIDY; Smith: MICHAEL GARNER; Pierre: FRANK JARVIS; Geneviève: TRISHA CLARKE; Jaqueline Leclerc: SHEILA WEST; British Signals Sergeant: JEFF WAYNE; Belgian Resistance Men: LES CONRAD, ROY POOLE; Barman: TONY STARR; Whores: MANDY LESLEY, KIM LESLEY, SUE WINKLER, LEE RICHARDS; Communists: BOBBY JAMES, BARRY SUMMERFORD; Stuntman: ALAN MORRIS

SYNOPSIS: Late afternoon, 3 September 1944. Vercors and his men hang a collaborator and have Albert lined up to be their next victim. Natalie and Alain return to the Candide with Major Turner and, after releasing Dr Keldermans, learn from Geneviève that Albert has been taken to the old works at Rue des Aarpes. The trio try to get across Brussels in Turner's Jeep, but their progress is impeded by crowds of joyful Belgians. Vercors introduces Albert to the wife of one of the men killed alongside Max. Albert is strung up just before Natalie and Turner arrive on the scene. He is in a bad way but still alive. Back at the Candide, Natalie is beside herself with worry about Monique's whereabouts, but Turner tells her he can't help until they know where she has been taken. Turner takes Reinhardt to Gestapo Headquarters and uses him to diffuse the bombs in Kessler's office, before revealing that he also wants his help in bringing Kessler to justice. Meanwhile, Kessler's car has run out of petrol outside of Brussels and he and Madeleine have to continue towards the German lines on foot. Hans van Broecken, who is accompanied by an evader, spots Kessler and Madeleine in the distance and becomes intent on catching up with the man he blames for his wife's death. Natalie barges into a meeting at Gestapo Headquarters and demands assistance with her search for Monique. Turner informs the gathered resistance leaders of the work of Lifeline. They are surprised and one of them, Spaatz, tells her where she can find Vercors. Albert is back on his feet, but so disorientated that he does not understand why Monique isn't there. Kessler and Madeleine witness an occupied Wehrmacht car being bombed by a British plane. Kessler subsequently shoots one of the dead occupants, a Major called Spitzwerg, in the head so that he cannot be identified, and swaps uniforms with him. Hans has made his way to Brussels, and tells Turner about his sighting of Kessler. Spaatz challenges Vercors as to what he knew about Lifeline. Madeleine sprains her ankle and she and Kessler take shelter in a farmyard barn. Natalie finds Vercors but he refuses to help her. Madeleine tests Kessler on Major Spitzwerg's background and worries about her own fate if he is captured and believed to be this man. Hans, who has been called back to Headquarters, advises Turner that Spitzwerg's body is not that of Kessler. Madeleine is adamant that Kessler should not use a letter from Spitzwerg's wife to authenticate his new identity and she burns it. Hearing some men whistling 'Lili Marlene', Kessler is tricked into coming out into the open by a troop of British soldiers. He explains that Madeleine was his hostage. While keeping up this pretence they secretly say their goodbyes to each other. Madeleine travels back to Brussels in the back of a truck, while Kessler is marched away by the soldiers.

REVIEW: *Days of Judgement* is quite simply one of the strongest episodes of the entire series. The development of Kessler and Madeleine's relationship as the couple find themselves 'on the run' is incredibly well-handled, while many of its location sequences are also worthy of particular praise. As we have come to expect, regulars Rose, Hepton and Hammond-Hill all excel, but it is Hazel McBride, who takes a meatier part in the proceedings than usual, who is an absolute revelation here as Madeleine.

From the episode's opening scenes, it is immediately apparent that this is going to be something very special indeed. The shots of: Albert having the chain put around his neck; the view across a derelict building (incidentally, the very same location where 'Mad' Mike Miller met his end in *A Safe Place*); the zoom in on the warehouse doors; Vercors's first victim being pushed off the platform; and, finally, Natalie, Alain and Turner's arrival at the Candide, are all accompanied by eerie and funereal musical stings, which create a deeply unsettling atmosphere and serve to emphasise the very real danger that Albert is in.

Although the hanging scenes themselves are not particularly gratuitous, they are nevertheless hard-hitting: satellite channel UK Drama certainly deemed them too graphic to go out unedited. As well as creating a high level of suspense; these scenes also allow Vercors not only to show the extent of his rage, but, more significantly, to present a more tangible reason for it – namely the death of (previously unmentioned) 'best friend' Guy Leclerc. To demonstrate the very real human effect of Albert's decision to betray Max and the rest of his *reseau* (besides the deaths of the men themselves), Vercors delights in introducing Albert to Guy's widow, Jaqueline Leclerc, who, according to his original script notes, Paice intended to come across as a 'symbolic Angel of Death' figure. The hanging is also notable for the presence of Reinhardt, especially as he observes the grim proceedings in silence. Although he has spent the previous ten episodes trying to crack Lifeline and therefore bring about Albert's downfall, now that he is set to witness the restaurateur's death first-hand he is clearly distressed by the turn of events. Ritelis's direction initially suggests that Natalie and Turner are too late to save Albert, as the camera-line slowly rises, representing his soul going heavenwards, and, after reaching the skylight, de-focuses into a white-out. However, the very next shot indicates that his time is not yet up.

Once again, Juliet Hammond-Hill displays absolute and total commitment to the role of Natalie. If only one word could be used to describe the young Dutch woman it would be passionate and she is never more so than here. The extent of Natalie's loyalty and love for her friends, especially Monique, who has become her closest friend and confidante, is not only demonstrated by her tears and distraught exclamations, but also by the way she takes command of the situations she faces. It is Natalie who: is instrumental in saving Albert's life at the warehouse; forces Major Turner to keep his promise to her to help her find Monique; and, most bravely of all, elects to confront Paul Vercors alone. It is notable that the various situations here in which Natalie becomes involved all emphasise the fact that all of the rules have suddenly changed. When rescuing Albert, she silently observes Reinhardt's presence, safe in the knowledge that he no longer represents a threat to her. Meanwhile, her decision to march straight into Gestapo Headquarters and specifically into Kessler's office – a place she must have previously hoped she would never see – presses this point home even further. It is interesting to note that many of the scenes involving Natalie were hastily rewritten just before rehearsals began for the episode on 31 August 1979. Whatever the reason for this, there can be little doubt that her revised role in proceedings provides rewarding character development and also benefits the narrative of the episode as a whole.

This is only the second episode in the entire series not to feature Monique, the first being the Series One episode, *Lost Sheep*. Despite this, her presence is still keenly felt as the objective of finding her before it is too late becomes one of the episode's key plotlines. Although this means neither vocal nor acting performances from Angela Richards, two of Monique's regular numbers, 'J'attendrai' and 'Je Suis Seul Ce Soir', are played during the scenes set at Vercors's local bar, the Caves du Souris, presumably to emphasise her absence from proceedings.

Several of the episode's plentiful location sequences deserve special mention. Paice had clearly reasoned, quite correctly, that the rescue party's progress across the city in the Jeep would be impeded by crowds of revellers, especially on their sighting a British officer, and this cranks up the tension considerably. The close-ups of Natalie and Alain desperately attempting to push away the locals – of which there are thankfully many – are particularly well-realised. On arrival at the old works, the Jeep's eye-view as Turner swings the vehicle around the access road also emphasises the urgency of their mission. Similarly effective is the low-angle shot in the derelict building, taken from ground level as Alain gives chase to the look-out. However, most impressive of all is the shot in which Turner drives the Jeep through the warehouse doors. The sequence is slowed down to maximise the impact of the stunt and the overall effect is pretty breathtaking. The decision to intersperse the shots of Van Broecken first spotting Kessler and Madeleine across the canal with close-ups of Kessler turning his face give the scene an unreal, dream-like quality. The judicious use of swirling mist in the air around the couple also suggests – although we know he is not – that Van Broecken is having some sort of ethereal vision. The mist is less natural than it first appears, and is in fact smoke left over from one of the seven explosions which grace the episode. This becomes apparent later on when Kessler and Madeleine become shrouded in the same 'mist' when approaching the wreckage of the bombed Wehrmacht car. The decision to approach this latter scene with a hand-held camera, as if from the perspective of the couple, also adds considerable atmosphere. The aforementioned explosions are satisfyingly meaty, and the shot of Kessler's and Madeleine's faces, lit up by one of the blasts from their position on the ground, is especially successful. The only superfluous shot here, akin to Ritelis's use of the black cat in *Not According to Plan*, features a group of ants going about their business in the undergrowth; however, it in no way detracts from the other location sequences on offer here, which are all uniformly superb.

Major Turner could have easily been a crass and irritating 'chocks away' character, but thankfully Paice's script and Jack McKenzie's performance ensure that he is both likeable and intelligent. The first opportunity where we get to see what he is made of is in his scenes opposite Reinhardt at Gestapo Headquarters. Turner correctly guesses that the Major is familiar with German booby traps and wisely elects to have him, rather than any of his own men, risk his neck, especially as "he's likely to be extra careful." After the first bomb is disarmed, rather than push for Reinhardt's cooperation in locating further devices, he comments about it getting stuffy in the office, an observation which is in fact a direct request to Reinhardt to defuse the device attached to the window. His exclamation of grateful thanks to the Major ("Splendid – you're going to save us an awful lot of time Major – I'm so glad you waited on for us!") is openly sarcastic and also suggests a man who knows what he is doing. Although it initially appears that Turner is seeking to pin on Reinhardt the deaths suffered by civilians in the very building they are standing in, the Luftwaffe Major soon realises that this is not actually his game at all. The astute Turner is effectively 'using a sprat to catch a mackerel' and his principal target is Kessler. Just as he seeks to use Reinhardt to his own advantage, later in the episode he is equally adept at dealing with the resistance leaders, throwing their complaint about not being told about Lifeline right back at them: "Did you tell the evasion lines who you people were?" Incidentally, continuity-wise, his subsequent sentence: "We used people who were least likely to arouse suspicion, just as you did," is not strictly true and would have Lisa Colbert turning in her grave! The idea that the British chose the Candide and its staff does not exactly match with the reality of the first series, which saw the Brits, represented by Curtis, trying to get in on the act, but, more often than not being shut out because they simply did not understand the game as well as the Belgians. Natalie, who is present when Turner makes this 'statement of fact' does not challenge his assertion, presumably because she is by this time far more interested in enlisting assistance to find Monique than in the finer details of Lifeline's history.

The episode's other British military personnel, although inevitably more stereotypical and less well-developed, also make their mark, due to their entertaining dialogue and manner. The poor bomb-detecting soldier who is taken aback by Reinhardt's sudden uniformed presence beside him ("Christ!") is amusing, as is the Cockney officer at the riverbank who is, quite understandably, not in the least bit interested in Van Broecken's information ("I don't give a damn if you've seen Hitler!"). However, most enjoyable is Michael Cassidy's Sergeant Major, who is everything a man of that rank should be: jumped up, overbearing and overly familiar. His cheerful words to Kessler ("Come on Spitzberger, right cock, your war is over") and advice to Madeleine ("Right miss if you want to go over there and kick Jerry where it hurts, no-one's going to notice") are a little hackneyed, but at the same time wonderfully British. It is especially difficult to begrudge him of his closing line: "Son, I could put you on a charge for what you're thinking!"

Bernard Hepton is required to give a very different performance to usual, as Albert slowly recovers from his ordeal in a state of bewilderment and distraction. Clearly suffering from what we would now readily identify as post-traumatic stress, his reactions to seeing the rope ties left on the counter and to hearing the radio announcement about public hangings are disturbingly well done. The former instance effectively prompts Albert to re-enact his recent suffering in such a vivid manner that the scene becomes far more harrowing for the viewer than the actual hanging, especially as in the earlier scene his head was covered. It is telling that, while in this deeply confused state, he is obsessed both with Monique's whereabouts and with not being able to open the restaurant. This behaviour strongly suggests that she and the Candide are indeed the key linchpins of his existence. However, one of these is due to take precedence over the other with far-reaching consequences and unfortunately, as Monique correctly observed in *Collaborator*, it is she who occupies second place.

The decision to bring back Hans van Broecken in an episode concerned with tracking down Kessler is a smart move. We last met him in *Weekend*, in which he also came across Kessler in the most unlikely of circumstances, when he ultimately lost his wife, Lena, due to the fear the (then) Sturmbannführer inspired in her. In this respect, Van Broecken has a very personal motivation for hunting him down. After he first spots him, he immediately dives into the canal to pursue him, despite the danger of the planes strafing the canal with bullets. His solemn statement, "I'm going to find this man," while he stands clutching his photograph, apparently unaware that he is soaked to the skin, also suggests an unshakeable determination to bring the man to justice. When Van Broecken later has to explain why he knows that Kessler, as an SS man, would not have been picked up by the Wehrmacht car, it is a nice touch that continuity is maintained in so far as the bargee is forced to reveal that he too is a German. It is an important lesson for Turner who, despite his intelligence, does not yet appreciate – as Brandt knew the British would not – that not all Germans are card-carrying Nazis. Gunnar Möller is thoroughly believable as the decidedly tragic figure of Van Broecken, once again imbuing him with the look of a man who has seen far too much during his life.

Given the overall quality of the episode, it feels churlish to mention the episode's few problems. However, one in particular does require some examination: namely the time of day at which its events are set. As this episode takes up the action exactly where *Collaborator* left off, we can assume that it starts at around 4.15pm in the afternoon (we know that Reinhardt revealed his hand in the Candide just after 3.50pm and that Vercors and his heavies arrived five minutes later, and Keldermans states here that Albert and Monique were taken 15 minutes ago). However, rather problematically, we later learn that Van Broecken first spotted Kessler and Madeleine at around 1pm. As we do not see this event until after Albert's ordeal at the warehouse, the only possible explanation is that Kessler and Madeleine's experiences are not contemporaneous with events back in Brussels and actually occurred earlier that afternoon, which ties in with the fact that they left the city at midday and did not get far before they ran out of petrol. This is all well and good, but it does not explain away Turner telling one of his colleagues by phone that Van Broecken saw Kessler just over two hours previously, making the time of this call just after 3pm, a full hour before Turner actually arrived in Brussels with Natalie and Alain! Although these timing problems are not exactly damaging to the episode, they are something of an avoidable shame.

The development afforded Kessler and Madeleine here is so well thought out and delivered that it is easily the most compelling component of the episode. Although their complex relationship has previously been examined in some considerable depth through their conversations at the Candide and her apartment, here, against the backdrop of their flight across Belgium, its foundations are tested afresh in a far more immediate and engaging fashion.

From the way that Kessler initially leaves Madeleine chasing after him with her two suitcases, it appears that the Standartenführer's overriding interest in his own survival will cause him to ignore her dire need for his support and reassurance. However, when she forces the issue, his response ("I love you Madeleine, more than my life") suggests that it is their joint survival that is consuming him. When the opportunity for a neat and incredibly timely change of identity presents itself, Kessler barely hesitates before killing off Ludwig Kessler and becoming Franz Spitzwerg. This expedient act is fascinating on several levels. On the one hand, it demonstrates just how far he is willing to go in order to survive ("I will do anything that's necessary for our survival"), in line with the disturbing moral code he outlined in *Sound of Thunder*, while on the other it displays a total lack of sensitivity to how Madeleine might feel about witnessing him blow a man's brains out without compunction! Kessler is presumably aware that Madeleine is seeing a very different side to him ("I don't think I know you at all!"), but his steely response ("Then you will have to learn"), together with his forcible command for her to get moving, suggests that he has little patience or interest in how she feels. This situation is made all the more interesting when it is learned that Clifford Rose and Viktors Ritelis fundamentally disagreed about the way in which Kessler should interact with Madeleine while the characters were on the run. While Ritelis felt that he would mistreat his mistress during this ordeal, Rose felt that Kessler had changed sufficiently in his personal life so as to behave more considerately towards her. This difference of opinion may well explain why Kessler is seen to veer between professions of love one minute and hurrying her along, as is if she were his prisoner, the next. However, by the time they reach the temporary safety of the barn, it is ultimately Rose's view which gains the upper hand as Kessler promises the injured Madeleine, rather romantically, that he will carry her not only to the German lines, but "to the Fatherland itself, if necessary."

However, the way Kessler treats Madeleine is only part of the story here. Equally as interesting is Madeleine's reaction to her lover's change of identity, especially in as much as it will affect her. The superbly acted scene in which she tests him on his new background before levelling the searching question: "If you are captured and you are a Major in the fifteenth artillery with a wife and two children in Travemunde, then who am I?!", proves that, unlike him, she has thought through the full repercussions of his actions. Her subsequent discovery that he has in his possession a letter from Spitzweg's wife sends her over the edge, on the grounds that she regards the letter as personal. His brilliantly scripted response – "There's nothing more personal than taking a man's identity!" – suggests that he views her concerns as rather like shutting the stable door after the horse has bolted. Given that the letter would prove invaluable in proving his identity and would help to further his survival, he is understandably reluctant to burn the letter as she demands. For this reason, especially given his deep-rooted survivalist instinct, it is hugely significant that he eventually acquiesces to her wishes and burns the letter, as it confirms, as he stated to her earlier, that he does indeed love her more than his own life. This is also supported by his attempts to reassure her about their future together: "When we reach Germany we shall be married. Somewhere a long way from all this and we too will have children." In these affectionate exchanges there is a definite sense that, despite their disagreements about his taking on Spitzweg's identity, above all else their experiences here have confirmed their love for each other.

The concluding set piece which sees Kessler tricked out of hiding and captured by British troops, is brilliantly conceived. The mode of his capture – the whistling of 'Lili Marlene' (which has effectively been the theme tune to the third series) – could not be more appropriate, while Kessler's joy at the possibility of a German advance, and his enthusiastic scamper out of the barn to meet them, is played just right. The decision to have Kessler and Madeleine ostensibly part company in the guise of captor and hostage makes their goodbye scene far more emotional and evocative than it would have been had they been able to part as lovers. Both actors judge the scene beautifully, as their characters' depth of feeling for each other is played out in their eye contact as much as it is through their verbal confirmation of love. Despite everything we know about Kessler, this scene in particular makes it difficult not to root for a future for him and Madeleine.

Days of Judgement is an almost perfect marriage of script and direction. Aside from the suspenseful resolution of the previous episode's cliffhanger, its undoubted highlight is the brilliantly constructed and depicted Kessler and Madeleine plotline, through which Rose and McBride succeed in engendering genuine sympathy for their flawed characters. Both actors are in such sparkling form that several scenes quite literally take your breath away.

HISTORICAL BACKGROUND

Greeting the Liberators

The welcome given to British troops on their arrival in Brussels was extraordinary. The city's civilians, who were besides themselves with joy, had dressed in their best clothes, were waving British and Belgian flags and shouted and cheered as vehicles made their way through the city streets. The Allied vehicles inevitably made slow progress and, on the occasions when they were forced to stop, their passengers were overwhelmed by citizens eager to shake their hands, kiss them and tell them how overjoyed they were to finally see them arrive. Younger members of the population also began to climb up on to the vehicles in order to take a more active part in the liberation parade, seemingly uninterested in where they would end up in the city. Over the next few days, the Allied troops were treated like royalty by the people of Brussels and there was a great deal of drinking, singing and general celebration in the city's many cafes and restaurants.

WHERE ELSE HAVE I SEEN..?

Roy Boyd (Spaatz)

Driscoll, *Doctor Who: The Hand of Fear*, 1976
Tilley, *Survivors: The Last Laugh*, 1977
Zukan, *Blake's 7: Warlord*, 1981
Paul 'Ferdy' Lamboit, *The Fourth Arm*, 1983
Lord Drinian, *Chronicles of Narnia: The Silver Chair*, 1990

Episode 12: BRIDGEHEAD

WRITTEN BY: Michael J. Bird   **DIRECTED BY:** Andrew Morgan

FIRST BROADCAST: 7.20pm, Saturday 8 December 1979

STUDIO RECORDING: 20 September 1979

VIEWING FIGURE: 14.3m

REGULAR CAST: Albert Foiret: BERNARD HEPTON; Monique Duchamps: ANGELA RICHARDS; Standartenführer Ludwig Kessler: CLIFFORD ROSE; Natalie Chantrens: JULIET HAMMOND-HILL; Alain Muny: RON PEMBER; Hans van Broecken: GUNNAR MÖLLER; Captain Stephen Durnford: STEPHAN CHASE

SUPPORTING CAST: Oberst von Schalk: PETER ARNE; Colonel Northwood: MICHAEL LEES; Major Scheer: DOUGLAS SHELDON; Werner Goetz: SIMON COWELL-PARKER; Otto Kaufmann: PAUL HENLEY; Lieutenant: JOHN GOLIGHLTY; German Captain: CECIL HUMPHREYS; Lieutenant Franz Nieman: RONALD FERNEE; Dutch Policeman: JOHNNY SHANNON; Barber: WERNER VAN DER SARREN; Singer: VALERIE MASTERS

SYNOPSIS: A mob of citizens have gathered in a Brussels square to witness the punishment of a group of women believed to be collaborators. The women, who are being held in a cage, are having their hair cut and then shaved off. Natalie arrives in the square and sees that Monique is one of these women. At the very last moment, Monique is spared the ordeal due to the intervention of a British Captain named Stephen Durnford. Durnford escorts a shaken Monique and Natalie back to Natalie's apartment. In Holland, after mooring his barge, Hans van Broecken discovers two young German deserters, Goetz and Kaufmann, hiding aboard his craft. At the Candide, Albert and Alain are discussing the fact that Monique is still missing, when Colonel Northwood of British Intelligence arrives. To Albert's surprise, Northwood hands over London's share of the Candide to him. Albert is overjoyed to be the sole owner of the Candide and at the prospect of holding on to the remaining Lifeline funds. At her apartment, Natalie tells Durnford about their work for Lifeline. Durnford seems particularly interested in finding out more about Monique. Goetz and Kaufmann explain to Van Broecken that they are attempting to get back to their home town in Germany. The bargee advises them to stay put for their own safety and agrees to hide them. Soon after his arrival at a Canadian-run holding camp, Kessler is forced to reveal his true identity to two German officers: von Schalk and Scheer. Von Schalk refuses to investigate the matter further, despite the fact that he knows Kessler to be a Nazi. Natalie tells Albert what happened to Monique and that she is not coming back to him or the Candide. When he presses her, she tells him that Monique does not want to see him and that he should stay away. Durnford calls on Monique, gives her some flowers and asks her to dinner. The next day, while on his way to visit Monique, Albert sees Durnford arriving just before him and he turns back. Monique and Durnford get to know each other better and she tells him that her relationship with Albert is over. At the holding camp, Kessler tells von Schalk that he is certain that Nazism will rise again. From the canal, Van Broecken and the deserters observe the battle of Arnhem. Meanwhile, in Brussels, Monique and Durnford continue to enjoy each other's company and appear to be falling in love. A British Lieutenant tells Van Broecken that the operation at Arnhem has been a disaster for the Allies and he refuses to take the deserters as prisoners. Albert is worried about Van Broecken's safety and speaks to Natalie about it, but there is nothing they can do to help him. A German Captain and a group of soldiers search Van Broecken's barge and find the deserters. Alain, Natalie, Monique and Durnford enjoy a day out in the countryside. Alain and Natalie discuss the happy couple and Albert's reaction to their affair. Van Broecken and the deserters are shot. Back at Natalie's apartment, an elated Monique accepts Durnford's proposal of marriage.

REVIEW: The penultimate episode of the series, *Bridgehead* is the only *Secret Army* script to be penned by Michael J. Bird, one of the finest writers of character-driven drama in the Seventies and Eighties. Although *Bridgehead* contains several successful plot strands – such as Monique's sensitively handled romance with Captain Durnford, Hans van Broecken's final tragic bow, and the continuation of Kessler's masquerade as Spitzwerg – this episode will always be remembered first and foremost for the incredibly resonant opening sequence, in which Monique faces the terrible prospect of having her head shaved in front of a baying mob of Brussels citizens. In fact, this might just be the most memorable *Secret Army* moment of them all.

The shaving sequence engages so completely because it is presented in such startlingly realistic fashion. This is primarily because director Andrew Morgan gets the very best out of his, thankfully numerous, supporting artists. Werner van der Sarren's almost demonic barber is particularly chilling, while the young Belgian woman who plays his first wretched victim is suitably shell-shocked by her experience. Although these two stand out, it has to be said that the entire crowd are disturbingly convincing, especially when they are united in their "Shave her!" chant. Of course the action of the scene is all the more compelling simply because it is Monique, of all people, who is under direct threat. However much the possibility was signposted in previous episodes, to see her in such desperate and undeserved straits, after all she has been through, is shocking and beyond unjust. According to both Angela Richards and Juliet Hammond-Hill, the atmosphere of high emotion, which is so tangible in the final broadcast version of this sequence, made for an extraordinary filming experience. Richards remembers feeling that the years had literally rolled back and that these events seemed almost to be happening for real, the crowd having somehow tapped into some latent emotion from the time.

As Monique has played an increasingly pivotal role in the third series's ongoing narrative, it feels only right that such a significant proportion of this penultimate episode should be given over almost wholly to her continuing story. Thanks to Richards's very human performance, it has always been easy to empathise with Monique's hopes and fears and *Bridgehead* is no exception. The episode offers a surprisingly complete journey for the character, as we follow her from the worst depths of despair to a moment of unbridled elation, as she finally gets the chance to accept a proposal of marriage. Stephan Chase is well cast as

Monique's new love interest, Stephen Durnford. After his first commanding scene, in which he heroically comes to Monique's rescue by tank – effectively his white charger – the British Captain is gradually revealed to be sensitive, affectionate and generous. As such, he is the complete antithesis to Albert, offering Monique everything that she has longed for. As he is also depicted as humorous ("I'm a very nice person"), endearingly romantic (e.g. when he waltzes alone), and possessed, almost permanently, of a twinkle in his eye, it's easy to like the man and understand why Monique falls for his charms. After their successful 'first date' at Natalie's flat, during which we get to see a playful and girlish side to Monique that we had almost forgotten existed, we are only permitted to catch glimpses of the couple's burgeoning romance. This is achieved via some beautifully filmed scenes shot in the Galerie de la Reine, in Brussels and at Waternewton Mill, near Peterborough. Both sequences are unashamedly romantic and have a definite peacetime feel which is immensely satisfying to witness after the preceding forty episodes of doom, gloom and uncertainty. The mill scene is particularly notable as it shows not just Monique and Durnford looking relaxed and happy, but Alain and Natalie too, as all four enjoy an idyllic day out in the country. As the episode reaches its conclusion, although it is great to finally see Monique joyfully accepting an offer of marriage (something for which she has waited for years), there is a slight sense that her story may have been resolved a little too quickly and neatly – her life has been turned around in the space of one episode after all. Nevertheless, thanks to eminently believable performances from Richards and Chase, we accept Monique's relationship with Durnford without question.

Presumably in order to strengthen the contrast with Durnford, Albert is seen to be at his most stubborn and insensitive here. Albert's first scene comes straight after Durnford's rescue of Monique, at a point when she is still believed by him to be missing, and as a result it is particularly difficult to stomach the sight of him chuckling away with Alain while swigging Cognac and giving evasive answers to the farmer's questions about whether he has been looking for her. By telling Alain that he has been out looking "every free moment [he's] had," but that he hasn't had "any free moments recently," he is effectively admitting that he has not been looking for her at all! Given that Monique is supposed to be the woman he loves and intends to marry, his behaviour in this regard is unconscionable, especially as he goes on to attempt to blithely excuse his neglect by citing higher priorities: the need to keep the Candide going and the "endless identity parades" he has had to attend! The uncomfortable truth levelled by Monique in *Collaborator* – that the Candide is more important to him than she is – does appear to be proven here once and for all. For all he knows he could be effectively putting his business before her life, especially seeing as she was taken by the heartless Vercors and his vile cronies who as Albert knows all too well, are perfectly capable of killing in cold blood. Given that he is clearly happy to attend identity parades and, as seen later in the episode, to cross Brussels by foot, he does not even have the plausible excuse that his recent ordeal has affected him in

461

such a way that he is too fearful to leave the Candide to look for her. This leaves us with only one vaguely excusable explanation for his behaviour, namely his possible fear that if he did go out and manage to find her, then just as Monique rejected him when they last talked about their relationship in *Collaborator*, she might do so again. Of course, his 'head in the sand' approach will have the effect of ensuring that she will not come back to him regardless, but maybe he is thinking that at least this way his pride is not hurt into the bargain? And pride has always been an ostensibly integral part of Albert's make-up.

Albert's reaction to the news brought by Colonel Northwood (a well-judged performance from Michael Lees) that he is now the sole owner of the Candide, is so euphoric that it is obvious that he is barely interested in Monique's continued plight. Like the viewer, Alain appears to be stunned that Albert can be behaving in this way, and especially by his line "We've survived!" which suggests that they are all safely accounted for when this is clearly not the case. And if any other evidence were needed that Albert does not value Monique highly enough, then his reaction to Natalie's news that she is alive and well is it: rather than immediately haring across the city to be reunited with his love, because the Candide is open for business and "packed out" he elects to visit her tomorrow! Even when Natalie makes it clear that: "Tonight might just make a difference. Tomorrow will be too late," he still does not seem to understand the gravity of the situation and refuses to accept the idea that she will not come back to him. The fact that this scene is underscored by the strains of a new singer in the Candide, who has clearly been employed to replace Monique, further emphasises Albert's callous response to her absence and that once again, as Natalie observes: "Business comes first, doesn't it Albert? It always has." When Albert does finally deign to visit Monique, en route to Natalie's apartment he cuts a somewhat pathetic figure, especially when he comes face to face with the young and dashing competition and it becomes obvious to the viewer, if not to Albert, that even if he was intending to win Monique back he might have a fight on his hands.

Bernard Hepton is faultless throughout as the flawed Albert, who infuriates and frustrates in equal measure. Despite everything we know Albert to be, we still want him to experience a sudden epiphany and try to build bridges with Monique. However, as the narrative progresses, it becomes ever clearer that this is never going to happen, and Albert's own, increasingly hollow, statements that "Monique will come back in her own good time," sound more and more like a triumph of hope over expectation. Natalie's last lines of the episode, about Albert not believing that Monique has fallen in love with Durnford, suggest that he continues to remain in a serious state of denial.

Despite the fact that he has been sent to a Canadian-run prison camp and immediately runs into two Germans who are aware that he is not Franz Spitzwerg, due to the intervention of one Oberst von Schalk it looks as though Kessler's fortunes are about to take a turn for the better. Von Schalk is no Nazi, in fact he believes that: "The whole National Socialist movement is scum"; however, he has reluctantly decided that Germany must maintain a united front against the Allies and that, to that end, it must appear as though there are no Nazis in the camp in which they are incarcerated. In this way, although he despises him and his kind, von Schalk effectively protects Kessler's lie. The quality of both the script and the acting as this complex scenario is carefully depicted is exceedingly high. Peter Arne is perfect as the pragmatic but war-weary von Schalk, who joins the ranks of sympathetic Germans in the series who know better than the Allies the terrible threat that the Nazis pose. In response to Kessler's unshakeable resolve, conveyed by the superb line: "When we rise from the ashes once more, as we assuredly will, you may be very glad you made this gesture, Oberst von Schalk," we believe von Schalk utterly when he states: "If I could believe for one moment that history would repeat itself and the Nazi sickness would rise again in my country, I would shoot you myself, Kessler." Nevertheless, there is the distinct feeling that the German will come to regret his complicity in Kessler's escape from justice, precisely because the sentiment behind his gesture does not matter to Kessler. All that matters to him is to survive by whichever expedient means present themselves, a fact which is immediately emphasised by his wonderfully curt reply to Scheer as to how Spitzwerg died: "Usefully, as every German should." Clifford Rose is at his chilling best here, as we once again witness Kessler taking on the German military and coming out on top. Kessler may be down, but he is definitely not yet out.

Hans van Broecken is arguably the series's most tragic character. As such, as soon as it becomes clear that his barge is moored fuel-less near Arnhem, it seems like a strong possibility that this may be his final episode. Fittingly, the circumstances of Van Broecken's increasingly inevitable demise are inextricably tied up with his past, and Bird finds the perfect narrative opportunity – Durnford's curiosity over a photo of him in Natalie's flat – to reacquaint the viewer with it, as Monique tells Durnford: that his wife was "one of Kessler's accidents"; that he is a German; and most significantly in terms of the situation the bargee finds himself in here, that he was a deserter in the Great War. Although Hans felt as though his past was catching up with him in *Second Chance*, when British deserter Finch came under his protection, here he is presented with the prospect of helping two youthful deserters who are not only German, but who even come from a place near to where he grew up. Although he tells the deserters that he is going to risk his life for them because he has "run out of hate," the cleverly-plotted truth is that he wants to help them because he himself was in their perilous position some 26 years ago. Given that he has been helping British evaders since Lena's death, the fact that the British soldiers retreating from Arnhem are unable to offer him the assistance he needs is ironic. However, even more so is the fact that he is eventually executed by his fellow Germans for harbouring German deserters, and nothing to do with British airmen! The bargee's quick and unceremonious end is appropriately hard-hitting and marks an abrupt end to Van Broecken's involvement in the ongoing narrative.

As well as the unqualified successes of the opening sequence and the 'peacetime' days out, Andrew Morgan makes some excellent directorial choices elsewhere in the episode. The shot of Kessler, half-shrouded in darkness, as he driven towards the prison camp is particularly effective, as is the German boarding of Van Broecken's barge, which is conveyed simply by a view of their boots as the soldiers swarm over the gangplank. The high-angle shot from above the table in the Candide at which Albert, Northwood and his Lieutenant sign the documents relating to the restaurant's transfer is also notable. However, it was with the realisation of the Arnhem battle sequences that Morgan was the most creative. For these he sought permission from Richard Attenborough to buy some off-cuts of unused footage from his feature film *A Bridge Too Far* for a small fee. The shots in question fits in very well with the action and duly, looking like the most expensive elements of the entire production, when in fact they were the cheapest.

Given that this is *Secret Army*'s penultimate episode, it is especially impressive that two newcomers to the series, Bird and Morgan, were able to deliver such a high quality and apposite final product as *Bridgehead*. However, the highest praise should be reserved for Angela Richards, who has by now engendered such understanding of, and empathy for, the character of Monique that it is increasingly obvious that saying goodbye is going to be very difficult indeed.

HISTORICAL BACKGROUND

Treatment of Collaborators in Belgium

Treatment of collaborators in Belgium has been reported as having been harsher

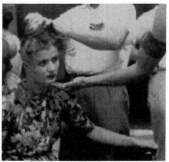

than anywhere else in Europe. Lawyer Paul Struye summed up the situation as the Occupation drew to a close as follows:

'Numerous collaborators with the occupier are attacked in their homes, in the street or in the countryside. Women figure in rather larger numbers among them. The reprisals are violent… The succession of bloody dramas has created in much of the country a veritable atmosphere of terror. The hatred which some Belgians manifest towards others at present is implacable and truly ferocious. It is infinitely more violent than that shown towards the occupiers.'[6]

Operation Market Garden

Operation Market Garden, which began on 17 September 1944, was the largest airborne operation of the war. In total, 1600 transports, 500 gliders and 900 fighters flew eastwards from England to the Netherlands, carrying the US 101st and 82nd Airborne Divisions and the British 1st Airborne. The aim of the mission was to secure bridges across the rivers and canals of the southern Netherlands, particularly the Rhine at Arnhem, and hold them long enough for the British

XXX corps to arrive from Northern Belgium. Although the operation met with initial success, with the capture of the Waal bridge at Nijmegen on 20 September, ultimately German forces were underestimated and the 1st Airborne Division failed to secure the bridge at Arnhem. On the evening of 25 September, the survivors of the 1st Airborne retreated back over the Rhine, having to leave their wounded colleagues to the mercy of their enemies. Of the 10,600 men of the 1st Airborne Division and other units who fought north of the Rhine, 1,485 had been killed and 6,414 were taken prisoner, of whom one-third were wounded.

WHERE ELSE HAVE I SEEN..?

Peter Arne (Oberst von Schalk)

Major Kitchener, *Khartoum*, 1966

Leonard Martin Pasold, *The Avengers: Room Without a View*, 1966

Captain of the Guard, *Chitty Chitty Bang Bang*, 1968

Dr Farrington, *To Serve Them All My Days*, 1980

Kevin Warrender, *Triangle*, 1982

Douglas Sheldon (Major Scheer)

Kirksen, *Doctor Who: The Daleks' Masterplan*, 1965

Brad, *The Avengers: The Forget-Me-Knot*, 1968

Driver, *Ryan's Daughter*, 1970

Arthur Parker, *Triangle*, 1982

Captain Rogers, *Appointment with Death*, 1988

Michael Lees (Colonel Northwood)

Albert Speer, *The Death of Adolf Hitler*, 1973

Phipps, *Nanny*, 1982-3

Colonel Jackson, *Tenko*, 1984

Governor, *Knights of God*, 1987

Mr Foster, *You Rang M'Lord*, 1990-3

Episode 13: THE EXECUTION

WRITTEN BY: John Brason   **DIRECTED BY:** Roger Cheveley

FIRST BROADCAST: 7.15pm, Saturday 15 December 1979

STUDIO RECORDING: 1 October 1979

VIEWING FIGURE: 15.1m

REGULAR CAST: Albert Foiret: BERNARD HEPTON; Monique Duchamps: ANGELA RICHARDS; Standartenführer Ludwig Kessler: CLIFFORD ROSE; Natalie Chantrens: JULIET HAMMOND-HILL; Major Hans Dietrich Reinhardt: TERRENCE HARDIMAN; Alain Muny: RON PEMBER; Madeleine Duclos: HAZEL McBRIDE; Dr Pascal Keldermans: VALENTINE DYALL; Captain Stephen Durnford: STEPHAN CHASE

SUPPORTING CAST: Oberst von Schalk: PETER ARNE; Staff Sergeant Drexler: JOHN RATZENBERGER; Canadian Commandant: SHANE RIMMER; Kapitan von Wolzogen: IAN BARRITT; Major Scheer (Defending Officer): DOUGLAS SHELDON; Major von Reitlingen (Prosecuting Officer): DAVID QUILTER; Duty Officer: DOUG LAMBERT; Corporal Lewis: STUART MILLIGAN; Canadian Officer: GORDON SHERIDAN; Sentry: IAN TYLER; Driver: COLIN REESE; Firing Squad Captain: CARL BOHUN; Leutnant Schober: JONATHAN HACKETT; Singer in Candide: JEANIE LAMBE; Leutnant Rosch: DEREK SUTHERN; Leutnant Stransky: GILES MELVILLE; Major Diffling: KEN TRACEY; Hauptman Swing: DOUGLAS AUCHTERLONIE; Oberleutnant Bahr: GEOFF WHITESTONE; Radio Announcer: LIONEL MURTON; Best Man: MICHAEL LEADER; Canadian Soldier: CHRISTOPHER GUINNESS

SYNOPSIS: Spring 1945. Major Reinhardt is among the new consignment of prisoners delivered to the Canadian-run warehouse cantonment in Brussels. Keldermans visits the Candide, which is doing good business. Albert tells him that Monique is not coming back to him. Kessler notices Reinhardt and asks him why he disobeyed his orders. Reinhardt describes what happened at the Candide that last day and Kessler is furious to learn that the Major surrendered to Albert. Albert discusses living arrangements with Natalie and, despite her protestations, questions her about Monique's plans to marry. Natalie berates him for his treatment of Monique when she needed him the most. Kessler seeks von Schalk's agreement that Reinhardt be subjected to a court martial. Albert gives Alain some advice as to what he should do with his share of the Lifeline money. Von Schalk informs Reinhardt that he will face a court martial in two days' time; the Major is put under close arrest until then. Monique and Durnford are enjoying tea together at Natalie's flat when Madeleine makes a surprise visit. After Durnford makes himself scarce, Madeleine tells Monique that she knows about Lifeline and asks for false papers for herself and 'her brother'. Monique agrees to help. Reinhardt's court martial begins. Alain provides the papers requested by Monique. Leutnant Schober interrupts the court martial to turn on the radio so that they can all hear the news that the Führer is dead and the German final surrender is imminent. Kessler insists that the court martial be resumed. Von Schalk agrees on the basis that it is their duty to examine the charges brought against Reinhardt. Natalie visits Monique and they talk about Durnford, Albert and her impending wedding. While the court martial continues, Madeleine pays a visit to the prison and bribes Staff

Sergeant Drexler with a necklace worth $35,000 in exchange for Kessler. Reinhardt is found guilty and is sentenced to execution by firing squad, but von Schalk is not prepared to act upon the pronouncement. Kessler protests and insists that the sentence be carried out within the next few days. Von Schalk reluctantly agrees to consider his demand and seeks an audience with the Canadian Commandant. The Commandant is astonished that they have carried out a court martial and that they are seeking firearms and bullets in order to carry out an execution. After warning von Schalk about what will happen if his trust is abused, the Commandant agrees to provide them with what they need. Von Wolzogen offers Reinhardt an opportunity to make an escape bid, but he refuses. Monique and Durnford are married at a local church. As the service ends, bells ring out across the city to proclaim that the war is over. There is a celebration in the street outside the church. At the prison, Reinhardt is executed by firing squad just before the sound of the church bells is heard in the prison yard. It is VE Night in Brussels and there is a big celebration at the Candide. Monique and Durnford arrive when the party is already in full swing. Monique introduces her new husband to Albert. Together with Natalie, Alain and Keldermans, they make a champagne toast to Lifeline and to absent friends. Drexler brings Kessler to the agreed rendezvous and, after handing over her necklace, Madeleine leads him away from the prison. Rather than going to Switzerland as she has planned, Kessler insists that they go instead to a 'new' Germany. At the Candide, Albert and Monique reflect on the demise of their relationship. Albert insists that she take her share of the Lifeline money. Durnford interrupts to tell Monique it is time for them to go. Albert asks her if she will sing for them before she goes. Monique agrees and decides to sing her signature number, 'If This is the Last Time I See You'. She sings the song with considerable emotion and everyone present is affected, especially her former Lifeline colleagues. At the end of the song she hugs and kisses everyone including Albert, but it is all too much for her. As she leaves the Candide, Albert sheds a tear.

REVIEW: Expectations of the last episode of any long-running drama series are inevitably very high indeed and *Secret Army* is no exception. Thankfully, however, John Brason excels himself with *The Execution* and delivers an evenly-paced and engrossing finale which in no way disappoints. As well as tying up all the remaining loose ends, the episode also manages to incorporate several genuine surprises along the way.

One of the reasons *The Execution* works so well is Brason's inspired decision to base a large chunk of the narrative on another real-life incident: the dramatic and surprising court martial and execution of a German officer in a POW camp by his fellow inmates, at Schellingwoude in Holland on 12 May 1945. Brason transfers the action to Brussels, with Reinhardt as the execution victim, and changes the date to 7 May 1945, chiefly in order to juxtapose this grim event with the joyful end-of-war celebrations.

Reinhardt's startlingly honest and laidback approach has always provoked Kessler's fury and as a result, throughout the final series, has often caused the latter to threaten revenge on the Major. Here, however, Reinhardt's unembarrassed account of his surrender to Albert ("There didn't seem any point in doing anything else") is finally set to have fatal consequences. Despite the fact that we can plainly see that Kessler is absolutely stunned by Reinhardt's revelation and that he regards his actions as utterly treacherous, given their status as prisoners and their current environs, the idea that he will be able to take any action over this matter does not even seem like a remote possibility. However, this is to underestimate Kessler's overtly zealous and determined nature and it eventually seems inevitable that, against all the odds, the Standartenführer will somehow succeed not only in having the Major tried, but executed as well.

Although Kessler brings the charges, it turns out that the most senior officer in the prison, Oberst von Schalk (once again superbly played by Peter Arne), will play a crucial part in sealing Reinhardt's fate. Although he despises Kessler and his kind, the Standartenführer's plea for justice and the rights of a German officer are, nevertheless, enough to convince the dutiful von Schalk to agree that a court martial should be convened. Later, when it looks as though the court martial may be suspended due to the radio announcement of Hitler's death and the German surrender, it is once again von Schalk's sense of duty that prompts him to insist on its completion. Although his outburst to Kessler ("I am reconvening this court martial, not because that megalomaniac is dead, nor because you are an incognito SS upstart") implies that von Schalk is a sane and reasonable man, both his willingness to convict Reinhardt on the Standartenführer's evidence alone and his decision to request weapons for the execution suggest otherwise. When he is standing before the stupefied Camp Commandant, who understandably thinks his prisoners are "crazy," von Schalk cuts a pathetic and pitiable figure who appears to be trapped by his adherence to duty, simply because it is the one thing that still helps him to make sense of an increasingly mixed-up world.

Reinhardt is presented as being just as stunned by the situation as the Commandant, responding incredulously to events as they unfold. Although the Major has clearly always had reservations about the Führer and the SS in particular, he has nevertheless always been depicted as carrying out his Luftwaffe duties assiduously; a fact which has suggested at least some loyalty to Hitler's Germany. Here, however, as his worst fears about the "insanity abroad in Germany" are confirmed, we witness a Major who is so disillusioned that when von Wolzogen assures him that "Germany will rise again" he tells him: "That does not make me want to stay alive." Even in respect of the manner of his death he seeks to distance himself, preferring a firing squad ("the way of a soldier") over von Wolzogen's very German method of being garrotted with cheese wire. Eagle-eyed viewers will notice that, prior to the action of this episode, Reinhardt has already discarded all of his medals and ribbons apart from his Knight's Cross; however, as the day of his execution looms, this last remaining decoration, presented to him by Hitler himself, also commands his attention, presumably as he reflects upon his own part both in the war and his discredited nation. When the end comes, Reinhardt's last quiet disbelieving words ("You're mad... all of you. Stark raving mad") not only echo the words of the Camp Commandant, but also the thoughts of the viewer. Reinhardt's death is brutal, pointless and unjust, and as such it is impossible not to feel some sympathy for this man who, aside from the fact that he has effectively been Lifeline's principal enemy during the final months of the Occupation, has for the most part come over as a relatively humane and charismatic individual.

While *The Execution* arguably confirms Reinhardt's sanity, it has the opposite effect where Kessler is concerned, as we once again witness his most blinkered and fanatical side. His determination to nail Reinhardt prompts him to use anything and everything to build a case against his former colleague. When telling von Schalk how Reinhardt gave himself up to the enemy after "making certain arrangements with a resistance organisation," which in itself is stretching the truth, he goes on to add that he now believes it to be significant that the Major failed to apprehend them! Kessler must know that this allegation is completely unfounded, especially as Reinhardt was so dogged in his pursuit of Lifeline and, if anything, it was he himself who was obstructive in this regard. When news of the Führer's death and the German surrender reaches the court martial, significantly it is Kessler who is the first to recover his composure, because he has realised that he can play on the reactions of those present to fulfil his current objective: "In the end he was betrayed, as all great men are. But are we, then, to wash our hands of it all and release yet another who betrayed him?" The obvious pleasure Kessler derives from the Major's eventual death is particularly disturbing, whereas his lone cry, just before Reinhardt is shot, of "Der Führer Gebehlt" (By order of the Führer), depicts a man who will, despite the loss of his leader, always remain a Nazi. The execution plotline ensures that a high level of suspense and tension is maintained throughout the episode, while simultaneously offering a welcome opportunity for a final examination of the contrasting characters of Kessler and Reinhardt.

Viewers hoping for a last minute reconciliation between Albert and Monique are going to be disappointed by the events of this final chapter in their series-long love story. However, the outcome that is presented is entirely in keeping with the sort of emotional complexity that has come to characterise *Secret Army*. Over three separate scenes, shared with three different Lifeline colleagues, Albert is presented in reflective mood as he finally starts to recognise that he has done wrong by Monique. In the first of these, Albert is visited by Dr Keldermans, who he tells about his sole ownership of the Candide and the fact that "the restaurant is coining money." Despite the success of his business, it is immediately clear from Albert's manner that this may not be enough for him, and by asking if there is any news of Monique, Keldermans correctly identifies what, or rather who, is missing from Albert's new life. Given that some seven months have passed since the events of *Bridgehead* – something which is rather belied by the fact that the majority of recent episodes have taken place over consecutive days – Albert's assertion that she will not come back is a rather safe bet! As he has done precisely nothing to attempt win her back during these seven months, it is difficult to feel much sympathy for him, and when it is Natalie's turn to talk to him, it is deeply satisfying that she does not hold back on this and other home truths. She responds to his excuse of not marrying Monique because of the uncertainty of the war, by telling him that it did not stop thousands of others from getting married. And his pathetic explanation as to why he did not look for the missing Monique – because he was afraid the Candide would be wrecked – she immdiately dismisses, making it explicit to him that his priorities are all wrong ("It was alright if they wrecked or even burnt the woman you so desperately wanted to marry?"). His face betrays the fact that he knows she is right about this, but it still does not prevent him from making a further feeble excuse: "I didn't know where she was" – a distinctly unwise thing to say to someone who also had no idea where Monique was, but nevertheless spent all her waking hours trying to find her anyway! By the time that we see Albert in conversation with Alain, it seems apparent that he may be seriously questioning the decisions he has made. When the farmer, who is talking about the war, states: "You haven't done too badly out of it," Albert's plaintive reply is: "I sometimes wonder whether I've lost more than I gained," and it is clear what is meant. However, when Alain reminds him: "You play your cards right, you're going to be a big man in Brussels," Albert's simple reply ("I intend to be") suggests that he has no intention of altering his present course and that rather than fighting for the woman he claims to love, he is content with seeking money and status instead.

Given the picture of domestic bliss which greets us at Natalie's apartment it is probably just as well that Albert isn't stirred into action, as it seems unlikely that he and Monique would ever be as happy or as relaxed around each other as she is with Durnford here. Monique's joy at the news that Stephen has already fixed both a date and a church for the wedding is obviously genuine and when Natalie later questions whether she really loves him, it is clear that she does. That Natalie feels the need to check makes complete sense narrative-wise, given that she is her closest friend; it is also important that, through their conversation, the viewer is assured that Monique is definitely doing the right thing, given all that we have been through with her, especially during this final series. It comes as no surprise when Monique tells Natalie that the end for her and Albert was the fact that he didn't come looking for her "when I was in that cage"; however, when she does finally see Albert again in the episode's final scene, she tells him that she knew they had no future together when he took his wedding ring off on the day of the landings (at the very end of *Day of Wrath*). Given that this is one of the very few scenes that conversely seemed to suggest that they may finally end up together, this is something of a revelation, although that is not to say it is invalid.

Monique and Stephen's wedding and the subsequent street celebrations are so infectiously joyful that they are in marked contrast not only to the sombre scenes which precede and follow them – which deal with Reinhardt's fate – but to the series as a whole. It is a much deserved and highly appropriate payoff for the loyal viewer that Monique finally gets to walk up the altar after all that she is been through. Despite the wartime utility and simplicity of the ceremony, the presence of a beaming Alain, who proudly gives Monique away, and a tearful Natalie – Juliet Hammond-Hill once again proving that she can cry convincingly on demand – heightens the emotion of a scene which is undoubtedly the happiest moment of the series so far. However, it is to be almost immediately surpassed in that regard by the scenes of unbridled elation that follow, as bells peal out all around the city signalling the end of the war, prompting Brussels's joyful citizens to celebrate with the wedding party in the street outside the church. This sequence is terrifically well put together, combining excellent location footage of the regulars and supporting artists (filmed on the Rue des Minimens in Brussels) with shots of the city's bells and bell towers, backed by a triumphal arrangement of the Toccata from Widor's Symphony No 5. The overall effect is suitably heady and evocative, and arguably one of the highlights of this final episode.

Perhaps the episode's most surprising plotline is Madeleine's plan to rescue Kessler, which is just as audacious as his plan to deal with Reinhardt. We last left Madeleine in the superb *Days of Judgement* being driven back to Brussels by Allied soldiers, having been separated from Kessler just after they had reached a new understanding. Here we learn that in the intervening seven months she has somehow managed to reconcile their vastly different moral codes and become consumed by the idea of a future with him. Madeleine once joked that if she discovered Monique to be the Queen Bee of the Belgian Resistance she wouldn't tell Kessler. When we meet her again here, we quickly learn that she now knows that this is exactly what her friend was and realises that she is the perfect person to help her! The scene in which Monique agrees to help Madeleine and 'her brother' is regarded as one of the most controversial of the whole series and continues to divide devotees of the series to this day. Does Monique know that Madeleine's 'brother' is Kessler? And if she does, how can she possibly think about helping him escape from Belgium? To my mind, it is quite obvious from the way that Madeleine's request immediately stops Monique in her tracks that she is in no doubt as to who the forged documents are intended for. The way she pauses to think and then adopts an artificially casual tone for her reply ("I don't see why not. Well, the war will soon be over. Anyway, who cares?") seems to confirm this; however, the final clincher is her intonation of the words "your brother" so as to suggest to Madeleine that she knows full well who her 'brother' really is. This being the case, how then can she have come to this decision? The most obvious explanation is that she agrees for Madeleine's sake, out of compassion for one of her few friends. Another possibility is that, as she is about to embark on an entirely new existence with Stephen, she is in the mood to forgive and forget, putting her old life firmly behind her. A further explanation is that the blithe reasoning she offers Madeleine suggests that she is simply choosing not to think too hard about what she is agreeing to.

Although there was a good possibility that Monique would refuse to help her, the second stage of Madeleine's plan is considerably less likely to succeed and far more risky. In her interview with Drexler she wastes little time in making her startling proposition clear: "I want to buy a human being" – offering her necklace from the Baron D'Aquise in exchange for the life of 'Major Spitzwerg'. Hazel McBride herself made sure that this particular plot development would make sense by insisting that Madeleine kept hold of her handbag while she was on the run with Kessler, the idea being that the necklace was inside it all along.

471

Although we can accept this, it is more difficult to believe that Drexler would have a jeweller's eye-piece in his desk drawer! Nevertheless, thanks to a steely performance from McBride and a believable turn from John Raztenberger as the greedy Staff Sergeant, the scene works very well indeed.

The idea that it would be Madeleine who would successfully deliver Kessler to freedom is a turn of events that would have seemed highly improbable before this episode began; indeed, Kessler's expression on his discovery that it is she who has saved him betrays understandable disbelief. That he immediately rejects her plan to go to Switzerland and instead insists on going to Germany despite Madeleine's protest that "it is in ruins" is perfectly in character, not only because it means that he is immediately taking over control of the situation from her, but also because it reaffirms his blind loyalty to the fanatical idea of a new Germany rising from the ashes, a future in which he is desperate to play a significant part. By having them walk away hand-in-hand into the night, Brason sets up the intriguing possibility of Kessler's return. However, for now this is a more than satisfactory and well thought out conclusion to his story. Although this 'day-for-night' sequence is beautifully lit and evokes a commendably realistic Forties feel, unfortunately, due to the dry river beds at the chosen location on the Thames, Kessler and Madeleine do not get to make a rather more romantic escape by rowing boat, as originally intended.

Fittingly, the episode's final scenes take place in the Candide and feature all of the Lifeline regulars as they celebrate VE day (or as Dr Keldermans renames it: "Lifeline's day") and as such it is a perfect end to the series as a whole. It is intensely gratifying to finally see characters who we have come to know so well, and who have been through so much, finally being able to let their hair down at last, and a believable party atmosphere backs up Natalie's observation that: "The whole world is happy tonight." It is a great relief to see Monique return to the Candide, because it suggests that the unfinished business between her and Albert will be resolved one way or another. First up, however, is the moment in which all of the surviving members of Lifeline come together one last time to toast both their organisation and absent friends, which is unfortunately marred a little by a very poor camera position which obscures both Monique and Natalie from view entirely. When the action resumes, we are finally given the essential heart-to-heart between Albert and Monique with which to conclude their series-long story. The fact that Albert is still asking "Why?" suggests once again that not going back to him was the right decision – as she plainly says: "If you don't know, Albert, nothing I can say will tell you." Although Albert accepts her subsequent assertion that it won't do any good to talk about it further, he is insistent that she takes her share of the Lifeline funds, the suggestion being that while he may have lost her, he is nevertheless determined that she will take something with her that makes her independent. He may never understand where he went wrong with Monique – no matter how much he has been told, by Natalie in particular – but it is obvious that he still cares for her very much.

The idea of concluding this final scene with Monique singing in front of her friends and the Candide's clientele for one last time is an inspired one, which succeeds in saying so much more than any amount of dialogue. The song she chooses to sing, 'If This is the Last Time I See You', manages to encapsulate all of the emotions of the moment so perfectly that it is hard to believe that it was not written expressly for this finale. On one level the words refer to the fact that this may be the last time she will see Albert and her Lifeline friends, while on another they emphasise to the viewer that this is the last time we will get to see these characters that we have come to know and care about. The lyric: "We said when we started our story," even seems to acknowledge that she and the others have simply been players in a drama and that this is *Secret Army*'s final goodbye. The final two lines of Monique's song "The summer may bring me a new love, but never a love like you," are just as appropriate, referring both to what she now has with Durnford and also to what she had with Albert and how much that meant to her. As the tears fall down Monique's face, she delivers the final line of the song with such depth of feeling that only the most hard-hearted viewer could fail to be moved to tears. The episode's final thirty seconds, which see Monique embrace Alain and a distraught Natalie, then her impulsive rejection of Albert's formal hand kiss in favour of a heartfelt hug before, overcome with emotion, she flees from the Candide, come together as a very true and incredibly moving scene which ends the series on exactly the right note.

One thing that is obvious from this last scene is that its recording must have been a very emotional experience for the series's regular cast, although considering they had all given three years of their lives to their roles this is hardly surprising. However, they all just about manage to hold it together before the end credits roll.

Given that much of *Secret Army*'s success undoubtedly arises from the quality of the ensemble cast, it is appropriate that every regular character that has made it through to May 1945 is given the opportunity for a suitable final bow. Ron Pember offers a convincing and charming portrayal as we witness Alain at his most elated and overcome, while Juliet Hammond-Hill is finally given the opportunity to present Natalie's happy and fun-loving side and it is a real pleasure to see it; however, there is little change to the number of tears she sheds! Clifford Rose, meanwhile, one of his most commanding performances as Kessler is presented here at his most fanatical and dangerous, while Hazel McBride offers such a resilient and determined Madeleine that there is a suggestion that she may just be the right woman for Ludwig after all. Terrence Hardiman is simply outstanding as the tragic and disillusioned Reinhardt, whose performance proves particularly affecting as he contemplates his impending doom. Bernard Hepton succeeds in further bringing out Albert's vulnerability as it finally dawns on his character that his priorities are distinctly awry. However, it is the decisions that Monique makes and the matter of her personal happiness which really drive the storyline. As this is the case, it seems clear that this final episode, like *Bridgehead* before it, is suggesting that *Secret Army* has really been Monique's story all along. She is certainly given the most complete journey of all the regulars and is arguably the character whom we have come to know the best. Angela Richards ensures that this emphasis is not misplaced by giving a breathtaking final performance.

There was a very real danger that, being the very last episode of the series, *The Execution* could have been both over-sentimental and over-played. Thankfully, however, it is neither of these things and instead stands as one of the finest examples of a series finale in television history.

HISTORICAL BACKGROUND

VE Day

Alexandra Fanny Brodsky, a Russian Jew who 'became a Catholic' for the duration of the German occupation of Belgium, recalls VE Day in Brussels: 'Church bells rang, the national anthems of the Allies were played in rotation over loudspeakers in the city's squares from morning till late at night, and the weather was glorious. Thousands of people stayed up all night. We walked for miles along the central arteries of the city, drunk with the thrill of having lived to witness the event.'[7]

SONGS IN THE CANDIDE

If This is the Last Time I See You (Richards, Osborne)

If this is the last time I see you
Then let's make the most of today
Let promises keep for tomorrow
When you will be far away

If this is the last time you hold me
Then hold me as never before
We said when we started our story
The future we'd just ignore

While I'm here in your arms
all my sorrows desert me
Only you and your sweet love
are the comfort I need

If this is the last time I kiss you
Then let it be tender and true
The summer may bring me a new love
But never a love like you

WHERE ELSE HAVE I SEEN..?

Shane Rimmer (Canadian Commandant)

Scott Tracy (voice), *Thunderbirds*, 1965-6
Seth Harper, *Doctor Who: The Gunfighters*, 1966
Kelly, *Space:1999: Space Brain*, 1976
Commander Carter, *The Spy Who Loved Me*, 1977
Secretary of State, *A Very British Coup*, 1988

John Ratzenberger (Drexler)

Major Derlin, *The Empire Strikes Back*, 1980
Cliff Clavin, *Cheers*, 1982-93
Rigger, *Captain Planet and the Planeteers*, 1990-3
Hamm (voice), *Toy Story/Toy Story 2*, 1995/9
Fred Doyle, *8 Simple Rules*, 2003

David Quilter (Von Reitlingen)

PC Tanner, *Softly, Softly*, 1966-8
The Tracer, *Blake's 7: The Traitor*, 1981
Chief Inspector Charles Parker, *A Dorothy L.
   Sayers Mystery: Strong Poison*, 1990
Mr Arnold, *Grange Hill*, 1994-2000
Greeves, *Doctor Who: The Unicorn and the Wasp*,
   2008

Ian Barritt (Von Wolzogen)

Ultra 3, *Blake's 7: Ultraworld*, 1980
Rancott, *Flesh and Blood*, 1980
Ian, *The Buddha of Suburbia*, 1993
Stanley Cooper, *Life on Mars*, 2006
Professor Peach, *Doctor Who: The Unicorn and
   the Wasp*, 2008

AFTERLIFE

AFTERLIFE

Secret Army has enjoyed a varied and interesting afterlife, quite unlike that of any other drama series, which has taken in the worlds of theatre, books and television. Despite this, and largely due to the debilitating effect of a certain BBC sitcom which directly spoofed the series, *Secret Army* has become what the writers of the *TV Heaven* compendium accurately describe as 'one of [television's] least remembered gems.'[1]

The Novels

The first item of *Secret Army* merchandise to be made available was a novel, simply entitled *Secret Army*, written by series script editor and principal scriptwriter John Brason, which he somehow found the time to write in the summer of 1977 despite his heavy involvement in the production of the first series. Brason decided to avoid the standard TV tie-in novelisation of transmitted episodes – initially at least – and write a rather unexpected prequel to the series instead, which was first published by the BBC in hardback on 17 November 1977, during the only week that autumn in which *Secret Army* was not broadcast (the series took a break between the transmission of *Identity in Doubt* and *A Question of Loyalty*). It seems likely that Brason took this approach as he could see that, as the action of the first series began some time after the founding of Lifeline and indeed after Curtis's first encounter with Lisa (this latter story being the subject of Wilfred Greatorex's unused script), there was an obvious story waiting to be told through the pages of his book. Like the series, Brason's novel is quite naturally a dark read in places, taking in as it does harrowing real-life happenings such as the German invasion of Belgium and fictional incidents including an attack on Monique in a Brussels' alleyway. The storyline which dominates the first third of the book is the displacement of the series's heroine from a happy life with her fiancé to a quite different existence where she is all alone in the world and, for a time, delirious. The second third of the book is taken up with the foundation of Lifeline, through Gaston's introduction of Lisa to Albert and Dr Keldermans. For its final third, the action chiefly switches to Curtis's journey through France with several fellow evaders, for which Lisa is his indomitable guide. The front cover showed a still of Lisa taken during filming of *Too Near Home* in Covent Garden, while the back cover another shot of Lisa, this time taken in Belgium during filming of *Radishes with Butter*.

In 1978, Brason followed up his prequel novel with a more standard TV tie-in novelisation, again published by the BBC, entitled *Secret Army Dossier*. The book covered four of his seven televised episodes from the first two series: *Good Friday*, *Be the First Kid...*, *Russian Roulette* and *Day of Wrath*. As Brason was only free to adapt his own television scripts, he had to try the best he could to make the period covered in the book (April 1943 – June 1944) coherent in terms of the ongoing narrative, with huge chunks of action and incident that had been seen on-screen necessarily missing. However, two chapters were to be entirely original. The first, entitled *Pastures New*, seeks to bridge the gap between the first and second series by explaining how Lifeline hit on the idea of setting up the new high-class Candide after the death of Andrée and the departure of Curtis. Although it is said that Curtis thought it would be a good idea for Lifeline to have a place where German officers could come and relax, it is Alain who crystallises the idea and also finds the new premises in the Grand Place. The chapter also explains why Jacques Bol doesn't make it into the second series – he is killed while helping a London paymaster, Henderson, to escape by Lysander – and dramatises Lisa's last fateful mission to St. Nazaire, with the chapter ending as she decides to shelter under a doorway as an Allied bombing raid begins... The book's second original chapter, *Phoenix*, which is set in December 1943, is likely to have started out as a script that Brason had originally written for inclusion in the second series. The story concerns the discovery of downed British flying ace Squadron Leader Aiden Coates, who is both too recognisable and too severely injured to be taken down the Line. Instead, Alain and an engineer called Caspar repair an old antique Stampe biplane, right under the noses of the Germans in a shed attached to one of their headquarters in the country, and it is flown out, with Coates aboard, by another evader, Roger Patrick, who is familiar with the type of plane. Despite several hair-raising moments, the Stampe makes it back to England safely. The fact that Coates is severely injured and also a flying ace means it shares elements of both *Little Old Lady* and *Prisoner of War*, which is perhaps why it was never progressed to become a part of Series Two. The book's final *Day of Wrath* chapter is notable for the fact that Rennert rather than Brandt dies at its close, as had been originally been planned in the series until Michael Culver announced that he was not planning on renewing his contract. *Secret Army Dossier* also includes dating that Brason seems to have relied upon when putting the third television series together, which crucially neglects to remember that Easter of 1943 fell in late April; this was to cause a whole heap of continuity problems for those paying enough attention. The book's cover was a photograph from *The Hostage* of Kessler about to interrogate Brigadier General Markham in his cell.

Brason's third and final *Secret Army* novel, *Secret Army: The End of the Line*, was published by Star books in the autumn of 1979. In the preface to the book, Brason described the real historical background to several incidents contained therein, commented on the number of favourable letters received from Belgium and the Low Countries about the series's 'startling authenticity,' and also took the opportunity to express his sincere hope that, during production or upon watching the series, 'no-one has been unduly distressed in reliving the happenings of the past.' The book chiefly novelises Brason's episodes from the third series – *Ring of Rosies*, *Just Light the Blue Touch-Paper* and *The Execution* – and once again seeks to fill in the blanks in between. The book ends, as the series does, with Monique's tearful goodbyes in the Candide, but there is no final rendition of 'If

This is the Last Time I See You.' Kessler once again adorned the cover of the book, this time with a head and shoulders shot with his eyes highlighted by a bright light, taken during the recording of *Lucky Piece*.

In 1981, Brason also chose to novelise *Kessler*, and due to the fact that he had written all of that series (bar episode three, but he was given permission to adapt it by its writer Gerry Glaister) was this time able to tell the whole story, albeit slightly truncated in places, leading to a larger page count. The novel's cover featured a swastika motif over a map of Paraguay and a BBC still of Clifford Rose, and was inspired by the cover of Ladislas Farago's book *Aftermath* (1975), which itself had inspired Brason to write the Paraguayan-set sections of *Kessler*. The book was divided into two parts 'The Eurocitizen' and 'A Place in the Sun'.

Kessler

Arguably the most significant *Secret Army* 'spin-off' was the six-part BBC serial *Kessler*, first broadcast in the autumn of 1981, which starred Clifford Rose, was written by John Brason and Gerard Glaister, and directed by Michael E. Briant and Tristan de Vere Cole. (For full details of the production of this serial - see the specific section on *Kessler*.)

The 'Glaister Repertory Company'

Kessler aside, many of *Secret Army*'s principal actors would regularly find themselves cast in subsequent Glaister dramas, as members of what effectively became an unofficial 'television repertory company'. Many of the series's writers and directors would also find their talents employed again.

Buccaneer (1980) 13 episodes

A drama series concerning the trials and tribulations of an air freight company called Red Air, which featured Clifford Rose as regular cast member Charles Burton, a crooked financier. Writers included N. J. Crisp, John Brason and David Crane, while directors included Andrew Morgan and Tristan de Vere Cole.

Blood Money (1981) 6 episodes

A thriller serial about the kidnapping of a young boy (originally a prince until Buckingham Palace intervened!) by a terrorist group, which boasted no less than three *Secret Army* regulars: terrorist leader, Irene Kohl, was played by Juliet Hammond-Hill; another member of her group, James Drew, was played by Stephen Yardley; while on their tail was Detective Chief Superintendent Meadows, played by Bernard Hepton. Also featured were Jack McKenzie (Major Turner in *Collaborator* and *Days of Judgement*) as Detective Inspector Perry, and Daniel Hill (*Too Near Home*, *The Big One*) as Inspector Clark. One of the serial's stars, Michael Denison, playing Captain Percival, would link *Blood Money* to two further Glaister outings. The serial was written by Arden Winch (*Child's Play*) and directed by Michael E. Briant.

480

The Fourth Arm (1983) 12 episodes

Another wartime serial, this time about the Special Operations Executive, and specifically a unit of agents led by Major Hugh Gallagher, a role played by Paul Shelley and not at all unlike his *Secret Army* character (as Shelley himself admitted in 2004: "You could see why Gerry cast me in that role – it was very Major Bradley") The series's writers included John Brason and Michael J. Bird, while directors included Viktors Ritelis and Andrew Morgan. Angela Richards co-wrote the title music.

Skorpion (1983) 6 episodes

Another Captain Percival thriller serial, principally set in the Scottish Highlands. As well as featuring Jack McKenzie and Daniel Hill in the same roles as they'd taken in *Blood Money*, it also starred Terrence Hardiman in the lead role of Chief Superintendent Franks. The plot concerns the investigation of an attempt to murder a French charity worker named Gabrielle. The series was based on a story by Arden Winch and was scripted by John Brason.

Cold Warrior (1984) 8 episodes

The final Captain Percival drama, *Cold Warrior* was a series rather than a serial. Guest stars in its different stories included: Ron Pember; Andrew Robertson (Kelso in *Little Old Lady*); and Michael Wynne (*Be the First Kid...* and *Prisoner*). The series was created and written by Arden Winch. Braason also contributed as a writer, while Andrew Morgan was one of two directors.

Morgan's Boy (1984) 8 episodes

A boy from the city goes to live with his Welsh hill farmer uncle. Stephen Yardley featured as Alan.

Howards' Way (1985-90) 78 episodes

Glaister's sea, sex and sailing drama, which ran for six popular series, saw him employ the talents of Stephen Yardley once again, this time as the scheming Ken Masters. There were other notable turns from Oscar Quitak and Ralph Michael (both regulars in *Kessler*) as Richard Shellet and Lord Rannoch respectively. *Secret Army*'s Timothy Morand, Ruth Gower and Michael Lees also made appearances. On the directing front, Glaister would turn to Tristan de Vere Cole (9 episodes), Michael E. Briant (6 episodes) and Roger Jenkins (3 episodes).

Trainer (1991-2) 23 episodes

This horse-racing drama (featuring Mark Greenstreet and Susannah York) was Glaister's final TV series. Once again, he chose Tristan de Vere Cole as one of the directors.

Repeats

Secret Army was repeated in the UK on BBC2 in the Summer and early Autumn of 1981. However, this was a truncated season of repeats, which only featured key episodes from the second and third series. Throughout this run, it was regularly the most watched BBC2 programme of the week. The short-lived satellite broadcasting company BSB showed *Secret Army* on their entertainment channel, Galaxy, in 1990. On 3 June 1994, as part of their commemoration of the D-Day landings fifty years previously, the BBC chose to show the episode *Bridgehead*, once again on BBC1. From the Nineties, the series has been a mainstay of the schedules of various UK satellite stations, beginning with UK Gold, then UK Drama and most recently, from November 2007, UK TV History. Due to daytime transmission slots, these repeats have often been heavily edited, notably affecting key scenes from the episodes *Day of Wrath* and *Days of Judgement*.

Transmission Overseas

The BBC sold *Secret Army* around the world, with many countries showing it in the early Eighties, shortly after its first run in the UK,. In Sweden, for instance, where the series was broadcast as *Hemliga Armén*, it aired between 1981 and 1983 and became a huge hit which reportedly 'cleared the streets' when the final series was shown. *Secret Army* was naturally very popular in Belgium (first transmitted by BRT on TV1 in 1979) and the Netherlands, but also found particular favour in Australia.

First Day Cover

One item of *Secret Army* merchandise would come about due to the initiative of the series's Technical Advisor, Bill Randle, as part of his fundraising role at the RAF Museum Hendon (where the *Secret Army* exhibition was housed): a philatelic First Day Cover issued on 31 May 1980. The item celebrated the 40th anniversary of the formation of the first real-life Secret Army and was titled Armée Secrète. In order to generate sufficient publicity and interest, Randle managed to gather together the series's principal cast and production team to a signing event at the museum. As a result, the First Day Covers were all signed by Gerry Glaister, John Brason and above their character names, by Bernard Hepton, Angela Richards, Juliet

Hammond-Hill, Ron Pember, Clifford Rose and Terrence Hardiman. Randle also added his autograph, but rather than in his capacity as Technical Advisor, he signed above the name Helmut Rath (his character in the episode *Collaborator*).

Au Café Candide LP

Back when the series was still in production and the songs composed by Angela Richards (in collaboration with Ken Moule and Leslie Osbourne) were becoming a more important component of the series, Gerry Glaister decided to explore the possibility of a merchandise spin-off with BBC Records. The result, *Au Café Candide* (an inaccurate title as the Candide was always a restaurant), was eventually released in 1981 on LP as BBC REC 412 and on Cassette as ZCM 412. It showcased the considerable talents of Richards and Moule, and on several tracks also incorporated the talents of Lennie Bush on bass and Alan Ganley on drums, The album comprised 14 tracks altogether, as follows:

Side One:
1. Je Suis Seul Ce Soir (Richards - vocal, Moule - piano, Bush - bass, Ganley - drums)
2. Memories Come Gently (Richards - vocal, Moule - piano)
3. Nuages (Moule - piano, Bush - bass, Ganley - drums)
4. Einmal Wirst du Wieder Bei Mir Sein (Richards - vocal, Moule - piano)
5. Lili Marlene (Richards - vocal, Moule - piano, Bush - bass, Ganley - drums)
6. That Lovely Weekend (Richards - vocal, Moule - piano)
7. For All Our Yesterdays (Richards - vocal, Moule - piano)

Side Two:
1. J'Attendrai (Richards - vocal, Moule - piano)
2. Blues in the Night (Moule - piano, Bush - bass, Ganley - drums)
3. I Bet You've Heard This One Before (Richards - vocal, Moule - piano)
4. Velvet Blue (Richards - vocal, Moule - piano, Bush - bass, Ganley - drums)
5. I'll Be Seeing You (Richards - vocal, Moule - piano)
6. If This is the Last Time I See You (Richards - vocal, Moule - piano)
7. When We Can Live in Peace Once More (Richards - vocal, Moule - piano)

Although the music production was excellent, the sleeve notes were rather less good. A large proportion of the LP's back cover text, penned by record producer Bruce Talbot, is highly inaccurate: notably a scene-setting opening paragraph about a typical night at the Candide in the Grand Place 'in October 1942' (almost a year before Albert and Monique moved there in the series) and a gaffe stating that Ken Moule rather than Stephen Yardley played piano player Max. However, what Talbot does say about Moule himself is worth repeating: that he was 'one of Britain's most individual and creative musicians.' Far more accurate was the contribution of Bill Randle to another column of text on the LP's back cover describing the work of the real-life Secret Army. Also included were the motto of RAFES ("Let us never forget those who helped us in our hour of need") and a very appropriate photograph of a Wellington Bomber that had been christened 'Blues in the Night' by its crew, who were themselves helped back home by the

Comète Line. The cover artwork was a shot of Angela Richards and Ken Moule in the Candide, taken during recording of the third series in 1979.

'Allo! 'Allo!

It is still difficult for *Secret Army*'s cast and production team to understand just why the BBC thought it would be acceptable to effectively choose to damage one of its greatest dramas by allowing the situation comedy *'Allo! 'Allo!* to go ahead in 1982.

Conceived by Jimmy Perry and David Croft, the series was a direct spoof of *Secret Army*, evidenced not least by its main character, café owner René Artois (played by Gorden Kaye, who has more than a passing, if unflattering, resemblance to Hepton's Albert (especially as he's wearing the same costume!)), who is trying to juggle his involvement with resistance activity with serving the German clientele at his café, who are unaware of his patriotic exploits. His wife Edith, who regularly bursts into tuneless singing, is partly based on Monique, while waitress Yvette is effectively Natalie, albeit with a different hair colour (Albert's affair with Monique is represented by his regular trysts with his waitresses). Michelle 'of the Resistance', with beret and beige raincoat, is undoubtedly Lisa, while Leclerc, who regularly delivers goods to the café and also plays piano, is a mix of Alain and Max. Herr Flick is the Head of Gestapo, clearly based on Kessler and played by Clifford Rose look-a-like Richard Gibson. General von Klinkerhoffen and Colonel von Strohm are amalgams of Brandt and Reinhardt, with the former being implicated in a Hitler bomb plot! Even Andrée is represented, by bed-ridden Madame Fanny, who regularly bangs on the bedroom floor to get René's attention. Two clueless British airmen, Fairfax and Carstairs, halfwits who consistently fail to get home, represent *Secret Army*'s evaders.

When *'Allo! 'Allo!* first went into production for the 1982 pilot episode, the designers assigned to create Café René were directed to cut corners by cheekily approaching *Secret Army*'s principal designer Austin Ruddy to see if they could use the plans he drew up for the original Candide: a request which, needless to say, he turned down flat. One particular episode of *Secret Army*, Paul Annett's *Weekend*, would be the direct inspiration for *'Allo! 'Allo!*'s most iconic prop/plot device: 'The Fallen Madonna with the Big Boobies'. In 1992, after ten years of exploding knockwursts and gateauxs, Café René finally closed its doors, having clocked up a staggering 85 episodes and has been a mainstay of terrestrial and satellite TV schedules ever since.

It has been reported that Kaye found himself playing opposite Bernard Hepton in a production of *Mansfield Park* at the time that *'Allo! 'Allo!*'s first series was in production, and that Kaye (who clearly knew that they were ripping off *Secret Army*) was understandably nervous about telling Hepton about the spoof. Apparently Hepton was "greatly entertained" by the idea. This may well have been the case back then, but it seems doubtful that Hepton remained as entertained when the comedy continued for a whole decade and went on to cloud viewers' memories of *Secret Army*, not only in the UK but throughout the world. Clifford Rose and Terrence Hardiman remember being rather less than entertained while visiting Sweden for a theatre production, soon after *'Allo! 'Allo!* reached those shores, and being forced to sit down in front of a crowd of people and watch an episode of *'Allo! 'Allo!*. The pair consequently had to be polite enough to appear to find the spoofing of their roles hilariously funny, for the sake of their insensitive hosts, when in fact they were dismayed by what they saw and, although they may not have felt betrayed by the BBC, very concerned about the long-term impact it might have on *Secret Army*. Gerry Glaister, on the other hand, did feel utterly betrayed, especially as the BBC had only been able to make *'Allo! 'Allo!* because he himself couldn't block it as he didn't have the status that should have been afforded him as *Secret Army*'s creator, due to the machinations of Ronnie Marsh back in 1977. Like Bernard Hepton, Jan Francis found the concept amusing at first, but by the time Rob Brydon asked her to contribute to his comedy series *Director's Commentary* in 2004 which covered *Secret Army* in one of its episodes, she was thoroughly "fed up of the piss being taken out of *Secret Army*." especially as the DVD releases were now prompting a re-evaluation of *Secret Army* as something more than just 'the show that inspired *'Allo! 'Allo!*'. Francis proceeded to firmly decline Brydon's offer. Juliet Hammond-Hill remains the most outspoken about her take on *'Allo! 'Allo!*, commenting that she finds it "completely mortifying." When interviewed in 2004, she stated: "It blackened our work – I do not understand why the BBC elected to deride one of its successes." Like Rose and Hardiman before them, Hammond-Hill and Richards had to bite their tongues when being interviewed on radio as part of the publicity for the release of the second series on DVD, as each interview inevitably, and sometimes immediately, came around to discussion of *'Allo! 'Allo!* rather than *Secret Army*, perfectly illustrating the impact that the comedy has had on television audiences. *Secret Army* is regularly conspicuous by its absence in lists of top TV dramas and most notably in the British Film Institute's TV Top 100, for which members of the television industry were asked to nominate the top television series of all time. Each chosen voter was given a list of likely contenders, compiled by someone who clearly knew their TV as *Secret Army* was on the list; however, the series was squarely ignored and not only failed to feature in the Top 100 list, but also in a Top 30 dramas list.

Any further doubt that *'Allo! 'Allo!* has managed to almost thoroughly eclipse *Secret Army* can be dismissed firstly by the fact that, when referring to the drama series, lazy writers consistently claim that it was inevitable that it would be spoofed, simply because of their post-*'Allo! 'Allo!* perspective (Jeff Evans in *The Penguin TV Companion* instead considers it, quite rightly, to be an unlikely TV series to be parodied) and secondly, by a quick surf to the Wikipedia entry on 'parody', where *'Allo! 'Allo!* is listed under the 'Reputation' section as a key example of a parody that has become 'much better known' than the creation that inspired it.

To add insult to injury, the comedy's 'creators', Perry and Croft, consistently refuse to admit that their series was a wholesale spoof of *Secret Army*. This is a position they adopt despite overwhelming evidence to the contrary; after all, the actors knew it, the audience knew it and the original set designers, who were instructed by the pair to get their hands on Austin Ruddy's Candide plans, certainly knew it!

However, the fact that Perry and Croft cannot admit this publicly is largely irrelevant – what matters more is that *'Allo! 'Allo!* remains an unfortunate barrier to *Secret Army* being recognised as a high-quality television drama by the general public. Even those who remember watching it in the Seventies cannot help but feel that it must have been rather po-faced and ridiculously stereotyped to have spawned the likes of *'Allo! 'Allo!* There is also the concern held by those coming to *Secret Army* for the first time that they won't be able to take it seriously due to *'Allo! 'Allo!* Thankfully, those who get this far soon find that *Secret Army*'s captivating plots and performances quash this fear, hooking them in and allowing them to reappraise the series on its own merits without any thought of, or reference to, a certain other BBC series.

A Spell in Sweden

Just as *'Allo 'Allo!* was reaching its peak of popularity in the UK in the mid-Eighties, many *Secret Army* actors were finding themselves in demand over in Sweden due to the success of the drama series there, for a run of theatre productions in Stockholm and Gothenburg. These plays were partly intended to be educational, by virtue of the fact that they brought the intricacies of the English language to the Swedish stage.

Blithe Spirit
An improbable farce
by Noël Coward

The English Theatre Company

© Christer and Ann-Sofie Berg

Blithe Spirit
by Noel Coward, directed by Richard Jacques
(September – November 1983, Regina Theatre, Stockholm)
Alison Glennie (Ingrid in *Kessler*) played the ghostly Elivira in this classic Coward farce.

Sleuth
by Anthony Shaffer, directed by John Chilvers
(November – December 1983, Nya Teatern, Gothenburg)
Terrence Hardiman and Ralph Bates played opposite each other in this psychological thriller.

Who Killed Santa Claus?
by Terence Feely, directed by Richard Franklin
(November – December 1983, Jarla Theatre, Stockholm)
Clifford Rose and Hazel McBride were reunited for this comedic thriller in which McBride was eventually revealed to be the murderer of the piece.

Sleuth
by Anthony Shaffer, directed by John Chilvers
(March – April 1984, Jarla Theatre, Stockholm)
This time Ralph Bates played opposite *The Onedin Line*'s Peter Gilmore rather than Terrence Hardiman.

Staircase
by Charles Dyer, directed by Richard Simpson
(February – March 1985, Princess Theatre, Stockholm)
Clifford Rose and Terrence Hardiman played two gay hairdressers who live and work together; a tragicomic study of shared loneliness.

Just a Song at Twilight: a Very British Cabaret
(October – November 1985, Princess Theatre, Stockholm)
Clifford Rose and Terrence Hardiman joined forces again to present readings from Dickens and Shaw and songs from Gilbert & Sullivan.

Season's Greetings
by Alan Ayckbourn, directed by Richard Franklin
(October – November 1985, King's Theatre, Stockholm)
Juliet Hammond-Hill joined two actors from Glaister's *The Brothers* (which was also popular in Sweden), Derek Benfield and Richard Easton, for this classic Ayckbourn comedy.

Video Compilation

UK retailer WHSmith released a 'double video pack' compilation of episodes from *Secret Army* in 1991 under their WHSmith Video Exclusive label, with a cover and spine featuring Monique, Albert and Kessler and a total runtime of 326 minutes. The compilation was edited by the infamous Margot Eavis who was responsible for hacking together many other TV dramas for VHS release at the time. The episodes represented were all from the second series with Eavis choosing to include those episodes that could not be missed if the ongoing narrative of the 1978 series was to make sense, rather like the schedulers had done when choosing which episodes to repeat in 1981.

After some amended opening credits which list all the main actors and the writers of the episodes featured on both videos, 'Part One' (on the first video) starts with *The Hostage*, which only runs here to around 35 minutes as Eavis removed all the scenes relating to Lisa. Eavis subsequently ignored *Russian Roulette* and *Lucky Piece* altogether, moving straight to *Trapped* instead, which is presented almost in its entirety. From the next episode, *Not According to Plan*, Eavis only elected to include two short scenes, both of which feature Vercors and the members of his cell, simply in order to reveal Max's Communist leanings and the potential threat to Lifeline. An almost intact *Scorpion* follows, then *Weekend*, albeit without its final ten minutes, concluding 'Part One' with Lena's death. Bizarrely, this last scene has been given new and particularly invasive incidental music that succeeds in robbing it of its original atmosphere. This first video ends with the Eavis trademark fade to black rather than any end credits.

'Part Two' (the second video) starts with a very brief reprise of the opening title sequence, before cross-fading to an early scene from *The Big One*, an episode that is not edited too severely. Skipping *Little Old Lady* and *Guests at God's Table* entirely, *A Matter of Life and Death* is next up, but only runs to 38 minutes. The next episode featured, Glaister's own *Prisoner of War*, is represented almost in full, before 'Part Two' concludes with the second series finale *Day of Wrath*. Eavis chose to cut to the final credits (which require the theme music to be played three times over in order for every credit to be included!) immediately after Albert and Monique hold each other, to avoid the final shot of the desk calendar showing the date to be 6 June 1944.

The reference on the back cover of this set to the track *Nuages*, composed by Django Reinhardt, may well have led to the mistaken belief that this is the name of the series's title music, as reported in various TV reference books. It is actually just one of the pieces played by Ken Moule for use in the series, for which clearance was required.

Books by Bill Randle

In 1999, Bill Randle, then 78 years old, released his first novel, *Kondor*, published by Independent Books, which drew heavily upon his own experiences as an evader and his time on *Secret Army*, and concerned German attempts to eradicate Belgian evasion lines. *Kondor* is unique in that it is written from a German perspective, specifically from the viewpoint of a character Randle had briefly played in *Secret Army*: Oberleutnant Rath. However, unlike his counterpart in the series (who is shot by Natalie), in this book Rath survives the war.

Randle followed *Kondor* with another novel, *Broken Wings*, in 2001, set during the First World War, before writing his autobiography, *Blue Skies and Dark Nights*, again for Independent Books, in 2002, which recounts his evasion experience in detail and later his experience as *Secret Army*'s Technical Advisor.

DVD Releases

In Spring 2003, the Harrow-based company DD Video first announced their intention to give the series a full commercial DVD release in the UK, under licence from the BBC (at that time the BBC were allowing DD to release several BBC series on DVD that they did not consider to be especially lucrative, other titles released by DD around that time included Terry Nation's cult series *Survivors*, the period drama *Fall of Eagles* and the comedy series *All Gas and Gaiters*).

Due to his work on the first DVD box-set for *Survivors*, writer Andy Priestner, a self-confessed fan of *Secret Army*, was approached by DD Video to work on their prospective *Secret Army* releases as well. Priestner, who began work on the Series 1 DVD immediately after signing off the *Survivors* DVD, was disappointed to learn that DD Video would not consider paying for a reunion studio day for *Secret Army* until the Series 3 release (provided, that is, that sales were good enough to warrant release of all three series), but heartened to learn that they were considering including the five-part 1977 *Behind the Scenes* series as an extra. Priestner set to work on a comprehensive 'Viewing Notes' booklet – which he researched by interviewing as many of the series cast and crew as he could locate – writing the text for the DVD and VHS sleeves and, in preparation for the DVD authoring, chaptering the series. He also advised on the release's artwork, deciding on photographic layout and producing a new map of the Lifeline evasion route. After viewing the first cover proof, prepared by design company Shoot That Tiger!, he noticed that one of the seven characters represented was Hugh Neville and that Monique wasn't present at all. He requested that this be changed but, as the cover had already gone off to various distributors this draft artwork still crops up on several online sites (notably alongside the listing for the Series 2 DVD on amazon.co.uk). As he was nearing completion of the booklet, Priestner was told by DD Video that they had unfortunately decided to drop the *Behind the Scenes* extra, partly because they felt sure that the BBC would charge 'over the odds' for it, but also because they had not realised that the first series ran to 16 episodes rather than the more typical 13, and at 4 episodes per disc there would be no room for it on the set unless another disc was added. The first DVD box-set was released in October 2003 and reviewed very favourably in Cult TV and general DVD magazines as well as on the Internet, notably by Graham Nelson on the DVDTimes website.

As they were feeling more confident about sales of *Secret Army* than they were *Survivors*, Priestner was almost immediately approached by DD Video to work a similar job on a DVD box-set of the second series with a release date of April 2004. This time around a little money was spent on publicity for the release, with Angela Richards and Juliet Hammond-Hill being hired to give interviews about their time on the series, at BBC Broadcasting House in central London, which would be heard on regional radio programmes around the country. A rather less than relevant extra, a documentary entitled *Resistance*, was included on the fourth and final disc alongside *Day of Wrath*, as DD Video did not need to pay anything to clear it. The release was again well-received and reviewed, notably on the BBC website.

Although it wasn't to be quite the complete package he was hoping to produce, the third series DVD box-set, scheduled by DD Video for release in October 2004, saw Priestner finally permitted to record some extras featuring the series cast. He had hoped to secure sufficient budget for commentaries on the classic episodes *Days of Judgement* (to feature Rose, McBride and Hardiman) and *Bridgehead* (to feature Richards and Hammond-Hill) but was ultimately denied. Nevertheless he did succeed in securing all five actors for interviews which would be recorded at the Sound Company studios, Gosfield Street, London. The studio day had an intentional reunion feel and incorporated a special lunch out at a nearby Italian restaurant at which the gathered cast and crew to a toasted absent colleagues and their producer Gerry Glaister, who was in

Juliet Hammond-Hill greets Clifford Rose

Godfrey Johnson and Angela Richards

Hazel McBride and Clifford Rose reunited

Angela, Hazel and Juliet

All photos this page © Marisa Priestner

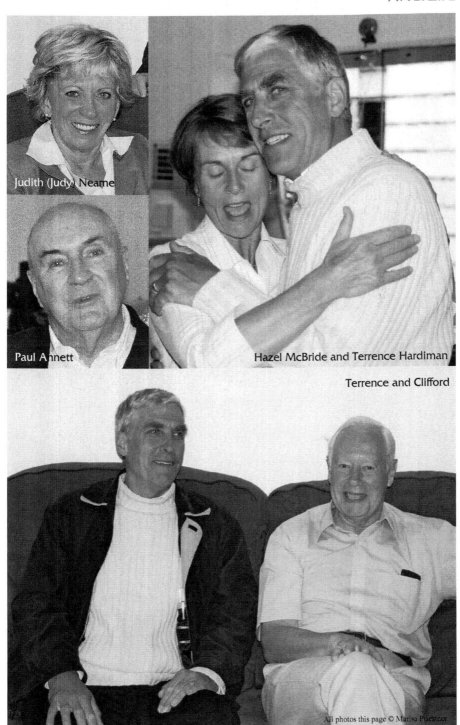

Judith (Judy) Neame

Paul Annett

Hazel McBride and Terrence Hardiman

Terrence and Clifford

All photos this page © Marisa Priestner

491

attendance with his wife Joan.

On receiving an edited cut of the interviews, Priestner was displeased with the way the interviews were lit, but soon discovered that this was the least of the edit's problems. He was scarcely able to believe his eyes when, instead of viewing footage of the reunion meal, the opening segment was interspersed with footage of several old women having a barbeque in their back yard! It transpired that the person who had been entrusted with the work had recorded over the precious reunion tape with some personal footage that had been taken since the studio day. Suffice to say the Priestner household was very much alive with expletives that evening. In complete contrast, Priestner was thrilled to receive Viktors Ritelis's retrospective documentary, *Remembering Secret Army*, from Australia, something which the director promised to 'cook-up' after speaking to Priestner by phone several times. Getting it past the BBC was a difficult task, largely due to their curious dissatisfaction with the fonts and music that Ritelis had used, but was eventually managed. The release's final extra was a slideshow of almost the entire collection of the BBC's own *Secret Army* publicity photos,

Michael E. Briant and Clifford Rose look through the Dorf family album

© Andy Priestner

supplemented by some black-and-white shots of the actors from the Seventies. In November 2004, a month after the Series 3 DVD release, DD Video also released a *Complete Secret Army* box-set containing all three series box-sets, with new sleeve notes, again by Priestner, and a new cover featuring headshots of all the series's regular characters.

The following year, by which time DD Video had become DD Home Entertainment, Priestner was approached once again, this time to produce a box-set for the serial *Kessler*, which was set for release in September 2005. For the, now standard, accompanying booklet, Priestner was once again to receive invaluable input from cast and crew, particularly Clifford Rose and directors Michael E. Briant and Tristan de Vere Cole. Enough funds were also agreed for a short documentary feature, to be directed by Priestner, entitled *Kessler Uncovered* (incorporating interview footage with Rose and Briant recorded at the Sound Company studios on Friday 13 May 2005) and a commentary on episode six, for which Priestner was again joined by Rose and Briant. The final extra was a rather special image collection of scans of the photos contained in the Dorf family album, many of which had been specially doctored back in 1981 to show Kessler with Hitler, which had been used in the serial and gifted to Rose at the close of filming on *Kessler*. After an unforeseen month's delay, the *Kessler* DVD became available in October 2005.

Websites

By the time that the first *Secret Army* DVD came out in October 2003, three separate *Secret Army* websites were in operation, including the now defunct *Circus* site, begun in 2001 and written by Chris Orton who had become a fan of the series after seeing *Secret Army* for the first time on UK Drama in 2000. As well as background information on the series, Orton's site included a lively message board. Another *Secret Army* site, part of the BBC's *h2g2* project (billed as 'an unconventional guide to life, the universe and everything'), offers information and images from the series. Finally, Andy Priestner's own *Secret Army* website, *Le Candide*, which went live in 2003, offers episode synopses, character information, a guide to filming locations in Brussels and the latest news on all things *Secret Army*.

TV Heaven

Although not an item of *Secret Army* merchandise in its own right, Jim Sangster's and Paul Condon's 2005 book *TV Heaven*, billed as 'An ultimate guide to classic telly, cult shows, one-hit wonders, soaps, TV firsts and forgotten gems,' is significant for its effusive celebration of *Secret Army,* which it describes as: 'The single greatest popular drama series ever produced by the BBC.' They end their four-page review by declaring that *Secret Army* 'deserves to be seen by everyone who enjoys quality television programming.'[2]

An Evening at Le Candide

One extra that Priestner had also tried but failed to secure the right to include as part of the final *Secret Army* DVD box-set was Angela Richards's *Au Café Candide* album from 1981. Knowing that there was significant demand to hear the music again, Priestner subsequently pursued the idea of a theatre evening at which Richards could sing her songs from *Secret Army* in front of an audience of fans of the series. Richards agreed to the idea and arranged for musician Jason Carr to join her at the piano. As she had been regularly playing at the King's Head Theatre in Islington, London, at the time (notably in *Dorothy Fields Forever* and *Call Me Merman*), Richards suggested the same venue. Once her fellow *Secret Army* cast members got to hear of the event, Priestner had little difficulty in persuading them to attend and agree to join Richards on the stage afterwards for a Q&A session. The King's Head Theatre is a dinner theatre and,

as a result, there were originally plans for a Candide-style menu, including traditional Belgian fayre such as cassoulet, but costs ultimately proved too prohibitive. Set to run over two nights, 26 and 27 March 2006, the evening, which was supplemented by a full-colour programme written by Priestner, essentially took the form of a one-woman show, as Richards reminisced about the series and sang all the familiar songs and some less familiar comedic numbers too. In order to give Richards an occasional break, Jason Carr played two wartime period piano solos which were also very well received.

Act 1:
Memories Come Gently
J'Attendrai
I Bet You've Heard This One Before
Medley: Je Suis Seul Ce Soir / Einmal Wirst du Wieder Bei Mir Sein / Lili Marlene
When We Can Live in Peace Once More
The Boys in the Backroom
Piano Solo: Warsaw Concerto
Just Another Rhumba
Too Marvellous for Words *(dedicated to the late Gerry Glaister)*

Act 2:
I'm Unlucky at Gambling
For All Our Yesterdays
Medley: Laura / Dream / Ain't Misbehavin' / I'll Be Seeing You
Piano Solo: The Leap Year Waltz
Velvet Blue
No One Man is Ever Going to Worry Me
If This is the Last Time I See You

The first night was attended by Michael Culver, Terrence Hardiman, Juliet Hammond-Hill, Paul Annett, Godfrey Johnson, and Joan Glaister with her two daughters, Morag and Isla; the second by Juliet Hammond-Hill again, Jan Francis and Hazel McBride. Clifford Rose was particularly disappointed not to be able to attend, but was tied up rehearsing for an RSC production of *Othello*, in which he was playing the Duke of Venice, which had recently transferred to London.

26 March 2006. Left to Right: Godfrey Johnson, Andy Priestner, Paul Annett, Terrence Hardiman, Juliet Hammond-Hill, Angela Richards and Michael Culver © Marisa Priestner

27 March 2006, 'Ladies Night'. Left to Right: Juliet Hammond-Hill, Hazel McBride, Angela Richards and Jan Francis © John Martin

An Evening at Le Candide on CD

In June 2006, a few months after the successful theatre evenings, Priestner invited Angela Richards and Jason Carr to record all the tracks – minus the piano solos – in a studio. The resulting 14 track CD, produced by Andy Park, with the same title as the theatre evenings, *An Evening at Le Candide*, was released in January 2007.

Further DVD releases

In Spring 2008, Belgian company, EIC, and Australian company, Umbrella Entertainment, both announced their intention to release *Secret Army* on DVD in their respective countries. The Belgian DVD release will be packaged by some distributors with the aforementioned *An Evening at Le Candide* CD.

AFTERWORD

AFTERWORD

Over the past few years there has been both a huge resurgence of interest in *Secret Army* and a definite re-evaluation of its place in television history, so much so that it is just possible that it may finally come out from behind the obliterating shadow of *'Allo! 'Allo!* in the near future. Recent appraisal of *Secret Army's* merits – no doubt encouraged by its increased accessibility via digital TV and DVD – has led to it being commonly described, in TV reference books, DVD magazines and online, not only as the best wartime drama ever broadcast, but, occasionally, even as the best drama series of all time.

Secret Army's rapidly increasing number of devotees most commonly cite three key components as significantly contributing to its unique appeal: excellent scripts; memorable performances; and the authentic recreation of the wartime period. Interestingly, all three are exactly the same factors that the series's audience repeatedly selected as its main strengths on first broadcast, suggesting that its approach is just as appealing – to some of us at least – some thirty years down the line (if you'll forgive the pun!). Part of this may well be due to the fact that its viewers, like *Secret Army's* very own Terrence Hardiman, find it riveting to see scenes "given time to breathe and develop" and "characters and relationships... time to expand," something that he has described as an "old fashioned virtue" that he'd like to see "a little more of... in drama today." That said, it is worth remembering that what may seem like breathing space and time for development today, apparently felt like break-neck pace back in the late Seventies if we are to believe TV critic Elizabeth Cowley, who complained about the final series's relentless barrage of plotlines. In fairness to Cowley, the third series does take the suspense levels up by several notches and the narrative can in places feel fast-moving even by today's standards.

One particularly striking element of *Secret Army*, which arguably makes it an almost completely unique specimen among wartime dramas, is its careful and three-dimensional depiction of its principal German characters. Rather than being written as stereotypical baddies with little or no redeeming features, Brandt, Reinhardt and even Kessler are presented as complex individuals with the same hopes, fears and ambitions as any other human being. The viewer is also repeatedly reminded that although the Allies are at war with Germany, not all Germans are members of the Nazi party; indeed, Brandt even considers becoming involved in a plot to assassinate the Führer. As well as the tensions that exist between the Luftwaffe and the SS, the series endeavours to depict, in the second series particularly, the specific strata extant in German society, which divide the two aforementioned groups along class lines (the aristocratic Junkers, represented by Brandt and his general's daughter wife, and the Nazis, represented by Kessler). In Kessler the series has perhaps its most memorable character, a factor that is due in no small part to an electrifying performance from Clifford Rose. Whether Kessler has cause to be commanding, cunning or even affectionate, Rose maintains his believability at all times. Through his relationship with Madeleine –

a master stroke of an idea from the production team – we have the opportunity to see his very different off-duty persona, a perspective that gives the character much needed light and shade, and which also has the effect of making his darker motivations and actions more difficult to comprehend by contrast. The input of John Brason and the other principal writers should also not be underestimated as they attempted to ensure that Kessler and the other lead characters were complex enough and therefore interesting enough to command the attention of the series's audience over 42 episodes. On the resistance side too were characters who were by no means straightforward action heroes: Albert for instance is not infallible, but instead is capable not only of making serious mistakes but also of often performing morally questionable actions. His personal and day-to-day working life also do not suggest an entirely pleasant man. The way Albert handles his relationships with both his wife and his mistress is not fair on either woman, while the priority he gives to financial considerations often mark him out as cold and heartless businessman, and yet he is one of the series's most courageous protagonists. Hepton always makes the morally troubled and weary Albert fascinating to watch and it is clear that he took the role very seriously indeed. The character of Monique, who becomes the series's female lead after the departure of Jan Francis, travels the longest journey of anyone in the series and is just as well drawn, through acting – an utterly believable performance from Angela Richards – and scripting, as Kessler and Albert. It is Monique with whom the audience are most likely to identify, as she asks the questions, levels the arguments and responds to situations in ways that we imagine we might. However, quite

© Henri Denis

brilliantly, after presenting her as opposed to the expedient actions of her lover, later on she too finds herself having to come to terms with making exactly the same sort of terrible decisions when she takes over the Line. Ultimately, it is both surprising and rewarding that Monique, a character who starts out with a fairly minor role in proceedings – who is often not even party to Lifeline's meetings – ends up as the ostensible lead character and one that we have come to know the best. The series's ingénue, Juliet Hammond-Hill's Natalie also makes a significant contribution to the show. However, critical comments about the character have often been limited to the simple fact that Hammond-Hill is a very attractive actress, rather than recognising both the authentically European flavour she brings to the series – a contribution for which Gunnar Möller and Brigitte Kahn should also be commended – and the interest Natalie adds to proceedings due to her passionate nature. Her character, which balances the formidable patriot who recognises the necessity for murder on the one hand with an intensely emotional person who feels everything so deeply on the other, is in many ways just as paradoxically fascinating as those of the Germans. Hazel McBride's Madeleine has been similarly overlooked and yet she becomes so much more than merely a means of glimpsing Kessler's tender side. Instead she develops into a character in her own right, who finds herself 'in too deep' with Kessler as the Occupation comes to an end and unable to decide whether to put her head, her heart, or even her country first.

© Viktors Ritelis

When selecting scenes that demonstrate the quality of the acting talent on show, *Secret Army* leaves the viewer completely spoilt for choice. All the cast are regularly given the opportunity to take their turn in the spotlight and prove that the series is blessed with an abundance of high calibre performers. However, Monique's heartfelt 'No compartments' speech (*A Question of Loyalty*), Albert's return from Kessler's garden party (*Russian Roulette*), Brandt's sudden grief-stricken spiral into violence (*The Big One*) and Kessler's rant at the hedonistically-occupied Glaub in the bierkeller (*A Safe Place*) are all particularly outstanding.

A factor that unites all of the series's principal performers is their obvious commitment to their characters and therefore to the series. Director Michael E. Briant recalls that: "The leading actors made it so real. They were prepared to try things and to take risks and, most of all, strive for the truth." It was an approach which he remembers made him feel "privileged to work with them" and that it was "a pleasure to come to work each day." Indeed, many of the actors tried so hard with their characters that they found it difficult to (or chose not to) put them aside while working on the series. In the case of Bernard Hepton, Robin Langford (Rennert) links this to the oft-mentioned cast divide, remembering that Hepton "took the role so seriously that I'm sure he considered it almost traitorous to fraternise with 'the enemy' in the canteen." Juliet Hammond-Hill also volunteers an extraordinary memory of her commitment to Natalie: "There was no other life for me at that time but her," although she is keen to ascribe this approach to the series as one shared by everyone who worked on it: "The passion, the commitment, the love, the experience, the expertise of all the people involved is just there to see." Of course, one of the most significantly committed members of the production team was Gerry Glaister himself. Briant muses that: "Producers come in three forms: the good, the bad and the very highly talented, and Gerry was definitely the latter. Gerry never felt it was necessary to say 'I am the producer and you will do what I tell you.' Gerry gave you the job and expected you to be able to do the job and be imaginative and creative, and do it within the bounds of the story." It was a hands-off approach that paid huge dividends, as so many accomplished directors were given the freedom to make their mark on the series, perhaps most notably Viktors Ritelis (whose filmic aspirations often lend the series an epic feel) Paul Annett and Briant himself. John Brason's contribution was also hugely significant, not only because he provided some of the series's best scripts (*Good Friday*, *Russian Roulette* and *The Execution* to name just three), but also because of his role as script editor. It is obvious when watching the series that there is a guiding hand making sure the series's scripts complement each other, that characters are sufficiently explored, that specific themes are developed and returned to, and that, for the most part at least, continuity is successfully maintained throughout. This guiding hand is Brason's, whose hold on the scripts was so strong that the cast and crew regularly remember that calls were put through to him when he was not present at rehearsals, even when all that was being suggested was that a solitary scripted word or line should be changed.

As with the actors, it feels unfair to single out other individual writers but, aside from Brason, N. J. Crisp (*Guilt, Trapped, The Big One* and many more) and Robert Barr (*Lucky Piece, A Matter of Life and Death, Prisoner*) deserve particular mention as they both provided several very memorable entries in the *Secret Army* canon, which arguably helped to develop and establish the series's iconic style and atmosphere.

Although *Secret Army* comes very close to getting almost every component element right, there are some inevitable shortcomings, the most obvious being the fact that its politics are often worn on its sleeve – a potent reminder that the series was made during the Cold War. This is most obvious in its portrayal of Communist characters, who, in contrast to their multi-layered German and Lifeline counterparts, are quite simply dimensionless ciphers who are rarely if ever given the opportunity to display anything other than negative attributes. The only exception is Prentis Hancock's Jacot, who assists Bradley with the release of Alain from captivity. Thankfully, Brason's original intention to preach in the series finale that the Communists have been responsible for far more evil than the Nazis was curbed by the decision to pull *What Did You Do in the War, Daddy?* Also a problem, but much less serious, is that of the series's internal dating continuity which, particularly in the final series, is often confused and contradictory; however, to be fair, the casual or indeed regular viewer might be hard-pressed to notice this. Those troubled by Seventies production values which of course utterly fail to seamlessly mix studio recording and location filming may also find fault with the series, but it is unreasonable to criticise what was simply the standard BBC house style at the time. Unusually for a series which runs for so many episodes and to which so many actors contribute, examples of poor acting in the series are few and far between, so much so that it really would be churlish to mention them.

One thing that is particularly striking about *Secret Army* is that it is quite unlike any other drama from the Gerry Glaister stable. Although its contrast with 'boardroom to bedroom' and 'sex and sailing' sagas *The Brothers* and *Howards' Way* are obvious, its differences from the acclaimed *Colditz* are much less apparent but arguably just as strong. Both series have a wartime backdrop and Allied and German characters – one of whom, played by Bernard Hepton, is not a clichéd Nazi – but this is where the similarities end. Although *Colditz* is unswervingly about escaping from Colditz Castle, in contrast *Secret Army* is quite simply not just about escaping airmen. Granted, *Colditz* has its occasional gripping and dramatic highpoints, such as John Brason's *Tweedledum* and Arden Winch's *Odd Man In*, but these are exceptions in a series which usually prefers to offer more linear action-adventure style plots which owe more to 'Boy's Own' than *Play for Today*. Put simply, what *Colditz* lacks and *Secret Army* offers in spades is emotional depth. For one thing, in *Secret Army* characters are consistently developed through their relationships with other characters, while we see a whole new side to Kessler through Madeleine, *Colditz*'s Kommandant is only permitted one episode which features his wife and, more to the point, her presence has no impact on his behaviour and tells us nothing more about him. Also, while *Secret Army* positively revels in presenting the majority of its characters as having flaws and foibles, *Colditz*'s inmates are all 'good guys' to a man, and furthermore – and perhaps in part due to this fact – it is very difficult to distinguish between most of them other than by their rank, looks and nationality. Also, unlike *Secret Army*, *Colditz*, due to its premise, is largely saddled with one solitary claustrophobic setting and as a result comes across as rather repetitive. Just how many times do inmates play ball in the courtyard in such a way as to distract the attention of German guards? Probably not every week, but the problem is that it starts to feel like it. *Secret Army* on the other hand has the freedom to choose new locations and new scenarios every week (although of course the Candide and the German offices are standing sets that appear throughout). Perhaps the most obvious difference though is that *Colditz* is a series that is about the war first and characters second, whereas conversely *Secret Army* is unashamedly primarily a drama about characters and, more broadly, the human condition in all its complexity, with the war providing the backdrop. Comparing each series's final episodes, *Liberation* and *The Execution* respectively, throws the vastly different approaches of each drama into stark relief. The former is an uplifting if anti-climactic and obvious end to the series which does exactly what it says on the tin: the Allies arrive and the castle is liberated and the inmates leave its confines. The latter, however, chooses to kill off one of its principal characters, have another bartered for by his mistress and yet another married off, before ending with perhaps the most emotive scene in any drama ever screened by the BBC. This isn't to say that *Colditz* is a bad series, but that *Secret Army* is its superior by a multi-layered country mile.

One other element that sets *Secret Army* apart from *Colditz* is its number of female characters. Furthermore, due to the strength and prominence of its women, particularly in the third series, it is tempting to suggest that *Secret Army* may even have a feminist agenda, especially as it is ultimately Monique's story that is played out in the most detail and as the final episode actually centres almost entirely upon the decisions that she and Madeleine make. However, one only has to consider the gradual sidelining of Lisa in the first series and the fact that, when Monique finally found herself in charge of the Line in the third, she wasn't allowed to run it alone for long – despite Richards's historically accurate protestations that there were more women doing that work than men in wartime – to realise that this probably wasn't a specific objective. Indeed, it is far more likely that Richards's prominence as the narrative draws to a close is to do with the fact that she was recognised to be a damn good performer rather than anyhting to do with her gender. Nevertheless, *Secret Army* does spend some considerable time fleshing out and developing its female characters, a fact that is all the more interesting because the production team was almost entirely male. Indeed, it is notable that although there were certainly female writers and directors around at the time, none ever worked on the series. Whether *Secret Army* is actually remembered for its depiction of strong women characters and made an impact on subsequent drama series is debatable. One of the most important women television writers of the Eighties, Jill Hyem, who would later help Glaister get *Howards' Way* off to a flying start but is best known for writing almost half of acclaimed women's POW drama *Tenko* (1981-85), recalls watching *Secret Army* avidly, but when interviewed about her inspiration for *Tenko* (as part of the BBC's *Drama Connections* series) she actually stated that *Secret Army* was solely about men. This is particularly interesting as the drama series that are most often – and quite rightly – considered to be most similar in style and tone to *Secret Army* are *Tenko* and LWT's *Wish Me Luck* (1988-90) for which the principal writer on its first two series was also Jill Hyem and which, like *Tenko*, had been created by Lavinia Warner. Apart from these two series, with the exception of the rather derivative Glaister/Brason drama *The Fourth Arm*, it is difficult to think of any series that either trod similar ground or took up the baton from *Secret Army*, particularly in terms of its emphasis on human drama. However, this may be due to the fact that it was broadcast at what many regard as the beginning of the end of an era of classic drama on television. The Eighties ultimately brought what actors, directors and drama enthusiasts alike universally recognise as the death of British television as we knew it by the end of the decade, as soaps, reality shows and much shorter and less in-depth dramas became the order of the day. However, there are now strong signs that the fortunes of television drama are slowly changing and that it has finally been recognised that viewers actively want to watch shows which put character, plots and scripting before vapid action and pace. Series like the new *Doctor Who*, which is more of a drama series than it ever was in its previous incarnation, *Life on Mars* (2006-7) and period pieces such as *Lark Rise to Candleford* (2008) are all getting the sort of care and loving attention (and, just as importantly, episode count) that TV drama rightly deserves. While the time might not be ripe for another World War II-inspired drama series (both *Island at War* (2004) – essentially '*Enemy at the Door* for the Noughties' – and a feature-length reimagining of *Colditz* (2005) were considered unsuccessful), despite the worrying fact that there is a generation growing up who know next to nothing about World War II and why its lessons must never be forgotten, there is at least hope that British character-driven drama is enjoying a revival and that the opportunity for engaging with a series as compelling as *Secret Army* is finally becoming a very real possibility again.

Although is it widely regarded as a classic television drama series, *Secret Army*, like many other avidly followed dramas, has never been classed as a cult series, perhaps because 'cult' is a term that has automatic connotations of science fiction and fantasy. Nevertheless, it is arguable that *Secret Army* has increasingly won a cult following which, as it has with more obvious cult shows like *Doctor Who* or *Blake's 7*, has caused its actors and directors to be surprised by: its continued popularity; the fact that it is still generating enough interest for a book, a CD and a theatre production to be economically viable; and, most of all, that they are finding themselves talking about a show that they contributed to some three decades earlier. It is a situation that suggests that maybe it is time for the merits of certain other drama series from the Seventies and early Eighties to be reappraised and examined in the same level of detail as I have sought to achieve for *Secret Army* through this book.

Secret Army's enduring appeal undoubtedly comes down to its excellent scripts, breathtaking performances and assured direction. Also, as Clifford Rose has perceptively said: "It's not sentimentalised, it's not romanticised and the characters are complex and believable human beings." Of course, as Angela Richards has observed, the series also stands, as a tribute to the real people who carried out the incredibly dangerous work of running evasion lines: "There were thousands of people who died and thousands and thousands of people who helped

RAFES plaque commemorating the work of the evasion lines during World War Two.

and supported and lived. It's a tribute and you can't forget it, you can't just say it was unimportant. It was hugely important." Bernard Hepton, meanwhile, remembers a directive that was never lost sight of when making the series: 'Gerry Glaister, our producer, directed everyone concerned, writers, designers, directors, actors et al., that "In war there are no heroes, no villains; everyone is a loser."' It is an objective that is wholeheartedly achieved and which helped to make *Secret Army* one of the most captivating and sophisticated dramas ever to be broadcast on British television.

LOCATION
GUIDE

Above: The archway through which the German vehicles pass in the opening scenes of LISA – CODE NAME YVETTE. Later seen in BRIDGEHEAD when Monique and Stephen climb aboard Alain's hay cart (Waternewton Mill, Waternewton, Cambs., UK).

Below: The exterior of Dr Keldermans's surgery, which Lisa visits with an evader in SERGEANT ON THE RUN. Also seen in SECOND CHANCE and other SERIES ONE episodes (37 Harrington Gardens, Kensington, London, UK).

Above: The bistro in which Walker and his fellow evaders eat in SERGEANT ON THE RUN (Argenteus and Octopus shops, Covent Garden Market, London, UK).

Below: St Catherine's Church as seen in SERGEANT ON THE RUN. In the cobbled square in front of it, Lisa passes Alain (who is manning a market stall there) a message (Place Ste Catherine, Brussels, Belgium).

© Andy Priestner

Above: The marble sculptures of Belgian notables that line the route taken by Sergeant Walker soon after his escape from Dr Bogaerde's surgery in SERGEANT ON THE RUN (Place du Petit Sablon, Brussels, Belgium).

Below: Two of the sculptures seen in close-up while Walker makes his way through the garden in SERGEANT ON THE RUN (Geographer Gerard Mercator and painter Bernard Van Orley, Place du Petit Sablon, Brussels, Belgium).

© Andy Priestner

Above: The canal-side Boulevard de Nieuport where Sergeant Walker is accosted by a group of drunk Germans who take him with them on an impromptu tram-ride in SERGEANT ON THE RUN (Boulevard de Nieuport, Brussels, Belgium).

Below: Another view on the Boulevard de Nieuport as seen in SERGEANT ON THE RUN looking towards the tramway with Klein Castle behind. Walker gets on and off the tram at exactly the same spot (Boulevard de Nieuport, Brussels, Belgium).

Above: The area beside the Place du Petit Sablon fountain where Curtis meets Albrecht Beerman in RADISHES WITH BUTTER (Place du Petit Sablon, Brussels, Belgium).

Below: The spot where Howson and his colleagues wait in the ambulance while their guides change over at the end of GROWING UP, and where Julius makes a run for it in TOO NEAR HOME (West Piazza, Covent Garden Market, London, UK).

Above: Where Natalie meets two evaders and Romsey misses the train in LOST SHEEP (Paddington Station, Paddington, London, UK).

Below: Julius's workshop which was visited by Lisa in TOO NEAR HOME and was subsequently ransacked by German soldiers (West Cornwall Pasty Company shop, The Cove, Covent Garden Market, London, UK).

Above: The spot where Natalie observes a rich couple celebrating in a car and an old man eating scraps in TOO NEAR HOME (Place du Petit Sablon, Brussels, Belgium).

Below: Albert surveys the square where his new restaurant is situated and purchases some flowers for Monique from a stall in front of the Hôtel de Ville in THE HOSTAGE (Grand Place, Brussels, Belgium).

514

Above: The new Candide in the Grand Place, first seen in THE HOSTAGE (No. 28 – La Chambrette de l'Amman, Maxim's Restaurant, Grand Place, Brussels, Belgium).

Below: Where Lisa meets a group of evaders and talks to Natalie aboard a train in THE HOSTAGE (Maria Leel stands in for Lisa, Platform 3, Wansford Station, Wansford, Cambs., UK).

Above: View from the Rue des Harengs into the Grand Place, at the side entrance to the Candide, as seen at the start of RUSSIAN ROULETTE when Alain arrives by bicycle with a box of vegetables (Rue des Harengs, Brussels, Belgium).

Below: The Galerie de la Reine where, after Max's tip-off, Claude Pelletain meets his end in RUSSIAN ROULETTE (Galeries Royale Saint Hubert, Brussels, Belgium).

Above: The farmhouse near Jauche where Natalie first meets Bradley in LUCKY PIECE (Whitelands, Old Sulehay Road, Yarwell, Northants., UK).

Below: The Cracheur ('Spitter') fountain near the Grand Place, which Natalie passes while being tracked by a Gestapo agent and Bradley in LUCKY PIECE (Rue des Pierres, Brussels, Belgium).

517

Above and Below: The steps of the Cathedral of St Michael and St Gudula where Natalie is tracked by Gestapo tail Helmut Schultz and Bradley in LUCKY PIECE, and where she later acts as bait in order to flush Schultz out so that she and Bradley can dispose of him (Cathedral of St Michael and St Gudula, Brussels, Belgium).

Above: The spot beside the tracks where Monique is shot in TRAPPED (Site of Old Castor Station, Station Road, Ailsworth, Nr Peterborough, Cambs., UK).

Below: The road, in TRAPPED, where Alain, Max, Natalie and the wounded Monique wait at the checkpoint in an ambulance while Kessler grows impatient at the other side (Old Sulehay Road, Yarwell, Northants., UK).

Above: The spot where the car in which Kessler and Horst are travelling is forced off the road due to the trap set by McGee and Harris in WEEKEND (Road near Top Lodge Farm, Upton, Nr Peterborough, Cambs., UK).

Below: The spot where Max and Monique park and switch the paintings over in WEEKEND (Entrance to Southey Wood, Nr Peterborough, Cambs., UK).

Above: The landing site of the scarred Wing Commander Kelso in LITTLE OLD LADY, where he is found by a group of patriots (Over the track from site of Old Castor Station, Station Road, Ailsworth, Nr Peterborough, Cambs., UK).

Below: The row of trees by which the Germans look for Kelso in LITTLE OLD LADY (Willow Row, over the track from site of Old Castor Station, Station Road, Ailsworth, Nr Peterborough, Cambs., UK).

Above: The river which Wing Commander Kelso and Natalie cross in LITTLE OLD LADY (Castor Backwater, between Old Castor Station, Station Road, Ailsworth and Waternewton Mill (in background), Waternewton, Nr Peterborough, Cambs., UK).

Below: The field which the Dutch saboteur flees across before being shot in LITTLE OLD LADY (Willow Row field, near site of old Castor Station, Station Road, Ailsworth, Nr Peterborough, Cambs., UK).

Above: The railway crossing where François meets his end while Natalie and Hervé look on in A MATTER OF LIFE AND DEATH (Wansford Station, Wansford, Cambs., UK).

Below: Bertrand Lecau's farm in PRISONER OF WAR. Later seen as the farm where Natalie leaves the evaders that she cannot take any further south in THE LAST RUN (Abbots Barn Farm, Southorpe, Nr Peterborough, Cambs., UK).

Above: The wooded area where Alain and Max swap Hauptmann Braun between vehicles in PRISONER OF WAR (Southey Wood, Nr Peterborough, Cambs., UK).

Below: The farm where Max and his comrades are killed in PRISONER OF WAR (Salt Box Farm, Woodcroft Road, Marholm, Nr Peterborough, Cambs., UK).

Above and Below: The building which became Gestapo HQ during the Occupation and was attacked from the air by Jean de Selys Longchamps, and the Longchamps memorial in front of it, respectively (No. 453 Avenue Louise, Brussels, Belgium).

Above and Below: A train that is seen pulling into the station, and one of the stations from which Natalie makes her abortive attempt to guide evaders down the Line, respectively, both in THE LAST RUN (Wansford Station, Wansford, Cambs., UK)

Above: The headquarters of the Reichskommissariat into which Kessler is driven at the start of REVENGE (Palais d'Egmont – behind Place du Petit Sablon, Brussels, Belgium).

Below: The Hôtel de Ville under which Bradley observes the Germans laying charges in SOUND OF THUNDER (Grand Place, Brussels, Belgium).

Above: The buildings opposite Le Candide in the Grand Place. Bradley walks under No. 8, known as The Star, while on his way to meet Brussels's resistance leaders in SOUND OF THUNDER (Grand Place, Brussels, Belgium).

Below: The bas reliefs of Charles Buls and Everard 't Serclaes under No. 8, which Bradley passes in front of in SOUND OF THUNDER (Grand Place, Brussels, Belgium).

Above: The market which Bradley walks through in SOUND OF THUNDER (Borough Market, Southwark, London, UK).

Below: The archway through which Bradley carries Lamotte's body in SOUND OF THUNDER (Green Dragon Court, Southwark, London, UK).

Above: The alleyway which Bradley carries Lamotte through in SOUND OF THUNDER (Montague Close and Montague Chambers, Southwark, London, UK).

Below: The spot where Bradley is killed in SOUND OF THUNDER ('Nancy's Steps', London Bridge, Southwark, London, UK).

Above: The building seen behind Albert (with a Nazi flag hanging from one of its windows) as he returns to the Candide after his prison term in COLLABORATOR (Residences of the Dukes of Brabant, Grand Place, Brussels, Belgium).

Below: The side wall of the Candide where the locals had painted the word 'Collaborator', which Albert tries to scrub off in COLLABORATOR (Rue des Harengs, Brussels, Belgium).

531

Above: Madeleine's apartment, which is ransacked by a group of locals in COLLABORATOR (Rue des Fleuristes, Brussels, Belgium).

Below: The small country road on which Natalie and Alain are stopped on their way to meet up with the advancing Allies (Southey Wood, Nr Peterborough, Cambs., UK).

Above: The farm at which Natalie and Alain meet Major Turner and from which they head off back to Brussels in COLLABORATOR (Salt Box Farm, Woodcroft Road, Marholm, Nr Peterborough, Cambs., UK).

Below: The farm buildings where Natalie, Alain, Turner and the British troops engage in a gun battle with Oberleutnant Rath and his soldiers in COLLABORATOR (Pellet Hall Farm, Woodcroft Road, Marholm, Nr Peterborough, Cambs., UK).

Above: The view seen towards the Candide and the Maison du Roi when Natalie, Alain and Turner rush out hoping to find Albert in time in DAYS OF JUDGEMENT (Grand Place, Brussels, Belgium).

Below: The small street on which Natalie, Alain and Turner are mobbed in their Jeep by joyful citizens in DAYS OF JUDGEMENT (Rue des Pigeons, Brussels, Belgium).

Above and Below: Natalie's apartment block in the Rue Therese near the Gare du Midi, which Captain Durnford visits during his courtship of Monique in BRIDGEHEAD (Rue Arthur Roland, Brussels, Belgium).

Above: The arcade through which Monique and Durnford stroll while courting in BRIDGEHEAD (Galerie de la Reine, Galeries Royales St Huberts, Brussels, Belgium).

Below: The back of the millhouse where Monique and Durnford stand while Alain and Natalie discuss Monique's intentions towards the Captain in BRIDGEHEAD (Waternewton Mill, Waternewton, Nr Peterborough, Cambs., UK).

Above: The church where Monique and Durnford are married in THE EXECUTION (St Jean et Etienne aux Minimens, Rue des Minimens, Brussels, Belgium).

Below: The front pew of the church in which Monique and Durnford are married, from which Natalie and the others watch the service in THE EXECUTION (Holy Trinity Church, Prince Consort Road, Kensington, London, UK).

Above: The aisle of the church from where Monique, Durnford and co. hear the bells chiming out the news that the war is over in THE EXECUTION (Holy Trinity Church, Prince Consort Road, Kensington, London, UK).

Below: One of the churches seen ringing out the good news in THE EXECUTION (Notre Dame du Sablon, Brussels, Belgium).

Above: The street in which Monique, Durnford, Natalie, Alain and Keldermans celebrate the liberation with their fellow Belgians in THE EXECUTION (Rue des Minimens, Brussels, Belgium).

Below: The warehouse cantonment in Molenbeek where Reinhardt was executed following the court martial led by Kessler in THE EXECUTION (New Crane Wharf, New Crane Place, Wapping, London, UK).

'We decided that – just as in *Secret Army* in which we endeavoured to base every happening upon reality wherever dramatically viable – we would continue that policy and investigate just what *did* happen to people like Kessler'

John Brason

KESSLER

(1981)

PRINCIPAL CAST

Ludwig Kessler / Manfred Dorf
CLIFFORD ROSE

Richard Bauer
ALAN DOBIE

Mical Rak
NITZA SAUL

Ingrid Dorf
ALISON GLENNIE

Franz Höss
NICHOLAS YOUNG

Colonel Hans Rückert
RALPH MICHAEL

Don Julian Yqueras
GUY ROLFE

Josef Mengele
OSCAR QUITAK

Hugo Van Eyck
JEROME WILLIS

José Garriga
JOHN MORENO

Karl Leider
ROBERT MORRIS

Albert
BERNARD HEPTON

Monique
ANGELA RICHARDS

Natalie
JULIET HAMMOND-HILL

Gidney
JEREMY WILKIN

Deakin
HAROLD INNOCENT

Maurer
ROYSTON TICKNER

Müller
GARETH MILNE

CREW

Series Devised by
GERARD GLAISTER and JOHN BRASON

Producer
GERARD GLAISTER

Writers
JOHN BRASON (1, 2, 4, 5, 6)
GERARD GLAISTER (3)

Directors
MICHAEL E. BRIANT (1, 2, 3, 6)
TRISTAN DE VERE COLE (4, 5)

Designer
CAMPBELL GORDON

Production Managers
IAN FRASER, RIITTA LYNN, WIM BERGERS

Production Associate
JOHN FABIAN

Production Assistants
WENDY PLOWRIGHT, CAROL BOLT

Assistant Floor Managers
PETER ROSE
LAURA GILBERT

Film Cameraman
GODFREY JOHNSON

Costume Designer
FIONA MATHERS

Make-Up Artist
TULAH TUKE

Sound Recordist
TERRY ELMS

Film Editors
ROBIN SALES, JOHN STOTHART

Videotape Editor
MALCOLM BANTHORPE

Studio Lighting
ALAN HENDERSON

Studio Sound
NORMAN CANLIN

Senior Cameraman
DENNIS CALLAN

Vision Mixer
NIGEL SHEPHERD

Technical Manager
JOHN MORRANS

Location Manager
ROBERTO PARRA

Graphic Designer
ALAN JEAPES

Properties Buyer
BRIAN READ

Technical Advisor
GRP. CPT. WILLIAM RANDLE CBE AFC DFM

Stuntmen
STUART FELL
GARETH MILNE

Music by
ROBERT FARNON

A BBC TV Production in Association with BRT Belgium

KESSLER - PRODUCTION

Whatever Happened to Kessler?

In the summer of 1980, some seven months after the third and final series of *Secret Army* had been broadcast, the Gerard Glaister-produced drama *Buccaneer* was in trouble. The thirteen-part series, devised by *Secret Army* writers N. J. Crisp and Eric Paice and script-edited by John Brason, was set in contemporary Britain and concerned an air freight company called Red Air. Its leading cast members were Bryan Marshall as a pilot named Tony Blair(!), Clifford Rose as JR-style financier Charles Burton and Pamela Salem as his wife Monica. Other key parts were played by Mark Jones, who had played Oberst Niedlinger in *Secret Army*, and Shirley Anne Field, best known for her film roles in *The Entertainer* (1960) and *Alfie* (1966). Despite scripts by N. J. Crisp, John Brason and David Crane and direction by Andrew Morgan and Tristan de Vere Cole, by the time the series's final episodes went out in July 1980, the BBC had already decided not to commission a second series, as it simply wasn't popular enough with the British viewing public. Rose, who had enjoyed playing Burton, believes that the relentless digs made by popular broadcaster Terry Wogan about the programme's cheapness (one such joke was that Burton smoked the exact same cigar week after week) had also contributed to it being axed.

Typically undeterred by the cancellation of *Buccaneer*, Gerry Glaister and John Brason (right) immediately began to discuss new projects. However, none appealed more than the prospect of a sequel to *Secret Army* which would investigate what had happened to Kessler since he and Madeleine fled from Belgium in 1945. They both felt that the fact that Kessler had been so popular meant that a follow-up was almost demanded of them, especially as he had 'entered the mythology of World War II in such a way as to be possibly more real and memorable than the persons upon which he was based.'[1] Soon entitled simply *Kessler*, the new six-part serial would be devised and scripted between late 1980 and early 1981.

Brason's initial ideas for *Kessler* included a stand-off for the former Standartenführer with the deceased Reinhardt's identical twin, who was seeking revenge for his brother's execution – a bizarre idea which got as far as Terrence Hardiman being asked if he was available but no further. However, the obvious genesis of the serial as it was finally produced, can be traced back to Brason's unbroadcast episode of *Secret Army*: *What Did You Do in the War, Daddy?*, in which the principal Lifeline characters are reunited and Kessler is, albeit briefly, seen to have successfully taken on a new identity as rich industrialist Manfred Dorf, head of Dorf Industries. As well as revisiting the idea of investigations into Dorf's true identity, Brason also elected to rework Lifeline's part in the proceedings – this time around they would be brought together in response to a direct invitation from a self-serving Belgian journalist called Van Eyck to view his footage of Dorf, rather than to enjoy a separate televised reunion in the Restaurant Candide. Crucially, Brason also decided to abandon the 1969 date of *What Did You Do in the War, Daddy?* in favour of an unspecified but more contemporary setting. Given the serial's preoccupation with the spectre of Nazism, Brason felt that a modern context would give *Kessler* a far more dramatic and unsettling edge. The fact that it would cost considerably less than a period piece was doubtless also an important consideration. A knock-on effect of this decision was the fact that both Kessler himself and his former enemies in Lifeline would be some thirty years older than they were in *Secret Army*, which would prove challenging for Rose and the serial's make-up artist in particular.

Despite the fact that the first episode relies heavily on the characters and familiar trappings of *Secret Army*, while devising their new serial, Brason and Glaister sensibly realised that if *Kessler* was to succeed in sustaining the viewers' interest then it had to introduce some strong new characters and scenarios which were unique and identifiable in their own right. The pair were also keen once again to achieve a significant level of realism: 'We decided that – just as in *Secret Army* in which we endeavoured to base every happening upon reality wherever dramatically viable – we would continue that policy and investigate just what *did* happen to people like Kessler.'[2] This starting point led them to explore the real-life activities of former members of the Third Reich and their presence in global society, the organisations in place to support such war criminals, their reaction to public revelation of their identity, and ultimately, as portrayed in popular films of the Seventies such as *The Odessa File* and *The Boys from Brazil*, the terrifying objective of a Fourth Reich.

War Criminals

At the time that *Kessler* was being written, the fate of Nazi Germany's two most infamous war criminals – Hitler's right-hand man, Reichsleiter Martin Bormann, and Auschwitz's notorious 'Angel of Death', Dr Josef Mengele – had increasingly come to command the fascination of not only the world's press, but also respected scholars and historians. Their whereabouts had also become an obsession for several Jewish individuals who displayed a missionary zeal in their dogged attempts to bring the men responsible for the Holocaust to justice, primarily in order to ensure that the full horror of what had taken place would never be forgotten. Foremost amongst these 'Nazi hunters' were Simon Wiesenthal, Tuvia Friedman (both of whom had written books about their endeavours, *Murderers Among Us* and *The Hunter* respectively), Dr Michael Bar-Zohar and husband-and-wife team Serge and Beata Klarsfeld. Best-selling books on the subject were also flourishing at the time, which typically promised to uncover the political conspiracies surrounding the continued survival in exile of Bormann (right) and Mengele, the nature and power of the protective Nazi undercover organisations and also the vast size of the Nazi fortune available to them. Brason seized upon all these elements in his writing.

Coincidentally, one war criminal in particular, Ernst Ehlers – who had been pursued by Serge Klarsfeld since 1962, when he had first been discovered working as an advisor to the Labor court of Schleswig-Holstein – was due to stand trial in Kiel, Germany, at the time that *Kessler* was being prepared. Ehlers was none other than the former Head of Gestapo in Brussels. A few days before the trial was due to commence, Ehlers committed suicide.

Unlike Ehlers, once he was unmasked, Brason and Glaister elected to have Kessler flee his native Germany and eventually arrive in South America, the final destination of many Nazis in exile. The writers incorporated the activities of the Kameradenwerk into their scripts in order to assist Kessler with his flight. Less well-known than the ODESSA (Organisation Der Ehemaligen SS-Angehorigen – 'Organisation of Former SS Members'), the equally secretive Kameradenwerk (literally 'Comrade Workshop') was believed to have possibly come into being after the ODESSA ceased operating around 1952. The Kameradenwerk, sometimes simply 'Kameraden', also sought to support the concealment and protection of Nazis overseas. According to journalist Ladislas Farago (author of *Aftermath: Martin Bormann and the Fourth Reich,* a source which appears to have strongly influenced Brason's writing), the ODESSA was 'actually little more than a shadowy consortium of a handful of freelancers and never amounted to much in the Nazi underground,'[3] whereas 'the Kameradenwerk was in fact what ODESSA was represented to be... financed lavishly from funds that [Colonel Hans] Rüdel, an unscrupulous fanatic, procured from his many friends among German financiers and industrialists... apprehensive lest their enormously profitable comeback be jeopardised if a rebuffed Rüdel exposed the taint of their Nazi past.'[4] During the war, Colonel Hans Ulrich Rüdel had flown 2,350 missions against the Allies and was considered to be the Luftwaffe's 'ace of aces'. Despite

losing a leg, Rüdel (left) continued to fly for his country and eventually, as the Wehrmacht didn't have an order high enough to do his much-vaunted exploits justice, Hitler himself created a new decoration especially for him which took eleven German words just to describe – even more in translation: Golden Oak Wreath with Swords and Diamonds to the Knight's Cross of the Iron Cross! Although Rüdel's flying achievements are well known, the zealous nature of his fanaticism for the precepts of Nazism and his post-war ambition to single-handedly assemble and lead the Kameradenwerk are far less so. The character and activities of Rüdel must have intrigued Brason, for in Kessler he was reproduced almost wholesale – give or take a few letters – as Colonel Hans Rückert.

The South American Connection

Ladislas Farago's incredibly detailed account in *Aftermath* of his protracted and dangerous search for Martin Bormann in South America, which first appeared as a series of articles in the *Daily Express* in November 1972, inspired much of the setup of the latter half of *Kessler*. In these articles he revealed that, despite the previously held – but unconfirmed – belief that Bormann had died in the streets of Berlin soon after fleeing Hitler's bunker, the Reichsleiter had in fact escaped to South America, where he had been living for the past twenty-four years. Furthermore, Farago claimed that he had met him and was even aware of his current living arrangements. A few days after Farago's articles were first published, German authorities of the State of Hesse suddenly announced that they had just found what they believed to be Bormann's skull and some of his bones in the precise location in West Berlin where seven years earlier an elaborate search for Bormann's remains had produced no results at all. Farago understandably considered their discovery to be dubious to say the least, especially as, just prior to the publication of his articles, he had offered the State of Hesse full access to the documentation he had obtained in South America (he was so confident that these materials proved that Bormann was alive that they were offered to the Hessian authorities in the hope that they might help them to finally apprehend him). In the introduction to *Aftermath* he sardonically states: 'I have authoritative proof that Bormann survived the war and went to Argentina in 1948; and obviously he could not have made the trip without his skull and bones.'[5] The pursuit of Mengele also receives considerable coverage in the pages of *Aftermath*, sometimes in direct connection with Bormann himself: 'During his stay in Bolivia, Bormann made several forays into Paraguay, showing up in Asunción to meet his friend Dr Josef Mengele.'[6] Farago also claimed that the Reichsleiter

550

regularly provided financial succour to his former colleague. Mengele's horrific crimes clearly made him a prime target for Nazi hunters and yet, unlike Bormann, there appears to be no question that he was alive and well in Paraguay, 'commuting between hideouts, always a step ahead of his pursuers, with an uncanny penchant for squeezing out of the tightest of situations.'[7] Brason clearly recognised the dramatic and atmospheric potential of the continued existence of this, at times, desperate individual, who lived in fear of suffering a similar fate to fellow Nazi Adolf Eichmann (who was abducted by an Israeli taskforce in May 1960 and later executed). Farago's frequent references to Paraguay and Asunción in particular, as well as that city's documented connection with both Bormann and Mengele, made it an appropriate and accurate choice as the location for the serial's finale.

Neo-Nazis

As well as the Nazi 'Old Guard', Brason sought to represent the equally disturbing new breed of Nazi extremism. To do this he elected to make Kessler and Madeleine's own daughter, Ingrid, a leading light amongst such a group. Ingrid would consider herself to take after her father, whom she deeply respects despite being frustrated by his connections with Bormann and the Kameradenwerk and their perceived lack of ambition beyond concealment in South America: "Does the Reichsleiter really think a new Germany will be built by inspecting fifty dagoes who fancy themselves in SS gear?!"

Provided in the narrative as a love – or at least sexual – interest for Ingrid is Franz, who is active in the same Neo-Nazi organisation, as well as being her father's manservant ensuring his personal security. In Brason's *Kessler* novel he is given the full name Franz Erich Melichar-Höss, although 'the Melichar part of the name Franz himself chose to drop... [it] had Jewish connotations that would have prejudiced his standing with the party.'[8] His name was perhaps chosen by Brason to provide added resonance, given its similarity to that of the commandant of the Auschwitz death camp: Rudolf Franz Höss. Franz was also a pseudonym that Mengele used during his exile.

New Avengers

In devising the serial's 'good guys' who would pursue Kessler throughout the narrative, Brason was similarly inspired by real men and women. In the preface of his *Kessler* novelisation, Brason states that the name of Bonn-based West German Intelligence agent Richard Bauer was 'not chosen by accident. 'Ricardo Bauer' was the favourite pseudonym, or alias, of Martin Bormann in South America. It is the author's quirkish sense of humour that uses it in its present context... it also helps to impress detractors who may think we have not done our homework.'[9] However, it is unlikely that this was the sole reason for the character's name, given the reputation of Dr Fritz Bauer, Prosecutor General of the State of Hesse who, for many years – before his mysterious and untimely death – sought to bring Bormann and other war criminals to justice (perhaps, given Bormann's choice of alias, he too had a quirky sense of humour?) Through Bauer's, and also his colleague Leider's, dangerous and repeatedly thwarted enquiries, Brason could dramatise the corruption and deception documented to have existed in West Germany due to the prevalence and power of former Nazis who had thus far escaped justice. It was this subject which was to later dominate *Radio Times* publicity for the serial.

Attractive Israeli Mical Rak, Bauer's eventual hunting partner, is perhaps more of a distillation of a variety of real-life female avengers such as Beata Klarsfeld, whom William Stevenson (author of *The Bormann Brotherhood*, another book used as source material for *Kessler*) described as 'a vital and good-

humoured young woman.'[10] It was Klarsfeld who smoked the infamous Klaus Barbie out of Bolivia, where he had turned himself into a respectable businessman, Señor Altmann. Brason may also have had in mind Nourit Haddad, who like Mical was a resident of Tel Aviv. Nourit risked her life by travelling to South America, taking on the alias Nora Aldot and gaining access to Mengele's inner circle while he was staying in Brazil. She passed for a German and Mengele (left), who had a weakness for women, soon fell for her and the pair became inseparable. However, her true intentions were discovered when Mengele's bodyguard located her Israeli passport under the false bottom of her suitcase. Nourit, who was hiking with Mengele up the Cerro Catedral at the time, was soon after dispatched off the edge of a cliff and her death recorded as an accident, despite the fact that it was later discovered that she was a member of the Israeli Secret Service. However, in *Kessler*, Mical Rak's vengeance would be personal rather than on behalf of Israel, a fact which did not convince journalist John Naughton when he came to review the series for *The Listener*: 'This lady protests that her interest is purely personal, but the way she kicks men in the balls and buries knives between their shoulder-blades suggests that she may yet be revealed as a Mossad employee.'

Other Characters

Of the other characters, Don Julian Yqueras (although of considerably lower status) is reminiscent of both the former President of Argentina, Juan Perón, a famous Nazi sympathiser who welcomed war criminals into his country and prevented their extradition and Paraguayan President Alfredo Stroessner – still in power in 1981 – who also allowed his country to become a haven for Nazi war criminals. Rückert's young Aryan SS-style security commander, Ulrich Müller, is no doubt named after the former Head of the Gestapo, Heinrich Müller, who at the time that *Kessler* was written was also still believed to be alive and well and residing with Bormann, coordinating all aspects of the Reichsleiter's security. While the choice of the first name Ulrich was due to the fact that it was Colonel Rüdel's middle name. Finally the surname of Mical's ill-fated travelling companion – Lieberman – was most likely derived from the 1978 film *The Boys from Brazil*, in which Laurence Olivier played a thinly veiled version of Simon Wiesenthal named Esra Lieberman.

Directors

As the six scripts for *Kessler* – which Brason considered to be 'much nearer the truth than has hitherto ever been portrayed' – neared completion, Glaister turned his attention to the production of the serial. The ever-busy producer was at the time just concluding work on *Blood Money* – a six-part BBC serial about a terrorist kidnapping, featuring *Secret Army* regulars Juliet Hammond-Hill (as chief terrorist Irene Kohl), Bernard Hepton and Stephen Yardley, and directed by Michael E. Briant, the lead director on the third series of *Secret Army*. The serial had originally involved the terrorist kidnapping of a prince and been titled *Blood Royal*, but Buckingham Palace intervened, making front page news in the process, resulting in the series being partially redubbed and renamed *Blood Money*. Nevertheless, the serial still held together well and Glaister was very pleased with Briant's work and immediately asked him to direct all of *Kessler* as well. However, as both series were scheduled for broadcast in late 1981, Briant remembers that: "I felt that the preparation time was simply not enough. I was coming off one very demanding show and, with no time to breathe, into another with the complications of extensive foreign filming for episodes that had not even been finished." He also judged that six hours was just "too big a canvas" for him to tackle. Another factor was that although he "had loved making *Secret Army* and had been very pleased with *Blood Money*," he "felt possibly that *Kessler* was going over old ground." Nevertheless, he was still keen to direct part of the serial and ended up handling four of the six episodes, including the crucial establishing instalments and the finale. For the remaining two episodes (four and five), both set in Paraguay, Glaister turned to another *Secret Army* stalwart – Tristan de Vere Cole, whom he had also worked with on *Buccaneer*. Rose was "extremely happy" to learn that Briant and De Vere Cole would be directing *Kessler*, as he counted them as two of his favourite *Secret Army* directors.

Returning Players

Casting was largely agreed upon by Glaister and Briant together, although of course several actors would be assuming the same roles they took in *Secret Army*. Clifford Rose, as the serial's title character, was of course totally indispensable. He was understandably very pleased to learn that Kessler's story would continue in a sequel serial; however, he remembers that the contemporary setting was a disappointment to him. Rose would have preferred to see Kessler and Madeleine's struggles in the immediate post-war period dramatised instead ("There was a great series to be made about that"), especially as it would mean that Kessler was still a comparatively young man and therefore would have allowed for the possibility of more than just the one series. Rose was informed that such an approach, which would have involved recreating 1950's Germany, would have been beyond the available budget. He was also disappointed that Hazel McBride would not be returning to the role of Madeleine, especially as he knew that the viewers had identified with the development of their relationship in *Secret Army*. Nevertheless, he was delighted that Brason would be scripting the serial, as they had had many previous discussions about his character and Rose knew that he would be keen to maintain Kessler's "redeeming human side, making sure he wasn't just a cardboard cut-out villain." Rose firmly believes that Kessler had "an integrity of his own – whatever you may think of him – he was true to his own principles and indeed lived by them" and that this was "down to Brason's writing."

© Carole Latimer

Several other *Secret Army* regulars were asked to return to their familiar roles, albeit for the opening episode only, including Angela Richards, Bernard Hepton, Juliet Hammond-Hill and Ron Pember. All of them accepted apart from Ron Pember, who was unavailable at the time of filming. As a result, Alain would not join in the reunion, although he is reinstated in Brason's *Kessler* novelisation, in which he is said to accept Van Eyck's invite principally in order to see Monique for the first time since the war. Despite these strong casting links with *Secret Army*, Brason and Glaister agreed that there was no place for Hazel McBride's Madeleine Duclos in their new serial; instead, viewers would learn that she died prematurely. Although McBride found this news disappointing, she still agreed to pose both alone and with Clifford for an extensive number of photos for the Dorf family photo album. The majority of these photos were taken in Chiswick – with McBride's six-week-old daughter Julia doubling for the baby Ingrid – and Richmond Park, while the remaining 'earlier' shots featuring Hitler were doctored by the BBC's graphics department to incorporate Kessler. This album and Kessler's enduring love for his late wife would prove to be crucial elements of the third episode, written by Glaister.

New Recruits

Undoubtedly the biggest name to be attracted to *Kessler* was Alan Dobie. Dobie was the first choice to play German agent Bauer and Briant remembers being "thrilled when he accepted." Dobie was best known for his self-confessed 'cornering of the market on Tolstoy,' having taken leading roles in *Resurrection* (Prince Dimitri Nekhlyudov) and the 1972 twenty-part adaptation of *War and Peace* (Prince Andrei Bolkonsky). He had also appeared in *The Planemakers* (David Corbett), *Diamond Crack Diamond* (John Diamond), Dennis Potter's *Double Dare* (Martin Ellis), *Hard Times* (Stephen Blackpool) and in the title role in the popular Seventies ITV

Victorian crime series *Cribb*. Dobie remembers being 'pleased to be playing a contemporary character for a change.'

When Juliet Hammond-Hill learned that Briant and Glaister were looking for an actress to play Kessler's daughter, Ingrid, she immediately thought of Alison Glennie and told them both that they must see her. Glennie remembers that: "We were both in the same episode of *Blake's 7* and she had become a very good friend." Glennie had started out as a child actress, appearing as: Jane Oakley in the Children's Film Foundation Cornwall-based film *Escape from the Sea*; as Lavinia in *A Little Princess* for the BBC; and as Katie in the first series of *Horse in the House* for Thames. She had also made appearances in *Thriller* (Annabella Tully in *A Midsummer Nightmare*), *Just William* (Moyna Greene) and with Alan Dobie in *Cribb* (Denise Winter in *Something Old, Something New*). Her *Blake's 7* episode, *Power*, in which she played Kate alongside Juliet Hammond-Hill as Pella, was broadcast in October 1981, a month before *Kessler* started to air. Once she was cast as Ingrid, Glennie recalls that she realised she would have to "play up a bit for the role. I was in my early twenties and I was supposed to be playing late twenties. But it wasn't too hard for me as I think I had the air of authority required."

Joining Glennie as Ingrid's lover, Franz, was Nicholas Young – another former child actor, best known for the role of John in the long-running cult Seventies children's series *The Tomorrow People*. Young, who had also appeared in *Blood Money*, remembers that he was a very late addition to the cast: "Gerry called my agent out of the blue a few days before filming. Either they had left the casting to the last minute or, as I suspect, the blue-eyed blond-haired Aryan actor they had in mind suddenly got a better offer!"

Briant recalls that casting Mical Rak was difficult, because of the specific requirements of the character – particularly her ethnic background and age. For

some time, Ishia Bennison (who would later play Guizin Osman in *Eastenders*) was considered for the role, but these plans were eventually shelved after Briant met actress Nitza Saul (left) (sometimes credited as Shaul). Army-trained Saul, who was well-known in her native Israel for playing ingénue roles in many Israeli films of the Seventies – such as *Hagiga B'Snuker* (Yona) and *Giv'at Halfon Eina Ona* (Yaeli) – immediately impressed Briant and the role of Mical was filled. However, Bennison didn't miss out entirely, being cast in the serial as Mical's ill-fated friend Ruth instead. Saul felt an immediate affinity for *Kessler*'s subject matter: "It isn't my life story, but it is something I know... I lost two aunts and some relatives [in the Holocaust] and my husband lost his grandparents and his uncle. It is part of reality in Israel. Knock on any door and you will find people who have lost someone."

Cast as the zealous Kameradenwerk leader, Colonel Rückert, was veteran actor Ralph Michael (right), whose career reached back well before World War II and who had actually been a Bomb Aimer during it. Briant had worked with him the previous year on a TV adaptation of *A Tale of Two Cities* (which Briant had written as well as directed) in which he had played Dr Manette. He was also known to Glaister for his work on an episode of *Colditz* (*Court Martial*). Briant considered many of the remaining supporting actors hired for the first three episodes, including Jerome Willis (van Eyck), Robert Morris (Leider), Jeremy Wilkin (Gidney), and Royston Tickner (Maurer), to be "old mates," adding that it was important for ongoing serials such as *Kessler* "to

have a mix of actors who are going to support each other and get on."

Tristan de Vere Cole was responsible for the casting of the new principal characters for the Paraguay-set episodes four to six. He chose Oscar Quitak – though a Jew – to play Mengele; Guy Rolfe, who had previously made a memorable appearance as Oberst von Elmendorff in the *Secret Army* episode *Russian Roulette* (and who had first worked for Glaister twenty-two years earlier on the six-part murder mystery *The Widow of Bath*), to play Yqueras; and John Moreno, whose most memorable role to date was that of the ill-fated Luigi Ferrara in the James Bond film *For Your Eyes Only*, for the role of José Garriga.

Aging Up

Before filming began, Clifford Rose remembers expressing some concern over Kessler's age in terms of "his viability as a lead character in a television serial" and also because he thought "it's very difficult to convincingly age on television." For this reason, he suggested to Glaister and Brason that "he still ought to be a man of some physical stature, not at all decrepit, and that it would be good for his first scene to see him swimming in a pool at his home or on an exercise bike." However, such a scene never materialised. Despite this suggestion, Rose would in general slow Kessler's movements down and make a great play of everyday activities like getting in and out of cars. The job of aging Rose, who was fifty-one at the time, to become a convincing seventy-seven year old (Rose has always believed that Kessler was born in 1900, which would mean that *Kessler* is set in 1977, rather than 1981 – he felt that an eighty-one-year-old Kessler would be much less believable) was down to make-up artist Tulah Tuke. Rose remembers that Tuke did some experiments at first "to see what would look best before finally coming up with what the viewers would see." The process, which Tuke took over an hour to complete, Rose recalls as "a real trial" as it involved "the application of scars to my forehead, work on my eyes and jaw-line, the scraping back of my naturally silvery-grey hair to give me the highest forehead possible and the addition of a moustache." Rose also elected to put on some weight in order to suggest that Kessler was not as fit or indeed as young as he was. He remembers putting on two stone in weight and that "while it was very easy to put on, it was much more difficult to take it off again!" For Kessler's costumes, Gerry Glaister instructed Rose to travel to Cologne – together with Michael E. Briant and costume designer Fiona Mathers – for a weekend prior to filming to make some purchases for the serial: "They were all genuine German clothes, including a black polo-neck sweater which all cultured Germans, such as Herbert von Karajan, seemed to be wearing at the time." Money was also splashed out on some special glasses for Kessler to wear: 'We found them in a wonderful opticians in Cologne – they were flat glass as I don't need them, but we wanted them to react to the light, so that when he's in South America they would be dark like sunglasses but when he was at home they were not. I felt they really added to the character."

557

Budget

As with all of his series, Glaister had insisted upon and managed to fund a very high ratio of film to studio, and planned to take the *Kessler* production team to Belgium, Germany, Wales, London and, for the episodes set in Paraguay, Almeria in Spain. Briant remembers that "The BRT co-production deal Glaister had negotiated was quite special as well... normally the co-pro company just put in the dosh, but in this case they provided all the motor cars... the BRT production manager, Wim Bergers, fixed and paid for all the locations, hotels, catering. They/he made a major contribution to the series." Nevertheless, there was not enough money to take a unit to Germany for several weeks as Briant would have liked, although they did go over the border to film in Aachen and Monschau.

Brussels and Beyond

Production began on 27 April 1981 with some brief location filming in the UK. Next up (from 6 May) was a return to the familiar environs of Brussels's magnificent Grand Place and specifically the exterior of the Candide. Arrival scenes were filmed at Brussels airport, and Albert and Monique's reunion was filmed in the foyer and lift in the Flemish part of the BRT television studios. As the Flemish division of BRT, rather than the French, was co-funding *Kessler*, there was some unhappiness with the foyer scenes in particular as they were filmed in the real Flemish reception area but incorporated French dialogue.

After Brussels, production moved on to the German city of Aachen – doubling for Bonn – where the principal scene was the demise of Hugo Van Eyck in the street outside Bauer's department. For the death, Brason had drawn upon the method by which Georgi Markov (a BBC World Service journalist and strong critic of the Communists) is believed to have been murdered in London in September 1978, via injection with poison from the tip of an umbrella. After Aachen, Briant and his team went on to the picturesque town of Monschau for the scene in which Mical purchases a rifle and is accosted by Leider. Briant recalls that, as the cast and crew didn't actually stay in Germany: "We used to go across the frontier every day with all our equipment. There would be six van-loads of gear to get through German customs at the beginning of each day." The filming block in Belgium and Germany concluded on 11 May.

The remaining locations for the first three episodes were all to be filmed back in the UK; as Briant recalls: "Anything that could be got away with at UK locations was excluded from foreign filming for cost reasons." However, before the UK work could begin, the production team ran into trouble trying to get back from mainland Europe. Instead of travelling by plane, the production team were driving back in the BRT-hired cars required for the next block of filming. Briant recounts that: "As the production people came off the ferry in Dover into customs, they were arrested for trying to import cars illegally into the UK!" The production crew were insured by the BBC, but crucially not registered as the hirers. The matter was eventually resolved after some five or six hours in custody, when production associate John Fabian called the BBC's legal department. They contacted the Head of Customs in London, made a large financial deposit and agreed a special deal. It was a shaken and fed-up team who were eventually permitted to return to London.

UK Filming

The first UK filming location was Brentford, where Bauer's arrival at the border post was shot and where Nicholas Young recorded his first scene for *Kessler* – Franz torturing Mical – on 13 May at the Docks. Young recalls that he wanted to make the scene 'as realistic as possible... Nitza was happy to spend time rehearsing so that the punches and the hits looked real. The rope round her wrists was very loosely tied and I made a point of hiding it with my hand when I released her.' Briant recalls that he had learnt from the SAS personnel he had met while making *Blood Money* that: "If you hang someone up like that by the arms, the beating can be less severe as it hurts more... Charming!" Young also remembers: 'I had not seen enough of *Secret Army* to register how Clifford was playing 'German'. He had a clever style of acting which was very Germanic. The inflections he uses makes you feel he is putting on an accent but in fact he is not. We met for the first time on location at the docks and I started off playing Franz with a German accent.' As filming progressed, Briant decided that "the base language was German and therefore without accent," and so Young was asked to

© Unknown

lose it, which is why, as filming was not done in sequence, Franz 'sometimes has an accent and sometimes not.' Alan Dobie muses that: 'It would have sounded very odd and probably difficult to listen to if we all had an accent.' Mical and Garriga would prove to be the only exceptions to this general rule.

Central London was the next stop, with locations including the exterior of the Hotel Russell in Russell Square and various busy London streets, for the sequences in which Kessler eludes his pursuers with the help of Ingrid and Franz. Clifford Rose recalls that the filming in London involved "going round and round Russell Square" and that the high volume of traffic – which the production team had no control over – proved problematic. Again because of his involvement with the SAS and professional security companies while making *Blood Money*, Briant remembers that "I was keen to use a modern system of surveillance, so a man outside the Russell Hotel keeping watch, became the BT van and its occupants." One of these men was actor Derek Martin, who now plays Charlie Slater in *Eastenders*. The scenes in which British agents Gidney and Deakin are introduced were also filmed on these days.

Clifford Rose subsequently returned to the Octagon Room at the Orleans House Gallery in Twickenham for the first time since filming scenes for the *Secret Army* episode *Revenge* there back in July 1979. In *Kessler*, the location would be used for the black-and-white sequence in which he is seen in his younger years meeting with Himmler when he was on his way up the ranks. Rose remembers that this was fun to do "because one had to look younger than one was rather than older" and was therefore in direct contrast to the requirements of the rest of the serial. It was during this shoot that several photos of the young dark-haired Kessler were taken for inclusion in the Dorf family album.

The final filming location in England was Stansted airport. Briant recalls "wanting Heathrow, as that was the only place that South American airlines operate out of, but the access fees and restrictions make it only viable for feature films." As a result, the Varig Airlines sign at Stansted airport was a BBC addition.

From there, the production moved on to two country houses in Wales on 18 May, which were to double for Kessler's homes at Schleiden See and Krefeld. Some key action sequences were filmed at these locations, both involving army-trained Nitza Saul. Alison Glennie remembers Nitza's background as "something that was amazing to me as a nice middle-class London girl... she had first-hand experience of weapons and was very familiar with that territory... whereas for me that was completely novel – I had no idea how to put a magazine into a handgun!" The majority of the BBC publicity shots were taken in the grounds of the 'Schleiden See house' (in reality a house in Cradoc near Brecon). However, during the fight scene here, Nitza twisted her ankle, which presented problems for her subsequently scheduled tussle with Franz outside Kessler's 'Krefeld home'. Briant's solution was to employ Ishia Bennison (Ruth) to be Nitza's double for these (thankfully night-based) scenes: "It is in fact only Nitza for the close-ups of the little fight on the patio; all the rest of the shots were doubled, so what was

Michael E. Briant (centre) directs the scene in which Mical Rak (Nitza Saul) meets Otto Dehmel (Nigel Lambert) in the grounds of Kessler's country residence

planned as a more extensive fight sequence became a kick in the pants!" These scenes were shot through a 'night image intensifier' and were one of the first times this had been used in television drama.

Other significant Welsh locations were Cardiff Airport, which doubled as Bonn in episodes two and three, and a factory at Abertillery which doubled as the Dorf Industries plant. Although the third episode pursuit of Leider and his visit to the service station were filmed in Germany, his final scene was also filmed in Wales. Briant remembers that it was difficult filming cars approaching as the British drive on the other side of the road and so he "flopped the film for that." He also recalls that he put down a 'bump' in the road, to represent Leider's body, for the car to go over, but that the BBC Head of Drama "cut that as soon as he saw it!"

Studio Recording

With all the film sequences for the first half of *Kessler* complete by 28 May, the cast began rehearsals on 1 June at the BBC's 'Acton Hilton' for the serial's studio recording. As on *Secret Army* a 'Producer's Run' was held at the end of each week, which involved running through all of the studio content for an entire episode in front of Gerry Glaister, who would watch each scene and then make any comments he felt appropriate privately to the director. Briant remembers that: "He seldom said much, so when he did comment on something it was worth taking note... Some producers would have several foolscap pages of detailed notes like 'He should lean on his left foot when he says that...' in order to feel they were in control. Gerry was always in control but knew that frequently less is more." After the 'Producer's Run' came the actual recording, but unlike *Secret Army*, this did not take place at BBC TV Centre. Instead, at the end of each week's rehearsals in Acton, the cast and crew would board planes or trains bound for Glasgow, as the studios allocated to *Kessler* were at BBC Scotland. The following day was reserved for camera rehearsal, while Friday was recording day, at the end of which everyone would travel back to London. Briant recalls: "Directors who failed to clear the studio so the cast and production crew could make the last overnight train were not flavour of the month." Nevertheless, he remembers that BBC Scotland's hosting of *Kessler* "had limited impact on the production... from a director's point of view it meant you could not have your favourite London camera crew, vision mixers, designers etc., but the enthusiasm and knowledge of the Scottish crews and staff more than made up for this. I particularly remember Campbell Gordon [designer] as being a pleasure to work with and very efficient and talented." Alison Glennie also has fond memories of the studio recording: "On a series you have the luxury of getting to know everyone really well, whether they be cast or crew, it engenders a good atmosphere and promotes better work."

The scenes featuring the return of the Lifeline characters were some of the earliest studio scenes to be recorded. Briant recalls their return as one of the best things about doing *Kessler*: "It was great to see Bernie and Angie and Jules greying up to reappear and to see that Albert was still running the Candide and film it again in the Grand Place." Echoing the views of many of the TV critics at the time, Briant also felt that: "It was nice for us all to get together again, replaying the *Secret Army* days," but "personally I would have liked to see it go on longer and to see more of the three of them." He also wondered if they could even have been involved in the hunt for the Neo-Nazis – a narrative option which Brason and Glaister had dismissed, but which for many years was regularly reported as what actually happened in the serial!

Immediately after one of the Glasgow recording days, Briant flew to Southern Spain then drove to Almeria – the location that had been chosen to represent Asunción in Paraguay for the final three episodes. West of Almeria, inland of El Palmer, was an area of dry and rocky terrain that had been used for many spaghetti westerns and was perfect for those scenes not set in Asunción. Briant arrived there at midday on Saturday and, after a brief recce, jumped on another plane back to London at midday on Sunday, so as to be back in the rehearsal room on Monday morning!

A Suitable End

Around this time, Glaister approached Rose to ask how he might feel about playing Kessler for a further series. Rose felt that as Kessler was as old as 77 in the new serial and that as "the hunting and pursuing theme had a limited life," there was little scope for such a venture and really nowhere for such a series to go: "All you could show was that he got away at the end and do it all over again." Given Rose's answer, Glaister therefore said to him that he thought Kessler really ought to be "finished off" in the current serial. There followed a lot of discussion about how he might die and for some time it was agreed that he would simply be shot by one of his pursuers (either Bauer or Mical), an ending for the character that Rose himself "didn't think was very interesting" and which led him to suggest that Kessler commit suicide instead. Rose though that "Being the man he was, for all his better qualities, he was still politically an absolutely fervent Nazi and utterly believed in that," and that he therefore "wouldn't want to live in a world without National Socialism" (a stance that was confirmed for Rose many years later when he watched the film *Downfall* in 2005, which depicted many suicides carried out for this exact reason). Set on the idea of Kessler's suicide, Rose then "remembered that the Captain of the German battleship the Graf Spee, who was called Captain Hans Langsdorff (right), scuttled his ship in Montevideo and committed  suicide," and that "he did it on the German flag." Rose mentioned this to Brason and Glaister who "thought it was a very good idea and so John Brason wrote the final script to incorporate that."

Handover

Of the mid-July handover to fellow director Tristan de Vere Cole for the rehearsals and studio recording of episodes four and five, Briant recalls that Tristan "was not very keen to discuss the earlier part of the show, as he felt once it got to South America it was a different pace. It certainly slowed down and became different, which is of course right and proper. A change of pace in a long running serial is valuable."

With a new director at the helm, Nicholas Young once again encountered issues with his character's accent. Although De Vere Cole was coming into the series midway through, 'he decided I was playing Franz too much like an English public schoolboy.' Young argued that it was too late in the day to change his portrayal of the character, and now muses that 'Some may argue there is not a lot of difference between a certain type of English public schoolboy and a Neo-Nazi!'

South America in Glasgow

For the studio recording of these later episodes, Clifford Rose remembers that "It felt very odd being in South America in Glasgow!", especially as the cast had not yet seen the location exteriors. Several important scenes during this block saw Rose play opposite Oscar Quitak. The pair enjoyed working together and, some time after *Kessler*, Brason wrote a two-hander comedy series for them about the Common Market; however, it never went into production.

Nicholas Young recalls that there was a mistake in the dressing of the Kameradenwerk's Paraguayan headquarters: "When I first saw the set I could not believe my eyes – the swastikas on the wall were back to front. Even Gerry (who I believe had shot one or two down during his time in the RAF) failed to notice. I'm glad to say that Franz saved the day by pointing out the error."

For the scenes in the final episode in which Kessler is seen playing Schumann's 'Scenes from Childhood' (Kinderszenen) at Yqueras's house – the piece that his mother is seen to play during the flashback sequence, and which Kessler had previously listened to in *Guests at God's Table* and earlier in this serial – Clifford Rose was determined to perform it himself. He remembers that: "I had learnt the piano as a small boy, but ended up asking my parents if I could stop" and that when it came to trying to pick it up again for *Kessler*, he found he "couldn't remember a note." Consequently he asked if he could have a music teacher. After this was agreed, Rose was tutored for an hour a day for three weeks at the Acton rehearsal rooms. He recalls that he learnt it "parrot fashion, adding two notes a day until finally I learnt it all." When it came to the recording, Rose played the piece right through without any problems, leading Michael E. Briant, who was not aware of the teaching he had received, to assume that Rose was an accomplished pianist.

Many years after *Kessler*, Alison Glennie would use a recording of Ingrid's death scene, which was filmed during this studio block, as a way of engaging the

© George Walker

interest of a group of teenagers in a drama class. She recalls that Gareth Milne dressed in a replica blue dress for the stunt: "I was all for trying it out myself being quite intrepid and a bit tomboyish, but I think perhaps they were worried about insurance costs."

Episode six's director, Briant, remembers that Ingrid's demise was by no means the only death performed by stuntman Gareth Milne. In fact, just as in his *Secret Army* episode *Ambush*, where everyone you see die was stuntman Stuart Fell, here in this final instalment – with the exception of Kessler – everyone you see die was Gareth. As well as Ingrid's shooting, he also performed Garriga's fall (pushed over the stairwell by John Moreno (left) in a blond wig, so that the actor in effect killed off his own character!), Franz's shooting and tumble down the stairs, and finally his own character's death when, due to Bauer's intervention, Müller's truck careers off the road and blows up.

One of the last studio scenes to be recorded, with Briant back as director, was Kessler's suicide scene in the Kameraden HQ set on 21 August 1981. Clifford Rose remembers that it was recorded as many as nine times, a situation at the time that made him wonder if he was doing anything wrong. He was subsequently reassured by Briant that the problems were due to the fact that the director was attempting to achieve a tricky wide-angled shot – which was causing lots of camera crane and sound issues – in order to give the scene sufficient dramatic resonance. Briant recalls that they were not permitted to use blood as part of Kessler's death scene, despite the fact that this final episode was ultimately transmitted well after the 9pm watershed, something which Rose feels makes the death unfortunately seem "slightly unreal".

With studio recording complete, the cast took ten days' break before departing for Spain on 4 September to begin location filming for episodes four and five, once again under Tristan de Vere Cole's direction, giving Briant an opportunity to supervise the editing of the first three episodes and to get ready for his final block of location filming. As he had suspected, if he had taken on all six episodes as originally suggested by Glaister, he would "have been exhausted and unable to prepare properly."

South America in Spain

De Vere Cole immediately faced unforeseen problems in Almeria when it became clear that the Spanish location 'fixer', Roberto Parra, could not 'fix'! He recalls that Parra 'was pretty hopeless and a total anathema to the local 'film mafia' who controlled filming in Almeria... it was a big mistake not to use a local fixer.' Parra aside, matters were made worse by the fact that this film mafia 'had an inflated idea of what they should get, having been used to the spaghetti westerns and films like *Patton*.' (As an interesting aside, *Patton* was based on a biography by Ladislas Farago, author of the aforementioned *Aftermath*). De Vere Cole remembers that they 'priced themselves out of the market, but at the time the BBC were committed' and so ultimately accepted the terms. Alison Glennie remembers hearing that in the end, "It would have been cheaper for us to have gone to South America!"

Despite these tribulations, De Vere Cole 'enjoyed getting atmosphere from the Almeria locations,' and although he was happy with the Kameradenwerk headquarters, he was not keen on the proposed spot (on a corner in a town) for Kessler's rendezvous with Bormann and Mengele. Together with his Finnish production manager Riitta Lynn, he elected to look for a location out in the countryside instead, and found the atmospheric deserted farmhouse that was eventually used. One part of the location, a wide, round, stone threshing area, looked to De Vere Cole to be 'perfect for a helicopter' – something which he felt would be a good addition to the conclusion of the rendezvous sequence; but when he sought John Fabian's approval he was told that he would have to make do with a plane fly-past. He pointed out that a helicopter booking from base to location and back to base of two hours would not have been costly, but to no avail. De Vere Cole muses that: 'The likelihood of our heroes missing a plane on a nearby strip seemed to me very unlikely. All that the production team had told me about the pay-outs to the local film mafia and the overspends on the previous episodes was being confirmed.' However, Briant does not think that there was any overspend at all and instead believes that John Fabian and Gerry Glaister denied De Vere Cole's request as it was not considered "value for money," and also that they "wanted to keep enough money available for me – for the stunt men and vehicle wrecks in the last episode. It was important that the show finished on a high."

Nicholas Young remembers having an enjoyable time in Almeria: "When we weren't filming we were in the pool... I was trying to improve my Spanish with one of the locals... the señorita spoke no English but we understood each other well enough for the purpose!"

When it came to filming the rendezvous scenes for episode five, Alan Dobie

© Unknown

recalls that the script originally required Bauer to be aiming a rifle at Mengele and Kessler: 'I persuaded the director I should use a telephoto camera instead, so that he's collecting proof of their existence.' Clifford Rose remembers the driving requirements of this episode as "exacting" due to the heat and the terrain, but that Tristan de Vere Cole's positive comments about his driving boosted his confidence. Rose was even required to drive the car during the windscreen-shattering sequence which he found "quite hairy!" De Vere Cole recalls that, on that same day, when 'filming Kessler driving down the dusty track to the rendezvous, I noticed the camera was tilting up and then that Godfrey Johnson, the film cameraman, was sliding down the tripod in a faint. 'Montezuma's Revenge' had struck and the crew were very grateful for my loo paper,' which Tristan produced from his ever-present 'Naval grip': a zip canvas bag in which he also carried his scripts, a pen-knife, string, a tape measure etc., and which had until this point been a source of amusement to the crew. Pretty much the whole cast and crew were affected and Oscar Quitak (below left) somewhat ironically became the unit doctor, handing out herbal remedies.

Johnson himself remembers that there was no way of getting electricians in Almeria and that they had to hire them – together with electrical gear – in Madrid. He also recalls that safety standards there were quite different and that "the Spanish electricians were quite happy to follow the actors around with great six-lighter lamps while they were on." These lamps were used to light the actors' eyes and were especially important because of the harsh overhead sunlight on location. Johnson also recalls that the location filming in Almeria was the only time that he came across a group of real-life Nazis: "Young men in brown-shirts, manning a recruitment stall at a festival."

After location filming on episodes four and five was completed, Michael E. Briant returned to Almeria for the first time since his whistle-stop recce, and remembers: "It was nice to be able to pick up the pace again for the last episode" Of his death scene, Nicholas Young remembers that, after Franz's fall down the stairs, there was no time to do the next shot in which Mical finds him, and so: 'For continuity purposes I had to stay put until after lunch (well that's what they told me anyway!), so I was stuck there without so much as a sandwich for a good twenty minutes! The later scene in which the armed Müller, played by stuntman Gareth Milne, is up on the roof opposite Garriga's hostel prompted a situation that Briant had not bargained on. He remembers that: "The production team had informed five out of the six police and national security organisations that we were filming and that there was to be a stuntman with a gun on the roof... the sixth organisation [the Guardia Civil] sent out snipers to shoot Gareth!" Godfrey Johnson, who was filming Milne at the time, takes up the story: "All of a sudden the square downstairs was full of policemen with proper guns and flakjackets. I bashed into the director [Briant] who was shooting out of the back door and we both walked around the front and pretended to be tourists!" Briant concludes: "Godfrey and I retired to a room in the hostel and had a few beers whilst we waited the couple of hours it took for the Spanish liaison guys to sort the problem." Despite this incident, Briant remembers that,overall, "I had a lot of fun with the action in episode six and was pleased to round the series off."

As the Spanish location filming neared its completion date (18 September), Gerry Glaister concentrated on the requirements for the serial's credit sequences. Once again, the talents of Robert Farnon (who, like Glaister passed away in 2005) were called upon for the title music – this time a reworking of his much-admired *Secret Army* theme. For the title images, Glaister elected to use a photo of Kessler in full Nazi regalia, over which a rostrum camera roved. For the final few frames of the closing titles, he chose a shot of Kessler 'today'.

Publicity

Leading up to the serial's broadcast, the British public were appropriately enough being treated to a re-run of a selection of episodes from the second and third series of *Secret Army*. Despite their transmission on BBC2, viewing figures were once again very favourable.

Although *Kessler* did not receive promotion for its opening episode on the front cover of the *Radio Times* – that honour was won by former *Secret Army* guest star Christopher Guard and Judi Bowker for the new four-part World War I serial *Love Story: Wilfred and Eileen* – it did receive a four-page feature incorporating large colour photos of Clifford Rose, Alan Dobie and Nitza Saul. However, the accompanying text, written by Tom Bower (author of *Blind Eye to Murder* – an account of the Allied treatment of Nazi war criminals and the failure to de-Nazify Germany), was only concerned with 'the many thousands of German war criminals who went unpunished'[11] rather than the serial itself.

The majority of pre-broadcast press publicity reported that it was the former Lifeline personnel who would be on Kessler's tail ('Old adversaries bent on making him pay for his crimes'), which made good copy and provided a stronger link back to *Secret Army*, but was not at all accurate. The serial was heavily promoted by *The Sun*, who previewed it on 7 November 1981 through an interview with Clifford Rose. The feature was titled 'Get Kessler!' and illustrated by a photo of a youthful-looking Rose in his garden at home. The interview concentrated on make-up requirements for the serial, the changes to Kessler's character since *Secret Army* and Rose's concern that 'we have to be careful not to glorify Nazis.' The *Daily Mirror* also interviewed Rose and revealed that many of the characters in the serial were based on real people. Meanwhile, in an article entitled 'Oh what a beautiful war!', the *Daily Mail* contrasted Nitza Saul's acting background with that of Emily Bolton, who was appearing as Christina Campbell in the first series of the BBC's *Tenko* at the time.

Broadcast and Reception

Kessler first aired at 8pm on Friday 13 November 1981, after the first episode of a new series of the long-running sitcom *Terry and June*. ITV competition included *Bruce Forsyth's Play Your Cards Right* and the Mollie Sugden comedy *That's My Boy*. Press reaction to the new series was mixed. Writing for *The Times*, Michael Ratcliffe considered that Clifford Rose, 'as the object of all the excitement, properly gives off the air of a man who has spent thirty years out of the fresh air in centrally heated boardrooms' and praised Alan Dobie as 'splendid.' Nancy Banks-Smith noted in *The Guardian* that 'Kessler will have to fight for his position as pre-eminent and terrible villain,' given the presence of both Rückert and Van Eyck, with the latter's callousness dominating her review. She was also fascinated by Rose's apparent ability to 'twitch invisible whiskers.' Writing for *The Listener*, John Naughton felt that the 'fast-moving and action-packed' series was 'as strong on technical detail – guns, surveillance gear, cars –

as it is weak on characterisation.' The *Daily Telegraph*'s Ronald Hastings, who had always been a loyal supporter of *Secret Army*, observed that it was ironic that the former series's villain was the 'one character considered popular enough to build a whole new series around' and was pleased – initially at least – 'to have the *Secret Army* setting and cast back.' However, after watching episode two, Hastings complained 'that you are rarely sure where you are' and that there was 'too little of Kessler himself' in the serial. The *Daily Mail*'s Mary Kenny was, like many critics, more interested in the *Secret Army* Lifeline regulars than the new characters and – despite their obvious departure from proceedings during episode one – hoped for more information on what had happened to Albert, Monique and Natalie in the intervening years in the remaining episodes. Unfortunately, *Kessler*'s later instalments were largely ignored by the press. One notable exception was Stan Sayer of the *Daily Mirror*, who described *Kessler* as 'a great thriller series,' although on 18 December he complained that there had not been enough action sequences during the run. *The Sun* was the serial's biggest supporter in terms of column inches and followed its pre-broadcast interview with Rose with three more mini-interviews throughout the run. An interview with Angela Richards accompanied the 13 November TV listings, in which she said that she found the aging-up for the serial a 'jolting experience... looking in the mirror was like taking a peep into the future.' Richards also revealed that this was 'positively the last appearance of Monique,' adding that 'I am sad to say goodbye to her because it has been a marvellous part.' On 11 December came an interview with Alison Glennie entitled 'Alison likes to turn nasty!' in which the actress explained that she 'would rather be evil than play the heroine' and mused that she had been 'a poisoner in *Cribb* and now as Kessler's daughter a political fanatic... because I have a rather deep voice and I tend to be a bit serious.' Finally, to accompany the serial's finale, a brief interview with Alan Dobie – the appallingly titled 'Snow-go for a Nazi hunter' – seemed to be more interested in the actor's recent encounter with a snow drift than it was with his role in *Kessler*. A rather late review of the serial in the 8 February edition of *Broadcast* by W. Stephen Gilbert argued that: 'While the subject matter was important and the moral issues complex, the series was, inevitably, thick ear and worse, hard to follow.' He concluded that 'Brason always airs his research but hard work itself is not enough.'

Viewing figures for the serial were good, with the opening instalment receiving 10.6 million viewers; a figure which dropped off slightly during the run to 9.3 million by the final episode. Audience appreciation, as measured by the BBC's Viewing Panel Report, was also positive. Over half the viewers surveyed had watched all six episodes and rated the serial with an 'A' grade, while the average audience Reaction Index score was a healthy 73.5. Although some viewers complained that they had 'been expecting *Kessler* to be more like *Secret Army*' and that 'the scenes in South America were considerably less interesting than those in Europe,' the majority view was that: the serial was 'exciting and believable'; the conclusion was 'particularly appreciated'; 'the camera-work had been excellent'; and that the whole cast gave 'convincing performances,' with both Clifford Rose and Alan Dobie being singled out for specific praise.

In Conclusion

Rose himself was relatively pleased with the final result but felt that the series didn't wholly do Kessler justice, principally because so many years had been missed out between then and the war; however, he felt that his dramatic exit was very fitting. Overall though, he felt that the production didn't quite realise its potential. Michael E. Briant also had his reservations, specifically with it being 'sold' as a sequel to *Secret Army* when, apart from the first episode, it wasn't that at all, but a new adventure in its own right, with a very different feel. When looking back at the serial in 2005, Briant, who now lives in France, considered that its theme of secret Neo-Nazi organisations still has relevance today: "There are a lot of very right-wing people out there and *Kessler* was beginning to expose this sore that runs through our society… and to address those problems. The Nazi party hasn't gone away, it hasn't vanished, the Kesslers of this world are out there and their sons and daughters are out there doing very well indeed. Le Pen in France is enormously successful and very popular. There are a lot of right-wing people in the European community and I think it behoves us to look at shows like *Kessler*… that was one of the reasons why it was good to do the show. It felt important at the time and it still feels important today."

John Brason's novelisation of the serial was published in hardback and paperback while *Kessler* was still being broadcast in late November, but the programme was never repeated by the BBC, although it was released in edited form by BBC Video in the early Nineties. Around the same time, satellite station UK Gold broadcast the series for the first time since 1981. DD Home Entertainment released the serial on DVD in 2005, together with a slideshow of photographs from the Dorf family album prop, an audio commentary on episode six and a documentary entitled *Kessler Uncovered* directed by Andy Priestner and featuring contributions from Michael E. Briant and Clifford Rose. The serial was repeated on UK TV History twice in 2008 due to popular demand.

KESSLER: Part One

WRITTEN BY: John Brason   **DIRECTED BY:** Michael E. Briant

FIRST BROADCAST: Friday 13 November 1981

REGULAR CAST: Ludwig Kessler / Manfred Dorf: CLIFFORD ROSE; Richard Bauer: ALAN DOBIE; Mical Rak: NITZA SAUL; Ingrid Dorf: ALISON GLENNIE; Franz Höss: NICHOLAS YOUNG; Colonel Hans Rückert: RALPH MICHAEL; Hugo Van Eyck: JEROME WILLIS; Karl Leider: ROBERT MORRIS

SUPPORTING CAST: Albert Foiret: BERNARD HEPTON; Monique Durnford: ANGELA RICHARDS; Natalie Chantrens: JULIET HAMMOND-HILL; Gidney: JEREMY WILKIN; Deakin: HAROLD INNOCENT; Maurer: ROYSTON TICKNER; Ruth Lieberman: ISHIA BENNISON; Leitgeber: HUGH SULLIVAN; Neumann: TERENCE CONOLEY; Frau Neumann: CYNTHIA GRENVILLE; Weber: MAURICE QUICK; Frau Weber: ELISABETH CHOICE; Graun: JOHN DEARTH; Helene: ANNA MOTTRAM; Agent: REG WOODS; Wim: MALCOLM BANTHORPE

SYNOPSIS: Present day Belgium. Journalist and documentary maker Hugo Van Eyck meets Albert at the Candide to ask him to help him his investigations into Nazi war criminals. German intelligence agent Richard Bauer arrives in Brussels to see Van Eyck about the very same matter. Two Israeli girls also arrive in the capital – Mical Rak and Ruth Lieberman. Mical also wants to see Van Eyck due to the fact that her late mother received a letter from him. Monique returns to Belgium for the first time since the war and is reunited with Albert and Natalie at the BRT television studios. Van Eyck asks them to view footage of an interview he conducted with a German industrialist called Manfred Dorf, who he believes to be Kessler. Monique and Natalie confirm his identity as Kessler but Albert claims to be less convinced. Mical meets Van Eyck and tells him that Kessler evicted her mother and her family from their house in the Grand Place and ordered them to be sent to Dachau, an experience from which her mother never truly recovered. Mical agrees to pass on any information she might find that links Dorf to Kessler in return for his home address. At his home in Krefeld, Germany, Kessler (Dorf) has obtained a VHS copy of the documentary programme that Van Eyck has made for Belgian television and watches it with his daughter Ingrid, assistant Franz, and old friend and German war hero Hans Rückert. Kessler is perturbed to find that the piece principally targets him and the subject of his true identity. After watching the programme, Albert, Monique and Natalie, who are having dinner in one of the Candide's upstairs rooms, discuss whether tracking down Kessler still matters. Their opinions are divided but they agree not to let it spoil their brief reunion. Rückert suggests to Kessler that it is time he went to ground and Kessler reminds him that he has "the key to the Kameraden money-box." Mical arrives in Krefeld with Ruth and pays a visit to Kessler's home. She is spotted prowling outside the house and is apprehended by Franz, but manages to make a getaway. Bauer is warned off from investigating the question of Dorf's identity by his boss and ordered to take two months' leave. Kessler, Ingrid and Franz arrive at the former's country retreat,; en route Ingrid shows her father that the Belgian papers' front pages are full of news stories about him and Van Eyck's revelations. Monique pays a brief visit to the Candide by taxi to say an emotional goodbye to Albert. Ingrid tries to convince Kessler that her group of young Nazis are more relevant and dynamic than the old men of the Kameraden and that they need his leadership. He thinks her group is no better than the Baader-Meinhof and rejects her suggestions. Mical discovers that Kessler has left his Krefeld home and upon returning to her hotel is appalled to discover that Ruth has been murdered and has had a Nazi swastika carved on her back.

REVIEW: The single biggest problem faced by *Kessler* is the fact that people have, and inevitably always will, come to it with preconceived expectations as to its likely content and approach, specifically the idea, nay desire, that it will be a true sequel to the wartime series that preceded it. On the whole, they can be forgiven for thinking this because, initially at least, *Kessler* actively seeks to secure this connection. The opening music is only a slight variation on Robert Farnon's *Secret Army* theme, the presence of no less than four of that series's regular actors in the opening titles of episode one, and the setting of some of the earliest scenes outside the Candide, all suggest that this will be a serial that will fully utilise its *Secret Army* trappings. However, as this episode progresses, it quickly becomes clear that these elements will actually have very little bearing on the serial – which has a completely different agenda and scope to its antecedent – and are here principally to remind us of Kessler's wartime career. If there was an element of the production team using the *Secret Army* brand simply in order to ensnare viewers, then who can blame them, as they were in the business of making popular television after all.

The Lifeline reunion is sensitively handled, underplayed even, a decision that was perhaps partly a reaction to the rather exaggerated emotion on display in the unbroadcast episode *What Did You Do in the War, Daddy?* However, this does mean that these scenes do fall a little flat in places. Although it is genuinely heart-warming to see them all meet up again, the time allocated to their reunion cannot begin to explore the impact that their wartime experiences have had on their lives. Thankfully, Brason elects not to even try to do this, perhaps having learnt from his earlier mistakes on the ill-fated episode 43, choosing to leave a lot of things unsaid and simply hinted at instead. Later that decade, the production team of *Tenko* wisely realised that they actually needed the luxury of almost a whole series in order to satisfactorily explore the after effects of the war on its characters and to observe them try, often unsuccessfully, to pick up their lives and move on.

The wonderfully-named make-up artist Tulah Tuke sensibly elects to choose a 'make-up lite' approach when aging the former *Secret Army* actors. Instead of the dubious flaky skin and heavy tans on offer in *What Did You Do in the War, Daddy?*, older hair styles and clothing are the main tools used to suggest the passage of time. As a result, the actors are relied upon, more than they otherwise might be, to act their age and slow themselves down. Due to his status as the serial's lead actor, Clifford Rose has the most to do in this regard and always ensures that Kessler makes a great play of getting in and out of cars slowly, walking less quickly and generally being less sprightly. He is largely successful in this regard, but it is perhaps not obvious just how difficult his task was until we see a thoroughly convincing pre-war Kessler standing before Himmler, looking as though he is in his early Thirties, which reminds us how young Rose still was in 1981. Only once in this first episode does Tuke's make-up appear overdone, perhaps due to changes made between filming and studio recording, in the scene in which Monique is seen for the last time in a taxi looking very pallid indeed. Of the *Secret Army* regulars, Natalie perhaps comes off the worst, looking like a cross between Miss Babs from *Acorn Antiques* and Simone de Beauvoir!

The first half of the episode is particularly well constructed as the serial's various protagonists converge on Brussels and more specifically the Grand Place, cleverly drawing the viewer into the story in the process. Given that the pair will team up later on, it is a particularly nice touch that Bauer is seen parking his car just before Mical walks into shot in the foreground.

One problem with this first episode (and with later episodes too) that was picked up on by critics at the time, is that it is not always entirely clear what country we are in at different points of the narrative. As there are such a large number of locations in the first instalment alone – Brussels, London, the German countryside, Krefeld and Bonn – James Bond-esque place, date and time captions would certainly have prevented the resultant confusion. Perhaps more perplexing though is some of the dialogue on offer. The conversations between the London-based double act, Gidney and Deakin, and later, between Maurer and Bauer, are reminiscent of the 'spy speak' which characterised the BBC's *Tinker, Tailor, Soldier, Spy* (for which the *Radio Times* felt compelled to provide their readers with a helpful glossary). While arguably there is a place for this in a serial like *Kessler*, especially as it bears hallmarks of an espionage thriller, the former pair's allusion to the fact that "the water is still warm", talk of associates being "on the fringe" and deciding to "push bait into a friend's court" are verging on the impenetrable.

Jerome Willis clearly enjoys himself as the ethically challenged journalist Van Eyck, a character who is startlingly honest about his selfish motives: "Personal crusades against a bunch of geriatric Nazis just don't ring the cash register." Tellingly, he doesn't react at all when Mical tell him about the horrors her mother endured in Dachau, immediately asking her an unrelated question rather than taking the time to sympathise with her. Although his morals appear rather dubious, Van Eyck is presented as one of the few characters in the serial who is not at all complacent about the very real threat that the Nazi movement presents to contemporary society (as he tells Albert, "Nazism exists today like a giant mafia throughout Germany and Europe!"), a threat that the serial is intent on exploring in some considerable detail.

On the subject of the continued existence of Nazism in Europe, the revelation towards the end of the episode that Ingrid is, like her father, involved in such a movement would have been considerably enhanced if, earlier in the episode, we'd seen her at a rally, say, or having a clandestine meeting with like-minded individuals, rather than strutting around in her high heels to no great effect. The fact that such a group exists, that she is crucial to its organisation and that they are looking to the likes of Kessler to lead them, should have been a revelation afforded considerable fanfare; however, in the event it is offered as almost throwaway exposition. This is by no means the fault of Alison Glennie, who in this scene offers the first real glimpse of just how chillingly resolute a character Ingrid will turn out to be: like father, like daughter. The Kameradenwerk itself, the old guard Nazi organisation which both Rückert and Kessler are very much a part of is, like Ingrid's beliefs, introduced almost in passing, as part of a conversation between Bauer and Leider. Both agents seem to be totally unfazed by its existence and talk about it as if it is NATO or the UN, rather than a supposedly top secret Nazi organisation! Although Brason was obviously totally *au fait* with the idea of the Kameradenwerk (or indeed with the proof of its existence), he should not have assumed that the same level of knowledge is held by the viewer. Neither should he have deemed it appropriate to introduce its existence in such a low-key manner.

The generation gap that divides Ingrid's Neo-Nazi movement from the elderly Kameraden is a fascinating one, which is set to be explored throughout the serial, and is set up in *Kessler* as early as Van Eyck's narration of his *In Our Time* exposé: "Is it a question of certain elements among the young wishing to assert themselves under the guise of National Socialism? Is it the latter day writhings of the old Nazi guard who survived the demise of Hitler's Germany?" Judging by Ingrid's condemnation of the Kameraden ("Do you think those old fools living in Brazil or Paraguay are ever going to do anything?") and her grave doubts that 'Der Tag' will ever come and, conversely, Kessler's description of Ingrid and her friends as "children without purpose" who have no hope of bringing Nazism back to Germany, the first indications are that there is a tough and bloody fight ahead. The fact that one faction is represented by Kessler and the other by his daughter is a dramatically interesting, if not ingenious, idea.

Clifford Rose is naturally superb, although in this first episode he does not yet have much of an opportunity to prove that Kessler's will is just as strong as it ever was. However, there are several important glimpses of the old mettle: when he exclaims that Graun is an idiot; his reminder to Rückert that he has the key to the Kameraden money-box and therefore should be protected; and his warning to Ingrid that her misplaced faith may cause him to disown her as a daughter.

Brason undoubtedly chose to create Mical Rak due to the research he had done about Jewish Nazi hunters, figures whom the general public would have been more familiar with back in 1981. Although, as Rückert asserts, Kessler had little direct involvement in the extermination of Jews (attentive *Secret Army* viewers will nevertheless remember that he was thoroughly aware of the Final Solution (*Guests at God's Table*), made his distaste of the Jewish race obvious (*A Safe Place*) and was obviously complicit with abhorrent wartime Nazi policy if not a fervent anti-Semite himself), Brason introduces the idea that he was nevertheless responsible for the death of Mical's mother and family, in order that he can dramatise the sort of story he wants to tell.

We see too little of either Mical or Bauer, characters who, Kessler aside, will become the series's main protagonists, to make a judgement as to their suitability for their roles. Despite this, Alan Dobie's calibre is still obvious, particularly in the scene when he is ordered to take leave by Maurer. Of the other supporting actors, Ralph Michael is good value as the rascally old Rückert, the original 'automatic pilot', while Nicholas Young's contribution is most notable in the scene in which Franz frisks Mical rather too thoroughly. *Kessler* will prove to be more sexual than *Secret Army* ever was and this scene is the first example of this approach.

Although Clifford Rose has always maintained that the serial is set in 1977, mainly because he didn't think he could pull off a believable 80 plus year-old Kessler (the character having been born in 1900), several design elements and props rather inevitably scream out that we're in the early Eighties: a top-loading video player, the passport control monitor and of course the type of clothing worn. There is also a surprising amount of product placement going on: if Sprite, Memorex and Lee Cooper were not paying for this advertising opportunity then they certainly should have been!

Although *Kessler* does not fully get going in this opening episode, it is nevertheless obvious that is going to be quite a different animal to *Secret Army* and, provided the viewer is willing to let go of the fact that our Lifeline heroes are not about to don their cardigans and zimmer after Kessler, there's the promise of much to enjoy in this serial.

KESSLER: Part Two

WRITTEN BY: John Brason   DIRECTED BY: Michael E. Briant

FIRST BROADCAST: Friday 20 November 1981

REGULAR CAST: Ludwig Kessler / Manfred Dorf: CLIFFORD ROSE; Richard Bauer: ALAN DOBIE; Mical Rak: NITZA SAUL; Ingrid Dorf: ALISON GLENNIE; Franz Höss: NICHOLAS YOUNG; Colonel Hans Rückert: RALPH MICHAEL; Hugo van Eyck: JEROME WILLIS; Karl Leider: ROBERT MORRIS

SUPPORTING CAST: Otto Dehmel: NIGEL LAMBERT; Gidney: JEREMY WILKIN; Deakin: HAROLD INNOCENT; Inspector: JOHN ROLFE; Agent: REG WOODS

SYNOPSIS: At his flat in Bonn, Bauer has begun his enforced leave and discusses being warned off by Maurer with his colleague Leider, before realising that someone has been through his possessions. At his house in the German countryside, Kessler learns from Rückert about the Jewish girl's death. They also discuss the need to stop Van Eyck's investigations and Kessler's intention to still go to a trade conference in London despite the recent news stories about his identity. Leider visits the crime scene at the hotel in Krefeld and learns that the murder victim was travelling with another Israeli girl. Bauer narrowly misses being shot in the street. Kessler arranges for new banker instructions to be taken to a Swiss bank, prompting Ingrid and Franz to wonder what he is up to. Mical has found Kessler's country retreat and begins surveillance of it. Kessler tells Ingrid that he has arranged for a heavy called Otto Dehmel to come and stay with them. She suggests that he and Rückert should take charge of the Kameraden, but he tells her that Reichsleiter Bormann will continue as its leader. Leider asks Van Eyck to meet Bauer at his flat. The pair meet and discuss exchanging information. Bauer tries to warn the journalist that he may be in danger. Minutes later, Van Eyck is murdered in the street with poison from the tip of an umbrella. Leider follows Mical to a German town where she has bought a hunting rifle and tries to warn her off from pursuing Dorf. Bauer also begins surveillance of Dorf's country residence, just as Dehmel arrives. Kessler learns of Van Eyck's death. Ingrid pushes him as to who will receive the monies held by the Kameraden. Kessler looks at photos of the time he spent in Nazi Germany. Soon after, he, Ingrid and Franz leave for Bonn airport and are followed by Leider and Bauer. Dehmel stays behind to locate Mical. They fight and Mical ends up killing him. Kessler goes to London via Zurich, while Ingrid and Franz go straight to London. After making love, Ingrid challenges Franz as to whether they are going to take on the Kameradenwerk. After Kessler arrives, Bauer is briefed by British intelligence agent Gidney about the recent money transfers that Kessler has actioned and that they want him to lead them to those in command of the Kameraden. Franz spots Mical on the street outside the hotel they are staying in. Kessler is determined to deal with Mical immediately and he and Franz abduct her. Meanwhile, Rückert makes a move on Ingrid at the hotel. Franz brutally tortures Mical before Kessler orders him to get rid of her by dumping her body in the Thames.

REVIEW: The most striking thing about *Kessler*'s second episode is just how violent it is. In *Secret Army*, violence was more often implied rather than shown, so it is shocking to see here, within the space of fifty minutes, a stabbing, a murder and a severe beating, especially as all three are horribly realistic. Their inclusion also reminds us that Kessler is not above ordering torture and murder if he deems there to be sufficient grounds for such action. While Kessler thinks that Rückert's "young Eagles" murder of Ruth Lieberman was "a little extreme," he nevertheless as good as sanctions Van Eyck's murder, ensures the presence of the vicious Otto Dehmel at his country retreat and later is directly responsible for Mical's abduction, subsequent torture and attempted murder. All of this is a reminder that, if his own survival is under threat, then Kessler will take extreme action to remedy the situation, and it should not be forgotten that although he is no sadist he is quite prepared to expediently spill blood.

Nitza Saul's military experience, Nicholas Young's motivation to spend sufficient time rehearsing with her, and Michael E. Briant's recently gained knowledge on torture techniques, (obtained while working on *Blood Money*), all result in several incredibly gritty and disturbing scenes. Van Eyck's death stands apart from the other violent moments as it is less gruesome and depicted more artistically, especially the excellent aerial shot which sees him stagger out into the main road before collapsing, dead.

The episode also demonstrates further that the serial is not afraid to include some sexual content, the majority of which seems to revolve around Ingrid's role in proceedings (although we do also learn that Gidney has a hankering after Franz, whom he considers to be a "pretty, young, German boy"). Firstly we get the indication, from a kiss, that she and Franz are lovers; there is a suggestion that she has been with Otto Dehmel from the way he greets her by holding her face in his hands; later we witness her and Franz after sex; and finally we see her allowing Rückert to kiss her. It is clear that Ingrid is fully used to using her sexuality in order to get her own way and quite willing to surrender herself, even to an old man, if it will get her the power she so keenly seeks. As such, Ingrid is presented as a force to be reckoned with, an impression that is further emphasised when she asks Franz: "Are we going to take on the Kameradenwerk?" She is equally fearless in the way she handles her father ("If the Kameraden are waiting for the Second Coming they are going to be as disappointed as the Christians!") and it seems highly likely that she only gets away with her frequent outbursts because she is his daughter. Perhaps another explanation for his patience is the fact that she is all he has left of the deceased Madeleine, whose framed picture he carries around with him (and was the first thing he attended to when arriving at his country retreat). As Ingrid has more to do in this episode, it becomes very apparent that Alison Glennie's intonation and delivery is very similar to Hazel McBride's, but by all accounts this was coincidental rather than planned.

The confirmation near the start of the episode that Alan Dobie's Bauer is actually a German character living in Bonn may come as a bit of a surprise to even the most attentive viewer, partly perhaps because Dobie is so quintessentially English, but also because this simply has not been made very clear before now. Dobie still does not have a great deal to get his teeth into here, although just as enjoyable as his more obviously dramatic dialogue to Leider about the pursuit of war criminals and the Austrian observance of Hitler's birthday, is his reaction to having to laboriously check his flat for bugs and his spotting of Mical in the grounds of Kessler's country house with the word "Snap".

Nitza Saul is better served than in the opening episode, making Mical pleasingly sarcastic and playful in the scene in which she is confronted by Leider. However, given the fact that her best friend has just been murdered perhaps this is a little overdone. She certainly goes through the wars here, and the fact that she doesn't throw the towel in after being attacked by Dehmel shows that she too, like Ingrid, is a very determined young woman. The fact that she kills Dehmel and subsequently hops on a plane to England in pursuit of Kessler suggests that she is also either incredibly brave or just plain stupid.

Although the Kameradenwerk are now an established element of the serial, albeit via exposition only, there is yet another startling revelation here which, as in episode one, is related far too casually: the survival of Martin Bormann, Hitler's private secretary, described as the current leader of the Kameradenwerk. Strangely, Brason also neglects to provide any exposition to relate to those viewers not in-the-know that Bormann is commonly believed to have died in Berlin in 1945. Either he judged this to be 'dumbing down' or he was too steeped in knowledge to consider that anyone might not be aware of this fact. The Bormann revelation aside, the issue of the transfer of money and the question of who has which pot and who has control of each, and indeed why, is a vexed matter. Even Ingrid and Franz admit to being confused, although they are certain about the fact that they want to get their hands on some of it!

There are the first indications here that, as Ingrid suggests, Kessler may well be too old a man to deal with the pressure of the situation he has suddenly found himself in, when he is seen drifting back to the 'good old days' in Berlin and has to be broken from his reverie by his daughter. Later, he is similarly lost in music when seen lying on his bed at the Hotel Russell in London. The music used for this scene is the same piece that we will see both his mother and himself play later in the serial, a piece that it has to be said he would have been very lucky indeed to find on his hotel radio.

Kessler's hi-tech surveillance at his Krefeld home reminds us that he has not lost his fascination for such equipment since its earliest days in 1944, when he optimistically sought to use it during the German Occupation of Brussels in the *Secret Army* episode *Day of Wrath*. Whether Brason remembered this and wrote it in for this reason is unknown.

This second episode of *Kessler* is as uncompromising as it is arresting, however, there is a sense that just because it elects to incorporate violence and (very mild) sexual content, it consequently thinks it is more grown up than it actually is. In contrast, *Secret Army* manages to be a very adult series without ever feeling the need to incorporate much of either.

KESSLER: Part Three

WRITTEN BY: Gerard Glaister   **DIRECTED BY:** Michael E. Briant

FIRST BROADCAST: Friday 27 November 1981

REGULAR CAST: Ludwig Kessler / Manfred Dorf: CLIFFORD ROSE; Richard Bauer: ALAN DOBIE; Mical Rak: NITZA SAUL; Ingrid Dorf: ALISON GLENNIE; Franz Höss: NICHOLAS YOUNG; Colonel Hans Rückert: RALPH MICHAEL; Karl Leider: ROBERT MORRIS

SUPPORTING CAST: Gidney: JEREMY WILKIN; Deakin: HAROLD INNOCENT; Maurer: ROYSTON TICKNER; Smithson: ANTHONY GARDNER; Frau Gerhart: SHEILA DUNN; Agent: REG WOODS

SYNOPSIS: Mical is dragged from the Thames. Bauer has been installed in a London flat by Gidney. The MI5 agent informs him that he is bringing Mical to him so that he can keep an eye on her. Kessler returns to the hotel with Franz and Ingrid reproaches them for their action, believing it could have jeopardised their safety. She and Kessler discuss Madeleine and new and old Nazism. Kessler defends the achievements of the Führer and the old guard. Mical is brought to Bauer's house and put to bed. She wakes and tells Bauer why she is pursuing Kessler. He reveals that he is with German Intelligence. Rückert calls the hotel and tells Ingrid that he thinks Kessler's actions were rash. Ingrid returns to bed with Franz and they discuss getting their hands on the Kameraden's money. The next morning, Bauer and Mical discuss Kessler, the Israeli's motives and the 'Nazi Fortune'.

Mical offers to work with Bauer and remains determined to pursue and deal with Kessler. She also puts him on to the idea that the late Madeleine could be the key to proving that Dorf is Kessler. Bauer calls Leider and asks him to search Kessler's home in Krefeld for relevant materials. Their conversation is recorded and subsequently listened to by Maurer. After Leider arrives at the Krefeld residence, two agents tamper with his car. Meanwhile, Leider obtains entry and locates the Dorf family photo album and takes photos of it with a miniature camera. The housekeeper, Frau Gerhart, makes a call to report on Leider's actions. Bauer pays a visit to Gidney, and Deakin arrives shortly afterwards. Deakin reports on Kessler's past and the possibility that he might have become Major Spitzweg and escaped imprisonment with Madeleine's help. It is also revealed that Kessler and Eichmann worked side by side and that during this time arrangements regarding the Kameraden money could have been made and Dorf Industries set up as a result. Gidney and Deakin want Bauer to see if Kessler will lead them to the Kameradenwerk. After leaving Krefeld, Leider records a Dictaphone message stating that he is being followed. Stopping at a petrol station, he posts the recording and the camera film before resuming his drive. Soon afterwards, the two pursuing agents take control of his car, and after making him pull over, drag Leider out, beat him up and finally run over him. Rückert learns that Mical's body has not been found. In order to avoid being tailed, Franz, Ingrid and Kessler leave the hotel in separate cars before meeting each other nearby. Kessler drives off to deal with some final monetary matters before leaving England. Maurer reports to Rückert in Bonn and orders that the photo album be destroyed immediately. Bauer receives Leider's tape and film. Mical offers to go out and get some shopping. Rückert admonishes Kessler for retaining the album due to the fact that it contains photos of him in uniform as well as shots of Madeleine and reveals that he has had it burned. Kessler is outraged and the pair argue. Rückert informs Kessler that it is time for him to 'disappear', but he is reluctant to do so. In order to persuade him, Rückert implies that Ingrid will be harmed if he does not cooperate. Arrangements are made for their travel to South America, with Kessler due to travel via Paris. Bauer learns that Leider has been killed. Mical follows Kessler to Paris. Gidney tells Bauer that he wants him to track down the leaders of the Kameradenwerk and he too sets off in pursuit.

REVIEW: In this third instalment, *Kessler* really starts to fire on all cylinders as a fuller picture is revealed of respective character motivations and relationships and of those elements that will drive the narrative in the remaining episodes. Glaister's script, the only episode not to be penned by Brason, is excellent, particularly as it finally offers the serial's actors some memorable dialogue, and the viewers, some much needed clarity.

Glaister chooses to have the spectre of the late Madeleine hang over the episode and although she does not feature in any flashback sequences, she remains a strong presence throughout. Indeed, Kessler's love for her ultimately proves to be his undoing: the fact that he has, for sentimental reasons, retained a photo album in which she features, leads to the confirmation of his true identity and the need for him to permanently disappear. That Kessler was shown in *Secret Army* to be capable of love and affection always saved him from being a clichéd stereotype and may even have engendered sympathy from some viewers. His grief at the news that his family photo album has been destroyed, emphasised by his line: "I have no record left of Madeleine," may also prompt such a response. The paradoxical nature of Kessler's character is both fascinating and intriguing, as Gidney reflects: "Curious man. Had men and women tortured to obtain information, Jews sent to concentration camps to die in gas chambers, yet loved his wife deeply." Although he may not have any possessions left to remind him of Madeleine, he still has a daughter and it is ultimately his desire for her safety that convinces him to leave for South America at the episode's close. The contrast between Ingrid and Madeleine is also interesting. Although their speech is similar, as Ingrid herself recognises, she takes after her father more than she does her mother. It is also apparent that she has much less time for her mother than he does, principally because she regards her "a bourgeois" who "didn't like National Socialism" and is not impressed by her father's defence of her ("She never wavered in her loyalty to me"). Unlike her father, who at least declares his love and loyalty to the late Madeleine, Ingrid is presented as a character with few, if any, redeeming qualities. Even when she defends Kessler to Rückert ("My father is used to making his own decisions"), it seems likely that she is merely relishing being confrontational with one of the 'old guard' rather than truly looking out for her father. Moreover, her single-minded certainty about the success of her Neo-Nazi organisation ("There'll never be a *Der Tag* for them. There will be for us.") is becoming increasingly chilling.

Mical's survival from her ordeal at the hands of Franz and Kessler, and latterly a freezing cold Thames, is rather less than believable, whereas her appearance after being transferred to Bauer's apartment is verging on the ridiculous: she wakes up *Dynasty*-style with her hair and make-up immaculately intact, with only the slightest cut on her lip. Nevertheless, Saul goes on to prove that she is much more than just a pretty face and even succeeds in stealing a scene from Alan Dobie, and not simply because of judicious leg-crossing while clad in just a pyjama shirt. The scene in question sees her playfully ignore Bauer's warnings about pursuing Kessler. Her wilful misinterpretation of Bauer's line, "If the Fortune, as they call it, could be somehow destroyed, the chances of a serious revival in Nazism would be over," as an invitation for her to help him ("Very well. I will work with you.") is glorious. Her subsequent, proudly stated, line, "I've had military training," is just as appealing and proves that she is, in her own way just as single-minded as Ingrid. When she says "I will get Kessler" it seems very likely; after all, she has not even been put off pursuing him after being tortured and left for dead in a river! Her determination is unquestionably proved once again when, without any hesitation, she follows Kessler all the way to Paris while Bauer thinks she is out shopping!

We learn a little more about Franz in this episode – none of it good. His patently false fascist bravado at the start of the episode ("Well, at least that's the end of the Jewish bitch") and later when in bed with Ingrid ("No Communists and Jews!") mark him out as a weak individual who is desperate to impress but way out of his comfort zone. As such, he comes across as an interesting if unlikeable character.

Both MI5 agent Gidney and MI9 agent Deakin have more to do here, with both Jeremy Wilkin and Harold Innocent proving to be entertaining if slightly superfluous. The best line of the episode is Gidney's terribly English warning to Bauer: "Those Nazis can be quite unpleasant," an understatement of epic proportions.

Leider's death is as brutal and uncompromising as we are coming to expect of *Kessler*, although by all accounts it would have been much worse had Michael E. Briant got his way and incorporated the sound of Leider's body being crushed! Keen-eyed viewers may notice that the actor playing the agent who works for Maurer, Reg Woods, also appeared as 'Natalie's tail' in *Just Light the Blue Touch-Paper*, while Smithson is played by Anthony Gardner who was Kupper in *The Last Run*.

The car-related subterfuge in Russell Square is good fun, especially Ingrid's treatment of the motorcyclist who is following them. However, the fact that the same red car is used later, for the journey from the hotel to the airport, seems to overlook the fact that the British agents know that Kessler had previously evaded them by making an excuse to leave that very car, so why would he willingly get in the same vehicle again?

One of the undoubted highlights of the entire episode is Kessler's confrontation with Rückert after he learns that his photo album has been destroyed, especially his exclamation: "You've never loved anyone. You have no real feeling!" Rückert's defiant reply gives us an insight into the Colonel's place in the Kameradenwerk, implying that, despite appearances to the contrary, Rückert is actually more powerful within that organisation. When Kessler complains that: "It's much easier to kill a man in battle than to sign his death warrant in your office," Rückert rounds on Kessler without hesitation: "Very well, my 'Desk hero'!" and proceeds to demand that he now must disappear from society. Rückert's subsequent threat to Ingrid's life is further evidence of his more elevated position within the Kameradenwerk.

Although this third instalment is easily the most dialogue-heavy thus far, it is nevertheless full of memorable moments and very neatly sets the scene for the remaining three episodes.

KESSLER: Part Four

WRITTEN BY: John Brason   **DIRECTED BY:** Tristan de Vere Cole

FIRST BROADCAST: Friday 4 December 1981

REGULAR CAST: Ludwig Kessler / Manfred Dorf: CLIFFORD ROSE; Richard Bauer: ALAN DOBIE; Mical Rak: NITZA SAUL; Ingrid Dorf: ALISON GLENNIE; Franz Höss: NICHOLAS YOUNG; Colonel Hans Rückert: RALPH MICHAEL; José Garriga: JOHN MORENO; Joséf Mengele: OSCAR QUITAK; Don Julian Yqueras: GUY ROLFE

KESSLER

SUPPORTING CAST: Vinding: RICHARD WREN; Brazilian: RICHARD REES; Chilean: LIONEL GUYETT

SYNOPSIS: Mical and Kessler arrive in Asunción, Paraguay, within minutes of each other. Mical spots Kessler, who is welcomed by Rückert. Mical calls Bauer, who is in Buenos Aires to tell him. Bauer gives her the details, obtained from Gidney, of a place for her to stay and suggests they make a plan of campaign there after he arrives. Ingrid and Franz are also in Asunción on their way to a rendezvous in a bar. Mical takes a taxi to a hostel run by the charismatic José Garriga, where she receives a warm welcome. Ingrid and Franz meet some neo-Nazi contacts. Ingrid tells them about the 48 billion Deutschmarks that her father is in the process of transferring to Paraguay and how she hopes to persuade him to release the money to them. She also reveals her plan to meet with her father's old friend Don Julian Yqueras, a wealthy aristocrat who, together with Perón, helped senior Nazis to settle in Paraguay after the war. Rückert and Kessler are driven out to the secret Kameraden Headquarters in the desert. Kessler is advised that he will be interrogated that afternoon in order that security can be assured. Garriga monitors Mical's movements as she makes her way around the city. Bauer arrives at the airport. Kessler is furious to learn that none other than Joséf Mengele is to head his interrogation, believing him to be a "sadistic mountebank". Mengele arrives and the inquiry begins. Bauer fills Mical in on Yqueras. Garriga reveals that he knows Gidney and that he is paid by him for information, and that no-one has managed to find the Kameraden HQ yet. Bauer asks Garriga about Yqueras, while Mical asks if he can get them some guns. At the inquiry, it is revealed that Mical is in Asunción. Mengele is terrified because she is an Israeli and may be intent on killing him. Kessler absent himself after being informed that he has to remain there for a few days. Mengele questions why Kessler has responsibility for the Nazi Fortune. Rückert reminds him of Kessler's lifetime of loyalty to the Fatherland. Mengele has a private meeting with Kessler at which he asks him for some funds because Bormann has become "difficult". Kessler, is disgusted by Mengele's wartime exploits, his obsession with his personal safety and his appetite for debauchery, but gives him access to some funds all the same. When Mengele talks about Germany's impending invitation for the old guard to return, Kessler puts him straight on the reality of the situation. Garriga brings Yqueras's address to Bauer and some flowers to Mical, and one of Yqueras's servants is paid off to pass on information to them. Kessler and Rückert visit Yqueras at his impressive residence. Kessler asks him to arrange a meeting with Bormann. Yqueras is reluctant, but Kessler convinces him. Garriga passes on information to Bauer and Mical of Kessler's planned rendezvous and the fact that both Bormann and Mengele will be there. Mical announces that she now plans to deal with both Kessler and Mengele. Garriga advises the pair on how to make their way to the rendezvous unobserved via horseback through some foothills. Ingrid reports to one of her contacts that everything has been arranged. Garriga brings Bauer and Mical suitable clothing for their trip together, along with weaponry. That evening, they set off towards the rendezvous and set up camp for the night when it gets dark. Ingrid pays a visit to Yqueras and tries to persuade him that it would better if the Nazi Fortune was handed over to her and the group she represents. Bauer muses as to how he has ended up "playing Cowboys and Indians" in the Paraguayan desert. Mical tells him she is happy of his company. Kessler tells Rückert about the transfer of monies from Switzerland and that it can only be withdrawn by himself and Reichsleiter Bormann. Bauer talks to Mical about the influence of possible Nazi Germans on global society and his feeling that he is not certain he wants to stop her killing Kessler. Kessler muses that he thinks that there will never be a Fourth Reich and that they are deluding themselves by thinking otherwise.

REVIEW: This fourth episode is undoubtedly the most accomplished and interesting episode of *Kessler* so far. This is largely due to several well-judged performances and a superior script. Aside from Clifford Rose, who thankfully has much more to get his teeth into here (putting us in mind of the Kessler of old), Oscar Quitak gives a startlingly watchable turn as the hideously craven Dr Mengele. The new geographical backdrop also adds considerable atmosphere as *Kessler* gets closer to its finale.

The difference in tone to the previous three episodes probably has less to do with the change of director from Briant to De Vere Cole and more to do with the switch to the 'South American' location. Paraguay is realised very credibly indeed. For the exterior sequences set in busy Asunción, De Vere Cole elects to include as much local colour as possible, as characters are seen to make their way through vibrant markets and charming back streets while its citizens are shown shopping, collecting water and preparing for the Ascension festival. In contrast, the unpopulated wilderness beyond is shown to be barren, colourless and forbidding. Easily the most impressive exterior shot is of the vista of hills and valleys that greets Bauer and Mical as they make their way towards their rendezvous. Unusually, for a drama of this vintage, the studio sets, designed by the talented Campbell Gordon, add to, rather than detract from, the overall look and feel. The interior of the Kameraden HQ, specifically the marble-floored corridor with its wooden slatted shutters through which sunlight floods, is particularly effective, as is Yqueras's comfortable lounge. Even for relatively insignificant sets, such as Mical and Bauer's room in Garriga's hostel, with its bright walls and striped bedspreads, care and attention has obviously been taken.

The early part of the episode, in which several regular characters arrive in Asunción, is cleverly constructed so as to depict contrasting motivations and perspectives. While Franz and Ingrid are openly dismissive of the locals, considering themselves far superior, Mical's outlook and approach couldn't be more different, as she graciously grins and charms her way to her room, enjoying the company of both her taxi driver and José Garriga along the way.

Gold-toothed Garriga is an interesting character, who adds real flavour to the episode. Despite his dodgy, and somewhat dirty, appearance, his smile is infectious and he somehow comes across as almost impossible to dislike. Even the naturally distrustful Bauer doesn't take long to warm to the man. Although the Speedy Gonzales-style accent which John Moreno has chosen to adopt becomes a little wearing after a while, the character nevertheless provides some important light relief in what continues to be a consistently dark and unremitting serial.

This episode sees the inclusion of two amusing in-jokes which are made at the expense of the production. The first comes when Mengele complains about how young Kessler looks: "You, Kessler, you remain young. Look at you. I'm so envious," a reference to the fact that Clifford Rose was in fact over twenty-five years younger than the character he was tasked with portraying! The second comes when Rückert and Kessler visit Yqueras's extravagant mansion of which we only get to see one moderate-sized sitting room, prompting Rückert to ask: "Why do you spend all your time in this one room, when you have such an enormous house?" Yqueras gives the rather unconvincing explanation that the room is set up with devices to give it perfect humidity, however the obvious answer is that the serial's budget simply could not stretch to more than one room!

If it were not for the fact that Clifford Rose delivers several stunningly performed speeches, this would undoubtedly be Oscar Quitak's episode due to his portrayal of Mengele. The actor is utterly believable as Auschwitz's horrific 'Angel of Death', ensuring that with every dragging step, sinister stare and unrepentant self-obsessed exclamation, the character comes over as as despicable and vile as one would expect him to be. Having previously passed up the opportunity to generate much dramatic value from the disclosure of the existence of the Kameradenwerk and the survival of Martin Bormann, the sudden revelation that Mengele is alive, and will be heading up Kessler's interrogation, sees the serial pull off its first real shock moment. Mengele's introduction and the inevitable references to his wartime career, butchering in the name of medical science, throw some interesting light on how Kessler regards his own wartime activities. Unlike Mengele, whom he considers to be "a sadistic mountebank" who "murdered thousands" and "was merely a butcher for his own perverted amusement," he considers that in his own case his actions were excused by his belief that "the end justifies the means." Although we may consider Kessler's argument to be dubious and untenable, there is no doubt that Mengele is in a different league when it comes to depravity. Mengele's thoroughly abhorrent nature is underlined when he tells Kessler how he would have liked to have had children and specifically by the disgustingly inappropriate line: "I would have liked to have given life." Kessler cannot stop himself from responding, with the most memorable line of the episode: "The world is full enough, Mengele. Besides the deficit you created more than compensated for credit entries in the Great Book of Life!" Kessler may be a dangerous and fanatical war criminal with plenty of blood on his hands but, unlike Mengele, he has never enjoyed torture nor put someone to death simply for his own amusement. Therefore, just as *Secret Army* sought to show that not all Germans were Nazis, *Kessler* seeks to depict the differences between the characters and objectives of the Nazi old guard, prompting consideration of the idea that it might be just as unsuitable to tar all Nazis with the same brush. This is not to say that Brason has a revisionist pro-Nazi agenda, but rather that, as his work on *Secret Army* also showed, he has no interest in dealing in clichéd absolutes.

A distinction between Kessler and his Kameraden counterparts that is particularly well developed throughout the episode is the former's absolute commitment – for the majority of the episode at least – to the establishment of a Fourth Reich. The Kameraden are portrayed as giving priority instead to the safety of their members, their objectives having been no doubt skewed by the presence among them of two of the most wanted men alive. Mengele's lunatic outbursts confirm all too clearly that he has become utterly obsessed with his own survival, due to the fact that he has been on the run for over thirty years. At one point, when he talks about how he has never been caught, he observes: "They always end up on the cold slab themselves," and almost sounds disappointed by this fact. He is also depicted as consumed with self-pity over his quality of life in Paraguay, and his pursuit of funds from Kessler, in order to supplement what Bormann gives him, is pitiful and shameless in equal measure. After Kessler succumbs to Mengele's demands (which he cuttingly observes will keep him "in cigars and little girls for at least another year"), he confronts him about the Kameraden's lack of action and is dismayed to learn that he and Bormann are foolishly waiting for an invitation back to Germany. As it gradually becomes clear to Kessler that the Paraguayan-based members of the Kameraden have no handle either on the currently prosperous state of their former homeland or of the methods that Kessler has learned to adopt to inveigle Nazism into modern society, he finally realises that the Fourth Reich may not be an achievable proposition after all, especially if he is just relying on the old guard Nazis. It is no accident that De Vere Cole chooses to marry Kessler's dialogue which summarises this state of affairs ("The tardy realisation that the dream is not to be fulfilled. There is no Fourth Reich, there never will be.") with a shot of Rückert's prosthetic leg to emphasise just how immobile the Kameraden are. The fact that Rückert has not even heard Kessler as he has already fallen asleep, also suggests that the Kameraden is simply too old to be instrumental in such an undertaking, an opinion that Ingrid has regularly forwarded throughout the serial.

Unlike her father, Ingrid has known from the outset that the possibility of a Fourth Reich lies with her and her young Nazi friends, and receives yet another evocative line to express her lack of regard for the activities of the old Kameraden: "Letting off fireworks on their way to the grave." During her initial meeting with local Nazi leaders, who are rather two-dimensional, she once again expresses her fanatical belief that "We are the New Day." The meeting is also notable for the fact that it seems that Franz is already known to those present, a circumstance that seems a bit unlikely given that, until now, he has hardly come across as a Nazi of international standing and rather more like Ingrid's inexperienced puppy dog. Ingrid's determined nature eventually leads her to an audience with Yqueras in order to make it clear that she and her fellow activists are the real future of Nazism, even though this means flying in the face of her father's plans. Once again, Brason forwards the view that young Nazis are a very real threat to modern society, a message that Michael E. Briant recalls as having attracted him to the serial in the first place. The idea of Ingrid and her group having DM 48 billion behind them is certainly a sobering one.

Guy Rolfe, who previously played Oberst von Elmendorff in *Russian Roulette*, effortlessly inhabits the role of aristocratic Nazi sympathiser Don Julian Yqueras, but has little to do in this episode other than to act as a go-between and to prompt Kessler to make impressive speeches about having given his life to National Socialism and how he is crucial to the release of the Nazi Fortune.

The episode's incidental music is worthy of note as it is hugely varied, both in style and suitability. The first Latino track we hear is intended to be evocative of South America in order to reinforce the new location, but is rather too jangly and invasive. A subsequent triumphal sounding track is pacey and dramatic and matches the action much better. The creepy piece that accompanies Mengele's introduction is well chosen, while the Spaghetti Western-style tune that underscores Mical and Bauer's trek is a bit daft.

From this episode on, Mical and Bauer are seen to form a friendship of sorts. While Bauer finds it hard to believe that he has ended up "playing cowboys and Indians in a desert in the middle of Paraguay with a very pretty ex-soldier from the Israeli army," Mical, as with all her previous experiences, takes it in her stride, but nevertheless lets Bauer know that she is glad of his company. As both characters are rather underdeveloped, their section of the narrative is arguably becoming the least convincing. Unfortunately, it becomes even less so when the pair don cowboy gear in preparation for their trek. As Bauer himself observes, he does look "bloody silly" in his get-up and as a result their mission is difficult to take seriously, especially when it is also accompanied by the aforementioned cowboy music, which seems to poke fun at their serious objective.

A terrific amount is packed into this one episode of *Kessler*, the majority of which is very well acted, particularly by Rose and Quitak, and makes for very classy and entertaining viewing.

KESSLER: Part Five

WRITTEN BY: John Brason   DIRECTED BY: Tristan de Vere Cole

FIRST BROADCAST: Friday 11 December 1981

REGULAR CAST: Ludwig Kessler / Manfred Dorf: CLIFFORD ROSE; Richard Bauer: ALAN DOBIE; Mical Rak: NITZA SAUL; Ingrid Dorf: ALISON GLENNIE; Franz Höss: NICHOLAS YOUNG; Colonel Hans Rückert: RALPH MICHAEL; José Garriga: JOHN MORENO; Joséf Mengele: OSCAR QUITAK; Don Julian Yqueras: GUY ROLFE

SUPPORTING CAST: Himmler: RICHARD ADDISON; Krebs: JIM BYARS; Rankl: ALAN BRECK; Radio Operator: PETER BERRY; Kessler as a boy: ALEXANDER BULLION

SYNOPSIS: Mical and Bauer watch the sun rise over Paraguay from their desert shelter. In Asunción, Ingrid wakes Franz and asks him to phone a German contact about her father's banking arrangements. Mical and Bauer resume their trek to the rendezvous point. Over breakfast, Kessler quizzes Rückert about Bormann's inactivity and his own refusal to ally himself with the young Nazis. Franz returns to Ingrid with information about Kessler's bank accounts. She has decided to wait for her father's disillusionment to be complete

586

before she makes another move. While Mical and Bauer stake out the rendezvous, Kessler journeys there by car. His arrival is observed and Bauer takes several photos. At the Kameraden HQ, Rückert gives orders to two of his men and tells them that *Der Tag* will be three months from now. Rückert goes to the conference room, dons his old flying jacket and looks at his Knight's Cross medal. A disgruntled Kessler is leaving his meeting with Bormann and Mengele when Bauer falls down a shaft in the ground. The group are alerted to their presence and Mical shoots at them. Kessler escapes by car, while a terrified Mengele, after being shot at several times, eventually gains entry back into the boarded up house where Bormann is hiding. Bormann and Mengele escape by plane. A shattered Kessler returns to the hotel in Asunción, tells Ingrid about Mical's appearance at the rendezvous and explains that he must remain alive in order for the Nazi Fortune to be released. They agree to have dinner together that evening. Yqueras is visiting the Kameraden HQ when Mengele radios Rückert to tell him about the ambush. Ingrid gives Franz instructions to alert all units for their *Der Tag* and reveals that she plans to deal with Mical personally. Back at their hostel room, a doctor sees to Bauer's injured leg. Garriga invites him and Mical to stay in his apartment to ensure their safety. Kessler and Rückert argue about the Kameraden's priorities again. Kessler declares that Ingrid was right about the 'old guard' and Rückert restates that the safety of comrades must come before the 'grand design'. Mical and Bauer settle into Garriga's apartment. However, they are soon at loggerheads over Germany's lack of pursuit of war criminals. Garriga explains the drumming schedule that is part and parcel of the Ascension Festival. At the Kameraden HQ, Kessler becomes lost in his thoughts and thinks back to his acceptance into the SS and the subsequent war years when Nazism flourished. Ingrid and Yqueras discuss the future of National Socialism. He refuses to give her the address of the Kameraden HQ, but they come to an agreement about their material interests. Ingrid returns to the hotel to find her father there in a bad state. She comforts him as he tells her how right she was about the Kameraden and that he has now decided to make the money over to her and her friends. He reveals that he already has Bormann's token and so is "ready to move." Ingrid is delighted by this turn of events and urges her father to lead them. He agrees just as the drumming begins, marking the start of the Ascension festival.

REVIEW: This fifth episode is most notable for the fact that it finally sees Kessler agreeing with what Ingrid has been saying about the Kameraden all along – a conclusion which not only prompts much soul-searching on Kessler's part, but also means that Ingrid and her young Nazis, with Kessler's leadership and the Nazi Fortune behind them, have suddenly become a very real threat to modern society. The prospect is a startling one and viewers back in 1981 may well have been rather more discomforted by the idea than those watching the serial over twenty-five years later, for whom the dramatic edge has been inevitably dulled by the fact that there has not been a Neo-Nazi resurgence on the scale that Kessler and Ingrid are envisaging here.

Alison Glennie has the opportunity here to make Ingrid much less of a stereotypical Nazi. After the ambush, it is Ingrid who Kessler goes to, telling her: "I just want to be with someone I love, someone I trust." Although her mind is clearly ticking over as to what this might mean for her personal ambition and her Nazi friends, she is nevertheless taken aback by her father's state and willingly and genuinely hugs him. She subsequently muses as to how her mother saved his life and how she might be able to do the same – by seeing to Mical herself – motivated by a desire for acceptance by him. In their final scene together Ingrid sheds a tear, not merely because her own hard fought dream might become a reality, but also because in such a gesture her father proves that he both loves and values her. The fact that Kessler feels the need to reassure her that he does have a heart, suggests that Ingrid has turned out the way she has because he has never given her enough love and attention and he knows it. This is excellent writing on Brason's part which reveals carefully plotted character development for the entire serial, an element which the earlier episodes do not always suggest.

The action sequence at the rendezvous hangs together well, although, given that we have been leading up to it since halfway through the last episode, arguably turns out to be a little less exciting than it has been set up to be. It does seem odd that the impulsive Mical does not shoot at Kessler and Mengele when she first gets the chance, but this can be forgiven as it is obviously dramatically necessary for Kessler to meet with Bormann in order for him to obtain his ring (half of the key to the Nazi Fortune). Kessler's escape is well handled, especially the shattering of the windscreen, while Mengele's attempts to get back inside the building are suitably pathetic and desperate. The fact that Bormann effectively leaves him to die outside perhaps suggests that, as well as having a determination to survive, he too cannot abide Mengele. That we are not introduced to Bormann is a clever (and inexpensive!) touch, which adds tantalising mystery to these scenes, and of course also means that we do not learn until the final scene of the episode that as a result of his meeting with him Kessler now holds all the cards. Bauer's fall is well executed and Nitza Saul proves incontrovertibly that she can handle a rifle. Although De Vere Cole was reportedly unhappy that he was denied the option of a helicopter for Mengele's (and Bormann's) escape, the plane fly-past does its job, although, as he thought at the time: where was the runway and why didn't Mical and Bauer spot it and the plane from their various vantage points looking down on the rendezvous?

Rückert's relationship with Kessler, which has been rocky ever since the former destroyed the Dorf family photo album, is put under further strain here as once again Kessler presses him on the Kameraden's priorities. His observation of the fact that even Rückert resorts to the French pronunciation of courage when looking to the future, suggesting that he does not truly want to face up to the building of a Fourth Reich, is an interesting one, especially as it is later revealed that the Colonel is secretly plotting a *Der Tag* of sorts. Perhaps this is because he sees no place for Kessler in his version of the 'grand design' as he feels threatened by him? He certainly sees no place for Ingrid and her group of "carpetbaggers" in such a design, believing them to be "...basically terrorists. Their pretence of love of the Fatherland is a front to make terrorism palatable." It is a stance that does not influence Kessler at all, as he is very frustrated by the Kameraden's lack of activity and has begun to realise of Ingrid and her fellow Neo-Nazis that "The life is in them, not in this charade here." When Kessler confronts Rückert later in the episode, he is doubtful of the Colonel's claim that the Kameraden could assume control in Germany within 48 hours, observing that they may have some muscle now, but in five years the majority of them will either be retired or dead. He even resorts to describing them in a similar way to Ingrid: "Strutting dagoes in fancy dress." Rückert does not let these comments go, and after pressing him for reasons why he did not return directly to the HQ after the ambush and why he is being followed by Mical, even threatens him if there is a special reason for the latter that he is not disclosing: "If there were, we would either have to kill you or abandon you to your fate." This statement seems very odd indeed and bears little relation to the Kameraden's primary policy of protecting its comrades above all else. After all, Mengele has done the Jewish people unspeakable ills, and yet he is not threatened in this way, in fact far from it. In this threat, the implication is that Rucker no longer regards Kessler as a comrade. Indeed, when Kessler reminds him that without him there is no money, he replies that it "does not matter compared with the safety of the Kameraden" and that "comrades come first." It is a response that prompts Kessler to turn his back on the Kameraden for good and it is easy to see why.

An earlier exchange between Kessler and Rückert, prior to the rendezvous, also deserves mention. In it, Kessler pulls up Rückert for using the phrase 'war criminal': "I do not consider myself a criminal, war or otherwise. I did my duty as I saw it to my Fatherland and my Führer. Where is my crime?" Rückert gives a surprisingly honest reply, stating that the Allied airmen "flew for freedom and democracy" and that the Germans instead "flew for supremacy," which does little to support Kessler's obvious argument that they have suffered because the winning side writes history.

Further definite contrasts between Kessler and Rückert are suggested by the way they behave when they each spend time alone in reflection. Rückert dons his flying uniform jacket and looks at himself in the mirror, before regarding his Knight's Cross with huge pride, and in this way is seen to reflect on his own personal glory. Kessler too, who has a more extensive daydream than Rückert, remembers his own achievements, specifically his admission into the SS, but also the wider glory and might of the Reich, emphasised by a rally in wartime Germany complete with swathes of swastika flags, goose-stepping soldiers, the Führer himself and a chorus of "Sieg Heil!". In his dreams he ultimately finds himself alone, the soldiers all gone, and looking up hopefully and expectantly at the place where his beloved Führer should be standing, suggesting that Kessler now believes that glory, and even Nazism, is over. It is a stance that perhaps even suggests that his ultimate transferral of loyalty to the Neo-Nazis is a last ditch triumph of hope over expectation.

Kessler's dream sequence is also notable for the fact that it shows him as a young boy listening to his mother at the piano playing 'Kinderszenen' by Schumann. The piece, and the scenario, is clearly Kessler's 'happy place' and obviously of huge comfort and emotional significance to him.

Mical and Bauer receive some further development here but, once again, very little compared to their Nazi counterparts. As well as an interesting discussion as to whether Germany should have done more, or be doing more, to put its house in order as regards pursuit of war criminals, a debate which sees them on opposing sides, conversely they are depicted as closer than ever after their hair-raising adventures in the desert. At one moment in particular, before leaving their room in the hostel for Garriga's apartment, they stop and look at each other in a way that, for the first time, suggests more than just friendship. Bauer is even seen to gently stroke Mical's hair, an action which she freely allows. As Bauer seems much more youthful in these later episodes than he did back in Germany, especially given his recent exploits in the desert, the idea of their relationship seems less distasteful than it would have done had it begun earlier; nevertheless, they could still be father and daughter.

Garriga once again provides some much-needed light relief, most obviously when he interrupts Mical's and Bauer's moment to cheerfully ask "We go now?!" He interrupts the pair again later on, brightly offering coffee in order to prevent them from arguing further. It is clear that Garriga finds Mical very attractive, indeed he even assumes that she and Bauer are together, something which neither deny, when he tells him: "You are a very fortunate man!" The fact that Garriga is a pigeon fancier and the scene in which he and Mical feed them seem like rather superfluous inclusions in the episode, but at least the activity gives the characters something to do while they converse with each other, as well as suggesting that Garriga is more nurturing than he might at first appear. However, it later becomes clear (in the final episode) that the pigeons were undoubtedly introduced in order to ultimately make Garriga's death, which takes place in the pigeon coop, more dramatically interesting.

Although he still does not feature very prominently in the episode, Yqueras is nevertheless increasingly revealed to be a rather duplicitous and self-serving individual. When he advises Rückert that Kessler is "too valuable to lose," it is not immediately clear that this is because he is concerned about access to the Nazi Fortune. This only becomes apparent when he meets with Ingrid later on and they come to an agreement based on their material interest in Kessler's safety. The way Yqueras raises his eyebrows after Ingrid leaves suggests that he thinks that in her he has met his match; either that or he has recognised a kindred spirit. We also learn from their exchange that Yqueras once tried it on with Madeleine, despite his friendship with Kessler, which does not suggest an altogether loyal individual.

The episode ends with the most effective cliffhanger of the serial so far, as Kessler's decision to ally himself with the young Nazis is underscored by the start of the dramatic drumming that not only marks the beginning of the Ascension Festival celebrations, but also the disquieting possibility of a new Nazi dawn.

KESSLER: Part Six

WRITTEN BY: John Brason   **DIRECTED BY:** Michael E. Briant

FIRST BROADCAST: Friday 18 December 1981

REGULAR CAST: Ludwig Kessler / Manfred Dorf: CLIFFORD ROSE; Richard Bauer: ALAN DOBIE; Mical Rak: NITZA SAUL; Ingrid Dorf: ALISON GLENNIE; Franz Höss: NICHOLAS YOUNG; Colonel Hans Rückert: RALPH MICHAEL; José Garriga: JOHN MORENO; Don Julian Yqueras: GUY ROLFE

SUPPORTING CAST: Ulrich Müller: GARETH MILNE; Krebs: JIM BYARS

SYNOPSIS: Kessler and Ingrid wake the next morning and discuss Madeleine, their plans to reshape Germany and their respect for the late Führer. At his apartment, Garriga warns Bauer of the danger that he and Mical are in. Mical returns and they arrange to stake out the hotel where Ingrid is staying. Garriga elects to find out where the Kameraden HQ is located. Kessler tells Franz that he knows he has been sleeping with his daughter, before getting down to the business of planning how they will take control of Germany. The pair agree that education and the trade unions must be their main targets and discuss indoctrination and intimidation techniques. Kessler takes Franz's car in order to visit the Kameraden HQ. Ingrid is dismissive of Franz's declaration of love for her. Garriga learns the location of the HQ. Rückert arrives there and orders his heavy, Müller, to get rid of Mical and her colleagues, and informs him of his plan to evacuate the hacienda. Ingrid and Franz discuss how they will dispose of Mical. Müller arrives at the hostel looking for Mical and throws Garriga over the stairwell, before ransacking his apartment. Garriga is left for dead in his pigeon coop. Müller leaves. Bauer observes Ingrid and Franz entering the hostel and stops Mical from returning there. Ingrid and Franz enter the room that Mical and Bauer had been staying in. When Ingrid goes to open the shutters she is shot by Müller, who believes her to be Mical, from his vantage point on top of an adjacent building. Ingrid dies instantly. Franz makes to leave but is shot by Müller and falls dead down the hostel stairs. Mical and Bauer enter the hostel and discover that Ingrid, Franz and Garriga are all dead. Bauer picks up the address of the Kameraden hacienda from Garriga's body. Yqueras receives a call from Rückert telling him that Mical is dead. Kessler arrives and questions him as to why he has had him under surveillance. After playing 'Kinderszenen' on the piano, he is asked by Yqueras not to sign the transfer. Yqueras explains his concerns about Communism and why he has allied himself with the Kameraden. Kessler reveals to him exactly how he is vital to the release of the Nazi Fortune – which requires Bormann's ring and his live hand-print – and that he knows that he has been plotting with Ingrid, before revealing that he has decided to release the money to the Neo-Nazis, a move of which Yqueras approves. Mical and Bauer arrive at the Kameraden HQ and observe the process of evacuation. Kessler arrives and tells Rückert how he is no longer able to accept the leadership and purposes of the Kameradenwerk due to their obsession with the preservation of the Nazi old guard. Rückert considers this a betrayal and tells him that the possibility of *Der Tag* no longer exists. Bauer stops the last truck in the Kameraden convoy from getting away by shooting at its tyres; it rolls over and blows up. Mical enters the hacienda and looks for Kessler. Bauer follows her in and soon finds Mical pointing a gun at Kessler. Kessler questions why they have been pursuing him and their intentions. After discussion of the Holocaust and Communism, Bauer states that

591

all of Kessler's defensive arguments are just words and tells him that Ingrid is dead. Kessler is stunned and asks them to kill him now before he can dwell on the news. Bauer refuses and, with a view to persuading Mical not to kill Kessler, argues that there is no cause or belief worth the taking of a human life. Mical finds she cannot bring herself to kill Kessler and the pair leave him alone. After laying out the Nazi flag, Kessler takes Bauer's Uzi and shoots himself. Bauer and Mical return to the room to find him dead, before leaving the hacienda together.

REVIEW: The final instalment of *Kessler* is a gripping and occasionally shocking piece of drama which rounds off the serial on an immensely satisfying high. By the end of the episode, which for the most part sees Clifford Rose play a disturbingly reinvigorated Kessler, the only truly viable conclusion is reached, as he finally meets his end and it is confirmed that this is indeed the end of the line for the character.

Given the loose ends that this final episode has to inevitably tie up, the narrative begins surprisingly slowly, with Kessler and Ingrid waking up and breakfasting together. In fact, the first twenty minutes of the episode are comprised almost entirely of dialogue-heavy static scenes, and as such, given the action-packed content of the final thirty minutes, embody the calm before the storm. This early part of the episode not only sets the scene for the dramatic and tragic ends of the majority of the regular cast – in the case of Ingrid's death, quite literally, as Mical is seen closing the very shutters that Ingrid will open just before she is shot – but also serves the purpose of recapping on recent events, loyalties and agreements.

That Kessler is finally depicted here as set on a definite course of action, having agreed to both fund and lead Ingrid's Neo-Nazis, makes the narrative much more straightforward than it has been up until now. Arguably, it also makes it much more entertaining, as it means that rather than seeing Kessler 'on the back foot', we are observing him on familiar territory, back on top, planning, manipulating and toying with his colleagues. This is most evident in the way he deals with Yqueras, who he knows has had him followed, has been plotting with Ingrid and, most importantly, is ultimately out for himself. Rather than just telling Yqueras that his allegiance to the Kameraden is at an end, he instead lets him sweat, even electing to calmly play the piano before getting down to business and reassuring the South American that they are on the same side after all.

An element of the serial that has often dominated proceedings is whether the much touted *Der Tag* – the new Nazi dawn – is actually a viable proposition. Here, Kessler and Ingrid seem to think so; indeed the latter even appears to survey the world from her apartment as if those beyond it are her prospective subjects, such is her confidence in her vision. As to Kessler, his arresting discussion with Franz about the practicalities of taking control of Germany affirms his belief strongly, especially as the pair casually talk about using an army of schoolteachers to indoctrinate the young, intimidating Trade Unions to make them comply and, most startlingly, eliminating troublemakers. That Kessler's conscience will allow all of the above – he only adds the caveat that Franz should take things slowly and carefully – is a reminder that Kessler is first and foremost a dangerous fanatic who thinks nothing of the loss of human life if it means achieving his dream of a Fourth Reich. Rückert, however, despite his statement in the previous episode that he has settled on a date for *Der Tag* (something that is ignored here and which presumably he was only using as a carrot to dangle in front of his younger Nazi followers), pronounces here that there is no real possibility of a new Nazi dawn, stating that "the parade has gone by" and that he does not pretend to himself anymore. His belief is cleverly emphasised by the marrying of this dialogue with his taking down of a Nazi flag. Rückert's reasons for this are fascinating. While he believes that only the old guard Kameraden are true Nazis, he recognises that he and his comrades are too old to build a new Reich ("We have nothing to give and nothing to take. We shall be dead soon anyway") and seems, for the first time, to be tired of carrying the burden of a Nazi future and of their criminal reputation ("Keep the anger of the world off my back and my comrades"). He symbolically passes the burden on to Kessler by draping the Nazi flag over his shoulder – a responsibility for him to take on, if he still wants it. Although Kessler is clearly shocked by Rückert's stance, it does not appear to dampen his enthusiasm for the cause he is now intent on backing. When Bauer and Mical corner him, he still speaks like a fanatic – "The true Germans are dispersed throughout the world, waiting to reassert themselves in a great new Reich!" – proving, as Bauer said earlier in the episode, that his kind of belief is "indestructible". Kessler only finally accepts defeat and the fact that his dream is beyond his grasp when he learns that Ingrid is dead. This is not just because of the loss of Ingrid's contacts and her similarly fanatical enthusiasm but, perhaps more importantly, because she was Madeleine's daughter and as such shared in what he describes at the start of the episode as his "unstinted love". It is clear from the fact that he does not want to dwell upon Ingrid's death, immediately asking Bauer to kill him, that the closeness that he sought with her, which he believed would be enhanced by their joint goal of reshaping Germany, was a hugely significant part of his renewed belief in a Nazi future, even if he was not aware of just how much.

Michael E. Briant ensures that the deaths of all concerned here are sudden and shocking. Ingrid's death is particularly surprising as the viewer does not see it coming, partly because we are only halfway through the episode, but also because we are not party, until the very last second, to the fact that Müller is waiting on the roof of an adjoining building. That Ingrid is killed because she is mistakenly believed to be Mical is suitably ironic, as instead of murdering a Jew, Müller has killed one of the only people in the world who could have played an instrumental part in the global rebirth of Nazism. Alison Glennie plays dead particularly well, her staring lifeless eyes, which Briant keeps on for some time, proving to be particularly haunting. Garriga's and Franz's deaths are similarly believable and startling and, given the lack of resources available to him, ingeniously directed by Briant, especially in the way that they fully utilised the talents of stuntman Gareth Milne. Although Briant's desire to end the series with a bang is understandable, of the action sequences on offer here, the careering lorry stunt is arguably superfluous, if impressively executed.

An element of the episode that puzzled Briant in 2005 when watching the series back for the first time in 24 years was the fact that the extras in Almeria were all dressed in their best clothes, something which he did not think was realistic given that the town was a relatively poor place back in 1981. However, it makes perfect sense if one remembers that in the narrative this is meant to be the festival of Ascension Day on which the locals would wear their 'Sunday best'. However, Briant can be forgiven for forgetting this fact as strangely, after laying the relevant groundwork so well in episode five – particularly with the atmospheric drumming at its close – Brason elects to make no reference to the festival at all in this final script. This is something of a missed opportunity, especially as it would have allowed a clever juxtaposition of the theme of ascension with the depiction of the total collapse of the Nazi dream.

Once again the matching of the Spanish exteriors with the Glasgow interiors is extraordinarily seamless, especially when Mical finally enters the Kameraden hacienda. The stained glass door and the light and shadows offer a marriage between location and studio rarely achieved in other dramas of this vintage.

The evacuation of the hacienda is well handled and not only visually depicts the Kameraden's need to move on again in order to preserve their safety, but symbolically signals the end of the road for the entire Nazi movement and, more specifically, for Kessler. The removal of items of furniture from the room in which Kessler and Rückert are debating is particularly effective, and is an activity which is also essential, in narrative terms, in order for Kessler to ultimately commit suicide more dramatically in an almost empty room.

Arguably the most fascinating element of the episode is the long-awaited confrontation between Kessler and his pursuers, principally because it provides us, for the final time, with a further insight into the workings of his mind. Although Kessler's fanaticism has rarely if ever been shown to extend to anti-Semitic action, he displays no feelings of guilt for the Holocaust here, in fact quite the reverse. Not only is he entirely dismissive of the activity of those Israeli's who have abducted Nazi war criminals in order to bring them to trial, calmly stating that: "A trial with Hebrew commercials in the breaks is more than I could stand," but he even tells Mical that: "Without the Final Solution, there would be no Israel. Never forget that. It was the guilt of the Allies that gave you your 'promised land', nothing else!" That said, his first reaction to Mical's mention of the Holocaust is to protest that: "I was not involved in that lunacy," however, his objection to it seems to have arisen from his opinion of its counter-productive effect on the Third Reich rather than as a reaction to its horrific immorality. Earlier in the episode, Kessler accused Franz and Ingrid of dubious moral behaviour, describing his own personal morality as antediluvian in comparison, but bizarrely he seems to make no connection between his moral standards and his culpability as a Nazi for the unspeakable Final Solution. It is an interesting paradox that perhaps just goes to show the hugely disfigured nature of the Nazi mind.

In the same scene, Brason is unable to stop himself from using dialogue that he had originally written for the unbroadcast *What Did You Do in the War, Daddy?* concerning the fact that the Communists have murdered more people than the Nazis. Thankfully however, this time around it is Kessler, rather than Natalie, who is given the argument, which in this context is used much more appropriately as a untenable defence of Nazi evil rather than as a dubious argument as to why the Second World War was not an especially important war to fight. In addition, the lines about the taking of a single life being a crime (originally spoken by Albert, albeit slightly reworked here) are given to Bauer: "There is no faith, no cause, no belief, worth the taking of a single human life." Once again, the lines are much more effectively used here, as Bauer is not just holding forth about his beliefs, as Albert was, but is instead actively seeking to prevent Mical from killing Kessler so that she doesn't ruin her life, showing that he has come to care deeply for this impulsive Israeli girl. That Bauer is so crucial to the final ten minutes, with Alan Dobie as believable as he ever was in Tolstoy, begs the question why his character has been arguably underused in the serial. The answer seems simply to be the fact that Brason elected unreservedly to give the meat of the drama to the serial's Nazi characters rather than their pursuers.

After Bauer has forced Mical's hand, preventing her from killing Kessler, and the pair leave him alone with the Uzi that Bauer has 'thoughtfully' laid against the wall, it is not immediately clear that the fight has gone out of Kessler, especially as he has just been expressing the view that: "It's the fate of the strong, the determined, to do what the weak know is a necessity and to be chastised for doing it." This uncertainty is briefly heightened when Briant has Kessler make for the door with the Uzi firmly in his grasp, suggesting for a moment that he might have chosen to try to live to fight another day. However, when Kessler closes the door rather than walking through it, it is clear that he has elected to take his own life. That he bows out in a style suggested by Clifford Rose himself, by committing suicide upon the flag of his party, seems entirely fitting and proves that, other than John Brason, no-one knows Kessler better than the actor who brought him to life. Kessler's demise is breathtaking, moving and, thanks to a wide-angle crane shot from Briant, sufficiently dramatic too. As Rose firmly believed, it certainly does feel like the right time for one of the most three-dimensional villains ever to grace our television screens to take his final bow.

Brason's decision to end the serial with Mical and Bauer left a little bewildered as to what to do next hits exactly the right note. The last thirty minutes have after all been a rollercoaster ride, and they and the audience are rather left gasping for breath. Although Bauer's line, "People in Germany don't want the Nazi's back," feels as though it is bordering on the glib, it is nevertheless an important message that, given *Kessler*'s prevalence of old guard and young Nazis perhaps needed to be said.

This final episode does a superb job of bringing all of the serial's plot strands together, in an eminently watchable fifty minutes which balance edge-of-the-seat action sequences with expertly written scenes of significant emotional depth.

AFTERWORD

Kessler is categorically not the serial that everyone hoped or expected it to be, a situation which has often led to it being very unfairly dismissed as unsatisfying as a result. Although it is often billed as such, *Kessler* simply does not fulfil all the criteria of a sequel. Sequels are generally defined as being set in the same universe as a previous work and continuing their story, typically with the same characters and settings. With the exception of Kessler himself, this serial quickly takes the risk of leaving all of the other featured *Secret Army* characters behind in order to develop new and untested characters in their place. The familiar Brussels setting is also quickly abandoned in favour of a broad, and occasionally confusing, European canvas, before the production uproots entirely and moves wholesale to Paraguay. Given these factors, it is far more appropriate to describe *Kessler* as a spin-off rather than a sequel, in that it derives elements from *Secret Army* but is offered as an entirely distinct product with a different pace, scope and agenda. If this distinction is owned and recognised and there is sufficient will not to constantly compare it to *Secret Army* then the serial can be truly enjoyed on its own merits. However, this is a feat that may not be easy for those who come to *Kessler* immediately off the back of the hugely addictive final series of *Secret Army*, who inevitably are seeking more of the same.

What is arguably most fascinating about *Kessler* is its depiction of the tensions, loyalties and allegiances that exist among the Nazi old guard, represented by the backward looking Kameradenwerk, and also their contrast with the young Neo-Nazi pretenders, who are dangerously eager for the National Socialist madness to be reborn. Kessler himself is placed in neither camp for the majority of the narrative as the chess game goes on around him, so that his decision as to which group to back can become the dramatic crux of the serial. Unfortunately, the Kameraden receive far more exploration than their Neo-Nazi counterparts, and the threat of the latter is dulled by the serial's unwillingness to depict their threat to modern society other than through the dialogue of two characters, of which only one, Ingrid, is sufficiently developed.

Thankfully the serial's characterisation is, with one or two exceptions, largely on a par with *Secret Army*. Clifford Rose copes very well with the demands of playing a man much older than he was at the time and is as convincing as ever as Kessler, particularly in the latter episodes in which he grasps the nettle again and briefly promises to become a far more significant threat to the world than he ever was in *Secret Army*. Ralph Michael is also excellent value as Luftwaffe hero Colonel Rückert, a man with more metal inside him than the Bismarck, who starts out as a loyal friend of Kessler and ends up anything but, subverting our expectations en route. The moments when he bares his steel (no pun intended!) are some of the most memorable of the serial. Alison Glennie does her very best to transform Ingrid into a three-dimensional character rather than a cliché, but is prevented from doing so for much of the narrative by virtue of the fact that she does not have enough screen time. Ultimately, however, she becomes a female version of her father, just as fanatical and yet capable of genuine affection (if not for Franz, who is clearly just a sex object to her, then for her father). Classical actor Alan Dobie, who occasionally gives the impression that he is a little mystified to be in the serial, is rarely given the opportunity to show off his acting credentials here, but nevertheless manages to make Bauer into an interesting individual, who journeys from grey civil servant to tanned action hero during the course of the narrative. Nitza Saul, an actress who was also a genuine army-trained Israeli, fits the bill perfectly as Mical. However, neither Mical nor Bauer, as the serial's pursuers, are developed enough for the audience to engage with them emotionally. Of the remaining regulars, Oscar Quitak also deserves particular mention for his believable portrayal of the unhinged and utterly vile Mengele.

The existence of the Kameradenwerk, the inclusion of Mengele and Bormann (albeit only his hand), the revelation that Kessler was a close friend of the late Eichmann, and the existence of a vast Nazi Fortune – are all part and parcel of Brason's attempts to place *Kessler* in as authentic a post-war 'Nazi landscape' as possible. Unfortunately, despite his protestations that the serial is 'closer to the truth than has hitherto been portrayed,' these factors can come across as rather unbelievable to the uninitiated who quite understandably have no book-knowledge of, say, Mengele's flight to South America or of the possibility of Bormann's survival post-1945. What is more, Brason makes few attempts to educate the viewer in these matters early on through the obvious mouthpiece for such exposition, Bauer, and instead they are introduced as accepted fact.

Kessler is also inevitably constrained by the fact that it is only a six-part serial and so does not have the luxury of time for themes or indeed characters to develop fully. As a thirteen-part series, it might have been a very different beast indeed, and judging by the amount of content that is packed into the serial that was made, it is plain to see that there would have been more than enough intrigue and action to fill it.

Wherever one stands on the quality, subject matter or chosen scope of *Kessler*, there is no question of it detracting from the series from whence it was born. This is largely because it wisely chooses not to attempt to recapture its style and approach, but is instead intent on ploughing its own dramatic furrow. *Kessler* may have its faults, but it is nevertheless an entertaining and unique drama serial which deserves appraisal on its own considerable merits.

APPENDICES

Appendix One:
GERRY GLAISTER

War Career

John Leslie Gerard Glaister was born in Hong Kong on 21 December 1915, the son of a Royal Navy doctor. After an education at Taunton School, he trained to be an actor at RADA and subsequently worked in repertory theatre. Shortly after his West End debut at the Whitehall Theatre, in Spring 1939 Glaister elected to join the RAF to train as a pilot, believing war with Germany was now inevitable. The following year he was posted to Norfolk and began to fly Blenheims. After early missions in Northern Europe, he led bombing raids over Tobruk and Derna in the Western Desert. A few near misses later, he went on to fight in the Italian campaign, in Greece and Crete. Glaister then moved on to the Photo Intelligence Squadron and began to fly daringly low reconnaissance missions and was subsequently awarded the DFC (Distinguished Flying Cross). He then returned to England to work as an instructor before joining the Air Ministry intelligence unit.

© Joan Glaister

Pre-*Secret Army* BBC CV

1957	Romantic Chapter (tv play) ~ director
1957	Uncertain Honours (tv play) ~ director
1957	Wideawake (serial) ~ producer
1958	Big Guns (serial) ~ producer/director
1958	Starr and Company (series) ~ producer/director
1959	The Widow of Bath (serial) ~ producer
1960	The Men From Room 13 (series) ~ producer
1961-2	Maigret (series) ~ director
1961-3	Tales of Edgar Wallace (tv plays) ~ director
1962	Dr Finlay's Casebook (series) ~ director
1962	The Dark Island (serial) ~ producer/director
1963	Moonstrike (series) ~ producer
1963	Kidnapped (serial) ~ director
1965-6	Dr Finlay's Casebook (series) ~ producer/director
1966	King of the River (series) ~ director
1966-7	This Man Craig (series) ~ producer
1967-8	The Revenue Men (series) ~ producer/director
1968-71	The Expert (series) ~ creator/producer/director
1970	Codename (series) ~ producer/director
1971	The Passenger (serial) ~ producer
1972	The Long Chase (serial) ~ creator/producer/writer
1972-4	Colditz (series) ~ creator/producer
1972-6	The Brothers (series) ~ creator/producer
1975	Oil Strike North (series) ~ creator/producer
1976	The Expert (series) ~ creator/director
1977	The MacKinnons (series) ~ producer/director

Appendix Two:
HOMING PIGEON by Wilfred Greatorex

The following is a full synopsis for *Secret Army*'s original episode one, written by Wilfred Greatorex in 1976 and abandoned in early 1977. Greatorex received a consultant credit on the series's closing titles for his contribution.

Autumn 1941. Flight Lieutenant Royce and his four crewmen are flying a Wellington Bomber at night over Occupied Belgium. Meanwhile, in the country's capital, 22-year-old orphan Lisa Colbert is playing bridge with her Aunt Louise and Uncle Gaston and a family friend. However, Lisa is distracted from the game by the noise of a bomber flying overhead. At Gestapo Headquarters, Major Kessler orders that a prisoner be brought to him for interrogation. Lisa elects to leaves her home, telling her relatives that it is "a night for her 'children'." After being stopped by a German soldier for her permit, Lisa arrives at the Candide, a busy restaurant-cum-bar. There she meets its proprietor Albert and his young mistress Monique. A German corporal takes an interest in Lisa as she makes her way to the Candide's back room, but Albert refuses to give the man her name. In the skies above Brussels, after being hit by a 'night-fighter', Royce's Wellington Bomber is in trouble. Meanwhile, Kessler interrogates a man called René. He threatens him with the firing squad unless he tells him about the people whom he works with. Royce and his crew bail out of the Wellington, parachuting down to the Belgian countryside below. At the Candide, the corporal who has taken a fancy to Lisa bursts into the back room to make a move on her, but is subsequently escorted off the premises by the Wehrmacht military police for causing a disturbance. Lisa proceeds to talk on the telephone with other members of the evasion network she leads – Lifeline – passing on information about evaders. As soon as she finishes one call, the phone rings again immediately. Royce and his crew have come down separately near the Belgian-Dutch border. A group of them are discovered by two Belgians named Louis and André. The next day, while Lisa is cycling across Brussels, Royce, who has been sheltering in a ditch all night, approaches a passing farmer. The man advises him to go back to the ditch, but Royce decides not to in case he is informed on, and instead makes his way to a barn where he falls asleep in the hay. He is found some time later by two men who proceed to interrogate him, but he refuses to give any more information than his name, rank and number. At the Candide, a young man named Alain tells Lisa that their colleague René has been shot, but thankfully the only person he knew in the Line was him and even then he didn't know his real name. Lisa gives Alain a piece of paper listing the names of three airmen – Sergeant Kenneth Godley, Captain Lincoln Willis and Flight Lieutenant John Royce. Alain leaves the capital by potato truck. Kessler interrogates an airmen called Peter Thomson (one of Royce's crew members), but he too will only give his name, rank and number. Due to his lack of cooperation, Kessler orders that a man be brought in. It is André, and he has been severely beaten. Kessler explains that he has been in a road accident and that he will receive medical attention if Thomson will identify him. Kessler believes André to be an evasion line 'collector'. Thomson states that he doesn't know him. Kessler advises him that if he identifies André then he will accept that he is an airman and therefore entitled to full protection under the Geneva Convention. Alain has joined the men who have been interrogating Royce and asks him several specific questions set by 'London'. A disorientated Royce answers them all correctly and Alain and the others accept that he is who hw says he is, explaining that the Gestapo have recently been trying to infiltrate the Line with fake evaders. Major Brandt of the Luftwaffe Police, who has managed to obtain Thomson from Kessler's clutches, asks him to plot a route on a chart for him, telling him he will return him to the Gestapo if he doesn't cooperate. Alain takes Royce to a safe-house where he is reunited with Willis and given instructions on his conduct while he stays there. Kessler interrogates André, specifically asking him if he is a member of Lifeline and who runs it. Meanwhile at the Candide, Lisa, Lifeline's leader, is talking with Alain about the fact that she knows that Kessler has André. Monique enters to tell Albert that his invalid wife is calling for him. Alain is very surprised to learn from Lisa that Albert is having an affair with Monique. Alain confides that he is not comfortable with her coming to a place like the Candide. Kessler oversees a brutal torturing of André. Alain brings another of Royce's crew, Godley, to the safe-house, where he is reunited with Royce and Willis. Lisa arrives as well and gives all three of them new identities. As Willis is American, she decides that he must pretend to be retarded otherwise he will give himself away. She goes on to give them advice about the right way to walk. Godley doesn't take her instructions very seriously and messes around, much to her annoyance. Royce finds that he is increasingly captivated by Lisa. The next day, after they have left the safe-house, Lisa diverts the attention of some Germans, stopping them from stopping Royce and Willis, by pretending she has caught her shoe in a pavement grille. At their new safe-house, Royce and the others are introduced to a monk called Père Michel who is there to coach them. Michel christens Royce 'Pigeon'. At her home, Lisa listens in to a BBC radio broadcast waiting to hear a specific message. Kessler continues to interrogate a now haggard André, asking him who Yvette is. At the safe-house, the evaders are miming eating food so that Michel can instruct them on how they should eat 'continentally'. After being dressed as Flemish salesmen, Michel takes them to Brussels Gare du Midi and onto a train bound for Paris. When they find themselves in a corridor full of Germans, Godley thinks it is a trap, but Lisa arrives and he calms down. She arranges to meet them at the arrivals board at Paris Gare du Nord. After a nerve-shattering stop at a customs checkpoint, the train continues on to Paris. Upon arriving at a Paris safe-house run by a woman called Marie, Royce talks to Lisa alone, but she brushes off his obvious interest in her without showing any emotion. At Gestapo Headquarters in Brussels, Kessler and Brandt are now interrogating another airman, called Jimmy Fender, who was found at a safe-house in Blankenburg that they think is run by Yvette. Louis, the Belgian man who was first seen with André, and who has also been beaten, is brought in to the room and Fender is instructed to identify him. When he too fails to cooperate, a furious Kessler strikes him and then makes for Louis too. Fender trips Kessler, grabs a desk lamp and is about to bring it down on Kessler's head but is prevented from doing so by Brandt who instructs Fender to put it down. Louis and Fender are taken away. Kessler is incandescent with rage, whereas Brandt has a much calmer take on the situation, advising him that he does not want Fender to be beaten as he needs him to be able to think and speak clearly. Lisa and the evaders are now on a train to Biarritz. Royce, Willis and Godley are distressed as they are having to share a compartment with several German soldiers. A German soldier is coming on to Lisa, but she politely declines his offer to meet up with her again. At one station stop, Royce observes three men out on the platform who are dressed almost exactly as they are, and therefore obviously evaders, who appear to be lost and without a guide. Lisa has noticed them too but elects to leave them where they are. Some time later, Lisa, Royce and the other evaders are riding bicycles on a mountain path in the foothills of the Pyrenees, being guided by a rugged Basque smuggler called Tollo, who is less than impressed with their levels of fitness. After a while the bicycles are abandoned and they continue on foot until they reach a farmhouse. After resting and eating, it is learned that a French Police patrol are nearby and so it is decided not to move on for a while. Royce asks Lisa about her involvement in evasion work and specifically why she left the three lost evaders at the station they passed through. She explains that one guide is worth a hundred airmen. Royce tells her he would like to be of some use after returning to England and she tells him he can best do that by coming back over Europe in a Bomber. She reveals that she lost her fiancé during the German invasion but refuses to answer any more of his questions. Later, the party make their way up another mountain path and have to take cover when an armed French patrol comes past, just inches from where they are hiding. They arrive at a river and although exhausted, make it across. Lisa tells them they are now in Spain. They shout in jubilation at this news, but she advises them that they are not safe yet. Suitably chastened they walk on. After another close call with a passing Spanish Army patrol, Lisa and Tollo try to encourage the flagging airmen to keep moving. However, they are completely exhausted and beg for time to rest. They are instructed to hide in a ditch and are covered over with scrub. Tollo is furious. Two hours later, the evaders are amazed to see Lisa return in a taxi which she has hired to take them all to the British Consulate in nearby San Sebastian. Royce is distraught at having to leave Lisa behind, having become very fond of her indeed. He complains that he will not know if she survives the trip back to Brussels, but she tells him that she will know that he is alright and affectionately calls him 'Pigeon' once again. He kisses her hand and makes to get in the taxi, but then thinks better of it and races after her, grabbing her face in his hands and kissing her on the forehead. He tells her once again that he must know that she'll be alright. She tells him she's sure he'll find a way. He and the others leave in the taxi. Several days later, in the Candide's back room, Lisa, Gaston, Albert and Alain are listening to a BBC radio broadcast. Lisa is waiting to hear a particular message. Meanwhile at Gestapo Headquarters, Kessler advises Brandt that he has written a report that makes serious allegations about him. The former is furious that Brandt has sent Fender to a prisoner-of-war camp behind his back. They too are listening to the BBC and hear the phrase "Le Pigeon est bien rentre," but unlike Lisa are unaware that it refers to the safe return to England of Royce. At the Candide, Lisa permits herself a slight smile but no more. Brandt describes Kessler's report as a fantasy and criticises his interrogation style as ineffective. The next day, Louis and André are blindfolded and shot, and their bodies are taken away. At the Candide that evening, Alain tells Lisa that he doesn't think André would have talked and that Louis was not one of their agents anyway. Lisa tells him that she may know of a possible replacement for André. Albert goes to draw the black-out curtains and expresses his frustration with how long the war is lasting. Alain and Lisa discuss the fact that Royce got home. Their conversation is drowned out by the noise of Bombers overhead.

Appendix Three:
From Script to Screen: **BRIDGEHEAD** by Michael J. Bird

Of all of the episodes of *Secret Army*, with the obvious exception of the very first instalment, the twelfth episode of the third series, had one of the longest journeys from original conception to script and then to screen.

During one of their earliest meetings about the third series Glaister and Brason agreed that the episode would see Lifeline remobilised in September 1944 in order to 'assist in the recovery of as many paratroopers as possible' after the disastrous Operation Market Garden at Arnhem. When it later became clear that neither Albert nor Monique could be involved in such an operation (the former due to Monique's continued absence and the fact that he was recovering from almost being murdered; the latter because she would be facing and recovering from an altogether different threat during the episode) the plot was refined to include only the efforts made by Natalie and her uncle, bargee Hans van Broecken, who would be approached to help out by the Allied forces in Brussels who receive news of what has happened at Arnhem.

However, by the time that the episode was eventually assigned to seasoned television scriptwriter Michael J. Bird, after Willis Hall, the writer originally assigned to the episode, dropped out, the brief for episode twelve was different again. It was now set to open a few days after the liberation of Brussels in early September 1944. In terms of content, Glaister and Brason required that it dramatised three separate strands: Monique's story following her kidnapping by Vercors and his cronies; Kessler's continued masquerade as Franz Spitzwerg at a Canadian-run cantonment (a temporary or semi-permanent military quarters); and Van Broecken's experiences near Arnhem. However, Gliaster and Brason specified that it was Monique's story that should take precdence, so much so that one of the episode's working titles was simply *Monique*. Nevertheless, the episode title eventually chosen ignores this fact and instead refers back to Glaister and Brason's original conception of an episode that solely centred upon Operation Market Garden.

There follows a full synopsis for Michael J. Bird's first draft script for *Bridgehead*, together with annotations in italics describing those scenes and elements that were different in the final transmitted episode that was directed by Andrew Morgan.

September 1944. On a street in liberated Brussels, a jubilant and vengeful mob of citizens are on the rampage, demolishing a small shop. They are watched by two policemen who are choosing not to intervene. A British armoured car enters the street and pulls up alongside the policemen. Sitting on the rim of the gun turret is Captain Stephen Durnford of the British Army. Durnford asks the policemen what's going on and they tell him that the Resistance say the shop was owned by

606

collaborators, but that they don't know that for certain. Durnford discusses it with his Sergeant, Friar, and argues that it could just as easily be about a personal grudge or "plain bloody hooliganism." As the armoured car moves towards the mob, they gather around it cheering. Some of the women climb up to try to kiss Durnford and he has to disentangle himself. After the armoured car leaves, the orgy of destruction continues.

> *This scene is entirely absent, probably due to the usual limitations on the amount of available location filming time, but also because it required the expensive demolition of a period shop. Unlike most draft scripts, at 88 pages, Bird's first stab is not overlong, so it is unlikely to have been dropped due to time constraints.*

In a square elsewhere in Brussels, an even larger mob is assembled in front of an imposing building where several women are imprisoned in an improvised cage. A dishevelled Monique is among them. One by one they are being dragged from the cage to have their hair cut off and their heads shaved. The crowd is delighted by what it is witnessing and those near enough also spit, punch and slap the women after they've been shorn.

These scenes are noticeably more violent. At the behest of Glaister's BBC bosses, several moments that were filmed by director Andrew Morgan were later cut, largely because they were considered to be too harrowing and graphic to be transmitted in an early evening time-slot.

Natalie arrives on the scene and, after pushing her way through the crowd, is horrified to see that Monique is in the cage. Eventually Monique sees Natalie, who is calling out to her. She tells her to go away as there is nothing she can do to help. Natalie ignores her and goes to speak to two men and a woman who seem to be in charge of this macabre sideshow, while another victim is barbered. Natalie tells the men that Monique is a friend of hers. They tell her that they know her too, describing her as 'the bitch who used to sing in the Candide." The man taunts Monique, calling her a little nightingale who used to sing her head off for the Germans but who won't sing for them. Natalie tells them they've got it wrong and that her singing was part of her cover and that she was with the Resistance. While one of the men tries to grope Natalie, the woman who is with them tells her that they all say that now and that if she is Monique's friend then she probably 'tarted' herself during the Occupation too. Monique calls to Natalie, urging her to leave again. Another woman is dragged from the cage. Durnford's armoured car pulls into the square and he observes with horror as the latest victim is shorn. One of the two men advises Natalie to push off, but the woman grabs her and calls to the crowd, telling them that she admits to being a friend of a friend of the Germans. The crowd chants that she should have her hair cut and shaved too.

Natalie's attempts to reason with the mob's ringleaders, and the subsequent danger of her meeting the same fate as that intended for Monique, were eventually abandoned.

Monique is taken from the cage and forced to sit in the wooden 'barber's chair', which is surrounded by a 'sea of hair'. The barber, who is enjoying his work, selects a lock of her hair and hacks it from her head.

To Angela Richards's disappointment, rather than hacking off a lock of her hair, in order to tone this sequence down, the actor playing the barber would be instructed by Andrew Morgan to gently snip off a lock instead.,

A distraught Natalie struggles to free herself and reach Monique. Durnford chooses this moment to intervene and shouts "That's enough!" but the mob take no notice of him and another lock of hair is cut from Monique's head. Durnford orders Friar to fire the armoured car's machine gun over the heads of the crowd. The crowd and the barber freeze. Durnford orders that they release Monique and Natalie and tells them that if the women have committed any crimes then the authorities will deal with them. The woman and the two men are still defiant calling them "whores" and "traitors", and urge the crowd to get Durnford to leave them to it. Once again, Friar has to fire in order to quieten them. Durnford begins to count down, giving them fifteen seconds to let them go. Friar shows they mean business by lowering the machine gun so that it is pointed at the mob. Their intent is believed and the prisoners are freed. Durnford orders the crowd to disperse. They still complain but the movement of the machine gun soon gets them on their way.

The crowd take much less convincing – Friar only needs to give one machine gun burst, but he still has to point the machine gun at them to make them finally disperse. The two men and the woman cited in Bird's script were obviously considered surplus to requirements and it is the barber who agrees to Durnford's demands, to the displeasure of the mob.

Natalie helps Monique from the chair. Monique tells her she doesn't want to go back to the Candide, so Natalie offers to take her to her apartment instead and escorts her towards the armoured car. Durnford becomes more interested in Monique as she approaches. They thank him. When he sees Monique stumble, he offers them a lift to Natalie's flat – on Rue Therese near the Gare du Midi – on the armoured car, despite the fact that it is out of their way completely.

There is no such discussion, instead Natalie instinctively decides to take Monique back home with her. Similarly, Durnford doesn't wait for Monique to stumble and immediately offers to give the pair a lift.

The armoured car leaves the empty square and a gentle breeze disturbs the pile of hair lying around the chair.

This is immediately followed by the first scene to feature Van Broecken, however in Bird's script Hans's scene doesn't occur until after Monique and Durnford have their first date. This may be because Bird knew that Van Broecken's storyline directly related to Operation Market Garden and so shouldn't begin until much later in September 1944 (the episode takes place over several weeks after all). The Van Broecken sequences were undoubtedly moved forward so as to be spread throughout the episode for the purposes of balance and pacing.

At the Candide, which is closed, Albert is serving coffee and cognac to himself and Alain. Alain asks after Monique and whether he has been looking for her himself. He confirms he has, along with attending endless identity parades at the Avenue Louise.

Alain is more confrontational than Bird's script suggests about Albert's interest in Monique's safety.

Alain thinks she'll turn up safe and sound, but Albert isn't so sure and refers to the fact that if it hadn't been for Natalie then he would have been lynched.

609

This suggests that it was originally intended that, of the Lifeline personnel only Natalie would be involved in rescuing Albert in Collaborator. As it turned out, Alain would also be with her, so this dialogue was subsequently altered. Bird's script also makes no reference to Albert's neck being sore or bandaged, which suggests that his lynching was not initially planned to go as far as it did. Albert's comment that he isn't sure about Monique's safety is also absent.

Albert tells Alain that he hasn't seen Natalie for three days. Alain makes a gaffe by saying to Albert that he thinks if anyone will find Monique she will. A Colonel Northwood of British Intelligence arrives, carrying a briefcase. He asks if Albert can spare some time. Alain takes the hint to leave and exits the Candide.

Northwood is accompanied by another officer, a Lieutenant, who is there to act as a witness, and Alain does not actually leave the Candide but instead makes himself scarce by going into the back room.

Northwood tells Albert that London asked him to get in touch to give him "a full assignment of London's sixty percent interest in the Candide" in recognition of his work for Lifeline. Albert is surprised that this has been settled so quickly. Northwood requests he signs the documentation he has brought. Albert immediately signs, stating that he is sure everything is as it should be.

More in keeping with the Albert we know, the restaurateur is much more reluctant to sign quickly and scans the transfer document, before being urged to get on with it by Northwood. There is also a reference to Albert's lynching, which Northwood already knows about.

Northwood compliments him on his restaurant. On his way out, Albert offers him a free meal as a guest and the Colonel tells him he may well take him up on that. After congratulating Albert again on his work for Lifeline and briefly discussing the fact that several "big fish" war criminals are still at large, he leaves. Kessler is seen standing in the back of a truck being taken to a Canadian-run cantonment in a warehouse.

Morgan chose instead to show a close-up of a moody and despondent Kessler inside the truck. As Alain has already left the Candide in Bird's first draft, there is no mention of the subsequent scene between him and Albert in which they discuss the news that Northwood brought and the fact that they can now divide the remaining Lifeline monies five ways.

Durnford calls on Monique but Natalie tells him she needs rest. She explains that Monique is not a collaborator and that they both worked for Lifeline. Natalie tells Durnford that she hopes no-one makes trouble for him given that he helped them. He leaves the apartment block. He gets back in the armoured car and drives off.

Once again this is a scene that would be followed by another scene featuring Van Broecken, but which Bird doesn't include in his draft until much later on.

At the warehouse cantonment, senior German officer, General-Leutnant von Schalk, is meeting newly arrived prisoners who are identifying themselves to him. An infantry Captain called Heinrich Niemann introduces himself. On his way out, he notices Kessler standing waiting in line and reacts to the unit insignia on his uniform. He tells Oberleutnant Scheer that another of "his lot" has just come in.

Scheer is a Major instead and is sat next to Von Schalk at a registration table. Niemann is not instrumental in revealing Kessler's true identity.

Kessler introduces himself to Von Schalk as Franz Spitzwerg and tells him he was captured at Oostmalle. Scheer approaches and tells Von Schalk that Kessler is not Spitzwerg, a revelation that causes a bit of a commotion, but Von Schalk subsequently tells him that he already knew this to be the case as they have met before. Nevertheless, for the benefit of the others present he asks Kessler to reveal his true identify.

There is no commotion as only Von Schalk and Scheer are present in the room and, as a result, Kessler only has to reveal his true identity to Scheer.

He does so and also states that Spitzwerg is dead. Von Schalk announces that Kessler must have had good reason for assuming his new identity and that, for the sake of Germany, he wants their captors to believe that there are no Nazis among them, merely Germans loyal to the Fatherland. Kessler is pleased with this turn of events.

Scheer is shown objecting to Von Schalk's acceptance of Kessler's false identity, but is silenced.

That evening at a very busy Candide, a woman singer is belting out a popular song of the day.

The popular song is 'You Must Have Been a Beautiful Baby'.

Albert is busy behind the bar when he notices Natalie arrive carrying a suitcase. She explains that she has found Monique and tells him about her ordeal. She makes for the door to the back room and he follows her. Natalie tells Albert that Monique is not coming back. Natalie is surprised that he doesn't understand why. He states that he will go to see her tomorrow, as he can't get away now as the Candide is too busy. Natalie tells him that tomorrow might be too late and that if he goes tonight it might just make a difference, before concluding that it is probably better for him to just leave her alone. Natalie asks if she can stay in the spare room for one night. Albert is offended that she even asks. She then tells him that she won't be long and that she won't even unpack. He doesn't understand her, until she makes it clear that she has come back as a waitress, telling him that there's "money to be made."

> *Natalie tells Albert that she will go upstairs and change but there is no discussion of the fact that she is returning to her job as waitress or that she intends to stay at the Candide.*

The next day, Monique answers the door at Natalie's apartment. It is Durnford with a bunch of flowers for her. She takes a while to place him but then warily lets him in. She is concerned that he believes the things that were said about her in the square, but he reassures her that he knows differently and specifically that he knows about her work for Lifeline. He tells her that Natalie told him and that a Major friend of his in Intelligence confirmed it.

> *At this point there is a moment, not found in Bird's script, during which the pair stop being cagey and introduce themselves to each other, giving their full names.*

He asks her to dinner that night, but she tells him she doesn't feel like going out anywhere. He then asks her if she can cook and suggests that he brings some food and drink and that they stay in.

> *Durnford doesn't have his flash of inspiration about eating in until Monique has already seen him out of the apartment.*

He promises just dinner and conversation and no "hanky-panky". She is confused and he explains what the phrase means by mentioning "funny business", "slap and tickle" and "chasing around the bedroom". They laugh together. She agrees to see him back there at 7.30pm.

> *There is no mention of 'hanky-panky' or any other euphemisms for sex and no laughter together either. In fact, Monique seems much more wary of him and the proposed date than in Bird's script.*

On a clock tower (Bird specifies 'ideally a well-known landmark in the city') the time shows 7.29pm.

> *Morgan chose the clock on the Hôtel de Ville in the Grand Place. This shot is followed by two brief scenes not in Bird's first draft: Albert buying some flowers in the Grand Place, not far from the Candide, by the distinctive steps of the Residences of the Dukes of Brabant; and Albert walking along a lane and noticing some graffiti on a wall which reads 'mort aux collaborateurs' (death to collaborators).*

Albert arrives in the Rue Therese and notices an army Jeep pass him and pull up outside the entrance to Natalie's apartment. He sees Durnford get out, carrying two large cardboard boxes of food and drink, and enter the apartment block. After hesitating about whether he should still call on Monique, he thinks better of it and decides to leave the street. In the Candide, which is still very busy, Natalie is supervising the staff and waiting at tables. Albert enters from the back room and goes behind the counter.

> *Albert comes in the front door instead, clutching his bunch of undelivered chrysanthemums. He notices that Colonel Northwood is dining that night and goes to say hello to him.*

Natalie crosses to him while he busies himself checking spiked paid bills and asks him how it went. He tells her he decided against seeing Monique and that he thinks she'll come back to him anyway, and that he's been to see a man called Jacques Clair about some new ovens for the kitchens instead.

> *The Jacques Clair lie is less convincing because he is carrying flowers.*

Albert comments that business is good and Natalie makes a dig, saying that if that is the case then why isn't he smiling. Albert asks her about the British officer who helped Monique as he is thinking of offering him dinner as a 'thank you'. Meanwhile, Durnford and Monique have finished dinner and are both relaxing listening to some music. She offers him some real coffee but he declines. Durnford is lost in the music which is one of his favourites. Monique also likes it and he thinks this means she must be a romantic like him.

> *These comments about their romantic natures are absent.*

He compliments her on dinner and she comments favourably on the sort of food he managed to obtain. Durnford makes an unwise joke, describing soldiers as "lambs to the slaughter" and Monique is not amused.

> *This joke is absent.*

She wonders whether Lifeline getting the men back home to fly again was better than them rotting in a POW camp. Durnford is sure that it was, but Monique is much less sure.

> *There is no mention of rotting in a POW camp.*

He tries to get her to be proud of her achievement and convince her that the only really important thing about war is winning. She agrees with him. To Monique's surprise, Durnford goes on to tell her what he heard from a Major Cox about how Lifeline operated, about Natalie, Alain and Dr Keldermans and also about Albert and the fact that he was Lifeline's leader and that she and him were very close.

He doesn't mention Alain and Dr Keldermans, but cracks a joke instead about how his colleague told her that Monique "had nice legs".

She admits that she was Albert's mistress but makes it clear that the relationship is now over. Monique goes to the kitchen, while Durnford switches off the gramophone, looks about the room and notices a photograph of Hans van Broecken.

Durnford puts a new record on the gramophone instead and begins to dance with an imaginary partner; he turns to see Monique watching him, before mentioning the photograph.

Monique tells him about Hans and the fact that he's Natalie's uncle, believed to currently be in Holland and that no-one has heard from him in weeks. Durnford thinks he looks like a survivor.

Monique tells him much more about Van Broecken: the fact that he is German, now has Dutch citizenship, and about the fate of his late wife.

Durnford then makes to leave and, after offering to help her clear up, thanks her for the meal and her company. He reminds her that he kept his promise of no hanky-panky. Monique asks him if he will be in Brussels long. He tells her he will and she is glad. Before he leaves, she agrees to see him again.

Monique doesn't respond to the fact that he is staying in Brussels, nor say anything about seeing him again, but she does allow him a brief kiss which ably communicates all this instead.

Hans van Broecken is walking along the towpath by a canal next to his moored barge. He meets a Dutch policeman who is cycling along. The pair have a conversation about the lack of fuel before they offer each other sugar and soap. Van Broecken goes down to the hold of his barge and retrieves some soap to trade with the policeman. While down there he finds two young German soldiers in hiding. He advises them not to make a sound and does not volunteer their presence to the policeman. At the cantonment, Kessler joins Von Schalk by a window and tells him that he would rather be in a regular POW camp. Von Schalk comments that he should be grateful, as the Canadians who run it have deplorable discipline and slack screening procedures.

This changed to Von Schalk saying that the Canadians have excellent discipline, but screening procedures which lack coordination with the Allies, a fact that might save Kessler's neck. Kessler also thanks Von Schalk for helping him to maintain his fictional identity, to which the latter comments that he is not sure that it is the best thing for Germany and that he has decided on maintaining a united front reluctantly and without enthusiasm. He also comments that he has observed Kessler

614

assiduously avoiding another SS officer with a new identity in the cantonment and that it amuses and disgusts him. He goes on to tell Kessler that he doesn't like his kind and that he and the whole National Socialist movement is scum, but that he wants no-one to point to the German military and say "we stabbed you in the back." Kessler responds by saying "When we rise from the ashes once more, as we assuredly will, you may be very glad you made this gesture." Von Schalk states that if the "Nazi sickness" was to rise again, he would shoot him himself.

Scheer hesitantly approaches and asks Kessler how Spitzwerg died. He replies "Usefully, as every German should."

Scheer is not hesistant and instead man-handles Kessler, much to his displeasure.

Back at the Dutch canal, Van Broecken asks the two German deserters when they last ate and their names, which they provide: Kaufmann and Goetz.

This scene features after Durnford first visits Natalie's apartment, rather than after the much later scene with Scheer and Kessler.

They are both under eighteen and have been in the army for just nine weeks, and were put in the front line a month ago. They tell him why they deserted and that they were making for home and have been travelling for about a week. Van Broecken learns that they came from a village close to where he was born. Kaufmann tells the bargee that he must have spent a lot of time in Germany because he speaks it so well. Van Broecken makes an excuse for this, before telling them that they have no chance of getting home.

Kaufmann makes no such comment, presumably because it would raise the difficult question of language, which for reasons of consistency Glaister always chose to avoid by having every character speak English.

He suggests they stay with him and, after the British come, go to a POW camp, which is better than being shot as deserters. Kaufmann is concerned that if they are found they might shoot Van Broecken too. The bargee explains that he has "run out of hate" and that he chooses to help them as they remind him of someone in the same fix a long time ago, someone who was too young to die.

Bird had peppered Van Broecken's dialogue with a 'bloody' and a 'hell', both of which were removed due to the episode's time-slot. Also, the bargee concludes his explanation of why he intends to help them without referring to the fact that they remind him of someone.

APPENDICES

At the Candide, Albert and Natalie are listening to a radio broadcast which reports that the Germans have stopped the British advance in Holland. Albert assures her that Hans will be OK. She reveals that the last time she heard from him he was near Arnhem. Alain is at his farm loading his van with produce when he is distracted by the sound of a mass of aircraft approaching. They come into view and are en route to set up the Nigmegen-Arnhem bridgehead. Alain watches with amazement as the aerial armada passes overhead and comments: "Whoever's getting that lot, sooner them than me."

> *This scene takes place immediately after the end of Monique and Durnford's date instead. Also, Alain is walking along behind a horse with a plough attached rather than loading up a van. He has no dialogue either and just looks up in awe.*

Van Broecken, Kaufmann and Goetz are taking cover in a ditch as several bombs drop on the area as part of the softening up of the German positions. They then observe many Allied paratroopers gliding down. Van Broecken thinks that their waiting is almost over. They make their way back to the canal.

> *Andrew Morgan chose to enhance this sequence by sourcing unused scenes from the movie A Bridge Too Far. He also chose to end it with another bomb exploding.*

At a fairground in Brussels, Monique and Durnford are riding about on a sparsely patronised roundabout while hurdy-gurdy music plays in the background. They are both enjoying themselves enormously. This is one of many outings they've made together. After the ride is over, Durnford breaks up a bar of chocolate and gives it to some children, and gives some money to the roundabout owner so that the children can have a free ride. Monique looks on approvingly, before she and the Captain stroll away. They discuss the bridgehead at Eindhoven and Nigemegen and the fact that the First Airborne are getting "a pasting" there. They talk about how happy they are with each other. As they kiss, two British soldiers pass and salute Durnford but are ignored. Durnford asks her what she'd like to do now. Monique doesn't need to spell it out. They leave the fairground area, where the children are relishing the roundabout ride.

> *Presumably due to the unavailability of a roundabout or a 'fairground area', Morgan chose to transplant this whole scene to the Galeries Royale St Huberts, principally the Galerie de la Reine. Monique and Durnford do not discuss the situation in Holland to the same level of detail and there is no specific mention of the 'bridgehead'. The two soldiers who observe the couple kiss in Bird's script do not appear at all.*

At the barge, the sound of gunfire and mortars is not too distant. Van Broecken is peering down the towpath when a column of Allied soldiers approach. The soldiers are clearly exhausted and battle stained.

616

Morgan starts the sequence instead with another explosion and the group of soldiers, who Van Broecken is due to meet, emerging from a field of wheat.

A lieutenant goes to speak to Van Broecken to ask if they can use the barge. He replies that he has no fuel and tells them about the deserters he has down below. The lieutenant tells him that the operation at Arnhem has been a disaster and that the Germans are only a quarter of a mile behind them, so the last thing he needs is prisoners.

The lieutenant states that the Germans are about a mile behind them.

He advises him to "use his imagination". When the bargee refuses, the lieutenant offers first his gun and then one of his men, Miller, to do the deed, but he declines. The lieutenant and his troops move off as the sound of gunfire grows louder. At the Candide, Albert is looking at a photo of Monique in the back room, while the sound of the restaurant beyond is more boisterous than ever.

Instead of a photo, Albert looks at the now dead flowers that he didn't give to Monique and bins them.

As Natalie enters, he slips the photo into a drawer. She tells him they are out of wine and she needs the keys to the store. He hands them over. She tells him that the customers are in high spirits celebrating the evacuation of Arnhem. Natalie wonders about how Hans is getting on. Albert reassures her that he can look after himself and that he will be fine.

The Candide's customers are not heard to be in high spirits and Natalie does not therefore have this dialogue. Soon after Natalie enters, Alain arrives to speak to Natalie to tell her that there is a rumour that the airborne operation has been a disaster and that he now knows it took place in Arnhem. Natalie is understandably distressed to hear this, given that she knows that this is where her uncle was. Albert tells her they can't help him if, as Alain says, the British troops are surrounded. Natalie is not satisfied by his answer and, after telling him she loves Uncle Hans, asks him to try to do something. Albert tries to call through to Holland but is told there are no civilian calls. Alain suggests getting in touch with Dirk. Albert tries to get through while Natalie tells a concerned Alain that her mother is staying in The Hague. Dirk tells Albert that there is no way in to the area. Alain tries to comfort a distressed Natalie.

A German army lorry pulls up beside the barge. Van Broecken goes to speak to the driver, purchases some fuel and then returns to the hold. Van Broecken tells Kaufman and Goetz that the Germans are moving all undamaged barges up the Rhine into Germany and that he will drop them off close to Cologne. He urges them to keep quiet while the fuel is loaded. Returning outside, the bargee is alarmed to see that another lorry and a motorcycle with sidecar have pulled up and a German Captain and his troops are fanning out and approaching the barge.

> *The German troops in fact remain in the transport lorry until the Captain orders that the barge be searched.*

The Captain asks Van Broecken for his papers. The Captain tells him they are looking for British stragglers in the area. Van Broecken tells him he hasn't spotted any strangers and that he is the only man on board and has his sailing orders and is getting ready to leave. However, as he has not taken his fuel on board yet, the Captain is suspicious and orders that the barge be searched. Three soldiers descend into the hold, locate Kaufmann and Goetz and bring them back up to the deck. Meanwhile, Natalie and Alain are setting out food and wine on a rug for a picnic lunch in the countryside. Monqiue and Durnford are not far away, strolling along the bank of a stream.

> *Morgan chose to set this scene by a mill instead and there is no picnic or rug. Instead, Alain and Natalie are on a horse-drawn cart carrying hay.*

Alain and Natalie talk about the couple and Albert's knowledge of the relationship. Natalie tells him that she believes Durnford is in love with Monique. Alain asks if Monique feels the same way but she says she is not sure. Natalie stands up and waves to the couple and asks them if they are hungry. They wave and begin to walk slowly across the field towards Alain and Natalie.

> *It is Alain who calls over to them. The couple make their way to him and Alain stops the hay cart so that they can get up on to the back of it, before setting off again.*

In a prison courtyard, a German firing squad faces one of the walls. Van Broecken, Kaufmann and Goetz are escorted into the yard. Van Broecken comments that he finds it ironic that he is going to be shot for sheltering German deserters. The firing squad are ordered to port arms, load, aim and, finally, fire.

> *Presumably for reasons of cost, Morgan chose not to set this scene at a new location but on the barge very soon after the deserters have been found. There is also no ceremony to their execution, which takes place immediately after the German Captain corrects Van Broecken, who has said instead that he has been sheltering German soldiers, by stating that they are German deserters.*

In the bedroom of Natalie's apartment, Monique and Durnford are in bed together having just made love. Durnford tells her how much he loves her and asks her to marry him. After hesitating briefly, she puts her arms around him and draws him to her and, 'looking happier and more at peace than we have ever seen her' says "Oh yes, my darling! Yes! Yes! Yes!"

> *During the Seventies, there was a bizarre BBC drama rule that if two characters were not married then they could not be shown in bed together. This would seem to be the only explanation for transplanting this scene from the bedroom to the kitchen, where Monique is seen preparing a hot drink when Durnford proposes to her. Monique's acceptance changes to the more simple line: "Yes!"*

Appendix Four:
WHAT DID YOU DO IN THE WAR, DADDY? (Unbroadcast)

WRITTEN BY: John Brason   **DIRECTED BY:** Viktors Ritelis

REGULAR CAST: Albert Foiret: BERNARD HEPTON; Monique Durnford: ANGELA RICHARDS; Ludwig Kessler/Ludwig Manfred Dorf: CLIFFORD ROSE; Natalie Chantrens: JULIET HAMMOND-HILL; Alain Muny: RON PEMBER; Stephen Durnford: STEPHAN CHASE

SUPPORTING CAST: Janet Stone: SARAH TWIST; Paul Durnford: MICHAEL VIVIAN; Louise: PETA BERNARD; Etienne: DAN GILLIAN; Interviewers: BRIAN JACKSON, JOHN BOWN, DAVID STRONG; Floor Manager: JEANNA L'ESTY; Master of Ceremonies: SEYMOUR GREEN; Air Vice Marshal: VERNON SMYTH; Group Captain Alwyn: PETER FONTAINE; Air Commodore: Robert MacLEOD; O.B. Director: JOE DUNLOP; Resistance Worker: MICHAEL GODLEY

SYNOPSIS: September 1969. Monique Durnford is at home with her son Paul watching a programme entitled *In Our Time*, which is documenting the work of the evasion lines to celebrate the 25th anniversary of the liberation of Brussels. The programme intends to focus specifically on Lifeline and begins with an interview with Monique. She is uncertain about the prospect of being reunited with her old friends at the forthcoming liberation ceremony, to be held in Brussels. Unable to watch any more, Monique turns the TV set off just as Stephen returns home from work. Monique leaves the room and Paul switches the television back on to watch more of the programme. Alain is interviewed alongside his two grown-up children, Etienne and Louise, and talks about his inability to settle down once peace came. Natalie is the next interviewee. She has become a freedom fighter working in the Far East and would rather talk about the Communist infiltration of Western countries than the Second World War, which she thinks has become too glamorised. The programme switches its attention to the enemies of Lifeline and specifically to Kessler who the documentary makers have tried to trace. In Augsburg they interviewed an industrialist called Manfred Dorf who they believed to be Kessler. Dorf, who is clearly Kessler, firmly denies the allegation. After the programme finishes, Paul asks his mother why she has never gone back to Belgium. Monique is upset by his lack of understanding, but reveals to him that she was suspected of collaboration and locked up in a cage with other women. In order to attend the liberation ceremony and reunion, Monique flies to Brussels and is met at the airport by a BBC employee called Janet Stone. Due to bad traffic they are late for the ceremony, taking place at a nearby airfield, at which Albert receives honours on behalf of Lifeline. Monique has asked to stop off at a cemetery to find Lisa's grave. She thinks back to the war and is moved to tears. She tells Janet that she cannot go through with the reunion after all. Back at the airfield, camera interviews take place with several people who were helped by Lifeline. The second *In Our Time* programme begins with discussion of Lisa. Natalie is interviewed about her reasons for joining Lifeline and the murder of François. A visibly moved and uncomfortable Albert is interviewed next. While the production team prepare the Candide for the final evening programme, Monique is at the airport. However, as her flight home is called, she changes her mind about leaving. Back at the Candide, the programme has begun and Albert is joined by Natalie and a disgruntled Alain. Monique makes an unexpected entrance and the ensuing reunion is recorded. After a shaky start, the evening becomes more relaxed and Monique is asked to sing again. After thinking back to her time at the Candide, she refuses. The programme finishes and the foursome are left to their reminiscences. Monique and Natalie mention the airmen they helped, while Albert can only remember those who died. Their memories turn to a mid-war birthday party at which Monique and Albert danced around the Candide. Later, the producer returns to thank them all for coming and asks them whether they think their sacrifice was worthwhile. Their responses are mixed. In the closing sequence, Natalie describes the Nazis as amateurs compared to the Communists, due to the numbers the latter have killed. Albert argues that the numbers are irrelevant and the taking of lives is the crime. He concludes that the sacrifice they made was worth it and will always be worth it...

REVIEW: As it misfires so badly, perhaps a better name for this unbroadcast episode of *Secret Army* would be *What Did You Do That For, Daddy?* – an alternative title suggested by a friend who had just seen a copy of the episode for the first time and could scarcely believe his eyes. Not only was said friend convinced that the episode should continue to languish in the BBC Archives, but he also suggested the additional security of an armed guard to ensure it stayed there! This may seem unnecessarily harsh, but it really is no exaggeration to say that the episode fails on almost every level and that, had it been transmitted back in December 1979 as the fourteenth episode of the third series of *Secret Army*, it would have been a truly disastrous finale that could well have tarnished the brilliance of the preceding thirteen, or indeed forty-two, episodes. So why and where does it go so wrong?

Admittedly, on paper it does sound like an excellent, if a little indulgent, idea to have an episode which revisits the Lifeline regulars twenty-five years after the liberation of Brussels for an anniversary reunion. Indeed the concept is so appealing that it was later used as the basis for the final editions of the equally popular *Tenko*, entitled *Tenko Reunion* (1985), although that would be (very sensibly) set just five years after the action of the series proper, in 1950. Unfortunately it is probably also the obvious appeal of the episode's basic premise that has led to *What Did You Do in the War, Daddy?* to being regarded, by those *Secret Army* fans who have not yet had the misfortune of seeing it, as the series's 'Holy Grail' – a status it most certainly does not deserve. The episode's writer, the late great John Brason, seems to have been a little mystified by its failure himself and went on record as saying that it "was one of my few things that looked better on paper than on screen," and it is difficult to disagree with him.

The episode begins weakly with a long shot of an aged Monique sitting in a bleak living room watching television, and therefore immediately misses the opportunity to reveal with any dramatic effect that she has aged significantly since we last saw her leave the Candide some twenty-four years earlier. The start of the *In Our Time* documentary in which we shortly see her interviewed does not bode well either, emphasising as it does the fact that Ritelis is just as interested in (what were then) state-of-the-art television production techniques as he is in presenting the storyline: the documentary's presenter rushes to remove sticky cut-outs of countries forming a map of Europe from a CSO blue-screen, in order to reveal black-and-white film footage running behind, while delivering scene-setting dialogue about downed aircrew and the work of Lifeline. The result is that the viewer becomes distracted by the activity, and consequently is more interested in seeing if he will manage to remove them all in time than in listening to what he is saying (he doesn't, and the fact that the tiny Luxembourg piece is left behind is particularly irritating). The screen showing the film footage is subsequently split down the middle to reveal the interviewer standing in a hall of Nazi pennants, again for no good reason. This is followed by the slow reveal of interviewee Monique from a photo of her taken during the war, the perfect opportunity squandered to show her at fifty plus years of age for the first time.

It is unsettling that Monique (and several other characters whom we have come to know and understand) does not behave in ways that we expect. Her confrontational manner when being interviewed seems out of character, and her bitterness – which is part and parcel of the sort of dialogue that Richards is given to deliver – is overplayed. What is immediately clear from Monique's first speech is that the episode will unwisely choose to use the series's regulars to hold forth about the rights and wrongs of war, rather than just having them react to these situations in character, or indeed as normal human beings. Monique would be far more likely to be polite and courteous, if a little guarded, during this interview, rather than aggressive and sullen as she is here. Furthermore, the fact that she mouths off about the similarities between the Weimar Republic of the Thirties and the Britain of today, a view far more likely to be expressed by an Oxbridge Professor of History than a British housewife – albeit of Belgian descent – also seems entirely out of character (Would Monique really have a handle on what the Weimar Republic was like?). That the episode's interviewers are such idiots is also a mistake. The fact that the first interviewer we see arrogantly states that Britain is too civilised for Nazism to develop there just seems silly rather than, as it is clearly meant to be, a point well made, by Brason, about how easily it could emerge anywhere at any time.

The fact Monique's husband, Stephen, does not make it back in time to see his wife on television suggests that all is not well in the Durnford family home and initially it seems that this will be the explanation for Monique's obvious unhappiness. However, his line to his son: "You've been arguing again, have you?" suggests that rather than there being problems with their marriage, Monique has more problems with her son, but this idea is introduced here without any adequate explanation. Later, Monique scolds her son for once having done something unspecified but unpatriotic to a British Army jacket – an act that she claims "insulted the men who died in the war" – and this is really the only evidence we have of Paul's behaviour having upset her. That Paul seems like quite an amiable and sensitive young chap who actually wants to know about his mother's wartime experiences makes her reaction even less fathomable. The idea seems to be that she is ascribing the problem with the youth of today – a view which Alain also shares: "The young generation don't understand" – to Paul, a reaction that would be far more understandable if he had been a more stereotypical teenager with little or no interest in his mother's welfare, rather than what he actually is: an uninformed but interested young man. With this, as with so many other aspects of the episode, there is no room for such antagonisms to be sufficiently explored or indeed explained.

When Monique so readily switches off a TV programme on which she is likely to see her former friends for the first time since 1945 it seems very strange, no matter how distressed she is to think about the war again. But odder still is the fact that she is sat back in the living room again less than a minute later (and that Stephen has also had time to quickly put on a fetching blue cardigan in the interim!).

Alain's testimony to camera about adjusting to life after the war is one of the better moments of the episode, engendering real sympathy and feeling quite genuine: "For a long time I couldn't settle. Peace – it wasn't easy to live with. All the time I kept waiting for something to happen – it never did." And the revelations from Alain's children that Albert now has six restaurants and a new hotel, and is mean as he ever was, also feel in keeping.

The introduction of Natalie to the narrative jars for exactly the same reasons as the earlier Monique interview. Moreover, this new Natalie, who is actually comfortable with being described as a 'freedom fighter' and is desperate to talk about "the Communist infiltration of every Western country," somehow seems too glib, as indeed does her severely shorn hair, accompanying utility headscarf and combat outfit. Yes, Natalie lost François to the Communists and yes, she rescued Albert from being hung by them, but the idea that these wartime experiences would result in her engaging guerrilla warfare which actively fights revolution and the Left just doesn't ring true. Instead it feels very much like Brason is not-very-expertly shoe horning his own political opinions into the episode via a character who was the only available mouthpiece for them.

Natalie's interview also throws up another huge problem with the episode in that it actually elects to criticise what *Secret Army* is essentially all about, namely making entertainment of the heroics of the people of Lifeline: "You are cashing in on yet another war story, full of heroics that just didn't happen like that. If you have to make war films, why make them seem marvellous and exciting? Why not tell people how ghastly it is?" While *Secret Army* arguably has done the latter, it has nevertheless also always sought to make its episodes – and therefore the war – exciting. As this is the case, why then does Brason seek here to throw into question the validity of their entire dramatic endeavour on the grounds that it is entertainment? This is an especially strange objective, given that this was intended to be the very last episode and therefore the 'last word' on the series, and so effectively damns everything that has transmitted before it. That the producer of *In Our Time* stops the programme in order to respond to Natalie (quoting well-worn arguments, as Glaister himself might well have done if probed: that young people need to be educated about the war; that reminders of the horrors of war are important; and that such programmes honour those who fought) does not alter the fact that a doubt over *Secret Army*'s worth has been planted in the viewer's mind – a doubt that is arguably all the more compelling because it has come from the lips of one of the series's protagonists, and not just any protagonist, but one that we have always trusted. It is a curious discussion that one cannot help but feel must have surely contributed to this episode's eventual abandonment.

The Manfred Dorf segment of the *In Our Time* programme sows the seeds for the *Kessler* series that would eventually follow in 1981. Interestingly though, there is a difference in his name: here, Dorf has rather unwisely retained the forename Ludwig. The ever-reliable Rose is on great form when being cross examined, particularly when he slips into Kessler-style fury at the interviewer's 'insolence'. However, it does seem strange that the interviewer has come to question Kessler armed only with what Dorf quite correctly recognises as a retouched photograph (it could even be an illustration!) of the wartime Kessler in uniform, and is especially odd as the viewer has just seen from the pre-interview sequence that the *In Our Time* programme makers already possessed a period photo of Kessler in uniform that clearly had not been tampered with.

The scene in which Monique reacts to seeing Kessler again neglects to reflect the fact that she was instrumental in his escape from Belgium; that is, if one believes, as Richards herself does, that Monique gave false papers to Madeleine in *The Execution* for two people out of compassion for her friend, knowing full well that she was going to take Kessler and not her brother with her. It also chooses to ignore Monique and Madeleine's friendship, in that there is no reaction from her to the news that Kessler's former mistress is now dead. Richards's performance goes up a gear when Paul questions her about her wartime memories, especially when she finally feels driven to reveal that she was one of the women who suffered treatment as a collaborator. As a result we are once again encouraged to contemplate just what has happened to Monique since the war, especially as we last saw her (in *The Execution*) – having seemingly got over the traumas of the Occupation and its immediate aftermath – at her happiest, despite her obvious sadness at having to say goodbye to her friends. As she is portrayed here as half the woman she once was, it almost feels as though this episode is now denying that happiness, calling it out as a sham and therefore robbing the preceding episodes of their genuine emotion and truth.

The airfield ceremony (filmed at RAF Northolt) with its superficial pomp and circumstance, seems to be an empty and soulless way of celebrating the bravery and sacrifice of the people of Lifeline, but perhaps this was the effect that Viktors Ritelis was attempting to portray. Those attending the ceremony subsequently lay wreaths at a memorial decorated with the words 'Pro Patria Mori', words which cannot fail to bring Wilfred Owen's most famous poem to mind, calling into question whether it is indeed a lie that it is sweet and right to die for your country. For once the episode seems to be raising a question that it is entirely valid to ask at this juncture.

624

The ceremony scenes are neatly juxtaposed with Monique's sudden mission to find Lisa's grave at a cemetery, where the rather clumsy message seems to be that no-one cares about the war dead anymore as said grave is due to be dismantled and destroyed. That Monique appears not to remember the names of Lisa's aunt and uncle when they are mentioned is strange, and once again Brason's dating is completely out. Here he seems to have suddenly decided that Lisa died in February 1943, thereby preceding his recently fudged date of 9 April 1943 for the great encirclement (as recounted in *Just Light the Blue Touch-Paper*) for which he should have certainly remembered that Lisa was still alive.

The episode's most effective and emotive scene occurs at Lisa's graveside as Monique thinks back to the war, represented by a sequence of footage which is hauntingly underscored by Angela Richards herself singing another of her own compositions, 'For All Our Yesterdays', followed by a tearful goodbye to Lisa before her grave is dismantled by the waiting workmen. The song is one of Richards's best, so it is a great shame that it is not used elsewhere in the series (however it does feature on her *Au Café Candide* LP and the 2006 CD, *An Evening at Le Candide*). Although the workman who begins dismantling the grave with a jemmie while Monique is still standing there, before thinking better of it, seems callous, it is as nothing to Brason's original script, which has a bulldozer crashing into frame and soil being scattered over Monique's feet!

A return to the *In Our Time* studio later in the episode for a further interview with Natalie – perhaps an unwise decision after her last outburst on the programme – once again sees her spouting anti-Communist rhetoric, in a speech which concludes with her describing them as "the most appalling canker mankind has ever faced." However, during the start of her interview we do briefly glimpse the real Natalie again, who talks of loving her country, hating the Boche and what it was like at the start of the war. In contrast to the way the character is portrayed in the rest of this episode, this is a rare and brief moment of truthfulness which Juliet Hammond-Hill looks far more comfortable delivering. After Natalie, it is Albert's turn in the hot-seat and, after his poetic allusion to their evasion work (like a light guiding Allied airmen to safety, as per the series's opening titles), Albert admits that without his fellow Lifeline colleagues he could not have functioned and the organisation would not have existed. It is a rare moment of genuine generosity from Albert which clearly costs the old man in the telling, but which suggests that he still holds a deep affection for his former colleagues.

This *In Our Time* section of the episode concludes with a sequence which exemplifies the busy mix of media that characterises *What Did You Do in the War, Daddy?*: photographs (concentration camp victims and massed Nazis in Berlin) cross-fades (from Albert sadly peering out of a window to the piano in the Candide) accompanied by an invasive multi-layered soundtrack (consisting of more 'For All our Yesterdays', a chorus of Sieg Heils and bomber flak). These moments suggest that Ritelis was having a whale of a time as director, as he was finally able to use all the techniques which were, for the most part, necessarily denied him when working on the rest of the series. The problem with them being allowed now (which of course they ultimately were not, at least as far as the series's audience was concerned) is that they not only detract from the content of the episode, but they also separate it stylistically from everything that has gone before, arguably too much so for this to coherently feel like the fourteenth episode of the third series.

One way in which Ritelis seeks to show that this is 1969, something which it has to be said is rarely achieved convincingly elsewhere in the episode, is the playing of The Beatles's 'Eleanor Rigby' in the Candide. Hearing this music while seeing the Candide again is incredibly jarring, which of course it is meant to be, and somehow the way it destroys the restaurant's period ambience seems almost disrespectful. The fact that the restaurant's furnishings have not changed at all since 1945 is also a rather surprising and unfortunate reminder that this is simply a set that was used last week for the party scenes at the end of *The Execution*. Meanwhile, the filming of the reunion on the Candide set does gives a unique, if brief, insight into how the recording of *Secret Army* was actually carried out, as we get to observe the *In Our Time* crew in action. However, this seems to rob the series of some of its mystique, again reminding us that the Candide is just a set even though the narrative is asking us to believe that it is a real restaurant.

The first guest to arrive at the Candide, is Alain ("Get a shot of that chap in the wheelchair!") and the scene that follows between him and Albert is uncomfortable to watch, not only because of the antagonism that now exists between the characters, but also because of the reunion set-up which makes it feel for the very first time in the series that Hepton and Pember are simply acting on cue. That they are made to wait talking together for the other guests to arrive seems very strange, especially as their conversation is being monitored by several silent witnesses and continues to be recorded despite the fact that it is clearly unsuitable for transmission. Natalie's arrival prompts discussion of Albert's time in jail in 1944, something which she claims to have forgotten – this seems unlikely to say the least given the extra pressure and danger it placed on both her and Monique at the time. Monique's arrival is curiously downbeat; she doesn't even appear to receive a hug or a kiss from Natalie, while, conversely, the reaction of Albert, who may feel he has more to be bitter about in respect of Monique, seems much more genial.

A flashback sequence in which Monique thinks back to her time singing at the Candide (calling for a welcome reprise of 'For All Our Yesterdays'), is notable for the fact that Richards sings directly to the camera, therefore breaking television's so- called 'fourth wall'. Oddly, as we cross-fade to Monique in 1969, the sequence ends for no apparent reason with the sound of a plane taking off: yet another moment for which no explanation is provided.

After the *In Our Time* programme has finished, the final scene is fittingly set around a table at the Candide with the restaurant now empty, although still full of abandoned television equipment, as Albert, Monique, Natalie and Alain think back to the old days. However, things are initially spoilt by the tracking shot over to their table, as when the camera makes its way across the floor it obviously moves a large cable en route, once again making it obvious that this is just a recording. The dialogue in this scene starts off well, as they share with each other how they have coped since the war and what they remember of the people they helped and those that died such as Yvette, Gaston and Max. One beautifully-scripted line delivered by Albert relating to those they have lost particularly stands out: "They come in to my room at night when I sleep badly and they look at me. And there's something terrible about that look. It seems to say 'Why? Why did we die? Was it worth it?' And I have no answer."

The mood switches with another flashback to a birthday party scene during the war, which is surprising on several accounts. For one thing, it starts with Natalie (who is unusually all smiles) making eyes at a young German solider and him doing the same to her, which seems unlikely and an odd moment to include here; while for another, Albert and Monique are seen to dance around the Candide as the dinner guests stand around them in a circle clapping in time to the music. Even a fully-uniformed Kessler is there joining in the fun. The overall effect is a scene that suggests that the Lifeline personnel got on rather better with their German clientele than was ever shown in any other episode in the series and dangerously hints at collaboration.

The final scene features each of the remaining regulars forced to respond to an awfully stilted question from the *In Our Time* producer, as to whether they think the work of Lifeline was ultimately worthwhile. This proves to be just another opportunity to show: how bitter and depressed the characters now are; to have another dig at *Secret Army* itself ("We look back on it with nostalgia but it was the most awful chapter in out history"); and for Natalie, or rather John Brason, to get back on a soapbox about the Communists, who "make the Nazis look like amateurs." Only Alain seems to speak for the average viewer, being – incredibly given what the series has been about up until now – the only one willing to defend their involvement in fighting the Second World War: "I don't know anything about history, but I do know that this was one of the few that had to happen... that was fought because evil was taking over, humanity was fighting for its life." Albert has the last word and it is a horribly moralistic one, once again emphasising that this episode has been all about speech-making and opinion rather than character and truth: "The taking of one life is the crime! Numbers only make it bigger... it is the same crime. We have learnt nothing! Even so, yes, the sacrifice was worth it. It will always be worth it." Even though the episode at least ends by confirming the validity of Lifeline, this is small consolation given the ham-fisted and inconsistent way in which the subject has been explored and particularly the way in which this message is delivered here. And just to make matters worse, for these arguably crucial final moments, from the point at which Natalie holds forth about the evil of the Communists, the four of them are suddenly, and very badly, CSO'd out of the Candide to float in front of a photograph of the 'Pro Patria Mori' memorial from earlier in the episode, once again fourth-walling and therefore preaching directly to the viewer. While this dialogue is delivered, this scene, which really has to be seen to be believed, sees all four of them first fill the screen, before rapidly shrinking until they occupy only a sixth of it at most. Incredibly worse is still to come, for after Albert ends his speech they all stop to look at each other, appearing confused as if they don't know what to do next, before electing to walk off screen in different directions, entirely abandoning poor old wheelchair-bound Alain in the process! The scene is wrong on so many different levels and the thought that it was originally intended to close the entire series is a thoroughly arresting one!

There is not room here to fully summarise why *What Did You Do in the War, Daddy?* utterly fails to be an appropriate last episode of *Secret Army*; suffice to say it is clumsy, out-of-keeping and depressing and, worse still, denigrates all that has gone before it. When the recording of the *In Our Time* programme is seen to conclude, the producer is heard to say "I wonder what the punters will make of it?" – a question that the series actual producer, Gerry Glaister, must also have been thinking. Quite rightly he decided not to find out and it is no exaggeration to say that, as a result, disaster was averted.

SONGS IN THE CANDIDE

For All Our Yesterdays (Richards, Moule)

For all our yesterdays
and the memories we share
A thousand other dreams
have gone astray somewhere
If we could live our lives
in two places at one time
I would live mine all with you
and leave the rest behind

All our yesterdays
for the honey and the wine
Now the summer sun is pale
and there is no more time
For all our yesterdays,
all our yesterdays, all our yesterdays.

The love of our lives
is made up of 'hellos' and 'goodbyes'
And then comes the day,
when one of you cries. You cry for…

All our yesterdays
for the honey and the wine
Now the summer sun is pale
and there is no more time
For all our yesterdays,
all our yesterdays, all our yesterdays.

Appendix Five:
POST-SECRET ARMY CREDITS

The following are a selection of post-*Secret Army* television, theatre and film credits for the series's principal actors. Pre-*Secret Army* credits are covered in the appropriate production chapters. Roles undertaken by the actors concurrently to their time on the series are also listed below. Credits are for television roles unless otherwise stated.

MICHAEL CULVER

Soon after *Secret Army*, Culver would work for Michael E. Briant again on *Breakaway* and play the ill-fated Captain Needa in the blockbuster *The Empire Strikes Back*. Other notable roles in the Eighties included Nick Hannah in the John Brason-scripted spy series *Chessgame*, Major McBryde in the Merchant Ivory film *A Passage to India*, the murderous Edward Symmington in *Miss Marple: The Moving Finger* and the loathsome Dicky Cruyer in Len Deighton's *Game, Set and Match*. The Nineties saw recurring roles as Sir George Bluff-Gore in *The Darling Buds of May*, crooked financier Ralph Saroyan in *The House of Eliott*, and Prior Robert to Terrence Hardiman's Abbot Radulfus in *Cadfael*. More recent notable roles have included that of Nazi Albert Speer in two acclaimed theatre productions (*Responses from Nuremberg* and *Albert Speer*), Sir William Macpherson in the similarly celebrated dramatisation of the Stephen Lawrence murder trail entitled *The Colour of Justice*, and guest appearances in *Spooks* and *New Tricks*.

Production	Role	Year
An Ideal Husband *(theatre)*	Cast Member	1979
Call My Bluff	Himself	1979
Breakaway	Ernest Clifford	1980
Heartland: Working Arrangements	Cast Member	1980
Dick Turpin	Colonel De Courcey	1980
Star Wars: The Empire Strikes Back *(film)*	Captain Needa	1980
Turtle's Progress: Box Eight	Joseph 'Joey' Chalk	1980
Shoestring: Room with a View	Stephen Brook	1980
Hammer House of Horror: Charlie Boy	Mark	1980
Rain on the Roof	Malcolm	1980
Second Chance	Richard Seymour	1980
The Bunker	General Mohnke	1981
Diamonds	David Kremer	1981
Fanny by Gaslight	Lord Manderstoke	1981
A Fine Romance: Unlucky in Love	Ben	1981
Minder: Poetic Justice, Innit?	Soames	1982
ITV Playhouse: The Reunion	Murray	1982
Squadron	Grp Cpt James Christie	1982

Foxy Lady	Nigel Cavendish	1982
The Professionals: Lawson's Last Stand	Lt Col Peter Lawson	1982
All for Love: Mrs Silly	John	1982
The Bounder: Third Party	Reggie Thorne	1982
The Battle of Waterloo	Duke of Wellington	1983
Chessgame	Nick Hannah	1983
A Passage to India (film)	Major McBryde	1984
Miss Marple: The Moving Finger	Edward Symmington	1985
The Return of Sherlock Holmes	Sir Reginald Musgrave	1986
Casualty: Blood Brothers	James	1986
Hannay: Death with Due Notice	Major Edmund Philipson	1988
The Little Heroine (theatre)	Cast Member	1988
Game, Set and Match	Dicky Cruyer	1988
Countdown to War	Lord Halifax	1989
The Justice Game	Brian Ash	1989
Saracen: Ratline	Sir Anthony	1989
Boon: Love Letters from a Dead Man	Greg Simpson	1989
TECX: A Soldier's Death	Mark Frobisher	1990
The Green Man	Dr Thomas Underhill	1990
Shrinks	Sir Hugo Dyer	1990
Zorro: The Whistling Bandit	Honorio Aragon	1991
For the Greater Good	Sir Christopher St Place	1991
The Darling Buds of May	Sir George Bluff-Gore	1991
The House of Eliott	Ralph Saroyan	1991-2
The Transmission of Roger Bacon	Roger Bacon	1992
Losing Track	Mr Gervaise	1992
Lovejoy: Members Only	Arnold Featherstone	1992
The Piglet Files: Guerillas in the Mist	Hugo Wittersham	1992
Inspector Morse: The Day of the Devil	Maugham Willowbank	1993
Growing Pains	Cast Member	1993
Cadfael	Prior Robert	1994-8
Half the Picture ('Arms to Iraq' Inquiry)	Sir Nicholas Lyell	1996
Neverwhere: Knightsbridge	Portico	1996
Responses to Nuremberg (theatre)	Albert Speer	1996
Touching Evil	Pathologist	1997
Victoria and Albert	Disraeli	1997
Wow	Cast Member	1997
The Colour of Justice (theatre and TV)	Sir William Macpherson	1999
The Queen's Nose: Harmony's Return	Cast Member	1999
Albert Speer (theatre)	Albert Speer	2000
Anybody's Nightmare	Lord Chief Justice Bingham	2001
New Tricks	Ian Lovett	2003
Spooks: Project Friendly Fire	Hugo Weatherby	2004
Derailed	Lord Cullen	2005
Good Girl, Bad Girl	Koslowski	2006
Murder City: Just Seventeen	Michael Anderson	2006
The Impressionists	Antoine de la Pailleterie	2007

VALENTINE DYALL

Dyall would take several further memorable roles after *Secret Army*, notably in the science-fiction genre: guesting in *Blake's 7*, voicing the Magrathean computer Deep Thought in the TV dramatisation of *The Hitch-Hiker's Guide to the Galaxy* and playing The Black Guardian in several *Doctor Who* adventures. He also appeared in *Nanny*, a *Miss Marple* and several plays in the *BBC Shakespeare* series, before his death on 24 June 1985.

Production	Role	Year
Doctor Who: The Armageddon Factor	The Black Guardian	1979
Q9	Norl	1980
All's Well That Ends Well	The Astringer	1981
The Hitch-Hiker's Guide to the Galaxy	Deep Thought (voice)	1981
Yours Sincerely: A Roman Gentleman	Zosimus	1981
Peter and Paul	Seneca	1981
Sapphire and Steel: Dr McDee Must Die	Radio Broadcast Voice	1981
Britannia Hospital	Bloss	1982-3
3-2-1	Guest	1983
The Black Adder: The Witchsmeller Pursuivant	Angus, A Lord	1983
Horizon: The Intelligence Man	Cast Member	1983
Doctor Who: Mawdryn Undead	The Black Guardian	1983
Doctor Who: Terminus	The Black Guardian	1983
Doctor Who: Enlightenment	The Black Guardian	1983
Coriolanus	Adrian	1984
Miss Marple: The Body in the Library	Lorrimer	1984
Love's Labour's Lost	Marcade	1985

JAN FRANCIS

After leaving *Secret Army* in 1978, Francis became a regular presenter on *Jackanory*, played Mina Van Helsing in a new film version of *Dracula* and the regular role of Susie Dean in the LWT musical drama *The Good Companions*, before going back to her ballet roots as Barbara Livesay in the love story *A Chance to Sit Down*. However, it was as uptight Penny Warrender in the popular sitcom *Just Good Friends*, opposite Paul Nicholas's dodgy Vince Pinner, that she would make her name. The series ran for four years over three series and two Christmas specials. The final episode, in which Penny and Vince eventually tie the knot, went out on Christmas Day 1986 and won over 21 million viewers. In the Eighties and early Nineties, Francis could be seen regularly on TV in a series of adverts for Lloyds Bank alongside Paul Eddington, Nigel Havers and Peter Bowles. Regular roles followed opposite Dennis Waterman in *Stay Lucky*, as Maggie in *Under the Hammer*, Grace in the bizarre *Ghostbusters of East Finchley* and Colette in the comedy series *Spark*. More recently, she has made guest appearances as interior designer Catherine Earlham in *Bad Girls*, treasure-hunting spy Kate opposite David Jason in the drama *Diamond Geezer*, and June Parker in *New Tricks*. Her most recent television role was in the BBC drama *The Invisibles*.

Production	Role	Year
Give us a Kiss, Christabel	Christabel	1977
Star Turn	Herself	1978
A Play for Love: The Party of the First Part	Susan	1978
Target: Rogue's Gallery	Jenny	1978
Jackanory: Shiva's Pearls	Presenter	1978
Stepping Stones	Presenter	1978-9
Dracula (*film*)	Mina Van Helsing	1979
ITV Playhouse: Casting the Runes	Prudence Dunning	1979
Jackanory: The Hobbit	Presenter	1979
Ripping Yarns: Roger of the Raj	Miranda	1979
The Racing Game: Horses for Courses	Kate Ellis	1979
The Good Companions	Susie Dean	1980
Love Story: A Chance to Sit Down	Barbara Livesay	1981
Jackanory: Bravo Baltasar	Presenter	1982
Tales of the Unexpected: Death Can Add	Leila	1982
Jackanory: Cap of Rushes	Presenter	1983
Jackanory: Five Children and It	Presenter	1983
The Plot to Murder Lloyd George	Hetty Wheeldon	1983
Jackanory: Peter Pan	Presenter	1983
Just Good Friends	Penny Warrender	1983-6
Aladdin and the Forty Thieves	Princess Balroubador	1984
Champions (*film*)	Jo	1984
Minder: Life in the Fast Food Lane	Sarah Bates	1985
Pob's Programme	Herself	1985
Call My Bluff	Herself	1985
The Children's Royal Variety Performance	Herself	1985
Disney Time	Presenter	1985
The Corvini Inheritance	Eva Bailey	1986
Lend Me a Tenor (*theatre*)	Maggie	1986
Highway	Herself	1987
Pob's Playtime	Herself	1987
Hay Fever (*theatre*)	Myra Arundel	1988
Call My Bluff	Herself	1988
Stay Lucky	Sally Hardcastle	1989-91
Jackanory: Birthdays	Presenter	1991
Comic Relief	Herself	1991
Under the Hammer	Maggie Perowne	1994
The Good Sex Guide	Cast Member	1994
The Ghostbusters of East Finchley	Grace	1995
Spark	Colette	1997
Verdict: Be My Valentine	Kathryn Lewis	1998
Sunburn	Rachel Dearborn	2000
Water Colour Challenge	Herself	2000

Porlock Calling Rockall	Cast Member	2001
Dr Otter	Voices	2001
Water Colour Challenge	Herself	2001
My Family: Age of Romance	Amanda	2001
Micawber	Lady Charlotte	2001
Call My Bluff	Herself	2001
Heartbeat: Love Hurts	Vivienne Keen	2002
Seven Deadly Sins, Four Deadly Sinners (*theatre*)	Cast Member	2003-5
The Alan Clark Diaries	Barbara Lord	2004
According to Bex	Sally	2005
Twisted Tales: Fruitcake of the Living Dead	Penny Merchant	2005
Monkey Trousers	Cast Member	2005
Where the Heart Is: Together	Jean	2005
Bloodlines	Elaine Hopkin	2005
Bad Girls	Catherine Earlham	2006
Comedy Connections: Just Good Friends	Herself	2007
Diamond Geezer: Old Gold	Kate	2007
The Return of 'Allo! 'Allo!	Herself	2007
New Tricks: Powerhouse	June Parker	2007
That's What I Call Christmas Television	Herself	2007
Seven Deadly Sins, Four Deadly Sinners (*theatre*)	Cast Member	2008
The Invisibles	Janet Rigby	2008
U Be Dead	Irene	2008

JULIET HAMMOND-HILL

Hammond-Hill followed *Secret Army* with a spell with the Royal Shakespeare Company, creating the part of Madeline Bray in *Nicholas Nickleby* (a role later taken by Harriet Walter). After a guest-starring role in *Blake's 7* as the self-serving telepath Pella, she would play the similarly villainous Miss Hawk in the educational children's series *Look and Read*. However, her most notable role in 1981 was that of German Irene Kohl, the leader of a group of terrorists in the thriller serial *Blood Money*. She would subsequently play Emilie opposite David Bowie in Bertholt Brecht's *Baal*, and antique dealer Miranda Davenport opposite David Jason in an episode of *Only Fools and Horses*. Under the name Juliet Hammond (having decided that her stage name of Hammond-Hill was too long) she would go on to make appearances in the drama series *Big Deal* and play Sarah Lee, an exotic prostitute, in the film *Ping Pong*. After reverting to the original French spelling of her first name, to become Juliette Hammond (her name before she started acting), she left the profession behind in 1989 in order to devote more time to bringing up her daughter. After studying Humanistic Psychology and Counselling, and gaining a PGCE in Education in the Performing Arts, Hammond is now working as a drama teacher and theatrical director in the South of England.

Production	Role	Year
Give us a Clue	Herself	1980
Star Games	Herself	1980
Nicholas Nickleby (*RSC theatre*)	Madeline Bray	1980-1
Blake's 7: Power	Pella	1981
Look and Read: Dark Towers	Miss Hawk	1981
Blood Money	Irene Kohl	1981
Kessler	Natalie Chantrens	1981
Baal	Emilie	1982
Only Fools and Horses: Yesterday Never Comes	Miranda Davenport	1983
The Balance of Nature	Cast Member	1983
The Case of Marcel Duchamp (*film*)	Cast Member	1984
Big Deal: The Z Team	Cast Member	1985
Big Deal: Playing the Ace	Cast Member	1986
Ping Pong (*film*)	Sarah Lee	1986

TERRENCE HARDIMAN

Since *Secret Army*, Terrence Hardiman has enjoyed a successful and extensive acting career on television, film and in the theatre. Some highlights from the Eighties include playing Inspector Foster in police series *Juliet Bravo*, Chief Superintendent Franks in the Glaister-produced thriller *Skorpion* and Bobby Bishop in the drama series *The Bretts*. The early Nineties saw him don German uniform again for the third and final series of another wartime drama series, this time *Wish Me Luck*, in which he played the much less sympathetic General Stuckler, and guest star in the *Poirot* tale *The Case of the Missing Will*, for which he was joined by his actress wife Rowena Cooper, playing his fictional wife. In 1996, Hardiman took on a role that he is now best known for: the title character in *The Demon Headmaster*, a BBC children's drama that ran for three series, several specials and a theatre tour. This role made Hardiman a household name for several years, and also led to several years playing pantomime villains, including Abanazer in *Aladdin*, King Rat in *Dick Whittington* and Captain Hook in *Peter Pan*. In the last few years, as well as more TV (including *Midsomer Murders*, *The Royal* and *The Worst Week of My Life*), Hardiman has won acclaim for his performances in theatre productions, in: *Called to Account*, a dramatised inquiry into Blair's decision to wage war on Iraq, at the Tricycle Theatre; the English Touring Theatre's Jacobean drama *The Changeling*; and, this year, *Never So Good* at the National Theatre, concerning the life of Harold Macmillan, in which Hardiman plays Neville Chamberlain.

Production	Role	Year
The Bunker	General Fegelein	1981
My Father's House	Alec Blake	1981
Loophole	David	1981

Lady Killers: The Darlingest Boy	Mr Cecil Whiteley QC	1981
Inside the Third Reich	Cast Member	1982
Juliet Bravo: Heat	Inspector Foster	1982
Gandhi *(film)*	Ramsay MacDonald	1982
Crown Court: Fair Play	Stephen Hardesty	1982
Crown Court: Brainwashed	Stephen Hardesty	1983
Skorpion	Chief Supt Franks	1983
Sahara *(film)*	Browne	1983
Fresh Fields: A Brief Encounter	Mr Frobisher	1984
Mask of Murder	Dr Paul Crossland	1985
Storyboard: Ladies in Charge	Charles Carmichael	1985
Bergerac: Avenge O Lord	Nigel Ripley	1985
God's Outlaw	Thomas Chomwell	1986
The Bretts	Bobby Bishop	1987
The Charmer	Sawyer	1987
Miss Marple: Sleeping Murder	Walter Fane	1987
Home to Roost: Getting On	Doctor	1987
John Bull *(theatre)*	Peregrine	1987
Hannay: A Point of Honour	Harman	1988
Inspector Morse: Last Bus to Woodstock	Clive Palmer	1988
Wish Me Luck (Series 3)	General Stuckler	1990
This Is David Harper: Partners in Crime?	Supt Carter	1990
Lethal Impact	Bill Donovan	1991
Der Mann Nebenan	Inspector	1991
The Adventures of Young Indiana Jones	Fitzgerald	1992-3
Moon and Son: Past, Present and Future	Herbert Bolland	1992
The Brittas Empire: The Trial	Prosecutor	1993
Poirot: The Case of the Missing Will	John Siddaway	1993
Grange Hill	Mr Cresswell	1993
Surgical Spirit: You Won't Feel a Thing	Douglas Endicott	1993
Death Train	Captain Wolf	1993
Keeping Up Appearances	Eric	1993
Casualty: Born Losers	Carlisle	1993
Prime Suspect 3	Commander Chiswick	1993
The Curse of the Werewolf	Cast Member	1994
Cadfael	Abbot Radulfus	1994-8
Goodnight Sweetheart	Wilson	1995
The Moonstone	Colonel Sir John Herncastle	1996
Circles of Deceit: Kalon	Military Officer	1996
Ruth Rendell: The Strawberry Tree	Solicitor	1996
Markurell *(theatre)*	Markurell	1996
The Demon Headmaster	The Demon Headmaster	1996-8
Ellington: Matchmaker	Stuart Graham	1996
Aladdin *(theatre)*	Abanazer	1996-7
Lady Audley's Secret *(theatre)*	Cast Member	1997
Crime Traveller: Jeff Slade and the Loop of Infinity	Guy Lombard	1997
The Demon Headmaster Takes Over TV	The Demon Headmaster	1997
Heartbeat: Appearances	John Upton	1998

Verdict: Split Second	James MacKenzie	1998
Jack and the Beanstalk (*theatre*)	Bad Fairy	1998-9
The Demon Headmaster (*theatre*)	The Demon Headmaster	1998-9
The Worst Witch	Grand Wizard Hellebore	1998-2001
Distant Shadow	The Svit	1999
Comic Relief Special	The Demon Headmaster	1999
Jonathan Creek: The Eyes of Tiresias	André Masson	1999
Dick Whittington (*theatre*)	King Rat	1999-2000
After the Fair (*theatre*)	Mr Harnham	2000
Blithe Spirit (*theatre*)	Charles Condomine	2000-1
Urban Gothic: Dollhouse Burns	Severin	2001
Twelfth Night (*theatre*)	Malvolio	2001
Peter Pan (*theatre*)	Captain Hook	2001-2
The Road to Ruin (*theatre*)	Mr Dornton	2002
Doctors: Blackout	Sir Bobby Hewitt	2003
Simplicity (*theatre*)	Sir John Hearty	2003
The Bill	Judge	2003
Midsomer Murders: The Fisher King	Dr James Lavery	2004
The Courtroom	Judge Garrett Warburton	2004
The Royal: Duty Bound	Dr Sedgewick	2005
The Slavery Business	Lord of Trade	2005
Bloody Sunday (*theatre*)	Michael Mansfield	2005
The Worst Week of My Life	Gerard	2005
French Without Tears (*theatre*)	Maingot	2007
Called to Account (*theatre*)	Bob Marshall-Andrews	2007
The Changeling (*theatre*)	Albius	2007
Never So Good (*theatre*)	Neville Chamberlain	2008

BERNARD HEPTON

Soon after *Secret Army*, Hepton played Det Chief Supt Meadows in Brason's *Blood Money*, voiced a scientist in the haunting animated feature *The Plague Dogs*, and returned to the role of Toby Esterhase in *Smiley's People*, the sequel to spy drama *Tinker, Tailor, Soldier, Spy*. Other highlights of the Eighties included major roles as Sir Thomas Bertram in an adaptation of *Mansfield Park*, Krook (a character who famously meets his end by spontaneously combusting) in *Bleak House*, the vengeful Donald Stimpson in the Allan Prior-scripted drama *The Charmer*, and landowner Sam Toovey in *The Woman in Black*. The Nineties saw him play Arthur Fleming in the wartime drama *A Perfect Hero*, Malcolm Cellan-Davies in the dramatisation of Kingsley Amis's *The Old Devils*, and Mr Woodhouse in a production of *Emma* with Kate Beckinsale in the title role. In 1995, he won a Sony Gold award for his performance in *Elgar's Third* on Radio 3, while in 1998 he put in a bravura performance as Harold Winstanley in the *Midsomer Murders* episode *Death of a Hollow Man*. After appearing as Soames in the 2002 film *The Baroness and the Pig*, Hepton retired to the Kent coast.

Production	Role	Year
Tinker, Tailor, Soldier, Spy	Toby Esterhase	1979
Blood Money	Det Chief Supt Meadows	1981
Kessler	Albert Foiret	1981
An Inspector Calls	Inspector Goole	1982
The Plague Dogs (*film*)	Stephen Powell (voice)	1982
Smiley's People	Toby Esterhase	1982
Gandhi (*film*)	G.O.C.	1982
Saturday Night Thriller: Broken Glass	Cast Member	1982
Mansfield Park	Sir Thomas Bertram	1982
Season's Greetings	Cast Member	1982
Dear Box Number	Walter Cartwright	1983
A Profile of Arthur J. Mason	Arthur J. Mason	1984
Shadey (*film*)	Captain Amies	1985
Bleak House	Krook	1985
Honour, Profit and Pleasure	The Bishop of London	1985
The Holcroft Covenant (*film*)	Commander Leighton	1985
Bergerac: Avenge O Lord	Sir Geoffrey Newton	1985
The Disputation	Raymund de Penjaforte	1986
The Life and Loves of a She-Devil	Judge Bissop	1986
The Lady's Not for Burning	Hebble Tyson	1987
The Charmer	Donald Stimpson	1987
One Thing More (*theatre*)	Bede	1988
Stealing Heaven (*film*)	Bishop	1988
The Contract	Henry Carter	1988
The Woman in Black	Sam Toovey	1988
Wolf at the Door (*theatre*)	Teissier	1989
Eminent Domain (*film*)	Slovak	1991
A Perfect Hero	Arthur Fleming	1991
The Old Devils	Malcolm Cellan-Davies	1992
Dandelion Dead	Mr Davies	1994
Emma	Mr Woodhouse	1996
Midsomer Murders: Death of a Hollow Man	Harold Winstanley	1998
The Baroness and the Pig (*film*)	Soames	2002

HAZEL McBRIDE

After *Secret Army*, McBride's television roles included Anne Mieggs in mental health drama *Maybury*, Louise Medway in the *Tales of the Unexpected* episode *The Luncheon*, and Jackie Ogilvie in the Scottish soap opera *Take the High Road*. She also featured in an England-set episode of *Hart to Hart*, entitled *Harts and Hounds*, in which she played Lady Claire Belgrave and Gordon Jackson played her husband. In 1989 she appeared in the infamous scene in *Only Fools and Horses* in which Del Boy memorably fell through the bar. More recently she has taken roles in the comedy series *Coupling*, in the episode *The End of the Line,* as the character (Giselle) who all the female regulars claim to be; the soap opera *Hollyoaks*; the Nicholas Lyndhurst comedy *After You've Gone*; Kevin Whately divorce drama *Who Gets the Dog?*; and an episode of *Midsomer Murders*. As well as acting, McBride has also written numerous scripts for children's television, including episodes of *Rubbadubbers*. McBride co-runs School English Scene, a new theatre company created to support the teaching of English in secondary schools, which is currently touring with *How Do You Solve a Problem Like GCSE Poetry?*, which she has directed and produced.

Production	Role	Year
Maybury	Anne Mieggs	1981
House on the Hill: The Mistress of the House	Cast Member	1981
The Professionals: You'll Be All Right	Liz Spalding	1982
Tales of the Unexpected: The Luncheon	Louise Medway	1983
Take the High Road	Jackie Ogilvie	1983
Hart to Hart: Harts and Hounds	Lady Claire Belgrave	1983
Rumpole of the Bailey: Rumpole and the Judge's Elbow	Mrs Addison	1987
The Mousetrap (*theatre*)	Cast Member	1988
Only Fools and Horses: Yuppy Love	Snobby Girl	1989
The Bill: Only a Bit of Thieving	Kate Power	1989
Coupling: The End of the Line	Giselle	2001
Hollyoaks	Mrs Green	2002
Hardware: Women	Woman Shopper	2003
After You've Gone: Lock Back in Anger	Mrs Campbell	2007
Who Gets the Dog?	Female Judge	2007
Midsomer Murders: Midsomer Life	Governor	2008

CHRISTOPHER NEAME

After taking one-off roles in police series *Target* and sci-fi favourites *Doctor Who* and *Blake's 7*, Neame's first post-*Secret Army* recurring role was as Mark Antony in *The Cleopatras*. After appearing in Civil War drama *By the Sword Divided*, Neame quit England for the United States and was soon winning roles in popular series such as *The A Team* and *The Fall Guy*. After a spell in the soap *Days of Our Lives* and further guest roles in a variety of series, Neame would appear in several films, most notably as Sho in the Patrick Swayze film *Blue Steel* and as Bernard in *D.O.A.*. After spells in super-soaps *Dynasty* and *Dallas* in the late Eighties, in which he crossed swords with Alexis and J.R. respectively, he continued to make guest appearances in numerous hit US shows such as *L.A. Law*, *MacGyver* and *Murder, She Wrote*. In the Nineties he returned to sci-fi with appearances in *Babylon 5*, *Star Trek: Voyager* and *Sliders*. He followed these with notable roles as DCI Collingwood in Lynda La Plante's *Killer Net* and Ben Duffield in *Trial and Retribution IV*, both for British TV. His most recent credits include the film *Species III*, two episodes of *Star Trek: Enterprise* and the thriller series *Vanished*.

Production	Role	Year
Target: The Run	Billy	1978
Doctor Who: Shada (*unbroadcast*)	Skagra	1979
When the Boat Comes In: Friends, Romans, Countrymen	Robin Cunningham	1981
Blake's 7: Traitor	Colonel Quute	1981
The Cleopatras	Mark Antony	1983
By the Sword Divided	Henry Snelling	1983
The A-Team: The Road to Hope	Jack Scarett	1985
The Fall Guy: No Rms Ocean Vu	Terrill	1986
Riptide: The Pirate and the Princess	Klaus Gunter	1986
Days of Our Lives	Ogden Vaughn	1986
MacGyver: Deathlock	Quayle	1986
Love Among Thieves	Ian	1987
Spies: The Game's Not Over, 'Til the Fat Lady Sings	Hans von Sykes	1987
Steel Dawn (*film*)	Sho (Hired Killer)	1987
Second Chance: Moving In	Cast Member	1988
D.O.A. (*film*)	Bernard	1988
Case Closed	Max Dolpho	1988
Transformations (*film*)	Calihan	1988
The Great Escape II: The Untold Story	Kiowski	1988
Dynasty	Hamilton Stone	1988-9
Beauty and the Beast: Arabesque	Collin	1989
MacGyver: Legend of the Holy Rose	Erich von Leer	1989
Licence to Kill (*film*)	Fallon	1989
Ghostbusters II	Ma□tre D'	1989
Mancuso, FBI: Conflict of Interest	Cast Member	1989
Life Goes On: Paige's Mom	Clive Graham	1989
Lady in the Corner	Charles Patrick	1989
Dallas	Gustav Hellstrom	1989
The Radicals	Ulrich Zwingli	1990
L.A. Law: True Brit	Alan Scott	1990
Superboy: Carnival	Deville	1990
Danger Team	Peterson	1991
The Flash: Sight Unseen	Brian Gideon	1991
Edge of Honor (*film*)	Blade	1991
Hunter: The Grab	Jan Velboon	1991
MacGyver: Good Knight MacGyver	Sir Duncan	1991
Suburban Commando (*film*)	Commander	1991
Diplomatic Immunity (*film*)	Stefan Noll	1991
P.S. I Luv U: An Eye for an Eye	Jack Truduae	1991
Parker Lewis Can't Lose: Geek Tragedy	The Warrior	1992
Boris and Natasha (*film*)	Fearless Leader	1992
Still Not Quite Human	Dr Frederick Berrigon	1992
Human Target: Designed by Chance	Deguerre	1993
Irresistible Force	James Barron	1993
Murder, She Wrote: The Legacy of Borbey House	Peter Jatich	1993

Street Knight (film)	Franklin	1993
Acapulco H.E.A.T.: Code Name: Archangel	Werner Steinholtz	1993
The Last Chance Detectives: Mystery Lights of Navajo Mesa	Karl von Paris	1994
Hellbound (film)	Lockley	1994
Babylon 5: And the Sky Full of Stars	Knight Two	1994
Northern Exposure: Zarya	Lenin	1994
Star Trek: Voyager: Heroes and Demons	Unferth	1995
Earth 2: All About Eve	Dr Franklin Bennett	1995
Project Shadowchaser III (film)	Renko	1995
Murder, She Wrote: Nan's Ghost.	Dr John Sullivan	1995
Deadly Games	Dr Kramer	1996
Sliders: Into the Mystic	Dr Manfred Xang	1996
Walking Thunder (film)	Ansel Richter	1997
JAG: Washington Holiday	Minister Vartan Kepish	1997
The Naked Truth: Going Mein Way	Dr Schmekler	1997
C-16: FBI: The Sandman	André Divak	1997
The Apocalypse Watch	Ulrich von Schnabe	1997
Killer Net	DCI Collingwood	1998
Seven Days: There's Something About Olga	KGB Captain	1999
Ground Zero (film)	Andrew Donovan	2000
Martial Law	The One	2000
Movie Stars	Gestapo Officer	2000
Highway 395	Klaus Hess	2000
Trial and Retribution IV	Ben Duffield	2000
The Invisible Man: Immaterial Girl	Dr Henrick	2001
It's All Relative: Thanks, But No Thanks	Urune	2003
Star Trek: Enterprise: Storm Front	German General	2004
Species III (film)	Dr Nicholas Turner	2004
Special Ed	Dr Davis	2005
The Prestige	Defender	2006
Vanished	Claude Alexander	2006

RON PEMBER

Pember's notable roles immediately after *Secret Army* included Mr Cleaver in the children's serial *A Little Silver Trumpet*, Poggio in Victorian drama *'Tis Pity She's a Whore*, Mike Connor in two series of the Peter Davison comedy *Sink or Swim* and DI Jarrold in Agatha Christie drama *The Girl in the Train*. Mid-Eighties highlights included a memorable turn in *Victoria Wood: As Seen on TV* as the uninterested father of Chrissie, an ill-fated cross-channel swimmer, and guest appearances in *Cold Warrior*, *Dear John* and alongside Jan Francis in *Just Good Friends*. In the late Eighties, Pember appeared as Ron in the film *Personal Services*, as a psychotic taxman in *Red Dwarf*, and as recurring character Denis Timson in *Rumpole of the Bailey*. Pember retired from acting after suffering a stroke in 1992. He is currently writing a book about the Mermaid Theatre.

Production	Role	Year
Murder by Decree	Makins	1979
Flambards	Drayman	1979
A Little Silver Trumpet	Mr Cleaver	1980
Play for Today: Murder Rap	Davy	1980
'Tis Pity She's a Whore	Poggio	1980
Rough Cut	Taxi Driver	1980
The Gentle Touch: Break-In	Charlie Parker	1980
Minder	George	1980
Sink or Swim	Mike Connor	1980-1
Hi-De-Hi!: No Dogs Allowed	Private Detective	1981
Strangers: The Flowers of Edinburgh	Mole	1981
Q.E.D.: Infernal Device	Cast Member	1982
The Agatha Christie Hour: The Girl in the Train	Det Insp Jarrold	1982
The Professionals: Foxhole on the Roof	Jack Cobber	1982
Only Fools and Horses: Homesick	Baz	1983
Bullshot (film)	Dobbs	1983
Footlight Frenzy (film)	Cast Member	1984
Ordeal by Innocence	Ferryman	1984
The Invisible Man	Mr George Hall	1984
Cold Warrior: Bright Sting	John Palmer	1984
The Chain (film)	Stan	1984
Victoria Wood: As Seen On TV	Cliff (Chrissie's Dad)	1985
The Bill: Death of a Cracksman	Harry	1985
Dear John: Death	Commissionaire	1986
The Witness	Arthur	1986
Just Good Friends	Arthur	1986
Bergerac: Fires in the Fall	Jack Plemont	1986
Suspicion	Ticket collector	1987
Filthy Rich and Catflap	Shopkeeper	1987
Personal Services (film)	Ron	1987
Rumpole of the Bailey	Dennis Timson	1987-92
Red Dwarf: Better Than Life	Taxman	1988
High Street Blues	Chesney Black	1989
Hannay: The Confidence Man	Charlie Peterson	1989
The Bill: Favours	Langden	1991

ANGELA RICHARDS

Since *Secret Army*, Richards has predominantly worked in West End musical theatre. In the Eighties, she followed Elaine Paige in the role of Grizabella in *Cats* (New London), was Olivier-nominated for her role in the revue *Side by Side by Sondheim* (Donmar), played Liz in an acclaimed production of *High Society* (Victoria Palace) and Mrs Johnstone in Willy Russell's *Blood Brothers* (Albery). In the Nineties she played Mother Midnight in the musical *Moll Flanders* (Lyric) as well as performing in the revue *A Swell Party* (Vaudeville) and as the dresser in *Enter the Guardsman* (Donmar). Along the way she has still made the occasional appearance on TV, appearing alongside Anthony Hopkins in *Across the Lake*, and in popular series such as *Minder, The Bill and Hetty Wainthropp Investigates*. Her more recent musical theatre roles have included Amy in *Putting it Together* (Library Theatre, Manchester), Dorothy Fields in *Dorothy Fields Forever* (Jermyn Street/King's Head), Ethel Merman in *Call Me Merman* and the revue *Kern Goes to Hollywood* (both King's Head). In 2007 and 2008 she played Fraulein Schneider in Rufus Norris's acclaimed production of *Cabaret* (Lyric) alongside Amy Nuttall and Julian Clary.

Production	Role	Year
The Songwriters (*theatre*)	Performer	1978
The Winslow Boy	Catherine Winslow	1980
Kessler	Monique Durnford	1981
Six Fifty-Five Special	Performer	1981
Marti Webb – Together Again	Performer	1982
Cats (*theatre*)	Grizabella	1982-3
Minder: Senior Citizen Caine	Sheila Jones	1984
Singles' Night	Pam	1984
How Lucky Can You Get (*theatre*)	Performer	1985
Side by Side by Sondheim (*theatre*)	Performer	1986
High Society (*theatre*)	Liz	1987
Sunday Premiere: Across the Lake	Tonia Bern	1988
Blood Brothers (*theatre*)	Mrs Johnstone	1989-90
A Swell Party (*theatre*)	Performer	1991
Moll Flanders (*theatre*)	Mother Midnight	1993
The Bill: The Right Thing	Maureen Connolly	1996
Hetty Wainthropp Investigates: Lost Chords	Glenda Jason	1997
Enter the Guardsman (*theatre*)	The Dresser	1997
Moving On (*theatre*)	Performer	2000
Dorothy Fields Forever (*theatre*)	Dorothy Fields	2002
Putting It Together (*theatre*)	Amy	2004
Call Me Merman (*theatre*)	Ethel Merman	2004
Kern Goes To Hollywood (*theatre*)	Performer	2005
An Evening at Le Candide (*theatre*)	Performer	2006
A Love Letter to Dan (*theatre*)	Performer	2006
Cabaret (*theatre*)	Fraulein Schneider	2007-8

CLIFFORD ROSE

Rose went straight from *Secret Army* into the Glaister-produced air freight drama *Buccaneer*, in which he played financier Charles Burton. He was also the principal guest star in the 1981 *Doctor Who* story *Warrior's Gate*, playing the unscrupulous Captain Rorvik. After reprising his *Secret Army* role in *Kessler*, he went on to appear in episodes of *Reilly: Ace of Spies*, *Bergerac* and *Crown Court*. He subsequently took on the regular role of the villainous Challon in zoo vet drama *One By One*, and playd Professor Gracey in *Fortunes of War* and Kammler in the series *War and Remembrance*. In 1989, as well as guesting in *Inspector*

Morse and *Poirot*, Rose also returned to the Royal Shakespeare Company, initially taking roles in *As You Like It* and *All's Well That Ends Well* and more contemporary pieces such as *A Dream of People* and *Moscow Gold*. In the Nineties, he continued to mix TV and RSC roles. On television he was seen in *GBH*, *Maigret* and *Kavanagh QC*, while in the theatre, notable roles included Tiresias in *The Thebans*, Scroop in *Henry IV Parts 1 and 2*, the Ghost in Kenneth Branagh's *Hamlet*, Antonio in *The Merchant of Venice* and the Duke of Venice in Sam Mendes's *Othello*. Earlier this decade, his theatrical roles included Lepidus in *Antony and Cleopatra*, the Schoolmaster (opposite Ralph Fiennes) in *Brand*, the Duke of Venice again in *Othello*, and Cicero (again with Fiennes) in *Julius Caesar* with the latter two highly-praised productions touring extensively beyond the UK after their first run, while on television he appeared in *Anybody's Nightmare* and as Admiral Raeder in the docu-drama *When Hitler Invaded Britain*. His most recent theatre roles include Francis Nurse in *The Crucible* (RSC), Pope Paul VI in the critically-acclaimed *The Last Confession* at the Chichester Festival, and the Judge in a successful revival of The Chalk Garden co-starring Margaret Tyzack and Penelope Wilton, while on television he has appeared in the period dramas *Wallis and Edward* and *Foyle's War*.

Production	Role	Year
The Devil's Crown	Stephen Langton	1978
King Richard the Second	Bishop of Carlisle	1978
Buccaneer	Charles Burton	1980
Doctor Who: Warrior's Gate	Rorvik	1981
Kessler	Ludwig Kessler	1981
House Guest (theatre)	Cast Member	1981
The Wall	Cast Member	1982
Storyboard: Secrets	Cast Member	1983
Reilly: Ace of Spies	Cecil	1983
Bergerac: Come Out Fighting	Senator Beasley	1983
Oxbridge Blues	Cast Member	1984
Oedipus the King	Chorus	1984
Crown Court: Dirty Washing	Judge Herbert	1984
The Cold Room	Moltke	1984
Last Video and Testament	Bennet	1984
Minder: The Balance of Power	Cooke	1984
Love's Labour's Lost	Boyet	1985
The Good Father	Judge	1985
One by One	Challon	1985-7
The Girl	General Carlsson	1986
Fortunes of War	Professor Gracey	1987
Gentlemen and Players: Stags at Bay	Cast Member	1988
War and Remembrance	SS Lt Gen Heinz Kammler	1988
Act of Will	Hospital Specialist	1989
Inspector Morse: Ghost in the Machine	Dr Charles Hudson	1989
Poirot: Four and Twenty Blackbirds	Makinson	1989

As You Like It (*theatre*)	Duke Senior/Duke Frederick	1989
All's Well That Ends Well (*theatre*)	Lafeu	1989-90
A Dream of People (*theatre*)	Sir Evelyn	1990
Moscow Gold (*theatre*)	Andropov	1990
GBH	Judge Critchley	1991
As You Like It (*theatre*)	Jacques	1991
The Thebans (*theatre*)	Tiresias	1991
Henry IV (*theatre*)	Scroop	1991-2
Hamlet (*theatre*)	Ghost	1992-3
Maigret: Maigret and the Hotel Majestic	Jolivet	1993
Murder in the Cathedral (*theatre*)	Second Priest	1993-4
The Merchant of Venice (*theatre*)	Antonio	1993-4
The Tempest (*theatre*)	Gonzalo	1993-4
The Taming of the Shrew (*theatre*)	Baptista	1995-6
The Painter of Dishonour (*theatre*)	Don Luis	1995-6
Richard III (*theatre*)	Stanley	1995-6
The Marat/Sade (*theatre*)	Asylum Director	1997
Othello (*theatre*)	Duke of Venice	1997
Kavanagh QC: End Game	Mr Justice Gelder	1999
All Forgotten (*film*)	Dimitry	2000
Henry IV Parts 1 and 2 (*theatre*)	Worcester/Lord Chief Justice	2000-1
Anybody's Nightmare	Mr Justice Wright	2001
Antony and Cleopatra (*theatre*)	Lepidus/Proculeius	2002
Brand (*theatre*)	Schoolmaster	2003
When Hitler Invaded Britain	Admiral Erich Raeder	2004
Othello (*theatre*)	Duke of Venice	2004
Julius Caesar (*theatre*)	Cicero	2005
Wallis and Edward	King George V	2005
The Crucible (*theatre*)	Francis Nurse	2006
The Last Confession (*theatre*)	Pope Paul VI	2007
Foyle's War	Bishop Francis Wood	2008
The Chalk Garden (*theatre*)	The Judge	2008

PAUL SHELLEY

Soon after *Secret Army*, director Michael E. Briant cast Shelley in the drama series *Breakaway* and in the dual role of Sydney Carton and Charles Darnay in a version of Dickens's *A Tale of Two Cities* that Briant himself had adapted. In 1983, Glaister turned to him to be the lead in another wartime series as Major Hugh Gallagher in the twelve-part SOE drama *The Fourth Arm*. By the mid-Eighties, with the exception of John Mortimer's *Paradise Postponed*, in which he played Fred Simcox, Shelley had begun to concentrate on acting in theatre, largely in the West End, appearing as Stephen in Anthony Minghella's first play *Made in Bangkok*, as Trigorin in *The Seagull*, and as Leontes in a much-praised version of Shakespeare's *The Winter's Tale*. He went on to perform opposite Penelope Wilton in David Hare's *The Secret Rapture*, which was heralded by many as the play of the year. As well as (on television) an *Inspector Morse* and reprising the role of Fred Simcox in *Titmuss Regained*, the Nineties saw Shelley take key theatre roles in *Hedda Gabler*, *The Crucible* and, for the RSC, *Les Liaisons Dangereuses* (playing Valmont), a production on which he met his future wife, actress Paula Stockbridge. He would also direct a production of *The Seagull* at the Orange Tree Theatre in Richmond, and appear in the original stage production of *Little Voice* with Jane Horrocks and in *Six Degrees of Separation* opposite Stockard Channing. However, it would be at the end of the Nineties that he would make some of his most notable performances, taking the title roles in *Macbeth* (Orange Tree) and *Julius Caesar* (Globe Theatre), and the part of Antony in an all-male version of *Antony and Cleopatra*, again at the Globe, with Mark Rylance playing the Egyptian Queen. In the last few years, Shelley's career in the theatre has continued to thrive, and he has won particular acclaim for the roles of Capulet in *Romeo and Juliet* (Chichester Festival), Polonius in *Hamlet* (Royal Theatre, Northampton) and Hale in *The Crucible* (Birmingham Rep), the same role he first played in 1990. His most recent roles have included the elder Kipps in *The Woman in Black* (Fortune Theatre), Sir Toby Belch in *Twelfth Night* and Duncan in *Macbeth* (both Chichester Festival).

Production	Role	Year
Breakaway	Peter Bradford	1980
A Tale of Two Cities	Carton/Darnay	1980
When the Boat Comes In: Flies and Spiders	Bauer	1981
Guerre en pays neutre	David	1981
Doctor Who: Four to Doomsday	Persuasion	1982
The Fourth Arm	Major Hugh Gallagher	1983
The Real Thing (*theatre*)	Henry	1984
Lace II	Christopher Swann	1985
God's Outlaw (*film*)	John Frith	1986
Made in Bangkok (*theatre*)	Stephen	1986
Paradise Postponed	Fred Simcox	1986
The Seagull (*theatre*)	Trigorin	1986
A Midsummer Night's Dream (*theatre*)	Oberon	1987
The Winter's Tale (*theatre*)	Leontes	1987
Major Barbara (*theatre*)	Adolphus Cusins	1988
The Secret Rapture (*theatre*)	Tom	1988
Hedda Gabler (*theatre*)	Tesman	1989
The Winter's Tale (*theatre*)	Cast Member	1990
Inspector Morse: The Sins of the Fathers	Stephen Radford	1990
The Crucible (*theatre*)	Mr Hale	1990
All in the Wrong (*theatre*)	Sir John Restless	1991
Titmuss Regained	Fred Simcox	1991
Les Liaisons Dangereuses (*theatre*)	Valmont	1991-2
The Rise and Fall of Little Voice (*theatre*)	Cast Member	1992
Six Degrees of Separation (*theatre*)	Flan	1992
Soldier, Soldier: Base Details	Lt Col Horwood	1993
The 10 Percenters: Galaxy Quest 8	Aubrey	1994
Revelations	Edward Rattigan	1994

Arcadia (*theatre*)	Bernard Nightingale	1995
In Suspicious Circumstances: Golden Goose	George Storrs	1995
What the Heart Feels (*theatre*)	Peter	1996
Lady in the Dark (*theatre*)	Kendall Nesbitt	1997
All in the Wrong (*theatre*)	Sir John Restless	1997
Caught in the Act (*film*)	Neville Goodenough	1997
Frighteners: Rose Cottage	Bill Turner	1997
Macbeth (*theatre*)	Macbeth	1998
Proposals (*theatre*)	Burt	1998
The Invention of Love (*theatre*)	Wilde	1998
Julius Caesar (*theatre*)	Julius Caesar	1999
Antony and Cleopatra (*theatre*)	Antony	1999
The Threesome (*theatre*)	Alphonse Marjavel	2000
An Inspector Calls (*theatre*)	The Inspector	2000
Further than the Furthest Thing (*theatre*)	Hansen	2001
So Long Life (*theatre*)	Greg	2001
On Wings of Fire (*film*)	King Vishtaspa	2001
King Lear (*theatre*)	Albany	2002
Heartbeat: A Girl's Best Friend	Ralph Harrison	2002
Romeo and Juliet (*theatre*)	Capulet	2002
Camille (*theatre*)	Duval	2003
Crossroads	Stafford Wynter	2003
Private Lives (*theatre*)	Elyot Chase	2003
Hay Fever (*theatre*)	David Bliss	2004
The Crucible (*theatre*)	Mr Hale	2004
Hamlet (*theatre*)	Polonius	2005
Doctors: Home Front	Alan Bellamy	2005
The Soldier's Tale (*theatre*)	Cast Member	2005
A Man for All Seasons (*theatre*)	Duke of Norfolk	2005-6
The Woman in Black (*theatre*)	Kipps	2006
Twelfth Night (*theatre*)	Sir Toby Belch	2007
Macbeth (*theatre*)	Duncan	2007-8

STEPHEN YARDLEY

Yardley followed *Secret Army* by appearing in a *Crown Court* storyline, several episodes of police series *The Gentle Touch* and, along with Paul Shelley, was chosen by Briant to appear in his BBC version of *A Tale of Two Cities*. 1981 was a particularly busy year for Yardley, which saw him appear in the first episode of *The Day of the Triffids*, in the Glaister-produced *Blood Money*, the ITV drama *Fanny by Gaslight* and, like Juliet Hammond-Hill and Christopher Neame, as a principal guest star in an episode of the final series of *Blake's 7*. After appearances in other popular dramas such as *Bergerac*, *Juliet Bravo* and *Doctor Who*, Yardley was cast by *Secret Army* director Paul Annett as a lead character, Vic Morgan, in Lynda La Plante's *Widows 2*. In the same year, 1985, Yardley was approached by Gerry Glaister to take on a role with which he will forever be associated: medallion-wearing womaniser and businessman, Ken Masters, in *Howards' Way*. Yardley played Masters in 78 episodes over six series, and met his second wife, actress Jan Harvey, while making the show. After *Howards' Way* finished, Yardley took the regular role of Inspector Cadogan in the oddball detective drama *Virtual Murder*, and appeared in the film *The Innocent Sleep*. In more recent years, after turns in *Dangerfield*, *Bugs* (both opposite his wife Jan Harvey) and *The Bill*, Yardley became a regular on the Channel 5 soap *Family Affairs*, playing Vince Farmer for several years.

Production	Role	Year
Crown Court: Baby Love	Keith Tate	1979
The Gentle Touch	Jed Blanden	1980
A Tale of Two Cities	Defarge	1980
The Professionals: Hijack	Swetman	1980
The Day of the Triffids	John	1981
Blood Money	James Drew	1981
Fanny by Gaslight	'Duke' Hopwood	1981
Blake's 7: Sand	Investigator Reeve	1981
Funny Money (*film*)	Ridley	1982
Break Point	Mr Grieve	1982
Jemima Shore Investigates: Death à la Carte	Cast Member	1983
Slayground (*film*)	Turner	1983
Bergerac: Tug of War	Ken Lewis	1984
Juliet Bravo: Attack	Brian Adler	1984
Morgan's Boy	Alan	1984
Doctor Who: Vengeance on Varos	Arak	1985
Widows 2	Vic Morgan	1985
The Doctor and the Devils	Joseph	1985
Howards' Way	Ken Masters	1985-90
The Corvini Inheritance	Knowles	1986
Remington Steele: Steeled with a Kiss	Sergei Kemadov	1987
Virtual Murder	Insp Cadogan	1992
I, Lovett: Crime and Punishment	Sergeant	1993
The Innocent Sleep (*film*)	Drago	1996
Misfits (*theatre*)	Huston	1996
Heartbeat: Who Needs Enemies	Arnold Sampson	1996
Dangerfield: Adam	Richard Gresham	1997
RPM (*film*)	Chiarkos	1998
Bugs: The Two Becketts	Matt Beckett	1998
The Bill: Judgement Day	Joseph Anderson	1999
Holby City: Taking It on the Chin	Gerry Conroy	2000
Family Affairs	Vince Farmer	1999-2003
Hex	Thomas McBain	2004

Appendix Six:
INDEX OF ACTORS

BROOKS, Tony	3.1	CORNISH, Richard	2.5
BROOME, Derek	2.2	COTCHER, Tom	2.1
BROWN, Abigail	1.1	COWELL-PARKER, Simon	3.12
BROWN, Michael Napier	1.1	COX, Michael Graham	2.11
BULLION, Alexander	K5	COY, Jonathan	1.4
BULLIVANT, Malcolm	1.13	COYLE, James	1.11
BURNS, Mark	1.1	CREWE, Derek	3.10
BURRELL, Michael	1.3	CROFT, Jon	3.4
BURROWS, Martin	1.2	CROSSLEY, Steven	3.3
BUTLER, Alan	3.5	CULVER, Michael	1.1-1.4,
BYARS, Jim	K5, K6		1.6, 1.8,
BYRNE, Michael	2.5		1.11-1.15,
BYRON, Kathleen	1.13, 1.14		2.1-2.6,
CANNON, John	1.10		2.8-2.13
CARSON, John	1.12	CURRY, Shaun	1.9
CASSADY, John	3.5, 3.8	DADY, Susan	2.7
CASSIDY, Michael	3.11	DAGLISH, Neil	2.13, 3.1,
CAVENDISH, Robert	3.3		3.3, 3.6,
CHARLES, Maria	1.1, 1.3, 1.4,		3.8-3.10
	1.9, 1.12,	DAHLSEN, Peter	3.1
	1.15	DARVILL, Jonathan	1.4
CHASE, Stephan	3.12-3.14*	DAVIDSON, Peter	3.3
CHASIN, Daniel	1.1	DAVIDSON, Roger	1.7
CHOICE, Elisabeth	K1	DAVIES, Robin	3.4
CLARKE, Trisha	1.3,	DAVION, Alex	2.1
	2.1-3.13	DE GOGUEL, Constantin	2.2
CLAY, Peter	1.1	DE GRUYTER, Dom	2.2
COBURN, Brian	3.7	DEACON, Eric	3.6
COCHRAN, Barbara	1.13	DEARTH, John	K1
COLLINS, John D.	2.1, 2.10,	DELHEM, Rudi	2.3
	2.12, 3.4,	DENHAM, Maurice	1.14
	3.5	DICKSON, Neil	1.1
CONNOR, Martin	1.6	DOBIE, Alan	K1-K6
CONOLEY, Terence	K1	DOUGLAS, Christopher	1.10
CONRAD, Les	3.11	DUFF, Norwich	1.6
COPLEY, Paul	1.5	DUNN, Sheila	K3

STARR, Tony	3.11	WEST, Sheila	3.11
STEWART, Reginald	3.3	WESTON, Graham	3.9
STONE, John	2.4	WHITE, Arthur	3.2
STONE, Marianne	1.5, 2.6, 2.7	WHITE, John	3.9
STOTT, Ken	1.4	WHITESTONE, Geoff	3.13
STRONG, David	3.14*	WICKHAM, Jeffry	1.4
SULLIVAN, Hugh	K1	WIGHT, Peter	2.3
SUMMERFORD, Barry	3.11	WILKIN, Jeremy	K1-K3
SUTHERN, Derek	3.13	WILKINSON, Nick	3.5
TARTTELIN, Fred	2.4	WILLCOCKS, Sheelagh	3.10
TAYLOR, David	2.6	WILLEMS, Arnold	1.1
TAYLOR, Mark	2.10	WILLIAMS, Emma	2.5
THOMAS, Damien	1.9	WILLIAMS, Nigel	2.5, 2.6, 2.9,
THOMASON, Reg	2.3		2.11
TICKNER, Royston	2.8, K1, K3	WILLIS, Jerome	K1-K3
TRACEY, Ken	3.13	WILSON, Judy	3.2
TRACY, Susan	1.6	WINKLER, Sue	3.11
TREVENA, David	1.5	WITHERS, Margery	2.6
TULLO, Peter	2.1	WOODS, Reg	3.8, 3.10,
TWIST, Sarah	3.14*		K1-K3
TYLER, Ian	3.13	WREN, Richard	1.11, K4
UBELS, Steve	1.2	WYNN, James	2.6
VAHEY, Robert	2.4	WYNNE, Michael	1.16, 3.6
VAN DER SARREN, Werner	3.12	YARDLEY, Stephen	2.1-2.12
VAN GYSEGHEM, Joanna	1.7, 1.8	YELLAND, David	3.7
VANHECKE, Bart	3.2	YOUNG, Nicholas	K1-K6
VARNIER, Keith	1.6		
VINCENT, Frank	2.4	[3.14* - Made but not broadcast]	
VIVIAN, Michael	3.14*		
WAGAR, Paul	2.7		
WALDON, John	2.7		
WALLIS, Alec	1.6, 3.1		
WAY, Eileen	3.10		
WAYNE, Jeff	3.11		
WEBB, Esmond	3.10		
WELLING, Albert	1.15		

REFERENCES

Introduction

1. Cornell, Paul, et al., *The Guinness Book of Classic TV* (2nd ed., 1996), Guinness, p.380

Series 1 - Production

1. *Behind the Scenes: "We are not writing Hamlet"*, BBC, tx. 13.11.77
2. *Radio Times*, 3-9 September 1977, No. 2808
3. *Behind the Scenes: "We are not writing Hamlet"*, BBC, tx. 13.11.77
4. *Au Revoir* (1 May 2007), http://thoughtwad.blogspot.com/2007_05_01_archive.html
5. *Behind the Scenes: "We are not writing Hamlet"*, BBC, tx. 13.11.77
6. Brason, John, *Secret Army* (1977), BBC Books, pp.39-40
7. Ibid. pp.59-60
8. Ibid. p.143
9. Ibid. p.73
10. Neave, Airey, *Little Cyclone* (1973), Coronet, pp.24-5
11. Brason, John, *Secret Army* (1977), BBC Books, p.73
12. Ibid. p.104
13. Ibid. pp.47-8
14. Warmbrunn, Werner, *The German Occupation of Belgium 1940-1944* (1993), Peter Lang, p.151
15. Brason, John, *Secret Army* (1977), BBC Books, p.14
16. Ibid. p.188
17. Ibid. p.190
18. Ibid. p.219
19. Ibid. p.190
20. Ibid. p.219
21. Ibid. p.188
22. Ibid. p.253
23. Ibid. p.72
24. Ibid. p.60
25. Ibid. p.62
26. Ibid. p.66
27. Ibid. p.74
28. Ibid. p.188
29. Ibid. p.18
30. Randle, Bill, *Blue Skies and Dark Nights* (2002), Independent Books, p.325
31. *Behind the Scenes: "We are not writing Hamlet"*, BBC, tx. 13.11.77
32. Theatre Archive Project – Interview with Bernard Hepton conducted by Kate Harris (6 April 2006), http://www.bl.uk/projects/theatrearchive/hepton.html
33. Ibid.
34. Ibid.
35. Ibid.
36. Ibid.
37. Memorable TV interview with Angela Richards (2004), http://www.memorabletv.com/onthebox/interviews/angelarichards.htm
38. Billington, Michael, *Moral reform with a knees-up, The Times* (28 July 1967), p.6
39. Anon., *School play set Clifford on the road to acting success, Hereford Times* (23 February 2006)

40. Ibid.
41. Ibid.
42. Ibid.
43. Ibid.
44. Media Studies: *Behind the Scenes* – Notes, BBC
45. *Behind the Scenes: "All those people were heroes"*, BBC, tx. 20.11.77
46. Ibid.
47. Ibid.
48. Ibid.
49. *Behind the Scenes: "A problem of authenticity"*, BBC, tx. 04.12.77
50. *Behind the Scenes: "I enjoy it when it's over"*, BBC, tx. 27.11.77
51. Ibid.
52. *Behind the Scenes: "A problem of authenticity"*, BBC, tx. 04.12.77
53. Ibid.
54. *Behind the Scenes: "A boy? A ten year old boy?"*, BBC, tx. 11.12.77
55. Ibid.
56. Ibid.
57. Ibid.
58. *Radio Times*, 3-9 September 1977 (No. 2808)
59. Ibid.
60. Ibid.
61. Ibid.

Series 1 - Episodes

1. Neave, Airey, *Saturday at MI9* (2004), Leo Cooper, p.22
2. Brason, John, *Secret Army* (1977), BBC Books, p.219
3. Randle, Bill, *Blue Skies and Dark Nights* (2002), Independent Books, p.110
4. Ibid. pp.115-6
5. Warmbrunn, Werner, *The German Occupation of Belgium 1940-1944* (1993), Peter Lang, Chapter 4
6. Randle, Bill, *Blue Skies and Dark Nights* (2002), Independent Books, p.121
7. Middlebrook, Martin and Chris Everitt, *The Bomber Command War Diaries: An operational reference book: 1939-45* (1985), pp.334-5
8. Randle, Bill, *Blue Skies and Dark Nights* (2002), Independent Books, pp.102-3

Series 2 - Production

1. http://www.michaelbriant.com
2. Ibid.
3. Ibid.
4. *Radio Times*, 23-29 September 1978 (No. 2863)
5. Ibid.

Series 2 - Episodes

1. Neave, Airey, *Little Cyclone* (1973), Coronet, pp.182-5
2. Ibid.
3. Moore, Bob (ed.) *Resistance in Western Europe* (2000), Berg Publishers, Chapter 2: Belgium by Pieter Lagrou
4. Butler, Rupert, *An Illustrated History of the Gestapo* (1992), Ian Allan Publishing, pp.116-131
5. Reid, P. R., *The Colditz Story* (1952), Hodder and Stoughton, pp.159-160

6. Bodson, Herman, *Agent for the Resistance: A Belgian Saboteur in World War II* (1994), A&M Press, p.78-9

Series 3 - Episodes

1. Neave, Airey, *Saturday at MI9* (2004), Leo Cooper, p.174
2. Fest, Joachim, *Plotting Hitler's Death* (1997), Phoenix, p.258
3. Warmbrunn, Werner, *The German Occupation of Belgium 1940-1944* (1993), Peter Lang, pp.96-104
4. Foot, M. R. D. and Langley, J. M., *MI9: Escape and Evasion: 1939-45* (1979), Book Club Associates, pp.145-6
5. Neave, Airey, *Saturday at MI9* (2004), Leo Cooper, p.278
6. Struye, Paul, *L'évolution du sentiment public en Belgique sous l'occupation allemande* (1945), pp.178-9
7. Brodsky, Alexandra Fanny, *A Fragile Identity: Survival in Nazi-Occupied Belgium* (1998), Radcliffe Press, p.290

Afterlife

1. Sangster, Jim and Condon, Paul, *TV Heaven* (2005), Collins, p.646
2. Ibid. p.649

Kessler

1. Brason, John, *Kessler* (1981), BBC Books, Author's Note
2. Ibid.
3. Farago, Ladislas, *Aftermath: Martin Bormann and the Fourth Reich* (1975), Pan, p.185
4. Ibid.
5. Ibid. p.15
6. Ibid. p.277
7. Ibid. p.313
8. Brason, John, *Kessler* (1981), BBC Books, p.70
9. Brason, John, *Kessler* (1981), BBC Books, Author's Note
10. Stevenson, William, *The Bormann Brotherhood: A new investigation of the escape and survival of Nazi war criminals* (1973), Arthur Barker, p.143
11. *Radio Times*, 31 October – 6 November 1981 (No. 3025)

BIBLIOGRAPHY

Anderson, Duncan, *The Fall of the Reich: from D-Day to the Fall of Berlin 1944-1945* (2000), David & Charles

Bodson, Herman, *Agent for the Resistance: A Belgian Saboteur in World War II* (1994), A&M Press

Brason, John, *Kessler* (1981), BBC Books

Brason, John, *Secret Army* (1977), BBC Books

Brason, John, *Secret Army Dossier* (1978), BBC Books

Brason, John, *Secret Army: the End of the Line* (1979), Star Books

Brodsky, Alexandra Fanny, *A Fragile Identity: Survival in Nazi-Occupied Belgium* (1998), Radcliffe Press

Butler, Rupert, *An Illustrated History of the Gestapo* (1992), Ian Allan Publishing

Cornell, Paul et al., *The Guinness Book of Classic TV* (2nd ed., 1996), Guinness

De Ridder Files, Yvonne, *The Quest for Freedom: a story of Belgian resistance in World War II* (1991), Narrative Press

Eisner, Peter, *The Freedom Line, the brave men and women who rescued Allied airmen from the Nazis during World War II* (2005), Perennial

Ellis, Chris, *A History of Combat Aircraft* (1979), Optimum

Evans, Jeff, *The Penguin TV Companion* (3rd ed., 2006), Penguin

Farago, Ladislas, *Aftermath: Martin Bormann and the Fourth Reich* (1975), Pan

Fest, Joachim, *Plotting Hitler's Death* (1997), Phoenix

Foot, M. R. D., *SOE in France: an account of the Special Operations Executive in France 1940-1944* (2005), Cass

Foot, M. R. D., *SOE in the Low Countries* (2001), St Ermin's Press

Foot, M. R. D. and Langley, J. M., *MI9: Escape and Evasion: 1939-45* (1979), Book Club Associates

Mazower, Mark, *Hitler's Empire: Nazi Rule in Occupied Europe* (2008), Allen Lane

Middlebrook, Martin and Everitt, Chris, *The Bomber Command War Diaries: An operational reference book: 1939-45* (1985)

Moore, Bob (ed.) *Resistance in Western Europe* (2000), Berg Publishers

Neave, Airey, *Little Cyclone* (1973), Coronet

Neave, Airey, *Saturday at MI9* (2004), Leo Cooper

Pitchfork, Graham, *Shot down and on the run: the RAF and Commonwealth aircrews who got home from behind enemy lines 1940-1945*, (2003), The National Archives

Priestner, Andy, *Kessler DVD Booklet* (2005), DD Home Entertainment

Priestner, Andy, *Secret Army Series 1 DVD Booklet* (2003), DD Video

Priestner, Andy, *Secret Army Series 2 DVD Booklet* (2004), DD Video

Priestner, Andy, *Secret Army Series 3 DVD Booklet* (2004), DD Video

Ramsden, John, *Don't Mention the War: the British and the Germans since 1890* (2006), Little Brown

Randle, Bill, *Blue Skies and Dark Nights* (2002), Independent Books

Randle, Bill, *Kondor* (1999), Independent Books

Reid, P. R., *The Colditz Story* (1952), Hodder and Stoughton

Sangster, Jim and Condon, Paul, *TV Heaven* (2005), Collins

Shirer, William L., *The rise and fall of the Third Reich* (1991), Mandarin

Shuff, Derek, *Evader: the epic story of the first British airman to be rescued by the Comète Escape Line in World War II* (2003), Spellman

Stevenson, William, *The Bormann Brotherhood: A new investigation of the escape and survival of Nazi war criminals* (1973), Arthur Barker

Struye, Paul, *L'évolution du sentiment public en Belgique sous l'occupation allemande* (1945)

Warmbrunn, Werner, *The German Occupation of Belgium 1940-1944* (1993), Peter Lang

Teare, Denys, *Evader: the compelling true story of escape and evasion behind enemy lines* (1996), Burford Books

ALSO AVAILABLE...

Angela Richards's songs from SECRET ARMY, including 'If This Is The Last Time I See You', 'I Bet You've Heard This One Before' and 'Memories Come Gently', are now available on a CD entitled 'An Evening at Le Candide' recorded in 2006.

As well as all of the songs from the series, this compilation includes comedy numbers and wartime favourites, with piano accompaniment by Jason Carr.

Buy online at: http://www.survivorstvseries.com/merchandise.htm
or email andypriestner@hotmail.com to order by cheque or postal order.

Track Listing:
1. Memories Come Gently
2. J'Attendrai
3. I Bet You've Heard This One Before
4. Medley: Je Suis Seul Ce Soir – Eimal Wirst Du Wieder Bei Mir Sein – Lili Marlene
5. When We Can Live In Peace Once More
6. The Boys in the Backroom
7. Just Another Rhumba
8. Too Marvellous For Words
9. I'm Unlucky at Gambling
10. For All Our Yesterdays
11. Medley: Laura - Dream – Ain't Misbehavin' – I'll Be Seeing You
12. Velvet Blue
13. No One Man Is Ever Going To Worry Me
14. If This Is The Last Time I See You

ABOUT THE AUTHOR

© Marisa Priestner

Andy Priestner has been a devotee of *Secret Army* since he first caught the 1981 repeat season at the tender age of nine. While freelancing for the DVD company DD Video in 2003 some 22 years later, the opportunity arose for him to produce special features to accompany their *Secret Army* boxsets and he leapt at the chance. While researching the booklets for the DVDs, Andy amassed more material than he could use, so the prospect of a full book on the series beckoned. The fact that, unlike sci-fi series, classic TV drama remains largely unexplored, has also encouraged him in this endeavour.

Andy is Head Librarian at the University of Cambridge's Judge Business School, where his job chiefly entails the smooth delivery of electronic and printed resources to the School's students, faculty and executives.

Andy categorically does *not* advocate working full-time, changing jobs, moving house (twice!) and having your first baby while attempting to write a book.

His first book, *The End of the World?* (ISBN:1845830016), co-authored with Rich Cross, examined the BBC TV series *Survivors* (1975-7), and was published by Telos in December 2005 to critical acclaim.

Right: The author competing in a Silver Jubilee fancy dress competition (the soldier, second left) on the afternoon of 7 June 1977, while the cast and crew of *Secret Army* were preparing to record the first episode at BBC TV Centre.